ART AND CIVILIZATION

Bernard S. Myers
The City College, New York

ART
AND
CIVILIZATION

McGraw-Hill Book Company, Inc., New York, Toronto, London

1957

for Peter
*and the other young people
who want to know why*

PREFACE

LESS than a generation ago, explaining the history of art in terms of its sociocultural background might have appeared to indicate an extreme attitude. At that time the popular books were those using the poetic approach, in which a vaguely defined "time spirit" provided the background for the arts; or those stressing climatic, geographical, and dynastic information. In neither kind was there a clear notion of how changes had taken place from one period to another; the first group left the artist in an idealistic vacuum, the second produced a mechanical and inconclusive relationship between an art and its epoch.

During the years that have elapsed since then, however, there has been a growing realization that the environment of a given period could be portrayed in a more affective relationship to the arts of that time. More recently, serious studies of different periods, and more general books as well, have sought to do this, e.g., Arnold Hauser's monumental work, *The Social History of Art,* from which the present author has learned a good deal.

This approach, which we propose to follow here, does not merely establish parallels between the plastic arts and other cultural phenomena of a period — although these are also treated in some detail. It tries to achieve a synthesis of social, political, and cultural phenomena in each era in the interest of explaining as far as possible how the first two elements affect the third. From what kind of society does the artist of a certain period derive, to what social group is he directing his art, and to what extent does this influence the way in which he expresses himself? Is there a direct relationship between the courtliness of Rubens's style and his social milieu? Is there a perceptible relationship between the religious anguish of the Mannerist artist and the distortion of his forms, spaces, and colors?

To the extent that we are willing to explore the operative factors and are not satisfied with a bare recital of available materials (i.e., wood, stone, and the like) or wars fought, we shall find that all cultures — at least where we know something about them — yield this relationship. The changes from one epoch in Egypt to another, from archaic Greece to classical Greece, from the Romanesque to the Gothic, from Renaissance to Mannerism, are invariably clarified through the additional social, political, religious, and other elements that constitute this synthesized approach.

We become aware of the fact that human beings made a particular kind of art object for a particular kind of public, both artist and public responding to certain conditions in that period. This is quite different from the school of thought which acknowledges the importance of the human equation by stressing interesting anecdotes from the artist's life to explain his work. What then is done with artists like Vermeer who have left no anecdotes or with unknown artists of ancient times whose names have long been forgotten?

There is no question that art has a history of its own like any other discipline, and it is that history which concerns us here. Stylistic traditions and technical devices have been handed on from century to century; and many artists today are still living within the shadow of *styles* (manners of expression) first produced in ancient Greece or Renaissance Italy. Similarly, graphic artists may be using etching, woodcut, and engraving *processes* of the Renaissance and Baroque periods; while mural painters may use the procedures of fresco artists of the Italian Renaissance.

But the fact that art has its own history does not mean, as had formerly been maintained, that we need not look beyond this golden path through the ages. Why, for example, does the mural painter in Mexico use fresco techniques of Renaissance Italy and perhaps even its aesthetic? Is there not some social as well as personal necessity that impels the artist to find a means of expression suitable to his needs, to find, in other words, his own aesthetic and spiritual level? However much we may think of the artist of today (or of any period) as rummaging casually through past styles to find what is suitable for him, we must also realize that he makes a choice and that his choice is related to the way he thinks and feels. The way he thinks and feels is, in turn, related both to his make-up as an individual and to his emergence from a particular milieu.

If there is a significant change from one epoch in Greece or Italy to another, do we have the right to say, as sometimes it still is said, that the later style is a "decadent" version of the former, or "more important," style? Moreover, what is the significance of this change—specifically, what caused it? For example, fifteenth-century Flemish painting fills what has been called by some writers a "cultural vacuum." Does this mean that there was no, or very little, previous art in the area and that then — presumably in response to some mystical impulse — the air was suddenly filled with paintings?

We shall attempt here to present as clearly as possible the general background for each stage in the history of art, keeping in mind always that our end product is to be some rational explanation of the "why" as well as the "how" of artistic being and artistic change. We shall endeavor to give each era its full importance in the story of the world's art, leavening the parochialism of Western culture by the inclusion of sections on the Near and the Far East. The various techniques and terminologies throughout are explained as they are needed in the text.

If we have stressed the fact that art is the mirror of history, we do not mean to imply that it does not have values of its own: aesthetic, philosophic, and purely sensuous. Those values we have considered and developed here, without losing sight of the larger cultural context in which appear the differences from one age to another and the reasons for such differences. Our purpose is to give through this history of art a sense of the past and a heightened awareness of the present, to show through the object of art the crystallization of man's thoughts and feelings about the world in which he lives and the realm toward which he strives.

ACKNOWLEDGMENTS

I wish to thank the many artists, museums, and collectors who have made their works available for publication here, as well as those individuals and organizations who have supplied me with photographs. In the case of museums and galleries I have indicated these credits on the actual pictures as reproduced herein; for the nonexhibiting agencies I offer a special detailed listing as follows:

American Airlines: figs. 173, 174, 175, 180, 405
Archaeological Museum, Tehran (courtesy U.S. Information and Education Services, Tehran): figs. 48, 49, 53, 260
Australian Information Service, New York: fig. 14
British Information Service, New York: figs. 293, 294, 297
Canadian Information Service, New York: fig. 15
Consulate General of Egypt, New York: figs. 20, 21, 22, 25, 30, 31, 252, 253
Department of External Affairs, Eire (courtesy Irish Information Service, New York): fig. 217
Embassy of India, Washington, D.C.: figs. 141, 142, 146, 147, 150, 151, 152, 265
French Government Tourist Office, New York: figs. 108, 248, 251, 267, 273, 279, 280, 281, 288, 289, 308, 340, 383, 384, 386, 410, 418, 419, 425, 454, 464, 473, 498
Inter Nationes (Bonn), Courtesy Roy Bernard, Inc., New York: figs. 46, 109, 116, 117, 224, 240, 243, 244, 276, 277, 292, 331, 362, 366, 370, 372, 373, 409, 411, 422, 423, 426, 428, 449, 490, 557, 558
Italian Tourist Information Service, New York: figs. 124, 126, 127, 128, 131, 133, 134, 201, 232, 238, 298, 299, 302, 304, 305, 306, 319, 321, 322, 323, 324, 332, 334, 335, 344, 345, 352, 354

Japan Travel Bureau, Tokyo: figs. 167, 168
Netherlands Information Service, New York: fig. 424
Norwegian Information Service, New York: fig. 214
Pan-American Grace Airways, New York: figs. 185, 186
Pan-American World Airways, New York: figs. 153, 177, 258, 266, 477, 568
Royal Greek Embassy, Washington, D.C.: figs. 55, 56, 70, 78, 82, 86, 87, 89, 92
Spanish Tourist Office, New York: figs. 254, 255, 256, 257, 381, 404
Trans-World Airlines, New York: figs. 18, 27, 29, 84, 132, 191, 215, 268, 274, 275, 397, 497
Trinity Church, Boston: fig. 500
United Nations, New York: fig. 565

The die-stamping on the cover was adapted from a Maillol illustration, "Dreaming Nude," for Ovid, *L'Art d'aimer*, published by Philippe Gonin, Paris and Lausanne, in 1935. The print was furnished by courtesy of the New York Public Library.

Particular thanks for photographic assistance are due my many friends at The Metropolitan Museum of Art and in The Museum of Modern Art library. Mr. Edward Plunkett of the department of art of The City College has also been helpful in this regard. Professor S. Lane Faison has been good enough to supply the German photographs reproduced in Chapter 23.

To my wife, special thanks for her help in gathering the material for the chapter on the early Americas, as well as for an extremely painstaking and very beneficial job of editing on the entire manuscript.

Bernard S. Myers

CONTENTS

xi

PLATES

Plate I. Stained glass window, Chartres Cathedral, Detail.
Courtesy, Dayton Art Institute.

Plate II. Botticelli: Head of Venus. Detail from Mars and Venus.
Reproduced by courtesy of the Trustees, the National Gallery, London.
Color plate courtesy, Fama, Ltd., London.

Plate III. El Greco: The Vision of St. Hyacinthe.
Courtesy, The Memorial Art Gallery of the University of
Rochester, New York. Color plate courtesy, Thomas Yoseloff.

Plate IV. Harunobu: Hobby Horse.
Color plate courtesy, Fama, Ltd., London.

Plate V. Vermeer: Young Lady Standing at Virginals.
Reproduced by courtesy of the Trustees, the National Gallery, London.
Color plate courtesy, Fama, Ltd., London.

Plate VI. Van Gogh: L'Arlésienne.
Bequest of Samuel A. Lewisohn, 1951;
courtesy, The Metropolitan Museum of Art.
Color plate courtesy, Thomas Yoseloff.

Plate VII. Toulouse-Lautrec: Moulin Rouge—La Goulue.
Color plate courtesy, Thomas Yoseloff.

Plate VIII. Matisse: Young Woman in a Peasant Blouse.
Reproduced by courtesy of Raymond and Raymond, Inc.
Color plate courtesy, Thomas Yoseloff.

1 / PREHISTORIC AND
MODERN PRIMITIVES

HISTORY is not always a matter of dates nor wisdom a matter of age. Since the beginnings of the era of exploration, modern man has constantly encountered cultures out of the past. Many of these cultures have long been dead, and now exist only in relics, but many are still alive today in the people and their objects of art. An ever-astonishing fact is the simultaneous existence of races on different levels of civilization — and sometimes within the same country.

When European expeditions began to explore the Western Hemisphere, for example, they were struck by the tremendous difference between their own presumably more civilized ways and those of the "savages." Some Indians of the North American continent (those on the Northwest coast) were living like prehistoric hunters of the Paleolithic, or Old Stone, Age; while others (in the Southwest) followed the customs of the more settled agriculturists of the Neolithic, or New Stone, Age. The cultures of Middle America (from Mexico down) and South America, however, approximated in some respects those of the civilized Orient by which they may at a remote period have been influenced.

The retarded development seen in parts of the Western Hemisphere was later found in other portions of the world. As Africa was explored, once again nomadic hunters of the Old Stone Age type were discovered living in modern times. In the Pacific area, also, among the diverse races of Melanesia, Polynesia, and Micronesia, many exist even today on levels which compare with those of prehistoric times.

Primitivism, then, is not so much a product of date; it is a state of mind and development stemming from geographical, social, religious, and other circumstances. The Australian aborigines, for instance, ended their Old Stone Age period around A.D. 1870. By the same token, powerful influences from primitivism have been at work on civilized artists of our own day who have found it necessary to refresh themselves spiritually at this spring.

1

A general cultural parallel may be established between the Paleolithic cultures of around 20,000 to 10,000 B.C. and those of the latter-day African Bushman, the North American Eskimo, and the Australian aborigine; here we find an actual artistic parallel. In the same way, the cultural level (including the arts) of the Neolithic period between about 10,000 and 4000 B.C. corresponds with those of West Africa, the Pacific area, and part of Indian America.

PALEOLITHIC ART (CA. 20,000–CA. 10,000 B.C.). It is assumed that the Paleolithic, or Old Stone, Age paintings of northern Spain, southern France, and other regions were done for some useful end. On the other hand, they have also been regarded as religious in purpose. Basically the two viewpoints are not divergent, if we realize that the primitives (and even many civilized peoples) practice religion to ensure some desired result. Since the great necessity of primitive man was success in hunting animals which would supply him with food, clothing, and fuel — indeed with life itself — every effort was bent toward that aim. In an age where immediate danger and necessity overruled every other consideration, it was natural that types of practical magic would be evolved.

The artist of the Paleolithic period apparently did not distinguish between the image he created on the walls of the caves and the reality or fact that was pictured. To him the image was reality, not a symbol or spiritual essence, as it would be later to artists of the Neolithic Age. Therefore the bulk of Paleolithic art is naturalistic in form and meaning, trying to bring the image into concurrence with the object portrayed, to create an identity that would help obtain the desired object.

Magic in this sense is a concrete thing; its intention is specific: to achieve the successful hunt of a desired animal or the death of a hated enemy. It is based on a belief in coincidence, i.e., that one thing happens in conjunction or parallel with another; that somewhere, somehow, a secret link between the two is determined by similarity or by previous contact which causes these parallel events to take place. Obtaining a piece from the enemy's body or clothes and destroying that item is supposed to cause the enemy's death; a vitally realistic picture of the desired animal will help cause the death of that animal.

We have contemporary instances of this sort, in the Caribbean voodoo priests who stick pins in doll images of a condemned enemy (cf. the arrow-studded paintings of Paleolithic animals) and in the Central African practice described by the anthropologist Frobenius. He tells of a pygmy tribe which, before an antelope hunt, cleared a space on the ground and on it made a drawing of the animal. Just before the start of the hunt at dawn, as the sun began to warm the picture, a woman rose and sang an incantation while one of the hunters shot an arrow into the neck of the drawing, after which three men darted into the forest to make the kill. Later they returned with an antelope they had shot in the neck. From this beast they took hair and blood with which to daub the picture. The magic process was thus completed.

The Paleolithic paintings of Altamira in Spain and those of Lascaux and Les Eyzies in France are perhaps the best known; such works may be found in a wide territory stretching from western Europe to southernmost Africa. In Europe practically all occur within limited areas of eastern and northern Spain and southwestern France. At times the resemblances between European (especially eastern Spanish) and African Paleolithic are so strong that scholars have assumed there was direct contact at some point in prehistory. Cultural and other interchanges between Spain and parts of Africa run throughout history.

The eastern Spanish, or Levantine, phase of the Paleolithic shows a series of silhouetted figures of both animals and men representing the actual act of hunting or fighting. Here on the walls of caves or outdoors on rocks and cliffs, the flat two-dimensional silhouette (fig. 1) is employed, in contrast to the three-dimensional outline drawings of the

Fig. 1. Cave painting, eastern Spain.

Fig. 2. Bushman painting, South Africa.

northern Spanish examples at Altamira (see fig. 3). But the compositions in the east are livelier, while the northern examples (often of single animals) show greater monumentality of form. Yet in both parts of Spain there is a stronger feeling of reality for the animals than for the men, who are almost invariably schematized into long-legged, long-armed, thin-bodied "stick figures" like those drawn by children today. It is almost as though the artist, feeling he must draw the animal convincingly in magic terms, was afraid to portray the man, who might thereby fall prey to an enemy. We also find these vitally expressive and realistic animal silhouettes and schematized men in southern Africa among the Bushmen (fig. 2).

The famous animals of Altamira in northern Spain (fig. 3) contrast in many ways with the flatly silhouetted Levantine figures. Naturalistic to a high degree, some of these northern works are painted on the irregularly bossed surfaces of cave ceilings and take on a curved three-dimensionality from those very projections. The colors are relatively rich browns, reddish browns, ochres, yellows, and reds. We may suppose, by analogy with primitive tribes of today such as those of Melanesian New Guinea in the Pacific, that each group or tribe had its own expert or artist who ultimately rose to priestly status because of his strange abilities. The chief characteristic of the polychromed animals is their impressively rounded solidity. Although not predominantly action pictures, whatever

4

movement they show is lifelike. Here again we may note similarities in style between these works and others found in Africa, this time in Basutoland.

Some of the northern Spanish caves extend far into the earth, where people would not ordinarily go without a compelling ceremonial or perhaps military reason. No evidence exists of ordinary human habitation of these caves but rather of their use as sanctuaries where magic rites of hunting, fertility, and the like were apparently practiced. One of the sites in northern Spain at La Pasiega is almost halfway up a cliff, from which one drops down through a vertical opening into a great maze of twisting passageways. By and large the pictures in these caves are more serious and much less lively than the imaginative and almost chatty art of the Spanish Levant.

In southwestern France we are taken back even farther in the history of man by a group of caves found deep underground in complete darkness. Here, in most cases, there has never been any natural light. Yet the colors of these cave decorations show the widest range of any comparable area; the hues include yellows of different intensities as well as reds, browns, vermilions, and blacks. In addition the choice of animals depicted varies more than in Spain.

The most recent discovery in the Paleolithic territory of France was at Lascaux in 1940. Like Altamira, Lascaux was uncovered quite by accident; here a group of boys, trying to enlarge a hole to find their lost dog, fell into what has proved to be the most exciting site in the pre-

Fig. 3. Bison. Caves of Altamira, Spain.

historic field. Its paintings portray powerful bulls, many stocky little horses (fig. 4) that suggest in a general way the stone reliefs of Han China, shaggy ponies, stags' heads, charging bison, and other figures. Most of the pictures, like those of northern Spain, are relatively static and, similarly, feature individual forms rather than compositions. Although this site was used at various dates, estimated as far back as 30,000 B.C., the majority of these works belong to the end of the Paleolithic period (ca. 10,000 B.C.). Other important sites in this part of France include Font-de-Gaume, La Mouthe, Trois-Frères, and Tuc d'Audubert, located for the most part in the foothills of the Pyrenees, south of Toulouse and in the *département* of Dordogne.

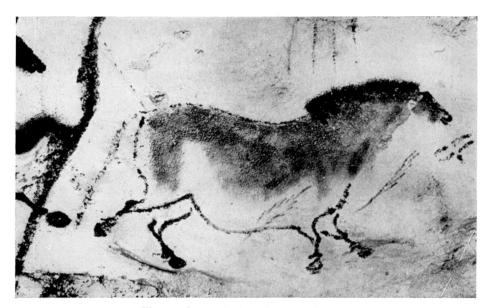

Fig. 4. Cave painting, Lascaux, France.

Most of the Paleolithic works so far considered belong to the Ice Age. With the end of this period a sharp break occurred, caused perhaps by changes in climate, vegetation, and animal life. This break, noticeable in the French and northern Spanish areas, did not affect the Levantine portion of Spain, where art continued gradually to change into a hard schematized formulation. After the Ice Age, animal portraits were still recognizable as such but had lost the vitality of the earlier style; so-called magic signs or symbols began to appear, especially on the painted pebbles of the time, very much like the *chirunga,* or sacred pebbles, of Australian aborigines.

From the symbols and schematizations of this transitional Mesolithic period (i.e., Middle Stone Age) the abstract art of the New Stone, or Neolithic, Age follows quite naturally. Here again is a far-reaching type of expression, found in different parts of the world, beginning at different dates in accordance with the lingering of Old Stone Age life. On this new level there are modern analogies in lands as far apart as the Pacific area, Africa, and North America.

NEOLITHIC ART (CA. 10,000–CA. 4000 B.C.). During the New Stone Age, man turned from the wandering existence of the hunter to herding and farming, a more stable life which involved community effort and craftsmanship and which enabled him to build in a rudimentary fashion. Now he observed that his crops, his herds, and his companions were recurrently affected by the elements and other obscure forces, good and bad. With this realization, man went from magic to the threshold of religion, to what we call *animism*. Special powers were attributed to gods who were responsible for different phases of life. The new attitude arose from the feeling that there were spiritual entities behind all living things — human, animal, and plant — in addition to their earthly forms.

Where hunting man had visualized in terms of the immediate physical need, the more settled farmer-herder projected himself beyond the everyday and came to see the world as both physical and spiritual. His cultural expression in art became more symbolic and generalized, with fewer details of natural forms; he placed greater emphasis on ideas and emotions than on facts. Since the new religion at this cultural level required symbols of actuality, of the forces that surround man constantly, he ultimately produced such forms as masks, totems, and idols. These forms are to be found not in the New Stone Age cultures themselves but in their modern counterparts in Africa or the Pacific.

Primitive forms of architecture appeared during the New Stone Age, such as the well-known *menhirs*, roughly equivalent to obelisks — enormous, almost casually shaped, upright stones that were revered in a fashion now unknown. More specific in function was the *dolmen*, a tomb of gigantic stones formed into a rectangular chamber and covered with one large slab for a roof. It was generally preceded by a small covered passageway, the entire complex covered with earth in mound form and surrounded by a circle of large stones as a kind of retaining wall for the earth. Today where these monuments are found they show only part of the burial chamber itself (fig. 5), which looks like some gigantic table — and occasionally some of the encircling stones as well, thereby recalling the general shape of a beehive. These dolmens have been discovered in an amazingly wide territory ranging from England, Spain, and the

Fig. 5. Neolithic burial chamber at Locmariaquer (France) known as *La Table des marchands*.

Balearic Islands in western Europe down into northern Africa, Egypt, and across into Syria and the territory of the Black Sea. The significance of this fact is that it lays a Neolithic groundwork for the emergence of civilization. This older culture, which is also referred to as Megalithic, i.e., of gigantic stones, is reflected in later forms such as the *Treasury of Atreus* at Mycenae (see fig. 63).

Within the New Stone Age tombs are found polished stone implements, particularly the triangular-shaped ax heads, or celts. These have a long history stretching from prehistoric times through the pre-Greek period in Crete and on the mainland of Greece up to Roman times and beyond. Wherever they are found, they appear to have been worshiped in some mysterious way. It therefore becomes clear that the shift from the Old to the New Stone Age is not only a change from chipped to polished stone implements. In the previous period the animal on whom life depended was the concrete and immediate object of primitive man's worship, whereas in this later period the ax was presented as a symbol of power, of life-giving force, and even as a kind of sex sign.

In addition these tombs contain a great deal of pottery, the most widespread art of the New Stone Age. Its ornamentation is almost exclusively geometric in character, a fact resulting from a number of practical and other circumstances. In some cases, for example, the pottery (and basketry) imitates earlier containers made of skins or rushes, retaining the original surface markings, textures, and parallel lines. Other types stem from involuntary markings made on the clay as it was being molded or coiled by hand in an era when the potter's wheel was still

8

unknown. A final and very significant type of ornament is geometric-symbolic in character. This is found in such designs as the Egyptian, Mesopotamian, and Iranian pottery of around 4000 B.C. (see fig. 6), in which Neolithic man attained some of his highest decorative achievements. Here we go beyond the mere technical causes and necessities which yielded the first two types of simple, unsymbolic zigzags or crosshatchings. Now we have living forms which, although not represented in the same clear realistic fashion as in Paleolithic art, do suggest specific objects and their characteristics. Probably made for some ritual and religious purpose, this kind of art differs from the purely ornamental and disinterested design application.

The New Stone Age artist (and his later African or Oceanic counterpart) did not try to remember the form of the horse, bison, or ibex as at Altamira and Lascaux; he was instead re-creating in artistic terms the idea itself, whatever it may have been. An earthenware beaker from Susa (fig. 6) excellently illustrates the transition from the representational to the abstract. The decorative band of flamingos around the top of the vessel is already reduced to a series of long parallel lines with smaller oblique lines at the bottom (the feet) and triangular areas above (the heads). This is one step beyond the still recognizable ibex which is well on the way to reduction into two triangles for its body and a double circle for its magnificent horns.

The geometry of the Neolithic level is also evident in the abstracted animals and birds of precolonial pottery and textiles in Latin America (see Peruvian pottery and fabric, figs. 183–184) and in North American Indian pottery and textiles. It occurs again in African and Oceanic art, where this extremely styl-

Fig. 6. Neolithic pottery from Susa (ca. 3000 B.C.). Paris, Louvre.

ized technique persists in bird-form mask ornaments from Senegal, in fish charms hung over the sides of boats by Society Island fishermen, and in other such manifestations.

AFRICAN PRIMITIVE ART. The African continent is in itself an example of the coexistence of Paleolithic and Neolithic levels in civilization — as witness the Bushmen of southern Africa and the West African Negroes. Bushmen in modern times have continued the nomadic lives of their ancient Paleolithic ancestors, still finding their food anywhere and showing no sense of community organization. Africa today contains examples of actual Paleolithic Bushman art and later, more contemporary examples on the same general level as the earlier work (see fig. 2).

The West African Negro, on the other hand, is part of a community cultivating crops for the common welfare and following a predominantly animistic religion in which all objects are endowed with souls. He believes in a world of mysterious powers that can only be conceived through the imagination. We therefore speak of his art (fig. 7) as an attempt to project in symbolic form the spiritual essence of those forces. Like modern Expressionist artists (cf. figs. 524–525) he tries to get beyond the mere physical appearance of things to their essential qualities. On the other hand, the modern Cubist (cf. figs. 517–518) has learned from the African sculptor to reduce shapes to a simplified form in which sharp divided planes become the visible material of the artist.

The mysterious powers which reside in wild animals, the enemy, fire, flood, or ghosts are very real to the West African. His abstract rendering of the idea carries great emotional strength and conviction. To him the sculpture not only represents an idea — it is the idea or the spirit itself. He does not make our distinction between reality and unreality; in creating sculptures, the African artist feels he is creating life itself. But while the masks and statues may be said to serve a utilitarian religious purpose, they never represent gods in our sense. The masks are used

Fig. 7. Ceremonial mask, Belgian Congo. Tervueren, Belgium, Museum of the Belgian Congo.

in a complicated series of rituals whereby the youths of the tribe are sub-
jected to ordeals in order to teach them not to fear the spirits of dangerous beasts, enemy tribes, and other forces — all this before their
ceremonial entry into the state of manhood. During this period the candi-
date is taken away from his home and his face painted with a thick layer
of white clay. The entire process is designed to incarnate in him a new
spirit of life, a vital power of manhood.

It is difficult to be more precise about the function of these masks, since the ceremonies are performed by secret societies whose procedures have
never become fully known. We can only guess that
the mask wearer is himself as frightened as anyone, although he acts as a kind of intercessor, as-
suming this temporary fearsome aspect to help
safeguard the members of the tribe. It does seem
clear, however, that the mask wearer thus aug-
ments his own vital force or soul, his *Nyama*.

It is often maintained that most African sculpture is magical in purpose. It differs in that regard
from our art which, though originally predominantly religious, has become in historical times
mainly an aesthetic activity. While the Africans
have a good many utilitarian art forms such as
pots, weapons, and other objects, these have carvings on them to protect the user or the article itself, and therefore also have ritual meaning. The
many statues of kings take on religious significance
to the extent that the king has attributes of divinity. In addition, some statues are used for healing
purposes, and others have commemorative functions.

Fig. 8. Ancestor cult
statue, Pangwe, Gabun.
Photo courtesy, Segy
Gallery, New York.

Emotionally the African sculptor is animated
by fear of the mysterious elements about him: fear
of the dead, whose good will is constantly sought;
fear of jungle beasts; fear of his fellow man; fear
of the forces of nature. But his motivations run into other channels as
well. His great interest in the souls of the dead and his strong efforts to
reinstall those souls among the living, through the medium of sculptured
forms, result in the many ancestor portraits found in this art (fig. 8).

The West African name for statue expresses the idea of "spirit trap" or "god trap" in which an abstract spirit is given corporeal shape or a home is provided for the spirit of an ancestor. Here the vital or life force, i.e., the soul, of an ancestor is held, and those of mythical animals that constitute the family totem. There are many aspects of life in which the ancestor's help is invoked, and so the statue containing his life force is kept available. It is problematical to what extent this custom is connected with the ancestor statue and its *ka*, or life force, in ancient Egypt's cult of the dead, but the resemblance is striking.

Another important drive toward sculptural form among the Africans, as among other primitives such as the Northwest American Indians, is totemism. This concept involves an identification between human beings and other living beings (sometimes even objects) which have meaning in the history of the human group or tribe. The Indian conceives of the animal as the founder of the clan; the African, as a helper or protector of the founder. Each clan has a different totem animal. Through this totem primitive man secures a certain release from fear by objectifying its power in living form. It also serves to give the possessor some of the qualities of the animal involved — its speed, strength, or aggressiveness. In the early days of social organizing, the identification of many individuals with the same animal brought them together as distinct from others with a different totem.

The aesthetic concepts implicit in African figure sculpture, whether of humans or of animals, involve a starkness of mood — as we have already noted in considering the fear-laden emotions of the creators and users of these objects. Always recognizable as a human body, head, or animal form, the African sculpture removes itself from naturalism by geometricizing each form and by relating one geometric shape to another. In many of the standing male or female figures, the artist projects a series of cones, cylinders, or other shapes, rhythmically arranged in sequences so as to emphasize some form or emotional characteristic of the object or the emotional idea the artist wishes to convey. While there is no lack of curved forms, even these have an angularity, a jerkiness of application and arrangement that characterizes the entire approach which is so much dominated by intense emotionality and fear.

Although these African parallels with New Stone Age society and culture are historically recent, the fact is that these sculptures now belong to a somewhat indefinite past. Most of the African objects found in the museums were made at least a century ago, and in some cases as long as three or four centuries before the penetration of the continent by Europeans. By the eighteenth century of our era, Negro art was already in a state of decline.

12

OCEANIAN PRIMITIVE ART. The term Oceania embraces Australia, Melanesia, Micronesia, and Polynesia (map, fig. 9). Each of these cultural areas shows certain parallels with at least one of the others, so that they form a related network — even though it would be difficult to find one stylistic feature common to the whole group. The various populations of this vast segment of the earth's surface are made up of the descendants of many waves of immigrants from the mainland of Asia. Those ancestors of the present inhabitants of Oceania had different racial origins and belonged to equally different levels of cultural evolution. The varying types of civilization now found in this region have grown up relatively undisturbed by outside influences (unlike those of Africa); but constant movement between the many islands has tended to diffuse cultural ideas, including art forms.

Originally all tools were made of wood with attached blades or heads of shell or stone. Livelihood was generally derived from agriculture or fishing; by the very nature of the small land areas inhabited, these races must be classified as settled and, in our terms, Neolithic peoples. Architecture, sculpture, and painting are of or on wood, and in some cases

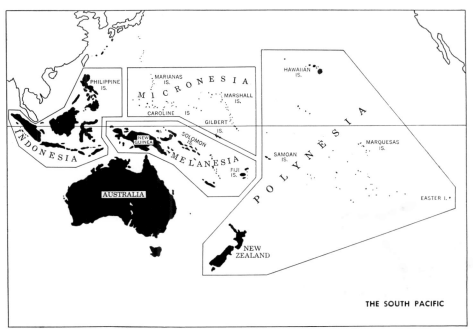

Fig. 9. Oceania. (Adapted from Paul S. Wingert, *Art of the South Pacific Islands*, New York, Beechhurst Press, 1953. By permission of the author.)

stone is employed. Often the three arts are combined, as in the elaborate carved men's houses and similar edifices; sculpture is usually colored with earth or vegetable pigments. Basketry is a widespread art throughout the South Pacific, but pottery occurs primarily in the Melanesian area. As in Africa, ancestor worship, animism, and totemism provide basic motivations for art, however differently expressed in the distant parts of this great area.

Although there are no precise limits to the geographical extent and character of the major art areas of Oceania, certain broad generalizations are possible. According to one system of classification, there are three broad stylistic trends. The first deals with highly simplified or abstracted natural forms in which any ornamentation derives from the function of the object and the technique by which it is made. This type occurs in Micronesia, including the Marianas, Caroline, Marshall, and Gilbert Islands. It may be illustrated by the house mask (fig. 10) from Mortlock Island, very reminiscent in form of the paintings of the modern German

Fig. 10. House mask, Mortlock Island, South Pacific. Philadelphia, University of Pennsylvania Museum.

14

Expressionist Jawlensky and the sculptures of the modern primitivist Modigliani. The intensity of expression in this and similar works results from the violent reduction of the human face to a series of elongated ellipses for eyes, mouth, and lips, as though the face were deliberately "tightened" for purposes of increasing tension and emotion. This mask served as a gable ornament in a "men's house," a ceremonial center and council house which was also used as social center by the men of the community.

A second area of Oceanic art is focused around Polynesia and includes the Hawaiian, Marquesas, and Samoan Islands, Easter Island, and New Zealand. Here the forms of nature are geometricized and embellished with involved surface decorations. This style may be illustrated by the well-known carved wooden clubs of the Marquesas Islands (fig. 11), whose tops suggest human heads. They are covered with a relatively complex Neolithic-type surface ornament, as well as a number of small human heads, the latter in a stark geometric simplified form. This kind of club was a regular part of every Marquesan man's equipment in a culture where the innumerable small tribes were at constant war with each other, because of the insatiable needs of their practices of cannibalism and human sacrifice. In everyday usage, the club could be leaned on while conversing. Other art objects in this society include demonic figures which were part of sorcerers' equipment for the trapping of souls.

Fig. 11. Carved club head, Marquesas Islands, South Pacific. Salem, Peabody Museum of Salem.

These are called *tikis* and may be of wood or stone, the chief materials available in this part of the world.

Although the cultures of Polynesia (like those of the rest of Oceania)

developed relatively unaffected by their more civilized neighbors, the original settlers had come from Indonesia, as is felt quite clearly in the sophisticated and involved art of the New Zealand Maoris. In richly carved canoe prows, house posts and lintels (fig. 12), war clubs, and other items, this proud warlike race has developed an art as intricate as the Neolithic Celtic enameled bronzes of the pre-Christian period in Europe or their later Irish counterparts (see fig. 217). Yet on further examination, the Maori objects reflect a relatively savage people; the conventionalized human and animal heads show overtones of fear as plainly as do the arts of Africa.

As in the Marquesas and other primitive societies, there are two different methods of expression among the Maoris: one involving the women's arts — the making of baskets, cloaks, mats, and the like, in which a rather simple angular geometric style appears; another the men's arts of wood carving of weapons, house decorating, and tattooing, where the style is curvilinear as seen above, with a wild exultant sweeping quality. Considering the high skill necessary for such work, we are reminded of the special status of the artist in primitive communities of this kind.

Fig. 12. Carved house post, Maori, New Zealand. Toronto, Royal Ontario Museum.

The third general stylistic type in the Pacific is found in Melanesia, a wide area covering a broad semicircle of islands northeast of the Australian mainland. These include New Guinea, New Britain, the Admiralty and Solomon Islands, together with the New Hebrides and New Caledonia. Basic to this art is a distortion of natural form and its arrangement in rhythmic curves. The style may be exemplified in a general way (there are many variations) by the dance mask from the Gulf of Papua in New Guinea (fig. 13). Such objects were part of elaborate ceremonials preceded at one time by human sacrifice, after which men appeared wearing huge bark-cloth masks from 9 to 13 feet long, the bark stretched over palm-wood frames. These large masks and the smaller type illustrated are not made by the professional artist but by the group which is entitled to the protection of the particular spirit portrayed. Our example characteristically emphasizes the large open mouth and menacing teeth; the rest of the face is divided into a series of organic or plantlike abstractions of eyes, forehead, hair, and other parts. Here we feel an affinity on the one hand with the folk-dance rituals of Mexico and Brazil, with their wickerwork frames to which large papier-mâché and other forms are attached, and on the other hand with those of Africa, with their analogous animistic and totemistic purposes.

Fig. 13. Dance mask, Gulf of Papua, New Guinea, South Pacific. Newark Museum.

The Australian aborigines were among the least developed of primitive peoples. When Europeans first came to that continent, the natives knew nothing of pottery or of houses in the conventional sense, often living in caves like Old Stone Age man. Their art, like that of the later Old Stone Age, may be placed somewhere between naturalism and the symbolic stylization of the New Stone Age; this would bring them within the orbit of some of our Oceanic peoples.

One of the most interesting art forms of the Australian native is the so-called "X-ray" painting on bark, in which vividly portrayed semi-naturalistic animal and fish forms are shown in outline with a clear but

Fig. 14. Mimi Spirits (bark drawing). Arnhem Land, Australia.

naïve view of their inner organs. Equally interesting are their portrayals of human beings and their preoccupation with the world of spirits. A bark drawing by an aboriginal artist from Arnhem Land in northern Australia (fig. 14) shows the mythical Mimi spirits who are believed to inhabit rocky caves in the west of that area. They are supposed to be so thin that they hunt only on calm days, since the lightest breeze can blow them away. In this painting they are shown holding a ceremony for a human whom they have lured to their camp. Frightening in a fanciful way that suggests the modern painter Paul Klee (see fig. 527), these works express a kind of naïveté and imaginative charm, the marvelous spirit world with which primitive man is constantly concerned.

PRIMITIVE ART OF THE AMERICAS. The Eskimos of northwest North America also belong to the world's primitive cultures. Unlike the Oceanic peoples, most of whom subsisted on agriculture and fishing in settled communities, the Eskimos of Alaska have no knowledge of agriculture. They live by fishing and hunting, eating wild berries, often moving from one area to another with the seasons or the movement of game.

Although a good many of their art objects are of bone and ivory, driftwood has enabled them to produce ladles, bowls, and ceremonial masks in wood also. Belief in a life after death induces a cult of the dead, and the profound belief in spirits is associated with the typical totemism of the primitive world. Their ivory carvings frequently show

18

very naturalistic animals such as bears, seals, walruses, and other beasts necessary for the continuance of life; these furnish food, clothing, and fuel for lighting. On this level the Eskimos may be said to approximate Old Stone Age man. Their religion, however, is that of New Stone Age man, with belief in animism and totemism and the need to represent in tangible form certain spiritual forces. In their ceremonial masks, rattles, and spirit catchers (in which the wandering souls of the sick are held until returned to their owners) the representations are abstract and fear-inspiring in the African and Oceanian sense. This is clearly illustrated in the brilliantly colored totem poles (fig. 15), which are genealogical summaries of each clan or grouping and contain powerfully emotive abstractions of human and animal forms.

Fig. 15. Totem pole, Thunderbird Park, Victoria, B.C., Canada.

In some parts of the Northwest an extremely skillful and fairly complex form of decorative abstraction has been produced by the Indians, the Thlinkit and Haida, for example. This type of ornament is characterized by squared-off sections of bold linear patterns with rounded edges, in which the artist never loses sight of his original beaver, raven, or other image. These Indians are also interested in portraying the internal structure of man and beast, frequently creating transparent forms that reveal various organs inside the body. Although there is no direct connection, this practice suggests the "X-ray" figures of Australian primitive painting.

The Indians of the southwest United States established settled communities a few millennia ago. So-called pueblos (many-storied houses) were built and were occupied by large numbers of people. These Indians had a highly developed agricultural system with irrigation ditches, as well as a fine geometrically decorated type of ceramic and textile art, completely typical of the Neolithic stage of man's development. The applied arts of the Hopis, Pueblos, and other tribes in the area north of the Rio Grande may be compared with those of the precolonial peoples of Middle and South America (see Chapter 9), whose works reflect a higher cultural evolvement.

We have seen that the periods of development termed Old Stone Age and New Stone Age follow different time schedules in different parts of the world. But in general the geometric abstraction — with or without symbolic meaning — typifies the latter stage. The worldwide extent of Neolithic culture, appearing among the distant peoples at varying times, stands as the foundation on which man in the next stage of cultural evolution builds his civilizations.

2 / ANCIENT EGYPT

EGYPT and the Near East, the starting points for the story of Western art, have their roots in prehistoric forms and ideas. The historical period of those civilizations begins shortly after 3000 B.C., but there is earlier and related material in predynastic Egypt, Neolithic Mesopotamia and Iran (see fig. 6), and the strikingly similar art objects found in ancient India.

The recorded past in Egypt and the Mesopotamian Near East goes back some five thousand years. By about 3000 B.C. the social order in Egypt had developed governmental forms, religion, and technical and cultural skills as elements of civilized living. These advances in community existence constitute a great step beyond the relatively primitive status of the preceding Neolithic period; and yet a great many ideas, particularly in religion and government, had evolved directly from those of the New Stone Age. For the arts this was of particular importance, since in most parts of the ancient world they were still used for glorifying the deified ruler and for ancestor worship and the cult of the dead. To that extent the arts would necessarily retain form ideas from the past.

RELATIONSHIP OF THE ANCIENT CULTURES. From the end of the New Stone Age (ca. 4000–ca. 3000 B.C.) to the beginnings of the classical age in Greece (ca. 500 B.C.), the arts of almost the entire ancient world were dominated by the decorative and abstract geometrical concepts of the New Stone Age. Specific similarities exist in Egypt, Mesopotamia, Persia, Crete, archaic Greece, and other Mediterranean cultures such as Cyprus and the Hittite lands. In this broad geographical and chronological area we find a constant tension between the naturalism of the Old Stone Age (which had never disappeared entirely) and the geometric style of the recent New Stone Age. Real things were still portrayed, but their forms were controlled and altered by the strong impulse toward abstraction. A similar set of circumstances conditioned the development of art in the Far East. One of the most striking evidences of this connection with a prehistoric past can be seen in the continuing difference between the naturalism of animal portrayal and the schematic and abstracted portrayal of human beings.

The growth of these ancient cultures in the Mediterranean had been abetted, at least in part, by military force and religious pressure; primitive kinship units had expanded into large social organisms through centuries-long conquest. In each case, this had produced a society which believed in the divine origin of its customs and attributed the success of its conquests to the old gods, who were henceforth considered infallible. As the earthly representatives of those gods (particularly the priesthood) grew powerful, there came into being an arrogance and intolerance, a demand for cultural homogeneity much like modern totalitarianism, that centered in a royal dynasty with both religious and secular authority. Accordingly, ancient Mediterranean civilization developed a monolithic social outlook, favoring long-lived and rigid political systems, religions, and artistic viewpoints. A reluctance to alter religious or social institutions found reflection in an unwillingness to change the artistic forms of expression dedicated to glorifying those institutions. Over an impressively long period of history, art was dominated by a fixed abstract geometric ideal, each area of the ancient world holding tenaciously to its own interpretation.

EGYPT: OLD KINGDOM. In Egypt the military-religious stage of civilization, the period of cultural homogeneity, fostered a professional class of artists catering to a sophisticated audience. At first an experimental attitude, with a new and higher standard of craftsmanship, produced more naturalism than the New Stone Age formal approach. But the increasingly rigid cultural attitudes of the ruling elite tended to suppress experimental vigor and to support a tradition-bound outlook. While the sculpture of the early Egyptian dynasties (Old Kingdom) had a strongly individualistic flavor, that of the Middle Kingdom and Empire periods gradually became formal and inflexible, the expression of an absolute society.

Pyramids and mastabas. The monuments of the Old Kingdom (dynasties III–VI, ca. 2700–ca. 2200 B.C.) are massive evidence of the profound Egyptian concern with life after death. The best resources of art and engineering were lavished on tombs and their decoration. Even more than in later periods, elaborate precautions were taken to preserve the body as a place of refuge for the *ka*, or double, a life force coexistent and identical in appearance with the body. The early Egyptians did not view the afterlife as a release from the travail of this world; they were interested in extending earthly existence by every possible means. Strong and even permanent tomb structures were built for the royal family and

Fig. 16. Pyramid of King Sahure, Abusir (ca. 2250 B.C.). Reproduction. New York, Metropolitan Museum of Art.

smaller mastabas for the nobility (*mastaba*, Arabic for bench, cf. figs. 16–17). These are provided with inaccessible coffin chambers from which the mummified body can be removed only with great difficulty. Every pyramid and mastaba also has a statue chamber, or residence for the ka, in which a stone statue is placed and to which the ka may return should the body be destroyed. The mastaba includes this statue chamber within the structure itself; the pyramid has it in an outside temple dedicated

Fig. 17. Mastaba model. New York, Metropolitan Museum of Art.

Fig. 18. The Sphinx and the Pyramids, Gizeh, Egypt.

to the buried king. Both pyramid temple and mastaba hold a third unit, the chapel where offerings were made to the ka; here paintings and reliefs are projected on the walls. These contain messages to propitiate the gods and scenes from the deceased's earthly existence, designed to help the ka in the next world (see figs. 23, 31).

It is logical to assume that the mastaba with its flat top, sloping walls, and generally modest size is an early tomb reflecting a predynastic stage of Egyptian history, before any one person possessed the enormous power necessary to build a pyramid. The so-called Step Pyramid of Zoser at Sakkara (early Third dynasty) seems to be an intermediate form. This large structure with recessed steps or setbacks, moving from a broad base to a narrow top, looks like a number of successively smaller mastabas piled on each other.

The classic pyramid, such as those of Cheops, Chephren, and Mencheres at Gizeh (fig. 18), belongs to the Pharaohs of the Fourth dynasty (2650–2500 B.C.) and reflects the solidification of royal power at that time. Thousands of workmen were needed to perform the enormous labor of dragging the huge stones to the spot and lifting them into place. The Great Pyramid of Cheops — an engineering tour de force — rises to a height of 475 feet from a square base measuring about 760 feet on each side; the massive blocks were raised into carefully calculated positions with the most primitive machinery. Originally sheathed in polished marble for enrichment and to help hide the tomb entrance (traces of the marble may still be seen at the top of Chephren's pyramid), none of these great tombs has been found in modern times with its contents intact.

In the pyramid temples and mastabas, the images of the deceased were in stone, as permanent a material as possible. These statues might be standing, sitting, or kneeling, but had to conform to the strictest geometric formality; their various parts were parallel to the vertical and horizontal lines of the original rectangular block and were contained within the dimensions of that block. The figure itself was so posed that it faced squarely front and could be divided into two equal parts. Sculptures like the *Menkure and His Queen* (fig. 19) and the well-known

Fig. 19. Menkure and His Queen. Courtesy, Museum of Fine Arts, Boston.

Fig. 20. Sheikh-el-Beled
(wood). Cairo Museum.

Sheikh-el-Beled (Sheikh of the Village, fig. 20) illustrate this prescribed arrangement: the head, shoulders, and hips are placed in parallel lines, and other parts of the body are made parallel to these. Arms are held rigidly at the sides; feet are set flatly on the ground, one before the other, in a formal rather than natural pose. Yet within these restrictions all three faces show a striking naturalism that is characteristic of earlier Egyptian art, more in the Sheikh (fig. 21) — probably an overseer or other minor functionary — than in the royal couple.

The reliefs, paintings, and painted reliefs on the walls of mastabas and pyramid temples exhibit the same conflict between Old Stone Age naturalism and New Stone Age

Fig. 21. Sheikh-el-Beled
(head). Cairo Museum.

26

formalism. This eternal problem is best seen in the portrayal of animal and bird forms, which maintained a high degree of naturalness throughout Egyptian history no matter how formalized human depictions became. The difference between human and animal portrayal is one of the distinguishing marks of the period between 3000 B.C. and 500 B.C., applying equally to Mesopotamia, Persia, and Crete.

The *Geese of Medum* (fig. 22), a painted panel from a tomb chapel of the Old Kingdom, has a real feeling for the form and movement of these fowl in spite of the formal composition and two-dimensional shapes. This sensation of reality recalls the cave paintings of the Old Stone Age, and yet the figures here are elegantly stylized with the outside and inside pairs neatly balancing each other in a highly decorative manner.

Fig. 22. The Geese of Medum. Cairo Museum.

More formal is the painted relief of *Ti Hunting the Hippopotamus* (fig. 23) from the mastaba of Ti at Sakkara. It typifies the Egyptian principle of "frontality" as applied to a painted or relief-carved human form, fulfilling the artist's compulsive, perhaps magic-conveying, desire for completeness. Ti's figure (far larger than that of the servants, since he is more important) is presented according to a visual formula characteristic of the ancient Near East as a whole, but especially of Egypt. Although the man is viewed from the side, the upper part of his body faces front, the shoulders brought forward and flattened against the wall's surface; and the eye is drawn in full, although the head is turned sideways. Since most of Egyptian art is made for life in the hereafter, the artist does not describe the *fact* of Ti hunting so much as the *idea* thereof, a symbolic and abstract representation which controls action and pose as carefully as the three-dimensional sculptures seen earlier. All forms are carved on the same level of low relief, frozen into permanent immobility as ideographs of actuality. The people who hunt with Ti are considered of little account, since they are socially inferior beings used for a specific purpose like the hunted animals themselves and similarly are shown with more naturalistic form and action.

Fig. 23. Ti Hunting the Hippopotamus. Relief sculpture from Tomb of Ti, Sakkara.

MIDDLE KINGDOM AND EMPIRE. After the Old Kingdom period the monarchy disintegrated into a group of autonomous regions or nomes. From about 2200 to 2100 B.C., during an era of feudalism, irrigation deteriorated and agriculture suffered. In Egypt, religion and the fertility of the soil were inseparable. The beneficence of the sun was worshiped as Ra, that of the earth as Isis, and that of the Nile as Osiris. Inevitably, then, the priesthood emerged as the great power, for they alone knew how to propitiate the gods. Religion finally became, and was to remain, the most important element of Egyptian life.

Valley of the Tombs. By the Middle Kingdom and Empire periods, 2100–1788 B.C. and 1580–1090 B.C., respectively, there was a marked change from the Pharaonic pyramids (symbols of absolute rule) to magnificent temple structures. Although life after death was still vital and every precaution was taken to ensure it, the approach was no longer overwhelmingly powerful. The Pharaohs now were buried in tombs deeply tunneled into the rock of the hills, in the Valley of the Tombs of the Kings beyond the cliffs on the western side of the Nile. Impressive mortuary temples were provided at some distance away, near the river, oriented directly on the tombs themselves, to serve in place of the outside chapels formerly attached to pyramids. Dedicated to the gods during the lifetime of the Pharaoh, the temple became a burial chapel after his death, bringing the king and the gods into a new, almost interchangeable relationship.

The most striking of these valley tomb-temples is that of Queen Hatshepsut, an Eighteenth dynasty ruler, at Deir el-Bahri (fig. 24). As reconstructed, this beautifully proportioned building is approached by a double row of sphinxes (each with the head of the queen) that leads through a ceremonial gateway or pylon into a tree-filled open court. Here the line of sphinxes continues up a gentle incline to the first terrace, which has in front an open colonnade of simple, geometrically shaped columns. At this level a more extensive columnar arrangement begins at the right, moves along the rear, and ends in a small temple at the left. A second ramp leads to the next terrace (more than 300 feet across) where another row of columns forms an enclosure containing an altar to the sun god and facilities on each side for worship of the queen's spirit. Within the cliff itself, a room held the image of the cow-headed goddess Hathor, the queen's special divinity.

The building has many effective aspects. Horizontal and vertical accents on the temple are counterpoised and have further relationship to the horizontal lines of the cliffs and to their vertical, almost columnar

Fig. 24. Mortuary Temple of Queen Hatshepsut, Deir el-Bahri. Model in Metropolitan Museum of Art, New York.

Fig. 25. Mortuary Temple of Queen Hatshepsut, Deir el-Bahri.

indentations (fig. 25). Designing this structure to fit into its natural environment is a conscious triumph of architectural planning. Just as remarkable is the delicate proportion of the whole extensive and panoramic arrangement, placed as it is against the gigantic cliffs into which we are imperceptibly led. Finally, the simple geometry of verticals, horizontals, open squares, and rectangles is beautifully balanced by the chaste simplicity of individual columns, either rectangular in outline or with beveled surfaces that anticipate the shape of later Greek columns.

The great temples. A more typical monument of the Egypt of that period than the tomb-temple would be a gigantic, outright temple — its great size being an index of the augmented power of the priesthood. The general plan and function of such a building may be seen in the *Temple of Khons at Karnak* (fig. 26), erected by Rameses III (1198–1167 B.C.)

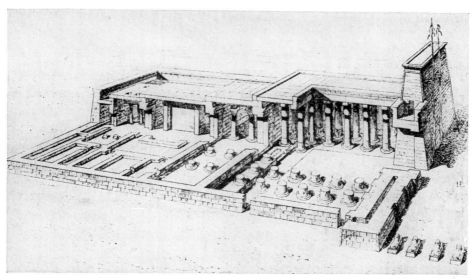

Fig. 26. Temple of Khons, Karnak. Reconstruction after Perrot and Chipiez.

during the Twentieth dynasty. Although not nearly so monumental as other structures of the Empire period, it is much more homogeneous than the larger temples to which many different generations contributed.

The approach to the huge pylon gateway is also through a double row of sphinxes (lion- or ram-headed, cf. fig. 27). It ends with a pair of colossal seated figures of the ruler and memorial obelisks describing his accomplishments, placed at either side of the pylon gate. The gateway

Fig. 27. Temple of Ammon, Karnak. Avenue of ram-headed sphinxes and pylon gate.

Fig. 28. Temple of Ammon, Karnak. The Hypostyle Hall. Model in Metropolitan Museum of Art, New York.

itself slopes from a broad base to a narrower top ornamented by concave molding. Upon entering, one arrives at a large, open, colonnaded court-yard — which is as far as the average unimportant individual was al-lowed to go. A more illustrious personage would have proceeded into the next section, a lower and roofed-over area supported by many rows of columns. This is the hypostyle hall, shaped somewhat like the later Christian basilica with relatively dark side aisles and a center aisle il-luminated by rays of light from a clerestory (a windowed section raised higher) above the columns. Finally, the last portion of the temple — dark, low, and mysterious — where the shrine of the god was located was reserved for the royal family and the priestly hierarchy.

We get a more detailed view in a reconstruction of the *Hypostyle Hall of the Temple of Ammon at Karnak* (fig. 28), a gigantic structure of the Nineteenth dynasty (1350–1200 B.C.). This section is about 330 feet wide by 170 feet deep, equipped with columns about 70 feet high and 12 feet in diameter. It is in its way fully as impressive as the pyra-mids themselves. The pyramids, though far wider and higher, are still inert masses of stone; the *Hypostyle Hall*, even without the rest of the temple, presents the spectacle of a huge building in constant use whose size dwarfs humankind into insignificance. From the reconstructed model we can see that the temple interiors were covered with painted reliefs extending over the entire surfaces of the central and side columns. These columns, much higher at the hall's center than at its sides, are topped by capitals whose shapes are generally derived from plant forms. The center capitals open up like the tops of lotus plants, so large that approxi-mately seventy men could stand on each; the side capitals are derived from papyrus buds.

Seen at close range (fig. 29), the columns of Karnak reveal some-thing of the Egyptian planner's almost frantic desire for all-over deco-rative effect combined with narrative needs. The result is a balancing of symbolic representation with hieroglyphic picture writing. If we can visualize the original luxurious (and to us perhaps garish) color on these incised forms, the music, incense, elaborate costumes and cere-monies, the constant striving for religious melodrama, we find a situa-tion comparable in effect to that of the great medieval cathedrals. In the Egyptian temple, as in those much later churches, there is the same impression of a ceiling lost in the upper reaches of the building; here the beams are hidden by the wide-spreading capitals of the central col-umns.

Yet the total effect of such Egyptian temples is neither harmonious in the finely proportioned and balanced Greek sense (see fig. 85) nor

Fig. 29. Temple of Ammon, Karnak. Detail of Hypostyle Hall columns.

dynamic and spacious in the rhythmical fashion of the Gothic (see fig. 270). It is often rather lumpy and heavy; the architect relied on mass rather than on space for his basic effect, adding a kind of ornament that frequently does not jibe with the general shape of the building — in contrast to the other systems just mentioned. Utilizing the simplest architectural principle, that of the post and lintel (two verticals capped by a horizontal), the Egyptian builder ended with a somewhat unsubtle shape in which the joining and fitting skill of the pyramids is no longer evident. Now the blocks are kept in place by sheer weight alone. In the same way, we may feel a certain inadequacy in a decorative system that treats the cylindrical columns as billboards: i.e., as surfaces to be plastered with reliefs, paintings, and hieroglyphics. The latter run in horizontal bands, negating the basic verticality of the columns, and cannot therefore be considered successfully integrated with the building as a whole. A final feature of disorganization is added by the fact that many Pharaohs wished to associate themselves with such an important building as the Temple of Ammon at Karnak. Over a period of about two thousand years, dynasty after dynasty left its mark on this increasingly complex structure by additions that would link their names with that of the great god. From the Middle Kingdom on, this had seemed the best way to immortality.

It is true that all Egyptian architecture does not suffer from these defects or to this degree. As we have seen, the tomb-temple of Queen Hatshepsut is a beautifully proportioned and designed structure. Similarly, in the neighborhood of Karnak is the great Temple of Luxor, also dedicated to Ammon. Here a more graceful and effective post-and-lintel arrangement utilizes a column based on a cluster of papyrus buds tied together below the top. This alone makes a harmonious vertical effect far different in quality from the relatively stumpy columns of Karnak.

Apart from this successful abstraction of a nature motif and the resultant vertical effect, however, the blending of painting and sculpture with the architecture again leaves something to be desired. Here at Luxor we are much impressed with the series of 20-foot-high sculptures of the great conqueror *Rameses II* (fig. 30); but once more we

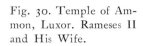

Fig. 30. Temple of Ammon, Luxor. Rameses II and His Wife.

do not feel any integral relationship between sculpture and architecture as in Greek or Gothic arrangements. The figures appear rather to have been pushed into open spaces between the columns; they could just as easily have been placed elsewhere. In contrast to the integration of arts achieved in later styles, it would seem that the Egyptian builder was primarily interested in permanence, and his decorative arrangements therefore were bound to be more practical (symbolically and religiously practical) than aesthetic.

Sculptures like the *Rameses II* at Luxor may be contrasted in a general way with such Old Kingdom standing figures as *Menkure and His Queen* (fig. 19). The latter, as already noted, contains certain naturalistic elements within the rigid and prescribed formulas and even a modicum of familial feeling. By the Empire period, however, Egyptian sculpture and painting had assumed a marked formality and actual courtliness, the naturalistic element dropping out almost entirely. Far more than before, the king was now a symbol of authority instead of a human personality. Even the traditional title by which he was known, Pharaoh, or "Great House," indicates the generalizing, the oblique importance of his position. The naturalism that had carried over from primitive times into the still fluid Old Kingdom — and further, into early Middle Kingdom (i.e., Twelfth dynasty) art — disappeared with the triumph of religion. At this point a symbolic rather than real Pharaonic representation seemed more desirable; naturalism continued only in animal portrayal, still under Old Stone Age influence. Finally, stereotyped royal figures could be turned out in profusion to supply the administration in various parts of an expanding empire.

In the *Rameses II*, it is difficult to discern any personal features whatever. Instead there is symbolic reference to his power and importance, to the fact that this is his part of the temple. His wife is reduced to a tiny figure about a quarter the size of the Pharaoh, whose calf she is touching. Here again, the importance of persons is indicated by their relative size, a device also used in Greek and medieval European art. This lady presents a marked contrast in social position to Menkure's queen. But the systematic frontality of the figure, the position of arms and legs, the width of shoulders, the parallelisms of various parts of the body — all these elements remain the same through the Old Kingdom, the Empire, and the period of Greek occupation of Egypt under the Ptolemies (323–30 B.C.).

In relief sculpture and painting also, the formal frontalized viewpoint is continuously maintained. The more directly a personage confronts the spectator, the more impressive it was considered to be. Reliefs of the Middle Kingdom and Empire periods show a high degree of abstract refinement that sums up the deliberately assumed artificiality of the Egyptian method. The rule of "frontality" is the product of a long evolution and is a conscious choice to fulfill a symbolic and hieratic social purpose.

A relief from the Temple of Seti I (the immediate predecessor of Rameses II) at Abydos, *Seti I with Horus and Isis* (fig. 31), exemplifies the delicate execution of the better reliefs. The tight smoothness of contour and essentially sophisticated simplifications of form demand from

Fig. 31. Temple of Seti I, Abydos. Relief sculpture with Seti I, Horus, and Isis.

the spectator, ancient or modern, a type of aesthetic judgment that is not required when looking at a naturalistic work. This factor, as well as the relief's traditional frontality, is an expression of the highly civilized and courtly society for which the work was done. It is by no means accidental that a modern symbolic painter like Paul Gauguin (see fig. 514) should have been directly influenced by the suave contours and abstractions of Egyptian reliefs and paintings. Through these consciously sought principles, together with the two-dimensional and flattened space, the modern painter also could try to control reality. Both ancient and modern artist would seem to have been well aware of what they were doing, and their art therefore must be looked upon as a purposely devised mechanism rather than as aberration or incompetence.

By adopting his artificial and conventionalizing devices, the Egyptian artist removed the accidental elements of naturalism and shaped his figures within the compass of very strict rules, while still exhibiting a personal skill which was undoubtedly appreciated by his patrons. He arranged and rearranged reality so that it became a symbolic and abstract quantity with lines and forms disposed completely by design. Seti, the great soldier-king, is seen in the center between the goddess Isis and her son, the hawk-headed sky god Horus, who holds in one of his hands a symbolic object which he is transmitting to the Pharaoh. In spite of the smooth outlines and the elegance of pose, however, even an unusually fine relief like this lacks a certain amount of balance, a characteristic defect of an art which was more practical in application than aesthetically integrated.

Akhenaton. For a brief period during the reign of Amenophis IV (or Akhenaton, 1375–1358 B.C.), the adherence to formal distortion was broken down. In opposition to the deeply ingrained idea of a widespread hierarchy of gods, Akhenaton (i.e., faithful to Aton) tried to substitute one god, symbolized by Aton the sun, whose life-giving rays shed their beneficence on all. But his new capital at Tel el 'Amarna was kept iso-

Fig. 32. Amenophis IV (Akhenaton) and His Wife Nefertiti. Berlin, State Museums.

38

lated by the powerful priests of Ammon-Ra at Thebes, the traditional center of the kingdom. After his death, Egypt slipped quietly back into its former habits. Akhenaton had sponsored a new style of painting and sculpture at Amarna, reflecting the changed attitudes of his court and time, but this art immediately yielded to the previous formalism as soon as its protector disappeared from the scene.

A characteristic and beautiful example of the short-lived style is the charming, almost modern limestone relief showing *Amenophis IV (Akhenaton) and His Wife Nefertiti* (fig. 32). We may readily contrast the informality of pose and personalized characteristics of this royal couple with the stiffness of position and purely symbolic attitudes in the relief of Seti I. Yet the conventions of frontality are still observed even in this strongly antitraditional work, producing a curious blend of formalism and casualness. The negligent pose of the Pharaoh, the simplicity of Nefertiti's gesture as she offers flowers to be smelled, the feeling of people out in a real garden — all these take place within the framework of frontality, of arbitrarily proportioned figures.

The influence of this breath of life, this new feeling for natural expression, carried over briefly into the reign of Akhenaton's son-in-law Tutankhamen, whose tomb was discovered by Carnarvon and Carter in 1922. A back panel on the throne of this ruler (Cairo Museum) shows a scene which is close in feeling to that of Akhenaton and Nefertiti.

But the retroaction soon set in. Egyptian art once more solidified in its rigid code, until after the conquest by Alexander the Great in the fourth century b.c. and the end of the Egyptian dynasties proper. The monuments of Egyptian tradition symbolize the cultural uniformity of this military-religious stage of human development, which encompasses the story of Egypt and its Mesopotamian neighbors.

3 / ANCIENT MESOPOTAMIA
AND PERSIA

IN the valley of the Tigris and Euphrates Rivers in western Asia — the area known as Mesopotamia — at about the same time as in Egypt and arising out of similar prehistoric circumstances, another monumental civilization appeared (map, fig. 33). Its religions also were based on nature deities — gods of the sky, air, earth, water, sun, and moon; but its basic outlook differed markedly from that of its neighbors to the west. The Egyptians labored endlessly to continue life in the hereafter, but the people of the Valley of the Two Rivers took a gloomy view of the shadowy next world and were less interested. While the Egyptian belief in an afterlife recurs later in the Christian faith, the Mesopotamian viewpoint reappears in the Greek Hades and the Hebrew Sheol.

The dynamic character of the Mesopotamian milieu partly explains this basic difference in attitude. Egypt was sheltered, enclosed, and static, conditions making for stability and continuity. Meanwhile its neighbor suffered perennial invasions from nearby land-hungry desert countries, and over the millennia the centers of power often shifted from north to south within the Mesopotamian area. The civilization of this valley was easily as old as that of Egypt, but by no means as polished. Forced by events into an aggressive pattern, it was more overtly militaristic and cruel, emotional and fatalistic, like the desert people from whom it perpetually defended itself. Control of the valley and its adjacent regions depended on a constant assertion of power.

The fluctuating situation prevented the undisputed rule of a Pharaonic "great house" with its immense building programs and precluded the sense of an unchanging and everlasting existence — even through death — which underlay Egyptian culture. The rulers of Sumer, Akkad, Babylonia, and Assyria emphasized not the permanent tombs and almost indestructible temples of Egypt, but practical and ephemeral brick structures for everyday use. They were content with unbaked (or

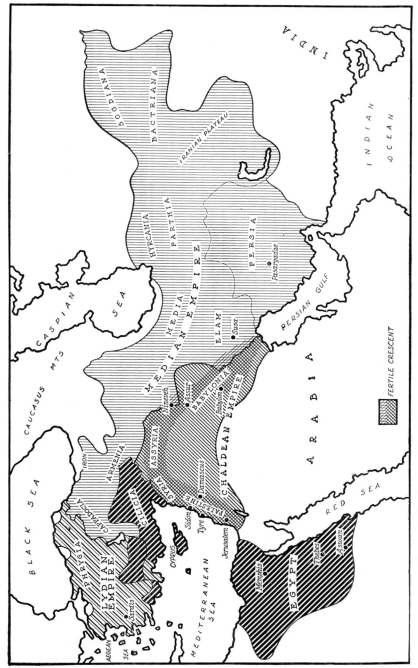

Fig. 33. The Ancient World. (From Henry S. Lucas, *A Short History of Civilization*, New York, McGraw-Hill Book Company, Inc., 1953. By permission of the author.)

Fig. 34. Ziggurat of Ur. Reconstruction by University Museum, University of Pennsylvania.

occasionally baked) brick, an extremely temporary material whose crumbling away complicates the problem of archaeology in this area.

THE SUMERIANS. Our first record of Mesopotamian culture is in Sumer and Akkad (ca. 3000–1900 B.C.). In an era of city-states ruled by deputies of the local gods, frequent conflicts developed military knowledge. Agriculture was the chief occupation, and they engaged in active commerce with foreign countries, an important factor in the dynamism of this culture. The Sumerians lived at the lower end of the Tigris-Euphrates Valley, where the rivers join and flow into the Persian Gulf. They influenced the evolution of banking and commercial practices, contracts, and standards of weights and measures and led the way in codifying civil law in written form. With constant usage, their writing moved forward from pictographs, or picture symbols, to a wedge-shaped, completely nonpictorial, and more utilitarian method known as cuneiform. It was indented on clay tablets with a stylus, and the tablets were preserved by baking. Around their nature gods were centered myths of the creation of the world, the deluge, or great flood, and the hopeless search for a future life — all three elements reappearing in the religion of the ancient Hebrews, who were later in the Assyrian sphere of influence from the ninth century B.C. onward and finally in exile under the second Babylonian kingdom of the sixth century B.C.

The typical Mesopotamian temple was the step pyramid, or ziggurat, which generally had two setbacks in a three-stepped arrangement. Like

42

other such buildings, the *Ziggurat of Ur* (fig. 34) was constructed of rough unbaked brick, faced by glazed tiles. At first an independent structure, the ziggurat was later made part of the king's palace (see fig. 40). Ramps usually connected one level to another; an altar would be placed on the topmost section. In form, the building suggests the intermediate mastaba-pyramid type of Egypt as well as much later Central American pyramids (see fig. 173).

Although contemporaneous with the striking Egyptian works of the Old Kingdom, early Sumerian sculpture was relatively rudimentary in form and execution. Yet it held to the laws of frontality that prevailed in the ancient Mediterranean world. Even more than in Egypt, works like the alabaster *Figure from Tell Asmar* (fig. 35) exaggerate conventionalization in the distended eye, angular elbows, and large nose. Frontality is clearly observed in the parallelism of the various parts of the body, and the limbs are carefully brought within the compass of the original block of stone. The general effect of such figures is expressionistic (i.e., emotionally expressive) rather than symbolic in the Egyptian sense, although this may partly be because of their undeveloped totemic crudity which is in sharp contrast to the sophisticated aesthetic purpose of Egyptian works.

From the same era comes the gold *Harp of Queen Shubad* (fig. 36) found in the royal tombs of Ur (ca. 2850–ca. 2450 B.C.). This metal musical instrument with inlaid mosaic work demonstrates the fine decorative skill of that age. The formalized head of a bull on this harp has great emotional strength in its abstractness; the pic-

Fig. 35. Figure from Tell Asmar (Sumerian, ca. 3000 B.C.). New York, Metropolitan Museum of Art.

tures on the mosaic plaque immediately below portray scenes from Sumerian mythology, conventionally frontalized (fig. 37). The upper section of the plaque is perhaps most interesting; here the god Gilgamesh seizes and subdues two human-headed bulls, representing the wild tribes conquered by the Sumerians. This is a slightly grotesque version of a legend that parallels the Biblical Samson story or the classical Achilles myth. The animals shown below in a variety of human activities suggest the bestiaries, or beast stories, of the Middle Ages, which are known to have come from the East.

Moving forward in time, the more sophisticated, free-standing form of the *Gudea of Tello* (ca. 2250 B.C., fig. 38) marks a high point in Sumerian civilization. While it is comparable in formality and frontality to earlier figures, there is less strain in the expression and greater smoothness in the articulation of body elements. This may be called the classical phase of Sumerian art. As in Egypt, the work of art is combined with written commentary or narrative, here on the lower part of the king's garment.

EARLY BABYLONIA. The first Babylonian Empire (ca. 1900–729 B.C.) brought a further evolution of Sumerian culture. Commercial expansion made for more complex administrative procedures like the epoch-making laws of the Code of Hammurabi. Under this king (ca. 1800 B.C.) the

Fig. 36. Harp of Queen Shubad. Reconstruction. Philadelphia, University Museum.

Babylonians conquered all of Mesopotamia, carried out important public works, and systematized civil law; in the latter field their work stood as a landmark until Roman times. Their god Marduk became the leader of the pantheon and was identified with the ancient Enlil (god of air and earth) as the Lord of Creation. Later he was known as Bel, or Baal, the Semitic word for master. Magical rites were practiced in religion; great attention was paid to omens derived from the movements of the planets (i.e., astrology), the actions of animals, and the appearance of their organs after sacrifice.

At the top of a black diorite stone bearing the inscribed Code of Hammurabi (fig. 39), a relief sculpture shows that monarch standing before the sun god Shamash (the Semitic word for sun) on a mountain, like the later Moses. Shamash, from whose form sun rays emanate, is dictating the laws to the king, whose hand is held to his mouth in a gesture of fealty. The frontalized arrangement, as in an Egyptian relief (fig. 31), emphasizes the ceremonial relationship between the king and the god in formalized gestures, feet placed before each other, full-face eye, and other similar details. The degree of carving, however, is considerably higher here, since Egyptian reliefs are generally modeled in low planes.

Fig. 37. Shell plaque from Gold Harp of Ur. Philadelphia, University Museum.

THE ASSYRIANS. The aggressive rise of Assyria in the north brought a third stage of development to Mesopotamia. Beginning as part of the Sumerian sphere, Assyria grew into a ruthless, land-hungry empire during the tenth century B.C. Culturally it continued Babylonian ideas but sur-

Fig. 38. Gudea of
Tello. Paris, Louvre.

passed them in architecture and sculpture as well as in military equipment
and imperial organization. During the ninth century B.C., this primarily
military empire extended as far as Phoenicia and Syria and moved shortly
afterward into Palestine and the northern half of Egypt.

The power and magnificence of the Assyrian Empire were glorified
in the splendid *Palace of Sargon at Khorsabad* (fig. 40) dating from the
late eighth century B.C. — a major expression of Mesopotamian architecture. Set into a city wall, the one-storied palace was placed on a typical
high platform, presumably to override the destructive floods of this
valley, which are often considered the legendary source of the Biblical
Deluge. The building could be approached on foot by the double stairway in front leading to the ceremonial gateway or by chariot through the
side ramp.

The Assyrian palace was constructed of unbaked brick covered with
glazed tiles that lent a brilliant gleam to the surface and shed water as
well. Its dominant note externally was the varied treatment of squared-

46

Fig. 39. Hammurabi and the Sun God (ca. 1800 B.C.). Paris, Louvre.

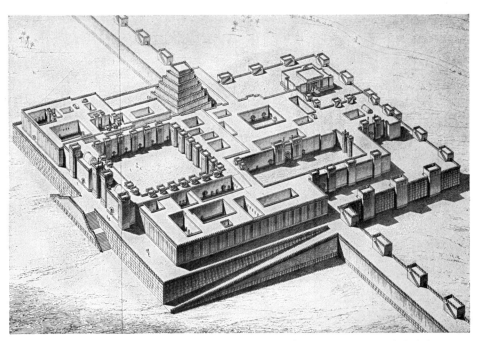

Fig. 40. Palace of Sargon, Khorsabad. Reconstruction after Perrot and Chipiez.

off geometrical elements: pylons, courtyards, ziggurats, wall buttresses, and crenellated walls behind which archers could be placed for defense. The last feature, which also serves the compositional purpose of breaking up the regularity of surface, was adopted by military engineers in the Middle Ages in Europe.

Perhaps the most significant innovation of the Assyrian palace was the arch and its related form, the vault. In Mesopotamia, where stone was unavailable and wood very scarce, the post-and-lintel method of the Egyptians was not practicable for bridging spaces between walls. An arch system was accordingly evolved, as seen in the main portal of Khorsabad (fig. 41). This was constructed on a semicircular wooden form; wedge-shaped bricks were pressed together by the weight coming from above — the more weight, the tighter the pressure. After the bricks were in place, the wooden centering was removed and the arch supported itself. In this massive gateway, a continuous succession of thin brick arches formed the canopy or vault through which one entered the main court of the palace. While there is reason to believe that the Egyptians knew about the arch

Fig. 41. Gateway of Sargon's Palace, Khorsabad. Reconstruction after Perrot and Chipiez.

and vault, their development must be credited to Mesopotamia. Here, centuries later during the Early Christian period, vaulted churches would be built which would influence the course of church architecture both in the East and in Europe. Although Assyro-Babylonian architecture is difficult to restore because of the perishable nature of brick, evidence indicates that the vault form was widespread. At Khorsabad, for example, remains of drainage vaults have been found with the bricks set up in semicircular and other arrangements.

Beyond the main gateway were the various parts of the palace with their respective functions. The ceremonial towered gate connected with a spacious entrance court which also had impressive towers. To the left were a series of temples apparently influenced by Egyptian architecture, flat-roofed structures preceded by open courtyards. Directly behind was the typical Mesopotamian ziggurat, here seven-tiered and with traces of four different colors still evident on the lower stages. The splendor and luxury of such a ziggurat may have been the source for the description of the Biblical Tower of Babel (i.e., Babylon). Further along on the same far side of the palace was the *hilani*, or judgment hall, a rectangular building with an entrance on one broad side, consisting of a two-columned porch flanked by heavy towers. Here the king, as head of both state and church, would render his judgments. This type of building appears to have had later influence, e.g., in the Roman judgment hall, or basilica. We may presume that in the *hilanis* of Assyria somewhat different judgments were rendered than in early Babylonia. In the earlier case the rulers had been highly civilized priest-kings; the Assyrian monarchs, on the other hand, were generals conducting the most systematic military conquest the Near East was ever to know.

The living quarters (seraglio) of the palace, right behind the entrance court, contained a special women's section, or harem. Stables were maintained directly off the side ramp of the palace in the service section, or *khan*, where chariots and horsemen could enter the palace complex.

Although the ziggurat at Khorsabad was part of the palace (a symbol of the king's omnipotence), there were independent temple structures in Assyria as in earlier Babylonia, with and without ziggurats. The ziggurats, in any case, were devices for raising the worshipers closer to the sky deities. Structurally they may be considered ancestors of the minarets on Islamic mosques from which the call to prayer was later issued to faithful Moslems throughout the Near East.

The typical Assyrian palace was decorated with two main types of sculpture: monumental guardians of the gateway, like those found at the Palace of Assurnasirpal II in Nimroud Calah (884–859 B.C., fig. 42),

Fig. 42. Guardian of the gate. Palace of Assurnasirpal II. New York, Metropolitan Museum of Art.

Fig. 43. King's Arms-bearer and Winged Being. New York, Metropolitan Museum of Art.

and considerably smaller alabaster reliefs showing religious and narrative scenes, placed in strips or bands on the interior walls to cover part
of the rough brick surface (see figs. 43–44). The great 16-foot-high
winged bulls with human faces, guarding the entrance to the palace, suggest the Egyptian idea of the sphinx, in which the man-king is endowed
with the attributes of the gods. Here the sky and earth are personified by
bird wings and the body of a bull. These combination creatures served
many functions: to support the brick towers, lend dignity to the entrance,
and drive away spiritual enemies. They blend compositionally into the
architecture through the emphasized verticals that accentuate the upward
movement of the towers.

Partly carved in the round and partly in high relief, the winged bulls
are designed with the most rigid frontality, so as to show the spectator
as much as possible. The use of five legs, two of these visible on the
narrow side and four on the long side, makes it possible to get a complete view either way. Some of the guardian figures have the human head
turned to the front and parallel with their main axis; presumably these
were meant to face the spectator as he passed through the archway. On
the portal towers at the sides, however, the creature's head was turned
at right angles to the body axis, thus facing the spectator from this position
also. The style as a whole is extremely conventionalized — especially in
the exaggerated eye and eyebrow accents, the precise carving of hair
ringlets and beard, and the beautifully patterned sweep of wings — but
the animal portion of the body, particularly the bull legs, exhibits strong
naturalism, even to reproducing the veins. Between each pair of these
guardians stood the figure of Gilgamesh holding a small lion in his power.

The smaller relief sculptures, in addition to the usual scenes of religious and magical rites, relate a number of worldly episodes indicating
the two chief occupations of this royal society: hunting and war. A religious portrayal is represented in the *King's Armsbearer and Winged Being* (fig. 43), a section of a larger relief from the Palace of Assurnasirpal
II at Nimroud Calah. The winged being, one of many such figures of
genii in the palace, holds a little container in one hand and what looks like
a lime in the other; he moves left toward a symbolic abstract tree above
which hovers the sun god. The genii are agents of fertility who help the
king to enrich his land. The magic rites involve a highly conventionalized
date-palm tree symbolizing the tree of life, here as in later Persian and
Early Christian art.

In comparison with the Egyptian *Seti I with Horus and Isis* (fig. 31)
which has serious gaps in the composition, the Assyrian relief possesses a
clearer and more balanced compositional quality. It leans toward greater

Fig. 44. Assurnasirpal II Storming a City. Relief from the Palace of Assurnasirpal II. London, British Museum.

naturalism, with the real distinctions made between right and left arm or right and left leg, seldom seen in Egyptian reliefs. Here also is added a linear accentuation of specific areas, e.g., eyes and leg muscles — a characteristic Assyrian technique.

Another relief from the same palace, *Assurnasirpal II Storming a City* (fig. 44), indicates the overwhelming importance of war in the Assyrian outlook, especially during the reign of this king who is associated with the rise of the Assyrian Empire. During his time its dominion was extended in all directions; many lands paid tribute under a highly efficient imperial administration and were held in check by a much improved military apparatus. Assyria in this period became a nation of plunderers, with its center at Nimroud Calah. Each spring after the crops were sown, the army would make a swing through the Tigris-Euphrates Valley and into Syria, Palestine, Phoenicia, and Egypt, reasserting its rights as conquerors, exacting tribute as it went, and ruthlessly suppressing the least signs of revolt. If a city would not submit and had to be stormed, "The Assyrian came down like the wolf on the fold," and terrible indeed would be the punishment of the conquered.

Although conventional in its frontality, this relief shows a highly realistic action as archers pour their arrows into the besieged city, destroy its walls, and throw enemy soldiers from the battlements. In comparison again, we have observed in Egyptian art a deliberate suppression of space which makes the figures exist in a kind of spatial vacuum; but the Assyrian artist, however formal his figure presentation, injects a feeling of distance. Objects begin to be seen behind each other, whereas in Egypt they are in registers, one directly above the other.

52

The Assyrian sculptor reached his greatest effectiveness in the area of animal portrayal. As with other ancient Near Eastern cultures, there was a distinct cleavage between animal and human representation, the first retaining its prehistoric naturalism and directness. This is even truer of the Assyrian than of many other ancient peoples, since they were so much addicted to hunting, as their palace reliefs clearly show. Among the numerous hunting scenes, the most celebrated is the *Dying Lioness* (fig. 45) from the Palace of Assurbanipal at Nineveh (668–625 B.C.). It is reminiscent in some ways of Old Stone Age cave paintings in which the hunted animal has darts stuck in him. But here we have the added elements of conscious design — aesthetic concern with the arrangement of various parts to occupy a space — and a tremendous emotional impact. The design quality is conveyed by the diagonal arrangement of the form as it cuts across from one corner to the other, the arrows so placed as to fill in (or imply the filling of) the empty spaces. Emotionally we are both attracted and repelled as the agonized beast drags its paralyzed body forward. The artist and the society he represented appear to have de-

Fig. 45. Dying Lioness. Relief from the Palace of Assurbanipal, Nineveh. London, British Museum.

lighted in the animal's suffering in this obviously popular pastime. This would seem to differ from the attitude of the Egyptian hunter (fig. 23), who engaged in refined pursuit for the sake of sport and exercise.

Assurbanipal was the last important king of this warrior-hunter nation, the armed camp known as Assyria. In 625 B.C. Nineveh was destroyed by a combined Median-Babylonian army, and the empire was divided between the two conquerors.

LATER BABYLONIA. The new Babylonian (or Chaldean) Empire was to last only until 538 B.C., when it would be taken over by the Persians. During its supremacy, however, the restored capital at Babylon became the center of the ancient world, ruling the same territory as had the Assyrians. But lacking the military dynamism of its predecessors, and with the increasing disaffection of conquered peoples (e.g., the Jews who were then in exile in Babylon), it was to succumb to the more aggressive Persians (fig. 33).

Nevertheless, in spite of its short life, this second Babylonian Empire was an important cultural influence with significant contributions in astronomy, mathematics, the arts, and business. King Nabonidus (555–538 B.C.), the last of his line, was interested in archaeological investigation and in restoring ancient temples. The splendidly revived Babylon, rebuilt under Nebuchadnezzar (the Biblical king, 605–561 B.C.), may be imagined from the reconstructed *Ishtar Gate* (fig. 46) which climaxes the Procession Street. In form it followed the earlier gateway of the *Palace at Khorsabad* (fig. 41), but the glazed tile had a new feature: it was in relief (fig. 47). This technique was used too for the rows of ceremonial lions on the walls facing the Procession Street; on the gates themselves were bulls and dragons in yellow and blue on a green background. Both arrays presumably guarded the city. The bulls showed the characteristic naturalism of all animals in this civilization; the dragons, as an imaginary conception, were considerably more abstract, combining a horned serpent's head and tail, lion's body and forelegs, and falcon's hind legs.

The sumptuousness of this fabulous city with its palace of Nebuchadnezzar and great ziggurat temple of Marduk is reflected in the Biblical Book of Daniel, which tells us about this king and his successor, Belshazzar (coruler with Nabonidus). Under the latter the Babylonian Empire passed into the hands of the Persians, who became the masters of the ancient Near East.

THE PERSIANS. Chronologically the Persian Empire lasted until 332 B.C. It represented the dominance of a group that had evolved in the highlands immediately to the east of the Tigris-Euphrates Valley. From

Fig. 46. Ishtar Gate, Babylon. Restoration in Berlin Museum.

Fig. 47. Bull design from Ishtar Gate, Babylon. Restoration in Berlin Museum.

there they not only overran the Assyro-Babylonian territory but moved far beyond it, east to the Indus River in India, northwest to include all of Asia Minor, and southwest to take in an additional portion of Egypt. Theirs was the greatest empire of the ancient world up to that point. Their administration was far more humane than that of their predecessors and also more efficient. Ethically and religiously they were much concerned with the problem of right and wrong; their chief gods were Ahura-Mazda, god of light (and goodness), and Ahriman, god of darkness (and evil). They considered the sensibilities of the people they ruled, permitting a certain amount of independence, particularly freedom of religious expression, and initiated the idea of an organized empire rather than a conglomeration of conquered peoples. To flatter their dominions, the Persian rulers styled themselves Kings of Babel and Kings of Egypt.

Although their ethical system is very important, their art offers little that is new; it depends on borrowed elements from such sources as Egypt and Assyro-Babylonia. The god of light was shown like the Babylonian sun god Shamash, enclosed in huge wings. The form of the *Apadana* (Audience Hall) *of Xerxes at Persepolis* (fig. 48) clearly suggests the forest of columns in the Egyptian temple at Karnak (fig. 28), though at Persepolis the various rows of columns do not differ in height. Like the

Fig. 48. Apadana of Xerxes, Persepolis.

later Moslems (who used a similar columned hall for the main part of their mosques), the Persians were clearly affected by the cultures they met and absorbed. This is evident, first, in the main outlines of this Egyptian-type structure with its Mesopotamian *hilani* function. The highly eclectic column (figs. 49–50) reminds us of Egyptian, other Mesopotamian, and even the contemporary Greek developments — magnificent bulls back to back for the capital, voluted (i.e., scroll-shaped) under-capital, fluted shaft, and floral base. The high platform on which the *apadana* is set and the winged beings of the *Propylaea of Xerxes* (fig. 51) bring to mind similar arrangements in the Valley of the Two Rivers (fig. 40).

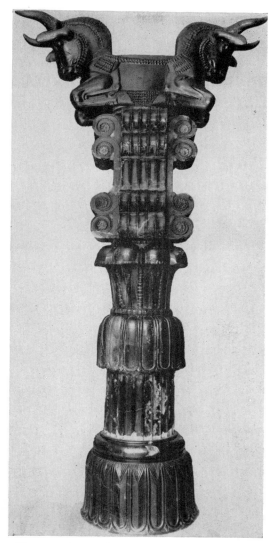

Fig. 49. Composite column, from Susa. Paris, Louvre.

The double staircase is directly comparable to Khorsabad, except that here it is covered with delicately executed reliefs showing subject nations bringing tribute to the "King of Kings" (fig. 52) and animal themes such as the *Combat between a Lion and a Bull* (fig. 53). The latter is a universal motif found in earlier archaic Greek art (see fig. 67), later Chinese metalwork of the Han period, equally later Scythian metalwork (see fig. 211), and the art of the Dark Ages in medieval Europe. The theory is that it moved from the Orient to the Near East and into Europe.

Fig. 50. Head of a Bull. Detail from capital of composite column. Apadana of Xerxes, Persepolis.

Fig. 51. The Propylaeum of Xerxes, Persepolis. Ceremonial gateway to the Palace of Persepolis.

Fig. 52. Tribute Bringers. Detail of outer wall reliefs. Apadana of Xerxes, Persepolis.

The reliefs of Persepolis bear a general resemblance to those of Assyria, with two significant differences: a distinct lessening of the effects of frontality (contemporary with the beginnings of the so-called Golden Age in Greece) and a new mood. We cannot arbitrarily set chronological limits to the idea of frontality, but it begins to disappear around 500 B.C.

Fig. 53. Combat between a Lion and a Bull. Staircase reliefs, left side. Apadana of Xerxes, Persepolis.

The majority of figures on these reliefs are seen from the side, but there is no discrepancy in viewpoint between the shoulders and feet, as earlier. Occasional figures are still frontal in the old fashion, however, and all the feet are directly in front of each other and flat on the ground.

The most meaningful change lies in a softer expression, a marked lack of the cruelty and harshness that had characterized Assyrian art. Quite possibly this reflects the spiritual outlook of the Persians, their awareness of good as preferable to evil. It might equally reflect the broader social outlook of this civilization. The dignity of movement in these reliefs, their delicacy of proportion, and their charming decorative quality affirm the high degree of Persian culture and sophistication at the end of this first phase of ancient history. Although contemporaneous with classical Greece of the fifth century B.C., the art of Persia was chiefly concerned with two-dimensional decorativeness, the appeal of a gracefully filled surface abstractly patterned in a manner traditional in the Near East for centuries afterward.

4 / CRETE AND MYCENAE

THE art of Crete stands vividly apart from the more rigid and repressed expression of Egypt and Mesopotamia. The formality and austerity of those contemporary cultures appear only in a surface resemblance in this island and its later settlements at Mycenae and Tiryns on the Greek mainland. The long Cretan figures with their broad shoulders and narrow waists, the frontality of shoulders, eyes, and placement of the feet, belong within the abstract formalism of the period from about 3000 to 500 B.C. Yet these forms possess an altogether different mood. They are part of a secularized approach and subject matter dealing primarily with the living human being, an exuberant joy in the facts of existence, expressed through brilliant decoration and improvisation.

Cretan culture (also called Minoan, after the legendary King Minos) reflects a different way of life from the Egyptian or Mesopotamian. Although it had similar agricultural origins, the hilly island of Crete was much less suitable for farming. Its strategic Mediterranean location within easy reach of the Greek mainland, Egypt, Asia Minor, and the coast of Italy made it a logical and important trade center. A fluid society came into being through constant contact with various peoples and cultures, in a commercial rather than military relationship (fig. 54). There are few decipherable Cretan written records, yet we know of actual trade connections with Egypt and with major islands such as Sicily and Cyprus. Crete may have been settled by refugees from Egypt around 3500 B.C.; from about 3500 to 2100 B.C. the island's independent city-states flourished; around 2000 B.C. this loose federation was replaced by the leadership of the kings of Knossos during the first climactic period of Cretan sea power.

FIRST PERIOD OF POWER; KNOSSOS. The extensive ruins at Knossos and Phaistos reveal a good many things about these people whose language we have only recently begun to interpret. There were no temple buildings and impressive sculptured gods. Religious worship in Crete was apparently conducted on altars and shrines within the palace (the domi-

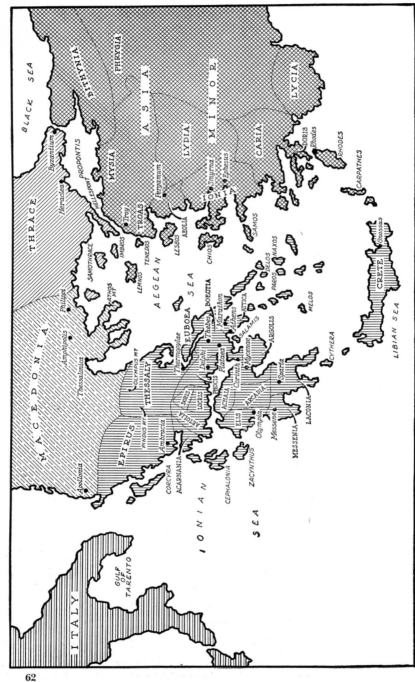

Fig. 54. The Mediterranean World. (From Henry S. Lucas, *A Short History of Civilization*, New York, McGraw-Hill Book Company, Inc., 1953. By permission of the author.)

62

nant building of this culture) and seemingly without the all-powerful priesthood of other countries. Worship was directed toward an earth goddess — as in other religions that are derived from New Stone Age ideas — here symbolized by a double-ax, or *labrys*, which was also used as a sign of royal authority by the priest-kings. Another symbol of abstract formulation is the pillar, or column, seen in its typical form in the halls of Knossos (fig. 55) and on the famous *Lion Gate of Mycenae* (see fig. 64). The lack of a priestly hierarchy of the Egyptian type allowed a more flexible cultural expression, while the absence of either human or animal deities added a certain informality to representations of living beings.

The naturalistic and secular viewpoint was fostered also by commercial activity and the consequently greater number of cities. Cretan society, in lively competition and relatively peaceful contact with the known world, reached a high degree of metropolitanism and luxury. The urban development, each town grouped about a local lord's palace, was the decisive element of this culture. In addition to impressive administrative centers such as Knossos, manufacturing towns and market towns met the nation's economic needs. Since the country depended on merchants and seamen to carry on its maritime trade, these occupational groups formed a uniquely important part of this society. For the same reason a prominent place was also occupied by the artisan class, fabricators of the beautiful

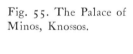
Fig. 55. The Palace of Minos, Knossos.

Cretan pottery and metalwork that were so essential to the export trade. Yet it must be remembered that the freer atmosphere was relative. However fluid and expansive it appeared by contrast to other nations of antiquity, the center of Cretan life was still the palace with its luxuriously furnished and frescoed rooms, its baths, and its elaborately dressed royal retinue.

The first important palace structures date between 2100 and 1600 B.C. They coincide with the assumption of leadership by Knossos, resulting from the important tin trade with the Danube Valley. In complexity of function they compare with Assyrian palaces, but they also differed in certain fundamentals. Similar to Assyria were the multiple residential apartments for the king, his family, and many retainers, around an open courtyard. In addition, there were places of worship (without the temple), storerooms, places of ritual such as the bull ring, a treasury and administrative facilities, and rooms for artisans, soldiers, and others (fig. 56). The multistoried open construction has progressed beyond the Assyrian palace; it could be built without regard to possible flooding (hence the absence of the Assyrian platform) or danger of attack (hence the absence of fortification).

In the earliest period of Cretan development, the so-called Kamares pottery of about 1800 to 1700 B.C. presents a close analogy with New Stone Age pottery (fig. 6), although it is more elegant in quality. The

Fig. 56. The Palace of Minos, Knossos. Rebuilt chamber with columns.

surface decorations on the gracefully shaped Kamares vessels are distinctly stylized or abstracted; the natural quality of the original flower or other form is secondary to the artist's decorative purpose.

REBUILDING THE CITIES; NEW HEIGHT OF POWER. A severe earthquake around 1600 B.C. put an end to the first phase of Cretan culture. But around 1625 B.C. the Greek mainland cities of Mycenae and Tiryns had been founded by the islanders; and during the next epoch the palaces of Knossos and Phaistos were rebuilt. The new palaces became focal points for Crete's greatest age of prosperity (ca. 1600–ca. 1400 B.C.). According to the later Greeks, whose gods were associated in legend with Mount Ida in Crete, human tribute had to be sent periodically to the island to appease the half-human, half-bull monster known as the Minotaur. This creature lived in an underground maze of rooms called a labyrinth (i.e., place of the labrys or double-ax), from which the legendary Greek Theseus was rescued by Ariadne, daughter of the Cretan King Minos. The Minotaur story reflects Cretan domination during this era of its highest ascendancy.

The so-called *Palace of Minos at Knossos* (fig. 55), excavated by the eminent archaeologist Sir Arthur Evans, belongs to this period of Cretan, or Minoan, supremacy. It has a markedly elaborate arrangement of buildings, as well as a more elab-

Fig. 57. The Cup Bearer. Wall painting from Knossos. Replica in Metropolitan Museum of Art.

orate lighting system, carefully fitted stone blocks, and wooden columns, tapering from wide top to narrower base (fig. 56), used to support ceilings or stairwells. Whereas Assyrian structures were somewhat disorganized in plan, Knossos has one large open courtyard leading to all parts of the palace. An advanced civilization is strikingly indicated in this and similar buildings, in one way, by very advanced sanitary provisions (they apparently had running water) and, in another way, by extremely luxurious, even chic, mural paintings and color reliefs. The murals display a special elegance of form and attitude, as in the painted *Cup Bearer* (fig. 57), a fresco detail from Knossos which depicts a typical tall, slim, broad-shouldered, narrow-waisted figure. His legs are firmly planted on the ground, one before the other, in the well-known frontalized manner of other ancient cultures, which is also seen in the profile face with fully shown eye and the maximum view of the shoulders.

This courtly bearing is repeated with variations in many other works of the period between 1600 and 1400 B.C., e.g., the effective painted relief of a priest-king from another wall in the same palace. They all show a vitality and movement, an elastic attitude far removed from the vacuum of Egyptian nonspatial representation or the tight cruelty of Assyrian art. As in other preclassical civilizations, the animal portrayals are more naturalistic than the human. The remarkable painted relief of a bull's head in polychromed stucco, the so-called *Bull of Crete* (fig. 58), is highly

Fig. 58. Bull of Crete. From Knossos. Cast in Metropolitan Museum of Art, New York.

Fig. 59. Octopus Vase. From Gournia. New York, Metropolitan Museum of Art.

simplified in outline, decorative background, and brilliant color, but it still conveys the vivid reality of the beast with its head lowered, tongue hanging out, and eyes bulging. Much smaller in size, though equally significant, are a number of faience (baked and glazed earthenware) plaques showing a variety of animals and fishes whose striking naturalism can only be compared with Old Stone Age art. Among them are a she-goat and her twins, a cow and its calf, and a number of tiny flying fishes so convincing that they were once mistaken for little fossils.

The pottery of this period is in its way as important as the other media. The highly stylized pre-earthquake decoration was replaced by a naturalistic rendition of forms in keeping with the cultural milieu of the time but definitely suited to the vessel's shape. Thus the well-known *Octopus Vase* (fig. 59) portrays a real creature of the sea, so arranged that its tentacles fall naturally and gracefully around the wide bulging surface.

The absence of monumental religious sculpture has been remarked; portrait sculpture similarly is missing. Three-dimensional expression seems confined to small figurines like the *Snake Goddess* (fig. 60), which demonstrates again the interesting blend of Cretan elegance and naturalism with Egyptian formalism and frontality. This tiny figure with serpents crawling up its arms represents a phase of snake worship connected with later Greek beliefs. The important symbols of Cretan religion, how-

ever, are the double-ax and the pillar, shown separately or combined (the latter occurs often enough for us to assume that there is some relationship).

THE MAINLAND CITIES: MYCENAE AND TIRYNS. During this final period of Minoan, or Cretan, development came the beginnings of the related mainland cities which by 1400 B.C. replaced Crete in leadership. At that date the palaces of Knossos and Phaistos were once again destroyed, either by Mycenaeans from the mainland or by Indo-European Achaeans, or possibly by both. (The Achaeans had been filtering into the Greek peninsula from the Danubian area since about 1800 B.C.) From about 1400 to 1100 B.C. the cities of Mycenae and Tiryns were the new centers of Minoan-Cretan civilization in the Aegean area.

The rugged and fortified architecture found on the mainland implies a harsher life, perhaps because of constant pressure from invading Achaeans and other Indo-European warrior folk who had wandered west from the steppes of Turkestan. In Mycenae and Tiryns there are extensive remains of the typical acropolis or hilltop palace (fig. 61) with huge walls about 20 feet thick. The chief element of a palace enclosure was the *megaron*, or king's council chamber (fig. 62), a rectangular-shaped structure. Its sometimes flat, sometimes gabled roof was supported by down-tapering columns of the Minoan type; the open porch at the short end of the building had two similar columns. The whole arrangement approximated the plan and elevation of later Greek treasuries (see fig. 75). These dwelling places of the Mycenaean and other mainland kings on their fortified hilltops were to become the legendary residences of the Greek gods in succeeding centuries.

The "beehive tomb," another type of architecture of this period, is a circular edifice in which the stones are not placed in the usual domical fashion of Mesopotamia but in a series of courses, one projecting out over the other up to the top (about 26 feet) in what is known as a corbeled vault. The so-called *Treasury of Atreus* (fig. 63), built into the side of a hill, is a classic example of this form. A high, narrow stone passageway led to the circular section — apparently used for ritual purposes. From here a doorway opened into a square burial chamber, cut out of solid

Fig. 61. Mycenae, general view. Reconstruction after Perrot and Chipiez.

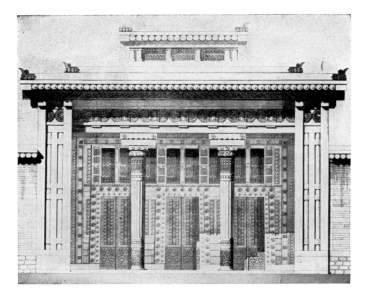

Fig. 62. Reconstruction of a Mycenaean king's council chamber, or megaron, after Perrot and Chipiez.

rock, where the treasure of gold masks, jewelry, and other precious objects was found.

Among the specific art forms carried over from Crete is the down-tapering pillar of the megaron described above. In the *Lion Gate at Mycenae* (fig. 64) this column is carved on a triangular stone slab above the main gateway to the city. Here, however, it appears as a religious symbol guarded by the two heraldically arranged lions that confront each

Fig. 63. The Treasury of Atreus, Mycenae.

other, their paws resting on the pillar's base. Murals found at Tiryns are very much like those already seen at Knossos.

A most effective metalwork also occurs in this art: the gold masks and dagger blades from the tombs at Mycenae, bearing incised and inlaid hunting scenes, and the wonderfully worked *Vaphio Cups* (fig. 65) showing naturalistic animal scenes. Each cup consists of an outer shell on which the forms have been beaten into shape from within (i.e., *repoussé*) and an inner smooth shell that protects the hollowed-out portions and makes an even surface inside the cup. These metal objects which show the hunting or snaring of animals have an extraordinary feeling for nature, a spontaneity and lifelikeness as impressive as anything in Crete itself. They sum up at the end of this entire development the character of the civilization as a whole.

The naturalism, life-enjoying qualities, and elegant courtliness of late Minoan style cut through, however briefly, the more formal hieratic and rigid art of antiquity. Actually, the Mycenaean phase coincided with the short-lived Egyptian style of King Akhenaton (1375–1358 B.C., fig. 32). Even before the Mycenae-Tiryns period, Egypt had come within the

Fig. 64. Lion Gate, Mycenae.

Fig. 65. Vaphio Cups. Reproductions in Metropolitan Museum of Art, New York.

Cretan trade orbit. After 1400 B.C. Mycenae and Tiryns, as the trading centers of the Mediterranean, reached every part of the ancient world with their wares: pottery, jewelry, cloth, and other manufactured goods. Several factors, however, prevented the mainland cities from continuing in this privileged position. They did not have a powerful enough navy to guard the sea lanes against piracy; they faced rising competition from the Phoenicians, an Asia Minor people previously controlled by Egypt; and finally they suffered further invasions from the north.

Earlier incursions by the Achaeans had led to a blending of the new-comers with the older Mycenaean civilization. By 1200 B.C. a second wave of invasion was under way, principally by the relatively uncivilized Dorians, another branch of the Indo-Europeans, racially and linguistically related to the Achaeans. Their usual trade destroyed, the Mycenaean-Achaeans undertook a series of raids on neighboring areas; one such episode was the famous Trojan War (ca. 1150 B.C.) later immortalized in Homer's *Iliad* and *Odyssey*. By 1100 B.C. Mycenae, Tiryns, and other pre-Greek centers were no longer in existence. The Greek "middle ages" had begun.

5 / THE COMING OF GREEK ART

THE civilization that came to flower in Greece — nourished by a grow-ing individualism and secularity — contrasted strongly with the military-religious despotisms of the Near East. Instead of a society with all-powerful priestly leaders and totalitarian expression, the lands of the northern Mediterranean evolved a socially dynamic and flexible con-figuration.

Lacking the relative economic security of fertile Near Eastern river valleys, the Greeks could not develop static social patterns. Their limited natural resources were not enough for self-sufficiency or what have been called "civilizations of ease of existence." A satisfactory economy could only be achieved by constant exertion, especially in the realm of trade, thus establishing a so-called "civilization of intercourse." As in Crete, the new elements of this younger culture were commerce, cities, and an in-creasingly vital merchant class. Through these factors the general standard of living was raised, and individual thinking and creativity reached higher levels than before, in what became primarily a secular rather than priest-ruled society. Crete had shown some of these features in its social out-look, but they were still conditioned by the dominant centralized mo-narchical system of the ancient Near East so that Cretan art took on an ambivalent half-stylized, half-naturalistic aspect.

With the Dorian invasion around 1200 to 1100 B.C., the Cretan-Mycenaean culture had come to an end. This second wave of Indo-Euro-pean folk — bringing Dorians to Greece and Italici into the Italian peninsula — had carried with it the less developed forms of tribal society characteristic of wandering nations. Those were now planted in the many small geographical sections into which Greece is divided by its mountains and seas. These manifold divisions, as much as the tribal background of the Hellenes, were responsible for the characteristic Greek separatism, mak-ing it virtually impossible to form an Eastern type of empire. The evolution of an individualistic trading society was made almost inevitable by the relatively arid soil conditions coupled with extensive commercial opportunities. Calm seas, numerous harbors, extensive seacoasts, the grain from nearby lands, tin from central Europe and Spain, and the rich markets of Egypt and the Near East were to offer a unique field for this activity. It has been noted that the most civilized Greek centers were to grow up on the seaboard (Athens, Corinth, and Miletus), while the inland cities would remain comparatively retarded and uncreative (fig. 54).

DORIANS AND IONIANS. The Dorians took over the large peninsula of southern Greece and penetrated into Crete, the southern Aegean islands, and the southwestern part of Asia Minor. Farther north the remnants of the Mycenaean-Achaeans, combined with Ionians, moved through Attica across the central Aegean islands into central Asia Minor. They were henceforth known as Ionians; from their settlements on the coast of Anatolia (Asia Minor) came the first important Greek aesthetic impulses. Traditionally we have thought of the Ionic culture as more refined and delicate, perhaps because of its association with the older civilization of Mycenae and also its proximity to the cultivated Near Eastern nations. The Doric, on the other hand, is regarded as simpler, more rugged, and reflecting to some extent the less sophisticated character of the people who produced it.

The Dorian invasion had brought destruction to the cities and their commerce and the temporary disappearance of arts and crafts. Its aftermath was social and political confusion. During this Heroic Age (ca. 1100–ca. 800 B.C.) marked by the emigrations into Asia Minor (ca. 1050 B.C.), there was a decided change in Greek social structure. The former clan monarchies were replaced by a feudal aristocracy of military leaders, who became great landlords at the expense of the poorer farmers. It was for this lordly class that the Homeric epics were set down about 800 to 700 B.C. as the crystallization of songs that had been delivered orally by many generations of Ionian bards.

BEGINNINGS OF GREEK ART. While the civilization of Ionia produced the *Iliad* and the *Odyssey* for a still heroic-minded noble class (whose ancestors had fought in the Trojan War and who themselves were now living in cities), the Doric mainland of Greece settled into a relatively simple feudal farming existence.

The geometric style. In this period (ca. 900–ca. 700 B.C.) art initially reappeared on the mainland by way of large ceremonial funerary urns such as the *Dipylon Vase* (fig. 66), which has highly schematic representations of funeral scenes. The broad-shouldered, wasp-waisted figures have the frontalized form of Minoan-Mycenaean art, but are drawn in

74

an abstract and decorative geometrical style that bespeaks the peasant and shepherd culture of the Dorians (cf. the geometric style of New Stone Age peasants, fig. 6). Yet here also are echoes of the Homeric age, not only in the schematized and wholly unnaturalistic Mycenaean influence, but also in the common customs that are revealed. The funeral games for the deceased recall those performed for the heroic Patroklos in Homer's *Iliad*.

The upper register of the *Dipylon Vase* shows the frontalized corpse lying on its bier, about to be burned (as in the *Iliad*), accompanied by animals killed for that purpose. A series of identical mourners tear their hair in the traditional gesture of sorrow. The lower register portrays chariots with horses and drivers as well as warriors with shields, prepared for the funeral games. Both upper and lower registers are surrounded by zigzags, crosshatchings, and other geometric ornaments that characterize a peasant and shepherd culture.

During this era, the land monopoly by wealthy nobles led to serious food shortages. A wide distress is reflected in Hesiod's *Works and Days*

Fig. 66. Dipylon Vase. New York, Metropolitan Museum of Art.

(ca. 700 B.C.), which is a pioneer, if calm, statement of the fact that the poor have often been oppressed by the rich. The very existence of such a poem is remarkable in view of the controlled nature of earlier Near Eastern civilizations. Similarly the Homeric poems, however aristocratic in feeling, are dedicated to individual glory and to human problems. At this early point in Greek development, these entirely distinct kinds of poetry already proclaim the constant and strongly differentiated characteristics of that society. Those characteristics and the emphasis on the human being are more fully expressed in the later course of Greek democracy and its culture.

The economic distress of the eighth century B.C. was one of the factors that helped inaugurate a period of colonization by the Greeks (ca. 800–ca. 600 B.C.). This process was encouraged first by the feudal aristocrats and later by the tyrants who ruled the growing number of cities and wished to be rid of malcontents and to profit from new trade possibilities. Colonization and commerce with other countries brought invigorating cultural contacts, along with increasing wealth for the colonizing cities and a new type of art patronage. During the late eighth and early seventh centuries B.C. architecture and then monumental sculpture appeared, in addition to the pottery which had been the sole evidence of aesthetic growth since the Dorian invasion. A system of coinage from Lydia and an alphabet from Phoenicia were adopted in the molding of new civilized patterns.

These patterns were shaped also by common religious customs, the first national literature (e.g., Homer and Hesiod), and the establishment of the Olympian games in 776 B.C. — the traditional start of Greek history and an important force in bringing together the various parts of the Greek world. Each city-state maintained its own local deities and usages, thus assuring a high degree of independence and individuality. But an over-all and unifying character was thereafter given to Greek life by its collective elements: methods of worship, language, and literature, shared shrines and sanctuaries (e.g., Olympia, Delphi, and Delos), conventions and ideas inherited from the Minoan–Mycenaean period, and Mediterranean-wide commerce.

ARCHAIC STYLE. After 700 B.C. the change from peasant to city life becomes visible in the alteration of the geometric Dipylon style into a more fluid and quasi-naturalistic one, even on the mainland. Such examples as *The Horses of Herakles* from an amphora (storage jar) of around 675 to 650 B.C. (fig. 67) show the spirit of an awakened Greece. Though still archaic and frontalized in outward aspect, this has a vigorous and natural feeling. The style and content of scenes like *The Horses of Herakles*, which comes from Attica, are shared by other city-states on the mainland as well as by those in Asia Minor (Ionia), southern Italy, and Sicily. The themes of gods and heroes become the chief subjects of Greek vase painting and sculpture.

The heroic ideal. The worship and admiration of heroic figures like Herakles (Hercules) or the superhuman gods of the Greek pantheon may perhaps indicate that these religious ideas were solidified during the period of aristocratic leadership of society. Greek gods, like those of almost all ancient peoples, originated as nature spirits. In this area they quickly became anthropomorphic (human in form) unlike those of the Minoan-Mycenaean culture which had been abstract. But the human form they took in Greece was considerably different from those in Egypt or Mesopotamia, for it was conditioned by two new factors. First, the general Indo-European (Asian-Indian, Celtic, Scandinavian, Greek, Latin) god-hero ideal involved a family of deities — originally nature spirits — which were concretized in human shapes with earthly weaknesses or virtues. Thus the elements common to Indian, Scandinavian, and other epics appear in Greek mythology in manlike gods related to each other by blood or marriage; they represent a higher and idealized type of human existence rather than the dark mysterious conceptions

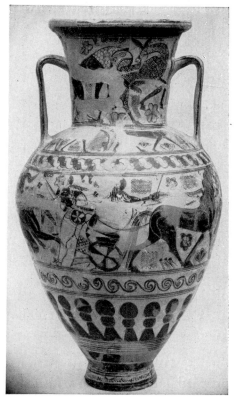

Fig. 67. Horses of Herakles. Detail from Combat between Herakles and Nessos. Greek proto-Attic amphora. New York, Metropolitan Museum of Art.

of Near Eastern religions. Second, the heroic element carried over from the same source was crystallized in the Homeric epics and finally translated into contemporary terms by the still dominant aristocracy of the seventh and sixth centuries B.C.

Although threatened in its power by the rising city-states with their middle class, the aristocracy remained important enough to stamp its character on the literature and art of these two centuries and even beyond:

from the courtly poetry of Anacreon to the odes of Pindar and the conservative philosophy of Plato; from the Hero type in sculpture of around 600 B.C. through the elegant figures of Praxiteles. This may explain an apparent paradox between, on one hand, the constant emphasis on nobility in Greek art, its straining after the beautiful mind in the beautiful body, and, on the other hand, the acknowledged democratic character of Greek society. The formulation of the Greek cultural and artistic ideal belonged to a predemocratic period and was to last into and beyond the period of democracy — which, it should be noted, was not democracy as we conceive of it today. Even during what has been termed the Golden Age in the fifth century B.C., Greek culture was still the creation of a limited number of people, a fact which the middle classes resented enormously, as witness the protests against expenditures for the Acropolis buildings and the traditional story of the imprisonment of Phidias.

Flexibility of Greek culture. It is significant, however, that by the late eighth century B.C., the names of individual artists and poets become known, so that this culture expresses the spirit both of the age and of the individual human being. Even more vitally different from the fixed, unchanging character of Eastern despotisms, Greek art and culture in general vary from century to century; we have already seen a change from the geometric style of the *Dipylon Vase* to the dynamic expression of *The Horses of Herakles.* From these beginnings through the Archaic style of the sixth century B.C. to the Classical style of the fifth and the more emotive expression of the fourth century B.C., we may trace the flexibility of this society, the true measure of its individualism.

The Archaic male figure. The *Kouros,* or heroized youthful athlete (ca. 600 B.C., fig. 68), summarizes in many ways the dissimilarity between early Near Eastern societies and the Greek city-states where this type of figure was widespread. Although clearly influenced in pose and proportion by the standing forms of ancient Egypt (cf. figs. 19–20, especially position of feet and arms, frontality, and body proportions), it differs markedly in its religious and social function. Egyptian sculptures were designed as shelters for the ka to ensure life in the hereafter and were influenced in their formal expression by the unchanging social order. Greek religion offered little hope of an afterlife for the majority of humankind, which was doomed to wander about an ambiguous region known as Hades. A limited number could become semidivine or heroized, securing a certain continuity in the form of a coiled snake that would remain in the funeral barrow or cave where their ashes were placed. This tiny group — the outstanding soldiers, the best lawmakers, and the most excellent athletes — would be buried with special honor. Their tombs were set in important locations like the town square (agora) or near the city gate, and a statue of each semidivine hero was made to preserve his memory. His tomb became a place of worship, and the snake in which his spirit took refuge was given annual offerings.

The Greek artist, faced with the problem of giving tangible form to his canonized heroes or his gods, turned to the outstanding three-dimensional art of Mediterranean antiquity. This accounts for the close similarity in outward form between the Hero portraits and those of ancient Egypt or Mesopotamia (the latter in stylized hair and accentuated muscles). But since the motivation was so different, it followed inescapably that Greek portrait figures would have a more human quality of expression and that as Greek society changed so would the forms of its art. The early statues are scarcely portraits in the modern sense but rather stereotypes in which the form retains much of the vigorous crudeness of *The Horses of Herakles*. In time, however, the growing demand for this kind of

Fig. 68. *Kouros* figure. New York, Metropolitan Museum of Art.

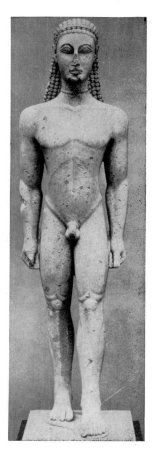

figure and the concentration on a limited number of types gave tremendous impetus to the art of sculpture; within less than a century, it reached a high point of development along entirely new lines.

Since the Hero figures were designed to give human beings an exalted, almost divine appearance and expression, we find from the outset a consistently idealistic rather than naturalistic point of view. Contrariwise, the gods and (later) goddesses of Greek art expressed semihuman strength and weakness and tended to be brought down to a less austere level than in Near Eastern societies. The gods and goddesses on Mount Olympus resemble a royal family more than a group of abstractly formulated and cold entities (see fig. 101). The worshipers who bring offerings display a dignity and serenity much like the idealized poise and nobility of their gods. The art of ancient Greece, therefore, less controlled by religious formalistic taboos than ancient Egypt and more interested in worldly considerations, brings the divine closer to the human and the human closer to the divine.

Secularism and individualism. A new and more worldly function attaches to the Hero figures (whether soldiers, athletes, or lawgivers), to the maidens presumably set up as votive offerings, e.g., *Acropolis Maiden* (see fig. 70), and even to the average pedimental figures in the gabled space of the temple. It does not arise from rigid adherence to a cult nor from a priestly or even royal commission. From a period as early as the *Dipylon Vase* and clearly felt in the age of the *Kouros* figure, the accent on secularization, the mingling of human and divine, is plainly indicated. In the Greek conception of godlike men and quasi-human gods, expressed in the *Iliad,* the personal presence of deities is felt in every human action and the gods themselves have human qualities. It is significant that a statue is erected to an athlete, lawmaker, or military hero not so much for a religious cult but as a form of appreciation for individual effort and accomplishment.

The fact that the artist himself is a known personality reaffirms that his work is no longer completely subservient to an all-powerful priesthood or god-king but is an increasingly human product created for the city-states, their rulers, or even for individual patrons. In sculpture, painting, and other arts man appears as a liberated creature, moving about freely in an idealized physical form and space rather than in the geometrically determined and rigidly controlled form-and-space environment of other ancient art.

At this early point, however (archaic period, ca. 626–480 B.C.), Greek art has by no means abandoned formal and purely decorative considerations. As we have observed, the basic form quality of the *Kouros* is Egyptian frontality; the athlete's body is enclosed within the rigid limitations of the original block. Moreover, the regularized ringlets of hair and the raised lines of the muscle and eyelid indications relate to the decorative abstraction of almost contemporaneous Assyrian art (fig. 43).

Early female sculptures. The same may be said of the initial examples of female figures, which began somewhat later (i.e., ca. 550 B.C.). These remain clothed, in contrast to the nude male figures which differ in this respect even from Egyptian male images. The female sculptures are either simply carved cylindrical shapes — like tree trunks — with no anatomical indications and highly stylized drapery; or Egyptian-type seated statues, closely related to the original rectangular stones; or winged-victory representations such as the *Nike* (Victory) *of Delos* (ca. 560–550 B.C., fig. 69). All three female types are severely frontalized like the *Kouros.* In the flying Victory, an important liberating element of motion is indicated by the kneeling, sideways movement of the lower part of the body, in contrast to the completely frontal upper portion. Here as early as the middle of the sixth century B.C. the Greek sculptor tried to break his way out of the original stone block and also (as in the *Kouros*) to achieve a certain amount of human expression in the face. Lips are drawn back into what is called an "archaic smile." In some

Fig. 69. Nike of Delos. Athens, National Museum.

opinions this is an unsuccessful attempt at expressiveness, but the very attempt is extremely meaningful in determining the humanistic direction of Greek art.

This archaic prototype of the later *Winged Victory,* with its strained frontal pose, decorative ringlets of hair, bulging eyes, and fixed smile, is the sister of the *Kouros* of a half century earlier. It is more conservative in the sense that it is draped rather than nude — Greek sculpture kept this convention until the fourth century B.C., perhaps because of the relatively secluded position of women in the community. But the *Nike of*

Delos has the virtue of movement, however ineffectual. Within a short time there appeared a large number of standing female figures, such as the so-called Maidens of the Athenian Acropolis (fig. 70), which date from the end of the archaic period, shortly before about 500 B.C. By comparison with the elementary cylindrical tree-trunk forms or the flying *Nike*, these young women have a charm and grace, an overt femininity, that recalls the smartness of Minoan wall paintings — a tradition carried to Ionia by the retreating Mycenaeans, now returning in the cultural cross currents of the sixth century B.C.

Damaged by the Persians during the Greco-Persian war, these attractive figures were swept up and buried by the returned Athenians preparing to rebuild their temples on the Acropolis. The Maidens may be divided according to costume: one group wears a simple Dorian *peplos*, a tunic tucked in at the waist, maintaining an architectural simplicity; the other group is dressed in the Ionian *himation* draped over one shoulder in graceful folds, covering an undergarment of wool. The coiffure and general expression are the same in both cases, as is the raised arm which has been freed from the body. Although the Greek sculptor would not

Fig. 70. Acropolis Maiden. Athens, Acropolis Museum.

82

show women in the nude for some time, he was definitely aware of the body beneath the carefully arranged drapery. It is noteworthy that here and in later Greek sculpture, color was used to heighten the appeal of the figures.

These *Korai* (maidens, singular is *Kore*) are evidence of the increasing humanity and nonformalization of Greek art — although we cannot tell just what they represent. Perhaps they were priestesses or sacred maidens whose function was sufficiently important to entitle them to canonization like their brothers the *Kuroi* (singular *Kouros*). Like most art of this period, however, the Maidens betray an almost Eastern decorative and conventional quality, in spite of their increased expressiveness of feature, giving the impression that they are meant to be seen from one point of view. To that extent they do not yet exist in a definite spatial environment as do later Greek sculptures. With the passage of time comes increasing three-dimensionality and movement, ever growing naturalness of anatomy and expression.

Archaic pottery. During this archaic period we also become aware of Greek painting, known to us almost exclusively through incised drawings on the surface of their widely exported pottery. These pottery vessels constitute one of the most important forms of Greek artistic activity. They were produced in a variety of graceful and functional shapes related to their utility. The subject matter of the painting is directly concerned with the function of each vessel; moreover, the figures, plants, and animals are so arranged that their outlines conform to the shape of that piece. Color schemes are usually simple and direct, the two chief types being black-figured and red-figured. As the name implies, the black-figured type refers to black forms outlined on the original red clay surface. The red-figured was made by first covering the red vessel with a "slip" or coat of black paint and then scraping away parts of this slip, exposing certain sections of the red undersurface, which make up the figures. Thousands of these pottery vessels have been found all over the Mediterranean world — to which the active Greeks exported them as containers for olive oil or wine and as objects of art.

One of the most beautiful examples of archaic black-figured pottery is the drinking vessel showing *Dionysos Sailing on the Sea* (fig. 71), done around 550 to 525 B.C. by Execias. In this art, as in sculpture, specific personalities appear early. These individuals, like the sculptors of the time, show a strong feeling for controlled decorative pattern; their works are consciously arranged in elegant two-dimensional surface compositions. Here the eye moves round and round following the layout of the dolphins, who symbolize the sea, or the grapes (representing Dionysos)

Fig. 71. Dionysos Sailing on the Sea. From a kylix painted by Execias. Munich, State Museum.

that spring from the top of the curved sail, which is in turn related to the countercurve of the boat's keel. Once again, as with the Minoan-Mycenaean ancestors of the Greeks, the decorative and formal is balanced by the naturalistic. The Greek artist retained the elegance and suavity of the earlier culture, applying them to concretize his new epic or religious aspirations, giving specific form to hitherto abstract or poetic ideas.

These formulations are particularly striking in their variability (or refusal to remain static), their secular character, and their increasingly personal and even aesthetic quality in the modern sense. Those factors lead further and further away from the purely ritualistic function of Near Eastern art. In *Dionysos Sailing on the Sea* the religious nature of the god's figure is less important than its use as an artistic motif. It becomes a portion of the design, subordinate to the artist's conception. Similarly in the *Kouros* or the Maidens, the conscious aesthetic arrangement of line and mass, of verticals and horizontals, seems more essential to the sculptor than the symbolic purpose of the Egyptian artist. *Dionysos Sailing on the Sea* also is beautiful for its own sake rather than for the magical or ritual meaning that suffuses every ancient Eastern work of art.

84

This does not mean that the Greeks were not religious; but their religious practices were tempered by the dynamism of Greek life and its many contacts with the outside world. Because the artist now worked for a particular city, nobleman, or even private patron (as in the pottery), he was no longer dominated by the priesthood. His themes were still the gods and the heroes, but they were presented from an enlarging humanistic viewpoint that helped make religion more alive and vital. The Greek citizen, seeing the impressive and serene sculptures of Olympia or Athens, was inspired, like the observer of thirteenth-century Gothic cathedrals in the Christian era, to a more exalted feeling for the deity.

Liberated from the totalitarian approach of ancient Near Eastern society, the Greek ventured into new paths of thinking and investigation of the nature of the world. His science, art, and philosophy did not have to be dedicated to solidifying tradition, whether religious or royal. The various intellectual disciplines were carried forward in a "pure" fashion, i.e., for their own sakes. It must not be overlooked that Greek cultural expression stemmed primarily from a leisure class that was also free economically to pursue its intellectual interests and ideals — scientific, artistic, and philosophical — without the necessity of a practical objective.

TRANSITIONAL PERIOD. From about 500 to 450 B.C. Greek art went through a transitional phase during which architecture, sculpture, and painting were concretized in the forms best known to us today. With the accumulation of wealth by the port and island cities, the building up of joint sanctuary cities, the increasing necessities and contacts of worldwide commerce, and the successful war against Persia (492–479 B.C.), the arts moved forward to their climax around the middle of the fifth century B.C. The change may be seen in the sculptures such as the *Warrior Figure* from the Temple of Aphaia (a Cretan-derived goddess) on the island of Aegina (ca. 500–480 B.C., fig. 72), representing generalized incidents from the Trojan War. Each pediment (or gable), as restored, shows groups of warriors in combat; Athena, the large standing central figure, dominates the two battles.

Individual and impressive marble figures preserved from the ruins of this temple are some of the earliest examples visualized and executed fully in the round. The beginning of a spatial approach and a relatively free movement of the human form is exhibited in the spirally arranged parts of a fallen warrior's body or the movement in the kneeling archer. The face of the Aeginitan soldier is still conventionalized and archaic in its stylized hair and beard, stiff expression, and deeply incised eyes (cf. fig. 68), but there is more direct observation of the human body, now studied both for itself and as part of a dramatic narrative in a specific

Fig. 72. Warrior figure from the pediment of the Temple of Aegina (500–480 B.C.). Munich, Glyptothek.

context and spatial environment. In this instance of the transition from archaic geometrical and decorative ideals, we see also an indirect allusion to the Persian Wars in which the soldiers of Aegina took a leading part at the Battle of Salamis, just as they had participated in the Trojan War.

Among the sculptors associated with Aegina is Onatas, famous for his bronze work and perhaps involved in the temple pediments whose liberated forms suggest a relationship to bronze casting. More definitely linked with Onatas is the wonderful nude *Zeus* (fig. 73) shown in the act of hurling his spear or thunderbolt. Here the technique of the hollow bronze enables the sculptor to liberate the free-standing and unsupported figure so that it balances its weight on the advanced foot without danger of breaking, since the stresses can be shifted as specific parts are strengthened or "loaded." Although there are still certain inevitable archaic aspects — notably in hair, beard, and facial expression — the sense of balanced movement, of force held in check, combined with the simple but powerful anatomy, makes this one of the most impressive figures of antiquity.

The great sanctuary cities. Aegina was one of the four preeminent religious centers of Greece. The other great national or Panhellenic sanctuaries were: the city of Delphi at the base of Mount Parnassus,

sacred to Apollo; the island of Delos, where the same god was worshiped; and the imposing center at Olympia (fig. 74), where Zeus was
glorified in a magnificent temple, together with the legendary hero
Pelops at whose tomb most Greeks made their reverences (in this city
the important Olympian — or Olympic — games had been held since
776 B.C.).

In addition to temples for the local god, these sanctuaries contained
a considerable number of votive monuments, places of recreation such as
stadiums for athletic contests and theaters for dramatic performances, and
small temple-shaped structures called treasuries. At the treasuries, visiting groups from various parts of the Greek world could congregate with
their fellow citizens and make special offerings. A line of these treasuries
can be seen in the upper center of the restoration of the Olympian sanctuary. The majestic *Temple of Zeus* stands near the middle of the sacred
enclosure, the altar to heroic Pelops behind it on the left, and a characteristic circular tomb farther to the left. The long building at top right is
an older temple dedicated to Hera.

The *Temple of Zeus* is an elaborate rectangular structure with columned porticos front and rear; a complete belt of columns encircles the
entire building (cf. *Parthenon*, fig. 85). The treasuries are much simpler;

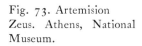
Fig. 73. Artemision
Zeus. Athens, National
Museum.

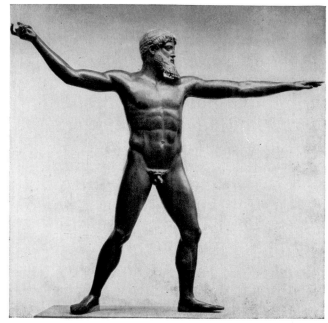

Fig. 74. Panhellenic sanctuary, Olympia. Model in Metropolitan Museum of Art, New York.

for example, the *Treasury of the Siphnians* at Delphi (fig. 75) is a small plain rectangle in plan with a two-columned portico only in front. These columns, however, unlike the conventional beveled cylinders of the *Temple of Zeus* or the *Parthenon*, are actually female forms. This is an Ionic device directly comparable to the Maidens of the Acropolis (fig. 70), while the simpler beveled columns of the Zeus temple or the *Parthenon* are in a Doric tradition. Another Ionic feature of the *Siphnian Treasury* is the continuous frieze of sculpture extending across the front of the little building, again in contrast to the Doric system of a horizontal band with alternating square reliefs (*metopes*) and simple vertical grooved members (*triglyphs*; see fig. 85). There is a general resemblance between this treasury and the presumable form of the Mycenaean megaron (fig. 62), as there is between abandoned palaces of pre-Greek kings and the Greek temples which often replaced them on the very spot.

Other important buildings of the typical sanctuary center included the athletic stadium and the theater. The stadium was a long hairpin-shaped structure, flat at one end and curved at the other to enable the racers to make a turn. At Olympia, where the most famous games were celebrated every four years like the modern Olympics, the stadium (*stadion*) was large enough to accommodate some 45,000 spectators. Along the center line of such enclosures many statues and votive figures were placed by the participants from different parts of Greece. As for the theater, this semicircular, unroofed edifice was usually built into the side of a hill so that it required no external supports, unlike the later

Fig. 75. Treasury of the Siphnians, Delphi. Restored. Delphi Museum.

Fig. 76. Temple of Zeus, Olympia. Restoration of west pediment showing battle between centaurs and Lapiths. Berlin, State Museums.

Roman theaters or their modern descendants, the football stadiums and baseball parks. A good example of a Greek theater still stands at the foot of the Acropolis in Athens (see fig. 92) where, as at sanctuaries, the religious-heroic dramas typical of Greek culture were performed.

The chief structure of each sanctuary was, of course, the temple. By the sixth century B.C. this had already assumed its characteristic shape and proportions, however refined these were to become in the next era when they would reach their highest form. At Olympia the rebuilding and redecorating that took place about 460 B.C., immediately after the destruction by invading Persians, evoked one of the last transitional types of sculpture between the archaic period and the so-called Golden Age. The pediments of the *Temple of Zeus,* as reconstructed, show on one side the legend of Pelops and Oenomaos, who engaged in a heroic chariot race for the hand of the latter's daughter Hippodamia; the other side depicts a combat between Lapiths and centaurs (fig. 76). These scenes, in both content and form, illustrate the constant Greek striving toward

90

balanced and poised expression. One pediment is quiet, representing the moment before the race; the other is dynamic, the half-human centaurs attempting to carry away the maidens from a wedding party. In both arrangements a typical solution for the triangular-shaped pediment has been found. The ever-present but invisible god and judge stands in the center — a larger, more impressive figure than the others — passing judgment on what he sees: Zeus decides whether the hero wins the maiden; and Apollo (fig. 77) stretches out his hand to denote that the human beings (symbolizing civilized Greeks) conquer the only half-human centaurs (symbolizing the aggressive Persians). In the corners of the respective pediments, figures may be seen lying down to fill the angles, one pair representing the local rivers, the other pair merely spectators.

In their balance of spiritual and physical qualities, the sculptures at Olympia express the Greek ideal. The magnificently controlled *Apollo*, still somewhat archaic in individual details (stylized hair, incised eyelids, stiff pose), shows a greater feeling for flesh than the earlier *Kouros* (fig. 68) or the Aegina figures (fig. 72); and yet the entire effect is one of

Fig. 77. Apollo. Central figure from west pediment of the Temple of Zeus, Olympia. Olympia Museum.

generalization and exaltation, of godlike human beings and of manlike gods who are still superior to those they judge. The exalted quality and reserved strength are characteristic of late archaic work, as seen also in the *Artemision Zeus* (fig. 73), and may perhaps place this earlier art on an even higher plane than the popularly esteemed product of the second half of the century.

Other details from the Olympia temple indicate the increasing naturalism of the middle fifth century B.C.: the older man seated in the right-hand angle of the Zeus pediment and the allegorical river forms. But all are within the harmonious clarity of the composition as a whole and its thoughtfully disposed effects. The centaur who clutches the maiden to the left of Apollo is a symbol of man's baser instincts (fig. 78); he has a more naturalistic facial expression than any encountered before. The maiden, however, even in the midst of violence, retains a certain detachment, as though the bride of a hero were above the expression of fear or even abhorrence.

Relief sculpture became a favored art among the Greeks of that period. In a still somewhat archaic piece known as the *Ludovisi Throne* (ca. 460 B.C., fig. 79) the decorative ideal remains paramount. Aphrodite, born from the sea and supported by two draped attendant figures, forms the center of a beautifully ordered pattern of arms, drapery lines, and subtly varied curves with predominantly aesthetic motivation. Because of the conservative convention, the artist represents even the newborn goddess as clothed. On the sides of the "throne" may be found two symbolic women: a chastely dressed housewife tending a lamp and, opposite

Fig. 78. Centaur and Maiden. From west pediment of the Temple of Zeus at Olympia. Olympia Museum.

Fig. 79. Ludovisi
Throne. Rome, Terme
Museum.

her, a courtesan type playing the pipes and shown nude. These are presumably the two kinds of love — both the province of Aphrodite.

Myron and Polycleitos. The end of the transitional development is reached with Myron and Polycleitos, whose work belongs to the middle of the fifth century B.C. Myron carried one step further the idea of movement expounded in the Aeginitan marbles and the bronzes of Onatas. His *Athena and the Satyr Marsyas* and his better known *Discus Thrower* (fig. 80) demonstrate passionate concern with the human body in violent action. In keeping, however, with the Greek idea of restrained emotional portrayal, the expression of the young athlete (with his slightly archaic and rather small head) is as neutral as that of the young maidens of Olympia. This figure is not so much a glorification of the athlete in the *Kouros* sense as the solution of an aesthetic problem. It is an appreciation of the human body in an intricately balanced pose, at the height of the athlete's swing, pregnant with power yet held back from either physical or mental explosion. Whereas the *Zeus* of Onatas is a symbol of movement, the *Discus Thrower* is movement itself and to that degree a step in the direction of naturalism. It is not accidental that the contemporary Eleatic philosophy emanating from southern Italy concerned itself with the qualities of matter and the characteristics of motion — not as applied science but as pure science, just as this is pure art. The *Discus Thrower* is not a conscious imitation of current literary or philosophical trends but a reflection of the general intellectual interests of the time.

The work of Myron, like that of Onatas, shows the importance of the bronze medium in enabling the sculptor to free his figure. Where

Fig. 80. Myron: Discus Thrower. Rome, National Museum.

the relatively brittle marble would have snapped off at the ankle because of the unwonted strain (marble copies usually have a decorative prop such as a tree stump carved at the danger spot), the bronze is more elastic. Its forms are hollow and therefore lighter, or loaded with additional metal where necessary. Moreover, the direct modeling of the clay original (as opposed to marble carving) likewise lends a certain naturalness to the bronze result.

Polycleitos, best known for his *Lance Bearer*, or *Doryphorus* (fig. 81), is also related to the bronze development, and brings to a climax the nude standing male athlete type. The *Lance Bearer*, identified with this sculptor's canon, or rule, is supposed to have contained the ideal proportions of the nude male athlete. It portrays a young man, lance on shoulder, advancing serenely into the arena. The simple yet graceful pose with the weight on one foot, the other slightly relaxed, is repeated in the artist's famous *Amazon* and in his *Fillet Binder*, another idealized

94

athlete shown binding the victory emblem about his head. Both the male figures (or their copies) still exhibit a certain archaism in the prominence of the muscles below the abdomen and around the chest. But the sense of freedom that pervades these sculptures (even in the surviving Roman copies) is significant of the new age, like the emphasis on contour rather than any blocklike architectonic or geometrical quality.

Both the *Discus Thrower* and the *Lance Bearer* are meant to be seen from various viewpoints, the contour changing with the position of the spectator even though the integrity of the original block is respected. Thus the movement of the *Lance Bearer* is contained within a limited area and consists of the contrast between the legs, the upward and downward movement of the arms, and the placement of the shoulders. The action of the *Discus Thrower* revolves within a circle, coming to rest as the result of opposing sweeps in motion. As to the so-called ideal proportions of the *Lance Bearer*, we should remember that there were earlier and different proportions among the Greeks, and we shall see later ones as well.

Fig. 81. Polycleitos: Lance Bearer. Naples, National Museum.

AGE OF PERICLES: *The Acropolis*. The highest part of the city of Athens, traditional home first of Cecrops (son of Earth) and Erechtheus (heroic ancestor of the kings of Athens) and later of Athena Polias, the Acropolis brings into focus the architecture and sculpture of the later fifth century B.C. (fig. 82). Famous as a religious shrine during Homeric times, it was razed by the invading Persians and then rebuilt in the great development of Athenian prestige and political leadership. Athens organized the Delian confederacy in 477 B.C. with regular levies made on some two hundred small states. Although democracy in Athens grew during this period, it was accompanied by this equally strong imperial-

Fig. 82. The Acropolis, Athens. Actual state.

Fig. 83. The Acropolis, Athens. Model by G. P. Stevens.

ism, which ultimately furnished the means for rebuilding the Acropolis. The great Athenian leader Pericles (in power 461–429 B.C.) moved the Delian treasury to Athens and appropriated its funds. The glorious artistic achievements of the late fifth century B.C. reflect the political eminence of Athens as expressed by a limited number of intellectuals led by the aristocratic Pericles. At the same time, this art contains a strong element of naturalism when compared with earlier stages, and includes perhaps the most typical examples of a balancing of the worldly and the spiritual, the specific and the general, the human and the divine, that characterizes Greek art and culture.

Under the direction of the famous sculptor Phidias, the work on the Acropolis buildings brought together the leading talents of the Greek world. In a reconstruction of this important hilltop shrine (fig. 83), the entrance is through a pylon gate below (not shown here), then up a flight of steps leading past a tiny Ionic-style temple set on a square mass of masonry and dedicated to Athena Nike (Victorious Athena). A temple-shaped ceremonial gateway, or propylaeum, stands at the head of the stairs. To the left behind the fortified wall is seen the famous *Athena Promachos* statue by Phidias. Initiating at the propylaea is the *via sacra*, the sacred way, leading past the chief building on this hill, the temple of Athena Parthenos, or *Parthenon*, dedicated to the virgin Athena. At the extreme left is the *Erechtheum*, a composite Ionic structure built after the time of Pericles and Phidias, in which the older gods of Athens — Cecrops, Erechtheus, and Athena Polias — were worshiped.

The Parthenon. The culmination of the Doric style of architecture in the relative subtlety of its proportions as compared with earlier examples, the *Parthenon* (fig. 84) today appears without its many different

Fig. 84. The Parthenon, Athens.

types of sculptural embellishment and final color effects on the sculptures and their backgrounds. This is particularly unfortunate since Greek temples, designed for outdoor worship, presented their most important aspects from the outside. A reconstructed model of this building (fig. 85) displays these elements as well as the proportions of the various parts in relation to each other. A slight outward curvature of lines compensates for any possible inward or downward bending appearance that could result from the visual impact of many downmoving or diagonal accents. The columns have a slight *entasis*, or gradual dilation, of about 7 inches to counteract the inward movement of their outlines, while the base, or *stylobate*, on which they rest is similarly raised in the center to overcome the continuous downward thrust of the columns which might make the base look as though it sagged.

Fig. 85. The Parthenon, Athens. Model in Metropolitan Museum of Art, New York.

The plan is rather simple: eight columns front and rear, and seventeen along each side, contain a rectangular structure with porticos in front and back. This long chamber, or *cella*, consists of two sections, the larger one for the gigantic figure of the goddess (by Phidias also) and behind it a square treasure chamber. Externally the temple presents a series of horizontals balanced by verticals and capped by the typical pedimented roof bearing sculptures. Two other forms of sculpture are found. One is in the square-shaped metopes above the columns that alternate with the slightly protruding beam ends (originally wood) called triglyphs from their division into three stone parts. The other is a long frieze on the outside of the cella, facing the ambulatory, or walking space, behind the columns (fig. 86). With the exception of the interior

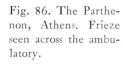

Fig. 86. The Parthenon, Athens. Frieze seen across the ambulatory.

figure of Athena, these sculptures were meant to be viewed from the outside in the clear Mediterranean sunlight and at varying heights and distances. Seen in the cold light of a northern museum, the colors used on the Greek temple might appear somewhat garish — like a gypsy skirt in a big city — but they were made for a brilliant sun by which they were tempered, while at the same time they heightened the visibility of the sculptures.

Doric and Ionic orders. A Greek temple in its entirety, whether Doric or Ionic (fig. 87), is an exterior expression of geometric proportions — a simplified and sculptured form to which other sculpture and painting are added. The chief parts of the Doric temple (e.g., the *Parthenon* or the

Fig. 87. The Doric and Ionic orders.

Temple of Zeus at Olympia) include first a base (stylobate) from which the columns with their beveled surfaces rise directly, the *shaft* enlarging slightly and then diminishing as it rises toward the narrower *necking*. Directly above is found a swelling curved stone cushion, or *echinus*, leading to a simple square *abacus* block, the final element in the sectionally built column. These three top elements form the capital of the column, effecting a gentle transition from vertical to horizontal: the necking because of its horizontal band; the echinus because of a curved, partly horizontal form; and the abacus block offering a miniature lintel on which the *architrave* rests. The latter, a plain undecorated continuous band of stone, forms the basis of the superstructure, or *entablature*, to which are added the alternating triglyphs and metopes and the pediment with its angled, or *raking*, cornice and flat, or ordinary, cornice. Not only the temple but also the propylaea on the Acropolis is of the Doric type, or *order*.

We may glance into the reconstructed model of the *Parthenon* (fig. 88) in order to visualize the essentially nonfunctional character of its interior. A mighty 40-foot ivory-and-gold figure of Athena dominated the space. Since worship was generally conducted out of doors, this crowding was not important, but proportionally it leaves much to be desired. Our information concerning the huge and long-since-disappeared Athena comes from literary sources, later and much smaller versions in marble, and from Athenian coins of the period.

In the Ionic style, the Acropolis possesses the small *Temple of Athena Nike* and the more complex and later *Erechtheum*. The former (fig. 89), although now without its gabled roof, shows the typical column and entablature (i.e., the order) features of this style. Taller and slimmer columns rise in grooves, or flutings, from their own bases; the echinus is decorated with egg-and-dart as well as bead-and-reel motifs; and a special double scroll or volute form is inserted as cushion between the echinus and the abacus block. The entablature consists first of a triple band of stone for the architrave, and above this a continuous sculpture frieze instead of the Doric triglyphs and metopes. Generally speaking, the Ionic is a more graceful, almost feminine style that may well be contrasted to the austere and simpler Doric.

In the *Erechtheum* (fig. 90) we find this embellished Ionic order on the north porch and an attractive variant of the mode on the so-called *Porch of the Maidens* (fig. 91), also seen in the *Siphnian Treasury* at Delphi (fig. 75). Here again female forms are used to support the entablature. A delicate balancing of directional thrust, typical of both Doric and Ionic architecture, emerges in the straight architectonic right leg or pseudocolumn opposed to the graceful feminine relaxation of the left.

Fig. 89. Temple of Athena Nike, Acropolis, Athens.

Fig. 90. The Erechtheum, Acropolis, Athens.

Other types of buildings of the Periclean period include the *odeum*, or concert hall, a circular, columned structure with a conical roof, and the theater, already mentioned in connection with the Panhellenic sanctuaries. At Athens the well-known *Theater of Dionysos* (fig. 92) is built against the base of the Acropolis hill.

Parthenon sculptures. The sculptures of the second half of the fifth century are richly represented by fragments from the *Parthenon.* From

Fig. 91. The Erechtheum, Athens. Porch of the Maidens.

the pediments, a number belong to the east façade, which showed a contest between Athena and Poseidon for the privilege of guarding Athens. On the west façade there was portrayed the birth of Athena full-grown from the head of Zeus. Typical among the fragments are the female group known as *The Fates* (fig. 93) and the so-called *Theseus* (fig. 94), both from the east pediment and both symbolizing the suprahuman idealization of Greek gods. The three fates, present at every birth, are heroic female figures combining extensive knowledge of the human form with a generalized interpretation. The handling of drapery, for example, displays keen observation and awareness of the body beneath; but the aim of the sculptor is never merely naturalistic — it is rather to raise these forms to a symbolic level above the human or specific. The woman at the left is about to rise, the central figure has her legs pulled in under her as she turns, the one at the right is in complete repose. Each movement is as assured and self-confident as the magnificent poise of the heroic male figure which the Greeks had been developing since archaic times, exemplified in the *Theseus*. His expression remains neutral, for the heroic-aristocratic ideal still allows only an unspecific and dignified use of the human body (the head absorbed into the over-all rhythm) to express the lofty sentiments of the age.

The same abstraction pervades the *Panathenaic Procession* relief (figs. 86, 95) on the outside of the *Parthenon* cella, a continuous band some 525 feet long and about 40 inches high. Here a distinguished procession of

Fig. 92. Theater of Dionysos, Athens.

Fig. 93. The Fates. East pediment of the Parthenon, Athens. London, British Museum.

the people of Athens moves toward the entrance of the building where, above the doorway, were represented the maidens who wove the ceremonial robe or *peplos* for Athena, the city fathers, and the gods who watched the concourse of people and the robe's presentation. Among these variegated and distinct types there is a uniformly quiet, dignified mood; with heads all on a level, they proceed in a completely neutral space whose unreality balances the strong trend toward naturalism. The metope reliefs show a series of Lapiths struggling with centaurs; these date from the beginning of the project and are still somewhat transitional in form.

Fig. 94. Theseus — also known as Mount Olympus. East pediment of the Parthenon. London, British Museum.

Although Phidias was director of the Acropolis works and we may assume that his style dominated the entire enterprise, there is no single piece that can definitely be attributed to him. The famous *Athena Lemnia* (fig. 96), of which copies still exist, is believed to have been executed by Phidias for the citizens of Lemnos for the Acropolis. Here are summed up the dignity, reserve, and powerful impersonality that pervade his semihuman, semidivine creatures.

Fig. 95. Horsemen from the Panathenaic Procession. North frieze of the Parthenon. London, British Museum.

THE NEW NATURALISM. The latter part of the fifth century B.C. was markedly influenced in a more naturalistic direction by the philosophy of the Sophists, which stressed the rational over the divine and accentuated the possibility of developing intelligent citizens by education rather than by birth (cf. Socrates). The questioning middle-class individual emerged in opposition to the long-dominant aristocrat. Instead of heroes,

Fig. 96. Athena Lemnia. Dresden, Albertina.

this fresh approach favored well-informed rational beings, heightened realities, and even emotions (however limited at first) instead of abstractions. Instead of seeking to balance the specific and the general, at the end of the fifth century B.C. and during the one following, art veered increasingly in the new direction.

Greek vase painting, because it was associated with utilitarian rather than ceremonial objects, moved toward naturalism and worldly expression sooner than the more formal temple sculpture. As early as the first half of the fifth century B.C. there had appeared innumerable everyday (genre) scenes such as *Women Putting Away Their Clothes* (fig. 97), where two nudes are shown in graceful attitudes that conform to the inside shape of a drinking cup (*kylix*), their bodies in trenchant outline. The sober elegance of the cup itself (fig. 98) illustrates a high point in the many varied Greek pottery shapes of that century.

Sculpture reached this stage of naturalism at the end of the century in such works as *Athena Tying Her Sandal* (fig. 99), a charming relief

106

from the *Temple of Athena Nike* in which the womanly goddess, her form vividly revealed by clinging drapery, performs the commonplace task of adjusting a sandal. Elsewhere the emphasis on the human rather than the divine, the beginnings of an interest in the emotions, may be represented by the soft beauty of the gravestone *Stele of Hegeso* (fig. 100). Here the deceased is in the act of choosing a jewel from a box held out by her maid as though Hegeso were merely going away somewhere, a restrained but poetic reference to death. This is a long way from the hero statues; now anyone could have a generalized portrait on a tombstone.

With the fourth century B.C. the influence of the rising middle class

Fig. 97. (Right) Women Putting Away Their Clothes. From a kylix attributed to Douris. New York, Metropolitan Museum of Art.

Fig. 98. (Below) Youths and Maidens. Painting on the outside of a kylix attributed to Douris. New York, Metropolitan Museum of Art.

Fig. 99. Athena Tying Her Sandal. Relief from Temple of Athena Nike, Acropolis, Athens.

and its rational Sophistic philosophy was increasingly felt in art through growing naturalism and emotionalism. The philosophy of Aristotle (384–322 B.C.), seeking the essence of life not in the absolute ideas of Plato but in the nature of things themselves, underlined the change. Portraits appeared in this period, while conceptions of space evolved from the limiting Polycleitan block to an outward-moving, space-engulfing form that included the spectator and the world. At the same time, there were the disordering consequences of the bitter Peloponnesian War (431–404 B.C.), in which Athens was defeated by Sparta but still remained the intellectual leader of Greece. Accordingly, in addition to the drive toward individualism and naturalism, we must consider the effects of an unsettled political situation and the disillusionment following defeat. This may help to account for the sensitive, inward-looking sculpture of Praxiteles, the dignified sadness of Lysippos' figures, the overt tragedy of the forms of Scopas. We speak primarily of sculpture in the fourth century B.C., since Athens no longer had the means for elaborate building projects, while its pottery trade that had carried Greek vases to every part of the Mediterranean fell off to a mere trickle.

Praxiteles. The career of Praxiteles reflected a kind of individualistic Bohemianism and the search for new types during his era. He is famous for the dreamy delicacy of such themes as the *Hermes and Dionysos* (fig. 101) and the *Cnidian Aphrodite* (fig. 102). At a time when no great temples needing pedimental sculptures were being built, artists like Praxiteles could turn to lighter things that expressed their own personalities in the modern sense. Instead of Olympian detachment (e.g., *Theseus*, fig. 94) a romantic introspection emerged with more human qualities in this sculptor's elegant *Hermes*, sensuous *Satyr*, and languid *Apollo the Lizard Sticker*.

Praxiteles was best known in antiquity for the *Aphrodite* done for the city of Cnidos (fig. 102). This is the first full vision of the feminine nude goddess and in many ways the most effective of the nude Aphrodites or Venuses of the next few centuries. It is identified through the coins of the city of Cnidos on which it is pictured. The goddess rests her weight on one foot as her body sways leftward in the characteristic Praxitelean "S" curve; balance is maintained and strain on the right foot is minimized by her arm's attachment to the drapery and the vase. Physically she is related to traditional art, but an already evident dreaminess, together with the original daring nudity of the figure, places her in a new category. Innumerable descendants of the type — draped, undraped, and partly draped — include the famous *Venus of Milo* of the Louvre and the *Medici Venus*.

Praxiteles' *Hermes and Dionysos* (fig. 101), one of the most beautifully surfaced marbles of ancient times, is also one of the few authentic works of an identifiable master. Here too the figure is supported by drapery as the messenger of the gods holds the child Dionysos on his left arm and in his right a bunch of grapes. Even more psychological than the *Cnidian Aphrodite,* Hermes reveals a complete self-absorption, a romantic inwardness as tangible as that of any nineteenth-century painter or poet. As in most of Praxiteles's figures, there is added slender-

Fig. 100. Stele of Hegeso. Athens, National Museum.

Fig. 101. Praxiteles: Hermes and Dionysos. Olympia Museum.

ness (the "ideal" proportion is changing), the typical body "S" curve for grace, a frank appeal to the senses, and a new type of face with a long straight nose coming directly out of the forehead.

Scopas. In contrast to the dreamy elegance of Praxiteles, Scopas offers a consistently tragic viewpoint, expressed in such figures as the head fragments from the temple of Athena Alea at Tegea (fig. 103), the heads apparently turned upward in their moments of pain and sorrow. Scopas was most famous in antiquity for a *Maenad*, an ecstatically mad figure holding up a kid as sacrifice to the god Pan. His interest in serious emotions led him to temple decoration, of which he was one of the last important practitioners. The existing fragments of his gods with their evident melancholy differ from the serene Phidian type of the previous century, for they now suffer as humans do. Scopas's name is associated with the *Mausoleum at Halicarnassus* in Asia Minor (building activity began to shift eastward in the fourth century B.C.), erected by Artemisia in honor of her husband Mausolus, King of Caria (fig. 104). Three other Greek sculptors collaborated with Scopas on the decorations for this monument to a Persian viceroy — one of the earliest examples of the

110

diffusion of Greek cultural ideas to non-Greek parts of the ancient world. Imitated in many modern derivations, the *Mausoleum* contained a sculptural frieze as well as colossal statues of Artemisia and *Mausolus* (fig. 105). Here the overt melancholy of Scopas's style is overlaid on a traditional Athenian type of figure with impressive draperies and relaxed pose.

Lysippos. Lysippos worked at the end of the fourth century B.C., with the beginning of the period of Alexander the Great, whose favorite sculptor he was. He expressed a dignified naturalness as well as a new concept of space. His best-known work, the *Apoxyomenos*, or *Scraper*

Fig. 102. Praxiteles: Cnidian Aphrodite. Draped original in Vatican Museum, Rome; undraped cast in Metropolitan Museum of Art, New York.

Fig. 103. Head of a Youth. From the Temple of Athena Alea at Tegea. Athens, National Museum.

Fig. 104. Mausoleum at Halicarnassus. Restoration.

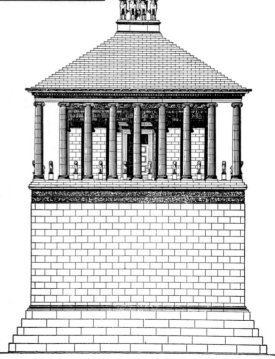

112

(fig. 106), comes down to us through the unfortunately usual and in-adequate means of a Roman copy, but certain elements are clear. First, in a mundane action the athlete is scraping dirt and oil from his body after exercise. Second, the proportions differ from the Polycleitan canon; the smaller head and slimmer form are executed more natural-istically than in the previous century, but are still far from photographic in effect. Third and even more important, a new dynamic spatial quality is implied in this and other Lysippan works. The figure is actually in motion as it stretches its arms toward the onlooker, seeming to break out of the rectangular block from which it was carved. The lower part of the body moves independently, swaying from one leg to the other and changing the direction of interest. This means not only that the figure can be observed from different viewpoints to get a change of silhouette,

Fig. 105. Mausolus. From the Mauso-leum at Halicarnassus. London, British Museum.

Fig. 106. Lysippos: The Apoxyomenos, or Scraper. Rome, Vatican Museum.

as in the motionless *Lance Bearer*, but that the spectator must move with the sculptor, first in one direction and then in another.

The elegant restrained silhouettes of Phidias and Polycleitos give way to this revolutionary concept of form. The outward-moving idea signifies the age of Alexander's empire, as the reserved and block-contained idealizations, the serene expressions of the earlier artists, had represented their period. In the sculptors of the fourth century B.C. — the sensitive Praxiteles and emotive Scopas as well as the naturalistic and space-enveloping Lysippos — are symbolized the qualities of a new era.

6 / FROM HELLENISTIC TO ROMAN WORLD EMPIRE

THE continuous Greek civil wars of the fourth century B.C. — reflected in the emotional seminaturalistic art of that period — came to an end through domination by the northern state of Macedon under King Philip. After subjugating the various city-states of Greece, Philip's son Alexander the Great moved on into Asia Minor, Egypt, Persia, and Asia itself as far as India, encompassing a greater empire than had any previous ruler (figs. 107, 54).

THE POST-ALEXANDRIAN WORLD

So vast a territory could not be held together after the death of Alexander in 323 B.C., when it separated into various major and minor kingdoms, chiefly the Greek mainland (Macedon), Seleucid Asia, and Ptolemaic Egypt, ruled by the leading generals of Alexander and their descendants. But a tremendous effect remained from this attempt to impose one-man rule on the whole world; the Romans, who would soon supplant the basically separatist Greeks, were to carry out that idea. The Macedonian scheme had provided first for a war against the rising Carthaginian power in North Africa. A great highway along the North African coast for communication between various parts of the empire, a continuous chain of temples for religious unity, great cities at strategic trade and military locations, and finally a mingling and mixture of the differing peoples were also projected. This boldly conceived international plan was destined to be fulfilled in all its major features by the Roman Empire.

THE HELLENISTIC WORLD OUTLOOK. After Alexander's time, Greek ideas were spread throughout the ancient world by conquest and the establishment of some twenty-five cities. This provided a surface unity which, though partial and even shallow in many respects, gave the period a completely new aspect. An interesting case of infiltration occurred as far away as northwest India, at Gandhara, where Buddhist sculptures were done under Greek influence (see fig. 145). The Greeks in turn were affected by these contacts; their religion changed from the simple Indo-European pantheon of earlier days to a more emotional and Eastern approach in the worship of the Asia Minor goddess Cybele, the Egyptian Isis, and the Persian Mithra. Changing his earlier role of individualistic city-state member, the Greek now became a citizen of a nation and even of the world. He lived under a government that, however dominating, considered his welfare and erected splendid buildings for his entertainment and use or as symbols of the power of the state. These included theaters and stadiums, concert and reception halls, as well as many new kinds of administrative buildings necessitated by new forms of political life. They were built either by kings or by the growing class of wealthy merchants.

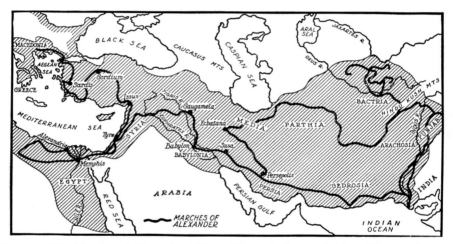

Fig. 107. The Empire of Alexander. (From Henry S. Lucas, *A Short History of Civilization*, New York, McGraw-Hill Book Company, Inc., 1953. By permission of the author.)

Business expanded in the most favorable circumstances. Conquest and unification of the empire brought to market the enormous treasures of the East and established easy communication, widespread colonization, and other conditions that created a new type of rich man and art patron. These factors strengthened the already existing tendency to minimize the importance of family background in favor of individual accomplishment, but they also left Athens and Greece itself in a declining economic position as young men went east for jobs and trade. Spiritually, however, Athens remained an important center where monuments were still erected by wealthy men and rulers from all parts of the enlarged Greek world.

116

In the Greek peninsula proper a new internationalism was reflected in such philosophical movements as Stoicism and Epicureanism which stressed the cosmopolitan rather than the individual viewpoint. According to one facet of these philosophies, man was now a creature without national or racial prejudice and more interested in economic status, which determined social and political importance. The Stoics recognized that all men possessed a reasoning faculty, which led them to the idea of the brotherhood of man above national, racial, or social distinctions. The Epicurean desire to free the mind from wrong was to be accomplished by attacking religion and superstitions of various kinds and by adopting a mechanistic, i.e., atomistic, explanation of the universe. In addition, there were the Peripatetic philosophers, followers of Aristotle, who were interested almost exclusively in historical and scientific research.

The rationalism of this so-called Hellenistic period brought about immense scientific advancement and an intensified naturalism in art. Hand in hand with the great discoveries of Euclid and Apollonius in mathematics, Eratosthenes in geography, Archimedes and Hero in physics, Herophilus in anatomy, and Hipparchus in astronomy went new anatomical, emotive, narrative, portrait, and genre interests in sculpture and painting.

CULTURAL EFFECTS OF INTERNATIONALISM. Culture itself became internationalized; scholars and artists were drawn to important political and business centers like Alexandria, Pergamum, and Rhodes, which were focal points for the new aesthetics of the monarchies and upper middle classes. The men of learning and the artists now worked on a different basis — not for the glory of a city-state fatherland or traditional gods but in the service of individual patrons in the modern sense who had to be catered to as rulers or wealthy personages. Moreover, the new internationalism added so much to scholarship and artistic knowledge, and business methods so rationalized procedures, that facts and styles were now gathered for their own sakes. Centers of learning were increasingly dedicated to the accumulation of data (which, however, did not reach the public as there were still no books) and became the haunts of pedants. As a result of the museums and art collections of all sorts, a wide variety of styles and subject matters appeared simultaneously, in contrast to previous epochs when styles were more clearly related to dominant social interests. This variety also implied a more fluid social pattern, a less stratified arrangement than before.

The art of the Hellenistic period, produced for specific national and municipal needs, reflects the relationship between state and individual, the international rather than local emphasis, an interest in the everyday

Fig. 108. The Winged Victory of Samothrace. Paris, Louvre.

world, and newer forms of religion. The conspicuous concern with the physical appearance and psychological character of the individual, both in literature and in art, comes very close to a modern approach. The constant theme of classical culture, the domination of man by the gods and his struggles against them, is now replaced by an expanding sense of man in and against his physical and social environment.

HELLENISTIC SCULPTURE: *Religious types.* Sculpture seems to have been the dominant art of the time between the death of Alexander (323 B.C.) and the conquest of Greece by Rome (146 B.C.). The influence of this Hellenistic interval would actually last well into the Christian era in some places, affecting among others the art of Rome. There was necessarily a continuation and development of Greek types of the previous age. *The Winged Victory of Samothrace* (fig. 108) is a product of the early Hellenistic epoch, presumably done for Demetrius "the besieger" (son of one of the generals of Alexander, whose wars dragged on for half a century). This is the climax of the development of the winged-victory type. Like late fourth-century B.C. sculpture, e.g., Lysippos, it moves powerfully out of the block. The goddess leans into the wind from the prow of a ship, her drapery clinging in dramatic naturalism that adds to the feeling of motion and brings the form into vivid relief under the many small folds. The sculptor seems interested in movement for its own sake rather than in symbolic considerations, a conscious aestheticism which is only occasionally evident in the classical era but very apparent throughout the duration of Hellenistic ideas.

This age was certainly less concerned with the conventional gods and goddesses, partly because of growing skepticism and vulgarity (which produced a series of erotic rather than symbolic Venuses) and partly because of the international mingling of divinities. Aristotle (who was Alexander's tutor), coming at the beginning of the period, tells us that the religious beliefs of men are apt to borrow their forms from political institutions. Indeed the world outlook now bore heavily on the old tribal and city-state gods — a much broader point of view was required. People often found that the various deities they encountered were very similar to each other; many bearded gods from this time cannot be accurately identified as Zeus, Dionysos, or Aesculapius. In Alexandria, the fusion of religious ideas or *Theocrasia*, the belief that there must be only one god under different names, produced Jupiter Serapis, a combination of a Greek element with the local Osiris-Apis-Horus mixture. This practical balancing of religion and universalism was accepted by all except the monotheistic Hebrews and Persians. It may be remarked that the worship of Serapis, a divine trinity, was conducted

Fig. 109. Praying Youth. Berlin, State Museums.

with ancient Egyptian interest in immortality, accompanied by the ceremonial burning of candles, offering of votive statues, and the prayers of monastic celibates with shaven heads. This important precursor of Christianity had spread through the civilized world by the first century B.C.

Religion in this period tended to be more and more the worship of a universal ruler, the symbolic vigorous bearded man. Its semimystical, semi-intellectual character is seen in the famous *Praying Youth* (fig. 109) which illustrates the philosophical, almost pantheistic devotion toward which men were turning. This work was presumably done by Boethus, a pupil of Lysippos. It recalls the latter's figures (fig. 106) in proportion and outward movement; but its positive overt religious aspiration differentiates it from classical statues and brings it closer to our own sense of worship.

Allegories. The concrete sculptural images of gods and goddesses appeared less often than abstractions and allegories — e.g., personifications of cities instead of the earlier patron deities. Thus the figure of *Antioch* (fig. 110), an embodiment of that magnificent Syrian city, is seated on a rocky hill, holding a few ears of grain in one hand and wearing a crown made of the city's walls and towers. At her feet a child form emerges from the earth, symbolizing the river Orontes which originates at this point. Another similar arrangement is the *River Nile*, a shallow Greco-Egyptian allegory showing a huge, bearded Poseidon type lying down; sixteen cupids (the 16 cubits which the Nile rises each year), a crown of grain, a horn of plenty, and the symbolic Egyptian sphinx complete the composition.

Genre types. Other new types developed during this era include idyllic subjects such as a child playing with a goose, children kissing

Fig. 110. City of Antioch. Rome, Vatican Museum.

Fig. 111. Spinario. London, British Museum.

each other, playful cupids of various kinds, and pastoral scenes. One of the best known, the so-called *Spinario,* or *Boy Pulling a Thorn from His Foot* (fig. 111), shows a very young runner performing this simple act and much concerned with himself. He is no longer a detached classical athlete such as the *Lance Bearer* or even the *Scraper;* the accent here is on charm and everyday activity.

Parallel in meaning with that piece are the many terra-cotta figurines first found in Greece at Tanagra and therefore called Tanagra figurines (fig. 112). These have an almost Rococo charm in the eighteenth-century mode (see fig. 456); they show women dressed in delightful costumes, nude Venuses, cupids, dancers, and a wide variety of other appealing themes. Reproduced by molds in apparently large quantities, these figurines are supposedly the equivalent of modern curios, or knickknacks; they give us an interesting picture of the contemporary tastes of relatively large numbers of people — something large-scale Classical art cannot do.

We have noted the vulgarized Venuses, which were part of a demand for luxury art that resulted in "unclassical" versions of the Praxitelean Venus such as the well-known *Medici Venus* or the plump *Capitoline*

Fig. 112. Woman. Tanagra-type statuette (terra cotta). New York, Metropolitan Museum of Art.

Venus whose additional flesh may be the result of Near Eastern taste. Venus (born from the sea) owed her popularity to the Epicurean philosophers who attached significance to anyone associated with water, which they considered the most important of the elements. For the Stoics, to whom fire was the most vital energizing element, the characters of Zeus (who built the world out of fire) and Dionysos (born when Zeus embraced Semele as a cloud of fire) were significant. Dionysos was one of the few god types perfected during this period of eclectic adaptation and alteration.

Naturalism. The most outstanding art trend of the age was toward naturalism, often running over into extreme exaggeration. Portraits, which had been infrequent even in the fourth century B.C., now became a staple item, symbolizing an interest in the personality of the individual and his accurate physical appearance. *Demosthenes* (fig. 113), the Athenian orator who had fought unification under Philip of Macedon, is shown as a thin, austere, almost fanatical type, holding a *rotulus* (scroll) in his hands. He reveals the strain of a dedicated individual,

122

his face lined and careworn, turned toward the audience. Detailed treatments of this kind would not have been possible in the more generalized art of the classical period. The Hellenistic epoch produced in the art of Alexandria a wealth of street types: beggars, urchins, singers, and peddlers, who are part of the same interest in personalities.

In a different vein, the naturalism of the *Marsyas Torso* (fig. 114) conveys an almost Baroque emotionalism (see fig. 396). The tortured satyr, hanged from his thumbs by Apollo, strains both face and body in his pain. This tour de force of psychological distortion displays anatomical knowledge and muscular tension. This kind of art was popular at both Pergamum and Rhodes. In the same general class as the *Marsyas* is a series of figures of elderly men and women, fishermen, shepherdesses,

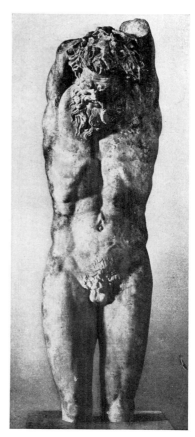

Fig. 113. Demosthenes (old version). Rome, Vatican Museum.

Fig. 114. Marsyas Torso. Istanbul, Museum.

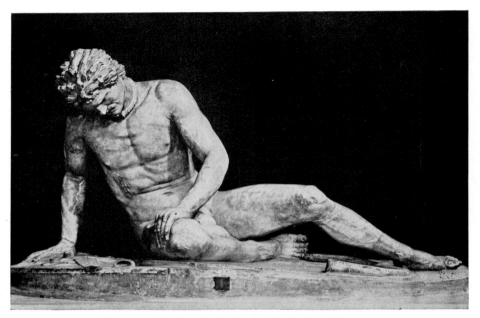
Fig. 115. Dying Gaul. Rome, Capitoline Museum.

and others with wrinkled faces and forms, stressing their most obviously ugly qualities — a far cry from the reticent art of the previous period.

Alexandria. There were, of course, artistic differences among the cities. It is difficult to ascribe specific innovations to Alexandria, since these seem to have been spread all over the Mediterranean and their points of origin are obscure. We may assume that the picturesque street types mentioned before belong to the Alexandrian area. Also, as the heart of the Ptolemaic dynasty, it is supposed to have had a highly developed taste for the sensuous figures discussed earlier — the erotic, plump Venuses and hermaphrodites.

Pergamum. In Pergamum we know much more about the local styles. Here a prosperous learned center grew up in a very small but intellectually superior state. When the Gauls or Galatians invaded Asia Minor, they were repulsed by the powerful mercenary army of the Pergamines, who set up a series of votive statues in the mother city of Athens (ca. 230 B.C.). Some of these have been preserved, e.g., the *Dying Gaul* (fig. 115) and the *Gaul Killing His Wife and Himself,* which show definite European types, perhaps resembling the modern French, in pathetic and heroic roles. In the latter scene, a defeated Gaul kills his wife and commits suicide; in the *Dying Gaul,* a barbarian warrior lies on the ground. This artistic descendant of the wounded soldiers of the Aegina pediment is no longer a heroic symbol but a sentient human being who engages our sympathies in the manner of Romantic art or literature (see figs. 480–481).

A second victory over the Gauls caused King Eumenes II to erect the famous *Altar of Zeus* in Pergamum (ca. 175 B.C., fig. 116). The three-sided open structure is approached by a flight of steps and embellished with a long high-relief allegory, the *Battle of the Gods and the Giants* (fig. 117). Again we may compare a Hellenistic with a classical treatment, the latter in the pediments at Olympia where Lapiths and centaurs meet. While the earlier work is arranged in terms of a charac-

Fig. 116. Altar of Zeus from Pergamum. Berlin, State Museums.

Fig. 117. Battle of the Gods and the Giants. Altar of Zeus. Berlin, State Museums.

Fig. 118. Laokoön (old version). Rome, Vatican Museum.

teristic magnificent restraint, the Hellenistic example shows conscious striving after melodramatic effects, as in the section where Athena grasps a rebellious suffering giant by the hair while his mother, the earth goddess, asks mercy for her errant son. In keeping with the contorted emotional attitudes, the musculature is tremendously exaggerated to show the superhuman power of the participants, but this very exaggeration is perhaps a measure of the lack of success of the 430-foot-long frieze.

Rhodes. The note of unusual pathos, though characteristic of the Pergamine style, is also found in one of the few works we can definitely associate with the school of Rhodes, *The Laokoön* (fig. 118). The prosperous island kingdom of Rhodes, balance wheel of the ancient Mediterranean world, is famous for its *Colossus* which bestrode the main harbor for more than half a century. The sculptures produced here are traditionally connected with the pupils of Lysippos. The *Laokoön* group, discovered in A.D. 1506 and influential in the work of Michelangelo and the early Baroque, is even more melodramatic than the Pergamine frieze — muscles distend almost to the breaking point, figures writhe uncontrollably, heads tilt sideways, and faces are distorted in terror. The boys are in mortal fear, and the Trojan priest, their father, suffers at his helplessness before the serpents sent by the gods to kill them. It is not

126

to be wondered that the Pergamine and Rhodian works seem so similar, considering the internationalism of the period and its easy communications. In the same way the charming Tanagra figurines and other types are found throughout the Mediterranean.

HELLENISTIC PAINTING. Wall painting was also widespread and not localized, running to comic and genre scenes with occasional touches of vulgarity, especially in the south Italian area at Pompeii where Hellenistic painting and sculpture had great influence. Stories of the gods are told with a new worldly quality and human emphasis that suggest Baroque or Rococo classical deities. In other instances, *Medea* is portrayed (Naples Museum) with the same desperately tragic quality of the *Dying Gaul*. The sense of receding space is particularly important in this art for its expression of the real and tangible world, a feeling that is transmitted to the slightly later painting of the Romans. In the famous *Odyssey Landscape* (ca. third century B.C., fig. 119) the painter conveys a sensation of aerial perspective (distance indicated by lessening the focus of distant objects) that will not recur until the modern era. A similar awareness of man existing in a tangible physical world is apparent in the

Fig. 119. Odyssey Landscape. Rome, Vatican Museum.

placement of individual figures within the picture space and the use of converging lines to show distance (linear perspective) in both painting and relief sculpture.

HELLENISTIC ARCHITECTURE. Architecturally the period discloses the same international and materialistic qualities. We have seen that many kings from outlying areas set up shrines at Athens — also at Delos and Olympia, the ancient sanctuary cities — just as later Roman emperors and men of wealth would do. A broader and more philosophical religious approach brought forth a great number of altars which became even more important than the temples. In such examples as the *Altar of Zeus* at Pergamum, the conception of this deity differs from his earlier association with a particular place or his chieftainship of the Greek pantheon of gods. Zeus in the broad philosophic terms of the Stoics is now regarded as the father of heaven and earth. The great *Temple of Zeus* in Athens (fig. 120), built by Antiochus Epiphanes in the second century B.C., is another of this sort, consisting originally of a gigantic double colonnade with no roof. In the eclectic columns the builder followed the Ionic separate base and channelings up to a Corinthian type of capital. Here an inverted bell form is surrounded by a double row of acanthus leaves with pairs of volutes (scrolls) at the corners supporting a broad flat abacus block.

Rational city planning appeared for the first time in this period, as at Priene in Asia Minor, which is laid out on a hill in a simple rectangular

Fig. 120. Temple of Zeus, Athens.

plan. On one side of the open _agora,_ or market place, a covered portico, or _stoa,_ offered a place where people could congregate out of the sun, like modern arcaded squares in southern European and Latin-American cities. Where the stoa had two stories, it became the _basilica,_ or place of contracts. Other buildings included the _bouleuterion,_ or council house (symbol of the autonomy of many Asian cities), the municipal library, the _gymnasium,_ or secondary school, the _odeum,_ or concert hall, and the theater. The last-named was generally more elaborate in shape and function than its classical predecessor and just as often out of proportion to the population of its city, a competitive gesture typical of the time.

Many features of Hellenistic society and art — their opulence, rationalism, international viewpoint — would be inherited and developed by Rome, which during this period was already an important force in the Mediterranean world.

ROME

The story of Rome is that of an agricultural-military people who expanded in successive stages from central Italy to the entire peninsula and into the rest of the Mediterranean world, northern and western Europe, and parts of Asia. An Indo-European race like the Greeks, they first appeared around 1000 B.C. During the sixth century B.C. they were dominated by Asian-Greek invaders, the Etruscans. That aggressive, capable builder nation transmitted to the Romans a strong impulse toward practical architecture (e.g., the vaulted great sewer in Rome), an anthropomorphic conception of the gods and their representation in sculpture and painting, and finally a strong mistrust of kingship.

After the Etruscan domination, the long period of the Peasant Republic (509–287 B.C.) formulated the pattern of Roman life: a constant struggle between upper and lower classes and absorption of other Italic peoples by Rome. Commerce and industry were not developed to any great extent — one explanation of later social problems and the purely military motives of Roman expansion. By 146 B.C. with the destruction of Carthage in North Africa and of Corinth, the last important Greek city, Rome had become the dominant power in the Hellenistic world. In 133 B.C. Attalus III, the last king of Pergamum, voluntarily bequeathed his empire to the Romans, and the imperial picture was complete except for northern Europe and some smaller parts of Asia added later (fig. 121).

The upper classes gorged themselves on booty; taxes on land were remitted after 167 B.C., while the constant stream of spoils camouflaged

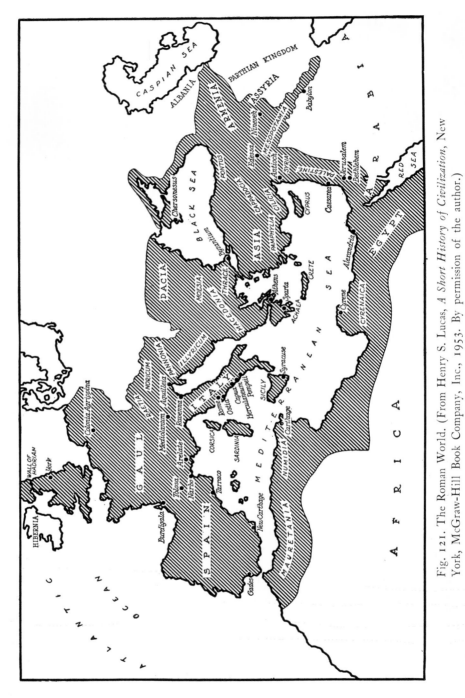

Fig. 121. The Roman World. (From Henry S. Lucas, *A Short History of Civilization*, New York, McGraw-Hill Book Company, Inc., 1953. By permission of the author.)

the need for constructive commerce and industry, until it was too late. During the second century B.C. people flocked to the city in increasing numbers, especially the poor farming class ruined by large slave-worked estates, creating thereby a landless, jobless proletariat — a city mob that had to be placated with the famous "bread and circuses," that is, free food and entertainment. The milking of the provinces went on unabated; patricians and upper middle classes lived luxuriously and threw an occasional bone to the increasingly hungry and restless mob. Although Rome was still a democracy, the deepening emergencies caused by its "predatory rather than productive" approach culminated during the first century B.C. in military dictatorship under Julius Caesar and finally in monarchy.

The ultimate downfall of the empire was to come about in large part through the failure to develop industry on a real scale and the elimination of a free peasantry. Other causes were the adoption of Eastern ideas such as traditional despotism as well as many supernatural, antirational cults, especially those emphasizing personal salvation. This last element was to be particularly influential, since the purely formal character of Roman state religion gave no comfort in times of increasing stress (the important side of Roman religion dealt with the cult of the household — the hearth — and family ancestors). As the crisis sharpened, the Roman and Greek state religions and their emperor worship would offer little solace, especially to the lower classes. For this mass of people (including the now harassed middle class) Stoic and Epicurean philosophies were to lose their appeal, while the idea of a better life in the hereafter was to become most attractive. By the fourth century of the Christian era it would be apparent that one of the new religions, Christianity, was destined to supplant Rome as a unifying force, at least in the Western world. In the East, Rome was to continue on a different basis.

ROMAN DEVELOPMENTS AND GREEK INFLUENCE. Creatively and aesthetically, Roman civilization cannot be compared with Greek; but in certain practical areas related to the administration and functioning of a great empire, the Romans were supreme. An exceedingly significant law code, engineering projects such as aqueducts and sewers, and the almost eternal Roman roads that still exist in some parts of the world typify their creative approach. In architecture, most impressive are the buildings destined for large-scale public use, such as baths, amphitheaters, and theaters, or those symbolizing the power and authority of the empire, such as palaces, triumphal arches, commemorative columns, and city gates. In the same way their sculpture is characterized by intense naturalism

Fig. 122. Etruscan Warrior (terra cotta). New York, Metropolitan Museum of Art.

and even practicability, its greatest expressions occurring in family or state portraits and in commemorative narrative sculpture.

Culturally Rome was an assimilator rather than a creator of unique forms in the Greek sense. Occupied with conquering and ruling the world in what it conceived to be its divine mission, Rome never developed beyond the cultural conservatism of an agricultural society. In most intellectual areas, including philosophy, science, and art, she borrowed rather heavily from classical Greek or Hellenistic sources whose Stoic and Epicurean viewpoints interested her practical-minded citizens. The former ideology attracted the upper classes because of its emphasis on restraint, discipline, and duty, while the latter interested the middle classes because of its pragmatic viewpoint.

Greek aesthetic ideals were first brought to Roman attention through the Etruscans, whose brooding archaic sculptures (fig. 122) correspond in form to Greek works of the early fifth century B.C. (see figs. 72–73). Etruscan tomb paintings of a slightly later period relate closely to Greek style at the end of the fifth century B.C., influenced perhaps by imported

132

Greek vases (a substantial percentage of the Greek vases known to us were found in Etruscan tombs). The deposing of the Etruscans did not end their influence but tempered it by the growing role of Rome in the Mediterranean. With the second-century B.C. conquest of Greece (146 B.C.) and the sack of Corinth, many Greek works of art came to Rome as part of the plunder, thus initiating a long period of Greco-Roman production in the various arts. So popular did Greek art become and so much in demand for the homes of the new rich that Greek artists were brought in to make copies of the great masterpieces, a circumstance to which we owe the many Roman copies of Greek sculpture.

Internationalization of culture, already clearly evident in Hellenistic times, reached new heights under the Romans to the degree that they coordinated the territory under them more successfully (even if not totally) and over a much longer period of time. Although there are certain marked distinctions between different parts of the Empire — for example, the enormous temples of the eastern portion as opposed to the smaller ones in Italy — we can speak of an Imperial style, reflected in the portrait busts of emperors distributed in all areas and the sculptural narratives carved on commemorative arches, columns, and other public structures. Even more significant from this standpoint is the profusion of aqueducts, arches of triumph, city gates and walls (the functional and administrative elements), as well as the adaptations of Greek architectural orders and ornament found throughout the Empire. Roman style would naturally vary from epoch to epoch, from the Ionic Greek inspiration of Etruscan art (purely local in effect) through the Etruscan-Hellenistic influence of the Republican period to the truly Roman works of the Empire and Late Empire periods.

Since the Etruscans were the first sculptors and builders in the Italian peninsula, we may assume their influence on the earliest Roman works of art — walls, aqueducts, and gateways as well as temple structures and bronze sculpture. The development of the vault, one of the most significant features of Roman architecture, is probably also due to the Etruscans and their Ionian, i.e., Asian Greek, connections.

REPUBLICAN ERA. Of the Republican period little is left today, since ambitious emperors wishing to achieve popularity through public works practically rebuilt the entire city of Rome. One of the few buildings surviving that period is the temple known as the *Maison Carrée* at Nîmes (fig. 123). Since public worship was less important than private, this, like most Roman temples, is relatively small — less than half the length of the *Parthenon*. It also differs from the Greek by its single flight of steps in front which leaves it on a high base. The columns are engaged, or

Fig. 123. Maison Carrée, Nîmes.

Fig. 124. Temple of Vesta, Rome.

partly embedded in the wall, on three sides of the building; only those in front are left free-standing, thus eliminating the ambulatory of the Greek temple with its dignity and impressiveness. We know from this and later examples that the Greek integrated sculptural decorations and painted surfaces were generally lacking in the Roman buildings, which usually seem somewhat cold adaptations.

Another early type is the circular temple such as the *Temple of Vesta* in Rome (fig. 124), possibly a version of the Greek circular design but preserved by the Romans as one of their most characteristic forms and transmitted to Christian architecture as the baptistry (see fig. 239). Again, like the majority of Roman temples, this is rather small.

In sculpture also the comparatively few early examples reveal Etruscan influence on the Romans. The *Portrait of an Unknown Roman* of the first century B.C. (fig. 125) reflects the uncompromising naturalism and psychological character that presumably come from Etruscan bronzes of an earlier period and that remain typical for Roman portraiture through most of its history — except for the idealizations of the Augustan age.

During the Republican period and again later, a number of factors in-

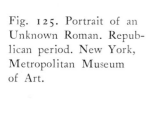

Fig. 125. Portrait of an Unknown Roman. Republican period. New York, Metropolitan Museum of Art.

fluenced the straightforward naturalism of the Roman portrait — this product of an ultrapractical society which stressed moral values and social decorum. Portraits were made of those who had given outstanding service to the state (the grave dignified consuls, censors, and tribunes) rather than for heroic and legendary reasons as among the Greeks. From earliest times, moreover, Roman portraits were part of the all-important household and ancestral worship, a private rather than public function which undoubtedly added to the naturalness of their rendition. Many of these ancestor portraits, judging from the sunken cheeks, were apparently made from wax death masks and consequently bound to be more naturalistic than idealistic.

THE AUGUSTAN AGE. Toward the end of the Republican period, with the growing influence of Hellenistic Greece and the rivalry of military leaders and important patrician families for public favor, the idea of refashioning Rome in the new style became increasingly attractive. From the Emperor Augustus (27 B.C.–14 A.D.) and his immediate followers down to the death of Nero, Rome was literally rebuilt in impressive marble under classical influence. In both architecture (temples) and sculpture, Greek forms were utilized in a more Roman, that is, practical and individual, manner. For instance, the temples reproducing Greek plans, like the Temple of Augustus at Ancyra in Asia Minor (Galatia), show a

Fig. 126. Sacred Procession. From the Ara Pacis. Florence, Uffizi Gallery.

Fig. 127. Augustus figure from Prima Porta. Rome, Vatican Museum.

new type of proportion and a distinctly individual handling of ornament.

In Rome the *Ara Pacis* (Altar of Peace) of Augustus seems to have been an open, colonnaded, late Greek-temple style (like the *Temple of Zeus* at Athens, fig. 120) with a Hellenistic altar set in the middle. This altar, symbolizing the era of peace under the beneficent reign of Augustus, was decorated with classically conceived relief sculptures (fig. 126) which show not merely the Roman sense of *gravitas* (dignity) but also their sense of history. An allegorical figure representing the Roman Senate makes sacrifice on one plaque; on another are allegorical representations, not of the gods but of the Stoic and Epicurean ideals of earth, air, and water — late classical in their rich forms but Roman in the naturalism of plant and animal shapes. The most interesting and perhaps original section of the sculptures is a procession, shown here, with Augustus in the costume of the High Priest, or Pontifex Maximus, accompanied by officials and members of his family (his wife, Agrippa, and Tiberius). In contrast to the *Panathenaic Procession* (fig. 95) these portraits of the royal family and its suite have historical immediacy instead of a completely symbolic and ideal approach. There is just as sharp a contrast between the nonnaturalistic space of the Greek frieze and the spatial devices employed here. The latter appear in the feet projecting over the ledge and the different heights of relief: high relief for the figures in the immediate foreground, medium for those further back, and low for those intended to be at a distance.

Portraiture during the Augustan age also bears the marks of Greek influence. Conceived along the lines of a very dignified naturalism, such figures as the *Augustus* from Prima Porta (fig. 127) may be compared to the style of Polycleitos in pose and general form (fig. 81) and of Lysippos in the half-naturalistic, half-idealized face (fig. 106). The emperor in the costume of a consul — his feet bare as a symbol of courage — is haranguing the troops, accompanied by the little family spirit at the left.

FLAVIAN-ANTONINE PERIOD. The next era of Roman history, the Flavian-Antonine period (A.D. 69–192), was an epoch of eastward expansion and was the age in which the most characteristic Roman forms in architecture and sculpture were developed, especially the great public buildings. These two trends are combined in the *Arch of Titus* (fig. 128) commemorating the Jewish War conducted by Titus under his father, the Emperor Vespasian, which culminated in the siege and destruction of the

Fig. 128. Arch of Titus, Rome.

138

Temple of Jerusalem in A.D. 70. The triumphal arch, an essential part of the "triumph" granted a victorious general by the Senate, became an increasingly common feature of Roman architecture, influencing modern forms in nineteenth-century Europe and America. This victory is represented allegorically on one of the reliefs inside the arch below the coffered vault. On the other side (fig. 129), portrayed with still classical restraint, the spoils from the destroyed temple are carried through a triumphal arch with spatial indications recalling the Altar of Peace. Later

Fig. 129. Spoils from the Temple of Jerusalem. Arch of Titus, Rome.

arches bear reliefs on their front and top portions as well, the style changing from the restraint of the late first century of the Christian era to an ever more pictorial, narrative, episodic manner that would be readily understood by the public.

This change may be seen in the commemorative *Column of Trajan* (fig. 130) of the early second century (A.D. 98–116), on which is unrolled a series of incidents from that Emperor's campaigns along the Danube. They ascend spirally around the surface of the column in what is known as "continuous narration," as though a picture scroll, or rotulus (the book of those days), had been translated from painting into stone. The figure of the chief character, the Emperor, appears some seventy times in the course of the different scenes. He is depicted in council, holding sacrifice, supervising the building of a camp, addressing the troops, and so on. Various aspects of the life of the Germans he was conquering are also shown. In this work (later hailed by Renaissance artists) we find the climax of the Roman naturalistic narrative style — its exciting realistic quality, filled with the drama of a great event and meant to catch the eye of the spectator and influence public opinion. Its continuous character is like so much of medieval art in which Christ is shown in different actions within the same picture (cf. the *Tribute Money* of Masaccio, fig. 334); but it is markedly different from the isolated timeless scenes in Greek art.

Fig. 130. Column of Trajan, Rome.

The great *Colosseum* (fig. 131) known as the Flavian Amphitheater was also built under Vespasian and Titus. It typifies the Roman building designed for mass entertainment, doubling the semicircular Hellenistic theater to make a full circle surrounding the performance — the ancestor of modern football stadiums and bull rings. Even today this gigantic ruin is one of the most magnificent sights in Rome because of its massive arched and vaulted construction. The vaults consist of poured concrete with brick and stone facing. On the exterior design (fig. 132), three rows of arches are framed by engaged Roman Doric, Ionic, and Corinthian columns in succession from bottom to top, proceeding from heavy to lighter orders and ending on the fourth story with an engaged and flattened Corinthian order without arches. There is conscious planning of horizontals against verticals: the heavy moldings on which the columns rest accentuate the circular mass of the building; the columns, one above the other, contribute a straight upward movement which helps to lighten the heaviness of the structure. This building is a brilliant example of Roman engineering.

140

Fig. 131. (Above) Colosseum, Rome. Aerial view.

Fig. 132. Colosseum, Rome. Side view.

Fig. 133. Pantheon, Rome.

Fig. 134. Pantheon, Rome. Interior view.

The famous *Pantheon* (fig. 133), built during Hadrian's reign (A.D. 117–138), underlines the formal character of Roman state religion in which the gods did not have the Greek familial relationship. In Greece the gods dwelt together on legendary but very real Olympus; here niches were provided for them in an impressively spacious public building. The outside of the *Pantheon* combines a dome-capped low cylinder and a Greek-type portico with porphyry columns. The inside (fig. 134) is one of the great triumphs of Roman domical structure. Concrete is poured into a framework of brick squares that lend support and elasticity, showing themselves in the square coffers of the underside of the dome. This marvelous ceiling is 140 feet in diameter, and it is about the same distance from the floor to the circular opening (*oculus*, or eye) at the top. The massive circular wall is about 20 feet thick and 75 feet high, supporting the dramatic dome whose full expanse can only be seen from the inside in all its space-enveloping effect.

LATER ROMAN ART. The *Baths of Diocletian* (fig. 135), built at the end of the third century, are another type of building emphasizing interior space, accommodation of large crowds, and concrete vault construction. Here the vaults are groined (i.e., two barrel-shaped vaults crossed at right angles) and faced with thin slabs of marble or molded stucco ornament for richness of surface. The impression of height is increased by the huge columns and their entablatures which are decorative rather than functional.

Fig. 135. Baths of Diocletian, Rome. Restored.

Whereas Greek architecture was primarily religious and symbolic in purpose, Roman buildings such as this have a practical character. These bath houses (*thermae*) were social and amusement centers; and basilicas were designed for business, legal, and administrative uses, e.g., the Basilica of Maxentius. Some of the greatest structural achievements of the Romans are exclusively functional with no aesthetic intention, as in the case of their aqueducts. Nevertheless these make a strong impression on the spectator because of their simplicity and power, rhythmic repetition of pier and arch, and varied proportions from one story to another. The *Aqueduct of Segovia* (fig. 136) exemplifies this form; its superposed arches support an open channel 100 feet in the air through which water was carried long distances to the Imperial cities. Many remains of these aqueducts, as well as the famous Roman roads and bridges, are still to be found in parts of Europe and North Africa.

In sculpture, the reserved naturalism of the Augustan age gradually reverted to the traditional lifelikeness of Roman household portraits during the Flavian period (A.D. 69–138). The Antonine era (A.D. 138–192)

Fig. 136. Aqueduct, Segovia, Spain.

144

Fig. 137. Bust of the Emperor Commodus. Rome, Vatican Museum.

Fig. 138. Head of Emperor Constantine. Rome, Capitoline Museum.

Fig. 139. Hercules and Telephos. Naples, National Museum.

shows increased pictorialism in sculpture; the hair is rendered in loose and flowing locks, carved with the drill to create additional light-and-dark effects, as in the *Bust of the Emperor Commodus* (A.D. 180–192, fig. 137). A contrasting smooth skin and carved indications of iris and pupil heighten the dramatic quality of these works.

By the mid-third century, Roman portraiture manifested a new and more powerful inner emotion and starkness of feeling, combined with simple vigorousness, as also found in the later *Head of Emperor Con-*

stantine (fig. 138). The de-emphasis of external form and concentration on inner mood approximate the modern Expressionist approach (cf. figs. 524, 547). In the early fourth century the spirit of classical Rome was clearly on the wane. Its straightforward naturalism yielded to a barbarian vigor and a greater spiritual quality that symbolized the unhappiness of the period and the oncoming conquest of Christianity.

As for Roman painting, its figure subjects such as *Hercules and Telephos* (fig. 139) clearly reflect the naturalism of Hellenistic art as well as the often serious, even tragic, mood. Much of the extant painting comes from Pompeii and Herculaneum, which also developed a series of semicommercial decorative styles whose Rococolike charm and ornateness mirror the luxury of those Roman vacation resorts in southern Italy. A variety of light and airy forms are painted on their walls in impressionistic fashion, like the countless Cupid figures (fig. 140). These exist side by side with more sculpturesque anecdotal and religious themes, like the *Hercules and Telephos*, charged with Hellenistic emotion. The loose style of the *Cupid Riding a Crab*, favored by the upper classes to make their homes attractive, would be adapted by Early Christians working in the catacombs during the first centuries of the Christian era. But they

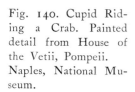

Fig. 140. Cupid Riding a Crab. Painted detail from House of the Vetii, Pompeii. Naples, National Museum.

would use it for a profounder spiritual purpose and would derive a more intense expression from the *Hercules and Telephos* style.

As Roman sculpture lost its material quality and moved away from the crispness and sharp outline of its earlier examples, Early Christian painting, developing at this same time, gradually took on a similarly increasing spiritual aspect. Its forms became lighter, thinner, and flatter — expressive rather than descriptive. It yearned toward the hereafter instead of being satisfied with the present. This hoped-for transition from one state of being to another would take tangible form in the art of the Early Christian period.

7 / THE ART OF INDIA

THE earliest remains of civilization in India reveal an art as ancient in origin as any the world has ever seen. It can be traced back to about 3000 B.C., at which time it shows certain similarities to contemporary Mesopotamian art, emerging from the Neolithic at a parallel point. The continuous history of India begins at 2000 to 1200 B.C. with a series of invasions by the warlike and pastoral Aryans coming from the Iranian plateau in the west to subdue the dark-skinned Dravidian inhabitants of the Indian peninsula (fig. 141).

From 1200 to 800 B.C. these Aryans — akin in race and language to the Indo-European invaders of Greek and Roman territory — lived as clans in small villages, worshiping vaguely personified natural powers that had to be appeased. Their famous Vedas, perhaps the oldest Indo-European religious treatises, contained sacrificial hymns to gods of the sky, sun, morning, storm, earth, river, and others. The chief deities were Indra, thunder god of the air and the storm; Agni, the sacrificial fire god; Varuna, god of the sky and guardian of cosmic regularity; and Soma, worshiped as the life-giving fluid drunk by all the gods. The early Vedic books mention no temples or images; not until much later, under Buddhism, do we begin to find images.

A transitional period (800–550 B.C.) produced two very important religious works — the Brāhmanas, which were commentaries on the Vedas, and the Upanishads, a series of philosophical teachings on which much of Indian thinking has depended. By this time also the division of Aryan society into four main castes was clear. There were priests (*brahmans*), warriors (*kshatriyas*), farmers and artisans (*vaisyas*), and slaves (*sudras*) — the last group segregated from the others. The system undoubtedly fulfilled a desire of the priests and noble warriors to perpetuate their supremacy over the darker Dravidians of the fourth caste.

The manifold services due the gods of the Aryan-Dravidian pantheon were described in minute and formalized detail by the Brāhmanas. The Upanishads, however, brought forth a more flexible outlook: the ideal of continuous rebirth (*samsara,* or reincarnation) which is conditioned by

149

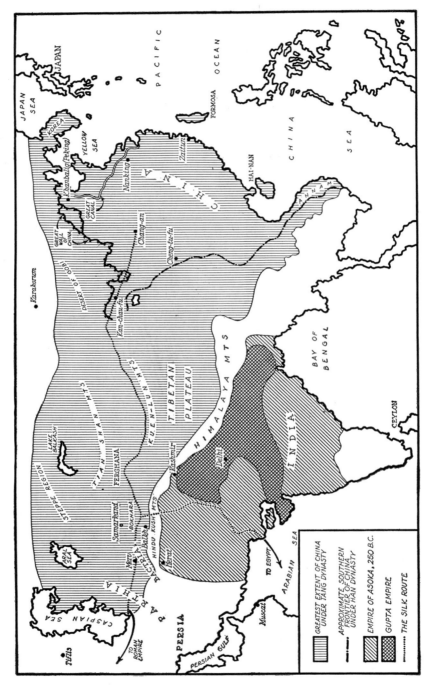

Fig. 141. The Orient. (From Henry S. Lucas, *A Short History of Civilization*, New York, McGraw-Hill Book Company, Inc., 1953. By permission of the author.)

the inescapable results of previous acts in other existences (*karma*, or causality, or heredity). The soul could avoid the unhappiness of individual existence by identifying itself with an impersonal cosmic soul, "the supreme soul of the universe," or Brahman. F. C. S. Northrop has defined it as "the ocean of being in which the transitory part of man is a wave. The wave comes and goes, but the ocean which is the immortal part of man never ceases to be. A man lives and dies but Brahman, his true self, is formless and timeless." From this formlessness man emerges at birth; to it he returns at death. One of the essential concepts deriving from the Upanishads is the Indian view that the material world is an illusion. The individual's knowledge of Brahman, or the Absolute, is not to be obtained from ritual or even learning but through grace proceeding from extended contemplation.

JAINISM AND BUDDHISM. During the sixth century B.C. there were other departures from the dry formalism of priestly ritual, among them the religions known as Jainism and Buddhism. Jainism, under the leadership of Mahavira, advocated a concrete program to free the soul from the material fetters of this world: to injure no life, to be truthful, not to steal, to possess no property, and to be ascetic and chaste. Buddhism, far more influential, was founded by the contemporary Siddhārtha (563?– 483? B.C.) of the Gautama clan and the Sākya tribe. Although it ultimately disappeared from India, Buddhism spread into the neighboring territories of Ceylon, Siam, Burma, Tibet, and, most important, China.

According to the preaching of the Buddha, or Enlightened One, suffering was inseparable from life, and since life originated in the will to life (or egoism) release could be obtained by destroying this self-assertion. When that was accomplished, the blessed state of nirvāna (release) would be attained. Since obviously this state could not be achieved by a man of the world, Buddha instituted a monastic order of wandering mendicant friars who were to follow a disciplined but not too ascetic existence. Sanctity was to be reached by following the Eightfold Path, the most important parts being right views, right conduct, and right trance.

Within a relatively short time this Lesser Vehicle, or early Buddhism, was replaced by a more formal hierarchical organization in which the Buddha was deified and the doctrine of Boddhisattvas, or saviors, predominated. A Boddhisattva was literally a "wisdom being" destined to become a Buddha at some future date after many successive lives of virtuous conduct. In this formalized system of Buddhism, the so-called Greater Vehicle, the great Boddhisattvas were those who gave up their opportunity of achieving nirvāna in order to help save the world. Although Buddhism began in the sixth century B.C., it did not arrive at images of its leader for many centuries. In a sense this parallels the evolution of the religion itself from an abstract ideal to a more concrete and formal basis.

CONTACTS WITH THE WESTERN WORLD. While Buddhism was spreading in India, the Persian King Darius I seized the northwest territory of Gandhara from the disunited Aryans and sent his Greek admiral Skylax to explore the Indus Valley. In the late fourth century B.C. Alexander the Great invaded the Punjab (327–325 B.C.), crossed the Indus River, and, after fighting one battle, withdrew his troops. During the Maurya dynasty (ca. 321–184 B.C.) there was further military contact with the Hellenistic world, and Megasthenes, a Seleucid (Syrian Greek) envoy to India, wrote an account — since lost — of that country.

The tremendous Buddhist missionary activity carried on by King Asoka (ca. 274–ca. 236 B.C.) was a key to further relationship between India and the outside world. Asoka tried to communicate his own fervor to such distant places as Syria, Hellenistic Egypt, Cyrene, Macedonia, and Epirus, and far more successfully to Burma and Ceylon. In addition, throughout his extensive kingdom he erected sculptured pillars with inscribed exhortations to be virtuous according to Buddhism. These pillars have a distinctly Persian style and may be compared in general form with the columns of Persepolis. Four lions (symbols of the leadership of Buddha in the Sākya tribe) placed back to back on top of a column recall the similar Persian practice (fig. 49). Below them, symbolic wheels represent the teaching of Buddha; animals between the wheels are allegories of the rivers of India and represent the many directions in which Buddha's

Fig. 142a. The Great Stūpa, Sanchi.

Fig. 142*b*. The Great Stūpa, Sanchi. North gate.

Fig. 143. Yakshī torso from Sanchi. Courtesy, Museum of Fine Arts, Boston.

law spreads. Although Hellenistic kings occupied part of the Punjab until the Christian era, for a long time after Asoka's death Buddhist art remained completely symbolic. Without reference to a physical form, the Buddha was symbolized as in the column just described or as in the flourishing and rich sculpture school of central India during the following Sunga dynasty, about 184 to 72 B.C.

BUDDHIST SHRINES AND SYMBOLS. This sculpture appears primarily on the railings and gates around hemispheric memorial mounds of earth covered with stone and known as *stūpas*. Mounds like the famous *Great Stūpa at Sanchi* (ca. 50 B.C., fig. 142*a*) or the one at Bharhut have an external stone railing with four monumental gateways called *toranas* at the main points of the compass, covered with luxuriant and typically lavish Indian sculptural ornament (fig. 142*b*). This ornament consists of allegorical and symbolic narratives dealing with the life of the Buddha, who never appears directly but only in oblique references such as the wheel of the law, the lotus of his birth, the tree of his enlightenment, the stūpa of his consecration, and the umbrella, symbol of his royalty, on top of the mound itself.

The decorative female nudes on the corners of the various gates (fig. 143) are perhaps the most interesting figurative elements. These lush little forms are known as Yakshīs or Yakshinīs (male: Yakshas). They are a prehistoric, animistic Dravidian contribution to Indian religious life, absorbed here into a Buddhist arrangement or elsewhere into orthodox Brahmanism — and later into Hinduism as well (cf. fig. 151). The Yakshī may embrace a tree as though she were part of it like a dryad, since in their most characteristic form Yakshīs are tree spirits. Like some animistic deities of Druid worship in the British Isles, they become Lords of Life, controlling all processes of growth and especially human fertility, particularly important to women desiring children. In both their female and male forms, these beings include a wide variety of types corresponding to the giants, fairies, gnomes, demons, and vegetation spirits of European mythology. In typical Indian legend these creatures had previously been human beings; they reached spirithood at death, and when their store of merit is exhausted they will be reborn as human beings.

In addition to shrines like Sanchi, the Sunga period also produced a series of temple halls in western India near Bombay, cut out of the rocky cliffs, perhaps to avoid the intense heat. One of the best known, the cave temple or *Chaitya Hall* at Ajanta (ca. 100 B.C., fig. 144), appears to reproduce in stone an earlier wooden form, as in the curved ribs under the vault of the ceiling that suggest bent bamboo sticks. The hall's impressive procession of columns and its apse end bring to mind the nave of an Early Christian basilica, although the ribbing and the clerestory over the entrance suggest a Romanesque cathedral (see fig. 228). The focal point of this interior is a carved stūpa at the sanctuary end of the building, similar in form to those at Sanchi and Bharhut.

Fig. 144. Chaitya Hall, Ajanta.

EARLY BUDDHA IMAGES: GANDHARA. The transition from symbolic representation of the Buddha to a more figurative conception came in northwest India — across the Indus River in Gandhara, which at an earlier date had been occupied first by the King of Persia and then by Alexander the Great and his successors. Their influence had persisted, more or less interrupted, over the centuries during which Buddhism had spread into that part of India. Between about 100 B.C. and about A.D. 50, the Gandhara school with its Hellenistic heritage of concretely represented gods seems to have stimulated the making of Buddha images. In this particular version they may be looked upon as easternized Greek art or, conversely, as westernized Oriental art.

In this borderland between East and West, the blending of ideas and forms was inevitable. A *Boddhisattva* from Gandhara (first-second century of the Christian era, fig. 145), in spite of its three-dimensional and solid "classical" character, shows not only the prescribed markings of its own religion but a mental attitude quite different from that of ancient Greek art. The distinguishing marks of the Boddhisattva, some of which are observed here, are laid out in the *Silpa Sāstras* (traditional manuals for the artist). They include the prescribed gestures (one hand held out in charity, the other held up in reassurance); the rich turban; and the jewelry in ears, around wrists, neck, and ankles, which indicates that he is still a prince and not yet a Buddha; the typical round Buddhist mark (*urna*) between the eyes; the elegant floating draperies; and the cloth wrapped about the waist.

Fig. 145. Boddhisattva Maitreya from Gandhara. New York, Metropolitan Museum of Art.

The psychological quality of such a sculpture is just as important as its Indian iconographic elements. On comparing it with a typical Greek figure, we find that the creator of the latter was concerned with an ideal state of form and being, outgoing and objective in its meaning, whereas the Indian artist has other interests. He is more occupied with achieving a certain inner vision. His withdrawal from the world is quite different in spirit from the serene untroubled attitude of the Greek who idealizes nature and builds up form on the basis of visual experience, refined into an ultimate, elevated version of life. The Indian craftsman is completely nonnaturalistic in approach — his point of view is conceptual rather than perceptual. He works not from nature but from a series of mental images achieved through contemplation and visualization; the proportions and content of his subject are already prescribed by handbooks and are actually the least important ingredients. When the craftsman is to make an image for a temple, he must go through a subtle process of worship of that deity and by means of *yoga* (contemplation) he must achieve a vision of and identification with the divinity. The yoga method has been characterized as "focused attention leading to the realization of identity of consciousness with the object considered." In both China and India the production of works of art is bound up with this system.

The form of the Indian image therefore is based on a mental conception of the object and has little to do with its relations to life. In the East far more than in the West, a sharp distinction is drawn between art and nature. Where the Western artist sums up a form or a series of forms, the Easterner sums up an idea — not a fleeting impression of dancing, for example, but an attempt to express the condition or state of dancing (see fig. 149). In this sense Indian art is neither naturalistic nor idealistic (i.e., descriptive or summing up from descriptions); it is ideographic communication based on a certain vitality and feeling. Indian art is not "fine arts" in the Western meaning, since nothing is purely ornamental; it exists to serve some practical purpose, to produce a desired state of mind or body.

The Gandhara *Boddhisattva* (fig. 145) may be considered to have classical influence in its strong feeling for form and the more or less naturalistic handling of the very tangible draperies that cling to and outline knees and shoulders. Yet the factor of design is far more important than representation. The arms, legs, base, head, and the rest compose a carefully controlled pattern of linear form that negates to a considerable extent the classical three-dimensionality. The seminaturalistic draperies swing back and forth with great elegance, calling attention constantly to the delicate and decorative nature of the folds arranged in parallel curves throughout. In its unity and abstraction, Indian sculpture here may be compared with that of ancient Egypt.

THE GUPTA PERIOD. The traditional "great" period of Indian history comes in the Gupta dynasty, A.D. 320 to about 535, in art to around A.D. 600. This empire of northern India was a truly eminent world power known from Persia to Egypt; it denoted an epoch of national expansion and cosmopolitanism, a mature and self-possessed culture. Literary evidences show the revival of Brahmanical worship, a series of brilliant courts, an age of luxury and patronage of all the arts. The period was marked by important religious foundations, by dramatic and poetic creations such as those of Kalidasa (India's most exalted poet and author of *Sakuntala*), and by scientific and mathematical research and compilation, the latter not without Greek influence. It was in this era probably that the great epics of India, the *Rāmāyana* and the *Mahābhārata*, received their final form.

Specific writings on the arts included the *Natryasudra*, a text on the technique of the drama, especially notable for its exposition of the language of gesture in theater, dancing, and painting. The famous *Kamasudra*, literally "the text of love," discloses the proper atmosphere for conducting a love session, as well as other important information on how to enjoy life. It makes reference to painting, whose "six limbs" are listed as the discrimination of ideal types, ideal proportions, emotional content, infusion of charm, color distinctions, and various poses (i.e., hieratic and secular). Even the actual painting technique is set forth in these books and may be observed in artistic practice. The *Silpa Sāstras*, connected previously with sculpture, in this period prescribed rules for architecture as well. The Buddha types now became more formal, sophisticated in shape and elegant in quality; they were destined to have considerable effect on the art of other countries where Buddhism existed. At this time Gupta culture was one of the most important in the Orient, in close contact with many different countries; pilgrims came by land and sea, carrying back to their own homes the images and texts. During the sixth century there was extensive influence on China and Japan; an Indian preacher founded Zen Buddhism in China.

GUPTA SCULPTURE AND PAINTING. In *Buddha Preaching in a Deer Park* (fig. 146), from the Gupta period, the various conventions have finally crystallized into an elaborately decorated figure with mingled delicacy and strength in both form and gesture. Even more abstract than the Gandhara *Boddhisattva*, it has different proportions and a more distinct linear, two-dimensional, and Oriental quality. In the earlier figure, bulk had only been overlaid with the decorative movement of the draperies; now the form as a whole conveys that patterning. It becomes an arrangement of gracefully attenuated and exaggerated lines and movements. Shoulders are wide, hips slim, arms and legs unusually long — conscious deformations in the interest of composition. This applies also to the fragile, egglike head and the tubular shapes of the other parts.

The painting of this era shows similar graciousness of form and attitude. Some of the outstanding wall decorations (fig. 147) were executed in western India in the caves at Ajanta, the site of a monastic community from before the Christian era through the Gupta period. Besides important examples of architecture and sculpture, within the often huge, hollowed-out rock chambers are the best preserved and perhaps most typical Indian paintings. In these and other Indian art forms, emotional meaning is not achieved through facial expression but through the disposition of arms and legs as though in dance movements, or in the ritual gestures of the Buddha. The painted panels contain a tremendous variety

Fig. 146. Buddha Preaching in a Deer Park. (The First Sermon.) Sarnath Museum.

Fig. 147. Fresco detail, Ajanta.

of pose and action, complicated architectural detail, rich color, and a dynamic restless motion. Even when the subjects are presumably still, as in some religious themes, the feeling of linear movement is always strong, because one's eye follows the decisive contour of the figure. The space may seem too tightly packed for traditional Western taste, since it is composed aesthetically rather than naturalistically; but similar conditions were operative in the ancient Mediterranean world and are again of great importance in twentieth-century art. The color ranges from black and brown through green, red, and white. Like Gupta sculpture, the Ajanta paintings are elegant and aristocratic, rich in decoration, costume, and architectural background. The lushness of the forms and their proportions may be compared with the native exuberance and vitality of the ancient Dravidian tradition seen in the *Yakshī* of Sanchi (fig. 143).

The bulk of Indian painting is mural decoration for walls in temples and palaces and on gateways. The technique is not true fresco (painting immediately on wet plaster); here, after the initial coat of plaster, there is a second plaster coat of priming, on which a pencil outline is drawn. From this a red outline is made; then the colors are applied, proceeding from underpainting as a base to the local colors of the subjects. A black

160

outline is added for final definition of the figure's contour. Indian painting may be classified according to theme: religious art; lyrical art dealing with everyday topics; and Nāgara painting, a courtly accomplishment
(generally portraiture) associated with love and pleasure. The last-mentioned type is the only one that appears on portable panels.

Although Buddhist works are typical of the Gupta period, the Gupta
rulers were not Buddhists but Brahmanists who permitted the other faith
to exist. For this and other reasons, from the sixth century onward Buddhism moved eastward into different lands where it struck permanent
roots, disappearing from India (Jainism, a somewhat similar religion, has
survived) to be replaced by the Brahmanical religion known as Hinduism.
Hinduism has remained the basic faith of India—except for the newer
Mohammedan portion — combining the elements of Aryan (i.e., Vedic)
and Dravidian (i.e., Yakshīs, serpents, and other animistic concepts) worship with the ability to absorb almost any cult or belief. Instead of the
abstractions of the Vedic period, the various nature gods are now represented concretely as personal forms of deity, to whom offerings and sacrifices can be made in their own temples.

HINDU WORSHIP. Hinduism is essentially monotheistic, in contrast to
the polytheism of Vedic times and the numerous Dravidian local popular
deities. It envisages God as a supreme being or overlord (Isvara) to be
worshiped directly and strives for identification with him as the ultimate
reality. Although there are different cults — Brahmā, Vishnu, Siva, etc.
— philosophically these are regarded as manifestations of the one God.
In fact, these three deities are spoken of as the Trimūrti, or Trinity, and
are often depicted as a three-headed figure; each avatār, or manifestation,
can be worshiped. The great variety of forms in Hinduism results from
the incorporation of local or tribal gods into the idea of the supreme godhead. Missionary work for other religions becomes difficult in India, since
any new faith, if acceptable in a moral and ethical sense, can be absorbed
into the general pattern.

HINDU SCULPTURE. The change from abstraction to concretion is illustrated in the Brahmā (fig. 148), a tenth- to eleventh-century image from
southern India which shows the ancient god with four heads, representing
the four traditional sacred Aryan Vedas, which are generally held in his
four hands. In form this sculpture suggests the proportions of the Gupta
figure of Buddha but accentuates power and monumentality rather than
delicacy. Nevertheless, as with all Indian sculpture, the element of design
is more important than representation; the various segments of the body
become parts of an in-and-out pattern. The left leg is bent in the direction of the double-lotus-leaf seat, the lower portion of the body repeats

Fig. 148. Brahmā (tenth to eleventh centuries). New York, Metropolitan Museum of Art.

the shape of the bottom of the base, and the upper body is a variation on the upper-base section. But this severe geometry is modified by a contrast between the relative lightness of the figure and the solidity of the pedestal, as well as by touches of delicate ornament.

The gods Vishnu and Siva and the goddess Devī are more frequently represented and more popular with the people at large. According to the allegiance of the worshiper, any of these might be regarded as the supreme deity, or Isvara. Vishnu had existed in Vedic times as one of many solar deities and was also associated with a definite being, possibly a teacher, who later became deified. He plays an important part as the divine hero-teacher in the *Mahābhārata* epic, where he is identified as the supreme god. In the *Bhagavad-Gītā*, perhaps the most widely read book in India, Vishnu is identified with Krishna, who is the great exponent of caste duty and the fulfillment of one's vocation (*dharma*). Krishna is only one of the ten *avatārs*, or incarnations, of Vishnu; Buddha has been accepted as another — a synthesis that came about during the ninth century.

Siva during the Vedic period had been regarded as part of or the same as the storm god Rudra and was afterward combined with older, wilder,

162

and mystical elements as well as with the cult of a goddess. In contrast to
the more beneficent Vishnu, Siva represents the darker powers of nature;
he is the destroyer, very often a naked and penniless creature, filthy and
lascivious. Yet in keeping with the Hindu need for the joining of opposites,
he is also the generative force, frequently seen in connection with phallic
images. As the divine dancer (fig. 149) he both creates and destroys; his
movement is the rhythm of the universe, opening and closing, growing
and decaying, rising and falling. His four hands represent the different
aspects of his being and importance. With one he holds a flame, symbol
of his destructiveness; with another, a drum to represent the first sound
to be heard in the universe, namely, the moment of creation. A third hand
is held up in a gesture of reassurance; the fourth points downward to the
dwarf on whom Siva dances, symbol of the many evils overcome by this
lord. The theology of Saivism (of Siva) is complicated, but it reduces
itself to the idea of a supreme undifferentiated godhead and of a personal

Fig. 149. Siva Nata-
raja. Courtesy, Mu-
seum of Fine Arts,
Boston.

god who appears as two-in-one, male and female, being and becoming, spirit and matter. Thus it is possible for the worshiper to think of Siva in his highest form as Mahesa, the direct agent in the various processes of creation, maintenance, and destruction.

Associated with Siva is his Sakti, or energy, the goddess Devī. Devī is followed independently by various Sākta cults which worship her as the Mother Goddess (a worldwide conception, extending from the Aegean to the Ganges). Many of the Dravidian nature manifestations (Yakshīs, etc.) are incorporated into this supreme feminine principle as a separate deity or, more popularly, as the wife of one of the other gods. She is the classical Magna Mater, the Great Mother, in a word Nature, both good and evil, and the source of all the other manifested deities. Her images range all the way from gracious and benign Umā and Pārvatī to Kālī, the lean, hungry, devouring ogress. In Bengal she is the most popular form of divinity in the guise of Kālī, from which is derived Kalighat, or Calcutta.

HINDU TEMPLES. The need for temples to honor the cults of Vishnu and Siva brought sculptors and architects together in a flowering of build-

Fig. 150. Lingaraja Temple, Bhuvanesvara, Orissa.

Fig. 151. Girl Looking into a Mirror. Detail from Bhuvanesvara Temples.

ing activity. The architectural types and their evolutionary steps are as diverse as the sculptures, but it is possible to differentiate the chief varieties of temples. The earliest free-standing Hindu type, after the elaborate rock-cut tombs of the eighth century, is the temple dedicated to Vishnu, usually found in northern India. In the *Lingaraja Temple* at Bhuvanesvara (fig. 150) of around the ninth-tenth century, a square shrine is covered by a high tower built up from a series of horizontal stone stripes so tightly compressed that they give the impression of verticality. Most northern examples, with their high ribbed domes (*amalaka*) shaped like a gigantic fruit, have this general form. The dome is capped by a flattened round element with a vase form on top of it. Directly in front of the elaborately carved vertical tower usually stands the pyramid-shaped assembly hall, or *mandapam,* often covered with lush and intricate carvings (fig. 151).

In southern India a totally different type of building is dedicated to Siva and other gods; here the dominant feeling is horizontal rather than vertical. The shrine is surrounded by an impressively large walled en-

Fig. 152. Thiruvannamalai Temple. View of entire temple with four main gates in typical south Indian style.

closure within which are pavilions, pools, chapels, and even living quarters to accommodate visitors to these pilgrimage centers. The most conspicuous architectural features of these complexes, apart from their low-lying horizontality, are the intricately carved gateways, or *gopura* (singular *gopuram*) which may be seen in the seventeenth-century example at Thiruvannamalai (fig. 152). The form is that of a pylon, or four-sided pyramid, in which architectural function is completely submerged by an overly lavish (even by Indian standards) type of sculptural decoration. The surfaces become masses of ornament where artistic achievement seems lost in an over-all continuity.

Another type of Hindu temple retains the general plan of the northern building but changes the square to a cross shape and incorporates the horizontality of the southern forms. This kind of temple is sometimes referred to as Chalukyan and is found in the Deccan region of south India.

DIFFUSION OF INDIAN IDEAS: CAMBODIA. In the later history of Indian art, the two most significant aspects are the impact of Mohammedanism (see Chapter 13) and the spread of Indian cultural influence to nearby and related areas — among the more important of these were Ceylon, Burma, Siam, Cambodia, and finally Tibet. The outstanding twelfth-century temple of Angkor Wat (figs. 153–154) in Cambodia was one of the many magnificent building projects of the Indo-Chinese Khmer kings. It consists of an elaborate, many-towered, square, walled enclosure, the main court dominated by a 200-foot-high central tower. The prolific narrative sculptural ornament is equally notable: Hindu gods, their wives, and retinues are portrayed in exceedingly delicate relief (fig. 155). Though clearly related in tradition and subject matter to Indian religious art, Cambodian sculpture has a native refinement and grace that distinguish it from the source. While there are literally miles of this complex and calligraphic flat relief work, it is at all times subordinate to the architectural concept of the structure as a whole.

A perspective view of Indian and Indian-derived art highlights its functional character within that culture. Accordingly, Western aesthetic standards do not necessarily apply to it. In the words of the distinguished Indian scholar Ananda K. Coomaraswamy: "Alien ethnic tastes and interests, like our own, are beyond aesthetic criticism; they certainly cannot be judged by our own, but must be understood and taken for granted

Fig. 153. Temple of Vishnu, Angkor Wat, Cambodia. General view.

Fig. 154. Temple of Vishnu, Angkor Wat. Close-up detail.

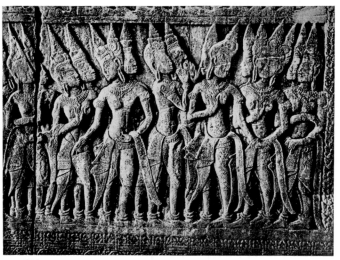

Fig. 155. Temple of Vishnu, Angkor Wat. Relief sculpture.

before the art can be studied as a stylistic sequence. . . . Absence of prejudice (provincialism) in matters of taste and ethics, which are not absolute, but relative to different times and races, is a prerequisite to taking pleasure in or deriving spiritual advantage from the study of any foreign culture. The greatest advantage to be derived from any such study is not the knowledge of the particular facts, but the ability to regard such facts impartially. To overvalue an alien culture, to regard it as perhaps superior to our own, is sentimental; to undervalue it, to regard it as necessarily inferior to our own, is provincial. Its perfection can only be judged in terms of the degree to which it realizes its own tendencies."

8 / CHINA AND JAPAN

IN the long and complex history of northern Asia, the two outstanding cultures are those of China and Japan. Both are important in themselves; particularly significant is China's decisive influence on the art and culture of Japan.

CHINA

Separated from India by towering mountain ranges and deep valleys, isolated in northern Asia by the dreary flatlands bordering Tibet and Mongolia, fertile agricultural China lay effectively sealed off for centuries from the rest of the world. The earliest center of Chinese civilization appeared in the valleys of its two chief rivers in the north, the Yangtze-Kiang and the Hwang-Ho, or Yellow River, both flowing west to east like the invading peoples that represented China's chief political problem. This rich land of north-central China, watered by the two rivers, enriched by deposits of soil blown from the Mongolian plateau, and moistened by monsoons blowing in the opposite direction, became the "Flowery Kingdom" — attracting to itself not only the primeval wanderers who became the future Chinese but many later invaders as well.

While there have been other long-lived cultures (e.g., ancient Egypt or the Hebrews and their descendants), China is today the outstanding instance of an uninterrupted and continuous civilization occupying the same territory for so long a time, that is, since the second millennium B.C. This deep-rooted continuity enabled the Chinese to withstand and even absorb their various invaders. But it also created a conservatism that ultimately stifled creativity and made it impossible for China over a period of centuries to keep pace with the progress of other countries.

EARLIEST CHINESE ART. The first artistic evidence in China appears in Neolithic, or New Stone Age, pottery, some of which is comparable to that of Mesopotamia — as were early Indian ceramics. Since Chinese civilization, like others, began on the hunting-herding-farming and family-clan level of Neolithic culture, it had many of the same aesthetic

170

motivations as ancient Egypt. The belief in an activating force behind the growth of crops and herds, the feeling of a spiritual power in nature, turned man from earlier magic practices to organized religion as individual nature gods were associated with different aspects of life. In the newer and more settled existence of the Neolithic era, we have seen that man visualized things spiritually as well as physically. Aesthetic expression took on a more conceptual and abstract character in place of its earlier representational quality. The Oriental artist, Indian or Chinese, who began to function during Neolithic times was therefore concerned with the spirit or essence of the thing portrayed, instead of an objective appraisal of its physical appearance. He devised ideographs of form which summed up each particular shape or idea. Because of the conservative nature of this basically peasant society, which remained unaltered in customs and manners even after the shift to town life (some parts of China retaining Neolithic customs to about 500 B.C.), Chinese art and culture preserved their conventions almost without change. Over thousands of years, Chinese art balanced the opposed tendencies of naturalism and abstraction in a fixed and immutable form of conceptual rather than representational expression.

The constant usages of a civilization in more or less the same area have tended to destroy and wear things out. As a result, relatively few abandoned sites or unused ruined buildings are found in China. Also, in spite of the profusion of stone, wood was preferred for building, which has affected the nature of the remains. Very early structures no longer exist, and although there is literary and other evidence of a highly developed and more ancient culture in China, we have no artistic relics of any consequence — apart from Neolithic pottery — before the Shang dynasty (ca. 1766–1122 B.C.). From this era come the oldest surviving important works of art, the ceremonial bronze caldrons (*tings*), tripods, beakers, wine vessels, and bells that were used mainly in connection with worship and burial.

SHANG DYNASTY. The monumental shapes and the intricate and abstract decoration of forms like the owl-shaped bronze *Wine Vessel* (fig. 156) argue a long period of previous development for this masterly casting technique with its sophisticated geometric ornamentation. There are two types of decorative motif: the regularly repeated abstract feather pattern (cf. feathers in the winged bull, fig. 42) with the "meander" pattern at the rear of the wing; and the pictograph form surrounding the meanders, expressing the skeleton idea of the object in moving, dynamic fashion. This latter motif is generally in higher relief than other ornaments on the bronze vessels; it also assumes different shapes, particularly the equally calligraphic curved-horn pattern. The actual bird portrayal

Fig. 156. Wine vessel shaped like an eared owl. Shang dynasty. Courtesy, Art Institute of Chicago.

on this *Wine Vessel* is distinctly secondary to the idea of a bold expressive form suggested by the bird's original contours. It may be compared with the lions capping the Asoka column in India and, later, the lions in the court of that name in the *Alhambra of Granada* (see fig. 258) and the *aquamaniles*, or water vessels, in animal shape produced by Moorish craftsmen in Spain.

In Shang times the importance of the family over the individual was already clarified as the basic tenet of Chinese life. The acts and habits of ancestors became established custom, and the whole fabric of society was maintained by pious respect for the spirits of those ancestors, who could also be petitioned for advice and aid. From this attitude as much as from any source, comes Chinese traditionalism. Other ceremonies and rituals developed during this period as part of an elaborate court life, remains of which have been found especially in the Confucian *Book of History*, supposed to have been put together by the great scholar and covering the years from about 2400 to 700 B.C.

CHOU DYNASTY: CONFUCIUS AND LAO-TZU. The life span of Confucius (551–479 B.C.) fell within the later Chou period (early, or Western, Chou, 1122–947 B.C.; later, or Eastern, Chou, 770–256 B.C.). By his time certain elements of Chinese society were clearly established: an imperial type of government; the main territorial or provincial divisions; reading of the stars; important social customs involving marriage, ancestor worship, agricultural development, and other activities; and the art of writing, or calligraphy. Under the Chou dynasty, candidates for public office were examined in horsemanship and archery as well as writing, reckoning, music, and ceremonial usages. The last are worked out in great detail in the somewhat later *Book of Rites* which describes in its account of government under the Chou dynasty sacrificial rites, divination rites, court regulations, and exact rules for government — all minutely catalogued in the interest of greater stability and public morality.

With the early Chou period, the Shang had been overwhelmed by relatively barbarian peoples from the west, who absorbed the customs of the conquered as well as their art. Later Chou was important for the development of new ideas, especially those of Confucius and Lao-tzu. Confucius, "the most sagely ancient Teacher, the uncrowned King," was destined to exercise great influence on subsequent Chinese thinking. He was not a religious leader or the founder of any cult, but a moralist and social philosopher. He was interested in reforming society rather than withdrawing from it as did many ascetics and religious figures in the feudal corruption and confusion of those times. His belief in the natural goodness of people led to the conviction that they would naturally conform to "right principles" if a good example were set by a just ruler. This example must be conditioned by filial piety, true reverence for lessons of the past, and a proper sense of ceremonial, for "all virtues have their source in etiquette." Confucius' approach was eminently rational, mixing common sense with decency; he paralleled the Socratic idea in his faith that men would do the right thing if they but knew it, and the Christian idea in his "What you do not like when done to yourself, do not do unto others."

Lao-tzu (meaning "old philosopher"), author of *The Canon of Reason and Virtue* (ca. fifth century ? B.C.), advocated an even greater confidence in mankind and its inherent virtue. Whereas Confucius relied on education, paternalistic example, and intellectual attainments, Lao-tzu felt it would be better to let people alone and they would be good by themselves. This implied that each person should live in the way that was most natural for him. The Tao, or "Way," that this teacher tried to communicate, the ordered system of the universe, the course of nature, meant getting as close to nature as possible, living a simple humble life, and even withdrawing from the world in order to find oneself. Although Taoism was ultimately overlaid with various magical and superstitious practices involving exorcism of evil spirits and malignant forces, it was vastly influential in the evolution of a significant Chinese nature philosophy and the nature poetry and painting that have stemmed from it.

The feudal era was brought to an end by the Emperor Shih Huang Ti (259–210 B.C.) of the Ch'in dynasty. He unified China by melting down weapons, standardizing laws and commerce, building the Great Wall of China against the Tartar invaders, and burning books which had been used by the enemies of his "new order." Ch'in (from which we get "China") made possible the four centuries of peace and prosperity under the Han dynasty (202 B.C.–A.D. 212). Paper and ink were in use by the beginning of the Christian era, a fact important for the development of painting and illustrated manuscripts. During this epoch Confucian ideals became firmly implanted. Meanwhile the nation expanded westward in military power and commercial relations, coming into contact with western nations via Chinese Turkestan. Through this same route Buddhism was later to come from India (fig. 141).

Fig. 157. Fight between a Man and a Tiger. Han dynasty relief. Courtesy, The Cleveland Museum of Art, J. H. Wade Collection.

HAN DYNASTY. There are no paintings extant from the Han dynasty; but many bas-reliefs tell interesting stories of either a Confucian or ordinary genre type and portray the life of the court. The *Fight between a Man and a Tiger* (fig. 157) shows the great skill of Han artists in depicting animals with emphasis on linear quality, paralleling the elegant Chinese handwriting (calligraphy). The abstractly flattened and dynamic forms move vividly across the smooth surface on which they are so well placed. Neither three-dimensionality nor naturalism is considered (this is true of most Han reliefs) but rather the smooth flow of tight outlines and the ideographic summation of the agility of the man and the fierceness of the tiger. In one way this composition may be compared with modern linear abstractions (Matisse, Brancusi); in another, its shorthand symbol of emotional quality compares with the *Dying Lioness* of Assyria (fig. 45). Other Han reliefs are even flatter in character and show no differentiation of height from one part to another (as in Egyptian examples); they give the impression of large woodblock surfaces that might be used for printing. Most of them, like Han sculpture generally, are funerary in purpose and hold valuable clues to the life of the time. It is believed that the predominantly linear nature of the reliefs indicates they were transcribed from painting or at least influenced by the linear character of Chinese pictorial art. Interestingly enough, they are often more legible in rubbings, which impress the design on paper.

Three-dimensional sculpture does not occur with any frequency in China until the fifth to sixth centuries of the Christian era and can be attributed, as in India, to the effect and necessities of Buddhism. During the Han era it is still confined to the tomb-guardian animal figures, such as lions and chimeras, or to little clay figurines put into the tombs to accompany the deceased in the future life, as in Egypt.

EFFECTS OF BUDDHISM. Buddhism was introduced into China as early as the first century of the Christian era, but it did not become a powerful force until the turbulent and disunited interval between Han and T'ang, the so-called Three Kingdoms (A.D. 220–589). During those years the desire for direct Buddhist knowledge and authoritative texts led at least eighty-two Chinese pilgrims to make the trip to India, including the famous Fa-hsien who crossed the central Asian desert and returned by sea (A.D. 399–414). Invading northern nomads, formerly held in check by Han emperors, had in many cases been converted to Buddhism by wandering missionaries and now brought their new faith with them during the troubled times. Toward the end of the fifth century these influences emerged in a flourishing school of Buddhist sculpture and painting, suited to the highly developed hierarchy of Boddhisattvas. Under the Northern Wei dynasty (A.D. 386–534) founded by the Toba Tartars, who moved the capital to Loyang in 495, work was started on the famous caves of Lung-men. These were decorated with figures of the Buddhist pantheon, exhibiting the extraordinary delicacy and spirituality characteristic of Chinese treatment of Buddhist themes.

T'ANG DYNASTY. The reuniting of the empire after 589 by the Sui emperors led to a long period of peace under the T'ang dynasty (A.D. 618–907) and increasingly active patronage of the Buddhist faith, which now became the common religion of all parts of China. In the new land of its

adoption, the faith of Gautama changed from its original emphasis on a series of reincarnations ending in nirvāna to more immediate aims. These involved direct aid from the guardian Boddhisattva Avilokatesvara — known in China as Kuan Yin and responsive to prayer like Catholic saints — equally direct access (via rebirth) into the Western Happy Heaven guarded by Amitabha Buddha, who welcomes all souls appealing to him, and finally salvation emanating from the coming Buddha Maitreya. Sectarian differences arose between Taoism in one group (Ch'an sect), which taught that the Buddha nature was in every man, and Confucianism in another (T'uen-t'ai sect), which believed in education as the means of reaching Buddha.

In T'ang sculpture the willowy *Boddhisattva on a Double Lotus Leaf* (fig. 158) retains the monarchical character of Indian Buddhist art with its elaborate headdress, jeweled costume, and almost diffident air. The delicacy apparent in the Indo-Chinese art of Cambodia at Angkor Wat emerges with full clarity in the ultrarefined, nonphysical delineation of this Boddhisattva. Unlike most Indian figures, it has no clearly indicated sex. The accent is on the outspread movement of the legs and even more on the gentle, sinuous curve of the arms connected by the necklace falling between them. Proportions dif-

Fig. 158. Boddhisattva on a Double Lotus Leaf. T'ang dynasty stone sculpture. Washington, Freer Gallery of Art.

fer also from the Indian ideal: the waist is placed much higher, and the shoulders are narrower and more delicate. Yet unquestionably such figures are affected to a considerable extent by Indian art of this and earlier periods. The total visualization of the artist is just as conceptual or non-naturalistic as in Indian sculpture; in fact, the Chinese is even less interested in the human form as such.

T'ang was an era of empire and expansion, development of elaborate trade relations with the West, and establishment of an administrative scheme that was to last into the twentieth century. (Chinese are often referred to as "the sons of Han and the sons of T'ang.") Sculptural and pictorial production responded to the popularity of art at court. Under the slightly earlier Sui emperors, more than 100,000 images had been ordered for the temples; through the cosmopolitanism of the T'ang ruler, T'ai Tsung, art was further encouraged. The traveler Hsüan-tsang returned from India with many Buddhist images and was made head of a commission to translate the sacred Sanskrit texts.

The brilliant court of Emperor Ming Wang the Great in the eighth century was notable for its painters and poets. Li Po, perhaps the most famous name in Chinese poetry, belongs to this epoch, as do many painters who took the first significant steps in a landscape art. In addition, many superb, extraordinarily delicate, and realistic clay tomb figurines come from the T'ang period; the most famous are the "horses of T'ang." Convincing camels, dancers, musicians, soldier types, and others also begin to appear. These are factual in approach and distinctly different from the formal Boddhisattvas. This disparity is analogous to the difference in Egypt between the abstract religious sculpture and the relatively naturalistic wooden tomb figures.

SUNG DYNASTY. The later *Lao-tzu on a Water Buffalo* (fig. 159), a small bronze of the Sung period (A.D. 960–1279), represents the Chinese tomb figurine — filled with charm and, in this type, a wonderful feeling for animals and their movements. The tail curling forward, the outstretched head of this animal (which is vital in the Chinese economy), the delicate movement of the legs, and the contrast between its bulk and the tiny figure of the smiling "old philosopher" are tribute to the sensitivity of the sculptor. Yet with all this great feeling for nature, the Chinese artist works within the sense of design and patterning that typifies Oriental art. This little sculpture therefore becomes a combination of curved forms: the small ellipse of the philosopher's body against the much larger ellipse of the water buffalo's form (with the outer parts — head and tail — shaped into the general outline) resting on the double triangles of the legs.

CHINESE PAINTING. Both the T'ang and Sung Dynasties are significant in the growth of Chinese painting, which had only begun during

Fig. 159. Lao-tzu on a Water Buffalo. Sung dynasty incense burner (bronze). Worcester Art Museum.

the Han period when ancestor portraits and other subjects were popular. No actual Han painting has survived; the only evidence for it is offered by the flat or incised relief. From the following Three Kingdoms there have been left the name and the work (in a later copy) of Ku K'ai Chih, a fourth-century artist who executed a long, horizontal scroll painting — the flowing, calligraphic, and delicate *Admonitions of the Imperial Preceptress* (fig. 160). In this series of illustrated maxims designed for the imperial concubines, he set forth the Confucian virtues of decency, truthfulness, family life, and loyalty to the emperor (whose life one of the palace ladies attempts to save by sacrificing herself).

Mural paintings of the fourth to tenth centuries are found in caves at Tun-Huang, an important oasis city along the trade routes of central Asia. These works show the accretion of influences from the West (and, in reverse, influence from China westward) as well as the growth of Buddhism in the East. Here during the fifth century, Chinese landscape art — the most significant pictorial contribution of that country — was first developed.

With the T'ang era (again according to later copies and literary references) painting became a meaningful art and part of a major literary activity, mirroring the poetic feeling of the writer in its content and his elegant calligraphy in its forms. Original works from before the tenth century no longer exist, except for the cave murals at Tun-Huang. The Sung painters mark the full rich climax of Chinese pictorial art and of Chinese humanism. This was an age of the diffusion of learning through printing and an epoch of scholar-statesmen like the Emperor Hui Tsung (reigned 1101–1125) who were at the same time poets, painters, and philosophers. A personal and even romantic note enters, where earlier the painter had been concerned primarily with Confucian moral precepts (cf. fig. 160), Taoist dragons, star-divinities, or the Buddhist subject matter of the T'ang period.

PICTORIAL SUBJECT MATTER AND APPROACH. Chinese painting in general is far more selective than Western art; nudes, for example, are rare indeed. On the other hand, while still life is a modern development in the West, it is ancient in China, though possessing different properties. The most important subject in Chinese art is landscape (the Chinese word for it means "mountains and water"). Unlike the classical or Renaissance ideal, man here is not the measure of all things but merely part of a larger universe. In the average landscape painting, either man and his works are totally absent or else so tiny that they are swallowed up in the overwhelming grandeur of nature, as in the horizontal *Landscape* scroll (fig. 161) by Tung Yüan (tenth century). Chinese painting is

Fig. 160. Ku K'ai Chih: Admonitions of the Imperial Preceptress. Detail. London, British Museum.

often mystical or emotional, and a good many apparently representational works are actually the expression of some emotion. Yet originality of theme is relatively unimportant; subjects are quite standardized, and painters consider it no disgrace at all to copy the old masters or to repeat their themes.

The Chinese painter is usually first a philosopher, then a poet, and finally a painter. In Sung times, for example, most painting was philosophical, and compared with Western art, paintings like the *Landscape* of Tung Yüan seem impersonal. Nevertheless from the poetic point of view these works show a great sensitivity to animal and floral forms, although landscape is preferred. The various elements of the scene are presented as ideographs, the spectator receiving an impression of the essentials of each object. In this sense, pictures are often incomplete and entail a certain amount of imaginative filling in by the observer. Contrasted with the vibrant lush richness of Indian painting and its sensuous forms, the art of China is extremely reticent, arousing in the onlooker the painter's own concentrated love of nature and his delight in it, as well as his philosophical probing of its deeper meaning. The tiny figures of mankind exist in a typically Oriental infinity — the philosopher sitting on the bank of a river or musing in the forest, the fisherman in his minute boat on a long winding river, his equally small house lost in the vastness of the pictured mountains. The actual process of painting is related to other Oriental (e.g., Indian) methods in that a long period of concentration and identification of self with the subject has to be undergone before the lightninglike outpouring of lines and tones.

EXECUTING THE PAINTING; SPACE AND COMPOSITION. The painter's themes, primarily genre or landscape, are put down on paper or silk

Fig. 161. Tung Yüan: Landscape scroll. Sung dynasty. Courtesy,

with ink and brush, the brush held downward in the fist rather than in the fingers. This execution, following the concentration process and acute memorizing, demands extraordinary spontaneity and manual skill, because there is no possibility of correction with the silk or paper material and the ink medium. The art of handwriting (and it is considered an art among the Chinese) and the art of painting are closely allied; the flowing quality of Chinese characters at the side of the *Landscape* scroll (fig. 161) may be compared with the movement of the vertically oriented mountains and the horizontally arranged lower and left-hand portions. The same swinging movements of the fist-held brush are used to make the outlines of the picture and the pictographic words.

Neither the space nor the composition of Chinese painting agrees with traditional Western concepts. Spatial perspective lines do not go inward to meet at a point, but come out toward the spectator (as in certain forms of modern art, cf. Cézanne), thus engaging the interest and participation of the observer to a higher degree. The composition is not concerned with a balancing of figures against each other or a "center of interest." The onlooker is introduced into the picture and then gradually led from the outstanding forms to those of lesser importance, as though his eyes were directed along a particular vista. Nor are the objects arranged behind each other with any particular emphasis on diminishing size (linear perspective) as in Hellenistic, Roman, or Renaissance art. Instead the comparatively two-dimensional planes are placed one behind the other, almost in the fashion of stage scenery. This is the Chinese manner of articulating space in landscape — different from the Western development but nonetheless a valid and systematic approach. Such a compressed

Museum of Fine Arts, Boston.

space is typical of both the Far East and the Near East and is a permanent part of Chinese visual interpretation.

In a philosophic, later Sung painting by the Buddhist Lu Hsin-chung (thirteenth century), *Vanavasi Gazing at a Lotus Pond* (fig. 162), a relatively flat space is filled in a decorative and asymmetrical fashion, somewhat like the Han relief seen earlier. As in most Chinese art, a great deal of observation is summarized in the forms: the nature of the leaves, the gentle fall of the self-absorbed individual's drapery, the forward movement of the servant at the left. All these are semiabstracted into two-dimensional form concepts that move into various areas of the composition. The large single curve of the tree, with the smaller curve added by the man's back, is balanced by a series of smaller curves at the left and by the left-curving branches. Unlike many other types of Chinese painting which are monochromatic, works of this kind add the factor of color balance — here a combination of red, blue, blue-green, pink, and gold.

THE SIX CANONS. The pictorial ideals of Chinese art follow the Six Canons of Hsieh Ho, a famous painter-critic of about A.D. 500. His first and most important precept is "rhythmic vitality." This has also been expressed as "the Life Movement of the Spirit through the Rhythm of Things." His second law deals with composition and lines and is called "the Law of Bones and Brush-work." According to this rule, the painter in putting his feelings into pictorial form must give that form an organic structure, achieved mainly through line and linear arrangement. Conformity with nature is placed third in the artist's rules; it is followed by "harmonious coloring," which means exactly what it says, that is, harmonious rather than naturalistic coloring. The last two laws deal with artistic composition and "finish." But the great power and attraction of Chinese art lie in its line and its line composition, each outline having an abstract beauty of its own just as does an ideographic word character.

Going forward in Chinese history, with the later Sung came a period of Mongol domination from the north under the Yüan dynasty (1260–1368) founded by Kublai Khan. This Mongol dynasty, ruling in China according to Chinese customs with Peking as their winter capital, was described by the great Venetian traveler Marco Polo, who was in the service of the Khan from 1275 to 1292 and who brought the first factual knowledge of the Far East to Europe.

MING DYNASTY: ARCHITECTURE. The following Ming dynasty (1368–1644) signified a return to native rule in China and was marked by an active centralization and expansion policy. Originally at Nanking, in 1421 the capital was shifted back to Peking, thereby ensuring the northern

Fig. 162. Lu Hsin-chung: Vanavasi Gazing at a Lotus Pond. Sung dynasty. Courtesy, Museum of Fine Arts, Boston.

Fig. 163. Pailou, Ceremonial Gateway. Peking.

Fig. 164. Pao He Ti'en Pavilion (Ming dynasty). Forbidden City, Peking. Rear view.

frontier for the next few centuries. Peking became a great administrative and cultural center with some outstanding examples of Chinese architecture.

Because of the Chinese tendency to utilize wood in their buildings in spite of the availability of stone, there is no surviving architecture before the T'ang period (seventh to ninth centuries). This art is as conservative in practice as the sculpture and painting; its types remain static throughout. Most characteristic is the wooden-walled, tiled-roof building — the roof edges curling upward in typical Chinese fashion on temples, pagodas, ceremonial gateways, and elsewhere. The roof in this "t'ing" type of structure is massive in proportion to the rest of the building (which consists of flimsy walls or short columns) and is often multiplied for additional effect. Its curved and multiple form may be seen in the Chinese-derived *Hōryūji Temple* near Nara, Japan (see fig. 167), whose buildings go back to the seventh century.

Later Chinese categories include the *Pailou*, or Ceremonial Gateway (fig. 163), the *Pao He T'ien Pavilion* at Peking (fig. 164), and the

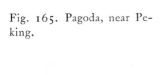

Fig. 165. Pagoda, near Peking.

Pagoda near the same city (fig. 165). The first of these may be related to the ceremonial gateways of India as at Sanchi (fig. 142*b*), although in China it is not used for religious purposes but rather as in ancient Rome (cf. fig. 128) to memorialize a famous individual. This "triumphal arch," about 100 feet wide, shows how pervasive the upcurved roof is in Chinese architecture. In the ceremonial hall the multiplied turned-up roofs are rectangular in their shape and still remain the determining factor of the structure. The elaborate, enveloping marble fences once more recall Sanchi with its equally important stone enclosure.

The pagoda, represented by the example here, is an upward-moving narrow structure in which the usually horizontal accent of Chinese architecture is changed toward the vertical. The jeweled pagoda is a Buddhist type of building, its top comparable to that of the *Stūpa at Sanchi* (fig. 142*a*), since the multiple roofs symbolize the royal umbrella of the Buddha. In the angular base are symbolized the guardians of the four quarters of the earth, here enshrined under the arches. The octagonal central portion represents the abode of the Boddhisattvas preceding their Buddhahood, guarded by the eight celestial deities. The building reaches its doctrinal climax in the upper portion, circular to represent the heavens where Buddhas dwell after achieving complete enlightenment.

POTTERY: MANCHU DYNASTY. Over the ages China has excelled in many varieties of pottery. The most refined and skillful is in porcelain, a Chinese invention based on a translucent white paste that when shaped and fired remains unaffected by scratches and resonant to the touch. Most eras of Chinese history since the Han have produced porcelain pottery — its diversity of shapes, surface colors, and ornamental patterns is so great that any single sample can give only a limited idea of it. Perhaps the best period is the K'ang Hsi (1662–1722) of the last, or Manchu, dynasty of China, exemplified by

Fig. 166. K'ang Hsi vase. New York, Metropolitan Museum of Art.

an elegant and gracefully formed piece showing a series of rich tree, flower, and insect forms (fig. 166). The decorations in bold patterns are painted in enamel colors on a white coating with a blue underglaze. While the vessel is shaped in fine but powerful straight lines and curves, it is the subtly textured glaze that gives the porcelain its most essential quality. In this area the Chinese craftsman reveals an originality and refinement that are almost unique in the history of the world.

JAPAN

The art of Japan, influenced in many ways by that of China, began considerably later. Its recorded history acquires elements of fact only during the third to fourth centuries of the Christian era. Early Japanese religion, known as Shintō, combined worship of nature deities (especially the sun goddess from whom the imperial family claims descent) with elaborate ritualistic observances and a mythology based on ancestor heroes. Buddhism was introduced from China via Korea by the fifth century, as was Chinese writing. Japanese society at this period consisted of numerous clans under priest-chieftains serving the clan gods, occupational guilds, and a small number of slaves. The imperial clan was the leader, its chief becoming emperor and its god the national deity, in a loose feudal system.

The effects of Chinese civilization on Japan (aided by an influx of immigrants from Korea) were, first, to win the nation over to Buddhism officially and, second, to weaken the clan system in favor of greater power for the imperial family, ultimately bringing about a complete economic and political reorganization along Chinese lines. The religious change was accomplished by the middle of the sixth century; the political, during the T'ang period. The first officially recognized monarch, Empress Suiko, reigned from 593 to 628 during this crucial transitional stage in Japanese history. A good many of the changes must be credited to the crown prince Shōtoku (d. 622), who is not only the real builder of Buddhism in Japan but also the founder of the great Buddhist monasteries of that early time.

ARCHITECTURE. Those monasteries, illustrated by the famous *Hōryūji Temple* near Nara (fig. 167), perhaps the world's oldest wooden building, show the close relationship between Japan and China during the first wave of Buddhist influence. This is apparent not only in the form and function of the building complex itself but also in the sculpture, painting, and other decorative features. As in Chinese archi-

Fig. 167. Hōryūji Temple, Nara.

tecture, whose early character can only be traced in these seventh-century Japanese examples, the outward-curving tile roof dominates the structure, completely overwhelming the façade.

Hōryūji was a combination monastery, school, and hospital with many buildings for its various functions, much like a medieval monastery in Europe. Within the square-walled enclosure stands the dominant shrine (*kondō*) hall with the pagoda directly behind it, an impressive gate building, and a lecture hall. Supplementary buildings are located outside this enclosure — all in the same general form with tile-covered roofs resting on beams supported by thick wooden columns. As in most Japanese architecture (in contrast to Chinese forms) there is delicacy in the proportions of the buildings and considerable refinement in the sweeping curves of their roofs. The wood and plaster walls have a characteristic light and open quality supplemented, as in residential buildings, by sliding screens.

Extremely conscious of nature, the Japanese architect always thinks of his building in terms of its environment and tries to fit it into the surroundings as gracefully as possible. Homes are designed in connection with a garden (fig. 168); the plan revolves around a large main room with a recessed space, or alcove (*tokonoma*), in which carefully selected family possessions may be shown — a hanging vertical scroll, or *kakemono* (a horizontal scroll is a *makemono*), or an outstanding piece of

188

pottery. Simple, severe, and with hardly any furniture, the rooms are separated from each other by the typical sliding screens, many decorated with painting. When these screens are pushed back, the inhabitants of the house seem to be partly outdoors. Beginning with the flat entrance stones at various points of entry, the view extends into the house garden and out to the surrounding countryside. Besides the large room with its alcove, the Japanese home contains smaller functional rooms opening off the main hall, as well as a more elaborate entrance porch for visitors.

In addition to the relationship between house and garden (even perceptible when the screens are closed and trees are silhouetted against them), Japanese architecture stresses certain functional and design relationships between the various parts. Wall spaces are plain, flat, geometric areas related in shape to the beams supporting the ceiling. Furnishings are austerely simple; cupboards are absorbed into the walls, and the few art objects are chosen with scrupulous care. This exceeding simplicity of form is accompanied by profound understanding of the possibilities and limitations of the various materials used. These elements and the relation of the building to the outdoors coincide with the expressed aims of many modern Western architects (cf. figs. 552, 559).

Fig. 168. Japanese home. View from garden.

SCULPTURE. Early Japanese sculpture, like its architecture, is based on that of China, particularly Chinese art of the sixth century immediately preceding the Suiko period in Japan. This Japanese sculpture is generally wood or bronze, because of the lack of stone. A *Kwannon* — the Chinese Kuan Yin — Boddhisattva (fig. 169) from the *Hōryūji Temple* dates from the seventh century. The elaborate Indian type of headdress and long ears are balanced by the Chinese tendency to minimize the importance of the body. In this case it is surrounded by the typically graceful and delicate Japanese draperies and halo, which in their sweeping curves dominate the form itself.

A second wave of Buddhist influence from China during the T'ang period resulted in a more plastic, or three-dimensional, approach, revealed in the religious imagery of this period and in the beginnings of a restrained but distinctly naturalistic art of portrait sculpture. The latter tendency is basically Japanese in character, as distinguished from the more abstract and China-Korea-derived religious sculptures, which remain symbolic and ideographic. An example of this trend is the much later work by one of Japan's greatest sculptors, Unkei, a portrait of the Chinese pilgrim and patriarch *Muchaku Zenji* (fig. 170), dating from the early thirteenth century. There is no question that this body exists beneath its drapery, nor that the drapery relates to the body rather than to a chiefly decorative pattern. The psychological character and physical qualities of the individual emerge with equal clarity.

PAINTING. During the Fujiwara period (866–1185) an elaborate and extravagant court life developed in Japan, with extensive cultural interests which produced fine poetry, painting, and other art forms. One of the most striking phases was the growth of a national literature in Japanese, especially the *Genji Monogatari* (ca. 1008–1020), a charming romance written by a lady of the court. Although the painting of the period was somewhat feminine in character, it marked the birth of a narrative and naturalistic style — first in the illustrations for the *Genji Monogatari* and also in the twelfth-century bestiary scrolls, attributed to Toba Sōjō, in which animals were used to satirize the affectations of court life. This popular style existed side by side with a long-lived formal style, derived from the Sung painters of China, whose influence reached great heights in the Kamakura period (1185–1333) during which many Chinese fled from Mongol invaders to Japan. The two trends, the formal and the popular, continued throughout later Japanese history.

The seminaturalistic genre style is exemplified in a later work by Sotatsu, illustrating the *Genji* romance (fig. 171). An exuberant sense of movement, of living beings in action, is tempered by the generalized forms, the linear flow, and the two-dimensional spatial quality of Oriental

190

Fig. 169. Kwannon (wood, sixth to seventh centuries). Yumedono Hall, Hōryūji Temple, Nara.

Fig. 170. Unkei: Muchaku Zenji (wood). Kofukuji Temple, Nara.

art. This might be compared with the abstract realism of Cretan art, where an analogous balancing of factors takes place. In the Kamakura epoch, other aspects of this popular form of expression included scrolls dealing with contemporary military events, such as the fine example at the Boston Museum, and portrait sculpture like the *Muchaku* (fig. 170).

During the Kamakura, when the armies of Kublai Khan were resisted successfully, and the following Ashikaga period (1336–1568), Japan entered a phase of military dictatorship based on a feudal pattern, which lasted into modern times. The increasing dominance of the warlike nobility was reflected in the building of fortified castles and in a simpler, less subtle approach to pictorial art. Decoration and genre quality became more prized than the delicate poesy of Chinese style. At the same time the growth of a middle class during the Ashikaga fostered a demand for art based on everyday themes and ideas. This developed during the next era, the Tokugawa (1600–1868), to which the Sotatsu painting (fig. 171) belongs.

Fig. 171. Nonomura Sotatsu: Scene from the *Genji Monogatari*. Tokugawa period. Japan, Iwasaki Collection.

JAPANESE PRINTS. Even more everyday in character and also part of the seventeenth- to nineteenth-century development was the colored woodblock print, a technique in which a design was printed on paper in many colors, using a different block for each hue. Among the famous masters of this new popular art were Harunobu, Utamaro, Sharaku, Hokusai, and Hiroshige. Workers, lovers, actors, geishas, landscapes, and genre scenes poured forth in great profusion, placed in the typically Oriental restricted space and dominated by its basic linear quality.

192

Fig. 172. Harunobu: Lovers under Umbrella in the Snow. New York, Metropolitan Museum of Art.

Harunobu's *Lovers under Umbrella in the Snow* (fig. 172) is a characteristic figure composition by the best-known portrayer of upper-class young ladies, outstanding for its varied colors, the extreme delicacy of its general form and individual detail. The Japanese decorative charm expressed in linear rhythms and bold flat color areas is perhaps less subtle than traditional Chinese style. But in the perfection of this particular medium (also inherited from China) the woodcut artists of Japan left an important heritage for European painters in modern times.

9 / ART AND CULTURE
OF THE EARLY AMERICAS

SOMETIME between the Old and New Stone Ages, successive waves of nomads from Asia crossed the Bering Straits into Alaska. Spreading through North and South America, they developed various stages of culture that ranged from the most primitive to a relatively high standard. Some advanced rapidly to the agricultural level, especially the inhabitants of the Valley of Mexico; others, such as the Incas of Peru, learned to use bronze. But some basic elements of civilization such as the wheel and the use of iron were unknown to the early Americans, and, except in Peru, there were no beasts of burden for transportation, commerce, or communication.

Yet without iron tools several groups in Mexico, Central America, and Peru achieved miracles of building and sculpture. Nor did the lack of a system of writing in Peru or means of transportation in Mexico prevent the formation of organized societies in those lands. When the Spanish conquerors arrived in the early sixteenth century, they found Aztec, Maya, and Inca cultures that represented advanced stages in the development of these peoples.

MEXICAN CULTURES: COMMON FEATURES. In Mexico the oldest evidence of a settled agricultural existence goes back to about 2000 B.C. The great civilizations of this land were based on the cultivation of maize (Indian corn), especially in the Central Valley where rich soil was produced by the natural filling in of lakes with silt from numerous mountain streams. In spite of primitive methods of agriculture, such richness made for a sure food supply and, consequently, leisure time for arts and crafts. In this farming economy, the regularity of life facilitated building and helped evolve the calendar; the deities that controlled fertility and growth were worshiped on magnificently constructed and enduring pyramids.

Most Mexican religious practices were associated with natural phenomena. Tlaloc the ancient rain god appeared at an early date; other gods represented the sun, the wind, fire, and the maize itself. Without

194

the metal tools that had been available to other races at this cultural level, the ancient Mexicans shaped volcanic stones in regular and often impressively large blocks for religious edifices and frequently carved the surfaces in intricate geometric patterns or abstract anthropomorphic forms. The basic architectural style throughout Middle America (in Mexico, Guatemala, Honduras) was the flat-topped pyramid, rectangular or square at its base with several stages of ascending terraces. One or more staircases led from the base to the flattened top, where there were temples with their idols (see fig. 181). In accordance with the elaborate Mexican calendar system, these pyramids were renewed every fifty-two years by adding another layer of stone to the previous surface. Thus they grew layer by layer, until in some cases they became the largest structures of their kind in the world. An early example at Tenayuca shows five superposed pyramids encompassing a span of about three hundred years.

Although social patterns differed among Mexican groups, religion was generally polytheistic with the priesthood exercising both political and religious influence. The number of gods tended to grow constantly; the Aztecs, for example, found a deity for every phase of life. The endless attention necessitated by such a complex system of religion seems to have hastened the downfall of this particular people.

The art of ancient Mexico, while differing markedly in character from that of Europe, shows a conspicuous vitality throughout its history, producing fresh, vigorous forms along conceptual rather than perceptual lines, much in the manner of Oriental art. Again as in the Orient (fig. 152), architecture was not an art of enclosing spaces but a process of erecting imposing masses of masonry covered with elaborate ornamentation. The vaulted structures developed in other parts of the world were unknown here. Nevertheless, most Mexican plastic art has the feeling of grandeur, deriving partly from its basic abstractness and partly from its exalted religious purpose.

Outside the Central Valley of Mexico there were smaller valleys, cut off for the most part from the main one except through a system of fast runners who carried messages. These areas showed the same basic agricultural civilization with some local variants, especially in sculpture and handicraft styles like the Oaxacan and Tarascan, respectively. The main cultures from north to south were: earlier, the Teotihuacán and the Toltec, each northward of Mexico City; later, the Aztec, associated with the site of Mexico City; and the Maya, which extended from Guatemala and Honduras into southern Mexico. (The Inca culture of Peru was a separate phenomenon.)

Certain usages were common amongst Middle Americans: the Aztec and Maya calendars were similar, although the latter was more elaborate; rites of human sacrifice, associated primarily with the Aztecs, were practiced everywhere; and the legend of Quetzalcoatl (called Kukulcán by the Maya) spread through most Mexican beliefs. He was the "feathered serpent" who combined in his person the *quetzal* bird and the *coatl*, or serpent. At a later date, and perhaps because of Spanish influence, he was visualized in human form, fair and bearded. A distinctly intelligent and magnanimous god, Quetzalcoatl was credited with banning human sacrifice, inventing the calendar, and teaching picture writing, the only existing form in ancient Mexico, as well as the teaching of weaving, pottery, stone- and metalwork, and the improvement of agriculture. Finally, after all these great accomplishments, he was said to have departed in a boat of snakeskins, sailing toward the rising sun; and although angry because of a widespread relapse into paganism, he promised to return when his children needed him. Worshiped throughout Mexico as the god of life and the morning star, in his two component parts of serpent (symbol of the earth) and bird (symbol of the heavens) he represented the life force.

MEXICAN ART FORMS. Definite aesthetic features were also shared by many Mexican cultures. First were the stepped pyramids, consisting of mounds of earth covered by sheaths of cemented stone. Unlike the Egyptian pyramids, these structures were used to elevate temples. In the Valley of Mexico the temples were built of wood and hence have disappeared, whereas in the Maya south they were made of stone and frequently survived. A second common feature was figure sculpture ornamented with nose and ear plugs (and occasionally lower lip plugs) — often elaborately carved and sometimes made of jade and other semiprecious stones.

Metals were widely used, but only for decorative purposes as in gold jewelry. Metals hard enough for carving or cutting stone were not known either in Mexico or Peru, so that sculpture (and architecture) had to be carried on with hard stone tools. Highly developed feather work was prevalent in most Mexican areas, especially for the headdresses and other ceremonial garments worn by priests and chieftains. Two other universal elements were pitchers and vases based on animal and human shapes, and corbeled vaults, stones laid in horizontal courses, each one out a little further over the opening until they met at the top (cf. fig. 63), used in both Mexico and Peru. The true vault built around a temporary centering or support, as in Roman or medieval buildings, was never developed.

TEOTIHUACÁN. The first of the four chief areas in ancient Mexico was Teotihuacán, about 30 miles northeast of the present Mexico City. This center, whose name means "place where all go to worship the gods," began its evolution some time before the Christian era and continued through various rises and declines until around A.D. 1100. Its craftsmen were best known for their skillfully designed pottery, stonework, and fresco painting; their products and cultural influence extended into most of Mexico as far south as Guatemala. Until recently it was believed that the Toltecs, who occupied it toward the end, had founded Teotihuacán, but several years ago an older, independent Teotihuacán culture was discovered on that site. Later civilizations felt a great religious respect for this place, associating it with the mystic presence of Quetzalcoatl and making their own additions to its pyramids and other structures.

Teotihuacán was no ordinary city; it was an outstanding religious center with an elaborate arrangement of plazas, pyramids, and other facilities for public worship. Sacred structures lined an elongated plaza, or avenue, known as the "Way of the Dead." Although the priests and nobles undoubtedly had their residences in the vicinity, the bulk of the population, the ordinary farmers, lived in cane and thatch huts in the surrounding countryside.

Many religious buildings are still extant. The largest is the 235-foot-high *Pyramid of the Sun* (fig. 173) — a terraced mass about 700 feet

Fig. 173. Pyramid of the Sun, Teotihuacán, Mexico.

square at the base with a steep stairway of 220 steps mounting one side. It is constructed of volcanic stones as carefully cut and fitted as those in the great pyramids of Egypt and was designed to raise a temple high in the air (cf. fig. 177). The angle of elevation is lower here than in the Egyptian buildings. Its staircase is quite steep, however, with risers higher than the width of the treads. The pyramid's profile flattens out more at each setback, a subtle gradation that makes the mass of stone seem much taller and bulkier than it actually is, and also gives it more unity. Originally the *Pyramid of the Sun* was probably covered with plaster and painted. Various buildings at Teotihuacán have recently yielded a series of multicolored murals with decorations of allegorical figures in brilliant colors, especially red.

Fig. 174. Feathered Serpent. Pyramid of Quetzalcoatl, Teotihuacán, Mexico.

Another important structure on this site is the early *Pyramid of Quetzalcoatl,* found behind a later complex of buildings known as the Citadel. The central altar of this complex has three stairways, each with fifty-two steps, representing the fifty-two-year calendar cycle. The *Pyra-*

mid of Quetzalcoatl itself is particularly noteworthy for its profusion of serpent heads and other carvings (fig. 174), most of which were probably painted. This pyramid too was originally decorated with colorful frescoes. The earlier walls are paneled with feathered serpent heads (symbols of Quetzalcoatl); and the balustrade of the staircase has the heads fitted into its masonry, unlike the later simple line of the Citadel's altar staircases. The serpent heads have an unusually effective abstract character as they project horizontally from the surface of the wall or balustrade, conveying a stark impression of their snake quality; the feathers are represented by necklaces of simple leaflike forms about their bases. Alternating with the feathered serpent heads are representations of another god, possibly Tlaloc, the god of rain. Other meaningful structures at Teotihuacán, though of lesser importance, are the Pyramid of the Moon and the so-called Temple of Agriculture.

THE TOLTECS. A second group of great civilizers and builders were the Toltecs, who flourished from about A.D. 800 to 1100 and from whom the later Aztecs took over their gods and many aspects of their social order. One of the most significant and cultured nations in the Valley of Mexico, the Toltecs left such a mark on the history of that area that the Aztecs considered a person noble if he possessed Toltec blood. The principal Toltec city was Tula, some 50 miles northwest of the present Mexican capital. Among their impressive creations were a massive but harmonious architecture, a series of magnificent warrior columns of almost classical simplicity, and flat carved reliefs, such as the animal frieze decorating the base of their Pyramid of the Treasury.

By the time the Toltecs abandoned Tula, their civilization had spread as far south as Yucatán, where it provided impetus for a Maya-Toltec renaissance. Their contribution may also be seen in the final layer of Mexico's largest pyramid, at Cholula, which is over 1,000 feet square at the base. Quetzalcoatl was considered a semilegendary leader of the Toltecs and worshiped as their principal god. As a result, there is profuse use of the plumed serpent in their decoration.

At Tula, unquestionably the most striking feature is the series of anthropomorphic warrior columns (fig. 175), comparable in their way to the gigantic ancient Egyptian sculpture. These figures served as supports at the entrances to Toltec temples. On the surface of each huge cylinder are carved the stylized features of a face, details of an elaborate costume, and simplified indications of torso and legs. Originally the figures must have had mosaics of obsidian and mother-of-pearl in the openings of the eyes and mouths. The sculptured reliefs on Toltec temples

Fig. 175. Warrior columns, Tula, Mexico.

and pyramids show animal friezes, human forms, and dancing and singing skeletons that suggest the skeleton puppets and toys used by Mexicans today on their Day of the Dead.

THE AZTEC EMPIRE. The third important nation in the Valley of Mexico was the Aztec, which arrived there from the north around A.D. 1300. Their coming is associated with the legend of a promised land where they would find a stone within a cactus plant and seated on the stone an eagle with a serpent in his beak. On the marshy shore of Lake Texcoco in the Valley of Mexico, this prophecy was said to have been fulfilled, and the spot was named Tenochtitlán, meaning "place where the god sits upon the stone in the cactus." At this site the newcomers moved in on peoples already dwelling there and founded the city which now lies buried 9 feet underneath present-day Mexico City.

An active campaign of attack to the east, south, and west made the Aztec nation dominant in the region. In the process of this conquest for plunder and sacrificial victims, the Aztecs like other victors (e.g., Romans, Japanese) were affected culturally by the conquered peoples as well as by earlier local traditions. The tribute they received as a result of their expansion consisted of foodstuffs, gold, silver, jadeite, turquoise, pearls,

200

and jewel-colored bird feathers. Their capital became an important center for trade and for the craftsmen of other nations who were brought in.

Tenochtitlán, as Spanish soldiers described it, rivaled many European cities in size and splendor. It was built in Lake Texcoco on filled-in terraces and artificial plazas of stone, cut through by many canals and minor waterways. For security, it was connected with the mainland only by three major causeways that were dotted with drawbridges as further protection against invasion. Its buildings, erected in the spirit of the earlier Toltecs, included flat-topped pyramids with altars and idols on their summits, palaces, dance houses, aviaries, and even zoos. The entire area of the city abounded in palaces and dozens of pyramids, large and small. Rising above everything was the great Teocali, or pyramid godhouse. On top of this huge central structure were two temples, one dedicated to Huitzilopochtli, god of war and chief deity, and the other to Tlaloc, god of rain, clouds, mountain springs, and hail — generally the most popular because he influenced the crops. These temples have disappeared completely, since they were constructed of wood.

According to an early chronicler, the special religious enclosure of Tenochtitlán held twenty-five temple pyramids, two oratories, fasting houses, sacrificial and penitential stones, seven skull racks, and two ball courts for ceremonial games. It also had a well, three bathing places, a dancing court, nine houses for the priests, and a prison for the captive gods of conquered nations. In addition, there were vast open spaces for the worshiping multitudes. Human sacrifice played an important part in the rites of the Aztecs, whose gods appeared to need blood to keep them strong and whose expansionist tactics were often associated with the need for new victims.

Next to the main temple was the palace of Montezuma, who lived there with his wives, courtiers, and attendants. The palace was richly decorated with fragrant carved woods, and its walls had luxurious hangings of feathers and furs. The great chief (not an hereditary king) dressed in bright garments; his fingers and arms were decorated with gold jewelry and precious stones; and the ensemble was capped by a towering headdress of brilliant plumes from jungle birds.

In spite of its many borrowings, Aztec art has an individual quality marked by strength and brutality and by effective balance of its elements, as shown in the awesome stone figure of *Coatlique* (fig. 176). A goddess of earth and death, *Coatlique* is also important as a mother of gods, especially Huitzilopochtli, the god of war. The two are sometimes shown in a mother-and-child arrangement. This massive "Lady of the Serpent Skirt" is a synthesis of well-balanced animal forms — the "head" con-

Fig. 176. Coatlique. (Goddess of earth and death.) Mexico, National Museum of Anthropology.

sists of two confronting serpents; the "skirt" is a series of snake shapes. Immediately below the head, a necklace of hands and hearts with a skull as pendant lends a grisly touch. This statue must have presented a fearsome spectacle in its original place in a dark temple interior with the light coming up from below — a temple before which the Aztec taste for human sacrifice was often satisfied.

EARLY MAYA CULTURE. In contrast to Aztec bloodthirstiness, the Maya civilization represents probably the greatest flowering of culture in early America. Its arts display a unique excellence of style and impressive mastery of composition, especially in sculpture and murals. The earliest Maya sites, going back to about 600 B.C., were city-states with distinct artistic personalities, some architectural and some sculptural, while within each site it is possible to find different stages of stylistic evolution. Their cities eventually dotted the jungle from Honduras and Guatemala to the southern Mexican regions of Chiapas and Yucatán.

There were basic similarities to the Valley of Mexico in the stone pyramids elevating temples and idols and the complex ceremonials dependent on an elaborate calendar — but a far more complete calendar than the Aztec. And in Maya numerical reckoning, the long periods of time were represented by *glyphs*, or stone forms consisting of human faces with different kinds of noses, chins, cheeks, and headdresses. Short periods of time were figured by a bar-and-dot system, each bar equal to the number five and each dot to the number one. An important innovation was the concept for zero — symbolized by the outline of an open hand (the Hindus in India were to achieve a different zero concept considerably later). Maya chronology was eventually recorded on carved stone calendars, and special events were commemorated on stone pillars, or stelae, with the date indicated by a series of glyphs and numerals. The exact relationship of the Maya calendar to our chronology is still undetermined, the earliest certain date being carved on a slab of jade, the "Leyden plate," corresponding to about the year A.D. 320.

As in the case of Teotihuacán, the Maya cities were great ceremonial areas of stone rather than population centers. They were monumental in appearance and comprehensively planned, with additions made according to a preconceived scheme. Their main features, as in other such cultures, were the flat-topped pyramids, here crowned by massive-walled stone temples divided into compartments (fig. 177). Typical of Middle

Fig. 177. El Castillo, Maya temple in Chichén Itzá, Yucatán, Mexico.

Fig. 178. Building, Chichén Itzá, Yucatán, Mexico.

American usage, the Maya temple structures were made to be seen from the outside rather than to enclose space as in classical, medieval, or modern architecture, and they lacked the true arch or any kind of vaulting system beyond the corbel idea. In general form they were masses of masonry with narrow rooms and considerable external ornament. Grotesque masks of cut stone were set into the walls of these buildings, and their cornices and doorways were ornamented with faces or geometric motifs (fig. 178). In addition to intricate stone surface decoration, the Maya pyramid temple was often capped by a "flying comb," or roof comb, a decoratively carved stone element that helped strengthen the vaults. The work of the Maya master stonemasons was much superior to the Aztec.

Some of the earliest Maya activity centered around Lake Petén in Guatemala, where later dates on the stone columns begin about the third century of the Christian era and cease about A.D. 900. This period, the "Great Empire" or "Old Empire," reflected an integrated and well-ordered society, a high degree of organization that made the various centers possible. This first Maya area included the northern part of Guatemala, the western part of Honduras, and the state of Chiapas in southern Mexico. Here pyramid temples, such as those in the holy city of Palenque in Mexico, conform to type — with the flying comb and extremely skillful masonry work of stone facing on concrete. Their figurative sculptural decoration is exemplified in the well-known *Lintel*

204

from Piedras Negras in Guatemala (fig. 179). As restored, this portrays an enthroned chieftain surrounded by seated and standing personages, the entire group wearing typical feathered headdresses. Like many Oriental reliefs, it balances abstraction and realism; the latter quality is particularly evident in the convincing movement of the subjects. The general effect of Maya relief work is rather luxurious; its main emphasis is on decorative filling of a space.

In the field of free-standing sculpture, however, the Maya artist of this period achieved a notable degree of decorative monumentality in an Oriental sense. The famous head of the *Maize God* from Copán in Honduras (fig. 180) has a brooding intensity, an inward-turning emotionality quite rare even in this culture. Curved forms sweep back from the strong oval block of the face, repeating their movements in the roundness of the earplugs. Once again the Maya comes close to the feeling of Oriental sculpture and its conceptual viewpoint. The figure of an astronomer in the Brooklyn Museum collection, though less intense, shows a similar grasp of the formal relationship of parts, the lower portion of the face absorbed into the curve of the arms, the upper portion combined with the upward sweep of the headdress.

Fig. 179. Lintel from Piedras Negras. Restoration drawing — Courtesy, American Museum of Natural History, New York.

Fig. 180. Maize God. From Copán, Honduras. Peabody Museum, Harvard University.

LATER MAYA CULTURE: TOLTEC INFLUENCE. Until recently it had been supposed that after about A.D. 1000 the Maya migrated from the Guatemalan highlands to the Yucatán peninsula of Mexico. The latest findings, however, indicate that the Yucatán Maya cities had existed previously and merely experienced a later flowering. At any rate, these centers have similar religious monuments to those already seen. Groups of buildings are usually found at each end of an artificial causeway on a north-south axis.

During this later period, Maya culture was affected by invasions from the Valley of Mexico. The Toltecs who came south were able to conquer the Maya because of their throwing-sticks and bows and arrows. This invasion produced a Maya-Toltec renaissance characterized by elaborate architecture and decoration. In their borrowings from Mexican style, the later Maya buildings at Chichén Itzá and elsewhere are far more ornate than before. In Chichén Itzá, which was occupied for many centuries, the changes in Maya taste are well reflected; Mexican and Maya elements appear in various combinations of pyramids, temples, façade masks, and towering roof combs. This center was the major religious site of its time; a century before Columbus, it must have been as impressive and brilliant as many European capitals.

One of its edifices, called *El Castillo* (fig. 177), was dedicated to Kukulcán (the Maya Quetzalcoatl) and shows Mexican influence. It is crowned by a chapel decorated in a rather harsh way that differs from the earlier lush Maya style. On each side of this pyramid are large central stairways that impart an imposing grandeur to the ensemble.

The famous *Temple of the Warriors* (fig. 181, foreground) is located on top of a large pyramid, at the foot of which is found the Hall of a Thousand Columns, originally a roofed market place. The temple derives its name from the reliefs of warriors carved upon piers which are arranged in rows on the pyramid and which were undoubtedly roofed over with wood like the Hall below. A number of mural decorations from this site (fig. 182) show among other things a seacoast village painted in two dimensions, the foreground objects at the bottom of the picture and the background forms at the top. The preliminary drawing in red, the flatness of the figures, and the final outlines in black bring

Fig. 181. El Castillo (background) and Temple of the Warriors, Chichén Itzá, Yucatán, Mexico.

Fig. 182. Mural from Temple of the Tigers, Chichén Itzá, Yucatán, Mexico. Copy in the Peabody Museum, Harvard University.

to mind the procedures specified in the handbooks of India. Although there is no apparent unity of composition, the little silhouetted abstract forms consisting of flat, contrasting color areas are held together by the over-all tonality of the wall surface.

The high state of Maya civilization is demonstrated by the round tower known as "El Caracol," designed as an astronomical observatory for the calculation of the equinoxes, solstices, and the paths of various heavenly bodies. Without any system of writing other than the hieroglyphics found in their charmingly painted codices, the Maya made important contributions to mathematics and astronomy and preserved most of their historical and religious traditions orally. But the Maya cities, once leagued together, ended by fighting among themselves; singly they resisted the Spanish, but their lack of unity doomed them to defeat.

SOUTH AMERICA: PRE-INCA GROUPS. On the upper west coast of South America the physical problems were considerably different than in Middle America. The Andes Mountains were higher than the Rockies, their valleys much drier and unsuitable for the easy farming carried on by the Mexicans. Andean culture was built up on the mountains, whose sides had to be terraced laboriously with stone walls to contain the earth. Some flat plains did exist, but on a higher level than the Mexican and therefore colder. Agriculture, for all these reasons, was far more complex and the task of mastering the environment quite difficult. The civilization of the Peruvian area ultimately became completely organized and unified; production and consumption were rationalized under a totalitarian form of society.

A sequence of peoples existed there before the triumph of the Incas (the most significant nation in that region) in both the mountain valleys and the coastal sections. Those who lived along the coast developed centers of culture like the early Nazca and the early Chimu; those inhabiting the highlands around Lake Titicaca produced the culture known as Tiahuanaco, with its highly developed irrigation systems. These various groups are often referred to collectively as pre-Inca, but they did exhibit separate and distinct cultural patterns, having the same kind of interplay and cross-influences found in the valleys of Mexico. Nazca pottery, for instance, is decorated with abstract patterns of highly stylized birds, flowers, and other forms in an extensive range of colors (fig. 183). The example shown typifies the rich polychromy, the stylization of the figure (far more evident than in Maya painting or sculpture), and the use of a simulated inlay type of decoration. Chimu pottery, on the other hand, presents a more naturalistic attitude in which the pottery shapes themselves are based on animal and human forms. They may be compared in this respect with many Mexican vessels. The highland Tiahuanacans are considerably important for their highly organized form of government, agriculture, and administration, their ponderous architecture which is really a form of engineering — all these elements blending imperceptibly into the Inca development which they made possible.

Fig. 183. Round bottom bowl. Nazca culture, Peru. San Francisco, M. H. de Young Memorial Museum.

THE INCAS. The appearance of the Incas may be dated about A.D. 1100, in the highlands around Cuzco. Beginning as a small nation, they gradually conquered their neighbors, spreading north and south to absorb the Nazca and Chimu as well. The conquered groups were generally relocated so there would be less chance of revolt. More and more peoples were vanquished until by the time of the Spanish conquest the Inca Empire encompassed over 5 million subjects.

According to their legends, the Inca, or great ruler, was descended from the sun, and, as in Japan, religion and government were one, the Inca chieftain being head of the state and god. The state was led by a small ruling class, supported by mobile military units, and administered with the aid of a tremendous network of roads, over which relays of runners kept open the lines of communication. Messages were sent in *quipu,* a system of knotted and colored strings. The actual administration of the Inca Empire, frequently described as socialist, was an extreme form of paternalism under which all crops were turned over to the state, kept in warehouses, and parceled out to the inhabitants. In this difficult environment the idea of storing food in good times against the all-too-possible coming of bad times seemed eminently practical. Politically the empire was a confederation of tribes (under the Inca) who enjoyed freedom of religion and customs with the sole proviso that the Inca sun god be added to their pantheon. Every worker's job was assured, just as every job had a worker provided, but private ownership of land and individual economic or other enterprise did not exist. Communal activities included not only tilling the soil, but also shearing the herds of llamas and alpacas whose wool was collected, stored, and doled out like the crops. A specific portion of each worker's time was allocated to the service of the church and the Inca, as in medieval Europe.

This paternalism, however, did not stifle the artistic ability of the Incas; that talent was most effectively shown in the field of textiles (fig. 184), in which this culture was almost unique. The techniques of weaving were extremely varied and best expressed in colorful and complex patterns based on "repeat" motifs that changed slightly but perceptibly from one area of the fabric to another. Animals, fish, birds, and human beings were utilized in abstract arrangements that recall the earlier pottery designs of the Nazca people. In Peru also the art of feather weaving reached truly remarkable heights.

From the Tiahuanaco, the Incas inherited their prodigious engineering skill, which was utilized on the gigantic fortresses whose huge remains may be seen today, as at *Sacsahuaman* and *Machu Picchu* (figs. 185–186). Here again incredible skill was necessary to cut and join

210

Fig. 184. Panel from painted fabric. Late Chimu period, Peru. Courtesy, American Museum of Natural History, New York.

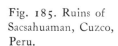

Fig. 185. Ruins of Sacsahuaman, Cuzco, Peru.

Fig. 186. Machu Picchu, Peru.

enormous blocks of stone without metal tools, but with a refinement matching that of any other culture. For the conquering Incas, these fortifications were a natural expression of their way of life, and they helped hold together the most developed political entity produced by the pre-colonial American world. Inca culture, unlike some civilizations in Middle America, survived until the advent of the Spaniards in the early sixteenth century.

212

10 / EARLY CHRISTIAN
AND BYZANTINE ART

THE Roman Empire finally reached a state of acute crisis in its political and economic life by the third century of the Christian era. With the swollen status of the army, the position of emperor frankly became a reward for successful generals from the provinces. To these men the only vital task was the defense of Rome's frontiers against the Germans in the north and the Persians in the east. This endless process drained the financial resources of the nation; heavy taxation, currency devaluation, levies of food and shelter were repeatedly applied. Since military affairs wholly absorbed the energies of the civil government, intellectual activity almost ceased. The unhappiness and hopelessness of the people were reflected by their seeking consolation in mystic Eastern religious cults. The visible evidence appears in later Roman art such as the *Head of Emperor Constantine* (fig. 138).

Had Rome's own religion offered sufficient spiritual comfort or direct communion between man and God, the situation might have been otherwise. As it was, the purely formal and mechanical character of state worship at a time of grave emergency turned the Romans — especially the poor — toward those Eastern religions which offered not only spiritual solace but hope for a better life in the hereafter. Of the many competing cults, Mithraism and Christianity were the most outstanding; the latter of course ultimately won out. By the turn of the fourth century, approximately 10 per cent of the population was Christian. Because they preached a world of the spirit rather than an earthly empire, because they refused to worship the emperor as the symbol of imperial authority, the Christians represented a serious challenge to the state. When legislation did not stem the tide, more active persecution was attempted, but this too failed; and by A.D. 313 the Emperor Constantine recognized Christianity as a legal religion. In 392 it was declared the state religion of the Empire.

Even with the support of the Church, however, the seriously weakened Empire could not withstand the increasing pressure of vigorous barbarian nations from both Europe and the East. When Constantine shifted the capital of the Roman world to Constantinople on the Bosporus, it was an admission that the West was doomed and an assertion of the stronger economic position and defensibility of the eastern part of the Empire. The West would soon fall prey to a constant stream of invasions, resulting in a long period of anarchy during which Europe would contain a group of unstable successor states with the Church as the only unifying element. In the East, in what came to be known as Byzantium, a new Empire colored with semi-Oriental splendor and dominated by a long dynasty of Christian priest-kings was to flourish for another thousand years.

Fig. 187. Jonah and the Whale. From the Catacomb of St. Calixtus, Rome.

EARLY CHRISTIANITY: CATACOMB PAINTING. Although we think of Rome as the center of early Christianity, this religion had been brought in from the Near East, where it had originated and had its earliest development. In Persia and Syria the new faith was already established by the second century, while important Christian centers also flourished in Armenia and Egypt. Those areas produced not only significant church architecture (Syria, Armenia, Egypt) but also manuscripts, textiles, and ivory and other sculpture. From Egypt came the institution of monasticism as well as the belief in a life after death.

The most extensive remains of the period of persecution are in the Roman catacombs of the first few centuries of the Christian era. During this underground phase, worship was presumably conducted in secret, and burial of the faithful (in many cases martyrs) was effected in the abandoned quarries known as catacombs. Some were buried in slots cut out of the tunneled corridor walls; others, such as elders and bishops, in special chambers — *cubicula* — set up at the crossing of two corridors. On these walls, working by the light of torches, the nonprofessional Early

214

Christian painter set down his emotive symbols of religious aspiration (figs. 187–188). The loose sketchy quality and weightlessness of the figures recall the light decorations of Rome (fig. 140), while their highly charged emotion and soulfulness point to the other side of Roman painting, which stems from Hellenistic sources (fig. 139). But the catacomb painter was not interested in pure decoration or romantic narrative; his purpose was to express religious truth through symbols rather than anecdotes. Like late Roman art itself (cf. fig. 138), the contemporary Christian expression utilized insubstantial, spiritualized, nonmaterial forms; in the catacombs this was part of the revolt against pagan materialism.

Christian art in the Eastern Empire, as we shall see, would naturally follow a nonclassical, nonsculpturesque, and two-dimensional path as the classical world yielded before ancient Oriental and Semitic abstract usage. The catacombs, however, stand between the two worlds: even if their figures take on the less substantial form and emotional quality of the East, they still employ the vocabulary of Roman art. Their dignified figures in the costume of the time retain the subject matter of classical expression, now turned toward Christian purposes. Consequently, the legend of Orpheus among the beasts became Daniel in the lions' den, Ariel and the dolphin became Jonah and the whale, in the long symbolic series concerning miraculous salvation (fig. 187). This pagan material

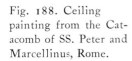

Fig. 188. Ceiling painting from the Catacomb of SS. Peter and Marcellinus, Rome.

was already familiar to the amateur artist of the catacombs, and the use of classical images may have enabled him to mask his purpose at those times when secrecy was necessary. Nevertheless, these are no longer classical allegories. Many images are projected from prayers for the dead in which the Lord is asked to preserve the soul of the supplicant as he saved Jonah from the whale, the three Hebrews from the fiery furnace, and performed countless other miracles. Different types of subject appear also — the souls of deceased persons (fig. 188) with arms generally raised heavenward in prayer and vivid, staring eyes; good shepherds carrying the symbolic lamb on their shoulders; the gathering of the grapes (a symbol of the sacrifice of the Lord); and others. In this early period of Christianity there were no direct representations of Christ or his sufferings but only such indirect symbolic scenes.

TRIUMPH OF THE EARLY CHURCH: ROME. When Christianity was named the state religion of Rome, it emerged from the catacombs; these became shrines over which in many cases churches were built. Christian burial, now respectable, developed richer and more elaborate usages, as shown by a detail from the *Sarcophagus of Junius Bassus* (A.D. 359, fig. 189). In the period of the Church's triumph, this object with its traditional Greco-Roman ornaments marks a reversion to antique ideals of

Fig. 189. Detail from Sarcophagus of Junius Bassus. Rome, Crypt of St. Peter.

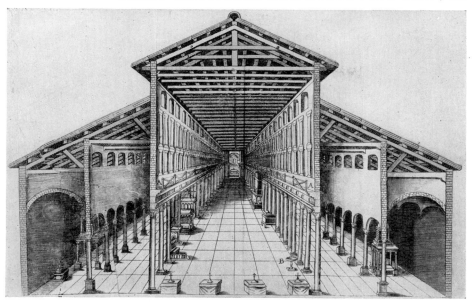

Fig. 190. Old St. Peter's (cross section). Restored.

form, applied to Christian subject matter. Set in niches separated by columns, the narratives include both Old and New Testament scenes emphasizing salvation motifs of the catacomb type; e.g., the beardless Christ transmitting the scroll of the law, or Daniel among the lions. There are a good many of these sarcophagi, dating from the fourth to sixth centuries. The modeling of their forms is slightly less crisp than in earlier classical sculpture.

Most impressive, however, were the basilicas of this period — the prototype of most later churches in Europe. The Early Christian basilica (fig. 190) usually consisted of a wooden-roofed nave, or center aisle, flanked by one or two lower aisles at either side connected to the center by open arches or by flat architraves. The far end of the nave from the entrance was completed in a semicircular portion, the apse, with a transept, or crossing section, before it, giving the plan of the building a rough "T" shape. Light was admitted through window openings in the nave walls above the level of the side-aisle roofs in a clerestory arrangement (cf. *Hypostyle Hall* at Karnak, fig. 28). To the front part of the basilica was usually added a large walled-in courtyard, or *atrium*, where those not yet admitted to membership in the Church could stand. At the building's exit to this atrium, as a lobby for the church proper, a vestibule,

Fig. 191. St. Paul's Outside-the-Walls, Rome. Rebuilt.

Fig. 192. St. Paul's Outside-the-Walls, Rome. Interior. Rebuilt.

or *narthex*, was placed for those who could witness the ceremonies but not enter.

St. Paul's Outside-the-Walls (fig. 191), built over the site of St. Paul's tomb near the Rome-Ostia highway, is prominent among these early basilicas from the time of Constantine. Its present reconstructed form reveals the splendor of an architectural type influenced by contemporary pagan basilicas and the open atrium (or patio) arrangement of the Roman residence. Inside (fig. 192) Corinthian columns support an imposing procession of arches moving toward the apse above a marble-inlaid floor. In contrast to relatively simple exterior treatments, the interiors of such churches displayed iridescent and striking mosaic decorations — also adapted from the Romans — along the nave walls, on the "triumphal arch" leading into the apse, and on the apse itself. In the nave the mosaics were chiefly historical in theme, showing saints or incidents from Scripture. On the arch an apocalyptic or visionary scene (e.g., the Last Judgment) foreshadowed the Paradise represented on the curved surface of the apse.

One of the finest early mosaics is in the apse of Santa Pudenziana in

Fig. 193. Apse mosaic. Santa Pudenziana, Rome.

Rome (A.D. 334–399, fig. 193). The church traditionally was built on the site of the home of Roman Senator Pudens, who is said to have sheltered St. Peter. In this work, against a perspectivized architecture of the New Jerusalem, or Heavenly City, a group of the Elect sit with judicial dignity and sculpturesque nobility around the throne of the bearded Christ. Here for perhaps the first time the Saviour takes the form in which he is henceforth to be known. The conception is distinctly classical in both shape and feeling and may be compared with the *Sarcophagus of Junius Bassus*. Yet these mosaics are an integral part of the church building, no longer confined to the aesthetic function of pagan art. Their chief purpose is to educate the illiterate masses by telling the story of revealed religion and to inspire them through sheer physical splendor. This basic didactic quality has remained part of Christian art down to the present day.

In addition to basilicas, the Early Christian period produced baptistries — circular buildings descended from the Roman round temple — to baptize converts to the new faith, as exemplified by Santa Costanza and San Stefano Rotondo, both in Rome and dating from the fifth century.

Fig. 194. The Ascension. Page from the *Rabula Gospels*. Florence, Laurentian Library.

EARLY EAST CHRISTIAN ART. During the fourth and fifth centuries, classical traits persisted in the Christian art of Rome and even Alexandria (e.g., the Joshua Roll of the Vatican). By the sixth century, however, a new conception of the human form emerged from the Eastern, or Byzantine, parts of the Christian world. Now the figure, though clearly defined, lost all its weight and was placed in an environment of ornamental forms instead of a real space. In an *Ascension* page of the *Rabula Gospels* from Syria (sixth century, fig. 194) the much softened images stand in mid-air as flat brilliant color areas forcefully outlined, emphasizing their emotional rather than structural possibilities. On another page, completely flat architectural elements — standing on a nonexistent ground line — enclose works from the canon table (concordances of important incidents from the Four Gospels). These religious manuscripts are different from pagan examples because of their book format, which replaced the scroll, and because of their greater importance as sacred objects, demanding ornate and splendid decoration in purple and gold. Luxurious covers were designed in ivory, precious metals, and jewels.

Fig. 195. Madonna and Child. East Christian ivory. Courtesy, Walters Art Gallery, Baltimore.

Monumental sculpture is nearly nonexistent in this early period, although reliefs on sarcophagi and various types of ivory objects are plentiful. In them also we see the anticlassical tendency toward weightlessness and higher emotive quality, as in the *Madonna and Child* ivory from Syria or Egypt (fig. 195). The direct and violent expressiveness of this summarized form carries an effect of emotional strain — typical of the mystical religious trend in the East Christian world outside Byzantium proper.

The stone architecture of this outer area of Eastern Christianity (Syria, Egypt, Armenia, and Persia) was developed before the Western church edifices and made an extremely valuable contribution. Here the first vaulted and domed churches were built. Outstanding were those of

Syria, where the lack of wood necessitated stone roofing or vaulting of basilicas as early as the second century. *Tourmanin* (fig. 196), a sixth-century monastery church, combines these features with triple-storied façade towers, buttresses, and corbeling, such as appear in later Romanesque architecture. The most important development in Syria was the dome on pendentives, or outward-curved and triangular corner pieces, a building technique which enabled the architect to put a hemispherical dome over a square space. It was especially influential in Byzantine architecture from the sixth century onward (see fig. 198). Significantly also, these Eastern builders produced a harmoniously designed and decorated exterior, which Western builders did not even attempt until the much later Romanesque period.

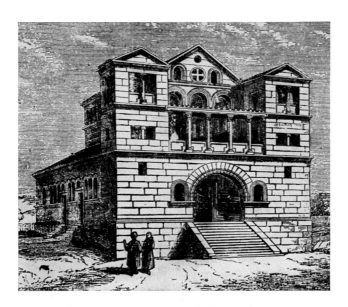

Fig. 196. Basilica of Tourmanin, Syria. Restored.

BYZANTINE EMPIRE. By the sixth century the Byzantine Empire under Justinian emerged as a reorganized state, strengthened to include Egypt, Syria, Armenia, and Greece, together with important parts of Italy (e.g., Ravenna), Sicily, southern Spain, and North Africa. This was accomplished in the face of Slav invasions of the Greek peninsula and Persian and Arab pressure from the east and southeast. The capital of the resurgent empire was Constantinople. This marvelous city with its huge population, splendid palaces, and colorful religious processions was the center of a state economic monopoly that helped support an efficient army and bureaucracy. It was the focal point of a system in which the Emperor

222

was the divinely appointed head of both state and Church and where Eastern qualities of absolutism appeared once more.

The Emperor's authority over army, government, and Church was a distinguishing mark of Byzantine civilization. It was manifested in a rigid, formal, politico-religious ritual clothed in colorful and impressive forms: ecclesiastical garments and implements, church mosaics and carvings — all the outward display of religious autocracy in which everyone and everything served the throne. The Byzantine nobility too were dependent on the state; their special rights stemmed from official employment rather than birth, and even the wealthy had to acquire government positions in order to have standing.

The identity of Church and state gave Byzantine art the formal unyielding character that had been associated with the codified, restricted culture of ancient Egypt or Mesopotamia. All art in Byzantium was subservient to the hierarchy and commissioned from that source. As long as the Church remained synonymous with imperial authority, art retained its primarily frontal view, its flat dehumanized forms and arbitrary proportions. Yet within these rigid regulations, the visible symbols of authority, the artist managed to express (as he had even in Egypt) a certain degree of naturalism in portraiture and anecdotal interest.

FIRST GOLDEN AGE OF BYZANTIUM: HAGIA SOPHIA. In the First Golden Age (ca. 525–725) Byzantine culture assumed some of its characteristic forms. To this period belong the great buildings in Constantinople and the Byzantine outpost of Ravenna in Italy — those following the traditional basilican shapes (e.g., Ravenna's Sant' Apollinare in Classe, cf. also figs. 190–191) as well as those representing the typical Byzantine fusion of Western and Eastern elements. Of the latter, the most impressive is undoubtedly the great Hagia Sophia (Holy Wisdom, figs. 197–200) in Constantinople, built under the direct supervision of Justinian from 532 to 537 by Anthemius of Tralles and Isidor of Miletus.

Hagia Sophia's basic aesthetic purpose, both inside and outside, is to support the magnificent dome (107 feet in diameter) which rises to a height of 179 feet from the floor. Although reminiscent of the domed Pantheon (figs. 133–134) — similarly contrasting a somewhat lumpy exterior and a soaring, exciting interior — there is a fundamental difference in construction. The Roman temple is a relatively static concrete structure, with the weight of the dome resting directly on a circular wall and thence on the ground. The more dynamic Byzantine dome is erected over a square area and, as in Syria, rests on curved triangles (the pendentives) inserted between arches rising from the square walls. The walls of Hagia Sophia, however, have arches and clerestory windows cut into

Fig. 197. Hagia So-
phia, Constantinople.
(Minarets from the
fifteenth to sixteenth
centuries.)

Fig. 198. Hagia Sophia, Constantinople. Interior.

the nave sides and outward-curving arcaded surfaces on the other sides; they obviously afford little support for the dome. But the pendentives rest on enormous piers standing in the four corners of the square central part of the church and offering a solid base. These piers have huge external buttresses affixed to them on the north and south sides of the exterior. On the east and west façades, the dome receives additional support through flanking and slightly lower half-domes. These latter are supported in turn by lower and smaller quarter-domes which finally "ground" the weight on those sides. Through this relatively dynamic system of weight and counterweight, the Byzantine descendants of Syrian builders solved for the first time the problem of keeping a broad floor space free of thick weight-carrying walls.

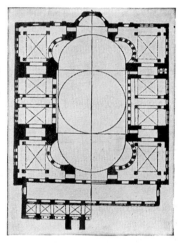

The plan of *Hagia Sophia* (fig. 199) follows in many respects the Early Christian basilica. It runs along an axis that includes the traditional atrium (no longer extant), a double narthex, a nave and aisle section with arcades and clerestory windows, and finally an apse. Its basic shape is a Greek (equal-armed) cross within a square, the dome covering the crossing of the two arms — poised above the entire mass as though suspended in air over a multitude of wall and window openings. The brilliant mosaics, which until recently were hidden under coats of whitewash applied by the later Moslem conquerors, would increase the sensation of lightness. Arcades and galleries are built of colored marbles and have flatly carved and perforated surfaces that heighten the impression of nonmateriality of the walls. The stone carvings (fig. 200) show a charac-

Fig. 199. Hagia Sophia. Plan. (From Henry S. Lucas, *A Short History of Civilization*, New York, McGraw-Hill Book Company, Inc., 1953. By permission of the author.)

teristic Eastern abstraction of natural forms akin to the arabesques in Moslem art (see fig. 261). Particularly striking are the completely nonspatial and flat character of such surfaces and the unusual shapes adopted for the capitals. These are variants of "basket" forms found in both Constantinople and Ravenna, with a special impost block inserted between them and the arch above. Cut out with a drill in alternating light and dark lacy patterns, these decorations give the area a sense of lightness and movement utterly unlike anything in classical or West Christian art.

Fig. 200. Hagia Sophia, Constantinople. Interior, detail of stone carvings.

RAVENNA: SAN VITALE. The rich and colorful mosaics of this period are illustrated by recently uncovered works in *Hagia Sophia* itself and better known instances at Ravenna on the east coast of Italy. At that city, during Justinian's reign, churches and mosaics were created in rich profusion. In addition to ordinary basilicas such as Sant' Apollinare in Classe and Sant' Apollinare Nuovo, which have Byzantine mosaics, there is *San Vitale* (fig. 201), a centralized type of building which had much influence later. Again all the architectural elements are grouped about a central dome, here resting on a drum supported by eight heavy piers in an octagon. The piers are tied together by seven skillfully arranged niches, or apses, that help maintain the dome, as do the half-domes and niches at *Hagia Sophia;* the eighth side constitutes the choir and main apse. To lessen the weight, the dome was constructed of concentric rings of terra-cotta pottery rather than solid units. Both dome and vaulted aisles are concealed on the outside by a tiled and timbered roof, whereas in *Hagia Sophia* the dome is clearly visible outdoors.

The severely simple exterior of *San Vitale* is in contrast with the glowing splendor of its interior mosaics (fig. 202), particularly the group scenes, *Justinian and His Court* and *Theodora and Her Retinue* (fig. 203). The first portrays the Emperor bringing rich gifts to the new church in company with Bishop Maximianus and a number of priests and soldiers. One of the latter bears a shield inscribed with the symbolic *XP*, the first two letters of the Greek word ΧΡΙΣΤΟΣ, or Christ. This mosaic sums up the Byzantine union of Church, state, and army around the person of the Emperor. In the second scene the Empress Theodora,

226

Fig. 201. Church of San Vitale, Ravenna.

Fig. 202. Church of San Vitale, Ravenna. Interior.

dressed in a richly embroidered robe (which depicts the Magi bringing gifts) and an elaborately jeweled headdress, is accompanied by her cortege of court ladies and gentlemen.

In both mosaics, all the personages face front in typical, stiff Byzantine attitudes, identically proportioned as though out of a manual and with their heads on the same level. Figures are flattened and elongated in the interest of two-dimensionality and are imagelike rather than naturalistic.

Fig. 203. Theodora and Her Retinue (mosaic). San Vitale, Ravenna.

The forms, especially the feet, overlap instead of being placed one behind the other, since space is arbitrarily reduced and atmosphere excluded by the neutral gold background. Yet within the rigid formulations and distortions of form and space, the characters in these two scenes are real persons who can be distinguished from each other — the purple-robed emperor with his slight smirk and tiny moustache, the austere bishop, the gaunt-faced empress with a high-cheeked, eager court lady at one side and a restless attendant at the other. As in ancient Egypt, the

228

outward forms are strictly observed; the methods of arrangement and proportion are carefully prescribed. And yet, as in that older despotism, the personality of the artist sometimes breaks through in manifestations of humanity and naturalism.

Byzantine culture undoubtedly was supremely traditionalistic, but, in the field of mosaic decoration and in architecture generally, some measure of experimentation was acceptable. Architectural adaptations of Anatolian, Syrian, and other devices yielded such different types as the domed basilica (*Hagia Sophia*), the centralized periapsidal church, i.e., with encircling apses (*San Vitale*), and the Greek cross with a dome over each arm as well as over the crossing (St. Mark's, Venice). Moreover, architecture, mosaics, and other art forms changed sufficiently from period to period so that one era can be distinguished from another, also like ancient Egypt.

ICONOCLASTIC CONTROVERSY. During the Iconoclastic controversy (725–843), when the representation of man in religious art was forbidden, the character of Byzantine art changed radically. Many persons, especially in intellectual and court circles, felt that the Church and particularly the monasteries had become centers of idolatrous image worship and, because of their great popularity, were rivals of imperial authority. In forbidding the worship of images, the emperor was cutting the ground from under the monastic establishments and strengthening his own power. The example of a dynamic and triumphant Islam (see Chapter 13) with its strictures against image worship may have had something to do with this movement, but in any case the effects of Iconoclasm in Byzantium are quite significant.

These persecutions, together with the oncoming Mohammedans in the Near East and in North Africa, forced many priests and artists into exile in Italy and northern Europe, especially England. In those places Byzantine religious art exerted considerable influence. Meanwhile at home there was a reversion to a more decorative and ultimately naturalistic Hellenistic style, which had been completely overwhelmed by formalism during the First Golden Age. The nonreligious art of Byzantium during the Iconoclastic period is typified by the ivory caskets showing animated and charming hunting, garden, and allegorical scenes (fig. 204). Apart from their pagan content and intellectual literary approach, these ivory reliefs have all the grace and three-dimensional charm of Pompeian cupids. For a brief moment, Byzantine formalism was arrested.

SECOND GOLDEN AGE. The Second Golden Age occurred from about 850 until the sack of Constantinople by the Crusaders and Venetians in

Fig. 204. Casket with mythological scenes (ivory). New York, Metropolitan Museum of Art.

1204. The lively expression of the Iconoclastic era carried over even into the religious revival of this epoch, saving it from the dryness into which it had fallen after Justinian's time. Interest in antique culture continued; in copies of ancient manuscripts, the non-iconic purpose was a softening factor. The religious manuscripts of this time took two forms: a so-called aristocratic style under classical influence (the aristocrats had been the iconoclasts) and a more rigid monastic type.

The mosaics of the period often introduce a combined classical and monastic quality, a balancing of West and East, of pagan form and Eastern abstraction and emotion. The center of this activity shifted from Constantinople to Greece, the Balkans, and Russia. A characteristic mosaic example is found in the eleventh-century Greek *Church of Daphni* near Athens. The story of *Joachim and Anna,* the parents of the Virgin, is told (fig. 205) through separate scenes in which they each enjoy an angelic visitation foretelling the birth of Mary. Anna's simple gesture of supplication, the timid servant at the left, the moody Joachim and the gracious angel at the right, are all elements of a strong naturalism, a distinctly human emphasis. The renewed feeling for form and space contrasts with the flat formalism of *San Vitale*'s royal presentations. An almost classical dignity appears in the relaxed positions of the characters, especially the standing angel who might be compared to the Roman *Augustus* (fig. 127). Yet however much it is affected by the renewal of interest in its classical heritage, Byzantine art even now shows different proportions and

230

Fig. 205. Joachim and Anna (mosaic, eleventh century). Church of Daphni, Greece.

Fig. 206. Church of Daphni, Greece.

Fig. 207. Last Judgment and Descent into Limbo (mosaic, eleventh century). Cathedral of Torcello.

232

handling of drapery and a more limited space. To that degree it is still Eastern and abstract.

The *Church of Daphni* itself (fig. 206) reverts to the Eastern Christian idea of a dome supported on squinches (slabs or arches placed across the corners of a square or octagon to bring that form closer to a circular base for the dome). It has, in addition, certain distinct Second Golden Age features — a narrower dome on a correspondingly higher drum, a reduced scale for the building as a whole, a more verticalized interior, and a clear external expression of the Greek-cross plan in the vault-covered arms of the clerestory. In churches of this type the spaces between the arms are often covered by shallow domes under sloping roofs. These high square structures now have a more decorative external quality through brick and stonework ornament, while the inside displays the usual colored marbles, bright mosaics, or frescoes. Among other building plans is the Greek cross within a square, which has been mentioned, each arm and the crossing itself graced by a dome — the five-domed type of St. Mark's in Venice.

BYZANTINE INFLUENCES. Many other parts of Italy, as well as northern European areas, responded to the stimulus of Byzantine architecture, sculpture, and mosaic works. A direct influence was exercised by the importation of Byzantine workmen; typical of this are the mosaics of the Cathedral of Torcello, an island not far from Venice. The awe-inspiring and monumental *Last Judgment* wall (fig. 207) from the eleventh century has a formalized delineation of the descent into limbo in the topmost section, and the rest of the wall is devoted to the *Last Judgment* itself — all arranged in accordance with the official Church *Guide to Painting*. This handbook prescribed not only the positions of the various scenes and the disposition of persons within those scenes but also their proportions and colors. It was symptomatic of the reversion to rigid ecclesiastical control in the post-Iconoclastic period. The *Anastasis*, or *Descent into Limbo*, takes a characteristic Byzantine approach to subject matter. Here the Christ rescues from that indeterminate region between heaven and hell those who were born before him and who had to await his coming in order to be saved — the patriarchs of the Old Testament, David, Solomon, and their like. The *Last Judgment* shows a liveliness and emotional expressiveness not unlike the contemporary Romanesque cathedral decoration in France and Germany.

With the exception of an occasional emperor portrait, Byzantine art did not encourage three-dimensional sculpture. In this medium it was confined for the most part to ivory plaques of various kinds. The well-

Fig. 208. Harbaville Triptych (ivory, eleventh century). Paris, Louvre.

known *Harbaville Triptych* (fig. 208) of the eleventh century illustrates the delicate workmanship and hieratic gravity of these works within their prescribed gestures, proportions, and themes.

THE FINAL PERIOD; SURVIVAL OF BYZANTINE TRADITION. In the final period of Byzantine art, from about 1260 to the capture of Constantinople by the Turks in 1453, the empire's limited resources dictated the use of mural painting rather than mosaic work. This new form, even more intense in spirit, was produced in a time of great political and social strain, with Byzantium hemmed in on all sides. A literary renaissance was accompanied by a distinctly humanistic and emotional art, as in the fourteenth-century paintings of the monastery at Mount Athos, the church at Mistra, and the mosaics of the Kahrie Djami at Constantinople (fig. 209). These works are a freer, more supple version of the mosaics of the Second Golden Age at Daphni; they have a broader, more diversified

234

subject matter and a restrained monumentality that almost suggests the contemporary frescoes of Giotto in Italy. Sometimes the artist strikes a note of sentimentality, at other times a more tragic note, but in all he betrays a new awareness of the world that helps break down Byzantine uniformity of expression.

The fall of Constantinople in 1453 did not mean the end of Byzantine tradition; it was continued in the lands subscribing to Orthodox Greek ritual, especially Russia. There the churches show the familiar square plan enclosing a Greek cross, with a very high drum supporting a narrow dome, as well as a standard Russian scheme with five domes — one over the crossing and one over each angle formed by the arms of the cross. The latter buildings feature a series of picturesque but unfunctional bulbous domes, unrelated to the interior of the church, which is usually very dark. In painting, Russian miniatures, icons, and murals are closely associated with the formal Byzantine procedures. This style survived in Russia until the Revolution of 1917.

Fig. 209. Virgin Receiving the Wool (mosaic, fourteenth century). Kahrie Djami, Constantinople.

11 / THE EARLY MIDDLE AGES IN THE WEST

WHILE Byzantium worked out its colorful fusion of Eastern and Western ideas, the Roman Empire in the West slowly crumbled and disappeared. Toward the end of the fifth century of the Christian era, the centuries-long infiltration of Germanic peoples reached a state of equilibrium. Barbarized Roman and civilized German, brought together under a rapidly growing Church, fashioned a new and supernaturally oriented society. Rome did not "fall" in the manner of other states. Its overstrained military and economic machine — superposed on a social order that excluded the masses of people from its benefits and offered merely a formal religion — was replaced by an ever-changing series of successor states. These were united only in their common Germanic vigor and their fervent Christianity. Such elements, together with the remnants of the Roman social system and population, formed the basis for the civilization of the early Middle Ages in the West.

In previous periods warrior nations had moved down from the north to alter the course of Minoan, early Greek, and Hellenistic history. Further waves of Celts, Germans, Slavs, and Scandinavians had come from a large area around the Baltic Sea. By 500 B.C. Celts had overrun Europe as far west as Gaul (France) and England, and as far east as the Black Sea; as Gauls they had attacked the Pergamenes (figs. 115–117). With the rise of Rome the European Celts had been subdued by Caesar's pacification of Gaul.

WANDERING OF THE NATIONS. Beginning with the Christian era, the main pressure against the empire had come from various Germanic tribes of the Baltic region. Their first wave of migrations had occurred around A.D. 200, when the Germanic Goths went south from the Vistula River Valley in northern Europe down to the shores of the Black Sea and the western end of the Scythian-Sarmatian area (which encompassed a good deal of Eurasia from southern Russia over to India). This had started a whole series of population movements against the frontiers of the Roman

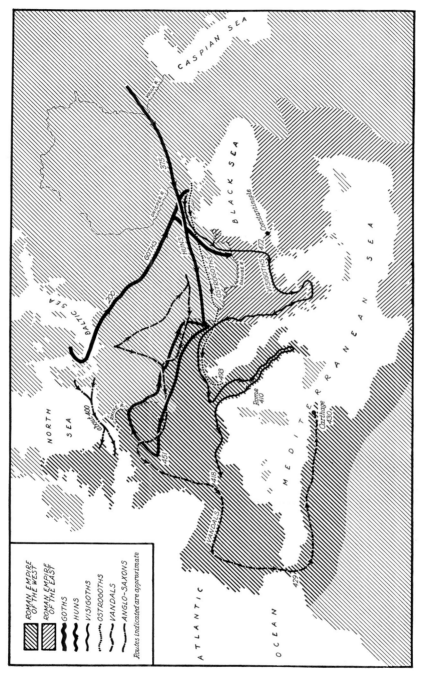

Fig. 210. Migrations of the Dark Ages. (From Henry S. Lucas, *A Short History of Civilization*, New York, McGraw-Hill Book Company, Inc., 1953. By permission of the author.)

Empire. By about A.D. 250, various groups had pushed forward into the Greek peninsula, Gaul, Spain, and northern Italy. Between this first invasion wave and the second (late fourth through sixth centuries), the Goths and other Germanic peoples were converted to Christianity (fig. 210).

In A.D. 375, Huns from the steppes of Asia — driven west by a China strengthened under the Han dynasty — appeared along the shores of the Caspian and Black Seas, setting in motion the second wave of migrations into the Empire. Visigoths, Vandals, and others were swept before them. The Visigoths sacked Rome in 410 and went into Spain, where they ousted the Vandals who had arrived there through France. Other groups pushed on by the Huns were the Burgundians and the Franks; the latter ultimately became the chief stabilizing force of the so-called Dark Ages. During the period of Hunnish supremacy (375–453) the Angles, Saxons, and Jutes began their forays against England, scattering the Celtic Britons and driving their priests and monks to Ireland.

ART OBJECTS OF THE WANDERING PEOPLES. The art of the wandering peoples was by definition an art of personal adornment, concerned with easily carried objects such as jewelry, weapons, harness trappings, and the like. Even during the relatively stable Frankish Merovingian period (486–751) there were still few buildings. The literary and artistic evidence underscores the great importance attached to jewelry. Warrior chiefs were buried not only with their horses but with their bracelets, fibulae (pins), necklaces, and weapons. In Roman and Hellenistic representations, "barbarians" are generally shown wearing jewelry; e.g., the *Dying Gaul* (fig. 115), an early Celtic invader of Pergamum, wears a gold necklace in the "twisted rope" pattern so popular later during the wandering-nations period.

Both Celtic and Germanic ornaments were highly abstract and non-figurative, offering strong and continuous opposition to Roman representational art. Germanic abstraction yielded to figurative ideas as the various parts of Europe were Christianized, but Celtic (or Irish) art continued its decorative path long after the triumph of the faith. In both cases the original tendency toward nonrepresentational expression had been related to two significant factors. First, the agricultural level of this new so-called barbarian society, as in New Stone Age cultures, had produced a craft approach with generalized rather than specific technique. Second, there had been various contacts with the East and its decorative viewpoint. The most important of these contacts had occurred around A.D. 150 between the Goths and the Scythian-Sarmatian folk inhabiting the tremendous area from south Russia to India.

SCYTHIAN-SARMATIAN INFLUENCE. Scythian-Sarmatian art may be placed roughly a few centuries before and after the start of the Christian era; it was unquestionably under the influence of nearby Persia. From this source (e.g., the Stairway of the *Apadana of Xerxes* at Persepolis, fig. 52, and the composite column, fig. 49) the Scythian-Sarmatian and related peoples seem to have borrowed the idea of using animals in abstract ornamental patterns — animals confronting and animals fighting each other (fig. 211). These conceptions were passed on to the Goths and

Fig. 211. Plaque (Scythian bronzework found in Siberia). Leningrad, Hermitage Museum.

Fig. 212. Frankish fibula (sixth to seventh centuries). New York, Metropolitan Museum of Art.

others, who also adapted the cloisonné technique for their jewelry from central Asian and Persian sources, either directly or through intermediaries (see fig. 212). This technique made it possible to set gems (or imitation gems) into a cloison or setting to which they were fused by heating. (There is also a mechanical cloisonné method which merely involves fixing the gems in mountings on the surface of the plaque.) Through the wandering of the barbarian nations, the cloisonné technique was carried all over Europe and remained an important part of medieval art as late as the thirteenth to fourteenth centuries.

BARBARIAN ART FORMS. A typical instance of the Germanic application of these Eastern ideas appears in the many fibulae, or brooches (fig. 212), of the "barbarian" type in Gaul. In addition to their sophisticated shapes, the stones and their settings are arranged in a variety of patterns. The surface ornamental motifs are rather simple, running to curvilinear designs. Yet barbarian art can have richness, as in the famous gold and jeweled *Crowns of Guarrazar* (fig. 213) made for the Visigothic Christian

Fig. 213. Crowns of Guarrazar (seventh century). Paris, Cluny Museum.

kings of Spain to hang over the altars of their churches. Barbarian art did not last long in Europe, for it soon gave way before the Christian need for images and an anthropomorphic conception.

In Scandinavia, however, where Christianity made slower progress (ninth to twelfth centuries), pagan motifs and ideas persisted. Even after the advent of Christianity, there were many applications of barbarian beast ornament and animal symbolism. A good example of the magnificent carvings of the Vikings is found on the *Oseberg Ship* (ninth century, fig. 214), which shows different types of animal designs: dragons in complicated abstract formulations curving back on themselves, or interwoven serpents arranged with a powerful feeling for constant rhythmic movement of the nonnaturalistic parts. Because of the extensive expeditions by these northern voy-

Fig. 214. Oseberg Ship. Detail from prow showing serpent head. Bygdøy Museum (near Oslo).

agers into all sections of Europe, their beast ornament became a staple feature of later medieval art through the Romanesque period.

IRISH ART. The Celts (as distinguished from the Germanic Goths) had made contact with the East long before the Christian era — for instance, in their attempts to invade Hellenistic Pergamum. As a result they had carried back the idea of perforated ornamental arrangements, spirals, and other elements which they transformed into their own characteristic patterns. Celtic Ireland, which lay off the beaten track of Roman conquest, was another area in which Early Christian representational art was strongly resisted. This might well have been a result of its long-established abstract ornamental style stemming from the Eastern influence, and even more of its essentially Neolithic origins. In spite of the relatively early Christianization of the Irish in the fifth century, they maintained their own aesthetic tradition, purifying and refining it into one of the

Fig. 215. Round Tower of Glendalough, Ireland.

finest expressions of decorative art in history. The use of a human image was eventually adopted, but not until somewhat late in manuscript and metalwork — and in a form consistent with the basic nonrepresentational and abstract approach of Irish art.

During the Dark Ages of the migration period, Ireland became a refuge for Christianity. Many monasteries were founded, and the writings of the Church fathers were studied and preserved for a future date when Europe would carry on its task of building the faith. Although these early monasteries have disappeared, their upward-tapering cylindrical towers still stand in many places (fig. 215). The characteristic Irish stone crosses dedicated to different saints are equally ancient. They bear relief carvings of interlaced knotwork patterns derived from the New Stone Age of Europe and some highly formalized human figures (fig. 216). Rising on a flat rectangular stem, the shaft here reaches a slender crossing, enclosed by a gracefully proportioned circle covered with ornamental detail. These crosses are also found in England, Scotland, and the Isle of Man, testifying to the early missionary activities of the Irish monks, who later established such renowned monasteries as St. Gall in Switzerland and Bobbio in northern Italy.

Metalwork and manuscript illuminations were highly perfected. The former took varying shapes — brooches to fasten cloaks, e.g., the *Tara*

242

Brooch (fig. 217); church articles like the famous Ardagh Chalice, the Cross of Cong, the Reliquary of St. Patrick's Bell; and a small number of book covers. The *Tara Brooch* is made of bronze but covered with gold plates, enamel areas, and pieces of coral. Its ornamental patterns include the characteristic interlace, "S" spiral forms, and a few abstracted dragons. In the Irish craftsman's tumultuous heaping up of decorative motif, there appears an all-over balance and controlling design — particularly if the brooch is considered without the diagonal pin bar. Its exuberance and sense of constant movement are equaled in the manuscripts, such as the famous *Book of Kells* (ninth century). The latter's initial page from the Gospel of St. Matthew (fig. 218) shows the same extraordinarily painstaking craftsmanship. Originally of Neolithic inspiration, these forms are raised to the highest and most sophisticated level of which medieval art is capable.

On this monogram page of the *Kells* manuscript are the Celtic trum-

Fig. 216. Murdoch's Cross, Monasterboice, Ireland.

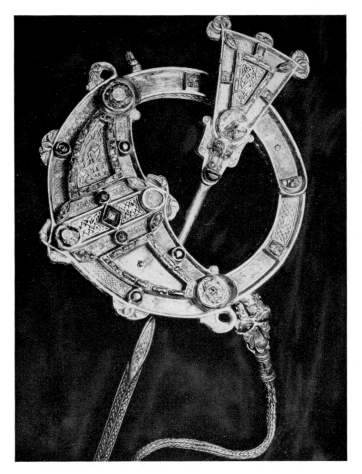

Fig. 217. Tara Brooch (A.D. 700–750). Dublin, National Museum.

pet and spiral, the complicated and endless Irish interlace, the key pattern arranged in diagonals, and the lacertines, or elongated and entwined animal forms, used rather sparingly here. This last motif may be a result of the original Celtic contact with the East or of the increasing influence of the Scandinavians in northern Europe. All this ornamentation is effectively integrated within a strongly dynamic conception projected by the grandiose sweep of the arms of the "X" — which, however, inevitably return to the points at which they began. In spite of the fantastic complexity that the eye finds difficult to follow, there is a total impression of graceful unity. On close inspection, human or animal representations may be made out here and there, as, for instance, at the end of the curve in the "P" form; but they are deliberately reduced to an abstract pattern, so as not to conflict with the decorative unity of the whole. Even on the Evange-

244

list pages, the full-length figures are hemmed in by complex borders and subordinated to the design movement up, down, and across. These faces and forms in Irish manuscript art are strikingly suggestive of playing-card types.

MEROVINGIAN STYLE. While the Irish would not compromise their nonfigurative approach or attempt a representational art — thereby retaining their strength of design — various nations on the Continent itself tried to reconcile the ornamental barbarian style with the figurative needs of Christianity. In this process neither style profited; the ornament of many Merovingian (Frankish) manuscripts, plaques, and other objects is distinctly coarse, and their figures are almost grotesque, though vividly emotional (fig. 219). The neutralization that resulted from this meeting of barbarian and Early Christian art would be resolved in favor of the

Fig. 218. Initial page from the Gospel of St. Matthew, *Book of Kells*. Dublin, Trinity College Library.

representational and classical viewpoint in the period following, the age of Charlemagne. During the Merovingian era, however (486–751), the indecisive half-representational, half-ornamental style reflected the decay of the classical Early Christian viewpoint within the less Romanized areas of Europe or those susceptible to barbarian influences (northern France, Spain, and northern Italy). Any comparison of a typical Merovingian ornament (generally an initial made up of bird and fish forms) with a contemporary Irish one demonstrates the low cultural level of the former as against the elegant suavity of the latter.

Monumental sculpture and painting vanished almost completely during this period in the West, while architecture was bound to be very sparse since city life had practically disappeared and there were no permanent royal residences. Churches were still built in the various separate kingdoms of Lombardy in northern Italy, Visigothic Spain, and Merovingian or Frankish France, but they were of the simplest type like the basilica of San Juan de Baños in Spain (661) or the Baptistry of St. Jean de Poitiers in France (also seventh century). A number of crudely ornamented stone fragments — railings, baptismal fonts, and capitals — show

Fig. 219. Cross page from Gelasian Sacramentary. Rome, Vatican Library.

the Merovingian conflict between two-dimensional and three-dimensional art.

THE AGE OF CHARLEMAGNE. The Frankish kingdom under Charles Martel repulsed the invading Moors in 732, and under Charlemagne in the Carolingian period (768–877) produced the first organized political entity since the fall of Rome. Charlemagne conquered western Germany and northern Italy, instituted a real administration, and received the title of Emperor from the Pope in 800. At Aix-la-Chapelle he founded a literary academy where sacred texts were edited and corrected and young men were trained for administrative careers under the new empire. There was also an art workshop where manuscript illuminations, book covers, and jewelry were fabricated in the various styles of the time.

Charlemagne's educational program, under the direction of the Irish scholar, Alcuin of York, was oriented toward a revival of classical antiquity — a corollary of his imperial political aspirations. Manuscripts and other objects of art were brought up from Italy. However, since these were not classical but Early Christian in origin, the Carolingian "renaissance" takes on that quality more than an actual antique flavor. The important point, nevertheless, was the shift from a mixed and indeterminate Merovingian art to one of three-dimensionality, now tinged with Celtic decorativeness and barbarian cloisons, animal ornaments, and the like.

CAROLINGIAN ART. Besides the monumental style of this period, as exemplified in the *Gospels of Charlemagne* (fig. 220), there was a sketchy impressionistic manner of handling the figure, as seen in the celebrated *Utrecht Psalter* (fig. 221). Thus the court style was contemporary with an informal and popular manner, the latter perhaps for some monastic rather than official purpose. The *Gospels of Charlemagne* is typical of the Palace School which produced luxurious objects of worship for Charlemagne's immediate circle and was closest in feeling to the antique. The increased naturalism of expression, posture, form, and even spatial indications is most significant. Certain other schools of Carolingian art showed the same tendency toward monumentality, especially the Ada Style whose draperies still suggest the Byzantine and whose flat architectural details recall the Syrian.

In the *Utrecht Psalter* of the Reims school, the essential component is a Germanic-Christian spiritualism that emerges in the loose, restless, jagged, linear forms. There is no question of classic dignity and restraint; instead, the underlying emotive and expressionist approach emerges in vivid narrative flashes whose dynamism is a pictorial equivalent of the restless but unified movement in Celtic ornament. An almost naïve but powerful directness is exhibited in the kings moving with their chains,

Fig. 220. Evangelist page from *Gospels of Charlemagne* (St. Matthew). Vienna, Schatzkammer.

according to the psalmist's verse: "to bind their kings with chains . . ." (Psalm 149). The symbolic realism of this school extended into the ecstatic and visionary art of the next epoch.

The books most often illustrated during the Carolingian period were Bibles, sacramentaries (containing the Mass, sacraments, and other rites), and psalters for the Psalms of David. They had certain features in common; the chief one was a dedication page on which the king or noble for whom the book was done appeared either alone or with his attendants, who were customarily made smaller. The Bibles habitually have an Evangelist page inserted before each Gospel, with a full-page miniature of the Gospel writer Matthew (fig. 220), Mark, Luke, or John. Full-page miniatures are often found with the Early Christian symbolic fountain of life (i.e., the Church) as well as pages of canon tables. The latter consist of four parallel columns of Roman numerals referring to coinciding passages in the Four Gospels, used by medieval priests as a kind of subject index of useful texts and concordances. During much of this era, the elaborate initial page was a constant practice, allowing play for the artist's decorative tendencies — especially the vestigial Irish interlace and barbarian beast ornament. In the psalters the large initial letter *B*

248

appears frequently to introduce the first psalm: *Beatus vir qui non* . . . ("Blessed is the man that walketh not in the counsel of the ungodly").

An interesting custom was prevalent in the various types of illustrated books in representing the Apotheosis, or deification of Christ. The Saviour is seated within an almond-shaped nimbus, or *mandorla,* surrounded by the symbols of the Evangelists (Man of Matthew, Eagle of John, Lion of Mark, and Bull of Luke) or by seraphim and angels. This composition — Christ in a *mandorla* surrounded by Evangelist symbols — was to become one of the commonest factors in later Romanesque art, as on the portal of *St. Trophîme at Arles* (see fig. 231).

Because of the basically still unstable conditions in a time when feudalism was just beginning to crystallize, Carolingian art did not produce any monumental sculptural works or outstanding architecture. Its chief products — manuscript illuminations, ivory book covers, and metalwork — were all small. Buildings were few and not significant enough to require large-scale sculpture. The Palace Chapel at Aix-la-Chapelle displays the typical Carolingian referral to Early Christian styles, in this case to *San Vitale* in Ravenna; Bishop Theodulf's church at Germigny-des-Près harks back to the Visigothic San Cristo de la Luz of Toledo in that cleric's native Spain. The buildings of the abbeys founded or reorganized by Irish

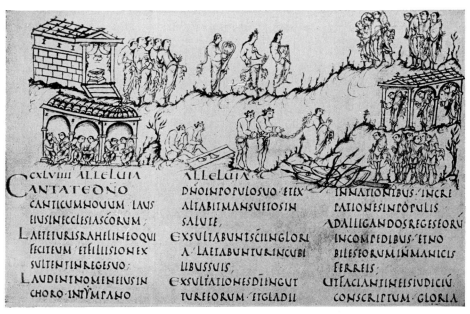

Fig. 221. Triumph of Israel page from the *Utrecht Psalter*. Utrecht, University Library.

Fig. 222. Carolingian book cover (ninth century). Four Gospels. New York, The Pierpont Morgan Library.

monks, e.g., St. Gall, Bobbio, and Fulda (in Germany), for the most part no longer exist, except in written accounts or illustrations such as the abbey plan from the Library of St. Gall in Switzerland. This is a complete plan for a monastic establishment, evidence of the already highly developed and self-sufficient form of these institutions as early as the ninth century. In addition to church and cloister, a systematic farming economy was carried on. The abbey church of St. Gall, like later German Romanesque buildings (see fig. 240), shows two separate apses, one at each end of the building.

Carolingian ivory carvings and metalwork, usually finer in quality than the manuscripts they might enclose, are exemplified by the gold and jeweled book cover of the Morgan Library (fig. 222). Although reminiscent of the agitated movements and fluttering draperies of the *Utrecht Psalter*, the figures on this magnificent book cover with its jeweled cloisons have more volume than the purely linear conceptions of the former manuscript. In this sense they also represent a step toward the future — toward the ecstatic religiosity of Romanesque sculpture, which often translates into stone the nervous movements of Carolingian manuscript painting.

12 / ROMANESQUE EUROPE

IN spite of the political and intellectual accomplishments of the Carolingian Empire, the economic foundations of early medieval society — already sadly deteriorated — collapsed almost completely in the ninth- and tenth-century period following. Commerce dwindled to a mere trickle as manufacturing became purely local, the large estates producing for themselves. Meanwhile foreign trade was cut off by the rising power of the Moslems in the Mediterranean area. City life nearly disappeared, populations decreased, and Europe turned more and more to the agrarianism and manorial life that marked the economic side of feudal existence.

Politically, Charlemagne's successors had divided the empire into a Frankish, a German, and an in-between, or Lotharingian, section combining Lorraine and northern Italy. The third area was soon divided among the Franks (French) and the Germans, who have been disputing over parts of it ever since. A series of terrible invasions by Norsemen, Slavs, and Magyars during the ninth and tenth centuries brought about the utter breakdown of imperial authority. "From the fury of the Northmen, good Lord, deliver us!" and "From the arrows of the Hungarians, good Lord, deliver us!" were regular prayers in this time. Strongly fortified castles were needed to repel these invasions from the north, east, and south (the last-named by the Moslems). And since the kings were unable to offer widespread safeguards, the feudal system of local protectors was further established — that is, lords or abbots furnished protection in exchange for services and feudal homage. By the middle of the tenth century, a certain amount of political stability was achieved on those terms.

In the post-Carolingian period the political center of Europe shifted to Germany, whose Ottonian emperors (ca. 950–ca. 1100) revived the idea of a universal empire, had themselves crowned in Rome, and attempted to control the thoroughly disorganized Church and papacy (fig. 223). This Byzantine attitude (Otto II had married a Byzantine princess) underlined the leading politico-religious problem of the era, the struggle between pope and emperor. But the weakness of the papacy until the end of the eleventh century was accompanied by an equally decisive growth

252

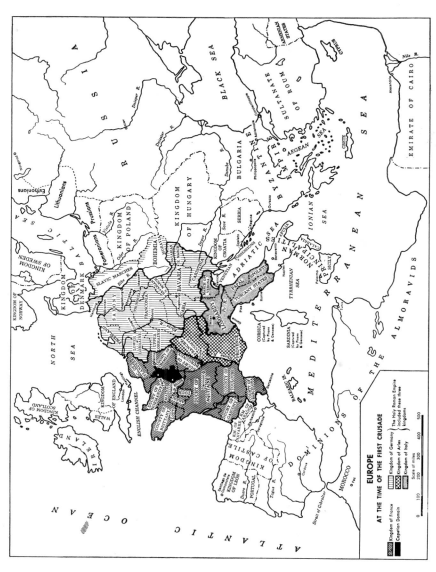

Fig. 223. Europe at the Time of the First Crusade. (From Carl Stephenson, *A Brief Survey of Medieval Europe*, Harper & Brothers, New York, 1941. By permission.)

of the monastic system in isolated feudal units which exercised their power over the minds of men as the castles controlled their bodies.

MONASTICISM AND FEUDALISM. The monastic element gave the culture of the Romanesque period its special character. It was, however, a thoroughly feudal monasticism in which the aristocracy (in addition to their own political role) also played an important part, occupying many of its chief posts. Similarly, many monastic foundations held their lands on feudal terms from more powerful lords or kings. And at the same time, monasticism furnished leading candidates for the papacy itself.

The monastic-feudal culture was only remotely related to the great masses of the people, who were oppressed by aristocracy on one side and the clergy on the other. The populace might enter the sphere of this culture as pilgrims or as beneficiaries of sermons and exhortations to crusade against the infidel (meaning anyone not a Christian and even in some cases an Orthodox, or Eastern, Christian). But basically the Romanesque culture was an entity created by monks for monks and clerics, as self-sufficient and unyielding as the inflexible social and economic scheme.

Just as there was no market for manufactured goods outside the manorial system, so there was no market for ideas outside the patterns laid down by the monastery and the Church. In an age of increasing supernatural beliefs, absolute faith was required of an individual; the fear of Satan and hell was made a stronger deterrent to evil-doing than the power of good. The moral and psychological control by religion was complete. In spite of struggles between Church and state, the Church's spiritual rule remained relatively unaffected. The idea that faith was more important than knowledge, that everything on earth was part of a fore-ordained plan administered by the Church, gave that institution the ability to dominate cultural expression. The conclusion that what was suffered here on earth was insignificant, compared with the joys of the hereafter, had been an important concept for early Christianity, but now merely helped to perpetuate the social and religious *status quo*.

OTTONIAN ART. During the Ottonian period, culture (especially art) still reflected a certain imperial splendor mingled with the growing visionary expression, the broadened emotional potential. Both manuscripts and ivories show an adaptation of Carolingian form ideas as well as Byzantine elements borrowed from manuscripts that were imported in considerable quantities. Painting was centered about the monastery of Reichenau, where these factors were blended with an intense emotive quality reminiscent of, but exceeding, the Carolingian *Utrecht Psalter.* Some of the restlessness of the linear Reims style is recognizable in the famous *Doubting Thomas* ivory from the end of the tenth century (fig.

224), raised to a higher, more intense, and almost psychotic level as the saint literally climbs upward into the wound of the Lord. This work differs from the former not only in its broader psychological range but also in its carefully organized architectonic composition. In that way it is a forerunner of the monumental sculpture on French, German, and other cathedrals of the Romanesque era.

The manuscripts of the Ottonian period were often under Byzantine influence, like the *Gospel Lectionary of Archbishop Egbert* (fig. 225). They show a new kind of emotion from that of the *Utrecht Psalter,* which had come primarily from the loose agitated drawing and restless movement of the figures. The Ottonian book displays a carefully finished painting that is almost soberly made. Its effects are owed to the Byzantine glaring of the eyes, the fluttering of drapery, the excited and dissonant color scheme, and the visionary arrangement and conception of the figures. We are often told that a good deal of tenth-century art was conditioned by apocalyptic prophecies of the millennium, the end of the world expected to occur in A.D. 1000. But since postmillennial art also envisioned agitating and frightening judgments, we must assume that the apocalyptic sense still existed during the eleventh and twelfth centuries and that artists

Fig. 224. Doubting Thomas (ivory, end of tenth century). Berlin, Deutsches Museum.

still felt — and expressed — this sensation of fear and imminent doom.

CLUNIAC REFORMS. During the tenth century, too, reforms within the Church by the Cluniac order of monks brought a new spirituality and

Fig. 225. Adoration of the Magi (tenth century) from *Gospel Lectionary of Archbishop Egbert.* Trèves, Public Library.

belief in the next world, fostering complete negation of worldly things in favor of escape into the beyond, even to death. It was this group that had preached about the millennium and the Last Judgment, that foretold terrifying punishment for sin, that organized crusades and sponsored pilgrimages — that, in short, gave Romanesque religiosity its fanatic character. From the year 1000 on, a unified and highly organized cultural approach expressed itself through the medieval cathedrals and their sculptured decorations.

BUILDING OF ROMANESQUE CHURCHES. The appearance of so many impressive churches after the turn of the eleventh century (and after so many centuries of architectural drought) was not caused by the mystic influence of passing the date 1000 without calamity. It was rather a symbol of the increased power and wealth of the Church Militant, the only segment of society that was in a position to give important commissions. The buildings themselves in their massive and static bulk mirror the centuries-long and inflexible character of the social and intellectual system that brought them into being; their decorations show the new religious fervor of the eleventh century. Although trade and town life had begun to reappear, foreshadowing changes in the next period, the art and culture of this epoch were primarily conditioned by its own religious and feudal requirements.

From the monastic cloisters (fig. 226) came the stimulus by which Europe learned to build and carve again. In these repositories of learning, the monks themselves were the chief workers and builders, although as time went by, lay workers and assistants were used and the knowledge so passed on to the next era. During the Romanesque period proper, the direction of large construction jobs was exclusively in the hands of the clergy, so that the buildings in their form and ornament represent the clerical viewpoint.

THE PILGRIMAGE ROUTES. As symbols of monastic power, the monastery churches were often much larger than might be indicated by their small communities. This impressive size and the brilliant interior color were also dictated in some cases by the fact that pilgrims, impelled by the fervor of the period, would come from all over Europe to pay their respects at a shrine holding relics of an important saint. There were a number of pilgrimage routes which the travelers could follow, banded together for safety and company, like those described in Chaucer's *Canterbury Tales* who were on the way to St. Thomas à Becket at Canterbury.

The chief roads led to Rome to the grave of St. Peter; to Santiago de Compostela in northern Spain to the grave of St. James the Greater; and to the Holy Sepulcher in Jerusalem, the traditional resting place of the Saviour. Generations of pious pilgrims, following these well-beaten paths, were put up at monasteries in an age when there were few cities and inns. Free-will offerings were made in return for the hospitality received and resulted in the accumulation of considerable wealth by those monastic centers, whose power was thereby increased. Pilgrimage routes of the Romanesque period would often become trade routes in the following Gothic era when cities grew and trade increased.

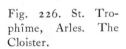

Fig. 226. St. Tro-phîme, Arles. The Cloister.

Fig. 227. St. Sernin, Toulouse. Apse exterior.

CLUNIAC CHURCHES. The most interesting route from an artistic standpoint is the "Way of St. James," organized by the reforming Cluniac order, for along its four roads are a whole series of so-called pilgrimage churches, with similarities in building style because of the movement of artistic ideas and of artists as well. Apart from Santiago de Compostela itself, the French cathedral of *St. Sernin at Toulouse* (fig. 227) has the greatest significance.

In addition to its starkly elegant sculptured capitals, *St. Sernin* exemplifies the changes wrought in the Early Christian basilican plan by Romanesque and especially pilgrimage cathedrals. In its cross-shaped plan the side aisles are extended beyond the transept (crossing) to provide an ambulatory, or walking space, around the choir. This made it possible for large numbers of pilgrims to pass around the altar without disturbing the services, and to visit the various side chapels which now radiated from the choir and were even added to the back of the transept, as can be seen from the outside of the building. These additional chapels

258

were needed to hold the saints' relics, to which prayers were offered. In the same way, the increased significance attached to the Mass and to ritual in general made for a larger altar area and choir (for an enlarged clergy). The vision of Christ as a personal deity, reachable by all, receded; the saints whose relics were here enshrined became intercessors with Christ for the supplicants.

The growing size of many churches as well as the need for fire-proofing (for some time there remained the problem of Norman pillaging and burning) gradually turned Romanesque builders from wooden to stone roofing. The interior of *St. Sernin at Toulouse* (fig. 228) illustrates the typical canopy, or tunnel-shaped stone roof, known as a barrel vault, which was used in the nave of one type of Romanesque church. Support for this half-cylinder of masonry is offered by small barrel vaults covering a new upper-story triforium gallery above the side aisles. The gallery usually has a series of often tripartite arcades (thus triforium) opening out into the upper nave from what was once a relatively un-broken wall. The small barrel gallery vaults lean against the nave vaults in one direction; in the other (see fig. 235a), they lean on extremely thick

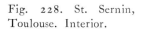

Fig. 228. St. Sernin, Toulouse. Interior.

outside walls that carry the combined weight to the ground. The nave vaults were frequently divided, as here, by transverse arches, or ribs, on their undersurfaces, thus forming independent square units, or bays.

The downward-curving shape of such nave vaults and their great weight generally made it impossible for the builders to use the old clerestory of Early Christian architecture, a fact which now resulted in a relatively dark interior. In the south of France, because of the sunny climate, this did not matter very much; but in the north the need for more light led architects to a form of vaulting that would permit piercing the upper walls. This is the groined vault seen at *St. Etienne at Caen* (see figs. 236–237), made by the crossing of two barrel vaults and inherited, like the barrel vault and dome, from Roman architecture — hence the term "Romanesque." Actually this form of stone roofing had been used earlier in the side aisles of southwest French churches (see figs. 229–230) and elsewhere also, but not until the Lombard architects at *Sant' Ambrogio in Milan* (see figs. 232–233) showed its potential as nave

Fig. 229. St. Pierre, Angoulême. Exterior view.

roofing did it become important in Romanesque building, and thereafter extended its influence in many directions.

St. Sernin is one of the most impressive types of French Romanesque in its size, complexity of radiating apse and transept chapels, and the fine balancing of elements within and without the building. It also exemplifies a change from the consistent horizontality of Early Christian interiors, with their procession of columns and arcades leading directly to the altar, to the beginnings of a vertical emphasis that will be fully exploited in the Gothic style. Already the division of the interior into separate bays, accented by the transverse arches of the vaults carried down into the nave, gives a feeling of upward movement rather than the forward motion of the Early Christian period.

PÉRIGORD CHURCHES. Another solution to the problem of a monumental structure in stone is offered by the churches of Périgord in southwestern France where, because of strong Byzantine influence, the naves

Fig. 230. St. Pierre, Angoulême. Interior.

Fig. 231. St. Tro-
phîme, Arles. Exte-
rior view.

are roofed with domes instead of barrel vaults. This may be seen in such
buildings as St. Front at Périgueux, whose five-domed plan is very
similar to that of St. Mark's in Venice, and in *St. Pierre* at Angoulême
(figs. 229–230), where the nave is covered by four domes on pendentives
with only the one over the crossing visible outside. The exterior of *St.
Pierre* at Angoulême is in many ways typical of the relatively heavy character of many French Romanesque buildings, their burly towers (cf.
Tourmanin in Syria, fig. 196) and the decorative arrangement of didactic
sculpture in round niches along various parts of the façade, as on Early
Christian sarcophagi (cf. fig. 189).

PROVENÇAL CHURCHES. A similar spirit of earlier style appears in the
architecture of the Provence region in the south of France, where the
simplest type of Romanesque and the most "Roman" was evolved. That
district had been well absorbed into the fabric of the Roman Empire;
there were (and still are) extensive remains of aqueducts, baths, amphitheaters, and arches of triumph. It is not surprising to find distinctly

classical features in such buildings as the barrel-vaulted *St. Trophîme* at Arles (fig. 231). The door jambs of the main portal are beautifully simple classic pilasters, while the whole arrangement of the doorway with its generous arch, its restrained dignified figures set into recessed niches, may be compared with a Roman arch of triumph — except for the gabled top. Here and in other examples (e.g., St. Gilles at Gard) the Provence style comes closest to justifying the terms Romanesque or "Romanish." *The Cloister of St. Trophîme* (fig. 226), noted for its fine carved capitals, not only typifies Romanesque monasticism but also demonstrates how an architectural unit may change in function from generation to generation. From its position in front of the church during Early Christian times, the atrium has now moved to the side of the church to be used as a place of meditation and relaxation.

THE LOMBARD CONTRIBUTION. The problem of lighting the French Romanesque church adequately within a vaulted system was ultimately solved by Norman builders in the north (see figs. 236–237) through their

Fig. 232. Sant' Ambrogio, Milan. Exterior view from the atrium.

use of a groined vault formed by the intersection of two barrel vaults. As we have indicated, this practice was begun by the Lombards of north Italy, although their solution was somewhat more rudimentary. In the church of *Sant' Ambrogio in Milan* (figs. 232–233), whose vaulting dates from the last quarter of the eleventh century, an imposing brick basilica is preceded by an elaborate atrium. The nave and aisles are covered by one gabled roof, the façade consists of open galleries, and the crossing is capped by an imposing octagonal lantern with open arcades. The open arcades of the lantern are typical of Lombard Romanesque, like the arched corbel tables (series of projecting supports connected by arches) of the façades and the free-standing square tower.

The important contribution of the Lombard builders was the use of the four-part, ribbed groin vault in the interior. This is divided by two supporting ribs running diagonally across the square vault section, two others running parallel with the axis of the nave (the longitudinal ribs), and two placed transversely across the nave and at right angles to it. Such an arrangement results in a humped, or domical, vault section; the outer edges are square because all the outside ribs are the same length, but the diagonal ribs are necessarily longer — thus raising the middle of the vault and keeping its sides down (figs. 234–235a). All these supporting

Fig. 233. Sant' Ambrogio, Milan. Interior.

ribs are brought down to the ground via the heavy, clustered, square floor piers, which alternate with lighter columns that carry the ribs from the aisle vaults. Since the aisle vaults are only half as long as the nave vaults and half as wide, some of their ribs are carried by the heavy piers and some by the alternating lighter columns; hence the name "alternating system."

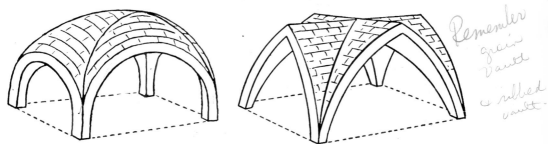

Fig. 234. Diagrams of Romanesque and Gothic vaults. *Left,* Romanesque groin vault. *Right,* Gothic ribbed vault.

Above the aisles in the triforium gallery are small groin vaults abutting or supporting the nave vaults. Here also so-called diaphragm walls help carry the thrust of each nave vault from its transverse arches (where it is concentrated) over the gallery vaults to the outside walls, there to be "grounded" by an attached outside buttress. The external, flatly attached buttresses are parallel with the heavy interior piers; and

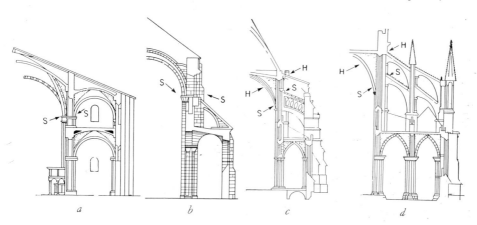

Fig. 235. Development of the Gothic flying buttress. From left to right: *a.* Sant' Ambrogio, Milan; *b.* La Trinité, Caen; *c.* Chartres Cathedral; *d.* Reims Cathedral. The buttress or buttressing agency supports the nave vault at the point of *S* (or springing) and later also at *H* (or haunch of the vault).

less prominent but similar props correspond to the alternating lighter columns (fig. 235*a*).

These reciprocal relationships between vaults, ribs, piers, and buttresses — establishing an organic or living balance — are a vital step forward in the evolution of medieval architecture. But the Lombard builder, anxious to ensure support for the heavy nave vaults, hesitated to insert a clerestory between gallery and main vault. Because of the triforium gallery vaults and the additional diaphragm walls, he had to rely for illumination on the light coming through the crossing lantern and the open arcade in front.

NORMAN STYLE. The defects of *Sant' Ambrogio* were overcome in the slightly later *St. Etienne* at Caen in Normandy (figs. 236–237), also known as the *Abbaye-aux-Hommes*. This building, like its sister church *La Trinité* (the *Abbaye-aux-Dames*), was ordered by William the Conqueror in 1064. It was first roofed in wood and then re-covered with six-part, ribbed groin vaults about 1125. The additional transverse rib across the center of the square nave vault gave sufficient security so that

Fig. 236. St. Etienne (Abbaye-aux-Hommes), Caen. Exterior.

Fig. 237. St. Etienne, Caen. Interior.

the Normans could lift the roof high enough to insert a small clerestory between gallery and nave vaults, admitting the light that was lacking in *Sant' Ambrogio*. Whereas in Lombardy the alternate column was used only to support ribs coming from the aisles, it now has the added function of supporting the new transverse rib coming from the nave vault.

Perhaps the most critical Norman innovation occurs in the gallery of *La Trinité*. While *St. Etienne's* half-barrel gallery vault is used as abutment along the entire length of the nave vaults, the builders of *La Trinité* (fig. 235*b*) realized that the concentration of nave vault thrusts at the piers made it unnecessary to have such long continuous abutment. Therefore, they used narrow half-arches to connect the piers in the nave with the flat buttresses attached to the outside walls. These new free arches, still covered by the roof of the building and somewhat too low to be entirely functional, are the ancestors of the flying buttresses of later Gothic architecture.

The pioneering character of Norman Romanesque is also visible on the exterior of *St. Etienne* (fig. 236), where soaring towers and a triple division of the façade by vertical buttresses give a feeling of upward movement that is generally associated with the Gothic style. The three doorways which result from the division of the façade have the effect of expressing externally the internal character of the building, another Gothic feature.

OTHER LOMBARD CHURCHES. In Italy, however, for the most part, the general Romanesque style is rather backward — in spite of the progressive Lombard architecture which may well have affected Normandy and certainly did affect other areas. Other important churches in Lombardy itself, except for San Michele at Pavia, are usually inorganic buildings such as San Zeno at Verona, with its typical Lombard gabled porch (the columns resting on the backs of lions), its simple basilican shape, a timber roof instead of vaulting, and the characteristic arched corbel tables along the cornice of nave and aisle roofs. A frequent feature of Lombard Romanesque, already noted in the lantern of *Sant' Ambrogio* at Milan, is the open arcade used on the façade, as at San Michele; this reappears with particular decorative force both in Germany and in central Italy, especially Tuscany.

TUSCAN ROMANESQUE ARCHITECTURE. In the latter area the *Cathedral of Pisa* (fig. 238), begun in the late eleventh and finished in the thir-

Fig. 238. Cathedral and Leaning Tower, Pisa.

teenth century, is a model to others as well as a tribute to the early prosperity of the Italian towns, brought about by traffic from the Crusades. In spite of its impressive scale and decorative brilliance, however, this and similar buildings are inorganic or static in construction, lacking the vaulting system of *Sant' Ambrogio*. A large cross-shaped basilica with a wooden roof, the *Cathedral of Pisa* emphasizes decorative quality both inside and out. Externally it has polished marble panels on the lower façade and four rows of open arcades on the upper, the arcades repeated on the famous *Leaning Tower* (1174–1184) and the baptistry. Inside, the walls are made interesting by alternating horizontal stripes of light and dark stone in the triforium and by a nave arcade resting on impressive Roman Corinthian columns.

In the Florentine area, the little church of San Miniato al Monte and the *Baptistry of the Cathedral of Florence* (both eleventh century, fig. 239) exemplify the unarcaded but richly surfaced style used here. Colored marbles are tastefully arranged inside and out, foreshadowing later Florentine buildings (cf. the cathedral, fig. 319) and the thirteenth-century decorative marble-plus-mosaic work of the Cosmati family in Rome.

Fig. 239. Baptistry of the Cathedral of Florence. (Cathedral in the background.)

Fig. 240. Cathedral of Worms.

GERMAN ROMANESQUE ARCHITECTURE. Just as Latin or Romance language dialects developed tremendous variety in Romanesque Europe, the styles of architecture in the formerly Romanized territories became diverse. For practically every political division of France and Italy there was a distinct architectural form. Germany, on the other hand, had a much more homogeneous style than either France or Italy, perhaps because of the continuity of Ottonian, Salian, and Hohenstaufen dynasties from about 950 to about 1175. This crystallized intellectually into the clearest national German style, lasting well into the thirteenth century.

Because of its historical background, German Romanesque combines Carolingian and Lombard elements, the latter because of the political linkage of Germany with Lombardy in the Holy Roman Empire. The Carolingian element is represented in the typical *Cathedral of Worms* (fig. 240) by the complex and picturesque doubling up of all parts of the church — as in the Carolingian monastery of St. Gall where there were two apses. The *Cathedral of Worms* has not only two apses but two lanterns, one over the crossing and one over the west end of the building (fig. 241), as well as paired towers at both ends. Lombard influence is shown in the Rhineland cathedrals (e.g., Worms, Speyer, and

Mainz) in the organic vaulting system, arched corbel tables, the liberal use of open arcades on the façade; and in Worms the arcaded lantern over the crossing is shaped like the one on *Sant' Ambrogio*. German architecture accordingly presents a significant aspect of Romanesque style, as does its sculpture.

ROMANESQUE SCULPTURE: GERMANY. The works of the Ottonian period in the first half of the eleventh century may be distinguished from those of the twelfth century which came under French influence. In the first and most characteristically Germanic group are the *Bronze Doors of Hildesheim Cathedral* (fig. 242), finished in 1015 for Bishop Bernward, the tutor of young Otto III. These doors are an outstanding example of the Saxon school of bronze casting which produced other famous works such as the Christ Column of Hildesheim (modeled on the column of Trajan in Rome, but depicting the life of Christ); the influence of this style lasted well into thirteenth-century late German Romanesque. It continued the Reims tradition of thin, agitated, nervous figures (fig. 221) with unexpected movements and fluttering draperies. With a literal-

Fig. 241. Cathedral of Worms. West apse.

Fig. 242. Bronze Doors of Hildesheim Cathedral (eleventh century).

ness derived from that early source and passed on to later German Gothic art, the angel (fig. 243) points accusingly at Adam and the unhappy Eve, who cover their nakedness as they move out of Paradise.

The most effective and moving work of the Saxon school is the bronze *Crucifix* of the monastery church of Werden (fig. 244) from the end of the eleventh century. Here the true inwardness of Romanesque feeling, the distortion of external naturalistic form to arrive at inner truth, is expressed through the stylization of hair, beard, moustache, and ears and the conscious distortion and enlargement of the eyeballs, nose, mouth, and forehead — all in the interests of greater expressiveness. The violent primitiveness of such a work might well be compared with that of modern Expressionists like Schmidt-Rottluff and Barlach (cf. figs. 525, 547).

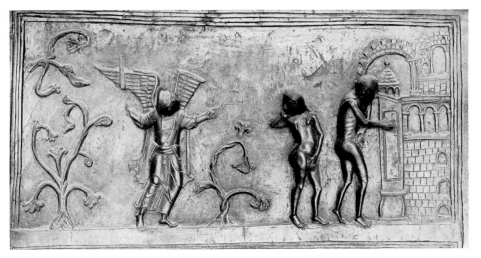

Fig. 243. Expulsion from Paradise, scene from the Bronze Doors of Hildesheim Cathedral.

ROMANESQUE SCULPTURE: ITALY. Romanesque sculpture in northern Italy, necessarily related to the art of Germany because of the political connection, reflects the more solid forms of Ottonian manuscript painting rather than the linear nervousness of Saxon bronze sculpture. In the works of an artist like Guglielmus on the façade of Modena Cathedral, the *Genesis Scenes* (fig. 245) show a similar heaviness of form, large feet with thick legs, and wide beards, but far less emotive or spiritual character. The Italian artist sought a three-dimensional expression of form rather than the mystic apocalyptic Ottonian utterance — a classical rather than a German quality.

Fig. 244. Crucifix (bronze, eleventh century). Abbey Church, Werden.

Fig. 245. Genesis Scenes. Reliefs on façade of Modena Cathedral.

274

FRENCH STYLES: PROVENCE. This heavy and serious side of Romanesque art, which ultimately resulted in an early classical revival in Italy
(see Niccolò Pisano, fig. 298), appears also in the southeastern French
school of Provence in the dignified and restrained façade figures of *St.
Trophîme at Arles* (fig. 231). Here in a heavily Romanized part of Gaul
which had not been affected by Carolingian emotionalism, the almost
classical togas, three-dimensional forms, architectonic relationship of figures to niches, and essentially static rather than dynamic conception reveal
a strong sense of antiquity.

In other parts of France, a far more impetuous and emotive art followed the great Cluniac reform movement that stimulated the building
of the cathedrals themselves. The conception is apocalyptic as in Ottonian
art but often more decorative and even elegant in quality, however much
mankind is threatened with the Last Judgment and the punishment of
hell-fire. Where German sculpture strews the figures about asymmetri-

Fig. 246. Scenes of the acts of St. Peter from the *Liber Vitae of Newminster*. London,
British Museum.

cally (reminiscent of the Carolingian *Utrecht Psalter*), the French seems to possess greater unity and organization. Yet it must be observed that the style of most French Romanesque sculpture is as much a transcription of manuscript drawing as that of the Hildesheim bronze workers. Its apocalyptic visions stem from the expressive Winchester school of manuscript illumination in England, which arose in the second half of the tenth century under the influence of such books as the *Utrecht Psalter* and during the eleventh century supplanted the Celtic illuminations. The preference for line more than color in early Romanesque English books, such as the *Liber Vitae of Newminster* (fig. 246) or the *Anglo-Saxon Psalter* of the British Museum, must be related to the Carolingian influence.

FRENCH STYLES: LANGUEDOC AND BURGUNDY. The two chief schools of expressionistic and linear sculpture in France during this period were those of Languedoc and Burgundy. There had been hardly any monumental sculpture before Romanesque times, but the wave of building — in the wake of the religious enthusiasm of the epoch with its late eleventh-century Crusades — also resulted in many examples of architectural sculpture. This may be traced partly to the survival of late antique art

Fig. 247. Last Judgment tympanum. From south portal, St. Pierre, Moissac.

276

Fig. 248. South portal from the right. St. Peter at the left of doorway. St. Pierre, Moissac.

in the south of France (e.g., the sculptures of Provence) but just as much to the inspiration of the agitated, nervous, linear Winchester style. Most of southern France and northern Spain were culturally and politically related during this era when pilgrimage roads extended across the Pyrenees to Santiago de Compostela; and there is a more or less homogeneous and expressive style. It is marked by agile and restless figures, their legs often crossed, draperies fluttering and carefully pressed into highly stylized folds. The whole is compressed into a space deliberately too small to hold the participants, so that they frequently seem to be bursting from their spaces and imply that if they were to stand up this would actually happen.

The main tympanum of the Abbey Church of Moissac in Languedoc illustrates the popularity of Last Judgment (fig. 247) and Apocalypse themes in Romanesque art, here expressed with monumental force. The crowned Christ (the feudal Middle Ages often represented Christ as King and Mary as Queen) sits in a shallow space, his face stylized in a fashion reminiscent of the Celtic, his draperies reduced to expressive patterns of two-dimensional form, very little related to the body they cover. Around this Christ of the Second Coming are to be seen in excited movement the four Evangelist symbols: the Man of Matthew at Christ's upper right (the place of honor), the Eagle of John at Christ's upper left, the Lion of Mark at his lower right, and the Bull of Luke at his lower left. Adjacent to these are two gigantic angels, their knees typically bent as though there were not enough room. This feeling is increased by the adoring four-and-twenty elders of the Apocalypse who are spread out over the rest of the two-dimensional space, all twisting their heads painfully to keep the Christ in view from beneath the heaving lines of stylized clouds which confine most of them. Their cramped positions are underlined by the raising of knees and crossing of legs.

On the lower section of this portal (fig. 248), the cusped edges of the door jamb increase the sense of agitation. A twisted, elongated prophet is portrayed on one side of the door (Isaiah, who foretold the advent of the Messiah), and a saint on the other side (Peter, the founder of the Church and the receiver of souls into heaven). The *trumeau*, or pier, dividing the doorway is covered with distinctly barbarian and exciting beast ornament.

The Isaiah theme with all its visionary implications may be seen in a famous example from the monastery church of Souillac (fig. 249). There also the fierce cruelty of animal ornament arises from the nervous Romanesque imagination with its sense of impending doom (both animals and prophet apparently done by a Moissac sculptor). The *Isaiah* figure stands out like some dematerialized and ascetic emanation of the monastic mind and its spirituality. He swings back and forth in religious ecstasy, pointing to the scroll of his prophecy foretelling the coming of Christ. His body is typically

Fig. 249. Isaiah. Church of Notre Dame, Souillac.

Fig. 250. Last Judgment tympanum. St. Lazare, Autun.

elongated, the ultralinear and graceful draperies clearly recalling the linear manuscript style which the artist attempted to transcribe here into stone. The true nature of the stone medium was ignored as the sculptor undercut the draperies to produce shadows, intent on the linear quality of his original model.

At St. Lazare in Autun is perhaps the most dramatic instance of a *Last Judgment* and a typical Burgundian tympanum treatment (fig. 250). The gigantesque Christ, far more terrifying than the visionary and symbolic figure at Moissac, is accompanied by a series of loosely formed, tortured figures with large heads — whose avowed purpose, according to the inscription of the artist Gislebertus, was "to let this horror appal those bound by earthly sin." Here we need not be told that the question of earthly sin and its punishment was one of the chief preoccupations of the Romanesque mind. This is spread out for all to see: the frightening Christ who causes Mary and John to shrink away from him up above; the archangel weighing souls to the left of Christ, while a demon attempts to pull the scales down on his side; and another devil nearby pushing the damned into the flaming pit with great delight. As the pitiful dead rise from their tombs in the lowest register, a pair of large demonic hands

Fig. 251. Last Judgment tympanum. Detail at left. St. Lazare, Autun.

reaches down (bottom right) to grasp a little soul about the throat in one of the most fear-inspiring moments of Romanesque or any other art. At Christ's right (fig. 251), Peter is receiving a group of pathetically expressive distorted figures.

In the baldest terms this age of religious fervor, of relic worship, of pilgrimages and crusades, of monastic thought control and pious hysteria called the world to judgment. Everything depended on the Church in this judgment — whether it would intercede or not, whether one could look forward to bliss or damnation — and in such scenes men's minds and souls were overwhelmed.

13 / ISLAMIC CIVILIZATION

THE intellectual and economic accomplishments of the Moslem (Mohammedan) world reached their height between 800 and 1300, a height
which the West was not even to approach until after 1500. It was
achieved while the Middle Ages in western Europe bred inflexible dogmatism and superstition, bleak feudalism and manorial isolation. And
contemporaneous with it were the Byzantine Empire's highly developed
political organization and commercial activity (Chapter 10). The Moslem synthesis of world civilization was to provide some of the cultural
stimuli toward European revival, through Spain — which was interrelated with southern France during the Romanesque period — and
through encounters with the Byzantines and the Crusaders.

The original impetus came in the seventh century from the Arabian
desert peninsula, where a former caravan manager named Mohammed
preached a religion based on one God (Allah) to the pagan folk of
Mecca. This town had been a place of pilgrimage for a long time; its
Kaaba, or sanctuary, contained many idols and a sacred black meteorite
that drew the faithful from the entire land. Since Mohammed's work
had brought him into contact with Jewish villages along the caravan
route, with Eastern Christianity, and with other faiths, his new religion
became a synthesis of Judaism, Christianity, and Persian religions, as well
as the traditional beliefs of Arabia.

In 622 Mohammed (called the Prophet of Allah) was forced to flee
to the city of Medina, where Jewish influence made his ideas of one God
more acceptable. The date of this *hejira*, or flight, marks the beginning
of the Mohammedan calendar. A few years later he returned to Mecca
as its master, and by 632 he was in control of all Arabia. The religion
he established is known as Islam ("to submit," i.e., to the will of God);
its followers are Mohammedans, or Moslems — those who submit
(Arabic, *muslim*). Its remarkably rapid success was a result of the land
hunger of the Arabs, their traditional organization for effective warfare,
and the disorganized condition of the empires about them. Most important, Islam as presented by Mohammed in the Koran (the Moslem

Life of Mohammed who he was, how he started religion, brief chron. of how religion spread.

scriptures) was a simple and clear-cut belief, compared with the complex Eastern Christianity, torn by abstruse, intolerant controversies, or the decayed Persian Zoroastrianism.

Judaism had through necessity made a kind of racial hoard of its God, whereas Islam — taking over many Judaic ideas (its ethic, its extensive system of precepts, and its monotheism) — was definitely interested in offering the new faith to all. At a time when Christianity confused the ordinary man with heresies, Islam originally preached a simple kindliness and brotherhood without the elaborate priestly mechanism. Mohammed's words: "Know that every Moslem is the brother of every other Moslem. All of you are on the same equality," were as appealing as the idea that divine mercy or punishment could not be given or withheld by any human being but only by Allah himself. Islam borrowed from Christianity the idea of a future life; but it differed sharply in clearly prescribing every act of worship and most other everyday acts for the individual, thus eliminating the necessity for a priesthood. It differed, further, by its belief in predestination, according to which the earthly fate of all persons, high or low, has already been decided by Allah. To this fate one necessarily must submit.

SPREAD OF ISLAM. In some ways the lightninglike spread of Islam can be regarded as a social and religious revolution. Within a century from the time of Mohammed's death in 632, his successors, or *khalifas*, (caliphs) had built an empire stretching from western Africa and Spain to the Indus River in India. The two chief Eastern powers, Byzantium and Persia, were too exhausted by wars to offer much opposition, although the former resisted until 1453, when it fell before the Moslem Turks. Other things apart, the spread of the Islamic Empire was greatly facilitated because the Prophet's followers allowed a conquered land to retain its own religion and culture, a policy which often prevented resistance. This further benefited the invaders by making available a variety of cultural traditions from which they could and did borrow. Like the ancient Persian Empire that had incorporated subject peoples on a similar liberal basis, Islamic culture became a synthesis of religions and of artistic, scientific, and literary lore.

Unlike the medieval Christians, the Moslems were not prejudiced against pagan learning and indeed profited enormously from it. In their conquest of Syria they met the Nestorian Christians, perhaps the most advanced group in the Christian world. These folk had preserved in both the original Greek and their own Syrian translations many significant ancient works. When Baghdad became the center of Islam (after 762), a magnificent court was gathered, inviting scholars, physicians, and other learned men. They translated into Arabic the Greek scientific, philosophic,

282

and medical authors such as Ptolemy, Aristotle, and Galen. Hindu books on mathematics were similarly translated. Arabic became the language of Islamic learning, though many of its practitioners were not Arabs but Syrians, Jews, Persians, and Moors. The mere existence of Baghdad, a great city of over 2 million people, far larger than Rome or Byzantium, was evidence of the administrative, economic, and cultural vigor of the Islamic Empire. The universities of Baghdad, Cairo, and Cordova (in Mesopotamia, Egypt, and Spain, respectively) were among the leading centers of research. Their attainments did not result from a unique genius on the part of Arab or other followers of Islam, but from a willingness to deal with outside elements and to develop them. In the transmission of this vast body of knowledge to western Europe, a leading part was taken by learned Jews in Moslem Spain who, acting in their traditional role of cultural intermediaries, translated from the Arabic into Latin for Christian scholars and, later, aided Western explorers by their navigational skills, derived from Moslem astronomy and mathematics.

The Moslem Empire therefore meant more than another new state and a new religion; it created the most advanced form of civilization in the Western world between the ninth and thirteenth centuries and made outstanding scientific, commercial, and administrative achievements. In the realm of ideas, of religious and other areas of tolerance, and also in everyday products (their wares were hawked from China to Spain), the Moslems surpassed many of the accomplishments of their Christian contemporaries.

ISLAMIC ART: DEVELOPMENT OF THE MOSQUE. On the other hand — notwithstanding the superiority of early Islamic textiles, metalwork, ivory carvings, rugs, and other luxury articles — the Koran's prohibition against images of living things placed a severe limitation on sculpture and painting in most of the Mohammedan world. Only in Persia and India was this prohibition avoided; even there, however, no monumental Islamic sculpture existed, and painting was confined to the pages of manuscripts. The most significant Islamic arts were architecture and architectural decoration, both influenced to varying degrees by the different cultures included within their scope. This borrowing from the diverse styles which Islam encountered — Byzantine, Persian, Visigothic, Roman, and others — was a natural consequence of the fact that there was no artistic tradition among the Moslems themselves.

From the very beginning this eclecticism became visible. Mesopotamia and Syria, the first countries to be overrun by the Arabs, were Byzantine provinces; from this area artists were summoned to help build the Mosque of Omar in Jerusalem (begun A.D. 687) on the former site of the Temple of Jerusalem. It turned out to be a typical centralized octagonal Byzantine building with two concentric aisles and a dome over the middle. The sacred rock under the dome marks the spot from which the Prophet is said to have ascended to heaven, and on which the sacrificial offering of Isaac by Abraham is reputed to have taken place.

Aside from this early example, however, most Mohammedan mosques revolve about a square open courtyard, as in Hebrew, Phoenician, or other Near Eastern temples where the sacred courtyard is the important element. The typical mosque form developed from a simple courtyard with a single row of arcaded columns on the side facing toward the holy city of Mecca. As the mosque evolved, it added further rows on the sacred side and decorated the remaining three sides with ordinary arcades.

Fig. 252. Mosque of Ibn Tulun, Cairo. Courtyard.

This stage is exemplified by the mosques of Damascus in Syria, *Ibn Tulun* in Cairo (eighth century, fig. 252), and Kairouan in Tunisia. In the order named, these show increasing elaboration on the side of the mosque facing Mecca, through the addition of rows of columns. By the time of the *Mosque of Cordova* in Spain (see fig. 256), following the westward sweep of Islam, the ratio of rows of columns to open courtyard would be reversed; the columns would now occupy the major portion of the space, and the courtyard would serve merely as vestibule.

In the center of the wall enclosing the sacred side, the builder inserted the concave *mihrab*, a highly ornamented apselike structure symbolizing the ancient *Kaaba* sanctuary in Mecca. Near the mihrab was placed the most ornately decorated piece of furniture in the mosque, the *mimbar*, a pulpit from which the weekly sermon was delivered on Fridays. Another feature of this side of the mosque was the *dikkeh*, a raised platform (similar in function to the Hebrew *bema*) from which various prayers and portions of the Koran were read. In the courtyard itself there would generally be a fountain for ablutions, since one could not enter unwashed. The exterior of these early buildings usually was severely simple with few or no wall openings and was dominated by a high minaret, or cylindrical ramped tower, from which the *muezzin* would call the faithful to prayer at appropriate times of the day. This tower may be an adaptation of the Assyro-Babylonian step tower, or ziggurat (fig. 34), whose tradition still existed in the Mesopotamia of that day, or of the Early Christian, Syrian church façade tower (fig. 196). Externally and internally, the mosque reveals a wider aisle leading to the mihrab (cf. the Christian basilican nave) as well as a dome placed over that aisle to increase its importance.

The *Mosque of Ibn Tulun* (fig. 252) represents the expansion of Islam into Egypt after the conquest of Syria and Mesopotamia and typifies the development of what is still the most characteristic Mohammedan city in the world — Cairo. Here, other and more complicated mosque forms were evolved on cruciform plans radiating from a central courtyard into four separate aisles, expressive of the four main rites of Islam. The main aisle, however, still has the typical mihrab, mimbar, and dikkeh, as in the mosques of *Sultan Barkuk* (fig. 253) and Hasan. Most Egyptian buildings of this type use the characteristic raised or pointed arch (resembling the arch in Gothic architecture) which derives from the Early Christian or Coptic buildings of Egypt (cf. fig. 260). Later examples show externally a picturesque pointed dome on pendentives or squinches, as in Eastern Christian forms, and are decorated with typical abstract "arabesque" ornamentation. Mosques like that of Hasan are part of an elaborate arrangement of buildings in which schools are attached to the corners of the court, a domed structure behind contains the tomb of the sultan, and various units include lodgings for pilgrims, hospital accommodations, and other housing.

ISLAMIC ART IN SPAIN. After taking over Egypt, the Arabs overran North Africa, crossed the Straits of Gibraltar into Spain, and moved

Fig. 253. Mosque of Sultan Barkuk, Cairo. The mihrab area with the mimbar in the rear and the dikkeh in foreground.

north through that country across the Pyrenees into southern and central France, where they were finally stopped by the Merovingian king, Charles Martel, at Tours in 732. Settling down in Spain, they built up the most enlightened cultural center of medieval Europe, utilizing as they had elsewhere structural and other elements already existent in that country. Certain early mosques seem based on Visigothic forms, especially in the columns and capitals. The great *Mosque of Cordova* (fig. 254), begun by Abd-er-Rahman II in 786, used the walls and columns of the Christian church of St. Vincent, which the Moors (Arab and North African Moslems) acquired peaceably from the Christians with whom they had shared it for a long time. In the spirit of the Koran (which enjoined religious tolerance) the Christians were permitted to build a church on another site.

Both inside and out, the *Mosque of Cordova* — prototype for most Moorish religious structures in Spain — shows the typical flat, flowing arabesque ornaments and the horseshoe-shaped arch, either single or crossed with others (fig. 255), a form which may have come from Visigothic architecture. Inside, the mosque is considerably different from *Ibn Tulun* and others in Africa and Syria; rows on rows of columns (fig. 256) have been added to form a veritable forest of cylindrical forms

Fig. 254. Mosque of Cordova, Spain. The façade.

Fig. 255. Mosque of Cordova. Façade detail.

Fig. 256. Mosque of Cordova. Interior.

Fig. 257. Mosque of Cordova, Villaviciosa Chapel. The maksurah.

supporting arches. Successive additions were made by rulers of the independent and highly developed Caliphate of Cordova; like the Pharaohs of ancient Egypt, the caliphs attested to their own importance and piety by augmenting the chief temple. Eventually more space was taken up by the rows of columns than by the courtyard, which made it necessary to raise the height of the roof in order to maintain agreeable proportions. A second arcade was placed above the first, somewhat in the manner of the Roman aqueducts in Spain (cf. the *Aqueduct of Segovia*, fig. 136). The only vaulted part of the building is the mihrab, which at Cordova has a special mosaic decoration, traditionally donated by the emperor of Byzantium, who was on good terms with the caliphs of Cordova. There is also a lavishly decorated approach, or vestibule, to the sanctuary, known as a *maksurah* (fig. 257), with typical Cordovan striped and cusped arches. The mihrab vault, carved from a single stone, carries a shell-like form enclosed in an octagon and resting on a decorative arrangement of four ribs laid out in a square and crossed at right angles with another set of four.

As with other Near Eastern peoples, the most important civil building among Arabs was the ruler's palace. Once more other cultures were drawn upon, since these seminomadic folk had no precedent of their own for palace architecture. Just as the interior of the *Mosque of Cordova* suggests the elaborately columned Persian hall (fig. 48), kingly residences like the *Alhambra of Granada* (thirteenth-fourteenth century, fig. 258) bring to mind the light, graceful, and complicated palace structures of Persia. Indoor pools and fountains satisfy the former desert dweller's hunger for the sound and sight of water, while gardens with delicate myrtles and rose bushes form an oasis surrounded by gossamer-thin walls that are covered with flat colorful ornament — recalling the Arab's accustomed tent where a brilliantly tinted carpet or other fabric was hung as temporary decoration.

The *Alhambra*, perhaps the best-known Moorish palace, is really a collection of halls and patios (cf. Khorsabad, fig. 40). These open spaces are enclosed by continuous two-dimensional decorations on thin plaster panels covered with colorful tiles, graceful stucco ornamentations, and picturesque stalactite forms suggesting cave growths. In both the Western and Eastern Islamic worlds (the latter Persian and Indian) the ornamental technique is very close to the Byzantine of *Hagia Sophia* (fig. 200), whose two-dimensional pierced stone drillwork, with its alternating light and dark accents, was a typical Eastern approach. This East Christian technique (certainly familiar to the Arabs) and that of the pagan

Fig. 258. The Alhambra, Granada. Court of the Lions.

East itself, exemplified in the eighth-century stone relief from the Palace of M'shatta (fig. 259), combine to form the two-dimensional ornament style found throughout the Moslem territory.

In Spanish Islam the injunction against portraying living things was more closely observed than in certain Eastern areas. Ornament tended to be primarily geometric and had few references to natural forms, even in an abstract version. The flowing cursive script of the Koran, the so-called Kufic lettering, plays an important role in this decoration, while continuously moving, flowing linear patterns weave in and out across the surface. Specific geometrical shapes such as the regular polygon represent the last step in this process of denaturalization of form. In the eastern part of Islam, however, there are more entwined leaves and flowers, as on the arcades of *Ibn Tulun* — abstracted, to be sure, but based on some form in nature.

ISLAMIC ART IN PERSIA. Further east, in Persia and India, Moslem art again takes on the character of those areas with an increasing tendency toward figurative rather than nonrepresentational forms. In Persia, instead of the religious coexistence that was allowed elsewhere, a scriptural misunderstanding had led the Moslems to force conversion on the populace. The Prophet had stated that "people of a book," i.e., a sacred book, were to be tolerated; it was believed that he referred only to Jews and

290

Christians and not to the Persians — who did, however, have their own sacred book, which may not have been known to the Prophet. Hence when Persia was overrun, it was forced into the faith of Islam, which did not make for unalloyed religious enthusiasm. Whether or not this was the entire reason for the ultimately different approach of Eastern as opposed to Western Islam, there was certainly a trend toward more figurative treatment in architectural ornament, manuscript illumination, pottery, rugs, and other forms of art.

The architecture of Islamic Persia, moreover, is more elaborate than that of Spain in both the forms themselves and the applied ornament. Where the Spanish Moslems used vaults and domes sparingly, the Easterners used domes in considerable quantity. Since there was no religious division in Persia between the conquered and the conquerors, the native inhabitants with their recent tradition of domed and vaulted structures were consistently employed in the building of mosques and other edifices. This pre-Islamic strain had been part of the late Persian, or Sassanian, tradition (A.D. 226–642); it is shown in the style of the Taq-i-Kisra Palace at Ctesiphon, which on the inside has domes and vaults and on the outside decorative arches, painted relief sculptures, and an impressively tall entrance archway. When Sassanian culture was superseded by

Fig. 259. Frieze detail from M'shatta Palace, Syria, built between fourth and seventh centuries of the Christian era. Berlin, State Museums.

Islamic, the new mosques and other buildings took over some of these ideas.

A typical instance is the shrine of the *Imam Rida* at Meshed (fig. 260), a fifteenth-century building dedicated to Persia's most significant religious figure after Zoroaster. The very high-pointed entrance arch recalls that of the Sassanian Taq-i-Kisra (literally the Arch of Chosroes) and its façade arches as well. Another resemblance is found in the profusion of external ornament, a sharp distinction from Egyptian and Spanish Moslem buildings. In the Persian shrine a clearly balanced and refined series of arcuated forms is set around the large center arch; an all-over decorative pattern of mosaic tiles in black, white, gold, turquoise, and emerald green covers both outsides and insides of these arches. The patterns are based on floral and animal forms as in most Persian decorations on architecture, rugs, and other objects. They may be exemplified by the arabesques on the columns of the *Masjid-i-jami* (fig. 261), which readily contrast with details from the *Mosque of Cordova* or the *Alhambra at Granada* in their figurative quality, their richer, more specific reference to living forms — flowers, leaves, and the like — as well as their plasticity.

From a purely architectonic viewpoint there would seem to be more ornamentation than necessary, swamping the strong outlines of the building. Here even the usual cylindrical tower is covered with applied ornament and has stalactite forms in its upper section. The intimation is that the architect has translated decorative patterns from handicraft arts such as carpets and manuscripts into the architectural realm; it adds to the impression given by Moslem architecture in Spain of structures without substance where the externals are more significant than the edifice itself.

Certainly Persian architecture as well as its other art reflects a luxurious civilization, a pleasure-loving society best known to the Western world through the poems of the skeptical and Epicurean Persian poet, philosopher, and scientist Omar Khayyam (d. 1123), who was also important for his work in the field of mathematics. The manuscripts of Persia, like those of India, deal with scientific material, history, scenes of the hunt and of war, the prince talking with his courtiers, delicate portraits, or decorative arrangements of the floral and animal abstractions.

Fig. 261. Masjid-i-jami (mosque), Iran. Mihrab and columns.

Fig. 262. Page from *Persian
Bestiary* (thirteenth century). New York, The Pierpont Morgan Library.

Fig. 263. Woman on Horse-
back. Rhages Bowl (Persian,
thirteenth century). New
York, Metropolitan Museum
of Art.

The thirteenth-century *Persian Bestiary*, or *Description of Animals* book (fig. 262), shows a typical combination of flat two-dimensional ornament, in this case based on the Kufic cursive script (also used extensively in Moslem Spain), besides a more figurative plastic style which depicts people, animals, and anything else necessary to the book. Delicacy and strength balance each other; the large but controlled area of gracefully strong lettering, completely abstract in character, is compensated by the heavier, more tangible forms of the animal and the tree arranged in sweeping dynamic curves. Coloristic charm and strength, deliberate two-dimensionality, linealism, and limited space, a free and spontaneous arrangement of the figurative elements — here and in the equally characteristic Persian pottery (fig. 263) — give the art of this country its special charm.

ISLAMIC ART IN INDIA. When the Moslem Moguls (from Persia) conquered India in the sixteenth century, Persian elements in architecture and the other arts were superposed on the native traditions of that land. A clear instance would be the manuscript illuminations of Mogul India, as in the sixteenth-century Indo-Persian painting *Prince*

Fig. 264. Prince Riding an Elephant. Indo-Persian miniature painting (sixteenth century). New York, Metropolitan Museum of Art.

Riding an Elephant (fig. 264). The elaborately dressed animal has a black body; its various ornaments stand away vividly from that powerful dark area, which moves up and diagonally across. The page is bordered by charming, delicate floral and other patterns. As in the Persian miniature, large bold color areas and asymmetrical figure arrangements are balanced against vernal border abstractions in a firm yet gentle manner.

Among the impressive aesthetic accomplishments of the Mogul dynasty in India was its tomb architecture which, unlike that of Western Islam, favored marble rather than stucco or gypsum for its carved ornaments. It was customary for a Mogul emperor to build a splendid palace for residence during his lifetime, afterward to be utilized as a mausoleum. The best known of such palace tombs is the world-famous *Taj Mahal* at Agra (fig. 265). As in this instance, they were generally set in large gardens with elaborate gateways, pools, and other embellishments. The magnificent *Taj Mahal* was begun in 1632 by Shah Jehan in memory of his wife. In general feeling and in some of its decorations the building reveals that this last highly cultivated Moslem society was already in touch with the Western world. Yet the form and arrangement of the arches still bear a real resemblance to the fifteenth-century shrine of *Imam Rida at Meshed.*

Fig. 265. The Taj Mahal, Agra, India.

The *Taj Mahal* is a large octagonal building set on an enormous platform more than 800 feet wide. It has four entrances and a huge pointed dome, similar in shape to others seen in Egypt, here set among four smaller domes that effect a transition from the pointed arches of the façade to the main dome. This arrangement, together with the four delicate minarets set at the corners of the building, suggests somewhat the Turkish Moslem adaptation of *Hagia Sophia* in Constantinople after 1453 (fig. 197). In *Hagia Sophia* the spacious narthex, orientation of the nave toward the apse, and other features made it easy to convert this Byzantine church into a mosque by the simple expedient of whitewashing over its mosaics and adding minarets on the exterior. As a result of the adaptation, other Turkish mosques of that type were built, e.g., the Mosque of Suliman I at Constantinople.

ISLAMIC STIMULUS TO EUROPE. The culture of Mogul India was the last great flowering of Islamic civilization on its own ground. Although Mohammedan ideas in general helped considerably to fructify the revival of learning in western Europe, in its own area it tended after the sixteenth century to become static. As various European countries assumed the character of strong national states, the power and prestige of Islam suffered accordingly. The initial impetus and fervor had long since disappeared; nothing could be done about it — "What is written is written."

It should not be forgotten, however, that from Moslem Spain, Christian and Jewish translators like Gerard of Cremona (d. 1187) and Moses Maimonides (1135–1204) had been able to spread the culture which Mohammedans had synthesized from antique remains and then developed on their own. During the thirteenth century, Jewish physicians trained in Spain founded medical schools at universities in France and Italy. From Islam also came the knowledge of paper making (learned from the Chinese) that would ultimately make possible the success of printing; the advances in astronomy and in nautical instruments which furthered map making and navigation and helped to bring about the European age of discovery; and many other vital ideas. Together with the expansion of Europe itself and the rise of the middle class, the impact of Moslem learning was among the most important forces in the subsequent growth of Western civilization.

14 / FROM CASTLE TO
COMMUNE: *The Rise of Gothic Art*

THE art of Gothic Europe brings with it the first real evidence of a growing fluidity and humanity which began to replace the fixed religious and social order of the Romanesque period. Both epochs, it is true, had profound religious faith, however differently expressed, a strong cult of the Virgin (Mariolatry), and deep-rooted superstitions, cruelties, and ignorance not easily eradicated. But the Gothic age introduced two other elements: the town and the new learning symbolized by universities. After the provincialism and localism of the Dark Ages — apparent in the many varieties of Romanesque expression — a national and even international complexion emerged. For example, there was now a French art where previously there had been Burgundian, Norman, Provençal, and Aquitainian.

The national character of the Gothic style was made possible by political centralization under kings who grew stronger as feudalism grew weaker. Even more striking is the supranational quality of this era. Through the Crusades (1095–1291), Europe came into contact with Byzantium and the Near East. Its horizons were further broadened by voyages of exploration undertaken by John of Monte Corvino, William of Rubruques, and the famous Marco Polo (1254–1324). Not the least significant aspect of the new internationalism was the diffusion of the Gothic style (primarily a northern French development) into the many countries of Europe as far east as Cyprus, Rhodes, and Greece, where crusading Frankish kings established themselves for a period.

The Crusades not only helped to widen the European outlook through encounters with Byzantine and Moslem civilization, they also aided the expansion of business and the growth of towns. Italian cities especially, because of their location on the route to the Holy Land, had opportunity for profit from supplying transportation and food, disposing of plunder, and opening trade agencies in the Levant (the eastern Mediterranean). Venice, Genoa, and Pisa were the first to flourish, and then

298

other Tuscan and Lombard towns. Through this stimulation of trade, town life in northern Europe also developed, and a money economy was instituted.

GROWTH OF TOWNS; THE CATHEDRALS. One of the chief effects of the Crusades was the serious blow dealt to the feudal system, destroying the lives and wealth of many nobles who took part in them. For two centuries feudal nobility was occupied outside of Europe; by the time they returned, town life was firmly entrenched. An old German proverb has it: *Stadt Luft macht frei!* ("City air brings freedom!"). To the oppressed peasantry of the Middle Ages, escape from semislavery under the manorial system into the towns offered the possibility of a new existence. The burgher, or trade, class became the fermenting element in medieval society, although it was an outside quantity in the fixed system of clergy, nobility, and peasantry. Yet allied with the kings, it provided — in addition to a new cultural climate — the means for subjugating the nobles and achieving a more stable society, which the burghers needed for their own development. Their instruments were the merchant guilds and craft guilds that became the basis of town government.

Towns grew as monarchies (e.g., French and British) strengthened and administrations centralized. Privileges were sold to the cities, uniform laws devised, parliamentary governments begun in the early town councils, and law courts set up with members drawn from the middle class. Between 1100 and 1300, towns increased tenfold, often causing serious conflict between the communes (town units) and the feudal bishops and lords who tried to restrict mercantile and industrial freedom or municipal independence. The city of Tours, for example, had to revolt twelve times before it could finally go its own way. The Gothic cathedral constituted the fullest expression of the new-found and still limited freedom of the era that gave it birth. Amiens, Reims, Beauvais, Soissons, Le Mans, Cambrai, Noyon, and Laon were some of the places that acquired liberty and new cathedrals at the same time — cathedrals built by the people of those towns.

THE NEW UNIVERSITIES; PRESTIGE OF PARIS. The Gothic cathedral (see fig. 268) reflects not only the fresh spirit of living in the communes but also the learning of the age and the growth of thought in general, which is so well represented by universities of the twelfth and thirteenth centuries. The movement toward secular schools instead of the earlier cathedral and monastic institutions had begun in twelfth-century Italy, but the most important center of scholarship was the University of Paris. This was formally chartered in 1200 and was soon followed by universities in other northern European localities (Oxford and Cambridge belong to this period). Paris, patronized by the increasingly powerful French monarchy, became the leading undergraduate school in Europe. Although they still maintained relations with church schools, the newer centers (e.g., Paris and Chartres) were relatively independent; they both furnished and stimulated the intellectual and spiritual climate of Gothic life.

The University of Paris owed its advantageous beginnings to the aid of King Philip Augustus (1180–1229), who established a unified monarchy in France. Through his sponsorship the city and its university became focal points of fashion and taste, arbiters of art and learning. The Paris text of the Bible came to be standard, and book illumination (see fig. 291), according to Dante, was known as "the art of Paris." So great was Parisian cultural prestige that it hindered the development of local styles in many areas; even in Italy, in spite of the strong classical currents evident at an early date, Gothic charm and decorativeness appear in the work of Giovanni Pisano and later sculptors like Ghiberti. French influence in art will be seen in architecture, sculpture (both monumental and small-dimensional such as ivories), manuscript painting, and other forms. German Gothic is a straightforward imitation; Spanish, a local variant embellished with native richness; English, very similar, in its evolution from English Romanesque, to the degree that England was French after the Norman invasion. Only in Italy is Gothic architecture almost completely alien except for certain "gingerbread" imitations, e.g., Santa Maria della Spina in Pisa and the Cathedral of Orvieto — although, as noted, Gothic sculpture had some effect.

Among the brilliant names associated with the University of Paris was Pierre Abélard (1079–1142). His refusal to accept theological authority by itself (in view of the many disparities between Church fathers) was not an attack on religion but an attempt to bring reason or logic to buttress faith. In this, Abélard — like the more scientific Roger Bacon — strengthened rather than weakened the medieval attitude; teaching this scholastic method became a foremost task of the medieval university. Thus the new towns and their burgher class existed side by side with the centuries-old faith and power of the Church. The Gothic cathedral and its sculptures, the greatest artistic fulfillment of Christianity, reveal a softer, more humanized religion that begins to consider life on earth while it still glorifies faith in God and heaven (see fig. 269).

THE BURGHER CLASS. There was nevertheless a challenge to constituted authority and custom in the burgher class and its culture; this is demonstrated by the change in literary interests. The vigorous chivalric *chansons de geste* gave way to lyric and tender poetry in the late twelfth and early thirteenth centuries, paralleled by a new popular literature of realism and satire such as the popular *fabliaux* and allegories of the period, which often ridicule chivalry.

CHURCHES AND SECULAR BUILDINGS. Within this new culture, towns competed in erecting cathedrals. It was often a matter of civic pride for the various guilds to contribute their services in either the actual building or financing of the churches. The craftsmen involved — stonecutters, stained-glass makers, masons, metalworkers — were laymen like the designers themselves. The guilds were memorialized in special chapels and stained-glass windows.

Fig. 266. Town Hall, Bruges. At right of main square.

Although the cathedral is the most characteristic structural form of Gothic art, other types emerged with the growth of cities and the burgher class: town and guild halls like the *Town Hall at Bruges* (fig. 266), city gates, market buildings, as well as elaborate private dwellings for the upper bourgeoisie. The *House of Jacques Coeur* at Bourges (fig. 267), built in the fifteenth century, indicates the status of its merchant-prince owner. At the same time, castle architecture also brought forth new styles, stimulated to a certain extent by contact with Byzantine and Moorish forms during the Crusades, e.g., the walled city of Carcassonne. These various secular buildings differ from the cathedrals in their lack of or-

Fig. 267. House of Jacques Coeur, Bourges.

ganic form; they utilize Gothic details such as pointed arches, gabled roofs, stone tracery, towers, and leaded glass as decorative elements. Other civic architecture includes the Cloth Hall at Ypres (a guild hall), the Porte des Allemandes at Metz (a city gate), the Charles Bridge in Prague, and the Beautiful Fountain of Nürnberg.

THE GOTHIC CATHEDRAL. Standing on one side of the market place, the Gothic cathedral (fig. 268) was the physical and spiritual focus of town life. People met there daily for worship and for other purposes. Mystery plays were performed before it; wandering preachers gave their sermons within its shadow — these were the entertainments of the Middle Ages. In its sculptures and stained glass the knowledge of the age was summarized for an illiterate public. In the church also, people were baptized, confirmed, married; from this point there still came the power for salvation.

It is little wonder therefore that the cathedral, symbol of the universal Church, dominated not only the town itself (even now it is the first thing one sees on approaching many old cities) but the aesthetic of the time as well. Every art in this period was subject to the architectural idea; even the pages in manuscripts are essays in architecture. Consequently, detail is subordinate to general effect in the ideal Gothic building. The figures on the column shafts are lengthened, as evident on the façade of Chartres, and so long as Gothic keeps this unified relationship it remains strong. A piece of Gothic cathedral sculpture is seldom able to stand by itself, since it is planned as part of a greater whole, differing from classical sculpture, which is often made to be self-enclosed (compare the *Beau Dieu* of Amiens, fig. 278, with *Hermes* by Praxiteles, fig. 101). In the thirteenth century both the mass and the shape of sculpture conformed to the building; in the fourteenth and fifteenth centuries the mass but not the shape conformed.

Emerging from the dark shadow of the monastic Middle Ages, ornament turned from geometric to naturalistic. For example, instead of the ever-present formalized acanthus leaf of previous periods, the actual flora of a given area was now reproduced in art. Although for the most part the Romanesque iconography and subjects of the monastery churches were retained, they were given a new naturalistic treatment. As early as the thirteenth century, nature and the physical world became part of theology — a significant change for all aspects of medieval life. Even historical subjects (e.g., Biblical and Roman themes) were given a certain contemporaneity of costume (fig. 269). The cathedral in this period epitomized the new secular spirit by its representation of scenes from everyday life and its generally humanistic approach. It appealed to the

Fig. 268. Notre Dame de Paris.

Fig. 269. Shepherds of the Nativity Led by an Angel. Chartres Cathedral.

senses through the use of color in sculpture, lambent stained glass, and rich complex sounds in the new polyphonic music.

GOTHIC CONSTRUCTION. Structurally the Gothic cathedral (figs. 270–274), while different from Romanesque (figs. 234–235), was an extension and outgrowth of the latter. The same basic physical problem remained: to build a large stone-vaulted fireproof structure. But the monastic Romanesque architects had been limited spiritually and technically to a static and massive conception, whereas their successors aspired to a more open, better-lighted, dynamic, and higher structure embodying the new striving and idealism, the mystic exaltation of the period. The physical and logical expression of this ideal constitutes the special character of Gothic building.

Dynamic in its total architectural effect, where the Romanesque church was static, the Gothic cathedral is thoroughly preoccupied with problems of space, both as means and as end. While the Romanesque in many cases seemed dark and low, this architecture achieves greater height and illumination, a quality of endlessness symbolic of newer feelings. The sense of infinity is lent in part by the repetition of small details and by avoidance of a terminus. More important, however, the vaults are raised to hitherto undreamed-of heights, a great number of windows are

304

cut into the walls, and the interior and exterior of the building are connected by the translucent windows and the general openwork character of the style.

From the outside of the church, its interior spaces can immediately be sensed, just as from the inside the exterior is implied. Instead of the earlier fixed dogmatism of heavy inert Romanesque vaults on massive unpierced walls, there is a delicately balanced organic system. The vaults are supported partly by ribs connected to the complex piers rising from the floor and partly by the solid stone outer buttresses rising from the ground. These buttresses are connected to the vaults and to the deliberately thin, window-pierced walls by stone braces called flying buttresses. The walls of the Gothic building are little more than stone curtains hanging from above, with large areas cut away for window openings and gallery spaces. The architect can raise his structure to grandiose heights be-

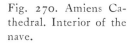

Fig. 270. Amiens Cathedral. Interior of the nave.

Fig. 271. The Gothic vaulting system.

cause of the dynamic balance engendered between the downward and outward thrust of the vaults and the upward thrust of the floor piers combined with the diagonal inward thrust of the flying buttresses. Through this triumph of logic, the Gothic builder produced a thrilling and inspiring religious structure in which the immense, sometimes invisible height of the vaults, the vibrating color of stained glass, and the rich music unite to achieve a more effective act of faith. Like Abélard, the Gothic architect brought logic and reason to buttress faith.

The Gothic style as described is most at home in the Ile de France region; in other countries it may either duplicate French efforts or use elements like the pointed arch in a decorative rather than functional manner. Gothic as a logical system of thrusts and counterthrusts is found in its most perfect examples in the northern part of France. Three important innovations led to this development: the use of a rectangular rather than square vaulting section, or bay; the pointed instead of round arch; and the external individual buttress placed against a concentrated point (or points) on the oblong nave vault section — this buttress replacing the Romanesque concealed half-arch under the roof (figs. 235, 270–271).

The oblong vault. By changing to an oblong vault (fig. 272), the Gothic builder overcame two objections inherent in the square Romanesque vault: a domical shape which carried the eye around and down its curve rather than continuously upward, and a relatively wide space between the supporting piers that led the eye horizontally along the nave floor in the processional manner of the Early Christian basilica. By narrowing the vault on the aisle side, the Gothic builder brought the floor piers closer together, thus leading the eye directly up to the vaults where the new pointing of the ribs would carry it even higher. Moreover, the nave now became wider.

The pointed arch. Through the pointed rib supports, the architect was able to choose an arbitrary radius that allowed him to erect the supporting ribs to almost any desired height and to make the various sides of the vault equal in height and level with the ridge pole. This would not have been possible in an oblong vault constructed on round arches, which are limited in height by their own radii. Not only did pointed arches automatically raise the height of the vaulting system as a whole, but they also made it possible to fabricate a more flexible, lighter, and more unified vaulting entity which appears to be tied together along the top as though by a stone spine running parallel with the nave floor (fig. 271).

Inner and outer supports; the flying buttress. Lifting the vault to the great heights envisioned by the Gothic builder (Paris, 112 feet; Reims,

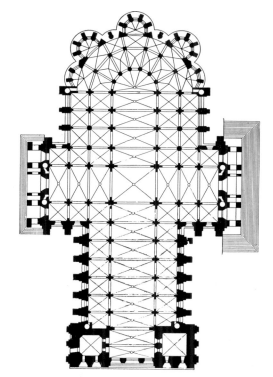

Fig. 272. Chartres Cathedral. Plan.

125 feet, Amiens, 138 feet; and finally Beauvais, 157 feet, see fig. 273)
made the question of support paramount. Here again earlier features were
utilized and developed. The round Romanesque column was elaborated
into a compound masonry pier (fig. 270) carrying thin stone ribs along
its surface up into the vaults; its shape was more complex, its height
greater, and its integration into the general plan more evident. Although
the ribs running down along the piers carried a good deal of the downward weight, it remained for external supports to counteract the outward
thrust of the vaults.

In Romanesque architecture the barrel-shaped vaults had been sustained partly by very thick side walls, as well as by small barrel vaults
over the triforium gallery and groined vaults over the aisles. This system,
as explained, limited both the height of the building and the amount of
light that could be admitted. The Gothic architect raised the height of his
vaults and practically eliminated the wall by means of a high pointed
nave arcade connecting the piers; a pointed open triforium gallery;
and enormous pointed stained-glass windows rising into the vaults. As
the process developed, other supports had to be found to replace the

Fig. 273. Beauvais Ca-
thedral. Vaulting of the
nave.

wall. Heavy stone piers were set up separately outside the building and were connected to those points on the structure where the vaults exerted their maximum outward thrust (fig. 271). Diagonal stone braces led from the outside piers to the significant points where these braces, or flying buttresses, could exert their counterthrust.

The flying buttresses replaced not only the Romanesque wall but also the small barrel side vaults, which in the course of development had narrowed to struts concealed under the roofing (e.g., *La Trinité* at Caen, see fig. 235), emerging finally in early outside applications as at St. Germain-des-Près in Paris. In this building the architect had used a single flying buttress. It was soon found, however, that there were two points of outward thrust: the springing (where the vault begins to rise) and the haunch (where the vault begins to bend inward). The buttresses were then doubled as at Amiens and Chartres.

This strategic placement of the individual-external-pier-and-flying-buttress combination (that admitted maximum light, contrary to the continuous Romanesque small barrel vault) was possible because the new vaults were shaped so that their thrust was concentrated at the desired points. While diagonal ribs were permitted to spread as they rose from the main impost, the two longitudinal ribs were run straight up for a way before springing inward and spreading, thus pinching the vault on the wall side into what is known as the ploughshare twist (see fig. 273). This narrower surface became the target of the pairs of stone braces, or struts, connecting the external supporting piers with the outside of the building, first, at the height of the vault springing, and, second, at the level of the haunch where the vault turned inward (fig. 271). With this dynamically balanced system developed in the Ile de France, the building might be regarded as a spidery stone skeleton, its spine parallel with the ground, its many clawlike arms supporting the transparent structure.

AESTHETIC CHARACTER OF THE GOTHIC CATHEDRALS. As the product of a relatively short historical period and a small geographical area, the Gothic cathedrals were bound to have a certain uniformity. The character of individual towns was nevertheless reflected in the stages of stylistic development and also in the differences between a large city church and a small-town building or a coronation church. The latter variations are more discernible in sculpture.

Paris, Chartres, Reims, and Amiens represent successive phases in the evolution of organic Gothic architecture. Although the façades of the first two bear vestigial traces of the Romanesque style (e.g., buttresses projecting from the façade), most thirteenth-century cathedrals in France have certain features in common. Viewed externally, such cathedrals as

Fig. 274. Notre Dame de Paris. View from southeast.

Amiens, Reims, or Paris (fig. 268) show a façade divided into three parts with a broader and higher central portal and often correspondingly lower and narrower side portals — but all open and inviting, like those on the two sides of the transept. These portals are recessed to contain a wealth of didactic sculptural detail along their sides and to move the eye both inward and upward: inward in search of the perpetual linking of interior and exterior; upward to pursue the vertical movement of the whole building. Above the portals are a row of "kings" set in their individual niches, open arcades, a rose-wheel stained-glass window, and openwork square towers planned to hold spires (see *Chartres Cathedral*, fig. 280).

The vertical motion created by straight up-and-down lines and pointed arches is repeated with variations along the sides and rear of the buildings (see fig. 274). Upward-thrusting, delicately ornamented buttress piers ascend gracefully to their climax far over the side aisles where the stone struts lean inward to fulfill their supporting function. The processionwise progress of piers around the sides of the Gothic cathedral is temporarily interrupted by the arms of the crossing — also built straight up and down

310

— which now occupies a position halfway down the nave length because of the elaboration of choir and apse-end, or chevet. The buttresses and their flying adjuncts continue their endless movement past the transept, marching along the choir and around the apse, where they spring over a complex webbing of vaults covering an ambulatory and a series of radiating chapels.

Whether or not they were planned that way, the sculptural ornament and stained glass (figs. 275, 276, 288) are vital elements in tying together the various surfaces that enclose the building. The repetition of full-length figures along the entrance portals unifies the doorways and at the same time relates them to the upper part of the building where there are free-standing figures in niches. In the same way, the repetition of trefoil (three-cusped shapes) and other ornaments on the façades, and finials and crockets (foliage ornaments) along the side of the building performs a similar function.

STAINED GLASS. Gothic stained glass, which replaces the Romanesque wall paintings, has a spatial as well as decorative function. It is decorative in its application of color areas tied together with pieces of lead and stone tracery. In addition, the large sections of glass, placed at regular intervals between curved portions of vaulting, link the interior and exterior by acting as a partly transparent wall (see fig. 288).

Although far more light than ever before is admitted through these immense translucent windows, the brightness is distinctly muted as it passes through small units of roughly blown colored glass, containing

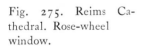

Fig. 275. Reims Cathedral. Rose-wheel window.

Fig. 276. Last Judgment portal. Reims Cathedral.

bubbles and other impurities. But it is a rich full light, which conveys a spiritual feeling. The lambent areas of mixed color are constantly in movement, activated by the juxtaposition of hues, the irregularities in shape, thickness, and purity of the glass itself and the connecting strips of lead. This subdued colored radiance does not always reach into the tops of the vaults, which are sometimes obscured in velvety shadows — thereby adding to the sense of infinitude and mystical aspiration that exists in the atmosphere created by the many-toned, vibrating luminosity and the polyphonic music. Interestingly, the Gothic glassmakers utilized the changing quality of natural light, which moves from the red to the violet side of the spectrum in the course of a day. The windows on the apse, or east, end of the cathedral are often dominantly red in tonality, while the rose wheel over the entrance, or west, end may be violet-hued, so that the sunlight can reinforce each as it moves from one end to the other.

Much of this early glass has disappeared, but there is still enough to give a good idea of the exalting effect it must have had on the spectators of that day. The best and most complete collection of Gothic glass is at *Chartres Cathedral*. Windows like the celebrated *Notre Dame de la Belle Verrière* make clear their multiple function of transparent wall painting, mystic inspiration, and didactic content. In the task of instruction, the stained glass joins with the sculptures, whose compositional and decorative values we have already considered.

GOTHIC SCULPTURE. Sculpture is in many ways the most revealing element in Gothic art. In both form and content it tells more about this latter portion of the Middle Ages than perhaps any other single cultural manifestation. It is not altogether accidental that the new-found serenity and idealism, the simple naturalism combined with spiritual aspiration, in Gothic sculpture differ so radically from the often spasmodic and nervous Romanesque art with its frightening detachment from life. In a remarkable and relatively rapid transformation, this medium discloses the altered face of European society, its changed mood. For example, a typical *Last Judgment* of the earlier period (see figs. 250–251) may be contrasted with the same subject found on the thirteenth-century Reims Cathedral (figs. 276–277). In the first instance there was a fearful and psychotic mood, especially in the detail showing the little naked soul hauled up so horribly by an enormous pair of hands about its throat. At Reims, on the other hand, there is a marked benevolence, a "sweetness and light," as in the lowest section of the story where the little souls are carried forward by smiling angels to be deposited in the bosom of a be-

Fig. 277. Last Judgment portal. Detail from upper section. Reims Cathedral.

nign Abraham. To the right of this idyllic scene, where the punishment
in hell is depicted, a group of people — significantly including a king and
a bishop — are being herded behind a rope by a pair of grinning devils
who supervise the boiling arrangements, while an angel urges them to
move along almost as though it were a waiting line in a theater.

The new kindlier flavor of the average Gothic cathedral sculptures
makes it possible to approach these buildings with an altogether different
attitude, undoubtedly felt by the people of that day. Such traditional
names as *Le Beau Dieu* (the beautiful God, fig. 278) or *La Vierge Dorée*
(the gilded Virgin, fig. 279) at Amiens betoken the affection in which
many of these figures were held. The conception of Christ as a benevolent
teacher, as in the *Beau Dieu,* is surely far removed from the apocalyptic
version found in the tympanum of La Madeleine at Vézelay or the one
at Moissac (fig. 247) which expresses punishment and menace.

Content of Gothic sculpture. Besides the stylistic differences, the content or subject matter of Gothic sculpture has its own special character.
According to the best authority, Emile Mâle, Gothic sculpture may be regarded as a sacred writing, a sacred mathematics, and a symbolic code.
In the first, certain conventions must always be observed so that sub-

314

jects are recognizable, e.g., holy people with halos and bare feet, or the nakedness of little souls. The second viewpoint, the mathematical, emphasizes position, grouping, symmetry, and especially number. Both the size and position of the chief figures are stressed, particularly of Christ, who is invariably centered and made larger. Figures around the Christ are grouped in order of their importance, the position on his right being the most favored, e.g., the Saved; the lesser personages, e.g., the Damned, are grouped symmetrically on his left. In a somewhat analogous fashion, the New Testament prophets are shown standing on the shoulders of their Old Testament predecessors. As for numerical symbols, such numbers as three (the Trinity), four (the elements, the New Testament Gospels), seven (sacraments, deadly sins), and twelve (apostles) have literary and representational meaning. Not only are the numbers important in themselves, but they represent combinations and derivations of each other (as four times three, four plus three), thus adding to their significance. All these factors are applied in the sculptural ornament of the Gothic period.

Fig. 278. Le Beau Dieu. Central portal trumeau. Amiens Cathedral.

Fig. 279. La Vierge Dorée.
Amiens Cathedral.

Consistent with the expressed and implied mysticism of this era is a
powerful belief in allegorical or hidden meanings in Holy Writ or
other sources, generally extracted by analogy. The most outstanding example is the symbolic import of the various steps in the Mass, which are
parallel to the important events of the Passion of Christ. On another level,
the figures in tomb sculpture almost invariably have their feet placed
on a lion cub to help the soul's resurrection, since the lion cub was believed
to have been born dead and, after a significant three days, breathed back
into life by its mother. Christ also came back to life after three days.

One of the most evident facts of thirteenth-century culture is its
encyclopedic tendency, manifested in the books of Thomas Aquinas that
bring together all Christian doctrine, those of Voragine on the legends of
the saints and of Guglielmus Durandus on the liturgy. Most meaningful for art is the monumental work by Vincent of Beauvais, "the devourer
of books," whose *Speculum Majus,* or *Great Mirror,* contains four separate "mirrors," or books: nature, morals, instruction, and history. The first
book deals with all natural phenomena created by God — minerals, vege-
tables, animals, the four elements, and man. The second book, really a
summary of Aquinas's *Summa Theologica,* classifies the virtues and vices;
it teaches that knowledge is a means to virtue and that to act is important.

316

The mirror of instruction deals first with the Fall and Redemption and the important idea that the human mind can redeem itself. It also instructs in different branches of knowledge, including the mechanical arts. Finally, the mirror of history (of course, sacred history is meant) goes through the two Testaments, the Apocrypha, saints' lives, antiquity, and the Apocalypse and Last Judgment.

These enormous compilations — Vincent's as well as the others — represent the systematic thinking, the logic buttressing faith of the late Middle Ages. The mirrors are also important because so much of their material is visible in the cathedral sculptures and stained glass of the period (figs. 275–289). These representations again underline the joining of theology with the various aspects of nature and the physical world. It is open to serious question whether the average medieval citizen was able to infuse all those meanings into his view of cathedral sculptures.

Fig. 280. Chartres Cathedral. View from west.

On the other hand, in an age when hardly anyone could read, the images must have served a useful didactic purpose; here the knowledge of the time was put forth in pictorial form. Just as we today understand certain cinematic, magazine, or other clichés, so medieval man recognized the meaning of these stone and glass decorations for which later generations are obliged to use guide books.

Changes in sculptural style; High Gothic. In the evolution of Gothic sculpture, the west front of *Chartres Cathedral*, done in the second half of the twelfth century (figs. 280–281), provides a good instance of a transitional form in which older stylistic elements exist side by side with newer qualities. Geometric ornament, schematic figures, ropelike beards, stylized drapery, and angular shoulders show the heritage from the Romanesque; but there is a new unity in the subordination of details to the whole. Although the figures on the sides of the portals (fig. 282) look none too secure in their positions as compared with later examples (see the *Beau Dieu*, fig. 278), yet they are designed for the space and for the portal scheme as a whole. The tympanum sculptures over the doorways retain traditional subjects — Christ in Majesty, the Ascension of Christ, and the Madonna Enthroned — but a distinct softening of forms and expres-

Fig. 281. Main portal. Chartres Cathedral.

318

sions, a new benignity in the face of the Christ, denote the humanization of the period.

The High Gothic style is part of the great religious enthusiasm of the first sixty years of the thirteenth century. So-called schools of sculpture

Fig. 282. Saints and royal personages. Portal of west façade. Chartres Cathedral.

developed at Paris, Chartres, Amiens, and Reims, where groups of stone carvers worked as individuals, yet with a common bond that gives the product of each center its own character. Paris, the big university city, seems to show an intellectual and dogmatic quality; Chartres, the small

Fig. 283. Virgin portal. Notre Dame de Paris.

country town, has a certain mystical and lyrical feeling; Amiens embodies the new bourgeois spirit of the times; and in Reims there is an almost classical aspect.

At *Notre Dame de Paris* the west front *Virgin Portal* (1163–1235, fig. 283), representing from bottom to top the prophets and kings, the Resurrection of the Virgin, and her coronation in heaven, carries a well-developed sense of anatomy and self-confidence; heads really look as though they belong on necks, and difficult poses are well executed. *Chartres Cathedral* displays the second and third phases of its development in the north and south transepts, respectively, from about 1210 to about 1275 — a slow growth compared to other centers — with preservation of old facial characteristics such as the long nose and face of the famous *St. Theodore* from the south porch (fig. 284). Here the mild and soft expression, the comparatively superficial modeling, seem to coincide with the more mystical character of the school. The sculpture of Chartres has an individual quality; its country types are affected by intense, unintellectual devotion. Without radical innovations, its figures are impressively monumental and controlled.

320

Amiens is one of those cathedrals built under the tremendous enthusiasm and community enterprise characteristic of the period; its whole effort was contained within the dates 1220–1236. As the typical bourgeois town of the Gothic age, its art exhibits a search for novelty, unusual effects of naturalism, and even smugness. Some of the finest figures are the apostles and saints of the main portal, e.g., *St. Firmin* (fig. 285), which are naturalistic and bourgeois portraits. The signs of the zodiac on the lower part of the façade depict appropriate activities for the various months and corresponding zodiacal symbols in a simple naturalistic fashion (fig. 286). *Le Beau Dieu* (fig. 278) shows a more advanced type of drapery than the Chartres figures, with deeper and more "interesting" undercuttings that suggest wood-carving techniques; but they are not organically related to the structure of the form they cover. The Christ is a dignified, pleasant teacher or paterfamilias with far less spirituality than *St. Theodore* or such Christ figures as at Reims.

The classical suggestions at Reims recall that Frankish kings during this period controlled certain Near Eastern areas, especially in Greece (until the end of the nineteenth century, the approach to the Acropolis

Fig. 284. St. Theodore (detail). Chartres Cathedral.

Fig. 285. St. Firmin. Amiens Cathedral.

in Athens was dominated by the Tower of the Franks). However this situation arose — and there is still a great deal of doubt concerning it — the fact remains that such figures as the Mary and Elizabeth in the *Visitation* scene (fig. 287) have a remarkable three-dimensional quality and an unusually strong relationship between drapery and the covered form. The naturalistic dignity of the older woman also suggests Hellenistic or early Roman types, and the gentle idealism of Mary again brings to mind certain Classical analogies. The contrast between the straight left leg and the relaxed right leg may suggest the stance of the *Lance Bearer* (fig. 81) or the caryatids of the *Porch of the Maidens* (fig. 91).

The development of medieval sculpture from the archaic and angular forms of the Romanesque to the half-spiritual, half-material Gothic ideal offers an interesting parallel to ancient Greek art from the sixth to the fifth centuries B.C. Although this similarity of evolution may be entirely accidental, the Reims women of the *Visitation* (who make the contemporary works of Niccolò Pisano look rather pale) or the figures on the *Last Judgment* portal (figs. 276–277) with their regular proportions, broad broken drapery folds, revealed anatomy, skillful flesh treatment, and regularly curled hair are far too specifically classical to be an accident. In the casual and straightforward handling of the nude and in such details as the burial jar, the Resurrection portion of this portal would seem to indicate some influence from Roman remains in the city of Reims itself.

Apart from its significance in the area of pre-Renaissance classicism, Reims was a point of departure for the later style of Bamberg and the school of Strassburg in Germany. The latter circumstance illustrates how wandering groups of sculptors moved from one place to another as jobs offered. This was one of the ways that the Gothic style in architecture and sculpture spread all over Europe; the currents could even reverse themselves, as happened when the early Reims sculptors came back from Bamberg.

Later Gothic sculpture. The later stage of Gothic sculpture is illustrated by the well-known *Vierge Dorée* (or gilded Virgin) of Amiens (fig. 279) who suits the bourgeois orientation of that city in her overly winsome and charming quality. The Madonna is undoubtedly more feminine than ever before and her relationship with the Child very warm and human as the artist strives for naturalism, but he ends up with a "cute" baby and a "soubrette of Picardy." Spiritual value has been sacrificed to everyday appeal; the desired emotional expressiveness of the Madonna is not quite achieved. Similarly, the figure's relationship to the design of the building is affected as she self-consciously looks sideways toward a Child held almost outside the protective covering of the canopy. The severely integrated relationship of the *Beau Dieu* and his architectural setting has been lost. The garrulous townsfolk, shown above the Virgin, also wander around loosely and aimlessly under their canopies.

These tendencies toward greater naturalism, toward artistic or aesthetic (they may also be termed "worldly") rather than primarily spiritual qualities, increased during the early fourteenth century with the natural evolution of the later Middle Ages. In a measure this was caused by the growing worldliness of the whole period, and in part by the injection of a certain courtly and aristocratic element. The latter was sometimes a

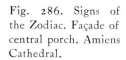

Fig. 286. Signs of the Zodiac. Façade of central porch. Amiens Cathedral.

Fig. 287. The Visitation. Reims Cathedral.

bourgeois affectation, but at other times signalized the reappearance of the upper class as a factor in Gothic culture. The centralization of monarchies that had begun in thirteenth-century France and England brought royal participation in the Gothic movement: e.g., the *Ste. Chapelle* (fig. 288) in Paris (1242–1247), built by Louis IX (St. Louis) as a repository for a Holy Thorn from the Crown of Thorns. The aristocracy adopted the style in their own fashion as, with the decline of the manorial system, many of them moved into the towns. The simplicity of thirteenth-century Gothic was diverted into new, more decorative and artificial channels by the upper classes. The burgher interest in naturalism continued and extended in an unorganic, unarchitectural manner, often influenced by upper-class luxuriousness, as in the art of Flanders.

The *Virgin of Paris* (fig. 289), carved in the early fourteenth century for the interior of the cathedral, indicates how far the mannerisms of the *Vierge Dorée* had gone. This posturized, elegant, overdecorated, and linear figure with a diffident expression, squint, and "Gothic swing" may be paralleled by the contemporary *Annunciation* painting of Simone Martini (1283–1344) (see fig. 302), who worked for a number of years in the papal court at Avignon. Far from spiritual, this statue is primarily aesthetic in purpose, an article of luxury rather than an image of faith.

GOTHIC IVORIES AND MANUSCRIPTS. The style of the *Virgin of Paris* is repeated throughout Europe in innumerable objects, both religious and nonreligious. For many artists it possessed a highly desirable elegance and smartness, a Parisian "chic" that was suitable for rich votive objects or ivory figurines and reliefs. Of these fourteenth-century ivories perhaps the most interesting is a series of scenes from the literature of chivalric romance, carved on the sides of jewel boxes, mirror cases, and the like (fig. 290). Aside from their characteristic elegance and swinging outlines, these are distinctly secular works unconnected with the previously dominant cathedral; yet a good many of the ivories (and manuscripts) of the early fourteenth century maintain some form of architectural background, even if mechanical rather than organic, as a decorative carry-over from the High Gothic.

The widespread use of chivalric literary themes in the ivories of the late Gothic period is tied up with the whole shift away from the shadow of the cathedral toward an advancing secular viewpoint. The so-called *matière de Bretagne* (i.e., the Arthurian cycle) and the equally popular Tristan legend had existed in literary form during the late twelfth and

Fig. 288. Ste. Chapelle, Paris. Interior with windows.

Fig. 289. Virgin of Paris. Notre Dame de Paris.

early thirteenth centuries. Marie de France and Chrétien de Troyes in France and the German love poets, Gottfried von Strassburg, Wolfram von Eschenbach, Walter von der Vogelweide, all show the strong interest in these themes on a courtly level. From this great chivalric movement grew a worship of woman, concretized in the elaborate codes of love used by these authors; it also took a form known as Mariolatry, the worship of Mary, illustrated by the *Songs to the Virgin* of Alfonso the Wise of Spain. Mariolatry had undoubtedly existed in the Romanesque period, just as chivalry had, but it was only during Gothic times that many cathedrals were dedicated to Our Lady of one or another city. During the later development of Gothic style from the *Vierge Dorée* onward (ca. 1280), the Virgin was increasingly

Fig. 290. Ivory casket (fourteenth century), showing the story of Lancelot, Gawain, etc. New York, Metropolitan Museum of Art.

portrayed as the Queen of Heaven. By the early fourteenth century, in religious ivories, as in the elegant paintings of Simone Martini, Duccio, and Cimabue, the idea of the Virgin holding court had become fairly well established. As the emphasis shifted from a dominantly architectonic art to a more decorative, nonfunctional, aristocratic expression, the popular chivalric material emerged in the luxury form of the ivories.

To this same period belong a series of suave manuscript illuminations, e.g., the *Pontifical of Metz* (1302–1316, fig. 291), which shows ornamental and now functionless architecture, the graceful swinging forms marked by a long curve from one shoulder to the opposite foot, and the initial letters beginning to be crowded out by the picture panels. The contrast between the formal attitudes of the bishop and his priests above and the playful, laughable little figures along the bottom floral spray — put in after the artist had fulfilled his duty to the Church — is paralleled in Gothic cathedral sculpture, such as the half-humorous "misericords"

Fig. 291. Bishop Dedicating a Church. From the *Pontifical of Metz* (fourteenth century). London, private collection.

under choir benches. Dogma exists side by side with the assertion of individuality and the emergence of living forms.

Through the military activity of Norman barons (conquest of Sicily, England, and parts of the Near East) and the equally significant movements of merchants and artist groups, the Gothic idea was diffused over all Europe. French architects and sculptors were in demand; French manuscripts, ivories, and enamels were popular for both form and content. The literary material of France (religious as well as secular) had its effect on other countries, as previously remarked, since many heads of foreign universities had passed through the University of Paris.

Fig. 292. Death of Mary. Strassburg Cathedral.

GERMAN GOTHIC. Germany was so heavily influenced by the French Gothic that it added few original features in its architecture. Its most famous building, the enormous Cathedral of Cologne, seems to have been planned by an architect who was either French or French-trained at Amiens. Like many German cathedrals, Cologne is embellished with a magnificent façade and high slender towers with fine stone tracery. A product of the thirteenth to fourteenth centuries, Cologne was worked on until the sixteenth and then, after a long interruption, finished only during the Gothic revival in the nineteenth century (1817–1880). German Gothic sculpture, because of the strong hold of the Romanesque in that country, came somewhat late and emerged on a rather high emotive and naturalistic level. Thus, while early Reims sculpture influenced Bamberg in Germany, the latter in turn influenced the sentimental character of later Reims, which in its turn affected the German school of Strassburg.

328

The relationship between the two countries may be illustrated by the *Death of Mary* tympanum of the Cathedral of Strassburg (fig. 292) where the rolling ground line, pitched heads, and the crossed legs of the figure at the foot of Mary's couch indicate clear Romanesque survivals. A certain individuality of face and gesture, ability to achieve characterization, and emotional outpouring are evident in these works, which, however, lack the French sense of organization or the relationship of figures to architecture. The dying Virgin seems to reflect the Virgin of the *Visitation* in Reims (fig. 287), part of her convulsive attitude stemming from the typical German emotive approach, and the rest from the use of a standing figure (one leg straight, the other slightly bent) for a lying-down pose.

ENGLISH GOTHIC. In England there is no French organic, or dynamically balanced, architecture; here they depend on Romanesque sturdiness for safety rather than on flying buttresses. The elevation of the English buildings, e.g., Salisbury or *Wells Cathedral* (fig. 293), is lower than the French; but that very fact, plus the narrowness of the structure, makes

Fig. 293. Wells Cathedral.

Fig. 294. Wells Cathedral. The façade.

Fig. 295. Exeter Cathedral. The nave (fourteenth century).

them seem longer. In English cathedrals the transept projects much more boldly and is usually doubled to give a double-armed cross effect on plan. The east, or apse, end is square rather than round, stemming from earlier Anglo-Saxon and Cistercian forms which exerted a strong influence even though early English Gothic was built under the dominance of the Norman-French style and government.

The great square tower over the crossing is a special feature of English Gothic, which in some ways is more complicated than the French, although less organic. Ribs are used in profuse decorative effect on the interiors for design rather than structural reasons (see fig. 295), while the equally unfunctional façades become decorative screens, hiding what lies behind them and relegating sculpture to an unimportant role (fig. 294). Because of the stronger hold of the monastic system in England, its churches were often set in the countryside, again differentiating them from the crowded town background of French buildings.

From the simplicity of Salisbury and *Wells,* English Gothic moved on to the so-called Decorated Style, exemplified in the nave of *Exeter Cathedral* (fig. 295) with its profusion of ornament and ribs, its enlarged openings filled with tracery designs. The climax of English Gothic was

Fig. 296. Chapel of Henry VII. London, Westminster Abbey.

achieved by the Perpendicular Style, e.g., the *Chapel of Henry VII* at Westminster (figs. 296–297) or the cloisters of Gloucester Cathedral, in which the native architect is most original — the complete accent on verticality, the ribs brought directly from the ground, and vertical tracery bars from bottom to top cutting up through very large window openings.

Fig. 297. Chapel of Henry VII. Interior.

The vaulting system has become so complicated that it would be difficult to distinguish the functional from the nonfunctional or purely decorative ribs. More accurately, there are no functional ribs; instead, ornamental ribs are carved fanwise out of the surface of the stones composing the solidly built vault. In English Gothic sculpture, the most important examples are found in a series of tomb figures, as in Westminster Abbey, and the alabaster relief carvings of the fourteenth century.

SPANISH GOTHIC. The Spanish were closer to French Gothic; buildings like the cathedrals of Burgos and León show the work of French sculptors and decorators. After a short period the Spanish gave these imported forms a somewhat vulgarized character, although the sculptors of Catalonia under the double influence of French and Italian art produced some fine pieces. A superior school of miniature painting existed at the thirteenth-century court of Alfonso the Wise in Castile, and another in Catalonia.

ITALIAN ARCHITECTURE. With Italy the situation was somewhat different; here the Gothic style found scarcely any welcome architecturally, except in bastardized, if decorative, buildings such as the Cathedral of Orvieto. Churches of this kind typify the superficial effect of the organic style in Italy, where a basilican form of building had been firmly entrenched since the Early Christian period, varied periodically in an ornamental rather than structural fashion. During the Gothic age it enjoyed pointed arches, finials, and crockets; at a later date classical ornament would be applied to the traditional structure. In the Early Christian era the large, unbroken wall surfaces of the Italian basilica had been advantageous for mosaic mural decoration; in Gothic times an art of wall painting replaced both the stained glass and integrated sculptures of the French.

ITALIAN SCULPTURE. Sculpture played an increasingly independent role in Italy, abandoning the architectural aesthetic of French art as well as its grayish stone. The Italian sculptor turned to marble, an easily available and more flexible medium which was now treated separately as in ancient art. Like the Italian painter of this early period (ca. 1200–1350), the sculptor became a clearer personality than did the anonymous group workman on the French buildings, who subordinated his personality to the character of the workshop or the town. Perhaps because of the earlier development of town life in Italy, the individual apparently had greater stature and social importance; contracts were made with individual artists whose origins and lives are recorded, and in some cases even their personal foibles.

Fig. 298. Niccolò Pisano: Pisa Baptistry Pulpit.

Fig. 299. Niccolò Pisano: Presentation in the Temple. Detail from Pisa pulpit.

For the most part, however, Italian art during the first half of the thirteenth century was inferior in quality to the contemporary art of France. It is customary to ascribe much influence to the sculpture of Niccolò Pisano (ca. 1206–ca. 1278) as a force in the reconstruction of the classical viewpoint in Italy, but the panels of his *Pisa Baptistry Pulpit* (figs. 298–299) appear less skillfully carved and composed than contemporary French works. While there is a striving toward monumentality — probably derived from the twelfth-century south Italian "classical" movement engendered by Frederick of Naples — the Reims school would seem to offer more effective classical comparisons. The work of Niccolò's son Giovanni Pisano (1250?–1328?), e.g., the detail from the *Pistoia Pulpit* (fig. 300), shows a different trend in its clear relation to the mannered French Gothic of the later thirteenth and early fourteenth century. Giovanni's graceful figures perform naturalistic activities with greater emphasis on everyday detail and narrative quality.

ITALIAN PAINTING. Although both these sculpture styles were to have their consequences in later Italian painting, during the first half of the thirteenth century that art presented a somewhat confused and often unimpressive character. For the most part, it was still dominated by the rigid hieratic and flat Byzantine mode, adroitly carried out in those instances where a Byzantine or Byzantine-trained artist was utilized, e.g., the mosaics in St. Mark's, Venice. In the course of the thirteenth century, with the rise of the humanistic ideal, this style and its provincial derivatives were undermined by a more sculptural conception, attributable both

Fig. 300. Giovanni Pisano: Nativity. Detail from the Pistoia pulpit.

to Early Christian mosaics (an important factor in the revival of form in Italy) and to the powerful French sculpture school of the time. Spiritually, this more humanistic approach was also affected by the Franciscan movement of the early thirteenth century, which softened to some extent the harshness of a period marked by constant struggles between the papacy and the Holy Roman Empire. The Franciscan belief in man's ability to commune directly with God was a tremendous factor in humanizing religion and religious art.

By the end of the thirteenth and beginning of the fourteenth century, these factors combined to produce a strong artistic movement. From a relatively provincial Byzantine type of painting there was gradual evolution in the direction of three-dimensionality and humanistic expression; the social and spiritual motivation of these paintings corresponded in many ways to the Gothic of France. Rome was relegated to a subordinate position during the greater part of the fourteenth century as a result of the struggles for power and the later captivity of the papacy in France. The center of activity moved first to Assisi and then to Florence and Siena, the first because the Franciscan movement centered there and the latter two because of their growing importance as great commercial and banking cities.

SIENA: *Duccio.* The two chief styles stemming from the Byzantine of the earlier thirteenth century are those of Siena and Florence, the latter also represented in the Church of St. Francis at Assisi. Siena may be represented by the work of Duccio (fl. 1278–1319) and Simone Martini (1283–1344). The former's great *Majestas* altarpiece (fig. 301) for the Cathedral of Siena, completed in 1311 and carried to the cathedral amid great rejoicing, characterizes Duccio's new manner in its peculiar combination of the formal and hieratic abstraction of the Byzantine with the more spiritual and lyric quality of French Gothic. Mary is seated "in Majesty" as Queen of Heaven surrounded by her court of saints and angels, altogether consistent with the artistically expressed cult of the Virgin seen in fourteenth-century France. Siena, a city dedicated to the Virgin, was necessarily more susceptible to this idea than many other centers. Simone Martini's *Madonna in Majesty* in Siena's Palazzo Pubblico is even more overtly aristocratic and courtly in character.

Duccio's forms, as in Sienese painting generally, are linear and two-dimensional — the Byzantine heritage — while their expression is spiritual and lyrical, conforming to the French Gothic ideal. The basic effect of these pictures is a monumental decorativeness (in contrast to the more sculpturesque manner of the Florentines) and a sweetness of expression that often descends to a chatty and garrulous manner, as in the series of panels telling the life of Christ, on the back of Duccio's altarpiece.

336

Here the subject matter is distinctly Byzantine, while the compositions —
although mildly preoccupied with questions of space — move the spectator's eye from one side to the other rather than from the outside in, as
with the *Majestas* itself. Though antinaturalistic in design, the life of
Christ is portrayed in the best tradition of medieval realism of effect and
emotional impact; in one panel, Christ in Gethsemane vividly conveys his
agony, and, in another, Peter his indecision when asked if he belongs to
the circle of the Nazarene.

Fig. 301. Duccio: Majestas. Siena Cathedral.

Simone Martini. Simone Martini, second important figure of the
early Sienese school, is one of the great virtuosi of line. His *Annunciation*
(fig. 302) marks a high point in Sienese two-dimensional decorative and
linear art. The Madonna shrinking away from the angel incorporates in
her form the Gothic swing, squint, and aristocratic diffidence noted in the
contemporary *Virgin of Paris* (fig. 289). The nervous elegance of her
attitude as she moves into the protection of the Gothic arch overhead, the
extraordinary gesture of the hand hooked into the neck of her gown, the
sensitive self-animated drapery unrelated to the body beneath, are as notable as the graceful floating motion of the angel coming to rest before
her. The basic decorative interest of the Sienese artist is combined with a
sensitively expressed emotional quality. The relationship between the
mannered French Gothic and Simone's painting is as clear as that between
the French and Giovanni Pisano, who during this period directed the
carving of the sculptures on the façade of the Cathedral of Siena. Simone's

Fig. 302. Simone Martini: Annunciation. Florence, Uffizi Gallery.

travels in southern Italy and to Avignon in southern France helped to spread these ideas and contributed to the International Gothic style of the late fourteenth century.

FLORENCE: *Cimabue*. From the very beginning of the late medieval Italian movement, Florence emphasized sculpturesque form and monumental restrained expression. The tradition of Niccolò Pisano and of the thirteenth-century Roman painter Pietro Cavallini formed an aesthetic background to the early Florentine movement. The initial two eminent names are Cimabue (1240?–1302?) and Giotto (1266–1336); Cimabue traditionally was supposed to have been the teacher of Giotto. Some of Cimabue's works, e.g., the *Madonna Enthroned* (fig. 303), may be compared in a general way with Duccio's panel paintings in their common derivation from — and softening of — the Byzantine style. Others, such as the *Madonna with Angels and St. Francis* (fig. 304), a fresco in the lower church of St. Francis of Assisi, express the new warmly emotional and rounded character of Florentine painting. In spite of conventional ar-

338

rangement of the personages, there is a distinctly new sculpturesque treatment of form; draperies are intended to reveal anatomy rather than to be independently stimulating and ornamental designs as in the Sienese method. The Madonna shows greater humanity and girlish charm than Duccio's Madonna, while the St. Francis at the right is a highly naturalistic conception, filled with a haunting, brooding sadness.

Giotto. The course indicated by Cimabue was fulfilled by the monumental and intensely humanistic painting of Giotto, in which the figures on the Gothic cathedrals seem to have stepped down from their niches to engage in their various activities. This great contemporary and countryman of Dante produced powerful three-dimensional forms placed in a perceptible, though limited, space — forms whose materiality is conveyed through the relationship between the drapery and the body be-

Fig. 303. Cimabue: Madonna Enthroned. Florence, Uffizi Gallery.

Fig. 304. Cimabue: Madonna with Angels and St. Francis. Assisi, Church of St. Francis.

neath. In such murals as the *Death of St. Francis* (in Santa Croce, Florence, fig. 305), the painter monumentalizes and ennobles his human beings to a degree far beyond French Gothic sculpture, setting them in a shallow but three-dimensional box, or artificial stage, within which they move parallel to the picture plane. The groups at either side point toward the central scene to achieve a concentrated impact. As in many later Italian works, the picture frame sets the limits; all parts are complete within this "closed composition." The figures with their backs turned illustrate how Giotto was able to convey the tactile, or touch, quality of a form without directly showing any part of it. The sensation of its actuality is achieved by tightening or loosening the drapery about shoulders, elbows, feet, and other portions.

Whereas Duccio and Simone Martini intensified the emotions of their characters, Giotto's presentations are almost invariably serene and controlled. This is admirably demonstrated by Giotto's series on the life of the Virgin, in the Arena Chapel at Padua. One of its most touching portions is the *Joachim and Anna at the Beautiful Gate* (fig. 306). Here the future parents of the Virgin, a middle-aged and hitherto childless couple, meet again after long separation. He among the flocks on the fields, she at home have both been favored by an angelic visitation foretelling the birth of a child. Avoiding the obvious melodramatic possibilities of such a situation, Giotto in his typical restrained but effective dramatic fashion has them touch one another gently, almost unbelievingly, understating instead of underlining the emotions. His eminent contemporary, the Florentine poet, Dante, also portrayed noble and dignified personages while never forgetting their humanity.

In this sense, Giotto in the fourteenth century took a great step along the humanistic path first indicated by the French Gothic sculptors of the thirteenth century. The combination of worldly and spiritual qualities which was characteristic of that earlier period is also evident in this early fourteenth-century Italian art, which is nothing if not religious in spirit, however much it bespeaks the reemergence of the individual. In northern Europe the new viewpoint was embodied primarily in sculpture; Italy, because of its continuing basilican broad-walled tradition, could project

Fig. 305. Giotto: Death of St. Francis. Florence, Church of Santa Croce.

it in murals. These wall paintings and such elaborate altarpieces as Giotto's *Madonna and Child Enthroned with Angels* (fig. 307) make clear the native Italian tendency toward monumentalism and generalized form that revived at the first opportunity. Such works measure the distance from the still-Byzantine treatment of the same theme by Duccio and Cimabue only a generation earlier.

The resurrected indigenous qualities of monumental form, powerful restraint, and humanistic characterization lost their early fourteenth-century impetus, however, during the troubles of the latter part of the century. The failure of important Florentine banks (the Peruzzi and Bardi, patrons of Giotto in the Santa Croce murals) in 1343–1344 was followed by a famine and the famous Black Death in 1347–1348. A war

Fig. 306. Giotto: Joachim and Anna at the Beautiful Gate. Padua, Arena Chapel.

342

Fig. 307. Giotto: Madonna and
Child Enthroned with Angels.
Florence, Uffizi Gallery.

with Milan, conflicts with the papacy, and finally the revolt of the poor
workmen (*ciompi*) in 1378 ended a long series of calamities. In the following half century of oligarchic domination of Florentine politics (1382–
1432), Italian art and civilization were to take their second step forward
in the period commonly known as the Renaissance.

15 / THE DECLINE OF FEUDALISM: *Fifteenth-century Flanders*

BY the fourteenth century, European commerce had once again reached the high level of Roman times. A marked increase of town life occurred in three major areas — northern Italy, southern Germany, and the Netherlands, or Low Countries (now Belgium and Holland) — each near an important trade route. While it was not comparable to modern population shifts, this fourteenth-century change from country to city life hastened the doom of the feudal system.

Between 1300 and 1500, also, royal authority was centralized, weakening feudalism perceptibly — almost causing it to vanish in France and England. The social position and economic power of the aristocracy, however, remained influential factors for a long time; serfdom and feudal land tenure survived for centuries, even in countries where the middle class became important. Where there was relatively little centralization, as in Germany and Italy, some features of feudalism continued for varying long periods. On a cultural and aesthetic level, this era retained many aristocratic elements in such forms of expression as the fourteenth-century ivory plaques with chivalric subjects and the International Gothic painting style which lasted into fifteenth-century Germany, Italy, Spain, and Flanders (roughly, modern Belgium).

The decline of the manorial system with its autonomous agricultural units was as important as the rise of the towns in weakening feudalism. In the expanded individualism of the new era, the peasant tended to move up from the serf class to become a freeholder or town worker. But in the cities themselves the communal guild system was gradually replaced by a more capitalistic conception, for all journeymen could not aspire to be masters, and most of them would have to work for someone else.

The authority of the Church was severely challenged in the fourteenth and fifteenth centuries and its power reduced in many directions, although it remained a strong moral and even temporal force. The heretical movements were symptomatic of its troubles — e.g., the Lollards under Wycliffe in England and the Hussites in Bohemia. The "Babylonian captivity" of the Church at Avignon in southern France (1305–1377) was followed by the great schism of 1378–1417 with its rival papacies; a series of councils between 1409 and 1449 tried to restore Church unity and abolish corruption. Torn by internal dissension and seriously questioned on matters of dogma and practice, the Church was approaching the crisis of the early sixteenth century: the Protestant revolt. In the face of a rising spirit of nationalism, a growing and independent burgher class, decline of the manorial system, and a generally more fluid and individualistic society, the theocracy of the Middle Ages was bound to be affected adversely.

Nevertheless, although the temporal power of the Church was lessened, religion still played a significant role in everyday life and in the art of this transitional period, however altered by the more worldly temper of the times. This worldliness, as it appeared in the miniatures, panel paintings, and sculpture of the fourteenth and fifteenth centuries, stemmed from two sources: the elegant court life of such centers as Paris, Dijon (the Burgundian capital), and Bourges (seat of the Duc de Berri); and a more down-to-earth naturalism developed in the commercial centers of the Low Countries.

RISE OF FLANDERS. It has already been apparent that French Gothic sculpture in the early fourteenth century, e.g., the *Virgin of Paris* (ca. 1320, fig. 289), had certain artificial and mannered qualities — a linear swing and elegance comparable to the courtly painting style of Simone Martini, who had worked at Avignon's papal court. This decorative tendency was now accompanied by a more naturalistic bourgeois quality deriving from the growing strength of the burgher class and receiving strong support from the great prosperity and development of Flemish trade. Flanders, having become independent of France in 1305, carried on extensive commerce with England and Germany. It reached a relatively high state of democracy at an early point and, enjoying the fruits of its trade boom, turned toward greater naturalism of expression during the fourteenth century.

In France the original impetus of thirteenth-century Gothic was lost in the course of the fourteenth century, when building and other important projects were hindered by the dragging Hundred Years' War with England (1337–1453). The Flemish provinces were taken over by the Dukes of Burgundy during 1369–1430. Flemish artists were brought to the courts of Paris and Burgundy (Dijon), and a Franco-Flemish style in sculpture (ca. 1370–1420) existed parallel with an International Gothic style in painting, also produced by this fusion. In this way the last flowering of French (and Burgundian) medieval art became the first step in the development of Flemish art.

Profiting from an advantageous geographical location and French political troubles, Flanders was to become a dominant influence during the fifteenth century. Its infusion into the art of France and Burgundy would ultimately return to the Flemish source as the luxurious naturalism and decorative splendor that were to mark fifteenth-century style in Flanders.

FRANCO-FLEMISH SCULPTURE. Transported to France, the new realism resulted in a series of individualized portrait sculptures, simple and serious, such as *Charles V and Jeanne de Bourbon* (Louvre, ca. 1370 — an earlier version, 1360, is on the Palace of Justice at Poitiers). Typifying the fourteenth-century development of portrait art, these figures provide an instance of the new naturalism and space interest, since they show both the old age of the sitters and the increasingly popular broad pictorial

Fig. 308. Claus Sluter: The Well of Moses (detail: Moses). Dijon, Chartreuse de Champmol.

346

drapery and solid form. The most famous example of the Franco-Flemish style is the so-called *Well of Moses* (fig. 308) of the former Carthusian monastery at Champmol, near Dijon. Its rich voluminous drapery and naturalism are characteristic of this school, which was in turn to affect Flemish painting, e.g., the van Eycks, Robert Campin, and many others. There is nothing vulgar or commonplace about the approach of these sculptors — Claus Sluter and his assistant Claus de Werwe; figures like the celebrated *Moses* embody a profundity and dignity unmatched at this point except in the contemporary early works of Donatello in Italy. These individual pieces of sculpture — the portraits of Charles V and his wife, and the *Well* (originally the base of an elaborate Calvary) — represent a distinct break with the predominantly architectural Gothic tradition and thereby reflect something of the lessened temporal significance of the Church.

INTERNATIONAL GOTHIC STYLE IN PAINTING. The painting of the late fourteenth century brought a parallel international phenomenon combining Italian — mainly Sienese — decorativeness (introduced to France by Simone Martini); the linealism of French Gothic manuscripts — e.g., the *Pontifical of Metz* (fig. 291); and the naturalism of the Flemish school, chiefly shown through an interest in nature, especially landscape. Although it was fabricated in France (Paris, Dijon, and Bourges), the style became sufficiently widespread to justify calling it International Gothic. Spain produced such outstanding examples as the fairy-tale-like *St. George and the Dragon* by Bernardo Martorel (ca. 1430, fig. 309). The lovely princess is draped in a Gothically swinging robe; the earnest, handsome saint and his horse, lance, and dragon are arranged two-dimensionally before a vertical landscape. This landscape is portrayed with coloristic charm and with that love of naturalistic detail so characteristic of the late Gothic. These qualities are universal, varying in terms of the backgrounds of different European countries in the early fifteenth century. They may also be found in the sweetly sentimental German *Paradise Garden* (Frankfurt), the analogous delicacy of Fra Angelico's early works (see fig. 330), or the paintings of Gentile da Fabriano with their rich decorativeness and linear rhythms.

In the Franco-Flemish territory proper, the *Très riches heures du Duc de Berri* (1411–1416, fig. 310) is one of the high points of the International Gothic style. It is a Book of the Hours of the Virgin, illustrated with activities appropriate to the various months. Evoking the richness and luxury of the court environment that sponsored it, this eminently worldly and unmystical devotional work sums up the transitional nature of the age. On the presumably religious foundation of a prayer

Fig. 309. Martorel: St. George and the Dragon. Courtesy, Art Institute of Chicago.

book, the artists have presented a series of everyday scenes — courtly processions and banquets of the nobles as well as peasant activities such as sowing, ploughing, and wood gathering. Even though the peasant activities demand more naturalism than the court scenes, both still retain a high degree of late Gothic elegance. The changing character of the period is indicated further by the fact that these manuscript pages could actually be panel paintings; they are waiting, as it were, to move from the pages of the book to the surface of a wooden panel.

FLEMISH PAINTING. If French Gothic sculpture had been the pre-eminent mode of thirteenth-century expression and Italian painting styles like those of Giotto and Simone Martini had dominated the fourteenth century, then in the next period supremacy was shared between Flemish painting of the fifteenth century and the burgeoning art of Italy. Returning from France to Burgundy and Flanders, the courtly naturalistic elegance of the Franco-Flemish style found a new home among the rich, powerful merchants of the Low Countries. Here, in response to highly developed materialism, evolved an art that combined the spirituality of the Middle Ages (still a weighty factor), the pageantry of court life, and the factuality demanded by the self-important burgher class.

Religious works still predominated, although now set in vivid naturalistic landscapes or vibrating atmospheric interiors. Portraits became more frequent, both as secular objects of social value and as "donor portraits" in which the patron appeared with Christ, the Virgin, or the saints. Objects of everyday use figured increasingly in the paintings; shown with all the beauty and material quality of perfectly realized still life, they were often used to symbolize — in a still medieval fashion — some aspects of religious truth as well. In this "transfigured symbolism" a bottle of clear water or a new spool of thread, for example, had a double function as ordinary still life in a photographically detailed interior and as a symbol of the purity of the Virgin. The Flemish painter of the fifteenth century may be said to have brought the heavenly element down to a mundane level and, at the same time, to have raised the everyday fact to a rarefied and symbolic plane. In such ways the continuing powerful spirituality of the late Middle Ages was accommodated to the character of a more worldly era.

Stylistically, Flemish painting of the early fifteenth century shows strong links to Franco-Flemish sculptures such as the *Well of Moses* (fig. 308), where a feeling of space resulted from broad draperies worked out in effective light-and-dark areas and naturalism was emphasized by the tactile, or touch, quality of cloth, hair, and other matter. The paintings of Jan van Eyck, for example (see figs. 313–314), have similar broad flowing draperies whose lights and darks achieve the same sense of occupying space. Just as sculptures like the *Well of Moses* approach the quality of paintings, some of the paintings show an intense desire for sculpturesqueness. The paintings often use figures placed in niches,

Fig. 310. Pol de Limbourg: *Très riches heures du Duc de Berri* (detail: February page). Chantilly, Musée Condé.

as though on the face of a cathedral, and may even be done in monochrome to further that effect. The Roger van der Weyden *Deposition* (see fig. 315) goes so far as to simulate the appearance of a late medieval wooden altarpiece.

Yet Jan van Eyck (1385–1441) and Roger van der Weyden (1400–1464) — however much they shared a predilection for sculptural effect and transfigured symbolism (Jan apparently influenced Roger in this regard) — represent two distinct stylistic trends in the Flemish painting of their century.

Jan van Eyck. The celebrated *Ghent Altarpiece* (fig. 311), begun by Jan van Eyck's older brother Hubert (d. 1426) and finished by Jan in 1432, demonstrates many of the general Flemish qualities. Its courtly figures in the upper panels of the opened altarpiece — the elegant choristers, the queenly Madonna, and the regal God — reflect the upper-class milieu of the Dukes of Burgundy, who were residing at Bruges in Flanders. Its insistence on naturalistic detail shows the more bourgeois side of this culture. The sculpturesque monumentality of the figures, their broad light-and-dark draperies, recall the forms of Claus Sluter in the *Well of Moses*. At the extreme ends of this series of upper panels, the figures of Adam and Eve are set into niches like sculpture but are treated with a particular, almost microscopic detail that reveals the skin texture, hairs, and other features in a merciless studio light. Directly above these two niche figures are little monochrome sculpturelike panels of the *Sacrifices of Cain and Abel* and *Cain Slaying Abel.*

The lower section of the opened altarpiece (fig. 312) displays the *Adoration of the Lamb* (from which its usual name, the *Altarpiece of the Lamb*), an apocalyptic vision of the Lamb on an altar surrounded by angels and symbols of the Passion. From the four corners of the earth — a beautiful idyllic conception of nature — come the various saintly and pious groups: just judges, knights of Christ, hermit saints, and pilgrims, to pay their respects to the symbol of Christ's suffering, a sacrifice necessitated by the original sin of Adam and Eve above. The elegance and miniature quality of the *Adoration* are reminiscent of illuminated manuscripts such as the *Très riches heures* (fig. 310) in the Franco-Flemish tradition which, together with the pictorial sculpture of Claus Sluter and his school, forms the basis for much of Flemish painting in this era.

The enamel-like finish on works of the Flemish school is the result of the use of oil-mixed paints, which were added to the traditional tempera technique that was still the base of pictures like this. Aside from their effect on the rendering of atmospheric landscapes and interiors, the oil paints unquestionably contributed to the luminosity of the robes of the Madonna, Christ, and choristers (especially their reds and blues,

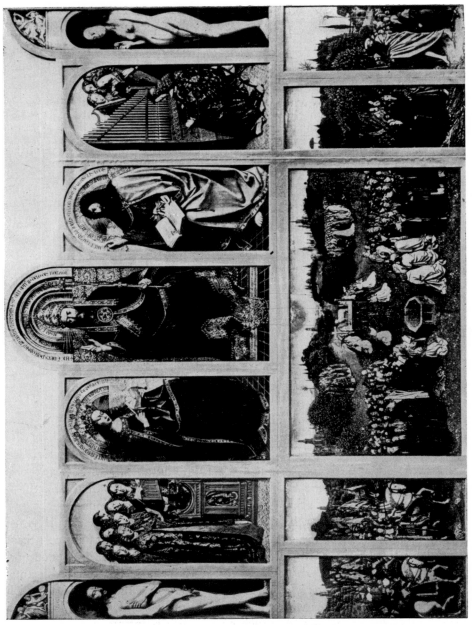

Fig. 311. Jan and Hubert van Eyck: The Ghent Altarpiece. Ghent, Cathedral of St. Bavo.

Fig. 312. Jan and Hubert van Eyck: The Ghent Altarpiece (lower center panel: Adoration of the Lamb).

Fig. 313. Jan van Eyck: The Arnolfini Marriage. London, National Gallery.

which glow with the intensity of stained glass) and the almost magical realism of the still life.

Jan van Eyck's *The Arnolfini Marriage* (fig. 313) is a symbolic betrothal scene between Giovanni Arnolfini, an Italian banker, resident in Flanders, and a local young lady. The characteristic atmospheric quality fills the air, pulsating with a warm light which flows into the room and joins interior and exterior in a way that foreshadows future Netherlandish painting (see fig. 429). In solemn hieratic fashion the two figures stand hand in hand, the man with a gesture of affirmation, or oath taking, as the solemn vow is made. This public avowal witnessed by the artist, who inscribed his name on the rear wall above the convex mirror in a Latin inscription translated: "Jan van Eyck was here," has all the seriousness and dignity of a religious portrayal. Van Eyck has typically presented a multitude of naturalistic details which, however, do not interfere with the unity of the work as a whole. This unity is accomplished by the dominance of the figures with their sculpturesque draperies and the palpable, almost vibrating atmosphere that envelops everything in the picture.

Symbolically, the bed in the corner of the room, like those used by Flemish masters in Annunciation scenes, has a broader significance beyond that of an object. The lighted candle in the chandelier, burning in broad daylight, refers to the presence of God (cf. Hebrew theology) and is often used in Annunciation and other religious scenes that require his implied presence. Thus too in a scene on the outside of the *Ghent Altarpiece*, a niche near the kneeling Madonna contains another such candlestick, while at her left there is a washstand with a shiny water basin, a ewer, and a spotless towel, all symbolizing her purity. These are commonplace items, and in later art they are merely that and nothing else; here, however, at the end of the Middle Ages, their function in a sacred moment gives them a special "transfigured" meaning.

The Madonna of Chancellor Rolin (fig. 314) by Jan van Eyck compounds an interior and exterior atmosphere seen as one continuous light vibration. In addition, it combines human and divine representation, so

Fig. 314. Jan van Eyck: The Madonna of Chancellor Rolin. Paris, Louvre.

common in this art and bequeathed to German, Spanish, and French art of the later fifteenth century. Flemish portraiture, judging from such examples, is serious in the same sense as the earlier cathedral sculptures; it is naturalistic to the level of ugliness but profoundly psychological at the same time, thereby showing the degree of humanistic interest which this era produced in Flanders as elsewhere.

Space representation, one of the chief preoccupations of Flemish artists, is achieved through the amplitude of the broadly draped forms and through the amalgamation of those forms with the atmospheric depth of the picture. An effect of movement into space is given by converging floor lines (linear perspective) and by aerial perspective in the background, whereby distant objects diminish in intensity of color (as well as in size). But pictures like this and the *Adoration* show a dogmatic rather than scientifically naturalistic linear perspective. Unlike the contemporary Italians who directed all lines to a single vanishing point on the horizon, the Flemish painter set up an imaginary vertical axis in the middle of his picture, toward which various pairs of lines came from the sides, to converge at points ranging from top to bottom of this vertical. By this method the Flemish artist exercised his own pictorial control; the composition, however, tends to tilt toward the spectator because it is viewed or scanned up and down, thus bringing the top further forward than in an Italian picture, which carries the eye back and inward to a single point.

Roger van der Weyden. Van Eyck's broad sculpturesque draperies, his atmospheric interest, piling up of detail on detail, and fusion of figures with atmosphere represent one stream of Flemish fifteenth-century style. Another distinct expression is found in the more precisely designed and linear paintings of Roger van der Weyden, with their emphasis on the movement of figures (lively or graceful) and their emotional intensity. The general tightness of Roger's style is revealed in the well-known *Deposition* (fig. 315), an almost musically composed work in which specific rhythms are repeated from one part of the picture to the other. Keeping in mind the idea of a group of carved figures set along the surface of a sculptured altarpiece, Roger defined the outer edges of the composition with two "S"-shaped forms: St. John at the left and the Magdalene at the right, the latter twisting her hands in the traditional gesture of sorrow. John supports the fainting Virgin, whose body repeats the posture of Christ's body descending from the Cross, one arm raised like his, the other moving downward in the same way. Further balance, though deliberately asymmetrical for the sake of surface movement, is supplied by the pairs of figures at right and left standing upright and the pair in the center behind the Christ.

356

Where van Eyck would have emphasized the breadth of drapery for spatial purposes, van der Weyden gives the draperies a nervous, linear, moving quality that complements the anguish and dramatic character of the personages. His style remains graphic rather than pictorial, which is one of the reasons it had such influence in those countries where the woodcut and engraving were later to flourish. Dürer, for example, was influenced by Roger's style more than half a century afterward, when he visited Bruges. What is more, the dramatics of such pictures — the weeping Mary at the left, the gesture of the Magdalene at the right, the swooning Virgin, the tense John — were bound to appeal to the period immediately preceding the Reformation of the early sixteenth century.

Other works by van der Weyden, although not nearly so dramatic as the *Deposition,* retain his neo-Gothic linealism and become more refined and ascetic, such as the famous portraits with their sensitive linear elegance, e.g., *Lionello d'Este.* Unlike Jan van Eyck's highly personal and therefore nearly inimitable manner, Roger's style had a wide following. Most Netherlandish artists of the second half of the century, as well

Fig. 315. Roger van der Weyden: Deposition. Madrid, Prado.

Fig. 316. Memling: Shrine of St. Ursula (detail: Madonna and Child). Bruges, Hospital of St. John.

as some Germans (e.g., Dürer and Martin Schongauer), French, and even Italians (e.g., Cosimo Tura), show some of his influence.

Hans Memling. Hans Memling (ca. 1435–1494), who may have worked in Roger's workshop around 1460, has little of the creative originality of either van Eyck or van der Weyden. Living artistically on the aesthetic ideas of the latter master, he added the simplicity and sweetness of his own nature to produce an essentially spacious and balanced art. In a very limited sense, he gives the impression of having combined Roger's linear elegance with the aerial depth of the van Eyck tradition. The *Madonna and Child* (fig. 316), from the famous St. Ursula shrine at St. John's Hospital in Bruges, shows Memling's characteristic refinement of drawing and serenity of expression, exemplified elsewhere in his numerous Madonnas. In the field of portraiture, *Martin Nieuwenhowen* (same collection) shows that gentleman in prayer before the Virgin, who is represented in a separate panel. Memling usually placed his sitter against a wall and often in the corner of a room, a device followed by later artists like Dürer in Germany.

Hugo van der Goes. The almost psychotic Hugo van der Goes (ca. 1435–1482) is one of the most interesting and problematic personalities of this school. Beginning under the influence of the aristocratic van der

Weyden style and its abstract linearism, he attempted to synthesize this frontal tight manner with van Eyck's broad spaciousness and infinite heaping on of detail. This task was clearly impossible to accomplish, except in the simple naïve way of Memling, and it tended to aggravate Hugo's already evident melancholy. In trying to reconcile linear exactitude with pictorial breadth, abstract generalities of form with minutiae of fact, the painter was in a difficult position — as he was through being the middle-class head of the painter's guild at Ghent and at the same time an unusual personality, perhaps even a genius. He retired to a monastery in 1475, his increased melancholia manifested in the terrifying and shrill paintings of his last few years.

Hugo's best-known work, stemming from an earlier period, is the *Portinari Altarpiece* (ca. 1473–1475, fig. 317), brought to Florence by its purchaser before 1485. The combination of large impressive forms (agreeable to the Italian temperament) with brilliant transparent color,

Fig. 317. Van der Goes: Portinari Altarpiece. Florence, Uffizi Gallery.

sensitive drawing, vivid sense of reality, and his own special brand of neurotic feeling gave this painting considerable influence. The ugly shepherds at the right turn up again in many Italian works of the end of the century, e.g., the Ghirlandajo *Adoration* (see fig. 341). It is not without significance that for the Italians one attraction of Flemish painting was its intense and traditional religious feeling, a quality that Italian art with its classical interests had begun to lose by the end of the fifteenth century.

JEROME BOSCH. That century also produced a number of Dutch painters in the Netherlands. One group included Dirk Bouts, Geertgen tot Sint Jans, and possibly van der Goes, who were part of the Flemish development by training; in another group were such masters as Jerome Bosch, who followed a more native and popular tradition. Bosch (ca. 1460–1516) presented a curious contrast to the thinking of the average Netherlandish painter who was absorbed by the problem of relating the earthly and the divine, raising or lowering each to bring them closer together and to effect a synthesis of new and old. Bosch, however, was more concerned with relating the real to the fantastic and the fantastic to the real. In his work phantasms are real, while reality becomes a mere phantom. Only an artist with a highly developed sense of reality could have made his improbable combinations of imaginary and everyday forms withstand the pressure of absurd and impossible appearance. Utilizing the atmospheric developments of his century, his backgrounds give as great an impression of actuality as the real-unreal figures.

Although some of his technical devices (verticalized perspective, old-fashioned costume) are deliberately archaistic to exaggerate the bizarre element, Bosch's manner of painting is generally loose and transparent, almost modern in feeling. This modernity is more evident in the content of his work, where he reveals himself as an amoral moralist, an irreligious theologian. Here at the close of the Middle Ages, the doctrine of the inherent goodness of man and nature — turned toward sin and degeneration by the Devil and helped by divine intervention — received a rude jolt. This period generally took sin less seriously than before, regarding it more in the light of foolishness, however Devil-inspired, which in the Renaissance would be counteracted not by Divine Grace but by Divine Reason. But Bosch, who chronologically at least stands between one age and the next, seems to deny both God and Reason, looking at the world as a domain of phantoms, making no distinction between actuality and imagination, between fact and hallucination. This may help explain his great appeal for twentieth-century Surrealists (see fig. 529), who are also interested in a simultaneous presentation of the real and the unreal with a very clear and heightened reality.

Bosch's *Temptation of St. Anthony* (fig. 318), typical of the phantasms he conjured up, indicates that in his view sin and temptation were not nearly so serious as they may have seemed in the early Middle Ages.

Fig. 318. Jerome Bosch: Temptation of St. Anthony. Lisbon, National Museum.

His monsters, combinations of human, animal, bird, and even imaginary components, are painted with an intense matter-of-factness that is most convincing. The border line between dream and reality, good and evil, living things and inanimate objects is thereby eliminated. Although Bosch did not live to see the Reformation, his art is a strong and critical affirmation of individuality. His monsters are a far cry from the demonic and frightening things of the Romanesque churches, which had already changed to half-humorous and fanciful conceptions on the Gothic cathedrals and manuscripts. With Bosch (and later with Bruegel in the sixteenth century) the satiric creatures of the Gothic period become philosophic and social symbols, criticisms of the age in which the artist lived, vehicles for a personal and meaningful statement. The haunted world of St. Anthony is meant to be that of each and every human being; man appears eternally restless and his folly incurable.

16 / THE RISE OF HUMANISM:

Fifteenth-century Italy

THE tide of worldliness had reached late medieval Italian art, like that of northern Europe, through the rising importance of the towns. Although the art of fourteenth-century Italy was still primarily medieval in feeling, it already showed a development of individuality in terms of the artist as a personality and from the standpoint of subject treatment. Even in the thirteenth century there had been a great humanizing factor in religion: the Franciscan movement, which emphasized the potentially close relationship between man and God. The effect of this force emerged in the art of Giotto, Cimabue, and other artists of the early fourteenth century whose work stressed a human quality for the personages of religious history (e.g., *Joachim and Anna*, fig. 306), unlike the more symbolic medieval treatment.

At the same time that artists presented a new outlook on religious matters, the painters and sculptors themselves came into the light of day as human beings in their own right. All through the thirteenth century, when Italy produced a school of painting in contrast to the prolific French sculptures of the time, the names of separate artists, climaxed by Cimabue and Giotto, are known to us and are connected with personality quirks and anecdotes. During this same period in France, on the other hand, we associate sculptors' workshops with particular cities as groups rather than individuals.

GROWTH OF ITALIAN CITIES. The sense of individual worth and enterprise, what the Italians called *virtù*, was related to the fact that the independent town had appeared earlier in Italy than in the north of Europe. The early existence of towns in northern Italy had initially been made possible by the influence of the Byzantine Empire in that area; the struggles between Byzantium and the Lombards gave the Italians (especially in coastal cities) an opportunity to expand on their own. The anarchy that followed the death of Charlemagne, the conflicts over lay investiture in the eleventh century, dissension within the Church, the struggles between pope and emperor for control of Italy, all made for greater freedom for the cities. As we observed, one of the most important factors in their expansion was the growth of trade opportunities, which stemmed first from the shipping and supply role of Italian cities during the Crusades and then from the early evolution of banking in Italy. The latter development was a result, at least in part, of the papal desire to use Christians in that role instead of Jews or Levantines. As early as the thirteenth and fourteenth centuries, Florentine and Sienese banks established branches in the Low Countries.

From Carolingian to modern times, there was no strong central government in Italy. This resulted on one hand in the later survival of certain medievalisms, while on the other hand the towns and cities acquired a degree of independence that was unparalleled elsewhere. By the early twelfth century, the bishops who had ruled the towns were deposed by communes which included resident nobles as well as tradesmen. It had already become possible to enter the nobility through commercially acquired wealth; and since birth and landed estates were no longer prerequisites for a coat of arms, Italy tended to develop a bourgeois aristocracy. Moreover, the Italian communes augmented this trend by restricting membership to the founding families and their descendants — only the richer merchants and artisans represented their class in government. This middle-class aristocracy in Italy was best exemplified by the Medici banking family of Florence which, in addition to its economic and political power, was also the great intellectual arbiter and patron of the fifteenth century.

Rivalries between the communes produced wars of trade or boundaries. The nobles who had been forced by the triumph of the burghers to become town residents built fortified castles inside the city walls and carried on their earlier feudal battles. Those nobles who had maintained their old castles outside preyed upon the cities. Within the towns, new guilds and workers clamored for admission to citizenship, adding to the dynamics of the situation.

IMPORTANCE OF INDIVIDUALISM. On every side and from every class of Italian society, the impulse toward the assertion of individuality grew stronger, crystallized in the ideal of *virtù*, of personal achievement in both thought and action. This urge became part of the rise of town life and the increasing dominance of the upper burgher groups who were important patrons of art in the fifteenth century. Politically it assumed the form of local tyrannies; certain families or individuals took forcible control of their communities — which they embellished with buildings, sculpture, and paintings in varying degrees of aristocratic taste. Intellectually, *virtù* encouraged the curiosity and investigation that became increasingly widespread during the fifteenth century. The desire to find out how things worked, to understand the nature of the universe, fostered experimentalists among the painters and sculptors of that century. Perspective, anatomy, mathematics, and other concrete studies were connected with the development of culture during this intellectual ferment.

The artist or writer studied the characteristics of the physical world, and he also studied his own relationship to that world. He was much concerned with problems of the individual (as Giotto and Dante) and his psychology (as Fra Lippo Lippi). Most of all, he was interested in the dignity of the human being. Where the Flemish painter of this period stressed the faith, mysticism, religiosity, and naturalism of man and his world, the Italian artist became increasingly occupied with a more abstract and generalized symbol of humanity: the human being as an ennobled creature in whom were epitomized the best characteristics of the race. The Flemish artist might pile up details for a compendium of fact, but the Italian absorbed these particulars in the course of his investigations and came forth with a summation of man or woman in which details were consciously subordinated to the monumental whole.

CLASSICAL INFLUENCE; SECULARISM. This monumentality was reminiscent of the sculpturesque forms of ancient, Early Christian, and Romanesque times which now strongly influenced Italian art; not only did it give this art its special form and character, but it also underlined the feeling for human dignity that grew stronger as time went on. The artists of Italy turned ever more toward classical borrowings which could help them express that ideal. In this classical land, so much ancient material was ready at hand, waiting to be used.

From about 1400 on, in Italy, these artistic tendencies accompanied the predominant philosophy of humanism in which classical education played a leading role, stressing as it did a secular approach, individuality, and the cult of beauty. The great interest in the classics interacted with the increased secularity of the age, each tending to strengthen the other. In this period when allegiance to the Church became formal instead of actual, men of culture eagerly welcomed those ancient writers in whom they found a similar viewpoint and social attitude. This attitude, it should be remarked, inclined toward the aristocratic rather than the democratic, toward the development of great individuals rather than great communities or classes, here again differentiating the Italian from his northern colleagues.

From evidence of the Gothic period, it would appear that some interest in the classics had existed long before the fifteenth century, e.g., in the cathedral schools of twelfth- and thirteenth-century France. The classical viewpoint in the plastic arts had been anticipated in the twelfth-century kingdom of Frederick of Naples and in the "classical" sculptures at Reims and Pisa (Niccolò Pisano) in the thirteenth century. These interests were broadened during the fourteenth century by artists like Giotto and writers like Petrarch; they reached their climax in fifteenth-century architecture, sculpture, painting, and literature. Classical artistic influence came from Roman or Roman-transmitted Greek sources, since the original Greek architecture and art were not known until the eighteenth century.

The study of ancient learning, however, had little to do with the development of scientific curiosity, which had been engendered in the later Middle Ages. This widespread inquiry concerning the world now sponsored the evolution of specific techniques and representational devices in sculpture and painting — anatomy, mathematical perspective (i.e., projective geometry), aerial perspective, and the like.

HUMANISM. Humanism helped bring forth an aesthetic attitude in which the contemplation of beauty was believed to offer a taste of beyond-earthly experience. In this so-called Renaissance, or rebirth, of classical ideas, an interest in humanity and love of beauty became substitutes for the supernatural beliefs of the Middle Ages. Classical, especially Greek, philosophy advanced the idea of living well on earth instead of waiting for salvation in the hereafter. Although this represented an important step away from medievalism, a great many humanists attempted to reconcile Christian and pagan thinking. This conservative process together with humanistic reverence for the past put the ideology of that day midway between the Middle Ages and modern times. Its chief attribute was the secular and individual viewpoint — an interest in the world of man but not an actual scientific approach.

It was essentially a transitional period. The newly developed individualism, unsuited to the collective thinking of the Middle Ages and without the future anchor of scientific fact, used vehicles of artistic expression. Poetry and art were considered devices of world understanding; in these media it was possible to absorb the multifarious phenomena of which man had just become aware and which were not yet subject to systematized categories. It was no accident that the greatest scientist of the fifteenth century was the painter Leonardo da Vinci, nor that the interest in such things as anatomy and mathematics went hand in hand with the development of sculpture and architecture.

Stylistically, whereas the Flemish bourgeois of the fifteenth century dressed his art in the courtly splendor of magnificently colored accessories which represented his aspirations, the Italian of this period moved toward an elegance derived from the dignity of classical models. For the middle class, these had all the appeal of tradition and respectability that modern men of affairs have found in them; for the "tyrants" or usurpers of the fifteenth and sixteenth centuries, classical forms lent stature and genuineness to their pretensions. These tyrants completely undermined the democratic tradition in Italy — an inevitable result of the anarchy and internecine warfare of the thirteenth and fourteenth centuries — yet they were important art patrons, since they sponsored all sorts of buildings, sculpture, and paintings to preserve their own fame and to aid genius.

ARCHITECTURE: *Brunelleschi.* The imitation of classical prototypes appeared in its most obvious and even mechanical aspect in architecture, where elements of ancient decoration emerged on medieval structures like assumed speech mannerisms. Such ornaments might be quite charming, but they had little to do with the original function of pediments, cornices, or pilasters, which were now generally applied for their decorative rather than functional possibilities, as in many buildings of our own era. Most of the architecture we see in cities like Florence, however, was the product of the medieval period, of late Romanesque or Gothic style, as in one of its most famous examples, the *Cathedral of Florence* (fig. 319). This impressive building, which still dominates the Florentine skyline, was begun at the very end of the thirteenth century and in the Tuscan Gothic

Fig. 319. Cathedral of Florence.

style with generous use of colored marble and superficial application of pointed Gothic arches. It was designed by Arnolfo di Cambio, who is also responsible for Florence's fortresslike Palazzo Vecchio. The *Cathedral* was finished in the early part of the fifteenth century by the distinguished sculptor-architect Filippo Brunelleschi (1377–1446), who created its soaring dome.

Although Brunelleschi spent a number of years in Rome studying ancient ruins in accordance with the vogue of that time, his dome is far

Fig. 320. Brunelleschi: The Pazzi Chapel, Cloister of Santa Croce, Florence.

more the result of medieval ideas than of antiquity. Compared with the broad squat roof of the *Pantheon* (fig. 133) or *Hagia Sophia* (fig. 197) whose height is apparent only from the interior, the dome of the *Cathedral of Florence* mounts majestically to 180 feet above the building's floor, creating its effect both internally and externally. In actual shape it is related to the domes over the crossings of such Romanesque churches as Pisa (fig. 238) or Angoulême (fig. 229). But this individualistic fifteenth-century architect, who refused to submit his plans to the building committee of the cathedral, also refused to abide by the earlier idea that the form of a building should relate to the structural method by which it was erected. Whereas in Gothic architecture there was always an awareness of the close harmony of form and structure, of vault and buttress, this newer dome rises much higher than anyone dared to build before and is supported by devices invisible to the spectator. In the masonry drum at the base of the dome, the architect buried girdles of timber and stone that hold the structure together at that point without sacrificing external appearance as the builders of the *Pantheon* and *Hagia Sophia* had been forced to do. This subordination of structural elements to visual appearance is characteristic of Renaissance architecture and is typical of most architecture since that time down to the modern period, which finally recovers the unity between form and function.

The use of classical ornament is revealed in Brunelleschi's treatment of the façade of the family *Pazzi Chapel* in the Church of Santa Croce (fig. 320). Here a wealth of Roman detail is applied to the surface of a masking wall placed before a Gothic dome on pendentives. This wall has the general outline of an arch of triumph set on Corinthian columns and broken architraves. Inside as well as outside, the architect utilized classical pilasters and other elements, both for their decorative two-dimensional effect and as devices for the delicate division of space, like his vault forms. He was mainly concerned with achieving a rhythmical relationship between linear and curved lines or between one open area and another. The sense of dynamism, of revealed function, does not exist here any more than in the dome of the *Cathedral*.

This feeling for abstract decorative design appears also in Brunelleschi's plans for churches such as the well-known San Lorenzo in Florence. On the traditional Early Christian basilica form he has grafted another series of cool restrained classical elements, such as the round arches of the interior that are made to descend on sections of ancient entablature. The monochromatic character of this building, like that of the *Pazzi Chapel* façade, and their common simplicity of effect stand in strong contrast to the coloristic richness and relative exuberance of the Tuscan Gothic style.

Michelozzo. Although Brunelleschi also designed palace buildings, it was Michelozzo Michelozzi (1396–1472) who produced the most typical example of this form. His well-known *Medici-Riccardi Palace*

Fig. 321. Michelozzo: Medici-Riccardi Palace, Florence.

(fig. 321) has the characteristic square plan around a courtyard like the medieval Italian palace. Through this open interior space one moves from room to room, and from here too light is admitted. Externally the *palazzo* shows its division into three stories, the bottom one finished in deliberately rough stone, the second in a smoother-textured surface (both with the joints showing, or "rusticated"), and the final story finished off smoothly. All three were originally equipped with windows consisting of paired round arches on colonnettes, deriving from medieval architecture.

The building is specifically classical in its general horizontality of effect, its cornice, and incidental details such as those on the colonnettes. Although the initial impression is one of ruggedness, in keeping with the tradition of the *palazzo* as an armed fortress — a style made popular by the warring nobility — the delicate sense of proportion and transition, the gracefulness of the windows and bands of Roman moldings that separate the floors, give this structure a new feeling.

Alberti. While Brunelleschi's adaptations of earlier ideas, medieval or classical, had shown a certain freshness owing to their very unlearned and even awkward quality, a distinctly altered attitude appeared in the second half of the century and the period following. As knowledge of the past increased, the tendency grew to utilize the vocabulary of classical art in a somewhat academic and conventional manner. This more learned approach is exemplified by Leone Battista Alberti (1404–1472), a distinguished Florentine humanist, scholar, and writer on architecture. In the work of such men it is often possible to see the direct source of derivation not merely of an element or an order of architecture but of the entire structural type. Alberti's still rusticated *Rucellai Palace* in Florence (fig. 322) uses the superposed orders of architecture of the Roman *Colosseum* (fig. 132). They are applied here with a studious grace and charm that suggest Brunelleschi's method on the façade of the *Pazzi Chapel*, but in a much more scholarly and archaeological fashion; by comparison, Alberti's treatment is academic rather than individualistic. In his Church of Sant' Andrea at Rimini, a somewhat similar system is followed in a full-scale façade adaptation of the Roman arch-of-triumph plan with three arches and engaged columns.

Alberti's treatise *Concerning Architecture* (based on the Roman writer Vitruvius), published in 1486 after his death, disseminated a textbook conception of building that came to dominate Western architecture. Instead of the excitement and freshness, the daring manner of handling elements, that were characteristic of the early fifteenth century, the treatment became increasingly formalized and cold. Similar changes were to occur in sculpture and painting.

Florence, at this time the chief cultural center of Italy, acted as breeding ground for the foremost fifteenth-century painting and sculpture as well as architecture. During the late Middle Ages, Florence had already become politically and economically preeminent in central Italy, over-shadowing such cities as Pisa and Siena, her former rivals. The democ-racy of that earlier age had been seriously compromised since 1382 by the oligarchical rule of a group of burgher families. Then in 1435 they were overthrown by Cosimo dei Medici, who substituted the benevolent despotism of his own clan. This supremacy lasted until the death of Cosimo's grandson Lorenzo the Magnificent in 1492. It was an interval marked by peace and prosperity, symbolized by extensive Medici patron-age of all the arts. One of its results has already been seen in the *Medici-Riccardi Palace.*

SCULPTURE. The painting of fifteenth-century Florence (as of other places in Italy) bore a sequential relationship to its sculpture. As sculp-ture moved forward in its grasp of form and space, so thereafter devel-oped the art of painting. It was almost as though sculptors, in the mount-ing trend toward the mastery of form and space, were able by the very nature of the medium to realize their aims before painters, who had to

Fig. 322. Alberti: Rucellai Palace, Florence.

Fig. 323. Ghiberti: Paradise Gates, Baptistry of the Cathedral of Florence.

devise illusionistic means for picturing a three-dimensional form on a two-dimensional surface. The connection between the two arts could be observed earlier in the precedence of Niccolò Pisano's sculpture before the painting of Giotto in the thirteenth and early fourteenth centuries. Now a group of sculptors led by Lorenzo Ghiberti (1378–1455), Jacopo della Quercia (1371–1438), and Donatello (1386–1466) foreshadowed certain aspects of the Italian school of painting in the fifteenth century. All three sculptors were influenced by the ever more popular art of antiquity, the influence varying considerably with each individual.

Ghiberti. In 1401, Ghiberti's victory in a national competition to design the bronze doors of the baptistry of the *Cathedral of Florence* gave him a lifetime job, while his chief opponent Brunelleschi went on to become the leading architect of the time. (It was not yet an age of specialization.) The first doors, ultimately placed on the southern entrance, were finished in 1423 and won the artist a commission for the second pair. Begun in 1425 and finished in 1447, these world-famous *Paradise Gates* (fig. 323) are on the eastern entrance of the baptistry. Although

Fig. 324. Ghiberti: The Creation. Panel from Paradise Gates, Baptistry of the Cathedral of Florence.

Fig. 325. Della Quercia: The Expulsion from Paradise. Bologna, San Petronio, façade.

Ghiberti changed from the medieval quatrefoil (four-leafed) panel shapes of his first doors, with their Gothically outlined figures reminiscent of Giovanni Pisano's swinging types, the second pair still retains some late medieval elegance. The prescribed subject for the first doors was a theological parallel of Old and New Testament scenes in the best tradition of the Middle Ages. The second doors, in ten square, picturelike frames, tell the story of the Old Testament from the Creation to the meeting of Solomon and the Queen of Sheba. Here, however, the accent is less on symbolism than on setting the Biblical story in a naturalistic environment through the newly evolved spatial devices of the time.

In the skillful aerial perspective of such scenes as the *Creation* (fig. 324) or the story of Abraham (top panel left and second from top at right), by diminishing the height of relief of the various figures, Ghiberti conveys the impression of forms melting into the atmosphere. In addition, in the two middle panels and the one at the bottom right, he achieves a masterly representation of linear perspective, by this means producing a deep spatial effect. Both techniques are worked out within the shallow depth of the eminently pictorial panels that almost ask to be converted into paintings. Basically this is a decorative accomplishment, affected to

374

a limited extent by the somewhat similar character of ancient relief sculpture but exceeding by far its naturalism. Yet the technical approach of the artist is linear rather than three-dimensional, as can be seen in the graceful aristocratic attitudes of many figures that evoke the fourteenth-century Gothic. Other figures set into niches, the medallion heads, the naturalistic floral ornament of the borders, are again echoes of antiquity but are technically in the same spirit as the panels themselves.

Jacopo della Quercia. Individual handling of antique ideas during this period also appears in the magnificent forms of Jacopo della Quercia on the main doorway of San Petronio at Bologna (fig. 325), where Michelangelo was to see them many years later to his own profit. Al-

though the sculptor was affected by classical generalizations of form and desire to monumentalize the human figure, the medieval linearism against a nonnaturalistic background is still perceptible. Like Brunelleschi in architecture and the contemporary sculptor Donatello, Jacopo's adaptations of the classical idiom were extremely personal. Here there is recollection of the curious strained quality of Simone Martini's fourteenth-century paintings (Jacopo was also a Sienese), but this quality is transmuted into a new and terrible grandeur that reached its climax in Michelangelo.

Donatello. An eminent adapter of ancient modes for contemporary purposes was the very influential Donatello, who must be considered a key figure in the artistic growth of this epoch. Like Brunelleschi, whom he accompanied to Rome, he was at first only lightly affected by classical ideas. His early *St. George,* for example (Or San Michele, Florence), is still mystical

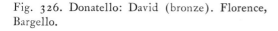

Fig. 326. Donatello: David (bronze). Florence, Bargello.

Fig. 327. Donatello:
The Gattamelata. Padua,
St. Anthony.

Fig. 328. Donatello: The
Gattamelata (detail: head).
Padua, St. Anthony.

376

and idealistic in the tradition of the *St. Theodore* (fig. 284) of Chartres. Donatello's subsequent debt to antiquity and highly personal rendering of its quality are revealed in many works, e.g., the bronze *David* (fig. 326). This interpretation recalls the curving sensuousness of the Praxitelean style (cf. fig. 101) in the generalized form, to which have been added the specific details of adolescent bony elbows, torn shepherd hat, and tangled hair.

Donatello's most famous work is the equestrian portrait of the mercenary general Erasmo dei Narni, better known by the nickname *Gattamelata* ("honeyed cat," fig. 327), a symbol of the constant warfare of the time and its hired soldiers. This revived an ancient type which the artist probably saw in Rome, e.g., Marcus Aurelius on horseback. Donatello added to the naturalistic accomplishment of Italian sculpture the element of anatomical knowledge (one of his chief contributions), both animal and human, which was to have a profound effect on the contemporary sculpture and painting. The *Gattamelata* shows, as do Donatello's other works, a blending of the all-over design (the triangular lines of the horse's legs and the man's body, the solid block of the head) with closely observed details of the human and the animal anatomy. The head of the soldier (fig. 328) reveals the sculptor's anatomical method, which is not based on precise knowledge gained by dissection (cf. the later Leonardo and Michelangelo) but rather on an inference of form. Just as Giotto conveyed the volume of a figure by stretching cloth over it (fig. 306), Donatello conveyed the underlying structure of forms by stretching or loosening skin on the skeletal framework. Psychologically this is a long way indeed from the generalized faces of antiquity and their pseudonaturalistic effects; this subject with his quiet force — even menace — lives up to his nickname of "honeyed cat."

Della Robbia. The monumentality of sculptors like Donatello and Jacopo della Quercia is balanced by a more lyrical type of sculptural expression which emerges in charming feminine portraits like those by Francesco Laurana, tender Madonna and Child scenes as found in the sensitive work of Desiderio da Settignano, or the colored terra-cotta plaques of the Della Robbia family (fig. 329). The last represent a kind of popular art, at once gentler and more understandable. It was also the more conservative side of Italian sculpture at this time and, because of the relative cheapness of the medium, easier to acquire or to give to parish churches. All the variants of this nonmonumental tendency show the characteristic Italian generalized form which remains a constant, no matter which area of expression the artist explores.

Fig. 329. Andrea della Robbia: Annunciation (glazed terra cotta). Casentino, Chiesa Maggiore.

Even at the end of the century when the continuous Donatello stream of naturalism reappears in the brilliant muscular studies of sculptors like Antonio Pollaiuolo, the main emphasis is on dynamism and movement — details are subordinate to the compositional effect. Donatello's influence, as will be apparent, extends equally to painting.

PAINTING: LYRICAL TRADITION. Italian painting in the fifteenth century, like its sculpture and architecture, is mainly that of Florence, with less important schools in other parts of the country. Its two chief streams parallel those of sculpture, divided again into a scientific monumentalism and a lyrical decorativism. The latter is the continuation of a more conservative medieval tendency, found in the works of Fra Angelico, Fra Lippo Lippi, Benozzo Gozzoli, and Botticelli, and carries through to the end of the century.

Fra Angelico. Fra Angelico (1387–1455) represents a clear survival of the medieval spirit into the fifteenth century. This gentle soul with his tender piety expressed an otherworldly sentiment that perhaps can best be compared with religious paintings of the International Gothic style (fig. 309). He retains the manuscript conception of an illuminated or decorated surface in such works as the *Annunciation* (fig. 330) from the monastery of San Marco, whose individual cells were decorated by

378

this monk. In characteristic fashion, Fra Angelico portrays a pair of figures outlined with the late Gothic swing, their tiny blond heads with blue
eyes set on tall graceful forms, the relationship between drapery and body
decorative rather than functional (cf. Ghiberti).

Although depth is specifically indicated in the recession of the vaults,
the dominant effect is two-dimensional. The eye moves across the surface
of the panel, led by the contour of the foremost arcade and by the oval
pattern which is described in a line including the angel's wing, the top
of the center capital, and the curve of the Madonna's back. The Madonna is set in another world, in the late medieval "closed garden" which
symbolizes her purity and untouchability.

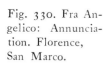

Fig. 330. Fra An-
gelico: Annuncia-
tion. Florence,
San Marco.

Fra Lippo Lippi. The basic two-dimensionality of Fra Angelico's
work is followed by the more worldly attitude of Fra Lippo Lippi
(1406–1469) in a less medieval but still effectively decorative manner.
One of his best-known works, the *Adoration* (fig. 331), continues the
fairy-tale backgrounds of Fra Angelico; the sacred scene is again removed
from the world, now set out in a flower-covered clearing of a forest.
But the Child is real, as is the young St. John at the left, while the
youthful Madonna has changed from an artificial, doll-like image to a
serious and thoughtful young woman. Like most of Fra Lippo's women,
this Madonna has been studied, almost psychologically; the picture is
therefore more worldly and subtle. This subtlety is especially apparent

Fig. 331. Fra Lippo Lippi: Adoration. Berlin, State Museums.

in the design: a light-toned oval pattern is created by the figures, and a darker background by the vertical trees that shut off the outside — presenting a theme in bass against which the bright melody is played.

Fra Lippo Lippi was more realistic in approach (anatomically, psychologically, and in landscape background) than Fra Angelico to the degree that he was influenced by the growing scientific accomplishments of his age. Yet the basic emphasis is on mood and on gentle linear rhythms that help express that mood. Many artists in different parts of Italy responded to the charm of Fra Lippo's manner, which may be compared in a general way with the lyrical sculptures of the Della Robbias (fig. 329); the latter also are colorful and decorative in intent. Fra Lippo's more intimate portrayal of feminine psychology is comparable to the sensitive works of Francesco Laurana, Desiderio da Settignano, and other sculptors of delicate mood.

Gozzoli. The linear decorative tradition in painting continues on a somewhat lower plane with Benozzo Gozzoli (1420–1497), whose *Jour-*

ney of the Magi (fig. 332) exemplifies the interest in harmony of shapes
and lines rather than in monumentality. Gozzoli's combination of the
sweet doll-like faces of Fra Angelico and an elaborately decorative processional effect with its landscape tilted toward the spectator — recalling
the processions in the *Altarpiece of the Lamb* (fig. 311) — expresses
something of the bourgeois-aristocratic quality of Florentine culture. The
entire picture, like many later works by Botticelli (the last of this group),
is a pretext for glorifying the reigning Medici banking family. Many of
its members are presented clearly and handsomely in the foreground.

Botticelli. Sandro Botticelli (1447–1510), who ends the linear tradition in Florence, belongs to the close of the century, in fact to the
beginning of the next period. Like his earlier colleagues in this vein
(especially his master Fra Lippo Lippi), Botticelli too was interested in
mood, in poetic expression, and in linear expressiveness — all worked
into a two-dimensional effect. In his art perhaps more than in any other
painting of the century, the literary humanism of that period appears
at its strongest. His *Spring* (fig. 333), *Birth of Venus, The Calumny of*

Fig. 332. Gozzoli: Journey of the Magi. Florence, Medici-Riccardi Palace.

Fig. 333. Botticelli: Spring. Florence, Uffizi Gallery.

Apelles, and others convey this literary sentiment in a unique and characteristic lyrical manner.

The *Spring* (or *Primavera*) may be a direct descendant of the isolated flowery glades of Fra Angelico and Fra Lippo Lippi, but it exists on a much more subtle and abstract linear level. It is at once a piece of visual poetry and a symbol of the doom hanging over the Florence of the Medicis toward the end of the century. The eye sweeps across the two-dimensional surface of the panel, whose personages are cut off from the world by the vertical accents of trees; it moves in a series of gentle rhythms from side to side. From the young Mercury at the left (Giuliano dei Medici), near the Three Graces with their undulating movements, to Venus in the center (the beloved of young Giuliano), and finally to the trio with the sad Flora and the only happy figures, Spring and Zephyrus, it encompasses an emotional gamut of melancholy, longing for past loves, and the hope of a new spring.

PAINTING: MONUMENTAL TRADITION. While the historical line from Fra Angelico to Botticelli represents the more lyrical and decorative side of Florentine painting, another vital development is found in the so-called monumentalists. This latter group begins with Masaccio and includes such figures as Uccello, Castagno, Veneziano, and Baldovinetti in Florence; Piero della Francesca, Signorelli, and Mantegna exemplify the non-Florentine areas. They constitute the scientific and monumental aspect of Italian painting. Toward the end of the century, the two streams mingle in the work of Perugino, Verrocchio, and ultimately Leonardo da Vinci.

Masaccio. Of the monumentalists proper, undoubtedly the most important is Masaccio (1401–ca. 1428), whose greatest work is a series of frescoes in the Brancacci Chapel of Santa Maria del Carmine in Florence. The *Tribute Money* section, for example (fig. 334), illustrates the great progress made by Masaccio in the sculpturesque tradition initiated by Giotto a century earlier. But where the earlier master had depended primarily on draftsmanship for his effects, Masaccio at the beginning of the fifteenth century invented a light-and-dark (*chiaroscuro*) method that accounts for the solidity of his forms and their existence in space. The large, tightly knit central group here stands solidly on the ground against a tangibly atmospheric landscape background; the figures at the right are

Fig. 334. Masaccio: Tribute Money. Florence, Santa Maria del Carmine.

seen against a carefully perspectivized building. The tightness and tenseness of individual heads are comparable to lights and hollows in the head of the *Gattamelata,* and the naturalistic environment suggests the contemporary accomplishments of Ghiberti in sculpture. The modeling effect of the light may recall how Jan van Eyck related his figures (see fig. 313) to their room spaces; Masaccio performed a similar task with his light coming from the right that simultaneously models the figures and relates them to each other.

With controlled power, the painter tells the story of Christ and his

disciples stopped by the tax gatherer demanding poll tax, the miracle of Peter's finding a coin in the mouth of a fish (extreme left), and his turning that coin over to the tax collector at the behest of Christ (extreme right). As in the other plastically conceived works of this youthful painter (he was only twenty-seven when he died), there is a characteristic realism of effect in which details are consciously subordinated to the general impression. Like most scientific painters of the period, Masaccio was intensely aware of the individual fact from which the general principle or effect was distilled. By this method the monumentalists gave their personages a sense of dignity suiting the humanism of the time; here it is at its best in the magnificent gesture of the Christ instructing Peter to catch the fish.

Fig. 335. Masaccio: Adam and Eve. Florence, Santa Maria del Carmine.

Masaccio's *Adam and Eve* (fig. 335) from the same chapel may be contrasted with those figures painted by the van Eycks in the *Altarpiece of the Lamb* (fig. 311), underlining the basic differences between the northern (and still medieval) approach and that of Italy. The northern work heaps detail on detail in the cold naturalistic light of the studio, and its people are entirely self-absorbed, symbolic images unrelated to each other in a human sense; the Italian artist has something quite different in mind. Masaccio's people, like those of Giotto before him and Michelangelo later, are characters in a great human drama, driven out of Eden by the splendidly serene angel and exhibiting their respective shame and anger as powerfully suffering beings. Their forms, however realistic the sense of movement and shape, convey these facts without insisting on the individual detail, which takes a lesser position in the broad general physical and psychological statement.

At one stroke this young man initiated a movement whose direct influence would die only with Michelangelo a century later; the indirect effects have lasted indefinitely. Transmitting and developing the late medieval humanism and sculpturesqueness of Giotto, Masaccio placed his personages in a more universally realistic background and devised a means of representation that was a challenge to artists for the rest of that century. The Brancacci Chapel for the next few generations became the unofficial academy of Italy; innumerable artists (among them Raphael, Leonardo, and Michelangelo) came there to learn his trick of light-and-dark modeling. There also they tried to discover his secret of combining the greatest tension with the greatest motor power in the figure.

Other Florentine monumentalists. Other Florentine work in this tradition may not be so impressive as Masaccio's, but it has significant elements. Paolo Uccello (ca. 1397–1475), well known for his experiments in linear perspective, was very much influenced by Masaccio and Ghiberti. Uccello in his Green Cloister frescoes of Santa Maria Novella in Florence, like his famous battle pictures (e.g., the National Gallery *Rout of San Romano*), was preoccupied with the technical question of diminishing the size of figures that are farther back in the picture space. These works are experimental — although the battle pictures have a decorative and abstract effectiveness. His equestrian portrait of *Sir John Hawkwood* (Cathedral of Florence, inner façade) reveals him as the plastic monumental follower of Masaccio; but here he was far less original than was the pioneer Masaccio or than were his own abstract pictures. In the battle scenes, Uccello employed the plasticity of Masaccio only in so far as it was useful to him, concentrating on pattern and limited space effects which are the best evidence of his creativity.

Andrea del Castagno (1423–1457), a more consistent follower of Masaccio (and of Donatello in anatomy), was not in full command of the earlier artist's light technique and produced relatively hard figures. He tended, moreover, as in his *Last Supper* (Sant' Apollonia, Florence) or the *Crucifixion* directly over it, to give a certain response to the moment, rather than the universality and symbolic command of Masaccio. His well-known series of Florentine historical personages, e.g., the *Pippo Spano* (fig. 336), reflects the plasticity of both Donatello and Masaccio but is primarily naturalistic and flashy in execution.

Domenico Veneziano (ca. 1438–1461) and Alesso Baldovinetti

Fig. 336. Castagno: Pippo Spano. Florence, Sant' Apollonia.

(1425–1499) are also connected with this style. Veneziano is noteworthy for his closeness to Donatello's linear quality — the line clinging to the muscle and bone — his delicate coloring, pioneering use of oil paints, and gentle emotion. His feeling for the recession of landscape space was unusual for Florence in this period and may be a result of influence from the Venetian school. In Baldovinetti (e.g., the Louvre *Virgin*) some of Veneziano's delicacy is mingled with an ability to monumentalize the figure by contrasting it with a deep space, as in the later *Mona Lisa* of Leonardo.

Piero della Francesca. Outside Florence within the orbit of the monumental tradition the foremost names are those of the Umbro-Florentine Piero della Francesca (1416–1492) and the Paduan Andrea Mantegna (1431–1506). Piero belongs to the monumentalist group by virtue of highly sculpturesque and powerfully articulated figures, presented in an abstract form that contains the most tensely controlled emotional strength in the history of art up to that point. The salient force of the ascending figure of Christ in *The Resurrection* (fig. 337) cuts straight up through the picture; it is related to the background through the vertical trees

386

and to the foreground sleeping figures through his arms, which become part of a rigid triangle. This work illustrates Piero's contribution to the scientific side of monumental painting, his interest in atmospheric effects — the glow of early dawn breaking over the hills and illuminating the tiny clouds against which the central figure looms up (cf. Orozco, fig. 532).

Mantegna. The Paduan Mantegna is historically interesting for two reasons: his pictorial equivalents of the sculpture of Donatello (whose *Gattamelata* and some other works are in Padua); and his influence on the Venetian school, especially the early work of Giovanni Bellini. The crispness and hardness of Mantegna's modeling of form in the *St. James Led to Execution* (fig. 338) show his relationship to Donatello. The unusual perspective angle reveals the painter's own originality. The best instance of this is his illusionary foreshortened ceiling of the bridal chamber in the Palace of the Gonzaga at Mantua, where he anticipated the ceiling virtuosi of the late Renaissance and Baroque periods. Man-

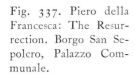

Fig. 337. Piero della Francesca: The Resurrection. Borgo San Sepolcro, Palazzo Communale.

Fig. 338. Mantegna: St. James Led to Execution (destroyed). Padua, Eremitani Church.

tegna's devotion to classical archaeology is evident in the *St. James*, which is filled with learned details of architecture and sculpture, the elements of arms and armor. One of the best-informed men of his time, Mantegna was also among its most significant and influential artists. His accomplishments included classical research, foreshortening devices, magnificent murals, and a whole series of etchings and engravings whose effect was felt throughout northern Italy and into Germany.

LATE-FIFTEENTH-CENTURY PAINTING: *Verrocchio.* The latter part of the fifteenth century brought a number of new trends. One of these was a fusion of the lyrical and the scientific streams, as in Andrea del Verrocchio (1435–1488), a versatile painter-sculptor and the teacher of Leonardo da Vinci. His *Baptism of Christ* (fig. 339), for which Leonardo is supposed to have done the angel at the left, shows a generalized, monumental, and yet very tender, sentimental Christ together with an anatomical Donatellesque John the Baptist, whose expression is equally gentle.

His emotional limitations are exemplified by the flamboyant *Colleoni* equestrian statue in Venice.

Ghirlandajo. Domenico Ghirlandajo (1449–1494) manifests a much worldlier quality than any other Italian painter of the time. His portrayal of upper-class patrons as participants in the *Life of St. John* and the *Life of the Virgin* (Santa Maria Novella, Florence), done for the Tornabuoni family, is analogous to the more intellectual pretensions of the Medici family, seen in the paintings of Botticelli during the same period. The bourgeois character of Italian art, as already noted, is tinged with a certain aristocratic quality; the smug ladies of the Tornabuoni family parading through the lying-in room of St. Elizabeth or St. Anne — seen on the fashionable walls of Santa Maria Novella — are elegant indeed. Employing the accumulated technical knowledge of his century, Ghirlandajo offers wide streets or interiors, atmospheric quality, strongly modeled figures, and the picture of a splendid mankind. The more naturalistic side of this painter under the influence of contemporary

Fig. 339. Verrocchio: Baptism of Christ. Florence, Uffizi Gallery.

Fig. 340. Ghirlandajo: Old
Man and Boy. Paris, Louvre.

Flemish art is shown in his justly famous *Old Man and Boy* (fig. 340), a
"corner portrait" in the northern tradition. In his equally reminiscent
Adoration of the Shepherds (fig. 341) the simple ugly shepherds recall
those of Hugo van der Goes in the *Portinari Altarpiece* (fig. 317). But
Ghirlandajo's half-sentimental, half-naturalistic *Adoration* with its patrician Madonna is depicted against an elegant background of classical
ruins with the medieval procession winding its way through an arch of
triumph. It was in this complacent painter's studio, curiously enough, that
Michelangelo was first apprenticed.

Perugino. Many late-fifteenth-century painters signalize a transition
to the next period. While Verrocchio in his fusion of the scientific and the
lyrical is a bridge to Leonardo, Perugino (ca. 1450–1523) accomplishes
a similar joining of influences and leads to another master of the so-called
High Renaissance, Raphael. Perugino came from the relatively provincial environment of Perugia, which in the late fifteenth century was
still suffering from intense medieval feuds and was dominated by an
extraordinarily unsophisticated piety. He expressed this extreme religious
sentimentality as well as the general scientific proclivities of the age. His

Christ Delivering the Keys to St. Peter (fig. 342) shows a characteristic series of ultrapious poses and facial expressions, but also a broad, spacious, typical Umbrian background, distinguished by Perugino's special brand of space composition. He leads the eye of the spectator from the forms in the foreground through a series of strategically placed figures and a building in the middle ground to the perspectivized triumphal arches in the third space area and finally into the landscape background. Here again, hill is placed behind hill, tree behind tree, to augment the feeling of movement into the picture. Such deliberate placement and spacing of forms is independent of the effect achieved by linear or aerial perspective, which add to the artist's tools for space movement. This was the device so frequently used by Perugino's most distinguished pupil, Raphael (cf. fig. 357).

Fig. 341. Ghirlandajo: The Adoration of the Shepherds. Florence, Academy.

Fig. 342. Perugino: Christ Delivering the Keys to St. Peter. Rome, Vatican, Sistine Chapel.

Fig. 343. Signorelli: Raising of the Dead. Cathedral of Orvieto.

Signorelli. Another type of painting that advances toward the High Renaissance is exemplified by the Umbrian Luca Signorelli (ca. 1441–1523), who brought together the monumental style of Piero della Francesca with a new interest in movement of the human form, developed by artists like the Florentine Pollaiuoli. Signorelli's best-known works are the frescoes in the Cathedral of Orvieto, e.g., the *Raising of the Dead* (fig. 343), done during 1504 to 1506. He was greatly concerned with emotional possibilities in poses of the nude human body — as Michelangelo and others would be. The preoccupation with sin and damnation and the generally tortured style of these works are part of the religious revival in Italy at the beginning of the sixteenth century, symptomatic of the need for reform as expressed by the Savonarola party in Florence and its "burning of the vanities."

A similar convulsive spirit appears in the religious paintings of Botticelli at this time, apparently for the same reason. Botticelli became a follower of the fanatic monk and reformer Savonarola, whose execution in 1498 fanned the zeal of many of his adherents. This later mysticism of Botticelli may be accounted for by these circumstances as well as by the death of his patron, Lorenzo the Magnificent, in 1492. That event marked for him, and perhaps for Florence as a whole, the end of an era.

17 / THE RISE OF HUMANISM:
Early-sixteenth-century Italy

THE second stage of Italian humanism — commonly called the High Renaissance — reached its climax during the first thirty years of the sixteenth century, corresponding in general with the transition from independent city-states to a broader pattern of rule, subject to the imperial rivalries of Spain and France. The hitherto latent nationalism of Italy emerged in the papacy's aspiration for political power, only to be crushed in a relatively short time by the stronger nations. By 1535 this short-lived but vivid stage in cultural history was over, brought to a close by the sack of Rome by the Spanish-Austrian armies in 1527, the installation of the Medici in Florence as hereditary dukes under the Spanish in 1530, and the absorption of the Duchy of Milan by Charles V in 1535.

IDEALISM AND INDIVIDUALISM. The end of Florentine cultural domination in Italy had followed the expulsion of the Medici in 1494 and the Savonarola reform movement which ended with his execution in 1498. Since the papacy had then become, however temporarily and unsuccessfully, the champion of Italian nationalism, the center of artistic patronage and production had shifted to Rome, which now drew artists to itself from all over the peninsula. There followed a marked change from the localism of the fifteenth century with its separate city-state culture, local traditions, workshop experiments, and the individual taste of benevolent and unbenevolent tyrants. The early sixteenth century produced an anti-naturalistic art in reaction against the "excesses" of fifteenth-century anatomy and perspective tricks. During this era of temporary national ambitions, artists were more interested in an impressive, even grandiloquent art seeking a universal ideal rather than a local or individualistic expression.

The individuality of the artist himself was not undermined; quite the contrary, he became a very significant figure indeed. He was no longer the simple guild artisan working for a local patron but more often an important social being, a free agent whose art (the product of his studio instead of his workshop) was much sought after by pope and prince. With this liberation from the guild, the object of art became an "aesthetic object" of interest to collectors and to dealers. The actual form that the artist sought was quite different from earlier experiments with reality — much had been accomplished along this line — and further in the direction of ideal statements. Historically this was the third formulation, in some ways the fulfillment of the Italian tendency toward large generalized shapes.

There were many "schools" of art during this era, centering about transcendent personalities like Leonardo da Vinci and Michelangelo rather than about workshops, but all had in common the aspiration toward an ideal human form and an ideal state of being. Grandiose general statements were made in sculpture and architecture that were destined to form the basis for later academic practice. Painting techniques became more standardized; these systematic procedures were also fated to be transmitted to future generations. In his attempts to control rather than to portray the uncongenial world of reality, the High Renaissance master had recourse to formulas of various kinds. Not the least of these was projective geometry, which became one of his chief sources for compositional and formal devices: triangles and pyramids, ovals and ovoids, circles and spheroids, squares and cubes, within which his personages were arranged.

Nevertheless, the master of this period could not escape his heritage of individualism. The conflict between that tendency with its naturalistic by-products and the new desire to generalize and to control the unhappy material world placed his art under a strain that could be sustained only for a short time and by outstandingly talented men supported by the unusual patronage of the day. With these conditions removed, the controlled art of the High Renaissance was to become the uneasy expression of the Mannerist period following.

RENAISSANCE CLASSICISM. It was this conflict that distinguished Renaissance art from that of the ancient world with which it is often compared and from which it undoubtedly derived great benefits. The idealism of ancient art was echoed in the Italian Renaissance, which naturally turned to the culture of antiquity because of its need for formal control and its humanistic interests. But the older art had a serenity that was in the main quite foreign to masters like Leonardo da Vinci, Fra Bartolommeo, and Michelangelo, just as it was to painters like Botticelli and Signorelli whose later work fell within the compass of the High Renaissance. For most of the great artists of this epoch, the classical spirit was tempered by unhappy political circumstances, by the mysticism of the dominant neo-Platonic school of philosophy which attempted to reconcile Christian be-

Fig. 344. Bramante: Tempietto. Rome, Cloister of San Pietro in Montorio.

lief with pagan feeling, and finally by the fact that their classicism was often a result of literary rather than artistic knowledge.

It was one thing to copy decorative ornament on architecture and sculpture from the ruins of ancient Rome — a first-hand though surface application; quite different was the book-derived classicism of Botticelli's *Spring* (fig. 333) or Signorelli's *Pan, God of Music* (Berlin, Kaiser-Friedrich Museum). In actual fact, ancient Greek art of the classical period was almost completely unknown to the Italians until the Renaissance was well on its way. The result was these "literary" paintings or other works that, however admirable in their own Italianate fashion, were basically attempts to approximate the classical spirit, like the paganism of Titian or Correggio. The closest to a pure classical art was Raphael, who was for a time in charge of archaeological excavations in the Roman area; but even with him the conflict between the Christian and the pagan was ultimately resolved in favor of the former, especially in the visionary works of his last period.

RENAISSANCE ARCHITECTURE: *Bramante.* The balancing of Christian and classical ideas is clearly seen in the field of architecture, where there was a shift from the fifteenth-century experimental and decorative use of classical elements (cf. *Pazzi Chapel*, fig. 320) to a more precise archaeological procedure. Donato Bramante (1444–1514) exemplified this shift in the *Tempietto* (San Pietro in Montorio, Rome), finished in 1502 (fig. 344). Roman Doric is used for the circular peristyle and the entablature above it, with the most scrupulous accuracy of detail, in terms of their original architectural function on a Roman circular temple. Whereas earlier structures like the *Pazzi Chapel* had stressed the façade of the building, the High Renaissance was more interested in questions of space and volume as in ancient buildings. Moreover, the architect turned toward a monumental, formal, and serious expression because he was now working either in Rome itself or under the leadership of the Church; many artists and architects coming to Rome were affected this way. Yet with all its classical dignity, the *Tempietto* (Little Temple) still utilizes the medievalistic and enlarged dome of Brunelleschi, once more balancing the pagan and Christian elements.

San Gallo. In domestic architecture, the *Farnese Palace* begun by Antonio da San Gallo (1485–1546, fig. 345) continues the fifteenth-century *palazzo* idea in both its hollow-square plan and elevation. It preserves the triple division of the façade with an impressive cornice, as in the designs of Michelozzo and Alberti, but does away with the rustication of the earlier buildings except for the entrance. San Gallo brought the windows above the surface to make them a positive part of the play of masses and relative proportions, in contrast to the textural surface effects

Fig. 345. Farnese
Palace, Rome.

of the earlier builders with their pilasters and rustication; but the total impression here is rather cold and formal. Classical elements are clearly shown in the pedimented windows of the second and third stories as well as in the coffered and vaulted entrance vestibule. The vestibule is projected forward to support a somewhat aristocratic balcony (capped by an elaborate coat of arms) from which the multitudes could be addressed. Symbolizing the spirit of the age, the stone used for this Renaissance palace was obtained from the ancient Theater of Marcellus and the *Colosseum*. The Roman theater also gave San Gallo ideas for the vault of the vestibule, and the *Colosseum* influenced the design of the palace's inner courtyard.

In this courtyard, San Gallo followed a three-storied arrangement with superposed engaged Doric, Ionic, and Corinthian orders like those of the *Colosseum*. On the two lower stories the columns are combined with arches; on the upper floor, with pedimented windows between which the columns have been flattened into pilasters. (The third story with its exterior cornice is by Michelangelo.) Although the *Farnese Palace* is not particularly different in approach from the palace designs of other architects of the period, it had a good deal to do with popularizing this type of building. It illustrates, especially in the courtyard, the growing monumentality of architecture, as well as the tendency toward direct borrowing and reproduction of antique forms.

Raphael. This last element is especially apparent in the architecture of Raphael, the nephew and protégé of Bramante, who succeeded to the latter's official architectural post upon Bramante's death in 1514. As archaeologist-in-chief for the Vatican, Raphael naturally came into more direct contact with the art of antiquity. His design for his own palace shows a combination of a rusticated lower story and an upper story endowed with coupled engaged columns of impressive dignity. The newly discovered Roman interiors inspired Raphael in designing the loggias of the Court of San Damaso in the Vatican, where he used the stucco decorations of ancient Rome. These charming arrangements of leaf forms, human figures, and medallions, which were to become popular in the works of his many followers, also enliven the interior of the Villa Madama in Rome.

LEONARDO DA VINCI. The High Renaissance spirit, well characterized in architecture, rises perhaps to its highest in painting and sculpture, through such overwhelming personalities as Leonardo, Michelangelo, and Raphael. Leonardo da Vinci (1452–1519) — a transitional figure from the fifteenth to the sixteenth century — has become the symbol of the investigating and searching character of the period as a whole. Summing up in his painting the accomplishments of the century into which he

398

was born, Leonardo moved forward into the new age with a series of works, however limited in number, that fulfill the pictorial achievement of the High Renaissance.

He was trained in the studio of the painter-sculptor Verrocchio, who had himself combined the fifteenth-century monumental and sentimental trends (fig. 339). Leonardo developed this idea further, while adding his own extraordinary perception and sensitivity together with the formal and idealistic needs of the new age. His *Madonna of the Rocks* (fig. 346), painted about 1482, brings together the scientific and the lyrical in a manner far more skillful and integrated than Verrocchio's. Following in the footsteps of Fra Lippo Lippi and Botticelli, Leonardo set his story in an unworldly romantic setting, against the rocks and waterfalls of north-

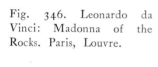

Fig. 346. Leonardo da Vinci: Madonna of the Rocks. Paris, Louvre.

ern Italy. He has filled the scene with a quality of mood, of suspended emotion — a tender graciousness in the adoration of the young St. John, the gentle gesture of blessing by the Child, and the protective hand of the Mother — making the picture part of the lyrical tradition. ·

Leonardo's scientific interests. Scientifically, the precisely drawn flora and rocks, foreground and background, illustrate Leonardo's intense preoccupation with such fields of knowledge and underline at the same time the close relationship between science and art in the fifteenth century. One cannot say which came first in his case — science as a stimulant to art or the needs of art as an incentive toward scientific investigation — but it is significant that apart from people like Leonardo and Michelozzo there were few scientists as such in this period. The art movement, in addition to its other virtues, was also the repository of scientific knowledge.

As a pioneer in this case, Leonardo used the previously individual monumental shape as part of a controlled and formal geometric group arrangement, which was not done to any extent before. There were undoubtedly a good many earlier instances of effective rhythmic form relationships in closed compositions, as in Botticelli, Piero della Francesca, and Masaccio. But Leonardo (and others after him) tried to contain his story within the framework of a clearly described three-dimensional geometric form, such as a pyramid, sphere, ovoid, or parallelepiped, symbolizing the rationality of life, its capability of being reduced to systematic explanation and arrangement. He transformed the separately monumental forms of a Castagno or Donatello into a higher, more universally significant expression, part of a broader plan and subject to what Leonardo called "the prime mover" or rational order. Once again, aesthetics assumes the role of a still nonexistent science.

Leonardo's technique. In the *Madonna of the Rocks* Leonardo's characteristic treatment of light and dark is also projected. A hazy, smoky element (*sfumato*) envelops the forms, adding to their essential plasticity and warmth of surface. The light seems to emerge from the center of the picture itself, rather than from any given source of illumination, and for the most part lends a subdued and relatively noncoloristic character to his painting. The poetic quality thus achieved was to affect the painting of Correggio and Giorgione in other parts of Italy.

An equally apparent, although more complicated, example of Leonardo's system of dignified, controlled form and composition appears in his famous *The Last Supper* (fig. 347). Like the previous picture, it was done during the artist's long stay at the Milanese court. *The Last Supper* is a large mural painted in tempera on a dry wall; it displays another calculated arrangement, confining the emotions of the characters within a specific geometry. Leonardo has chosen to present the highly dramatic

400

moment: "Verily I say unto you, that one of you shall betray me." In contrast to the chattiness of Ghirlandajo's *Last Supper* or the anatomical straining of Castagno's version, Leonardo has stripped his painting of all unessential details and set his figures within an austere geometrical framework in which all the visible lines converge at the Saviour's head. The Christ is portrayed in firm triangular form against an open rectangular window and expresses a gentle abnegation. His electrifying statement causes waves of feeling to flow from one group of disciples to another. Their four groups move rhythmically back and forth, both physically and emotionally, with gestures leading from one trio to the next and helping to define the respective reactions of these twelve individuals.

Fig. 347. Leonardo da Vinci: The Last Supper. Milan, Santa Maria delle Grazie.

Leonardo, unlike earlier painters of this theme, was less interested in naturalism than in universal truth. His characters therefore sum up different types, presented in terms of noble tragedy and in the best Florentine tradition of Giotto and Masaccio. But where Giotto was still medievalistic in both outlook and composition and Masaccio carefully balanced an expressed scientific interest with generalized statement, the artists of the High Renaissance led by Leonardo completely assimilated the factual side of nature into a statement of godlike truth. What is best, most dignified, and yet most characteristic of the human race is presented in this and other High Renaissance summaries of fact, emotion, and appearance. The thirteen personages of Leonardo's *Last Supper* are less religious portrayals as such than studies of mankind, humanistic and sympathetic portraits of anger (Peter), love (John), cupidity (Judas), and other universal emotions that the painter has tried to epitomize in attitude and gesture.

Critics have questioned the success of this admittedly studied and somewhat theatrical composition; but its exposition of the possibilities of symbolizing human emotions through calculated gestures lays the basis for a great deal of High Renaissance mural and other decoration. The rich complication of this composition, its amazing balance between the static and the dynamic, between the violently emotional and the relatively calm, the subordination of all these elements to Leonardo's basic geometry, have made it significant for wall painters from Raphael to Diego Rivera.

If the *Madonna of the Rocks* brought to painting a mysterious technique of light and dark and *The Last Supper* a more subtle type of emotional portrayal, the *Mona Lisa* (fig. 348) may be regarded as a step in

Fig. 348. Leonardo da Vinci: Mona Lisa. Paris, Louvre.

the history of portraiture. In spite of all that has been written about this picture (and *The Last Supper*), an objective appraisal will clarify certain fundamental facts. The half-smiling and reserved face of the *Mona Lisa* expresses somewhat the introspective psychological quality of the Fra Lippo Lippi school, but much more the detached, questioning, even cynical personality of Leonardo himself. It is surely like most of the women's faces in Leonardo's works (cf. *Madonna of the Rocks*), reflecting his own attitude rather than the personality of Mona Lisa Gioconda — the gentle, sad lady who had lost a member of her family just before Leonardo began to do her portrait around 1505. Not a portrait in the strict sense of the word, it becomes an idealization of this woman (and perhaps of woman in general), placed pyramidally and firmly against the romantic landscape with its winding river and typical Leonardesque atmospheric haze.

Ideal estimates of this kind are characteristic of the period as a whole, differentiated by each artist's own personality and philosophical approach. It would be a mistake, however, to assume that the people portrayed — or the artists, for that matter — partook of the apparent serenity of the pictures. The very opposite may be assumed in this case, for Leonardo was a disillusioned man in his fifties at that point, a perpetual wanderer who had been driven out of Milan by the French invasion to follow Cesare Borgia's armies in their ruthless attempt to achieve control for the Papal States in confused and unhappy early-sixteenth-century Italy. In view of these circumstances, the so-called serene portraits by Leonardo and other painters may be regarded as attempts to detach themselves from the times (cf. Michelangelo's symbolic portrait sculptures in the Medici chapel of San Lorenzo) rather than to reflect them directly.

The *Mona Lisa* exists in space, first, because of a subtle modeling emphasized by the smoky light about the cheeks and throat; second, through its sculpturesque form (cf. late-fifteenth-century portrait busts); and finally, through the contrast between the monumental verticalized figure and the inward-moving landscape (cf. Baldovinetti's *Madonna*, Louvre). Its combination of monumentality and lyrical sentiment recalls again that Leonardo brought together the two chief currents of fifteenth-century art and synthesized them in terms of the new ideals of the High Renaissance. For better or worse, painting would not be the same after his time; his influence would last for hundreds of years.

MICHELANGELO. The second great personality of the epoch, Michelangelo Buonarotti (1475–1564), was a mystical, tragic figure whose life symbolizes the instability and insecurity of an age in which his greatest projects could not be realized. Whereas Leonardo's world vision, including all the scientific knowledge of that day, could not find an adequate artistic form, Michelangelo's huge conceptions were larger than the uneasy politics of the time allowed. Unlike Leonardo's universal science absorbed into questioning symbols of emotion, Michelangelo's giant forms — rooted in the art of sculpture — combine the idealism of antiquity with the profoundly religious spirit of the man himself and the increasing neo-Platonic mysticism of the era. His feeling for sculpture, evident from the beginning of his career, is manifest throughout, even in his paintings and architecture.

He is at once a link with the late medieval past and a clue to the gigantism and exaggeration of the Baroque period. More than most other artists of his time, he imparts a sense of dislocation, of the individual breaking loose from the patterns of the guild and plunging into the highly competitive life of the artist in modern society. Driven back and forth by political difficulties between the papacy and Florence, his life reveals this insecurity as well as a deep dissatisfaction stemming from the frustration of his grandiose schemes and from his own neurasthenia.

Michelangelo's sculpture. Michelangelo's sculptured *Pietà* (1501, fig. 349) is a late medieval northern subject, similar in mood to the later painting of Botticelli, and may also reflect the Savonarola reform movement that had just ended. The small size of the Christ in relation to the monumentality of the Virgin is a feature of Gothic German sculpture at

Fig. 349. Michelangelo: Pietà. Rome, St. Peter's.

this time. But the simplicity of effect as one form is absorbed in another, the concealed strength of the youthful Madonna, with her almost Leonardesque expression and turn of head, are part of the new trend toward generalization. This last is particularly noticeable in the assimilation of details into the total conception, though they are clearly visible at close range — e.g., the veins in the arm of the Christ.

The *David* of 1501–1504 (fig. 350) exhibits another and equally important side of Michelangelo's art, his feeling for the gigantic, as projected by this colossal naked youth (ca. 18 feet tall). Although this interpretation still relates to fifteenth-century ideas in retaining some naturalistic detail, it is quite different from earlier renderings such as the Donatello example (fig. 326). Here is a giant, where before there was a dreamy adolescent; here is a generalized idea in the nude, where earlier there was naturalistic interest in the torn hat, the sword, rock, or head of Goliath. Michelangelo's figure also possesses a significant new quality

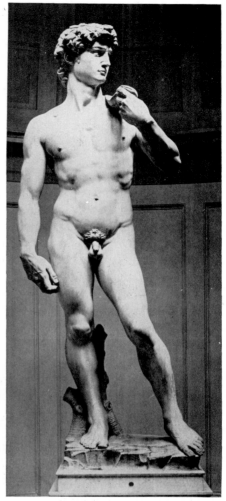

Fig. 350. Michelangelo: David. Florence, Academy.

of *terribilità*, or "terribleness," expressed through the challenging, flashing glance of the youth and his overwhelming size.

The inherent tenseness of the artist's style causes a tremendous emotional energy to be contained within the outside dimensions of the original block of stone or form space (a consistent practice of Michelangelo's sculpture and painting). The figure seems to be trying to break out of the space; the upper part of the body moves in one direction and the lower portion in another (*contrapposto*), while the upward movement of the flexed arm is opposed to the downward movement of the hanging arm. Since the figure cannot actually burst out of the space allotted to it —

Michelangelo believed that a piece of sculpture should be so tightly organized that it could roll downhill without any part breaking away — it can only emerge from its confinement through a spiral movement which carries the eye up, around, and vertically out into space. This principle, effectively illustrated in his famous *Bound Slave* of the Louvre (see also fig. 353), exemplifies the straining for emotional release that moves hand in hand with the self-imposed geometrical limitations of this period, and which is transmitted to the artists of the following Mannerist style — e.g., Giovanni da Bologna and Jean Goujon.

From this legacy it would appear that Michelangelo, like Leonardo, contained within his work the germs of an artificiality and a mannerism that were to plague art for a long time to come. In these two unusual men the various tricks of style are expressions of great personalities, but in later artists they often become empty formulas reproducing the barest externals without inner meaning. Michelangelo's later sculptures, such as the two tombs in the Medici Chapel of San Lorenzo, Florence, also introduce these strained qualities together with a symbolic meaning which foreshadows the intellectual aims of the next period. His synthesis of sculpture with architecture in these works prefigures analogous effects in the Baroque style.

Michelangelo's painting. The painting of Michelangelo also shows the same elements of monumentality, *terribilità*, yearning for beyond-earthly values, as well as the strain brought about by formal restrictions. Like his sculpture and like the work of many contemporaries, Michelangelo's painting presents magnificent godlike human beings, whose emotive power and meaning are expressed through the pose of the body, especially the nude.

His best-known achievement in painting is the Sistine Chapel ceiling (fig. 351), on which he worked between 1508 and 1512, perhaps the greatest singlehanded accomplishment in the history of that art. Called away from his project for Pope Julius II's immense tomb which he was fated never to finish, Michelangelo applied himself somewhat unwillingly to this new tremendous undertaking which almost inevitably took on an exceedingly sculpturesque quality. In keeping with the expanding literary interests of a period when patrons maintained favorite humanist scholars, Michelangelo used in this work a combination of Biblical, classical, and Dantesque sources to aid his personal interpretation of the Creation, the Fall of Man, and man's ultimate salvation.

On a curved surface some 50 feet from the ground and covering an area of around 155 by 45 feet, the artist laid out a huge panorama of incidents and people. Hundreds of heroic forms, most of them over life-size and nude, move across this surface without once repeating a pose.

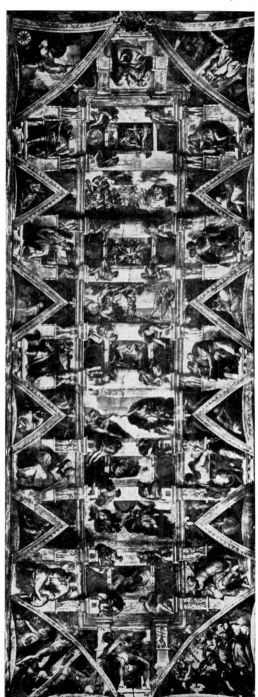

Fig. 351. Michelangelo: Ceiling fresco. Rome, Vatican, Sistine Chapel.

In the center of the space there are nine rectangular panels, beginning at the entrance and moving down to the altar end of the room. These are reserved for the Creation, Fall, and Deluge incidents as recounted in the Old Testament. At the corners of the ceiling the painter has placed four Old Testament scenes of valiant deeds which helped save the Chosen People; these show David and Goliath, Judith and Holofernes, Moses and the Brazen Serpent, Esther and Ahasuerus.

Turning to the New Testament, a succession of bronze-colored medallions bear scenes that forecast Christ's Coming and the Redemption; and a group of triangular spaces along the sides of the ceiling portray the "ancestors of Christ." The final element in this elaborate literary-artistic allegory is the series of niche-enclosed figures placed between the ancestor triangles on the long sides of the picture space. These are Old Testament prophets and pagan sibyls, or prophetesses, whose utterances are said to presage the Coming of Christ — the characteristic High Renaissance blend and balance of pagan and Christian ideas.

The ceiling itself gives the impression of an architectural-sculptural combination rather than a painting. Because Michelangelo had done no ceiling painting before, he was apparently not aware of devices already developed by Mantegna and Melozzo da Forlì for the effective representation of figures overhead. Although Michelangelo contrived a brilliant solution for the space involved, he painted it as though confronting a wall — which was actually the case as he lay on his back for months on a scaffold just below the ceiling. Today in the Sistine Chapel the viewer is forced to lean far backward in order to see the frescoes properly.

A typical section from this extraordinary mural is the *Creation of Adam* (fig. 352), the sixth of the nine central panels. The series of nine demonstrates how the artist's style broadened and simplified after the *Drunkenness of Noah* and *The Deluge*, which were painted first, at the entrance end of the chapel. Those first scenes give the effect of complicated bas-reliefs with many figures. The *Creation of Adam*, painted later, features two colossal figures on which interest is concentrated — forms that are predominantly three-dimensional in effect. In the scenes he did last, Michelangelo shows single figures emerging from the inchoate mystery of the beginning of all things — *God Separating Light from Darkness* and the *Creation of the Sun and Moon*. These finally expose the mystical depth of the artist's nature.

The *Creation of Adam* has a sculptural crispness of form and a magnificent linear contour that describes form, although the basic arrangement is still that of relief sculpture in the simpler fashion of Jacopo della Quercia's work in Bologna (fig. 325), which Michelangelo undoubtedly saw. In a general way, the recumbent Adam suggests the *Theseus* (fig.

94) of the *Parthenon*, but there is a great difference between the serenity and poise of a Greek fifth-century work and the spirit of a High Renaissance work which seems to be striving toward something. Adam is about to rise as his arm is lifted to the outstretched finger of God. The figure of the Deity, surrounded by seraphim as he rushes forward, is a dynamic contrast to the still unactivated man. Their finger tips almost touch, as though the spark of life were jumping the gap between them. Here, as much as in the artist's sculptures, tremendous power is held in check — power expressed through the tense contours of Adam's body, the flexing of the knee, the arm bent and supporting the giant twisting frame, the gentle yearning head inclined forward along the curving line of the dramatically posed arms.

Fig. 352. Michelangelo: Creation of Adam. Detail from Sistine Chapel ceiling.

The accessory figures of the ceiling may be represented by the *Libyan Sibyl* (fig. 353), a deceptively thoughtful and lyrical figure typical of the 12-foot-high men and women prophets that line the sides of the work. She is conceived as a seated sculpture on a pedestal, enclosed in a niche that is flanked by nude decorative cupids in high relief. Holding the book of her prophecy, she turns her body in Michelangelo's typical spiral movement, accentuated by the tucked-under left foot with its bent big toe and the swing of the magnificently muscular shoulders. As the body twists in its restricted space, the arms lift upward in two directions; and with the book they carry the eye into the corners of the niche, to stop there and return via the curves of the arms and body. In the prophet-sibyl series Michelangelo has summed up his use of the human body as a vehicle for the emotions; the prayerful outward-moving exaltation of the *Libyan*

Fig. 353. Michelangelo: Libyan Sibyl. Detail from Sistine Chapel ceiling.

Sibyl, the downward sweep of line in the dejected *Jeremiah,* the vertically upward-moving gesture of the inspired *Isaiah* typify this symbolic function of the figures in High Renaissance art.

Architecture of Michelangelo. The story of *St. Peter's* in Rome is part of the tragedy of Michelangelo's disappointments as well as a link between this period and the next. This greatest church in Christendom was first planned by Bramante. It was begun in 1506 to house Michelangelo's gigantic tomb for Pope Julius II, which was not destined for completion (the *Moses, Dying Slave,* and *Bound Slave* are its most important fragments). After Bramante's death in 1514, work on the cathedral was continued by his associates Giuliano da San Gallo, Fra Giocondo, and Raphael. Between 1520, when Raphael died, and 1546, when Michelangelo was called in as chief architect, the building's design had been altered by intervening architects, but Michelangelo restored Bramante's original Greek-cross plan and himself laid out an enormous dome over the crossing that would dominate the building from any point of the compass (fig. 354). At the time of Michelangelo's death in 1564, only the outer walls and the inner supports of the dome had been finished. His conception may be judged from the apse end of the church, since

410

the front of the building was later considerably changed. The dome was carried out in slightly modified form by Giacomo della Porta; but the extension of the nave in 1605 brought the façade so far forward that it destroyed the planned domination of the dome from the front of the building. During the Baroque period, long colonnades designed by Bernini were extended forward from the sides, ending in semicircles enclosing St. Peter's Square.

The magnificent dome rises to a height of 450 feet from the ground; its integrated relationship with the pilasters on the rear walls measures the control that even yet existed in late Renaissance architecture. As an amplification of Brunelleschi's dome on the *Cathedral of Florence* (fig. 319) in shape, relationship of an inner and outer shell, and the tying together of the base by artificial tie-chains imbedded in the masonry, this structure climaxes the development of the dome. Echoes can be found in the centuries following; *St. Paul's* in London (fig. 431), the *Panthéon* in Paris (fig. 451), and the Capitol in Washington, D.C., show the persistence of this impressive formal shape. Among Michelangelo's other architectural works are the subtly balanced staircase of the Laurentian Library in Florence and the handsome palace-enclosed square known as the Campidoglio in Rome.

Fig. 354. St. Peter's, Rome. Air view from the apse.

RAPHAEL: *Paintings*. Raphael (1483–1520) is perhaps the best balanced personality of the three great High Renaissance masters. A pupil of the sentimental space-composing Perugino (fig. 342), Raphael offers the warmest, most human feeling of the time, with figures skillfully placed in geometric and recessive space. More than most of his contemporaries, he demonstrates the essential worldliness of Renaissance art. In his pictures also are foreshadowed the academic and eclectic practices of the late-sixteenth-century Bolognese masters.

He is best known for his eminently human and appealing Madonnas, stemming from the style developed by Leonardo shortly before the ambitious young Raphael arrived in Florence. The warmth and pyramidal composition of Leonardo's *Madonna of the Rocks* (fig. 346) are reflected in many of Raphael's famous triangular Madonna and Child compositions: e.g., *La Belle Jardinière* and even later ones like the *Sistine Madonna* (fig. 355) in which the emotionalism of the end of the High Renaissance already appears. In this visionary scene where the Madonna floats upward and forward flanked by St. Sixtus and St. Barbara, there is still a geometrical limiting element, this time a diamond shape.

Fig. 355. Raphael: Sistine Madonna. Dresden, Picture Gallery.

Although influenced by Leonardo's composition and mood, Raphael is much more of a colorist, remaining unaffected by the older man's mysterious smoky shadows which he avoids in favor of a frank and luminous tonality. But his draftsmanship and compositional skill are the real contributions of his art. The two elements are combined in such pictures as the *Sistine Madonna*, where the body of the Child is gracefully and sinuously absorbed into the arms of the Madonna.

The warm humanity and linear fluency of the painter are further illustrated in the celebrated *Madonna of the Chair* (fig. 356), a slightly later work confined within a *tondo*, or circle composition. Every com-

Fig. 356. Raphael: Madonna of the Chair. Florence, Pitti Gallery.

ponent part is made to conform to this outline — the inclination of the Madonna's head, the curve of her shoulder, the turn of young John the Baptist's head at the right, and the placing of the Child's feet. The sweet simplicity of the Christ Child's expression and his relationship to the somewhat idealized peasant Mother, with her colorful scarf and shawl, are features that have given Raphael his enduring popularity over more than four centuries. The truly valuable aesthetic elements are the placement of various parts to fit the *tondo* and the graceful linear movements, exemplified by the arms of Mary enfolding the body of the Child, the lines moving continuously back and forth across the surface of the panel.

Murals by Raphael. For qualities of space composition and literary humanism, the *School of Athens* (fig. 357) is an outstanding instance. This is one of a series of murals painted by Raphael in the papal apartments of the Vatican while Michelangelo was at work on the Sistine ceiling nearby. Raphael, in whose eclectic career the entire Renaissance is mirrored — the sentiment and space composition of Perugino, the sculpturesque form of Donatello, the geometric design and dramatic action of Leonardo — now turns to the symbolic human figure as interpreted by Michelangelo.

The most significant room in this papal suite is the Stanza della

Segnatura (Signature Room, thus named because official papal documents were signed and sealed here) where Raphael painted a compendium of the intellectual interests of the time. One wall portrays the so-called *Dispute of the Sacrament,* a discussion of the significance of this vital portion of the Mass. This is the medieval and theological side of contemporary knowledge in which theologians, doctors of the Church, prophets, and saints participate. The figures are disposed in masterly fashion, and the composition is further held together by a subtly varied tonality of color. But on the opposite wall is achieved Raphael's greatest effect.

Fig. 357. Raphael: School of Athens. Rome, Vatican, Papal apartments.

There the *School of Athens* shows the humanistic counterpart of Christian theology, a characteristic High Renaissance antithesis presented through a series of idealized ancient philosophers. In the center of the composition, Plato and Aristotle advance toward the edge of the steps. The former points heavenward in a Leonardesque gesture (he actually looks like the elderly Leonardo) signifying the nonmaterial nature of his philosophy; the latter extends his arm in an earthly gesture signifying his more mundane approach. To left and right are grouped philosophers representing the theoretical and the practical disciplines, e.g.,

414

theorists like Socrates and Pythagoras on one side, and empirical thinkers like Euclid (demonstrating a proposition), Zoroaster, and Ptolemy on the other side. The friezelike assemblage occupies the top of the stairway, while the skeptic philosopher Diogenes rests comfortably on the steps connecting the two foreground groups.

Whereas the *Dispute of the Sacrament* is a formally organized composition, the *School of Athens* — symbolizing the spirit of investigation and thinking rather than fixed dogma — is freer in arrangement, and its spatial indications are accordingly more far-reaching. Here Raphael brings to a logical climax the space-composition ideas of his teacher Perugino (fig. 342); he proceeds farther and farther back into the picture space by the placing of individual forms like Diogenes, by the successive vaults with their intervening domed spaces, as well as by ordinary linear- and aerial-perspective effects.

Raphael's relationship to Michelangelo at this point is found in the pose of individual figures, especially those in the left foreground, who suggest the prophets of the Sistine ceiling, and the Apollo in the niche at the top left, who has some of the feeling of Michelangelo's *Dying Slave*. In this mural and others in the papal apartments, Raphael also reveals a more dangerous kind of influence from Michelangelo, that of painting away the architecture and in a sense going beyond the function of the mural as a decorative part of the wall surface. The other walls in this room contain an allegory of Jurisprudence and a grouping of the muses on Parnassus. The latter is one of this period's closest approaches to the spirit of classical antiquity — far closer than the purely imaginative poetic yearning of Botticelli.

Brilliant decorator though he was, Raphael did not have the original mind or searching temperament of Leonardo or Michelangelo, whose forms rather than spirit he so readily absorbed. More directly classical than either of the others, mirroring clearly the interests of his humanist friends, Raphael's work is more poised and serene, nearer the ideal of the time. But the norm of any period is not necessarily its greatest production; that distinction may be reserved for the seekers after new worlds of the spirit, who are discontented with the repetition of successful formulas. Nevertheless Raphael's aesthetic personality, though it took easily all impressions made upon it, still leaves the feeling of a fine human being, joyous and well balanced. Yet toward the end of his short career, even he realized that all was not well with the world, and his art responded to the imminent crisis of the times, as in the visionary *Transfiguration* which already sounded the note of the Reformation and the tensions of the oncoming Mannerist era.

Fig. 358. Andrea del Sarto:
Madonna of the Harpies.
Florence, Uffizi Gallery.

DEL SARTO. Another idealizing painter, the Florentine Andrea del
Sarto (1486–1531), is best known as a follower of Michelangelo. His
famous *Madonna of the Sack* fresco of the Santissima Annunziata in
Florence recalls the Sistine ceiling. Andrea's altarpiece, the *Madonna of
the Harpies* (fig. 358), contains all the devices of the so-called classical
Renaissance style: the pyramidal composition, statuesque pose of figures
with the tops of their bodies turned in an opposite direction from the
lower portions, the dignified and large folds of drapery. It has, in addition, a definitely unified tonality, resulting from a diffusion of soft warm
light and rich color. Del Sarto's rich hues, different from the relatively
de-emphasized color of most Florentine painters, are closer to those of
the Venetian masters.

VENETIAN PAINTING. The essence of Venetian painting is poetic rather
than intellectual; moreover, it reflects a culture dominated by a stronger
regard for luxury and materialism than existed in Florence. An active
center of world trade, Venice was a great intermediary in many senses.
It not only acted as commercial go-between for East and West, but also
combined the luxuriousness of the East with the highly developed bourgeois-aristocratic Italian culture of the time and its hallmark of dignity
and consequence. Venetian art, with its splendid pageants and richly
dressed paraders, glorifies material rather than spiritual values. This city

416

did not attract the concourse of philosophers and humanists who came to Florence or Rome, nor did it have too many of its own artists. From the time when it brought in artisans for the mosaics of St. Mark's, Venice left the impression of a wealthy commercial city to which architects, sculptors, and painters were drawn. This was true down through the High Renaissance.

Judging by the art of this commercial oligarchy, its chief preoccupation was to be powerful and impressive, to live well. This was a culture dedicated to good-looking men and women, fine clothes, religious and other processions, middle-class ostentation on its highest level. Unhampered by the intellectual concerns of Florentine masters who — because of humanist influence — felt they must be versatile "universal men," the Venetians stuck primarily to the business of painting, translating the Italian mode into more readily usable as well as sensuous terms. Where Florentine painting is the art of drawing, that of Venice is primarily coloristic; where the former produces sculpturesque forms as in Michelangelo and Raphael, the Venetians have richly glowing light-absorbing and light-reflecting color areas. The Florentines developed fresco painting for walls and tempera for panel pictures (oil came later); in Venice,

Fig. 359. Giovanni Bellini: Portrait of Doge Loredano. London, National Gallery.

because of the damp climate, fresco could not be used. For this reason and through the demand for a luxurious and material expression, there was a high development of the oil technique.

Giovanni Bellini. Venetian Renaissance painting begins with the Bellini family in the fifteenth century, especially Giovanni Bellini (ca. 1430–1516). His connection with the early Renaissance emerges through the tragic works of his early period, e.g., the *Agony in the Garden* (London). With their lavalike rocks, rigid draperies, and crisp bronzelike figures, these works reflect the influence of Bellini's brother-in-law Andrea Mantegna (fig. 338). More characteristic, however, are the mature, womanly Madonnas (see fig. 360) that introduce a type quite different from the usual Florentine Virgin who is generally younger and more girlish. The *Madonna of the Trees* (Venice, Academy) is one of dozens of the new kind of picture done by Giovanni Bellini; the self-absorbed Madonna is shown half-length against a bit of rich fabric and a subdued landscape background, her expression adult and wistful at the same time. The dreamy, suspended quality can be seen in the *Portrait of Doge Loredano* (fig. 359), a work of the early sixteenth century in which great

Fig. 360. Giovanni Bellini: Madonna Enthroned with Saints. Venice, San Zaccaria.

418

dignity and firmness are mingled with the inherently poetic character of Bellini's expression.

This poetic character is also found in his many splendid altarpieces in which saintly personages are brought together in the same room, flanking a Madonna and absorbed in their own thoughts. In these scenes no one looks at anyone else, even though the arrangement is commonly called a "sacred conversation." The *Madonna Enthroned with Saints* (fig. 360) from the church of San Zaccaria is an impressive example of this form. In the midst of a wonderfully shimmering and atmospheric light, four monumentalized saints stand about the Madonna's throne looking neither at her nor at each other, while she has her own thoughts, and a charming angel sits at the foot of the throne making music.

Giorgione. The lyrical quality was transmitted to Bellini's two great followers, Giorgione and Titian, who brought to a climax the High Renaissance in Venice. Giorgione (ca. 1478–1510), a romantic and somewhat mysterious figure, emerged from the Bellini circle to produce one of the most poetic and individualistic arts of the entire age. Among the

Fig. 361. Giorgione: Concert Champêtre. Paris, Louvre.

Fig. 362. Giorgione: Sleeping Venus. Dresden, Picture Gallery.

very few works that can with some measure of certainty be attributed to him are the other-worldly *Concert Champêtre* (fig. 361) and the supernally beautiful *Sleeping Venus* (fig. 362). The first picture shows two young men (clothed) and two young women (unclothed) against an Arcadian background, a shepherd and sheep at the right, and a luminous, typically Venetian landscape — typical in its painting, for Venice itself has no landscape. The young men gaze into each other's eyes; one of them, holding a lute, has his hand suspended as though about to strike a chord or perhaps just having struck one. A nude woman with her back to us holds a shepherd's pipe near her lips, about to play or just having stopped, while at the left a handsome nude female figure pours water idly out of a crystal pitcher into a fountain. Away from the mundane world, the poet-painter builds this lyrically symbolic structure — this dream world that is held in suspended animation as its characters seek to recover the past.

In the *Sleeping Venus*, Giorgione has placed his superb nude outdoors against a landscape similar to the *Concert Champêtre*, her flesh tones contrasted to the crimson velvet cushion and the creamy white satin cloth on which she lies. This work has little to do with classical mythology, in spite of the title. Like the previous painting, it is an exercise in pictorial romanticism, in the evocation of mood; the undulating form of the woman becomes part of the curved lines of the landscape background and is absorbed in the general light and color of the composition. Here, as in the regrettably small number of other works identified with this painter, the personality of the artist and the mood he is trying to evoke override the subject matter itself. What he paints is far less important than how he paints it.

Titian. The career of Titian (ca. 1477–1576), one of the longest and

Fig. 363. Titian: Madonna of the Pesaro Family. Venice, Frari.

most fruitful in art history, spans the grand manner of the High Renaissance, the more nervous and elegant Mannerist period, and the pre-Baroque style at the end of the sixteenth century that foreshadows such masters as Rubens and Rembrandt. A pupil of Giovanni Bellini, whom he succeeded as leading painter of Venice, Titian's early style is associated with a poetry similar to that of Giorgione and stemming from the same source.

In the second part of his career, Titian's inherent vigor and masculinity emerged in such pictures as the *Madonna of the Pesaro Family* (fig. 363), a characteristically splendid Venetian work, glorifying its patrons. Grouped at the left and right, the latter are presented to the full-blown and womanly Virgin by St. Peter and St. Francis, respectively; behind the left-hand group is an armored warrior carrying a flag with the family coat of arms and leading a conquered Turk — a reference to Venice's victory over the Turks. The accoutrements and background, especially the high columns, evidence the Venetian love of display which appears

Fig. 364. Titian: Bacchus and Ariadne. London, National Gallery.

422

Fig. 365. Titian: The Young Englishman. Florence, Pitti Gallery.

in so many of their official as well as family portraits. By this time the religious element of Venetian art hardly existed at all, for this is essentially a worldly picture. Asymmetrically balanced, with the Virgin high up at the right and placed on top of a receding compositional pyramid, the work is equalized by the flag moving diagonally left and by the high-reaching and stabilizing columns which return to the center and also go off into space.

Titian's feeling for antiquity is different from that of his Florentine or Roman contemporaries whose works may present the studious academicism of a Raphael or the pensive yearning of a Botticelli. Without the aid of scholarly humanism or exact reference to ancient texts, Titian in such pictures as the *Bacchus and Ariadne* (fig. 364) conveys the full pagan quality of ancient life. The splendor of his color, its transparent reds and blues, the sheer carnality of Bacchus and his riotous group sweeping forward to take in the hesitant Ariadne at the left are far more expressive of that spirit than any amount of learned reference could be. Yet it should be noted, too, that compared with the relatively calm classical subjects of painters like Raphael this work (ca. 1523) is already complicated in the oncoming Mannerist sense.

The portraits of Titian may be represented by a later one, *The Young*

Englishman (fig. 365), which expresses the magnificent conception of humanity memorialized in Titian's art. In comparison with the portrait of *Doge Loredano* by Giovanni Bellini (fig. 359), the forty or so years that separate the two paintings make the difference between the calm detached quality, the almost abstract confidence of the Doge, and the penetrative psychological quality of the later picture, its awareness of the world. The execution of Titian's work shows the technical direction in which Venetian painting was moving. The figure is visualized through successive layers of translucent oil paint on a darkish red underpainting; the underpainting absorbs the light that cuts through the outer layers, to create the ever richer and more mysterious depths. By varying the thickness of each layer of paint, the artist could control the degree to which the light was permitted to come through — whether it would be absorbed by the underpaint or reflected back to the spectator.

In the works of Titian's last period, this diffuse rather than linear technique was applied on an increasingly spiritual and emotional level as the crisis of the sixteenth century (religious, political, and economic) deepened. Paintings such as *The Entombment* (Prado, Madrid) or the *Crowning with Thorns* (Munich, ca. 1570) become abstract patterns of light and color which dissolve the form and at the same time describe it. More important, they take on a new religious — almost medieval — significance, far different from the exuberant pagan quality of the *Madonna of the Pesaro Family*. In the full swing of the Counter Reformation, Titian's religious paintings have the ecstasy and profundity of Baroque expressions, anticipating the brilliant color designs of Rubens and the dematerialized forms of Rembrandt.

18 / THE REFORMATION

FOR MAY 16th

IN the Protestant Reformation of the early sixteenth century, the new national powers of northern Europe made a conclusive attempt to separate from the body of the international Church. They also wished to do away with the special economic privileges of the clergy and the heavy burdens these imposed. Intellectually the Reformation was sparked by a strong religious mysticism that repudiated the process of salvation offered by the Church and the system of priestly mediation between man and God. The movement was not skeptical, however; the leaders of the Reformation were men of extreme piety — indeed less worldly in outlook than the contemporary Italian clerics and scholars. Although in the beginning at least the revolt did not go beyond the mild satire of an Erasmus, this piety finally encouraged large-scale rejection of holy relics, the sacraments, and the idea of "good works" to purchase salvation.

In economics the Protestant development coincided with the beginnings of modern capitalism, which became increasingly impatient with the unique privileges of the Church and its growing sale of indulgences and sinecures. The special situation of the Church weighed heavily on all classes, since not only were they taxed by it, but the amount of money drained out of various countries by tax-free clergy was an additional financial handicap. At the same time, the more ethical approach of the Church with regard to such things as interest rates made the new capitalists anxious to remove those restraints. The answer to all these problems lay politically in shaking off the authority of the Church, thus enabling the nascent monarchies to centralize their own power and control the religion of their subjects. This effort led to the bitter religious wars of the sixteenth and seventeenth centuries.

The religious mysticism which was the impetus of the Reformation differed substantially from the mystic humanism of Italy. The latter had been based on neo-Platonism and the Hebrew *Cabala,* while the new Germanic form stemmed from the pious mysticism of the later Middle Ages. As a result, in the wake of the Protestant movement came a revival of medievalism, superstitions, and intolerance. In the successful

425

campaign to do away with relicmongering, salvation by good works, image worship, and pilgrimages, Protestantism fell into a kind of religious bigotry that almost paralleled the Inquisition on the Catholic side. There was little to choose in that period between Protestant miraclemongering, belief in witchcraft or diabolism, and Catholic relic worship, sale of indulgences, and the rest.

It is important to realize that the first reformers considered themselves zealous and loyal Catholics trying to repair the Church from within. On the other hand, in spite of their real corrections of Church practices, the ascendancy of certain forms of Protestant fundamentalism (i.e., absolute reliance on Biblical, especially Old Testament, authority) and religious intolerance were serious hindrances to intellectual development. Luther's denunciation of universities and of any education not intended for the development of faith and his open opposition to the Copernican theory of planetary rotation are only two instances of the discouragement of liberal thought and scientific progress by the early Protestants. Aesthetically this attitude resulted in such acts as the burning of the pictures of saints in Wittenberg, Germany (1521); the Swiss Zwingli's persuading the Zürich city council to remove and destroy works of art from the churches (1524); and the wanton destruction of images under Henry VIII in England.

MEDIEVALISM VS. CLASSICISM: *Architecture*. The conflict between the medieval and the humanistic classical culture, already noted in connection with fifteenth-century Italy, reappeared overtly in northern Euro-

Fig. 366. City Hall (portico), Cologne.

426

pean art of the early sixteenth century. In spite of the new piety of the late fifteenth century — medieval in its intensity — the artist of Germany and the Low Countries could not help being influenced directly and indirectly by aesthetic and humanistic ideas of southern Europe. But this influence most often took the shape of external elements, as in architecture, or remained part of an unresolved disparity, as in the painting of the time.

The Old Chancellery at Bruges and the *Portico of the Cologne City Hall* (1569–1573, fig. 366) typify the accretion of Italian Renaissance detail on a characteristic northern European gabled town house. Here, as in the background of many paintings of the period, the borrowed details are more florid, less crisp and neatly carved than would be the case in the original culture. Because of its increasing authority and fashionableness, classical ornament was bound to infiltrate the late Gothic environment of northern Europe, but it would do so as an outside element and only in terms acceptable to the recipient. French Gothic of the early sixteenth century, for instance, shows round windows and pilasters on a medieval foundation. This problem is as readily traceable in painting and the graphic arts, even more dramatic in its implications of conflict arising out of transition.

GERMAN PAINTING AND GRAPHIC ARTS: *Schongauer*. German painting, the most important of the early sixteenth century in northern Europe, is a direct outgrowth of the Flemish-influenced art of the fifteenth century. The Flemish relationship is clearly apparent in Martin Schongauer (ca. 1430–1491), one of the outstanding painter-engravers of the fifteenth century. His *Annunciation* (fig. 367), a poignantly cut line engraving, may be compared in its breadth of sculptural drapery to the work of the Jan van Eyck circle a generation earlier in Flanders (cf. figs. 312–313). In keeping with the feeling of wood sculpture, a distinctly carved quality adds to the drapery's rippling, flowing independent movement. This independent motion of the cloth surfaces, especially in the banner flowing about the angel's cross, is evidence of the deep spirituality, even mysticism, animating such late medieval art. It is combined with a simple bourgeois conception of the Madonna and the continuously, though less effectively used, transfigured symbols (lilies of purity, bridal bed, closed garden). The engraving thus sums up and reasserts the juxtaposed materialism and spirituality of the fifteenth-century Flemish tradition.

Dürer. Albrecht Dürer (1471–1528), perhaps Germany's greatest artist, formulated the transition to the next period. Dürer was characteristic of an age struggling to tear itself away from the past and project

itself into the future, an era troubled by the contending loyalties of Catholics about to break away from the Mother Church. Although Dürer never actually made the break, his art reacted quite clearly to the intellectual strain and confusion of the times. Far more tense than Schongauer's, Dürer's art shows the stigmata of the age even in works done before the turn of the century, e.g., *The Large Passion* series of woodcuts from around 1498. Like the famous *Apocalypse* woodcut prints done shortly before that date, these represent a high point of revived Gothic feeling, in great measure because of the beginnings of the reaction against worldliness.

Dürer's best-known plate from the *Apocalypse* series, *The Four Horsemen of the Apocalypse* (fig. 368), treats an old theme with renewed and prophetic fervor, anticipating — as artists often do — the suffering and turbulence of the period immediately following. His vision of Death, War, Pestilence, and Destruction is Gothic not only in its complexity of detail, which is piled up in the overdecorated manner of late Gothic sculpture and architecture, but in bringing back a spirit that had not been felt in art for a long time. Significantly, this same decade in Italy produced the agony of the Savonarola reform against the "vanities," the reaction against the worldliness of that culture, seen in the *Last Judgment* frescoes of Signorelli (between 1499 and 1505, fig. 343) and the spasmodic later paintings of Botticelli such as the *Entombment of Christ* (ca. 1505, Munich, Alte Pinakothek). This new Gothic agony of the spirit had occurred in Italy even earlier, especially in the northern and Venetian areas, as in the art of Cosimo Tura.

But Signorelli's frescoes are splendid decorations for a church and Botticelli's art is a sophisticated personal expression, the one leading to Michelangelo and the other to later courtly Mannerism; whereas Dürer's work is part of a book, designed to be read by ordinary people and therefore part of a more realistic tradition. Although less plastic in its form than Italian Renaissance art, *The Four Horsemen* is emotively far stronger than most other art of the time. It is this emotional component more than anything else that German art, then and later, has to contribute. The degree to which Dürer speaks of people's fears and anxieties,

Fig. 368. Dürer: The Four Horsemen of the Apocalypse (woodcut). Courtesy, Museum of Fine Arts, Boston.

Fig. 369. Dürer: The Knight, Death, and the Devil (engraving). New York, Metropolitan Museum of Art.

their worries about life and death, war and disease, is the measure of his success in these works. In a period when Italian art turned to the expression of a fixed humanistic and theological system (as in the papal-apartment paintings of Raphael, fig. 357), Germany was expressing itself in the anguished terms of this and similar works.

In this print may be recognized the two-dimensional, multidetailed manner of Roger van der Weyden (fig. 315), his linear nervousness, the suffering of specific figures such as the curvilinear woman directly under the hooves of Death's horse — adapted by Dürer from the woman at the right of van der Weyden's *Deposition*. This style is revived and strengthened to meet the needs of a new period and represents the typical expressiveness of the entire German school of that era. The later works of Dürer achieve greater monumentality and simplicity of form, but they are never more effective and emotionally direct.

His conflict with and relationship to the art of the Renaissance may be seen in a series of works dating from the first decade of the sixteenth century, the result of his continuous study of contemporary Italian art. They begin with the *Adam and Eve* engraving of 1504 in which the forms show definite signs of generalization, especially the figure of Adam which suggests the recently done *David* of Michelangelo (1504, fig. 350); after this a succession of works bears the Renaissance relationship. But the influence of Italian forms on Dürer and his contemporaries is adapted in terms of Gothic restless movement and is surrounded by the many-detailed evidences of that style with its basic emotional character.

One of the best known examples of the stylistic fusion is Dürer's engraving of 1513, *The Knight, Death, and the Devil* (fig. 369). Here the courtly ideal of the Middle Ages is used in this neo-Gothic period to denote the power of individual moral strength in its silent conflict with the forces of darkness. Seated firmly on his well-proportioned horse (the result of typical Renaissance proportion studies, as in Leonardo), the Knight brings to mind fifteenth-century equestrian figures such as those of Donatello (fig. 327) and Verrocchio. But the generalized form of the horse and, to some extent, the rider is overbalanced by the endless piling up of Gothic detail, a rich naturalism in which the human being becomes only one of many important factors. Unlike the Italian contrast between an isolated human being and the natural environment (see *Mona Lisa* and *Madonna of the Rocks*), German masters of this period attempt to fuse humanity and nature in a romantic rather than classical expression that repeats itself in modern times (cf. Schmidt-Rottluff, fig. 525). The Italian and German attitudes at this point are also different in the over-

whelming emotional emphasis of the German, his insistence on the demonic and picturesque.

Dürer is more classicistic in some of his paintings. The *Adoration of the Magi* (1504, Florence, Uffizi) seems clearly affected by Leonardo's pyramidal compositions, background riders, and architecture — as in the Italian master's composition of the same name — even to the figure of the old king kneeling before the Christ Child. A more powerful and expressive example of Dürer's Italianism is found in the double panel showing St. Peter and St. John on one side and St. Paul and St. Mark on the other (fig. 370). By this time (1526) Dürer had been to Italy twice, the second time to Venice to visit Giovanni Bellini. The effects appear in this composition through an increased monumentality, especially in the magnificent folds of drapery reminiscent of Bellini's *Madonna Enthroned with Saints* (fig. 360). While Dürer's left-hand panel shows some

432

of the Italian's restrained mood and thoughtfulness, the right-hand side with Paul and Mark shows the typical Germanic expressiveness of face, particularly the staring eyes which have a frightening, almost mad quality. Generally speaking, color is less important in the art of Dürer than his extremely personal and forceful line.

Grünewald. This is not the case with Matthias Grünewald, a mysterious figure of the early sixteenth century (ca. 1468–ca. 1531). The most important work attributed to this painter is the *Isenheim Altarpiece* (fig. 371), whose *Crucifixion* section is perhaps the most violent expressionistic statement of the period. While the *Nativity* section of this same work depicts a homey Gothic environment with a Madonna and Child surrounded by everyday objects and a naturalistic landscape and sky, the scene of the *Crucifixion* becomes a realistic (in impact) rather than naturalistic testimonial to the sufferings of mankind as symbolized in the sufferings of the Redeemer. His enlarged form with its great pathos and emotionality — the fingers still twitching in a last agony — is so overpowering that the arms of the cross sag beneath its mighty weight. The gray-green body, presumably painted from actual sick models in St.

Fig. 371. Grünewald: Isenheim Altarpiece. Colmar Museum.

Anthony's Hospital, shows livid marks of the disease of ergotism (St. Anthony's Fire). The Madonna fainting into the arms of young St. John is dressed in a brilliant blue-white robe which stands out against the red robe of the saint. Between them and the cross an anguished Magdalene raises her twisted hands toward the Saviour; the unpleasant and deliberately dissonant combination of flowing yellow hair and pink robe furnishes another emotive accent.

A more violent protest could scarcely be made against the cult of the beautiful, as applied to either German or Italian religious art. Spiritually, the picture goes further; it symbolizes the protest of the whole Reformation and the desire for a more realistic outlook. Placed before a hopeless blue-black sky, this scene with its agonized spasmodic figures represents the increasing misery of the age, the social and economic inequities which the Reformation was to bring into the open but could not yet cure. All is not negative in Grünewald's presentation, however, for in the *Resurrection* panel of this revolutionary artistic monument he portrays a vivid dematerialized Christ soaring heavenward in a supremely visionary moment, so overwhelming that it leaves the tomb guardians in various attitudes of convulsive wonder. Only in El Greco (see fig. 382) later in the sixteenth century or Kokoschka in our time will its artistic like appear.

Altdorfer. A leading figure of this period in Germany is Albrecht Altdorfer (ca. 1480–1538), who illustrates a tendency already evident in the art of Dürer, the love of nature for its own sake. Dürer's innumerable watercolor studies of plants, animals, and scenes from Italy compare with Leonardo's approach. But the German artist's heritage from the Gothic and especially from Flemish painting of the fifteenth century (cf. figs. 309, 311, 317) makes this interest more meaningful. Nature is not merely a foil for the monumentality of the human figure, as in High Renaissance art, but is either combined with the human form as in Dürer or, as in Altdorfer, raised to a higher level of importance than the human being.

Altdorfer's *Rest on the Flight* (fig. 372) has all the charm of Grünewald's Madonna and Child scene as well as a monumentalized Madonna in the new Italianate manner; but the eye is drawn irresistibly back toward an endless landscape with a picturesque town set against mountains and water in such a way as to emphasize nature rather than man or religion, both of which now become pretexts for the portrayal of nature. Altdorfer and Dürer began to move away from the serene assumption of the Italian Renaissance that man is the center of the universe. Even though humanism is prevalent in Germany also, it is different in basic direction; through its more universal viewpoint, man becomes part of a larger world entity rather than its main element. Only in contemporary Venetian painting is there a similar change of relationship between man and his world. There it is symbolized by the smaller figure against a large landscape background, by the fact that the actions of many figures are no longer exclusively religious but poetic in meaning and part of the mood the painter wishes to express.

Baldung. Hans Baldung Grien (ca. 1480–1545) combines the emotionality of the German style with the increased monumentality and generalization of Italian art and directly reflects some of the crisis feeling of the epoch. His *Three Ages of Man* (fig. 373) is typical of this painter's insistence upon the fleeting nature of time, upon the fact that death is always waiting. He stresses here the change from childhood to blooming youth and old age; in other pictures he shows death standing behind a beautiful woman — presenting this theme again and again.

Fig. 372. Altdorfer: Rest on the Flight into Egypt. Berlin, Kaiser-Friedrich Museum.

Fig. 373. Baldung Grien: Three Ages of Man. Madrid, Prado.

Titian's *Three Ages of Man* (London, Bridgewater House) compared with Baldung's is poetic in a gently pagan and worldly manner, while the German is a prophet of doom. The period reflected in these pictures already felt the convulsive upheaval of the Reformation, which Baldung lived through. That he expressed such ideas with Italianate forms in this painting does not alter the basic difference between his emotional outlook and that of many contemporary Italians. Yet at the same time in Italy, which had also begun to respond to the impending crisis of the early sixteenth century, artists borrowed from the increasingly popular Dürer to help express their own changing emotions.

THE LOW COUNTRIES. The combination of Gothic naturalism and emotionalism with the generalized forms and classical ornament of Italian art is found in other areas, particularly the Low Countries. A relatively simple example is an engraving by the Dutch Lucas van Leyden (1494–1533). His *Rest on the Flight into Egypt* (fig. 374) is expressed with dignity and restraint, while the figures themselves are large and generalized in the Italian sense and the composition unified. Yet the faces are broad and simple, peasantlike rather than aristocratic, while the earnestness of the colloquy between the two is a further testimonial to the northern source of this work. It has much in common with artists like Dürer, who dominated the graphic arts both then and later in the north. The forms here, however simplified in the Italian style, show certain detailed crinklings of drapery (particularly the Mary), an insistence on background narration and representation, and a close form relationship between the characters and the background itself — as in the

436

Fig. 374. Lucas van Leyden:
Rest on the Flight into Egypt
(engraving). New York,
Metropolitan Museum of
Art.

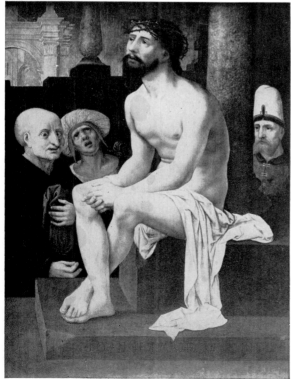

Fig. 375. Gossaert (Mabuse):
Ecce Homo. Antwerp, Mu-
seum.

curved Joseph figure continuing the line of the bent tree and the leg of the woman completing the general circular pattern.

In another part of the Netherlands — Flanders — Jan Gossaert (called Mabuse, ca. 1478–1533) was one of many so-called Italianate Flemings whose art, although influenced from the south, retained certain quite concrete native elements. His *Ecce Homo* (fig. 375) shows a nude Christ seated at the top of a short flight of steps against an Italian type of building. The recessive and diagonal composition is backed up by a vertical column as in Titian's *Madonna of the Pesaro Family* (see fig. 363), and the Christ form is reminiscent of the sculpturesque linear figures of Michelangelo. But a grotesquerie in the spectators at the left and a seriousness, even tragedy, in the man at the right testify that this is a product of the Reformation in the north, that the influence of Italian art arrives coincidentally with a great religious upheaval.

It is this agonized mystical element that changes the character of the mixture, that forces a resolution of the conflict between Gothic emotionality and broad Renaissance form in the direction of exaggeration of gesture and proportion. Forms will grow longer, hands and feet twist and turn in an effort to find a way out of the dilemma. Space in the old sense will be negated or distorted in a series of artificial patterns and expressions that will characterize the latter part of the century, the era of Mannerism.

19 / THE MANNERIST CRISIS

FOR some centuries the art of the post-Renaissance period was considered decadent and artificial, a series of exaggerated and unsuccessful imitations of that golden age of the High Renaissance, which for many people still remains the high point of European culture. But each epoch has its own aesthetic standards and aims, and artists at the middle and end of the sixteenth century were not necessarily unable to create masterpieces of the High Renaissance type — indeed it was much too late for that. They were compelled to find an art to express their own spiritual dilemma. If there had been reasons for the somewhat uneasy classicism of the earlier Renaissance period, there were now equally cogent reasons for the increased spiritualization and depth of religious feeling, for the somewhat affected and abstruse intellectuality of this new era. The simultaneous attempt to keep the vocabulary of classicism while rejecting its proportions and calm space is evidence of profound mental and social imbalance, of a desire to cling to some form of security and yet escape from the unpleasantness of the current environment.

By the middle of the sixteenth century, Italy had been invaded by the French and the Spanish. Rome had been sacked in 1527 and the great school of Raphael dispersed forever. The Reformation had been launched in Germany a decade earlier, and the power of the Church was seriously menaced. Economic as well as political and spiritual power began to pass into the hands of the new monarchies — Spain, France, England, and Germany. There was no longer any secure background for the artificially maintained and expressed stability of the High Renaissance, which had been supported by the temporary patronage of Rome.

During this new period the art of Italy (still important culturally) subsisted in petty courts which had been taken over either by Spanish viceroys or by local families acting for them. Florence, Ferrara, and Mantua were ruled by members of the Medici, Este, and Gonzaga clans — the previous bourgeois aristocracy — as deputies of Spain; Naples and Milan were under Spanish officials. Throughout this time of change, when the independent Italian city-states became portions of the Spanish-

Austrian empire and experienced the early stages of the great religious upheaval, their art took on a new elegant courtliness, a mannered expression of uneasy and troubled religiosity, a sense of impending doom.

SPREAD OF POST-RENAISSANCE ART. At this point in history, the various courts of Europe, still looking to Italy for aesthetic if not spiritual leadership, assimilated their particular versions of post-Renaissance art. The process had begun somewhat earlier, at least in France, whose King Francis I had sheltered the aged Leonardo and invited Andrea del Sarto. But the full realization of this trend had only come about with the invasion of the Italian peninsula and the stationing of imperial representatives in such places as Milan and Florence. What the court painters of the new Medici dukes transmitted to the School of Fontainebleau in France, to the court of Philip II in Madrid, to the various courts in Germany, Austria, and England, was not the art of Raphael, Leonardo, and Michelangelo but rather the more refined, attenuated, and elegant art of Mannerism — which actually was better suited to those places at that time. Some of them, especially the smaller German and Austrian principalities, found particularly fitting the intimate and highly intellectual culture produced in the Medici court. Even in Spain and France there was a certain insulation of the court, which had not yet become a great cultural force in the new nationalism of the time. For the most part, the courtly centers represented the intellectual aspirations of a limited group of people. Theirs was a polished and extremely esoteric culture, although the movement as a whole was made possible by the rise of the monarchies and existed only under their protection.

The average Italian artist's feeling of isolation was readily transmittable to the painters of northern Europe, because the latter were predisposed to it — apart from the question of fashion, which would dictate imitation in any case. The position of the individual artist was changing from that of a guildsman or a liberated creator (à la Raphael) to that of court pet. This was the beginning of a long period of protective custody for European art, in which the practitioner would be guaranteed a livelihood but intellectually and morally restrained from full individual expression.

Religious problems were far more serious and concrete in the north than in Italy where everyone was still Catholic. And all of Europe suffered in the economic sphere. The financial "crashes" of 1557 and 1575 affected Spain and France directly and the rest of the Continent indirectly. Thus, although the courtly art of Spain, for example, presented certain differences (even strong ones) from that of France, the general cultural viewpoint was more pervasive than during the Renaissance.

Italian religious art in this period communicated the need for a genuine, i.e., medieval rather than classical, Christian feeling. Its attenuated figures and tense complicated surface compositions (two anti-Renaissance qualities) were therefore easily imparted to the artists of the north. Because of the bloody religious wars, the latter too were under strong compulsion to produce a strenuous and profound religious formulation. This would have been accomplished in any case — as the Reformation art of Germany had shown — but it came to northern artists at this precise moment in Italianate form. Mabuse's *Ecce Homo* (fig. 375) marks the transition from a purely northern form to a more fashionable, although by no means insincere, Italianism.

The contemporary religious feeling of Italy, stimulated primarily by the danger of the Reformation, was part of a reform movement led by enlightened humanists who wished to improve things from within. In Rome, for instance, there was the intellectual circle in which Michelangelo moved during the late 1530s and 1540s, a group dominated by the noble lady to whom his sonnets were dedicated, Vittoria Colonna. From this influence derive the sculptor's deeply religious later works and his *Last Judgment* on the altar wall of the Sistine Chapel (1535–1541). Michelangelo's feelings about necessary reform within the Church are well known; they find an outlet in the punishing anger of the Christ in Judgment as well as in the actual words of his sonnets.

ITALIAN MANNERISM. This search for a deeper religious experience by Mannerist artists (cf. Pontormo's adaptations of Dürer) is accompanied by an intenser form of intellectualism — already felt in Raphael — interpreted now through deliberate deformation of reality, a cult of the bizarre and the esoteric shown in unusual space effects and abstruse cultural references within the picture itself. The accent is most often on subtlety and elegance of form and expression. All these things lead ultimately to abandonment of classical forms and balance; and yet in the final analysis, despite the anticlassical protest implicit in this art, it depends on the formal accomplishments of classical art which it consciously and intellectually adapts to its own purposes. In this sense Mannerism is as "modern" as late-nineteenth-century post-Impressionism. Its desperate effort to reinterpret older values in an age of chaos is as understandable as post-Impressionism's psychological straining to express its own inner conflict.

Bronzino. Florence, as one chronicler records, "when her liberty was lost was full of such sorrow, of such terror, of such confusion, that it can hardly be described or even imagined." In the courtly environment established by the new vice-royalty, the sense of isolation is well expressed in the portraits of Bronzino (ca. 1502–1572). Court painter to the dukes

of Florence, Bronzino did such characteristically aristocratic works as the *Portrait of a Young Man* (fig. 376) with its inherited contrapposto and monumentality of design. But there is a new uneasiness and self-absorption in most portraits of the period (Italian and others), a coldness of color — greens and blacks, for example — and an equally deliberate cold background architecture suggestive of buildings like the *Farnese Palace* (fig. 345).

Pictures of this kind, and indeed all Mannerist portraits, blend an abstract quality of design and relatively two-dimensional arrangement with an insistence on tiny photographically seen details (cf. Holbein, Clouet, Cranach). The abstract quality is conveyed by the overlapping of the various space areas in a series of flattened rectangular background shapes and by a tense linear contour, rather than three-dimensionality, in the figure; both factors are contrary to High Renaissance practice. A certain naturalism is shown in the crisp modeling of the foreground decorative details on the arm of the chair and under the table as well as in particularized elements of costume.

Not only are space and form altered (the latter also through the conscious elongation of the body and hands and reduction of head size),

442

but the very essence of the composition has been changed. The patterning of the human form is now complete and self-contained, but the space within which it is set is endless. Instead of being limited by the picture frame, the space moves off to left and right with the table and chair, which are only partially seen, as is the case with the architectural background. This is no longer the traditional Italian closed composition, i.e., the entire visual presentation completely seen. Here and in the next phase in the history of painting, the Baroque, there is a deliberate incompleteness of form which draws the spectator into visual participation by projecting his eye in imagination along lines that are begun but not ended.

Mannerism changes the conception of space in other ways. Previously, in a deep geometrical space, a monumental and controlled form was made the focus of attention through effective proportion or through the convergence of all lines toward a central point; now there is no longer a receding perspective box as in the *School of Athens* (fig. 357) or *The Last Supper* (fig. 347). In Bronzino's portrait the background, reduced to bare simplified surfaces overlapping each other, is joined with the foreground through the young man's flattened form; his horizontal hand flows into the line of the table, which in turn parallels the various horizontals of the background. Most significant, however, the previous form of composition with all the lines converging to one spot has given way to another type in which separate sets of lines may have their own meeting places — usually outside the picture space. The net result is to diffuse the accents along a primarily two-dimensional surface. The earlier concentrated directional indications are broken down into a series of differently directed groups of lines which the artist has deliberately set in motion in this new, increasingly restless conception of the world.

The young man himself is noteworthy for his elegant bearing, more affected than the essentially self-confident High Renaissance portraits (cf. Titian's *The Young Englishman*, fig. 365) and by the same token more human and psychological in character. He is not a man of action but of thought, in this case a reader of books; another sitter may appear with a cameo or statuette from his collection. The Italian nobleman of this period is inactive because his function has been usurped by the conqueror. He turns in upon himself; his pictured personality, like his earlier three-dimensionality, is subdued in favor of the abstract pattern made by the sweep of arms and shoulders in a consciously aesthetic design of curves set against straight horizontal and vertical lines.

Parmigianino. The majority of these court portraits, however, are necessarily formal in function and more controlled in spirit than religious works, which give a much clearer reflection of the conflict between emotion and fact. In Italy the two foremost religious masters are Parmigianino (1503–1540) and Jacopo Pontormo (1494–1556). The peculiar sensitivity, unhappiness, and insecurity of the Mannerist artist is illustrated by the fact that Parmigianino veered back and forth between painting and alchemy and ended his life as a melancholiac and eccentric. Pontormo was morbidly sensitive about his art, questioning his own ability, refusing to part with pictures done for patrons, and badly needing the reassurance of the world. A third painter, Il Rosso, was a strange mixture of violence and timidity and finally committed suicide. Against the background of the first steps in the Counter Reformation — establishment of the Jesuit order in 1534, reestablishment of the Inquisition in 1542, and book censorship in 1543 — the religious art of this period brings forth a series of tortuous unmaterial forms. These are at once a negation of increasingly repressive reality and a recognition of the necessity for a more genuinely spiritual religious attitude.

Pictures like Parmigianino's *Madonna with the Long Neck* (fig.

Fig. 377. Parmigianino: Madonna with the Long Neck. Florence, Pitti Gallery.

377) have the same courtly elegance as Bronzino's young man — tall figure, tiny head, long tapering fingers, aristocratic gesture. Like the other painting, too, the figure is clearly patterned into an abstract and rhythmical surface arrangement. But while the young man is shown in a calm dignified manner, however broken his spatial environment, the figures here crowd together at the left in a tense nervous fashion, accompanying the inquietude of the Madonna's gesture, her apparent floating in space, and the uneasy way in which the Child is placed in her lap. This contrasts, for example, to the slightly earlier *Madonna of the Pesaro Family* by Titian (fig. 363, 1519–1526). There the Madonna was the climax of a recessive pyramid, balanced by the figures at the left with their banner; and the entire composition was stabilized by the impressive columns behind. The morbid Parmigianino, on the other hand, creates a deliberately twisted and restive space with two different perspective viewpoints, one for the front figures shooting off to the left and the other for the curious background column. That column, traditional symbol of despair and ruin (as in Poussin and the modern de Chirico), is emphasized by the lean and ragged prophet below, his scroll foretelling the imminent catastrophe that hangs over the land. High Renaissance space existed as a symbol of the world mastered by man; Mannerist space is employed as a more overt emotional device expressing the artist's search for escape, for spiritual profundity, or for mystic identification with the infinite.

Fig. 378. Giovanni da Bologna: Mercury. Florence, Bargello.

Giovanni da Bologna. In this light the endless twisting movements of these paintings or of such sculptures as Giovanni da Bologna's *Mercury* (1567, fig. 378) become more than mere stylistic aberrations or affecta-

Fig. 379. Tintoretto: Last Supper. Venice, San Giorgio Maggiore.

tions. *Mercury*, the messenger of the gods, strives for the most positive upward movement and is detached from the earth — resting only on the puff of air that comes from a mask representing one of the winds. Giovanni, originally Jean de Boulogne (1529–1608), also utilizes the elongated Mannerist forms with their essentially linear emphasis, their physical and emotional strain. Contrasting with Michelangelo's prescribed block form that struggled for release, the *Mercury* uses the Renaissance upraised-finger gesture (cf. Raphael, fig. 357) to help overcome gravity, to escape from the world.

Tintoretto. Even relatively isolated Venice responded to the uncertainties of this epoch, troubled as a great mercantile power by the bankruptcies of France and Spain in 1557 and the second Spanish catastrophe of 1575. These circumstances add to the worried looks in portraits of the time, e.g., those of Lotto and Moroni, while the religious crisis is mirrored in the art of Jacopo Robusti, called Tintoretto (1518–1594). His *Last Supper* (fig. 379) with its supernatural light and diffused diagonal perspective effects may be opposed to Leonardo's painting (fig. 347) with its controlled realism and concentrated linear emphasis. Like other Mannerist works, Tintoretto's version destroys single-point perspective, stresses the spiritual over the rational, and transforms the balanced, closed

446

composition of the Renaissance into a deliberately unbalanced, infinitely extending space in which figures assume uneasy agitated postures.

Tintoretto's desire to transcend the physical limitations of space and of gravity is also expressed in those compositions where he shows figures flying gracefully through the air to effect their particular missions. The St. Mark in the *Miracle of the Slave,* who swoops out of the sky to save the slave from the hammer of the executioner, the marvelous grace of the Venus who brings the couple together in the *Marriage of Bacchus and Ariadne* (fig. 380) as she turns from limitless outer space toward the spectator, are examples of this technical tour de force. Tintoretto's figures are drawn with reminiscences of Michelangelo's proportions, just as his colors suggest the later work of Titian, but the conception is generally more human in its sympathies than either precedent. Titian's Bacchus (fig. 364) shouts his sensual message; Tintoretto's pleads and comforts.

In his religious works, Tintoretto felt the need for a stronger expression, in common with most artists of this era. He not only changed the forms and the space relationships in his pictures, but altered color considerably away from the enamel-like surfaces of Giorgione and early Titian or the later Titian richness of coloring. Tintoretto's significant contribution here is a broken, highlighted, and spontaneous handling of paint that often helps to convey a more emotional, even expressionist

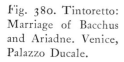

Fig. 380. Tintoretto: Marriage of Bacchus and Ariadne. Venice, Palazzo Ducale.

mood in which reality is destroyed to arrive at the underlying truth. Works like the *Christ on the Sea of Galilee* (Washington, National Gallery) with their spottily applied white highlights and deliberately atonal color combinations express an emotive quality in keeping with the Mannerist agony. They also foreshadow the most spiritual of the sixteenth-century painters in Spain, El Greco.

MANNERISM IN SPAIN. In this period Spain represented an even higher level of religious feeling than Italy. In addition to the universal problems of the Reformation, she also had the question of the recently and forcibly converted Moors and Jews (many of whom still retained their original beliefs in secret) and the revolt of the conquered Netherlands. Thus the soil was prepared for Mannerist expressiveness. Court painters of the time clearly resembled contemporary Italian masters like Bronzino, e.g., the portraits of the *Infanta Isabella* and the *Infante Don Carlos* by Sanchez Coello (ca. 1515–1590) in the Prado Museum, Madrid. Their unquiet glances, elongated figures with tiny heads, long oval faces, and long tapering moving fingers show the relationship to Mannerist style in general.

On the religious side is the work of Luis Morales, extolled as "El

Fig. 381. Morales: Madonna and Child. Madrid, Prado.

Divino" (ca. 1509–1586). His *Madonna and Child* (fig. 381) stems from the smoky painting of Leonardo, diverging toward a profound and yearning spirituality that emerges through the back-and-forth unbalanced movements across the picture surface. The painter deliberately emphasized these nonspatial qualities and a kind of endless motion and interaction in the uneasily moving parts.

El Greco. With these forms as background, the art of El Greco (ca. 1541–1614) fits more readily into the Spanish historical pattern and need not be explained solely on the basis of inherent Spanish mysticism. Originally Domenico Theotocopuli, El Greco ("the Greek") went to Italy from his native island of Crete where he had been under the influence of the austere, elongated forms of Byzantine art. In Venice he came in contact with the rich throbbing color of later Titian and the dematerialization of form in Tintoretto's flickering expressive colors. In Rome he was attracted by the later phase of Michelangelo's art with its intense spiritualization and distortion. Around 1576 he came to Spain, probably because there was employment to be found there, and settled in Toledo at the height of the Spanish Counter Reformation and Inquisition.

The violent religiosity of El Greco's art in its highest nonmaterialistic expression is seen in *The Nativity* (fig. 382). Space is compressed into a succession of two-dimensional movements of flickering, twisting flame-like forms that carry the eye upward and outward into some heavenly sphere. To maintain this arbitrary surface quality, the figures are placed one above the other in registers rather than in a receding Renaissance space. The center figures, moreover, are turned upward and defy the laws of gravity. Distortion of space is further effected by the fact that one cannot be altogether sure of where the various persons are standing and that some figures appear much larger than those next to them.

This arbitrary handling of space (cf. Bronzino and Parmigianino) is only one of the devices used by El Greco to increase the feeling of emotional disturbance. Form is equally distorted and expressive, with proportions willfully altered in the interests of heightened emotive response, again in the best Mannerist tradition. The shape of the Madonna here may be compared with those of earlier Mannerist works; the figure at the left, in his upward, almost flying movement, recalls the sculptured *Mercury* (fig. 378).

The third arbitrary and expressionist element in El Greco's art, the handling of color, places him closer to the Venetians (especially Tintoretto) than to artists like Bronzino. Instead of the cold clinical light of the latter, El Greco developed an intensification of the white-highlighting technique of Tintoretto, a sharpening of the latter's color contrasts —

Fig. 382. El Greco: The Nativity. New York, Metropolitan Museum of Art.

again for impact. The form becomes increasingly transparent through the method of paint application; and finally, there is a denial of local or original color of the objects or people. These elements together result in an almost complete dematerialization of form which, in terms of the comparable modern Expressionists, enables the artist to arrive at the spiritual truth that lies behind the mere appearance of things.

MANNERISM IN FRANCE: *Architecture and sculpture.* Other countries show evidence of the Mannerist style. France, which had been interested in Italian art since the fifteenth century, arrived at a significant absorption of that art during the reign of King Francis I (1515–1547). Under this monarch the aging Leonardo spent his last years in France, Andrea del Sarto was briefly employed, and architecture was encouraged in a combined late Gothic–High Renaissance style as in other northern countries. Buildings like the chateaux of *Chambord* (fig. 383), Chenonceaux, Blois, or Fontainebleau show clear infiltration of Italian motifs, which are superposed on older Gothic structures to create a tension of their own. With the first building of the Louvre palace (1541–1548) by Pierre Lescot (fig. 384), the new style was already overwhelming the old. The Louvre would be elaborated and ornamented by subsequent monarchs but would still remain Lescot's conception. With the aid of the sculptor Goujon, Lescot laid the foundations of French classical architecture, which was destined to be so influential throughout Europe. At this point it was still a rich Mannerist complex of friezes, pilasters, and architraves playing sensitively across the surface of the structure.

Jean Goujon (ca. 1510–1568) is a clearer instance of a French artist fitting into the Mannerist category. His extraordinarily graceful nymphs from the *Fountain of the Innocents* (Paris, fig. 385) are a characteristic adaptation of Italianate art with French grace and charm. Proportions, contrapposto, and surface interests evoke the international Mannerism of the sixteenth century, but the wonderful feeling for the body and its relation to the covering drapery are more local in quality and more genuinely classical than Italian practices at the time.

French painting. Although Francis I was unable to graft the High Renaissance art of Leonardo and Andrea del Sarto onto French culture, he did succeed in acquiring for the French court the services of Mannerists such as Il Rosso and Primaticcio, who founded the elegant and somewhat artificial school of Fontainebleau. These artists and their French followers produced frescoes and oil paintings typical of the slightly distant melancholy of the Italian courts, which because of their emphasis on the new classical culture and general aristocratic refinement were very welcome in France.

Fig. 383. Chateau of Chambord.

Fig. 384. Lescot: The Lescot Wing of the Louvre, Paris. (Detail.)

452

The Clouets. More than anything, the French court of this time sponsored the production of gallant and elegant portraits, delicately colored and sensitively drawn, in which Flemish fifteenth-century realism was tempered by the refinement of the Italo-French court. Whereas fifteenth-century French portraits had shown ugly people, as a rule those of the sixteenth century, the product of a more cultured and refined society, presented another version of the human face. The Clouets, father and son, are perhaps the most important portraitists of the period, and may be represented by the *Francis I* (fig. 386) of Jean Clouet, the Flemish-born father (active ca. 1516–1546). Again the typical blending occurs of large, relatively flat abstract forms with many realistic details in costume, so many in fact that the sleepy-eyed king is almost lost beneath them. François Clouet (ca. 1505–1572) made a series of more sensitive

Fig. 385. Goujon: Fountain of the Innocents (detail: Nymphs). Paris.

Fig. 386. Clouet: Francis I. Paris, Louvre.

and delicately executed red-chalk drawings of members of the court that established a long-lived tradition in French art down through the portrait drawings of Maurice Quentin de La Tour in the eighteenth century to Ingres and Degas in the nineteenth.

MANNERISM IN CENTRAL EUROPE: *Holbein*. Early-sixteenth-century German painting had already been affected by the Reformation (Chapter 18). On the Mannerist side was the work of Hans Holbein the Younger (1497–1543), born in Augsburg and brought up in Basel, Switzerland, one of the great centers of northern humanism. Although the talented Holbein was able to master both the northern and the southern manners of painting (the first illustrated in his famous detailed Flemish-influenced *George Gisze*, the second in his serenely balanced *Madonna of Burgomaster Meyer*), the latter style came to him too late. The crisis of the Reformation made it an open question whether any sort of art could survive in the Germanic countries, and Holbein left for England in 1526 at the suggestion of the great Erasmus, who recommended him to Sir Thomas More, author of *Utopia*.

In England, Holbein soon became court painter under Henry VIII, for whom he painted various members of the royal family as well as personages of the court. Typical of this important period in his life is the portrait of *Jane Seymour* (fig. 387), which may be compared with Clouet's *Francis I,* Bronzino's *Young Man,* and other Mannerist portraits. In his characteristic fashion, Holbein concentrated upon an abstract linear theme into which the human being is fitted and against which the elaborate costume plays its contrapuntal melody. The open, angular headdress is balanced by the pattern of the arms, with subordinate and related designs offered in the tapering bodice, tapering necklace, and reverse panel in the skirt. The face, as almost always in Holbein's paintings, is rather neutral in quality, at least at first glance, and has little of the outgoing character of High Renaissance portraits. There is an intimate intention in these works that again fits into the general tone of the period.

A more conventional type of Mannerism in Germany is found in the work of Lucas Cranach the Elder (1472–1553), who, in addition to court

Fig. 387. Holbein: Jane Seymour. Vienna, Kunsthistorisches Museum.

Fig. 388. Bruegel the Elder: Huntsmen in the Snow. Vienna, Kunsthistorisches Museum.

portraits, also produced a number of pseudoclassical allegories to please noble ladies and gentlemen. The forms are long and slender, their gestures affected, their physiognomies distinctly Germanic.

MANNERISM IN FLANDERS. Flemish Mannerism has been referred to in connection with Mabuse (fig. 375), whose work reflects not only the influence of Italy but the religious doubts and problems of the entire epoch. These difficulties reached a climax in the Netherlands with their revolt from Spain in 1568 — caused by the occupation by Spanish troops, the constant threat of the Inquisition, and the severe punishments for heresy. The northern, or Dutch, provinces, which had turned to Calvinism, ultimately secured their independence by the beginning of the seventeenth century; the southern, or Flemish, provinces remained Catholic and were part of the Hapsburg empire for a long time. In this era of adjustment, it was not yet possible for the fiercely Protestant Dutch to develop an art. Flanders (or Belgium) was brought back into the Spanish fold by the promise that its ancient democratic privileges would be restored; it did not forswear the older religion with its artistic tradition and continued to produce important paintings.

Bruegel. Most expressive and meaningful in revealing the social and spiritual struggle of the mid-sixteenth century is the work of Pieter

Bruegel the Elder (ca. 1525–1569). Although at first glance remarkably different from the courtly and even artificial style of the Mannerists, there are certain qualities that Bruegel shares with them. His conception of the world is as self-conscious as theirs and as different from that of the High Renaissance. For example, the space conception of the *Huntsmen in the Snow* (fig. 388) may be compared with that of Tintoretto's *Last Supper* (fig. 379); in both a deep, diagonally conceived space is seen over the heads of figures in the foreground, while balance is established by reconciling different directional thrusts. They are both universal in viewpoint rather than generalized in the Renaissance sense and manage to bring together the ideals of realism with larger and more significant truths.

In the *Huntsmen in the Snow* the small figures, increasingly typical in the sixteenth century (cf. Altdorfer, fig. 372), move into an endless vision of nature — which in Bruegel's philosophy (and he has one as much as any of the intellectual Mannerists) is far more significant than had been the case in the Renaissance. Time and again he portrays the

Fig. 389. Bruegel the Elder: The Wedding Dance. Courtesy, Detroit Institute of Arts.

cruelties of the age, but in allegorical fashion, since there was danger from the occupying and ravaging Spaniards against whom most of those pictures were directed. Man's inhumanity to man and other frailties, as in the *Massacre at Bethlehem, The Blind Leading the Blind, Magpie on the Gallows, The Unfaithful Shepherd, Daedalus and Icarus*, become symbols of the transitoriness of human activity — and the contrastingly eternal beauty of nature.

His peasant paintings, e.g., *The Wedding Dance* (fig. 389), are usually considered to indicate his interest in simple people and their customs, showing his fundamentally democratic character. Yet Bruegel's peasant themes are historically in line with the northern tradition first expressed in the *Très riches heures* done for the Duc de Berri in the early fifteenth century (fig. 310), which included representations of various simple farm activities, and the later tapestries also intended for court use, which mingled in the same way aristocratic and peasant elements. This fact certainly does not preclude a sympathetic viewpoint on the part of the artist. What is important here is the change from the particular (the specific peasant dance) to the universal — the constant endless movement, the symbolic dance of life, worked out in a series of semiabstract circular surface patterns that communicate this concept.

Individual details are invariably subordinated to the allover design, however many details may be shown, and the artist expresses himself not so much through the particular fact (any more than in the *Huntsmen in the Snow*) as through the universal truth which he tries to convey in aesthetic terms. This is Bruegel's interpretation of reality rather than the reality itself. In that sense the painting is as modern as Munch's *Dance of Life* or Matisse's *La Danse* in the twentieth century, as much an expression of the artist's own age.

20 / THE BAROQUE AGE

CONDITIONS were ripe for the appearance of a new style at the end of the sixteenth century; three operative factors combined to determine its course. The Catholic Church provided a major element by adopting a policy of art as religious propaganda — art to make worship more inviting. Secondly, there was a general broadening of man's earthly horizons. And thirdly, increased centralization and political stability were offered by the burgeoning monarchies.

BIRTH OF BAROQUE STYLE: ART AS PROPAGANDA. Within the Church proper, one of the most important reform activities had been a program elaborated by successive sittings of the Council of Trent, held between 1545 and 1563 and directed by the Jesuits. Recognizing that it was too late to stop the Protestant Reformation, they had decided to try to check its further spread. Although the meetings had coincided with the strained unhappy art of Mannerism (distinctly, if somewhat psychotically, motivated by religious conflicts), the Council now set forth an actual program for animating religious art to attract worshipers to church. This program, expressed in the impressive, sensuous, dynamic, and emotive style known as Baroque, came into being toward the close of the century as the Church's positive answer to its great problem. In this new form, art found its release from the tense inward-looking Mannerist style and became an expression for the many instead of, as earlier, for the few. The Baroque approach with its ornate and spacious churches, its attractive and emotionally appealing forms, also figured in the extension of the Church outside Europe to Mexico and Central and South America as the boundaries of the Western world expanded.

The flow of Church influence in the only direction that it could move was connected with the broadening of social horizons. The explorations of the sixteenth and seventeenth centuries were pursued, we are told, for "gold, God, and glory" — gold for businessmen, God for the Church, and glory for the still dynamic soldier and noble class seeking outlets for its energy. These explorations offered additional territory for Baroque architecture, sculpture, and painting through countless churches and monasteries established in the New World by Spanish, Portuguese, and French colonists (see fig. 405). In a sense they were one source of the new breadth of style. The expansion was augmented by non-Catholic countries such as Holland and England with their commercial East India companies.

SOCIAL EXPANSION. The opening up of the New World was a step toward demolishing the limited insular ideas that had dominated for so long. With it came the knowledge of new people, their languages and social customs; with it came the development of science, especially mathematics, optics, and astronomy. It is not accidental that the theory of Copernicus (1473–1543) came forth early in this era and ultimately transformed the world outlook, from the belief that the earth was the center of the solar system to the understanding that the sun is its central point. From that very time, man's notion of himself as the center of all things was doomed. There came into his cultural expression a strong feeling of endless rather than tightly controlled space, already noticed in the art of the sixteenth century. This phenomenon — together with the change from a large-size figure against a landscape to a relatively smaller figure — reached its logical climax in the art of the seventeenth century.

The Copernican revolution had been significant for the art of the Baroque age even in exchanging the respective positions of sun and earth within our solar system. The next step was taken by Giordano Bruno (1548–1600), who imagined a universe of infinite size (with many solar systems) and without fixed center, the free movement of heavenly bodies in space, and also the existence of many universes — all guesswork, to be sure, but "dangerous" enough to get him burned at the stake. Johannes Kepler (1571–1630) postulated the great laws of planetary motion and asserted that planets move freely in space in elliptical orbits. There were many other giant thinkers in this period, such as Galileo Galilei (1564–1642) and Sir Isaac Newton (1642–1727), all contributing to a permanently broader conception of the universe that had its effect on every aspect of culture.

The new viewpoint not only subordinated man to the cosmos but also described the universe as being without center, as consisting of equal and homogeneous units in a uniform but infinite system. Although man became a very tiny factor in this new scheme, his awareness of its infinite extent gave him a new-found confidence, particularly as he realized the interdependence of man with this endless cosmos and its various parts. Aesthetically this change is marked in the difference between the monumentalization of the Renaissance figure in or against its landscape [cf. *Mona Lisa* (fig. 348), *Concert Champêtre* (fig. 361), or *Sleeping Venus* (fig. 362)] and the increasingly small and de-emphasized figure of later post-Renaissance landscapes, e.g., Altdorfer (fig. 372). The tendency to "lose" the figure in the landscape background, to achieve a sense of infinity in both psychological and spatial terms, is fully developed in the landscapes of the seventeenth century, e.g., Poussin, Claude, or Ruisdael (see figs. 415, 416, 428).

On another level, the Baroque feeling of infinite extension into space is perceived in the mysterious unending shadows of a Rembrandt or in the dynamic endless space indications (begun during the Mannerist period) of a da Cortona. Even in Dutch painting, clear and contained though it seems (e.g., Vermeer), there is constant reference to people looking out of windows into the distance, to a relationship between indoors and outdoors, to simple spatial and linear extensions within and without the house.

It has often been noted that Baroque art is a reflection of the interrelated character of life and the space in which it moves, that it responds to the infinitude of that space. The individual works, conceived as homogeneous totalities with all their parts equally alive, underline this relationship. In Baroque architecture and sculpture, each part is equally necessary to the composition and has little existence outside that totality. Many Baroque paintings, especially by Rubens, display not only this homogeneous conception in which parts and whole are interrelated, but also a centrally focused composition wherein the various elements revolve about a central point like planets around a star. This may be illustrated also by some of Vermeer's compositions, e.g., *Girl at a Casement Window* or *Officer and Laughing Girl* (fig. 429), whose central point unites the different radiating elements, while the total effect includes both homogeneity and extension into space. The latter quality is strongly reinforced by the preponderant abrupt diagonals that dominate Baroque composition, the violent foreshortening effects that carry the eye rapidly into a given area, and the mysterious endless space of Rembrandt and countless others.

MONARCHIES AND MIDDLE CLASS. The third background element affecting the new style (in addition to Church policy and the broadened cosmic outlook) was the centralization of monarchies. This process, begun during the previous century, now came toward fruition. The establishment of national dynastic states — England, 1485; Spain, 1556; France, 1589 — owed much to the cooperation of the monarchies and the rising bourgeoisie against the nobility. The middle class, worn out by the religious wars of the sixteenth century, needed a degree of peace and security for the development of trade and commerce. It accordingly favored — and profited by — the establishment of strong national states. For art, this resulted in the creation of a new patron class as early as the seventeenth century.

This bourgeois factor accounts for two important aesthetic elements: rationalistic support for the underlying classical tendencies of the century, as expressed in Poussin (a favorite with the upper middle class); and a continuous pull in the direction of naturalism, as in the Le Nains, Latour, and others.

In monarchical countries these two elements are subordinated by an impressively attractive (even sensual) emotive and monumental style that combines the aristocratic and the religious — as in Rubens, a noble courtier who attended Mass every day and whose religious art testifies to that fact. In a bourgeois country like Holland, where there was no court in the same sense, the naturalistic factors are accentuated, the middle class is exalted instead of the aristocracy, and various treatments of infinity (landscape, architectural interiors, mysterious lighting effects) take the place of overtly religious and conventionally Baroque subjects. Conversely, it is possible to find in Dutch art a certain aristocratic character which became increasingly popular toward the end of the century. And the naturalistic element, so strong in Dutch art, appears in Italy, France, Spain, and Flanders as a parallel to the courtly formal manner.

ITALIAN PAINTING: *The Carracci.* In Italy, the ideological and stylistic source of the courtly sensual Baroque, there also may be seen the naturalistic side of the period. The two directions are represented in the academic (i.e., backward-looking) art of the Carracci family and the progressive painting of Caravaggio. Both forms, however different in character, are

Fig. 390. Annibale Carracci: Diana Visits Endymion. Panel from the ceiling of the Farnese Palace, Rome.

dedicated to arousing religious sympathy and exaltation; the former is considered more acceptable by the Church itself, since it derives from the grand tradition of the High Renaissance, whereas Caravaggio's characters, however pious they may be, are inspired by life.

The Carracci have influenced the history of art, first, by initiating a grandiose yet appealing conception of religion (cf. Domenichino's *Last Communion of St. Jerome*, fig. 391), and, second, by establishing the practice of dipping into earlier styles as part of a regular academic procedure. The academy they set up in Bologna in 1583, in opposition to the still powerful Mannerism of the time, became the precedent for similar academies in late-seventeenth-century France, eighteenth-century England, and other countries. They formed the static background against which the more progressive development of art would enact its role down through the nineteenth century.

The mural decorations (fig. 390) of Annibale Carracci (1560–1609) and his assistants in the *Farnese Palace* in Rome illustrate the academic process of borrowing from the past those elements which the painter finds most useful or congenial to him and utilizing them in a relatively conventional rather than original fashion. Thus, ideally, the power of Michelangelo, the suavity of Raphael, the color of Titian, and the sensuousness of Correggio should form a perfect blend; but one can readily see how artificial and uninspired such an aggregation could become. Moreover, the controlled art of the High Renaissance, which the Carracci regarded as desirable, was actually unsuited to the overtly emotive requirements of the new age.

Although for the most part the painting of the Carracci and their followers could not afford much comparison with the presumed sources, it was still extremely useful in its post-Renaissance type of lavishness for promoting the official and propaganda side of Italian Baroque art. Its real mistake, as with most academic work, lay in a too close imitation of the past; other artists of this period such as Rubens, starting from the same premise, used the art of the past as a jumping-off place from which they embarked on individual forms of expression. Yet the Carracci offer a starting point in the new Baroque splendor. In their curious blending of architectonic, sculptural, and pictorial effects in the *Farnese Palace* murals, they present one of the main characteristics of the courtly Baroque style: its denial of the boundaries that ordinarily separate the various arts. It will be seen that a good deal of Baroque architecture and often its sculpture has a pictorial quality.

Domenichino. Domenichino (1581–1641) is among the more important followers of the Carracci. His *Last Communion of St. Jerome*

Fig. 391. Domenichino: Last Communion of St. Jerome. Rome, Vatican Museum.

(fig. 391) exemplifies an art of melodramatic appeal as distinct from an art of grandeur. Its theatrical quality, like that of much Baroque religious painting and sculpture, is distinctly outgoing, whereas the High Renaissance form and content aimed at a contained effect. Its sides and top deliberately cut off, as opposed to the previous closed compositions, the picture moves into space laterally and into the infinite distance. Instead of elements symmetrically balancing each other (except in a general way), the group of angels comes in from the upper right, while the large candle

464

at the left moves directly upward without any actual compensating factor on the other side. Most significantly, the composition is circular in shape; forms move around the symbolic wafer in the center of the picture, making the centrifugal arrangement described earlier.

Many other Italian painters worked in this vein; but one of the most striking aspects of Baroque art in that country appears in the mural and ceiling decorations of such men as Andrea del Pozzo (1642–1709) and Pietro da Cortona (1596–1669) who carried the illusionistic principle to its logical conclusion, broadening the procedures begun by Mantegna and Correggio. Paintings of this type (fig. 392) have a deliberate infinitely reaching effect, as forms move higher and higher overhead to disappear ultimately into the clouds. At the same time they deny the validity of architecture as such; often the walls are extended by painting architectural elements into the vault or dome itself, so that it is difficult to tell where the walls end and the roof begins.

Caravaggio. The more directly naturalistic side of Baroque art also has its origins in Italy in the work of the exceedingly influential Michel-

Fig. 392. Pietro da Cortona: Detail from fresco in salon of Palazzo Barberini, Rome.

angelo da Caravaggio (1573–1610). At the very beginning of the new era, Caravaggio set the pattern for two kinds of everyday art: a poetic and lyrical naturalism as in the *Bacchus* (fig. 393) and a more melodramatic and appealing realism as in the *Death of the Virgin* (fig. 394). In the first and earlier category, a definitely outlined form in a limpid, clear atmosphere is surrounded by articles of everyday use shown with precise clarity. Colors are cool and bright, the form monumental in the late-Renaissance tradition, sentiment poetic in the Venetian sense, but the totality is one of warm reality, interior space, and a general awareness of the world. This phase of Caravaggio's work affects the more objective side of Dutch painting, as in Vermeer (fig. 430), and constitutes a link in the chain of clearly illuminated forms seen by direct light that carries down through Velásquez to Manet.

The second type of painting, shown in *The Entombment of Christ* (Vatican), *The Calling of St. Matthew* (San Luigi dei Francesi, Rome), and the *Death of the Virgin* (fig. 394), is another phase of Baroque realism. Abandoning the soft clear light of the *Bacchus* with its still-life details and gentle mood, the artist reveals his own faithful adherence to Baroque religious aims in an operatically illuminated scene, an accent on

Fig. 393. Caravaggio: Bacchus. Florence, Uffizi Gallery.

Fig. 394. Caravaggio: Death of the Virgin. Paris, Louvre.

extreme pathos, and most meaningful in terms of his own contribution, a deliberately lower-class realism. Instead of the Renaissance-derived glorifications of artists like Domenichino and the Carracci (figs. 390–391) with their officially sponsored formalism, Caravaggio's religious painting is the art of the common man — so simple and straightforward that, although it found little favor with the official clergy, it attracted generations of European artists. Ribera in Naples, Zurbarán in Spain, Le Nain and Latour in France, and Rembrandt in Holland all disclose the effect of his dramatic realism, his arbitrarily rather than naturalistically lighted figures, his controlled spotlight bringing into relief the details the painter wishes to emphasize.

Caravaggio's influence thus extends technically over two distinct areas: the clearly painted, muted early pictures with their emphasis on still-life effects and the later, more characteristic dramatic-spotlight pictures which establish a Baroque form of the earlier chiaroscuro of Leonardo and Giorgione. He is, further, one of the first leading painters of everyday, or genre, subjects (e.g., the *Card Players*, *Fortune Teller*); his so-called "pot-house" scenes reflect the Bohemian environment in which the artist moved, first in Rome and later among the villainous characters of Naples. It is by no means unusual that a man like Caravaggio, though he summed up the most typical elements of the culture in which he lived — its direct appeal to religious sentiment (even to showing simple and dirty peasants worshiping the Madonna) and its tremendous urge toward naturalism — should be rejected by that society. Nevertheless in the Rome of the early seventeenth century, as the papacy was rising toward a new goal, artists from all over Europe congregated to learn the message of Italian art. From the Carracci school on the one hand and from Caravaggio's followers on the other, the streams of influence flowed north.

ITALIAN SCULPTURE: *Bernini.* In Baroque sculpture, which developed somewhat more slowly than its painting, the outstanding name is Gian Lorenzo Bernini (1598–1680), also one of the leading architects of his century. Trained by an able sculptor father, young Bernini produced a number of Baroque works that reflected the diverse influences on the movement at its beginning. Among his early works is the brilliant *Apollo and Daphne* (ca. 1622, fig. 395), which inherits the upward movement and straining away from the earth of Giovanni da Bologna (cf. fig. 378) and the still strong feeling for antiquity that runs through Baroque art. What seems new, however, is the melodramatic idea of portraying the nymph turning into a tree as the elegant Apollo (i.e., the sun) touches her. The transformation is shown with intense realism as the sculptor tries "to mold his marble like wax." Even more striking is the Baroque mixture of pain and ecstasy, more apparent in the Daphne than in the somewhat languid and Hellenistic Apollo (cf. *Belvedere Apollo*, Vatican). The diagonal composition, expressed through a single curved line into which the parts fit indissolubly, is a typical Baroque arrangement.

A more fully developed work, and more characteristic of the international Baroque formulation in which Bernini had so important a role, is the *Ecstasy of St. Theresa* (fig. 396). This projects his general attitude of attempting "to synthesize to some extent painting and sculpture" and offers pictorial effects in sculpture plus an architecture that is both sculpturesque and pictorial in character. Color plays a large role in the contrasting effect of the marble columns and the gilt areas, especially the rays descending behind the angel and the saint. These personages are placed in a monumental columnar niche, capped by a typically broken curved pediment and based on a vertically effective altar that blends with both the columns and the base of the wall and niche. Everything is designed for a specific place in this operatic presentation of the dream related in the saint's book. An angel has pierced her breast with a golden arrow, causing her ecstatic look of pain, that signature of a good deal of Baroque emotionalism. The saint swoons and falls away from the smiling angel, who hovers over her with the symbolic arrow. The draperies take on a life of their own filled with passionate and dramatic movement, not describing the figure beneath but submerging it in

Fig. 395. Bernini: Apollo and Daphne. Rome, Borghese Gallery.

a whirling, tossing mass of symbolically agitated forms, suggesting parallels to the draperies of late Gothic art (fig. 311).

Even within the small compass of a portrait bust like the *Louis XIV* or *Pope Innocent X*, Bernini gave his forms pictorial breadth. He set the figure in motion through different directional thrusts and surrounded it

Fig. 396. Bernini: Ecstasy of St. Theresa. Rome, Santa Maria della Vittoria.

with swirling, dynamic, dramatically undercut patterns of hair and cloth. This conception of "sculpture as painting" reversed the High Renaissance idea of painting as dominantly sculpturesque, e.g., Michelangelo. Even in architecture this pictorial approach became very important, and, once more, as in the *Ecstasy of St. Theresa*, it is difficult to draw the line between various arts.

A transitional form between sculpture and architecture is found in Roman Baroque fountains executed by the overwhelmingly influential Bernini and other masters. In this embodiment, which combines the two arts picturesquely, water plays an interesting but independent and natural role, unhampered by the architecture in which it presumably operates and as important as either the sculpture or the architecture. This may be seen in the well-known eighteenth-century *Trevi Fountain* by Nicola Salvi (fig. 397).

ITALIAN ARCHITECTURE. The two most typical Baroque buildings are the church and the palace — the former, profuse in Europe and the New World as symbols of ecclesiastical activity; the latter, evidence of the increasingly powerful monarchies. It is in France, England, and Spain that the Baroque palace as such emerged. In Italy, since there were actually no monarchs as yet, the most important domestic building was the villa with its extensive gardens that, from the end of the sixteenth century on, tended to grow less formal in their lavishly applied sculpture decoration, artificially placed rocks, and other arrangements. Italy, however, contributed the form and spirit of the Baroque church, as exemplified by Borromini's *San Carlo alle Quattro Fontane* (fig. 398) and Bernini's Sant' Andrea al Quirinale or his magnificent colonnade for *St. Peter's* in Rome (fig. 354).

The effort to reach men's hearts in order to save their souls took the form of a more deliberately imposing building, elaborately decorated with every conceivable kind of painting and sculpture in varying combinations. The architect aimed at length and breadth — these buildings are designed to hold large numbers of people — somewhat like medieval cathedrals rather than the often more centrally planned Renaissance churches. In the interests of impressiveness, dimensions were increased, and individual elements such as columns and pilasters were multiplied, running up on the building to great heights without the sober and interrupting stringcourses of the Renaissance building. These gigantic colonnades, often rising two and more stories, signalize the flamboyance of this

Fig. 397. Salvi: Trevi Fountain, Rome.

Fig. 398. Borromini: San Carlo alle Quattro Fontane, Rome.

style in churches and its potential monumentality in either church or palace.

Detail is piled on detail, not in any coordinated scheme but in a subordination of individual parts to a larger whole that evokes once again the universal and infinite implications of this culture. Light and dark in an almost pictorial manner give the façade a sensation of movement and depth, a sense of drama. The façade has little if any functional meaning; it acts as a sort of false front, an artificially created entity designed to stimulate excitement like a musical chord or a series of lines and colors in a painting. The artificiality of this exterior is accentuated by its lack of relationship to the open and spacious interior; there is almost no way of telling from the outside what is on the inside. The thing exists for itself like the drapery of St. Theresa or, better, for what it can accomplish in creating religious receptivity. From the tight smooth façades of the early Renaissance, architecture had moved toward the more sculpturesque and monumental forms of the High Renaissance. In the period of Mannerism (fig. 384) there began that play back and forth of protuberances to produce a tension between the two-dimensional and the three-dimensional. With the Baroque age these tensions, like those of sculpture and painting, poured over into the exaggerated light-and-dark effects that

472

characterized the entire culture, a mysterious and moving chiaroscuro that became an important buttress of religion during this era.

SPANISH PAINTING. The two streams of pictorial and sculptural church art — the elegant monarchical form and the more bourgeois dramatic-realist type — soon spread to the countries of Europe and America that were dominated by a monarchical Catholicism: Portugal, Spain, France, Flanders, and the Spanish and Portuguese colonies in the New World. In Spain, painters like Ribera and Zurbarán show the effect of Caravaggio's shadowy manner, while Velásquez seems to follow that Italian master's early interest in clear light. But all three Spaniards show the strong hold of realism in their country, where middle-class feeling remained an important factor even after the economic disasters of the sixteenth century and after the conservative alliance of clergy and monarchy in the seventeenth century.

Ribera and Zurbarán. A significant aspect of Spanish art is represented by Jusepe Ribera (1591–1652), who brought the message of Caravaggism from Naples for the portrayal of his morbid martyrdoms, and Francisco Zurbarán (1598–1664), whose melodramatic light-and-dark effects were applied to paintings of the ever-increasing class of monks. They retained an earlier rebellious and popular mysticism of the

Fig. 399. Ribera: Martyrdom of St. Bartholomew. Madrid, Prado.

Fig. 400. Zurbarán: Monk at Prayer. London, National Gallery.

previous century (El Greco, Morales), expressed now in terms of natural-istic details of suffering. This transpired directly in the case of Ribera's *Martyrdom of St. Bartholomew* (fig. 399) and psychologically in Zur-barán's *Monk at Prayer* (fig. 400). The first work in its remorseless rendition of particulars of suffering — the painter's specialty — has an almost sadistic quality as it displays the tortures to which the saint is sub-jected. Although related to Caravaggio's second manner, Ribera's work is more emphatically and exaggeratedly Baroque in the accepted religious sense, but it shuns the formal standardization of the Renaissance-derived official tradition which will be seen in Spain in the painting of Murillo (see fig. 403).

Zurbarán's preference for the monk theme cannot be looked upon as accident or caprice but as the reflection of a characteristic feature of Spanish society. He portrayed self-absorbed monks, brooding monks, monks at prayer — and often with a curious combination of realism and mysticism. The use of the spotlight technique in his art, as in that of Ribera, helps to strip these pictures of the conventional and approved idealization, to re-

474

duce them to the lowest common denominator. Like Caravaggio before them, the Spanish artists frequently placed their religious personages on a low social level, even showing them as beggars. Zurbarán, whose monks and nuns cannot be beggars in the usual sense, used a variety of very commonplace, lower-middle-class folk as participants in holy narratives, e.g., his *Annunciation* (Seville) or *The Young Virgin* (Metropolitan Museum), one of the best examples of *petit-bourgeois* religiosity in modern times.

Velásquez. These painters prepared the way for Diego Velásquez (1599–1660), whose transcendent art, in spite of his job as court painter, retains a genuine and sharp sense of reality in some ways more effective than theirs. Velásquez's feeling for the commonplace in religion is reflected in an early work, *Christ in the House of Mary and Martha* (ca. 1620, London, National Gallery), in which Christ is visible only in the background of the picture, through the open doorway of a kitchen where two simple women are preparing food. His pictures of philosophers in

rags (e.g., *Menippus*) or classical characters as everyday people (*Forge of Vulcan, Bacchus*), while again echoing similar tendencies in Caravaggio, underline the general quality toward which Spanish art at this point still strived. As the century moved on, however, and Velásquez with it, such "vulgarizations" become less and less acceptable — especially in religion, with the absolute ascendancy of the clergy. Yet the impact of this painter's naturalism is none the less extremely significant both for its own aesthetic effect and for its place in the seventeenth century.

Velásquez is perhaps best known for his work at court, where he did innumerable portraits of King Philip IV (fig.

Fig. 401. Velásquez: Portrait of Philip IV of Spain. New York, Metropolitan Museum of Art.

401) and the latter's wife and children. Even in these official works it seems difficult for the painter to assume the aristocratic role one would expect in such portraits (cf. Rubens or Van Dyck, fig. 410). He remained almost always the startlingly lucid portrayer of facts as they appear in a clear light. *Philip IV*, for example, emerges as a relatively two-dimensional dark silhouette against the contrasting light behind him — as would indeed happen if such a form were to become visible against a light background. Generally the only portions of the figure that have any real three-dimensional quality are the uncovered parts such as the face and hands, the former especially, since it necessarily receives more attention.

With Velásquez, as with Hals in Holland, the path of the paintbrush becomes increasingly apparent; and he stresses what the artist sees directly before him rather than (the Renaissance practice) what he knows to be there. This method is not a linear refinement of endless anatomical, perspective, and other studies, as with Leonardo or Raphael, but instead is a highly spontaneous and — in certain measure — even improvisatory manner. Lines as such do not appear, but the artist's brushwork moves on until the end of a given color area — as in the dark clothes — and then continues in another hue for the background. The flat appearance may be partly the result of this method as well as of the often dark costumes of the men, which would come out flat; the elaborate costumes of the women, frequently painted without their owners' presence, also emerge in two rather than three dimensions. The two-dimensionality and immediacy of visualization in so many of Velásquez's pictures descend through the late-eighteenth-century Goya (fig. 478) to Manet in the nineteenth century (fig. 490). Conversely, the limpid, clear coloring may be traced back to Caravaggio's first style (fig. 393).

The most atmospheric Velásquez art emerges in another and just as important style, shown in his *Las Meninas* (fig. 402). Here and in the equally well-known *Tapestry Weavers* (Madrid, Prado), the artist has filled the interior scene with an almost tangible atmosphere that surrounds the figures and gives them form. The painter himself stands behind a huge easel in the act of painting a double portrait of Their Spanish Majesties, who would be in front of him about where the spectator of the picture stands; but they are visible only through a mirror in the rear. In the foreground is the little Infanta, together with her young ladies (*meninas*) and other companions, visiting her parents while their picture is painted. She and her two maids of honor wear the elaborate costume of the time, that hides rather than reveals the body. As in the contemporary paintings of Holland (cf. fig. 429), light enters the picture through a natural source and builds up the forms in a specifically naturalistic fashion. This procedure may be contrasted with the spectacularly dramatic effect of Caravaggio's chiaroscuro illumination (fig. 394), which is far more arbitrary — yet less naturalistic — since there light is used not so much to describe as to single out certain features.

Fig. 402. Velásquez: Las Meniñas. Madrid, Prado.

Baroque light. However different the results, Baroque painting in general is dominantly influenced by light effects: Caravaggio, Velásquez, Rubens, Vermeer, and Le Nain, to name a few characteristic representatives of different countries. In painters of the Caravaggio-Rubens-Rembrandt persuasion, the light is dramatic in function; in the Velásquez-Vermeer branch, it is primarily descriptive. Light had already begun to play an important role in Mannerist painting, e.g., Tintoretto and El Greco; but it still emanated from the object itself, in a kind of nervous or magical illumination. With the Baroque period, emotionality produces a dramatic, operatic, or theatrical light; the feeling of aspiration toward infinity causes it to be used for destroying rational boundaries, for extending space into infinitude as with Rembrandt. Even without the religious drama or profound spirituality (as in *Las Meniñas* or Vermeer's interiors), a feeling of extension into space is conveyed by the light coming through the window from a distant place.

Murillo. A more conventional Baroque expression is found in the paintings of Bartolomé Murillo (1618–1682), a slightly later painter whose work is emotionally superficial, yet recognizably middle class. Pictures like his *St. Thomas of Villanueva as a Child Distributing Clothes*

Fig. 403. Murillo: St. Thomas of Villanueva as a Child Distributing Clothes. Cincinnati Museum of Art.

Fig. 404. Ribera: Hospicio de San Fernando, Madrid.

(fig. 403) illustrate his characteristic emotional quality and his reliance on standard Italian techniques.

SPANISH ARCHITECTURE. Spanish architecture of the Baroque age was at first strongly influenced by Italian Baroque, as a reaction against the previous formal and severe Spanish style of the later sixteenth century under the melancholiac Philip II. During the first half of the seventeenth century, Spanish building was dominated by a group of Italian architects, as in the Jesuit collegiate church at Loyola. Toward the end of the century, this already enriched type of building was affected by the lushly ornamented style of the Spaniard José Churriguera (1650–1723), which gave to Spanish Baroque an altogether unique quality. This is exemplified in Pedro Ribera's façade of the *Hospicio de San Fernando* at Madrid (fig. 404) with its accentuated doorway and windows, its abundance of exaggerated and writhing ornament that gives the sensation of living forms of vegetation, like some elaborate garden set in motion. These pictorial and hence typically Baroque architectural and sculptural forms had a profound effect on the buildings of Spanish America: Mexico, Peru, Chile, Bolivia, Argentina, Ecuador, Colombia, and Cuba. These and other

Fig. 405. Ocotlán Cathedral, Tlaxcala province, Mexico.

centers were to produce various mixtures of their earlier plateresque, or silversmith, decoration with the classical, unadorned sixteenth-century mode and the elaborate Churrigueresque late-seventeenth- and early-eighteenth-century style.

In Latin America there is an interesting and austere treatment in the sixteenth century — especially in Mexico, e.g., Cathedral of Actopan — which for some critics is the most important aspect of Spanish American colonial architecture. This simple, relatively undecorated style had not yet experienced the Baroque. But the Baroque movement was especially well developed in the late-flowering eighteenth-century examples of Mexico and Peru. These show the effect of the Churriguera carvings on doorways and columns and the absorption at the same time of a native Indian tendency toward allover decorations on buildings, as in the *Cathedral of Ocotlán* (fig. 405) in the Tlaxcala region of Mexico or La Compañia at Quito, Ecuador.

FLEMISH PAINTING: *Rubens.* Seventeenth-century Flanders offers the best example of courtly Baroque painting. During the religious wars of the previous century the Dutch had broken away from Spain, but Flanders remained within the orbit of the Spanish Empire and the Church. Ruled by a Spanish viceroy, Flanders had its court life as well as typical formal religious observances. Rubens, the greatest Flemish painter of the period, was an important courtier and diplomat and also a devout Catholic.

Peter Paul Rubens (1577–1640) was not only the most notable painter of the southern Netherlands, but perhaps the leading Catholic Baroque master of Europe. After a long period in the Italian courts and galleries — he was in Rome during the lifetime of Caravaggio — Rubens returned to his native land. His artistic ambassadorship was not confined to religious interpretations; he showed in unmistakable terms the classical undercurrent in Baroque art as well as its striving for infinite distances, especially in landscape painting. In him are summed up the most characteristic manifestations of Baroque expression.

His Italian experiences brought Rubens in touch with the new currents in that country (the eclectic formulas of the Carracci and the dramatic realism of Caravaggio) besides the contributions of the High Renaissance masters from Leonardo to Tintoretto and Veronese. In some ways Rubens's art is a mélange of all of these; and yet because of the overwhelming personality and intellect of the man himself, his works bear the undeniable stamp of his own creativity. Similarly, although he established a kind of picture factory in his studio to cope with the tremendous number of orders and employed specialists to do animals, still lifes, or landscape backgrounds, his own artistic character is still evident in all the works that were turned out.

In both his personal life and his art, Rubens summarized the outstanding trends of the period. His career coincided with the diplomatic chess games between the great monarchies, Spain, France, and England, where Rubens functioned at various times as the ambassador of Flanders or Spain. The artist and the diplomat are not always separable; one opened doors for the other through such royal commissions as the paintings for Queen Marie de Médicis of France in the Luxembourg Palace and those for King Charles I of England in Whitehall Palace's banqueting hall. In these works Rubens projected the sumptuous allegories of Baroque art, symbolic compositions dedicated to the glory of a particular dynasty. For his Flemish patrons he performed this same feat as well as the creation of magnificent and typically Baroque altarpieces for various churches; the churches themselves are often in the new flamboyant, pictorial architectural style of the period, e.g., San Carlo Borromeo in Brussels.

A relatively early work, the *Descent from the Cross* (fig. 406), is one of the best examples of his Baroque religiosity. The central panel of

an impressive triptych whose wings show upper-class types of saints, the *Descent* is composed like a flaring "X" with a long single curved diagonal (cf. Bernini's *Apollo and Daphne*, fig. 395) moving from lower left to upper right. This area is artificially and melodramatically lighted, in the manner of Caravaggio's works, as the Christ is lowered between the darker straining figures about him. Not only does the typical dynamic curve move upward and outward into infinity, but every one of the figures is in motion. Yet the multifarious moving parts, dependent on each other in the Baroque fashion, come to some sort of rest pictorially as they balance and compensate one another.

Rubens has achieved here a representative yet entirely personal interpretation of the necessary Baroque religious pathos and dramatic suffering. It combines the realistic elements of Caravaggio's operatic approach with the formal qualities of official Church art as set forth by the Carracci and their followers. Rubens did not imitate the Carracci method as such but made a similar adaptation of standard Renaissance masters

482

(eclecticism). From those sources he borrowed what seemed most suitable: the Tintorettesque form at the upper left; the Titianesque figure on the ladder; the man supporting the Christ from below, who suggests Andrea del Sarto (fig. 358). Their appearance of upper-class well-being brings to mind the pseudoreligious compositions of the Venetians, particularly Titian (fig. 363) and Veronese; Rubens worked in a courtly milieu that made this quite natural. Although the shining satins of the two Marys at the lower left with their beautiful golden hair may be far removed from fact, they satisfy the courtly requirements which Rubens also fulfilled in other pictures — hunting scenes, aristocratic portraits, and various classical allegories.

A later work, the *Judgment of Paris* (ca. 1636, fig. 407), shows a much more subdued attitude, abandoning the previous Italianate excitement in favor of a broader treatment. Instead of the abrupt diagonal thrust, there is now a continuous gentle movement in the composition, achieved through its flow of line and color, the changing over from light to dark accents. The figures are arranged like an ancient relief and are blended into the curvilinear movements of the landscape, in a sense ab-

Fig. 407. Rubens: Judgment of Paris. London, National Gallery.

Fig. 408. Rubens: Garden of Love. Dresden, Picture Gallery.

Fig. 409. Rubens: Landscape with Rainbow. Munich, Alte Pinakothek.

sorbed by that nature of which they are a part — albeit on a most elegant and courtly level. This phase of Rubens's painting relates to the general esteem in which the antique was still held and more specifically to a somewhat similar feeling in Titian, who conveyed a high degree of pagan sensuousness without archaeological detail. The Italian artist, however, was more freely imaginative and produced a directer poetic emanation of the past, whereas Rubens's lush nudes (a signature of his style and perhaps of Flemish robustness in general) give the impression of court characters posing for their pictures. In fact the central figure in this trinity of goddesses is actually the youthful second wife of the painter.

Rubens's well-known *Garden of Love* (fig. 408) dates from the same period in his career (ca. 1635) and is again important for its idealized picture of contemporary court life. It is an allegory brought up to date by the costumes of the ladies and gentlemen disporting themselves in the garden before a typical northern Baroque building with its heavy banded columns. From the base of the foremost of these, the forms seem to radiate outward, flaring into the four corners, yet without the violence of the *Descent,* since this picture — and the period itself in Rubens's evolution — calls for a gentler, more integrated conception with the various parts playing back and forth against each other. Compared to later versions of such themes in the eighteenth-century Rococo style (cf. fig. 453), this work carries the wonderfully vibrant and robust quality of Rubens's art. He is not only a skillful painter in the sense of subtly adjusted color and linear compositional relationships, but also a man who imparts a high degree of his own vitality and poetic insight.

Rubens is often thought of as a courtier going from country to country, painting elegant portraits of the aristocrats with whom he came into contact or allegories on the glories of kingship. Yet neither this impression nor that alone of the faithful son of the Church embodies the complete man. A person of powerful intellect, he associated with the best minds of his time, reading omnivorously and expressing himself in every conceivable type of artistic medium. Rubens's sensitivity is revealed at its highest level in landscape painting — from the early ones exploiting Baroque diagonals and violent light-and-dark contrasts (e.g., *Landscape with Ruins of the Palatine,* Louvre, 1618–1620) to the later broader, more serene pictures, such as the *Landscape with Rainbow* (fig. 409). As with the *Judgment of Paris* and other works of the last decade of his life, these last landscapes move toward greater breadth and poise, expressing their relationship to the Baroque in a reaching toward infinity. By comparison with the earlier and specifically picturesque works, the landscape now becomes flatter, the view more distant, and the horizon lowered.

Fig. 410. Van Dyck: Portrait of Charles I of England. Paris, Louvre.

Rubens's stillness in this period (shared by his allegories and religious paintings) was caused partially by a uniform painting technique that was to affect the slightly later Dutch school of landscape and the nineteenth-century French Barbizon tradition which stems from that source (fig. 485). Replacing the picturesqueness of painters like Adam Elsheimer (who had founded the romantic landscape tradition in Rome in the sixteenth century) and his followers such as Salvatore Rosa in the seventeenth century, Rubens now developed a newer conception of landscape. Nature became philosophical rather than purely emotive, although the latter element was never absent. It is interesting to note that Rubens considered his landscapes relatively unimportant next to his other works; they were done entirely for personal amusement and relaxation.

Van Dyck. Closely related to the courtly art of Rubens is that of Anthony Van Dyck (1599–1641), who, although he practiced allegorical and mythological painting, is better known for his portraits. Lacking the personal and stylistic vigor of the leader of the Flemish school, Van Dyck's distinctly Baroque subjects seem more patently eclectic than those

486

of the older man. In the portraits, however, his own personality found its logical outlet, as in the well-known *Portrait of Charles I* (fig. 410), which has some of the decorative flair of Rubens but far less of his energy and overt power. Actually, Van Dyck strove for an aristocratic gentility in the Venetian mode, which was to be carried over by his ardent English admirers in the eighteenth century, notably Gainsborough (see fig. 438).

Van Dyck, with his tall elegant men and women of extreme refinement and even affectation, with their luxurious garments and exaggerated proportions, may be said to have founded the portrait tradition of England through his long sojourn there as court painter. Together with the Dutch Peter Lely (1618–1680) and the German Gottfried Kneller (1646–1723), he represents the continuing English importation of painting talent from the Continent (cf. Holbein, Chapter 19). Facile rather than penetrative, languid rather than forceful, he personifies one aspect of aristocratic Baroque art.

Jordaens. The courtly function of both Rubens and Van Dyck with its effects on their art should not obscure the fact that the Flemish tradition was an earthy one. Fifteenth- and sixteenth-century masters had established a type of robust realism and humor that was not obliterated by the requirements of aristocratic painting. There was also a powerful

Fig. 411. Jordaens: The King Drinks. Antwerp, Museum.

middle-class feeling in Flemish life which emerged in such painters as Jakob Jordaens (1593–1678), the direct opposite of a man like Van Dyck. Jordaens's famous eating and drinking compositions, e.g., *The King Drinks* (fig. 411) or *The Bean Feast* (Braunschweig), while reminiscent of Rubens in their lavish outpouring of flesh and compressed action, have a rank grossness that is quite different in meaning. Physical rather than spiritual — there is almost always a dining table between his characters — Jordaens epitomizes the more naturalistic side of the Baroque, reversing the elegance and courtliness of the other Flemings with a king of the feast who is crowned because he can eat or drink more than the others. This crude peasant quality finds its outlet in Flanders and across the border in Holland with Jan Steen, Adriaen Brouwer, and Adriaen van Ostade among others. But the richness of form and color in Jordaens, the constant movement, are as Baroque as anything in Rubens, whose influence extends into this area as well as the sphere of the courtly Baroque where he had his greatest effect.

FRANCE IN THE SEVENTEENTH CENTURY. In France, the sixteenth century had brought a steady increase in the power of the monarchy, supported by a rising middle class which needed stability for the accomplishment of its own aims. This process was augmented during the first half of the seventeenth century as the higher bourgeoisie were admitted into the ranks of the nobility and figured increasingly in the culture of the time. Their rise took place at the expense of the hereditary nobility, whose function during that period became more and more symbolic rather than actual, although the nobles were still an important group having great feudal estates, tax exemption, social prestige, and the highest political appointments. But the wars of the sixteenth and seventeenth centuries were taking their toll. The landed aristocracy became more and more impoverished; many drifted to the court for sustenance and moral prestige. The business of the nation, and a good deal of its positive accomplishment, fell into the hands of the upper middle class and the newly ennobled. Rigaud's *Portrait of Président Hébert* (see fig. 452) exemplifies the new man of this era.

The first part of the seventeenth century, the period of Louis XIII and Cardinal Mazarin, divulges in its art and literature this recently achieved importance of the middle class. It is an art of realism, of Baroque sentiment and individualized expression. After 1661 and the accession of Louis XIV, the government became completely centralized and autocratic. In place of the earlier Baroque feeling and naturalism, a stiff formal classicism now bespoke the authoritarian viewpoint and prescribed glorification of the king. The dynamic and forceful courtier of an earlier period (cf. Rubens, *Garden of Love*, fig. 408) is tamed and courtbroken, foreshadowing his comparatively negligible role in the eighteenth century (see fig. 453, Watteau). Government, art, and culture in general are "coordinated"; the Academy has the special function of exalting the monarchy. Artistic individuality suffered enormously under this restraint, and it is fair to say that creativity during the second part of the century is not in any way comparable to that before 1661. Certainly in art the great figures — Antoine and Louis Le Nain, Georges de Latour, Vouet, Poussin, Claude, Le Sueur, Callot — either were dead by the time of Louis XIV's accession or so far along in their development as to be credited to the previous era. The same may be said of the important literary figures who, although generally considered in *le grand siècle*, "the great century" of Louis XIV, really belong to the age of Louis XIII. Descartes, Corneille, and Pascal were part of this earlier time, while La Fontaine, Molière, La Rochefoucauld, and others were already mature men by 1661.

The expression of individualistic aspirations during the first portion

Fig. 412. Le Sueur: Death of St. Bruno. Paris, Louvre.

of the seventeenth century took two main forms: a bourgeois-naturalistic tendency in the genre art of the Le Nains, Latour, Callot, Bosse, and their like; and a more poetic, although carefully organized and classicistic, landscape art as in Poussin and Claude Lorrain. A third and here perhaps a less important manifestation was the religious Baroque emotionality stemming from Italy, in the work of Le Sueur and La Hyre. This last appears in the well-known *Death of St. Bruno* by Eustache Le Sueur (1616–1655, fig. 412), displaying a fervent, statuesque kind of Christianity. Its balance of the monks' gray robes against the bareness of the cell is as striking as its melodramatic Caravaggesque light that raises the emotional tempo to an unusual height. Pictures of this type have little to do with the academic Bolognese tradition of the Carracci, and by their evident sincerity must be considered part of the middle-class feeling.

Le Nain. In the work of the Le Nain brothers, Latour, and a number of other provincial artists, the simplicity and realism of the northern Gothic tradition emerge again. Of the three Le Nain brothers, the most important is Louis Le Nain (ca. 1593–1648), who is well represented by *The Forge* (fig. 413). In this, as in the majority of his works, a mag-

Fig. 413. Louis Le Nain: The Forge. Paris, Louvre.

nificent monumentality and seriousness is bestowed on the participants.
The typical Baroque light has the perceptible effect of animating the interior and increasing the spiritual feeling expressed in the repose and
quiet of the figures. Le Nain's peasants are more immediately impressive
than those of Brueghel, since they are not so much parts of a symbolic
design as they are individuals with important feelings of their own. By
the same token, their grandeur and dignity are significantly different
from contemporary Dutch or Flemish peasant pictures (cf. fig. 423,
Brouwer). Le Nain was the ancestor of the eighteenth-century Chardin
and the nineteenth-century Courbet.

Latour and other genre artists. Compared to the formal dignity of
such pictures, the work of Georges de Latour (1593–1652) looks provincial and somewhat forced in manner, particularly because of the artificial candlelight with which so many of his paintings are illuminated and
the rather stiff forms of the figures with their simple, sincere expressions.
A characteristic religious work is *The Newborn Child* (fig. 414), in which
the candle becomes a central source of light that falls on the white front

Fig. 414. Latour: The Newborn Child. Rennes, Museum of Fine Arts.

of the person holding it and the wonderful reddish robe of the mother. The sculpturesquely carved faces, their stiffness of expression and simplicity, give this picture its religious, even medieval, quality, although there is no indication that this is *the* Child.

On a more overtly upper-middle-class level, the engravings of Abraham Bosse, with his little genre pictures of Parisian activities, and the grisly "observations" of Jacques Callot (1592–1635), called *The Great Miseries of War,* are testimony to the essential fluidity and energy of the art of the period.

Poussin. The other chief trend of painting during this epoch involves the spirit of logic and balance that is associated with French seventeenth-century culture. But the logic — or classicism — is tempered by profound feeling and in this way typifies the bourgeois honesty of sentiment and need for a rational mode of living and thinking. It is not altogether fortuitous that the middle class showed greater enthusiasm for the art of Nicolas Poussin (1594–1665) than did the aristocracy. This painter is commonly looked upon as the essence of French *raison,* or logic, the exemplar of the French classical point of view; but true as this is, it must be qualified by comparison.

Pictures like the *Orpheus and Eurydice* (fig. 415) contain a carefully constructed and balanced series of forms that move with inevitable logic from foreground to background. The composition is divided into the traditional foreground, middle ground, and background, the latter closed

Fig. 415. Poussin: Orpheus and Eurydice. Paris, Louvre.

and final. One of many similar works painted during Poussin's long stay in Rome, this reflects the painter's attempt to resuscitate the Early Christian or the pagan past. Tiny legendary figures lie or sit about against a background of ancient buildings characteristic of the Roman landscape; man is insignificant in the face of time and nature. The workings of time are visible in the buildings about the ancient heroes, the force of nature in the great trees that balance each other right and left and the deep vista that swallows the works of man, however powerful or clearly defined.

Poussin's classicism — evident in the clarity of his forms, the balancing of parts like the trees, the recourse to ancient ruins and buildings, and the division of space into three clear sections — is counterbalanced by a romantic projection of the individual into the past. Through this double offering of logic and emotion, he attracted the middle class of his day. His formality, here compensated by genuine and lyrical emotion, was to be stiffened and artificialized by later painters into the pomp and circumstance of the Louis XIV period, which began just a few years before the death of Poussin. In that period they took the ancient and Roman components of his art with its fine drawing and exalted them into a cult of form and balance, as represented by Le Brun and his coterie.

Claude Lorrain. Together with Poussin may be classified the more openly romantic Claude Lorrain (1600–1682). This painter's compositions have a good deal of Poussin's formality and logic, softened by a shimmering light and atmospheric effects that place Claude in a unique but by no means un-Baroque position in French art. *Ulysses Returning Chryseis to Her Father* or the *Embarkation of the Queen of Sheba* (fig. 416) demonstrates how little the so-called subject counts for in landscapes of this period. The religious or classical theme was a pretext, making them publicly acceptable, since landscape art alone was still not too highly regarded. Compositionally these works compare with those of Poussin in bringing the actors "downstage" and making them as small as possible in contrast with the impressive inward projection — as from the wings of architectural stage sets — and the equally effective distance of the horizon. Even the light coming across the water through the center of the picture is an element of so-called logic and balance; but the painter's interest in this directly observed atmospheric effect is unusual for his time. Here and in other less carefully or obviously balanced works (e.g., *Morning, Hagar and Ishmael*) Claude's interest in light was very specific, almost impressionist; he tried to create the sensation of various times of day and of the sentiments appropriate to them. In a sense he was the first genuine Romantic painter (cf. figs. 482, 483, 485).

Fig. 416. Claude Lorrain: Embarkation of the Queen of Sheba. London, National Gallery.

LOUIS XIV AND THE ROYAL ACADEMY. During the second part of the seventeenth century, a centralization of cultural authority occurred. Upon the death of Cardinal Mazarin, Louis XIV took charge of his own government with the famous statement: "I am the state." Helped by his Director of Buildings, Jean Colbert, he embarked on a centralized building and rebuilding policy, together with sculpture, painting, tapestry, and other decorations, that soon channeled all the artistic energies of the nation in this direction. A government subsidy for the Royal Academy of Fine Arts (founded 1648) put that body directly under the official guidance of Charles le Brun, the King's First Painter, who in addition became head of the French Academy in Rome (founded 1666). Through the Gobelin tapestry factory, the Manufacture des Gobelins, which also fell to Le Brun, all art works necessary for the building program (including the Louvre, Versailles, the Invalides, and Val-de-Grâce church) were produced under the same auspices.

The Royal Academy of Fine Arts was transformed into a completely authoritarian institution under Colbert and Le Brun (Boileau set up a somewhat similar rule over literature). Artists were forced to conform

494

to a pattern laid down by higher authority, since the Academy was the source of scholarships, prizes, exhibitions, teaching privileges, commissions — in short, of livelihood itself. Undertaking its elaborate program of monarchical glorification, the government became the chief if not the only patron; the middle class (and the nobility for the most part) was excluded from this activity. But the strict formal rules laid down by Le Brun soon engendered a reaction from those who felt themselves oppressed by these procedures, by the linear formalism derived from the Italian Renaissance. Painters favoring a more colorful art (and a more liberal viewpoint generally) arose in opposition to the linearists and ultimately in the early eighteenth century were to win out.

The chief projects of this period (built 1661–1708) were the *Palace of Versailles,* whose rebuilding was begun in 1668, and the *Palace of the Louvre,* similarly enlarged and reworked from 1661 to 1674. Concentration on works of this kind, with the tremendous energies and money necessary for their completion, was made possible by the absolutist conditions of the time, which the buildings themselves symbolized. It is significant that during the previous period private chateaux had still been fairly common, e.g., those at Maisons-Laffitte and Blois; but now both the upper middle class and the old-line nobility were put into the shade by royal projects. Indeed, Colbert felt it necessary for the king to have such an impressive city residence as the Louvre.

Palace of the Louvre. The *East Façade of the Louvre* (fig. 417) was begun by Claude Perrault (1613–1688) in 1667, two years after the

Fig. 417. Perrault: East Façade of the Louvre, Paris.

design of the brilliant Italian sculptor-architect Bernini had been rejected. This façade sums up the character of the Louis XIV style. Far more severe and formal than Italian Baroque architecture, the dignified imposing composition with its gigantic columnar structure still embodies the Baroque. The largeness of conception, as in Italian churches of the period, the light-and-shade treatment with typical doubled columns moving forward, the variation of projections between the outside wings and the center portion, the elaborated entranceway, and finally the dynamic balance of the building as a whole all bespeak its Baroque character. The last-mentioned quality may be understood in terms of each part depending on the other; unlike early Renaissance designs, for example (fig. 321), the removal of any one part would work serious damage on the balance of the composition. Side wings with attached pilasters project forward; the adjacent inner sections with separate monumental double columns recede backward; and the central portion comes forward again, accented by the sculptured pediment above, but with the columns not so far out from the surface. In this way the Baroque architect once more effects a continuous backward and forward movement as well as a light-and-shade surface treatment which, while contained within the strict academic framework of the time, still express the sculpturesque character of this architecture.

Versailles Palace. In many ways the *Palace of Versailles* (fig. 418), then the real center of French government, represents the period even better than the Louvre. Built primarily because the king preferred this location, its exact planning is characteristic of an era when whole cities were laid out with precision and clarity. The formality and balance of individual parts extend here to the surrounding garden system. These elaborate and carefully tended gardens with their involved water displays are universally typical of the age (cf. Italy, where fountains and gardens play a major role in seventeenth-century buildings). The approximately half-mile-long façade is laid out so that a hollow square, open at one end, is flanked by two long straight wings. From the rear, the side facing the gigantic garden arrangements, this gives the effect of a projecting center and two receding sides somewhat like the Louvre and many contemporary Italian buildings. Individual parts such as the huge columnar orders and the traditional division of the façade into a ground floor for service, a second floor for the residents, and a third, or attic, floor for servants suggest similar features at the Louvre. The "pomp and circumstance" of its interior is seen in the splendor of the *Hall of Mirrors* (fig. 419).

Certain points — moldings, columns, and other details — underline

Fig. 418. Palace of Versailles. Princes Wing.

Fig. 419. Palace of
Versailles. Hall of
Mirrors.

the basically Italianate and derivative nature of this architecture, heavily influenced by the writings of the Italian Palladio, which were made available to French architects from the middle of the seventeenth century. The grafting of Italian cultural ideas on French civilization had already been evident in the early sixteenth century when their artistic elements began to appear as ornaments on French chateaux of the time (cf. fig. 383); and pictorial and sculptural ideas had been borrowed from Italian Mannerism, as noted. The interdependence of various parts in Versailles and other contemporary French designs is just as Italianate. Like the odd-numbered sections of the typical Italian villa of this period or the dynamically balanced Baroque church in Italy or Spain, both the Louvre and Versailles are arranged into a pattern of interrelated threes, fives, or sevens including a central point, or pivot. The façade of the Louvre, for example, consists of five sections; that of Versailles has three main sections, each of which divides into similarly odd-numbered groupings — some of the parts receding, others moving forward, in a consistent and logical plan.

From the standpoint of its general cultural significance (apart from the eclecticism and formalism implied in the wholesale adoption of foreign aesthetic ideas), the *Palace of Versailles* sums up the great power of the king. Built to accommodate the entire court — an increasing neces-

Fig. 420. Coustou: Louis XIV Crossing the Rhine. Versailles, Palace Chapel.

sity because of the growing absentee-landlord class of noblemen who were flocking to court — this project was so tremendous that only an absolute despot could have forced his country into the financial danger brought about by its completion. Figuratively and actually, Versailles was made to be the center of its environment; roads and avenues of trees radiated from and led to it. The existence of a private theater and church within the plan are additional symbols of the importance of the king and of the restrictive or nonpublic nature of this great structure.

French sculpture under Louis XIV. In the sculpture of the period, the work of Antoine Coysevox (1640–1720) reflects somewhat the alert characterizations of Bernini, especially in portrait busts like *Le grand Condé* (Louvre). This relationship is particularly evident in the brilliantly undercut and shadowed surfaces, as seen in the treatment of hair. An interesting example of the specific monarchical contribution of contemporary sculpture may be found in the declamatory relief by Nicolas Coustou (1658–1733), a nephew of Coysevox, showing *Louis XIV Crossing the Rhine* (fig. 420). In an atmosphere of florid gesture, the bas-relief of the so-called "Sun King" symbolizes his triumph over the Germans across the Rhine. It suggests in a general way the Italian Baroque fountains, with its allegorical water god, and also Roman arches of triumph on which the hero general is often crowned by a figure of Victory. Again it may be observed how the arts of this time tend to overlap. Here the sculpture is as pictorial as possible, having delicate gradations of relief in the background.

French painting under Louis XIV. Monarchical painting can well be represented by the all-powerful Charles le Brun himself (1619–1690), who for about twenty years directed the artistic destinies of France. The seriousness of his royalist art and its aims are illustrated in the tapestry designs for the history of Alexander, a rather obvious (although one can never be too obvious in cases like this) allegory on the conquests of that modern Alexander, Louis XIV. A typical one, the *Entry of Alexander the Great into Babylon* (fig. 421), is a pompous victory procession showing the impressive Louis-Alexander in his chariot against a background of classical architecture, soldiers carrying spoils, and spectators. Arranged in bas-relief fashion (just as, conversely, Coustou's sculpture is pictorial), it recalls the classical archaeology of Mantegna, the complex post-Raphaelesque compositions of Giulio Romano, and the elegant forms of Veronese. The "logic" and necessities of this job of glorification have brought the painter to a typical academic combination of borrowed Renaissance elements. His search for classical dignity and formality rings hollow when compared with the personal poetic evocation of the past

Fig. 421. Le Brun: Entry of Alexander the Great into Babylon. Paris, Louvre.

that had come from painters like Poussin in the years before art became codified and controlled.

Through these procedures of borrowing and formalization, the royalist culture of this period (the aristocratic Baroque) was designed for the relatively few who could understand its increasingly limited meanings. Nevertheless, although French society presented externally the spectacle of two widely separate social classes — the aristocracy and the poor — the ever-growing bourgeoisie, whose presence had already been felt in the culture of the age, was destined to provide the stimulus for continuation and enrichment of that tradition in the century following. The cultural triumph of the middle class is clearly anticipated in the Holland of the seventeenth century, which represents the other side of the Baroque, its Protestant phase.

21 / THE PROTESTANT BAROQUE

THE Dutch painter of the seventeenth century offers our first view of an artist working under a system of free competition and possessing freedom of aesthetic initiative. His situation in the dominantly bourgeois and individualistic environment of Holland was substantially different from that of the French artist restricted by a tightly organized state machine. The successful revolt of the northern, or Dutch, Netherlands against the Spanish monarch — and the Church — had put into power a conservative Protestant middle class. The geographic advantage of the Low Countries commercially was augmented in the late sixteenth century by the financial crises in central and southern Europe. These events shifted the financial center of the continent from Italy and Germany to Holland.

The new society and its art were therefore shaped by two important circumstances: a Protestant rather than Catholic religion, and a bourgeois rather than courtly viewpoint. The first meant a change from a primarily Church art to one concerned with the everyday world; the second, from court elegance to middle-class seriousness. Yet even without the religious element as such, Dutch seventeenth-century painting manages to infuse deep meaning into commonplace material, as in Vermeer and others, to project the spiritual on an everyday level, as in Rembrandt. In addition, the aristocracy was not entirely eliminated as a cultural force. They intermarried with the wealthier bourgeoisie and carried on commerce themselves, while the upper middle class took on the character of an aristocracy of wealth (as in Renaissance Italy). This is reflected artistically by a subdued richness of form and costume, even in middle-class pictures. Nevertheless Dutch art, unlike others of the period, is principally bourgeois in its outlook and clearly reproduces the national viewpoint and status. The Dutch artist no longer relied on church or aristocratic patronage; he was increasingly dependent on a new class of patron. In the next century other countries — especially England — were to present analogous situations; by the nineteenth century it would be a universal condition.

Besides being on the open market with his work, the artist was also

501

in the position of choosing (within the bounds of social acceptability) the subjects he wished to paint and to a more limited extent the manner in which he painted them. Dutch art during this period was an art of land-scapes (independent of religious or other pretexts), homey interiors, genre scenes, still-life pictures, and other evidences of everyday reality, plus an occasional classical or literary subject for the educated upper classes and a few religious themes. All these subjects, divorced from the aristocratic, voluptuous, or Catholic side of Baroque, were still done within the compass of the general Baroque concept, which has a strong realistic component along with its other qualities.

Aesthetically this relationship with the Baroque is expressed through the use of Caravaggesque techniques of clear objective portrayal, as in his *Bacchus* (fig. 393), and elaborate dramatic lighting effects, as in his *Death of the Virgin* (fig. 394). Morally the Baroque viewpoint is shared in conceiving art as a conquest of reality, by employing those techniques. The limpid clarity of the first lighting method appears in the meticu-lously viewed interiors of Vermeer (fig. 429); the dramatic effects of the second are reflected in Rembrandt's *Man with the Golden Helmet* (fig. 426). The latter type of light also functions in many genre pieces of the time, although in a descriptive rather than melodramatic fashion, e.g., the peasant pictures of Brouwer (fig. 423). This atmospheric light was also used by the Spanish painter Velásquez (fig. 402), whose more objective approach (fig. 401) emphasized what can be seen immediately in a form silhouetted against its background — comparable to the imme-diacy of Frans Hals's manner (fig. 422).

POSITION OF THE ARTIST. Undoubtedly different social groups pre-ferred different kinds of Dutch painters in respective degrees of formality, seriousness, or simplicity. That same variety signifies the great popularity of art among these new patrons. Ultimately, of course, under the rising prosperity and patronage of the middle classes, art became a commodity like anything else, with an increasing number of dealers and more artists than the market could absorb. For perhaps the first time in history there was a surplus of artists and actual poverty for many of them. Although there was more apparent freedom for the individual, he was limited by public taste, extent of the market, and the growing demand for typical works by each man — as ordered by his dealer, who now stood between the painter and the new public. When a given type of subject matter or portrait was popular, the painter was bound by this, as by court society in other countries. That Hals died in the poorhouse, that Rembrandt found himself out of step with public taste and forced into bankruptcy after a period of success, are only two instances of a generally bad situa-tion.

Many Dutch painters, because of the oversold market, had to adopt a side line in order to make a living. To the painter of the twentieth century, this does not come as a surprise, but to Dutch artists of the seventeenth century, emerging from the tradition of church and court employment and of guild protection, the struggle for economic security was unfamiliar. In other countries, e.g., France, Flanders, or Spain, the artist was still an integrated member of society under acknowledged restrictions, some worse than others. In the final analysis, neither position was to offer an adequate solution to the artist's problems.

HALS. Frans Hals (ca. 1580–1666) belongs to the early part of the Dutch development. His many commonplace scenes — drinkers, happy young couples, smokers, and other types of genre — are allied to Caravaggio's tavern pictures. Hals's works differ in their distinctly nonclassical technique, comparing with modern Impressionists like Manet in the absolute spontaneity of conception and execution. A figure such as *Malle Bobbe* (fig. 422) is seen from close up in a very informal pose; the upper part of her body moves in a different direction from the lower, as though she were turning suddenly in response to a call. Like Velásquez, the

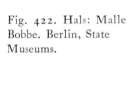

Fig. 422. Hals: Malle Bobbe. Berlin, State Museums.

Dutch painter reveals the path of his brush and builds up the form in terms of loosely applied strokes of paint that abruptly cause it to take shape.

Such pictures by Hals give the impression of having been painted directly on the spot, which may well have been true; there is no record of drawings for them, such as the studied and formal preparations for Renaissance paintings. This rapid procedure does not lend itself to profound psychological penetration in the work of Hals any more than in the work of Velásquez. Both masters evolved their technique to meet specific needs. Even the portraits from which Hals made his living show a similar objectivity. These individuals or groupings of charitable, social, and other organizations had themselves painted in order to gratify the middle-class aspiration to social standing.

The art of Hals, like that of many early-seventeenth-century contemporaries, stands in strongest opposition to the elegancies and formalities of the conventional Baroque style. The unaristocratic nature of Dutch expression is indicated by the popularity of Caravaggism and the even

Fig. 423. Brouwer: Operation. Frankfurt, Städel Institute.

harsher uncompromising character it assumes here. Often the Dutch seem to go out of their way, in an almost revolutionary manner, to assert their down-to-earthness. The unceremonious approach of Hals's portraits contrasts sharply with the polished elegance of Rubens or Van Dyck. Nowhere outside of Holland would a businessman be portrayed holding up — as the symbol of his occupation — a herring.

BROUWER. Related to this feeling is the work of Flemish-born Adriaen Brouwer (1606–1638), a lusty, earthy personality who also produced spontaneously viewed and painted genre, somewhat more elaborate than Hals's works but still looser than Dutch art generally. Brouwer's deliberately vulgarized peasants are not only a less heroic and formal conception than that of the Frenchman Louis Le Nain, but more significantly are an anticonventional version, almost a parody, of the Baroque. His *Operation* (fig. 423), in this early rebellious phase of Dutch art, transforms the usual Baroque martyrdom scene into something comical, the victim making faces, the torturer reduced to a vulgar barber of the time, and the eager crowds to a typical old hag who watches with great relish. Much as he parodies the conventional didactic pictures illustrating the senses, here and in other works such as the amusing *Smoker* (Louvre), Brouwer often reaches a height of effective spontaneous paint application comparable to Hals's and likewise in opposition to formal painting. The handling of landscape in such artists is similarly anticlassical and anti-Baroque, forcing the spectator away from broad infinite vistas toward a more drab, plebeian viewpoint.

REMBRANDT. The early career of the great Rembrandt van Rijn (1606–1669) also belongs to this phase of Dutch art. His genre religious pictures at this point have an earthiness and strained naturalism combined with the popular Caravaggio lighting effects. This is probably a result in part of the provincial background of the painter, but owes as much to the prevailing taste for melodramatically lighted and vulgarized themes of all kinds. In his treatment of the classical subject of Ganymede carried away by the eagle (Dresden, 1635), an overdramatically illuminated fat, blond child, whose rump faces the audience, scowls not uncomically as he is carried off. The whole is deliberately anticlassical in viewpoint and execution.

Like Hals, Rembrandt made his living for a long time as a portrait painter, achieving considerable financial success with detailed honest portrayals in which there is unquestionably more psychological probing than in Hals's works. Rembrandt's conventional interpretations are represented by the well-known *Anatomy Lesson of Dr. Tulp* (Hague, Mauritshuis, 1632), the successful medical practitioner giving his obligatory annual lecture-demonstration for those who had not gone to medical school. This is again reminiscent of the Baroque martyrdom picture in the irregular group and the spotlight falling full on the corpse (cf. figs. 394, 399). Although the composition is centralized through the interest focused on the cadaver, it seems rather forced in effect and posed; some of the characters do not know quite what to do with themselves.

Fig. 424. Rembrandt: The Night Watch. Amsterdam, Rijksmuseum.

Like Hals in his long series of shooting-club pictures, Rembrandt was confronted by the widespread demand for group portraits of all sorts: families, charitable organizations, business groups, military associations, and others. For a long time painters and clients had been satisfied with a conventional approach; handsomely dressed people were brought together and surrounded by their necessary insignia but not organized in any special pictorial form, since the important thing was to give each person his due. The problem is given new interest in Rembrandt's so-called *The Night Watch* (1642, fig. 424), the most famous of these group portraits, which marks a serious advance over earlier ones.

This is no longer a visual stroll over the surface of a food-, drink-,

506

and hero-strewn interior. It is a powerful effort — through the use of controlled glowing shadows rather than an arbitrary spotlight — to focus attention on a dramatic situation, in place of a series of convivial toasts. Instead of posing his sitters amiably, as in Hals's shooting-club series or his own *Anatomy Lesson,* the painter has given heightened meaning to the group by having them respond to a common stimulus. During a visit to Amsterdam by Marie de Médicis (Rubens's patroness for the Luxembourg Palace decorations), the riflemen's guild under Captain Banning Cocq comes out of the city gate to greet the queen. Compared to the earlier pictures, this is a more elegant, even courtly demonstration, a parade in the Rubens sense, with far less attention paid to the individual member of the guild than was customary and socially required. It denotes a stage in the creative growth of Rembrandt; however surprised some of his clients may have been at their subordinate positions, the picture was well received.

From the Baroque point of view this painting depicts a state of becoming rather than a state of being; men rush forward to assume their places, arriving from all directions and from outside the picture space. The two leaders, the captain and his lieutenant, are carried on the crest of this wave. The spatial as well as dramatizing force of Rembrandt's glowing shadowy light already reaches an infinite distance out of the everyday world.

During this period, because of his ripening talents combined with unhappy personal circumstances, Rembrandt's art became more and more profound psychologically. It progressed from generalized themes such as *The Night Watch* to subjects of universal significance, religious motifs such as *The Good Samaritan* (Louvre) and *The Supper at Emmaus* (1648, fig. 425). In these pictures Rembrandt turned from magnificent light-and-dark spectacles to deeply meaningful works, dramatizing the spiritual attributes of pity, faith, or suffering — always in terms of the warmest human sympathy and understanding — using the Old and New Testaments as sources. An interior like *The Supper at Emmaus* elevates the genre picture to a magnificently restrained classical treatment wherein the naturalistic material is reduced to an incidental role. But the people and the space, the material and the spiritual, are united in a way reminiscent of Jan van Eyck in the fifteenth century — without the latter's transfigured symbolism. Christ and the two pilgrims who suddenly become aware of him are simple people, entirely spiritualized by the transcendental golden light that floats about them and ennobled by the architectural background. The technique may recall the later works of Titian in which

Fig. 425. Rembrandt: The Supper at Emmaus. Paris, Louvre.

light and straining emotion perform a somewhat similar task; but Rembrandt's profound feeling and universality of emotion are wholly personal and unlike any other painter's.

Rembrandt's ability to evoke spiritual contemplation, to fathom the depths of the soul and its identification with the universe, is felt in such a work as the celebrated *Man with the Golden Helmet* (fig. 426). Here an elderly man is posed in steel cuirass and golden helmet, close to the spectator and dominating the picture space like many of Rubens's figures. This is no mere portrait; it is an allegory of despair and inherent tragedy. The hard-bitten, disillusioned professional soldier seems weighed down by the size and tangible gold of the helmet, whose heavy paint rises

508

above the surface of the picture and makes his already dark grayish face even bleaker by contrast. It is an entirely imaginary conception for which the painter's brother Adrian, a miller by profession, apparently posed. In a purely technical sense it may be distinguished from contemporary figure paintings in other countries by its use of little pinpoints of light that still suggest a considerable mass, although they break up the surface of the form; they seem to come from within the figure, heightening its spiritual and emotional qualities.

Rembrandt also painted a number of landscapes, some like *The Mill* (National Gallery, Washington, D.C., ca. 1650) with the same immeasurable reaching out and symbolic aspect as the contemporaneous *Man with the Golden Helmet*. This relatively late and broad dramatic style may be contrasted with an earlier sensitive etched landscape, the well-known *Three Trees* (1643, fig. 427). The latter, though more conventionally composed, is filled with a poetic mood. A heavy foreground side element,

Fig. 426. Rembrandt: Man with the Golden Helmet. Berlin, State Museums.

the trees, is balanced against a diagonally receding landscape that supplies the necessary amount of weight to stabilize the picture. The vastness of nature, its force and overwhelming power, are indicated by the endless space, the movement of clouds, sun, and wind, and most of all by the contrast between the small human beings at extreme left and the extent of the natural elements. Here may be sensed the poetry of the contemporary French landscapists, though Rembrandt is neither classicistic like Poussin nor atmospheric like Claude. His pictures of nature, whether in oil or in this delicate etching medium — where he is one of the world's greatest masters — are parallel in meaning with the deeply searching quality of his figure pieces, their sense of the infinite universe and man's part in it.

VAN RUISDAEL. Dutch landscape is an important factor in the art of that country. It may generally be divided into a romantic treatment, in which emotion figures largely, and a more spatial type; works such as Rembrandt's *The Mill* and *Three Trees* are most characteristic of the two treatments. The romantic category is also exemplified by Jakob van Ruisdael (1628–1682), who represents a later stage of Dutch art; he reached maturity at the same time that Rembrandt went into his advanced phase. Ruisdael's *Jewish Cemetery* (fig. 428), done around 1675, after Rembrandt's death, must be looked upon as a reflection of the older master's later and more lyrical expression, his profounder psychological attitude and awareness of the conflict between the individual and society. Ruisdael liked to show windmills rearing their lonely sails against the sky or grayish trees bending wearily over dark forest swamps. The *Jewish*

Cemetery strikes the mood of things gone by, of the transitoriness of existence, as the artist takes us into the dreary burial place of the Jews who were exiled from Spain and given shelter in anti-Spanish Holland. With the ruined buildings, tombstones, and gray-green tonality, he creates a mood of romantic despair in which man is noted only by his absence and by the symbols of his dissolution.

VERMEER. The latter part of Dutch seventeenth-century painting, however, is usually less spiritual in its outlook than either Rembrandt or Ruisdael. Pieter de Hooch (1629–1684), Gerard Terborch (1617–1681), and the masterly Jan Vermeer (1632–1675) brought a distinct lessening of Baroque excitement and romantic or transcendental feeling, which diminished almost to the vanishing point. These later painters took the genre interior of Rembrandt, e.g., *Supper at Emmaus*, and placed it in a clear, material rather than transcendental light. They were not

Fig. 428. Ruisdael: Jewish Cemetery. Dresden, Picture Gallery.

concerned with profound expression of personal or universal disturbance; their task seems to be the quiet, restrained glorification of middle-class and upper-middle-class patrons whose lives, works, and days are celebrated in their pictures. Calm and dignity have been substituted for emotional depth; in place of the symbolic darkness of Rembrandt that transformed the material into the spiritual, there is a far-reaching linear perspective in de Hooch or the implication of space through open windows and doors in de Hooch, Vermeer, and others.

Vermeer's *Officer and Laughing Girl* (fig. 429) is typical of this reduced spiritual potential, however beautifully painted and light-conscious. The figures are characteristically placed at the center of a radiating composition through which they are connected to the table, the wall map, the window, and the chairs. The forms are silhouetted carefully against the wall in a limpid light, much like the early works of Caravaggio and their similar themes. Vermeer deliberately creates compositional interest by turning the nearer chair at an angle so that it juts forward and diagonally out of the picture. In fact, all the elements are cut off as they are brought very close in modern Impressionist fashion (fig. 493) and at

Fig. 429. Vermeer: Officer and Laughing Girl. New York, The Frick Collection.

Fig. 430. Vermeer: Young Woman with Water Jug. New York, Metropolitan Museum of Art.

the same time projected out of the space. The window and map become devices for infinite projection, the window breaking down the barrier between the inside and outside of the room; the map in such pictures often represents the great distances of the earth conquered in that century, the colonies in America, and the activities of the Dutch East India Company. Aspirations toward infinity have come down to movements in tangible space.

In the same way, the dematerialized form of Rembrandt's *Man with the Golden Helmet* is changed to a highly materialistic conception, of which Vermeer's impressive interiors are the outstanding examples. The concentration on tactile quality of substances — cloth, wood, metal, skin — is one of the foremost characteristics of this style. Also significant is the light which falls on an object and is reflected upon something adjacent to it, as in the *Young Woman with Water Jug* (fig. 430).

The themes — a lute player, a girl reading a letter or standing before a window (another echo of distances), a couple having a drink — are relatively inconsequential as compared with religious or historical subjects. This is the beginning of a general trend toward the idea that what the artist paints is less important than how he paints it. Yet it is undeniably true that Vermeer and his colleagues in the second half of the seventeenth century were a mirror of the social aims and aspirations of the conquering merchant class. All the activities of this class, however commonplace, are magnified and treated with ceremonial seriousness, perhaps a natural thing in the absence of religious art as such. It is a return in a sense to the traditional meticulous character of Netherlandish art of the fifteenth century, without the religion and almost without aristocratic pretension. All energies are engaged in monumentalizing and memorializing the newly important group, shown most often in their leisure-class pursuits. Not until the following century in France was there to be an art similarly oriented toward glorifying the man of the middle class and his home life.

22 / FROM ABSOLUTISM TO FREE THOUGHT: *England and the United States in the Eighteenth Century*

T H E face of the Western world in the eighteenth century was shaped by many new features: the end of absolute monarchy, increasing power for the middle class, development of science, and the diffusion of rational thought. In the arts nothing is more striking than the interchange of relations between the upper and the middle sections of society. As the former lost its vitality and importance, the latter gained in strength and self-assertiveness, altering the character of eighteenth-century culture by a potent infusion of middle-class feeling into art and literature. Portraits, genre art, landscapes, plays, poetry, and novels respond to the sentimentality, the new-found sense of virtue and morality, the self-conscious worthiness of the bourgeoisie. These stand opposed to the artificiality, luxury, idleness, and licentiousness of the upper classes. Ultimately the aristocratic group tended to adopt the sentimentality of the newly rich, while conversely the upper middle class adopted some aristocratic coloration.

The first step in the new direction had been made in England, fully a century before the French Revolution, when the historic Bill of Rights of 1689 enumerated the basic privileges of Englishmen. Perhaps the most famous defense of the rights of the middle class, John Locke's *Second Treatise of Government* (1690), had inspired American and French revolutionaries. In spite of obvious defects and abuses, early eighteenth-century England was far ahead of the rest of Europe along the path of democracy in both government and social life. The long period of peace following the Glorious Revolution of 1688 solidified the power of the British bourgeoisie. A large number of fine town and country houses were built, stocked with graceful furniture and paintings — especially portraits. With these impressive symbols of well-being came

515

a taste for culture and general education. Books were bought, particularly English editions of the classics such as Pope's translations of the *Iliad* and *Odyssey*, which opened the doors to classical education, a mark of the true gentleman. Classical preferences were shown in the design of official and domestic buildings.

In this atmosphere culture became democratized. The writer working for this public no longer had to fawn on aristocratic patrons, and the painter soon also found himself in an increasingly favorable position. Many of the newly rich in their desire for gentility and pride of accomplishment wished to have their portraits painted. From this group and the still-influential aristocracy a broad market awaited the artist for the traditional formal portrait. The growing sentimentality, moral interests, and socially critical attitudes created even wider outlets for his energies. In response to these developing tastes a sentimental kind of portrait was to appear (Hoppner, Romney) as well as a forthright, rugged type of characterization (Hogarth). Sentimentally illustrative and genre pictures acquired a certain importance (Devis, Highmore), while caricature and moralistic paintings and engravings (Hogarth) initiated a new, distinctly British form. Landscape, like portraiture, catered to both the older aristocratic viewpoint and the more sentimental reactions of the bourgeoisie.

The fairly popular art of landscape painting signified a deep interest in nature in eighteenth-century Europe, especially England. The scientific discoveries of the period immediately preceding, particularly those of Newton, had brought a conviction that nature obeys invariable laws. The rationalistic belief that through the study of nature order could be brought back to human affairs is expressed in the often quoted lines from Pope's *Essay on Criticism:*

> *First follow Nature, and your judgment frame*
> *By her just standard, which is still the same;*
> *Unerring Nature, still divinely bright,*
> *One clear, unchanged and universal light.*

This worship of nature, rational rather than romantic, is the basis of the natural philosophy known as Deism (popular with eighteenth-century liberals like Jefferson and Paine) which sought the First Cause of the physical world. Politically it was related to Jean Jacques Rousseau's social-contract idea of government, which offered a "natural" explanation of the origins of the state, stressing mutual responsibilities and duties of the governing and the governed rather than absolutistic privilege.

CLASSICAL INFLUENCE. In literature and often in art of the eighteenth century, "truth to nature" meant studying the classical authorities, who were believed to have followed her ways most accurately and from whom the rules for imitation of nature were to be ascertained. There were such works as Pope's translations of Homer, his *Essay on Criticism* (derived from Horace's *Ars poetica* and the seventeenth-century Boileau's *L'Art poétique*) — and a continuity and strengthening of the classical tradition in general, particularly in architecture.

Each age has its own version of the classical attitude. Eighteenth-century English architecture, for example, moved from a late Renaissance — actually Baroque — classicism to a lighter, more gracious use of classical elements in the Georgian period, and finally into the more specific and accurate antique forms of the Revival at the end of the century. This evolution was paralleled in France and to a certain extent in other parts of Europe.

Classical tastes and education had been prerogatives and hallmarks of the aristocracy, but with the democratization of culture they were adopted in various ways by the rising middle class. Early in the century the aristocratic French Rococo works of Boucher are classical only in theme, while luxurious and decorative in design and color. The century later produced the increasingly sentimental or bourgeois classicism of Fragonard and Hubert Robert, who still retained strong Rococo elements.

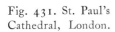

Fig. 431. St. Paul's Cathedral, London.

Fig. 432.
House in West Street, Chichester.

The sensuous Rococo was finally overwhelmed by the tide of middle-class feeling in the bourgeois tragedy, the tearful comedy, and the declamatory paintings of Benjamin West in England, Greuze in France, and others. Classicism takes on a stern and even harsh quality as in David, a distinctly moral rather than pleasurable meaning. This later classicism differs not only in mood and quality but also in form, based now on the real material of antiquity from new excavations in Italy and explorations in Greece.

ENGLISH ARCHITECTURE. English architectural classicism progressed from the Baroque *St. Paul's Cathedral* by Sir Christopher Wren (1632–1723, fig. 431) and Blenheim Palace by Sir John Vanbrugh (1666–1726) to the simpler, less grandiloquent Georgian homes of the wealthy merchant class, such as the *House in West Street* at Chichester (fig. 432) or the more elaborate houses at Bath built by the Woods family. The latter type may be considered a form of protest against the pompous Baroque with its absolutist connotation. The interiors of the Georgian period — although quite different in many ways from contemporary French Rococo — share with that style a lighter, more graceful and decorative quality so unlike the heaviness of the Louis XIV era which had seriously affected English work during the seventeenth century.

Like England's poetry, its architecture in the eighteenth century was much concerned with a rather academic search for rules, the "just standard" of "unerring Nature." Toward the end of the century this search was reinforced by the more accurate knowledge of ancient architecture, manifested in an authentic neoclassical revival. In the designs of the Adam brothers, e.g., *Home House* in London (fig. 433), the details are genuinely classical (Robert Adam had taken part in an archaeological expedition in Italy), not merely derived from the usual Renaissance sources. By the early nineteenth century, English, American, German, and other architects were reproducing complete classical buildings instead of decorative details — utilizing these forms somewhat incongruously for banks, schools, and other modern needs.

ENGLISH PAINTING. The formal or semiformal English building was often embellished with copies and casts of ancient sculpture, while the paintings preferred were Italian. This is not too remarkable, since there had been no native English school of art since the late Middle Ages. During the sixteenth, seventeenth, and even early eighteenth centuries upper-class portraits had been supplied by imported artists: German, Dutch, and Flemish painters such as Holbein, Rubens, Van Dyck, Lely, and Kneller. Other kinds of art were furnished by academic imitators of late-Renaissance masters. By the second quarter of the eighteenth

Fig. 433. Adam: Home House, Portman Square, London.

century, however, England began to produce painting which responded to the great changes that had occurred. Each category — genre, landscape, and portrait — was necessarily derived from older types of expression but was transformed by the tastes and requirements of an increasingly fluid society. Most striking and original was the English portrayal of manners and morals in paintings and engravings.

The many examples of social satire in eighteenth-century European art — Longhi in Italy, Greuze in France, Goya at the end of the century in Spain — were preceded by William Hogarth (1697–1764) and the English school. Earlier and more widespread than in painting, social criticism had existed in literature, which democratized itself sooner than the fine arts where royal patronage and academic tradition were restraining influences. Writers were able to respond more directly to the social changes of the early eighteenth century. Pope's *Rape of the Lock* (1712) represented an anti-aristocratic tendency, while John Gay's *Shepherd's Week* and *Beggar's Opera* (1728) ridiculed the conventional pastoral and the flamboyant Italian opera, respectively. Middle-class virtue was extolled by Richardson in *Pamela* and *Clarissa Harlowe* (novels much admired by contemporary French moralists), while Fielding's *Joseph Andrews* (1742) was intended as a satire on *Pamela*. The turbulence of the age, its rough-and-tumble individualism, loose morals, violent contrasts between riches and poverty, and its essential fluidity and critical attitude are all visible in the brilliant novels of Fielding, Smollett, and Sterne. Playwrights like Goldsmith and Sheridan portrayed the gayer side of that life.

Hogarth. William Hogarth, definitely a man of his time, gave as vivid and complete a picture of this era as Daumier was to do for the nineteenth century in France. In a pictorial equivalent to much of the literature of the period, Hogarth attacked not only a foppish and idle aristocracy, particularly for its affectation of French manners, but also false cultural standards, drunkenness, corrupt parliamentarians, the degradation of the lower classes, and the common social cruelty of the age. The broad spread of his subject matter covers the moral attitude of *The Four Stages of Cruelty* and *The Idle and the Industrious Apprentice* as well as a more adventurous, picturesque approach dealing with licentiousness in *A Rake's Progress* and *A Harlot's Progress* (fig. 434).

In works of the second type the moral touch is less obvious but exists none the less. The harlot is a victim of circumstances, having come to London and been seduced by her employer, so that her ultimate fate in Bridewell Prison is not so much a punishment for sin as an exhibit of man's cruelty. Similarly the artist considers the rake a foolish, unfortunate young man rather than a sinner, delineating the unusual and exciting

520

things that happen to him and taking the opportunity to lampoon the disgusting habit of fashionable folk who visit Bedlam insane asylum for amusement.

Hogarth the reformer was very much concerned with the viciousness of English public institutions at that time. In this sense, certainly, he was more than an entertaining portrayer of manners and customs; he became a social critic on a high level, although not as politically conscious as later artists. The fact that his enormous subject matter contains criticism against any violator of the decencies makes it difficult to maintain that he is for one class against another; yet Hogarth was a product of the new middle-class honesty of sentiment, the right to speak up against iniquity in any form.

His position in eighteenth-century art is illustrated dramatically by the fact that his stories of the harlot or the rake, originally paintings, were engraved and sold to the general public at a shilling apiece in quan-

Fig. 434. Hogarth: The Harlot's Progress series (Arrival in London). New York, Metropolitan Museum of Art.

Fig. 435. Hogarth: William James. Worcester Art Museum.

tities sufficient to support him comfortably. His portraits, on the other hand, e.g., *William James* (fig. 435), in spite of what today seem wonderful forthrightness and naturalism, were not popular; they had to compete with the prevailing factory-made Kneller type of portrait or the post-Venetian aristocratic Flemish manner practiced by the eighteenth-century descendants of Van Dyck. The so-called art lovers of the day refused to recognize Hogarth as either a portrait painter or a painter of history, while Hogarth refused to acknowledge their right to criticize on the basis of their presumable acquaintance with Italian art. His struggle against the little-informed conservatives and the art dealers of his time was part of the centuries-long conflict between the old art world and the new, and here again Hogarth's middle-class expression signified the new.

Though it may be pointed out that his compositions in the satirical engravings are crowded and overdetailed, it must be remembered that a great deal of this detail — which now seems bric-a-brac — was necessary and proper to the eighteenth-century audience for complete understanding. His contribution to the field of social criticism is considerable; it forms the basis for many developments in the second half of the eighteenth and the first half of the nineteenth century.

Highmore. Less important an artist or innovator than Hogarth, Joseph Highmore (1682–1780) equally indicates the new middle-class viewpoint. This member of the Hogarth circle is best known for his illustrations for Richardson's *Pamela*, which are as virtuous as their inspiration and typical of the eighteenth-century vogue for sentiment.

Wilson. Most English painting of the period did not depict life in Hogarth's direct manner, but presented landscapes of mood or semi-aristocratic portraits turning toward sentimental and even declamatory expression. Landscape painting of the time, however, also illustrates the conflict between the old and the new. Richard Wilson (1714–1782), often referred to as "the father of the English landscape," was not a popular success in this field. After a period in Italy, where he came into contact with the work of the Frenchman Vernet and the Venetian Zuccarelli, Wilson returned to England to find that a landscape painter was expected to put together conventionally the stock elements of trees, mountains, water, etc., with fragments of broken columns and ruined buildings — the last thin remnant of what has been called the picturesque-classical style, initiated by Claude.

This academic approach, lustily fought by Hogarth, was also impossible for an original painter like Wilson, whose pictures were usually based on personal experience rather than earlier engravings or other people's ideas. His *River Scene* (London, National Gallery) and *On*

Fig. 436. Wilson: On the Wye. London, National Gallery.

the Wye (fig. 436) show a new breadth and a fresh feeling for nature, far removed from the conventionalized pictures of Hubert Robert, Zuccarelli, or similar painters who were then popular all over Europe. Without breaking entirely from the accepted pattern of contemporary landscape, Wilson succeeded in injecting a poetic emotional element into his personal summations of the scenes, an attitude that was transmitted to landscapists of the nineteenth century from Crome to Turner. This element may be regarded as sentiment or as what was later Romantic feeling; it probably had aspects of both.

Fig. 437. Gainsborough: Landscape. New York, Metropolitan Museum of Art.

Gainsborough. Whereas Wilson's landscapes can be considered ancestors of the Romantic movement, those of Thomas Gainsborough (1727–1788) are distinctly sentimental in mood as they are fuzzy in form and artificial in quality. While based to some extent on the picturesque-Baroque tradition of generalized emotional reactions to nature (with some of the ragged contour and rhythmic quality of Rubens's land-scapes), their additional delicacy and suavity of color and form, especially for the people in the pictures, suggest the contemporary Watteau in France. Yet in such pictures as the *Landscape* (fig. 437), besides the over-all rhythmic elements there is a distinct mood of evening melan-choly, literary in character and symbolic of the end of day in the sense of Gray's poem *Elegy Written in a Country Churchyard*.

Transitional between Gainsborough's landscapes and his graceful, charming portraits are his modish characters of Rococo elegance, in the outdoor environment of fashionable London or Bath, e.g., *The Mall* (private collection, United States), and pseudocountry types before thatched cottages or in wagons, as in *The Cottage Door* (Mr. & Mrs. Charles F. Williams Collection) or the *Market Cart* (London, National Gallery). These would-be farmers are parallel in meaning and expression

Fig. 438. Gainsborough: The Honorable Frances Dun-combe. New York, The Frick Collection.

with the refined shepherds and shepherdesses of the period of Louis XVI in France and equally filled with a tender feeling for nature.

Gainsborough is best known for his elegant and sensitive portraits, painted on the main aristocratic level of English portraiture but with far greater delicacy in color, drawing, and expression than any of his rivals exhibited. Here again a self-made rather than academically trained painter brings forth a significant art form. Although his early portraits had been based on the serious conversation groups of the Hogarth circle, it was in the fashionable environment of Bath, where he met the pictures of Van Dyck and Rubens, that Gainsborough's characteristic style emerged. He elaborated and attenuated the Van Dyck manner, giving it even silkier form and color and expressing infinitely more sensitivity than the Flemish painter. Although Gainsborough had few illusions concerning the job of painting his sitters, he remains in many ways the most graceful, the deftest, painter of his period. Pictures like *Mrs. Graham* (National Gallery of Scotland) or *The Honorable Frances Duncombe*

Fig. 439. Reynolds: Sarah Siddons as the Tragic Muse. San Marino, Huntington Art Gallery.

Fig. 440. Reynolds: Commander Keppel. London, Tate Gallery.

(fig. 438) exemplify the grace and charm of his style, the aristocratic manner lightened and sensitized by his own unusual personality.

Reynolds. Sir Joshua Reynolds (1732–1792) represents a more academic and formal point of view, based directly on the Italian Renaissance as well as on Van Dyck. After three years in Italy, Reynolds returned to England and became the most successful society painter of his time. In 1768, when the Royal Academy was established, he was elected its first president. Judging by his letters and discourses delivered before the Academy, Reynolds apparently believed that it was possible to become a successful, if not great, artist by imitating masters of the past. Though he himself practiced this eclectic procedure, his works often reveal an originality and variety belying it. Obvious tricks may mar his *Little Miss Bowles* with its triangular Renaissance composition or the all-too-melodramatic *Sarah Siddons as the Tragic Muse* (fig. 439) and other, even more exaggerated allegories; but there is a magnificent bearing and authority in the *Commander Keppel* (fig. 440) or the *Dr. Johnson.*

Fig. 441. Raeburn: Colonel Alastair Macdonell. Edinburgh, National Gallery.

Raeburn. Other portraitists of the period — George Romney, John Hoppner, Sir Thomas Lawrence, and their like — leave stylish mementoes, little else. Only Henry Raeburn (1756–1823) in Edinburgh, away from the fashionable environment that spoiled so many others, produced a portrait art worthy of the name. His *Colonel Alastair Macdonell* (fig. 441), his *Scott, Hume,* and many other Italian-influenced works show a good deal of the power of Reynolds, whose career Raeburn followed in many respects. His mood in its directness and simplicity evokes that of some American portraitists of the eighteenth century.

THE AMERICAN COLONIES: ARCHITECTURE. The European colonies in America necessarily shared the cultural traditions of their respective mother countries. The Spanish Baroque had been echoed in the architecture of North, South, and Central America, however mixed with native ingredients (fig. 405, *Ocotlán Cathedral*). In North America, apart from the continuity of Spanish culture in Mexico, the Louisiana Territory, California, and Florida, other artistic influences had appeared — French, Dutch, and especially English. Canadian seventeenth-century buildings of the French Louis XIII type, New Amsterdam structures with the stepped gables and red brick of Holland, were part of the early colonial picture. In the seventeenth century also, the first English-derived structures appeared in the New England and southern colonies; the *Capen House* at Topsfield, Mass. (1683, fig. 442), may be compared to the late medieval architecture still dominant in Britain until the end of that century. The high peaked roof, overhanging upper story, Tudor chimney, and the ornamental pendants carved on the lower ends of the second- and third-story beams (cf. fig. 296, pendants in *Chapel of Henry VII*) show the relationship to English forms.

In the eighteenth century with the colonies' increasing prosperity came a more elaborate architecture. As the entire Atlantic seaboard fell under British control, a more uniformly English style (especially that of Christopher Wren and Inigo Jones) began to emerge. This process was helped in no small measure by the publication of handbooks on architecture (also on furniture) which displayed the necessary broken pediments, bracketlike decorative consoles, and ornamental doorway and cornice carvings of Georgian usage. Typical of this change is the *Longfellow House* at Cambridge, Mass. (fig. 443), exemplifying the delicately carved moldings, the well-designed cornices, the pilasters and pediment of the Georgian style. In the southern colonies a more elaborate, even feudal, mode of living fostered buildings reminiscent of the splendid English country houses of James Gibbs or the *House in West Street* at Chichester (fig. 432). Westover in Virginia, built around 1730, has loggias that con-

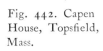

Fig. 442. Capen House, Topsfield, Mass.

Fig. 443. Longfellow House, Cambridge, Mass.

Fig. 444. First Baptist Meeting House, Providence, R.I.

nect the main house to related and balanced outbuildings in the Gibbs manner. The broken curved pediment and Renaissance carved doorway flanked by pilasters are important decorative elements of this style.

A close parallel between colonial and British architecture is found in the many churches of the period, e.g., the *First Baptist Meeting House* of Providence, R.I. (1775, fig. 444). Like the well-known St. Paul's Chapel in New York and others, they present a more advanced classicism in the use of a free-standing entrance or side portico with classical columns and pediment. A further and even more striking English element may be seen in their steeples, which derive from such across-the-seas examples as St. Mary-le-Bow by Wren and St. Martin's-in-the-Fields by Gibbs.

As in England, colonial architecture toward the end of the eighteenth and the beginning of the nineteenth century turned to a more specific and academic classicism. The imminence of the American Revolution may be regarded in the same light as the advance of the middle class in various European countries as they struggled out from monarchical control. The rise of the bourgeoisie in America also took on a neoclassical character, associating the ancient past with democracy and individual freedom. Shortly after the Revolution, Thomas Jefferson, one of the chief formulators of America's republican ideas, designed the initial Virginia State Capitol after the *Maison Carrée* at Nîmes (fig. 123), replacing the Corinthian order by an Ionic portico and the engaged pilasters by windows. Among Jefferson's most impressive adaptations of classical monuments is the *Rotunda of the University of Virginia* (fig. 445), a replica of

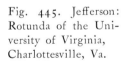

Fig. 445. Jefferson: Rotunda of the University of Virginia, Charlottesville, Va.

the Roman *Pantheon* (fig. 133). The colonnades and high porticos of the University itself likewise attest to his profound feeling that classicism and democracy were related.

In the years following the establishment of the United States, there were many such adaptations of Greek and Roman buildings in the new Federal style. The United States Bank in Philadelphia took the form of a Doric temple; the similar Subtreasury in New York City and countless others illustrate the spread of this fashion. Athens in Georgia, Troy, Ithaca, and Syracuse in New York State, and Ypsilanti in Michigan were among the scores of classically named American cities during the early nineteenth century, when classical republicanism was further stimulated by the Greek war of independence against the Turks between 1821 and 1827.

AMERICAN PAINTING: *Copley and Stuart.* The pattern of American painting in the eighteenth century is again like that of England — with certain significant differences. The upper classes in America, namely, the wealthier planters and merchants, were in the market for the courtly type of portrait produced in the mother country. Unfortunately, however, most American artists stemmed from their earlier tradition of self-taught

Fig. 446. Copley: Nathaniel Hurd. Courtesy, Cleveland Museum of Art. John Huntington Collection.

Fig. 447. Stuart: Thomas Jefferson. Courtesy, Bowdoin College Museum of Fine Arts.

journeyman portraitists (the limners) and were unable to meet a high professional requirement. Painters like John Smibert and Robert Feke represented the best of the average colonial portraitists, but they were not up to the standard of their European contemporaries. Feke's portrait of *Isaac Royal and His Family* (1741, Harvard University), in spite of its obvious symbols of wealth, does not give the sitters a convincing lifelike quality.

Unquestionably the best of colonial portrait painters and in many ways a rival to the English was John Singleton Copley (1737–1815), a Boston artist. Copley was a relatively provincial painter, devoid of the graces of London society work; but pictures like *Nathaniel Hurd* (fig. 446) or *Mr. and Mrs. Isaac Winslow* (Boston Museum, Karolik Collection) have a strength and integrity not to be met outside the portraiture of Hogarth and the French Chardin. It is noteworthy that an American painter isolated from the main stream of European art (except for what he could absorb from second-raters here and from books) arrived at such a high degree of formal strength, rich color, and psychological insight.

This was possible perhaps through the very fact that Copley long worked outside the aristocratic and academic British tradition and for the self-consciously worthy upper-middle-class Americans. It is certainly true that after 1774, when Copley went abroad to England, where he lived for the rest of his life, his style became more facile and charming, lacking its original integrity.

The conventional and English side of American painting is exemplified by Gilbert Stuart (1755–1828), best known for his many portraits of George Washington. Stuart belongs to that group of Americans who went to London to study with their eminently successful countryman, Benjamin West, who had succeeded Reynolds as president of the Royal Academy. When Stuart came back to America in 1792, he had already absorbed the fashionable London technique. His more charmingly colored and easy portraits — the *Thomas Jefferson* (fig. 447) or the many versions of Washington — do not have Copley's perceptivity, colonial simplicity, and strength. Perhaps by the 1790s, with the Revolution won and the period of struggle presumably over, it was time for the sort of aristocratic ease and charm represented by Stuart. The combination of Raeburn's brilliant technique with Lawrence's charming manner was to prove the favorite portrait recipe for the increasingly prosperous republican era.

23 / FROM ABSOLUTISM TO FREE THOUGHT: *France, Italy, and Germany in the Eighteenth Century*

ACROSS the channel from England, French intellectuals were still fighting the influence of the Church and the power of the absolute monarchy, problems which no longer concerned the British. England produced modern democratic forms and their culture early in the eighteenth century, but France had to wait until many years later for such developments. Voltaire's *Lettres philosophiques* (1734) were so favorable to the English way of life that they were forbidden by the French monarch; presumably an account of Voltaire's exile in England, they were certainly evidence of the influence of the "freethinkers." A mighty fighter for freedom, Voltaire lived a good part of his life in Switzerland, from where he sent his famous literary attacks across the border into France. It was only on the death of Louis XV that the writer appeared in Paris in 1778 to receive his well-earned acclaim.

The nonrevolutionary Montesquieu masked a criticism of French society in the *Persian Letters* (1721); his *L'Esprit des lois* (*The Spirit of the Laws*, 1748) was a calm and reasoned approval of the English system of government and affected the structure of the American republic. A whole generation of French writers under the influence of Montesquieu formulated the great *Encyclopedia* (1751–1772), which concerned itself, among other things, with the perfect state and with the rights and duties of citizens. Although they were not primarily political or reformist, these philosophers led by Diderot faced constant government opposition. More than any other group in France, they helped to sweep away the remnants of medieval superstition and monarchical absolutism.

The propagandistic character of French eighteenth-century literature and social theory resulted in part from English influence; in the slower

535

social evolution of France, certain forms and ideas took longer to express themselves, especially in art where a still important court and aristocratic patronage tended to retard the process. Artistic social criticism such as Hogarth's did not appear in France until the time of the Revolution proper and then only in the form of handbills. French art itself, however, is easily the most aesthetically significant and influential of the period; in addition, it clearly shows the gradual change from an aristocratic expression to one increasingly charged with sentiment and then with declamatory virtue.

In the French theater, the "tearful comedy" of La Chaussée in the thirties was evidence of the expanding status of the middle class. Such plays — affirmations of bourgeois virtue like the later moral paintings of Greuze in the fifties — were indirect attacks on the aristocracy. In the plastic arts, even at the end of the century there was nothing so bold and forthright as Beaumarchais's *Marriage of Figaro* (1783), which, in Napoleon's famous phrase, was already "the Revolution in action." Figaro symbolizes the rising bourgeois who mocks and deceives the aristocratic characters. When he says in the famous monologue: "Because you are a great lord you think yourself a great genius — you have taken the trouble to be born, nothing more . . . ," he sounds the death knell of privilege and caste.

FRENCH ARCHITECTURE; ROCOCO STYLE. This development was reflected in architecture as in the other arts. The end of the long reign of Louis XIV terminated the vogue of the splendid seventeenth-century Baroque of Versailles and the Louvre. During the Louis XV period (1715–1774), instead of the previous magnificent royal palaces, French architecture emphasized the private mansion, the *hôtel*, much more modest in size if not always different in detail. These town and country houses, built by both the nobility and the new bourgeoisie in various parts of France, are a tangible sign of the breakdown in the absolutist system of the Grand Monarch.

The powerful and dynamic seventeenth century, in many ways the apogee of French history, yielded to a period in which the nobility became increasingly nonfunctional and decorative like its art, while the middle class figured more and more in the culture of the time as its social and economic importance mounted. The less meaningful role of the aristocracy was mirrored in the Rococo style (ca. 1715–ca. 1745), whose most patent manifestations in France are in interior decoration, in the irregular arrangement of rooms and the cursive flowing character of ornament, the curved delicate shapes of graceful, intimate furniture, and the charming gold, pink, and white tonalities that predominate. These lighter elements contrast sharply with the heavy formal character of designs of the preceding Louis XIV period, whose splendid *salons* (e.g., *Hall of Mirrors* at Versailles, fig. 419) give way to the intimate and cozy boudoirs that figure so prominently in Rococo painting. The *Monkey Room* of the Hôtel de Rohan in Paris (fig. 448) is one of the best examples of this mode. Although its primary expression in France is found in interiors rather than on exteriors, away from the capital there are Rococo exteriors also. At Nancy the style breaks out on many façades, on iron gates, and on mythological fountains that suggest Boucher landscapes.

Fig. 448. Cabinet des singes (Monkey Room). Hôtel de Rohan (now the National Printing Office), Paris. Paintings of monkeys, "oriental" figures, etc., by Christophe Huet.

Outside of France this gracious expression was applied to both interiors and exteriors, especially in Germany. The central pavilion of the *Zwinger Palace* in Dresden (fig. 449), Sans Souci Palace near Potsdam, and the Amalienburg near Munich are good examples of that exuberant architecture. Others are the Schönbrunn Palace near Vienna and the Drottningholm Palace near Stockholm, with varying amounts of indoor and outdoor Rococo treatments. France exported this fashion either directly through French architects looking for work (as were many French

Fig. 449. Pöppelmann: Zwinger Pavilion, Dresden.

painters) or through locally developed foreign talent. Every ruler in Europe seemed to want a reasonable facsimile of the newly decorated Versailles, in which the splendid formality of the Baroque seventeenth-century building was combined inside with many Rococo curves in plan and elevation, while formal columns were replaced by more intimate and delicate panels, flower-decorated scrolls, and various irregularly shaped ornaments. Special small paintings were designed for some of the panels, against which exquisite furniture was placed.

In many display cabinets in palaces throughout Europe, orientalia appeared in considerable quantity. These bright-colored, finely designed objects known as *chinoiseries* were brought into Europe by an expanding mercantile economy. They fitted perfectly into Rococo backgrounds and had a direct effect on the art of the period, e.g., furniture design and the paintings of Boucher, Huet, and others (cf. fig. 448).

NEOCLASSICAL ARCHITECTURE. By the middle of the century, French Rococo began to be replaced by serious and direct imitation of antique styles. These were made familiar to artists through the expanded knowledge of history and archaeology, one of the many results of eighteenth-century rationalism and scientific curiosity. This renewal of classical interest after the partial excavation of Herculaneum (1738), the investigation of the Greek temples at Paestum (1750–1751), and the excavation

538

of the city of Pompeii (begun in 1763) must also be attributed in part to a revulsion of feeling against the luxuriousness of the Rococo manner. Further, the "naturalness" of the classical style and its severity of form became increasingly related in the public mind to the severe and useful morality of the middle class. In painting, revolutionary sentiments were expressed in the language of antiquity — with its overtones of a golden age — rather than the multigestured sentimentality of a Greuze.

This return to classicism during the late Louis XV and early Louis XVI periods is illustrated in the well-known *Petit Trianon* built for Mme. de Pompadour at Versailles (1762–1768, fig. 450). Exterior and interior both show a distinct trend toward simple and restrained forms, a much quieter color scheme, and less ornate rectangles and squares replacing the lush and curvilinear Rococo style. Although the building's delicacy and charm still carries over from the Rococo, it has an added dignity. More specifically neoclassical in feeling and style are such buildings as the *Panthéon* (1755–1781, fig. 451), which reproduces Wren's dome on *St. Paul's* but also brings back the high Roman portico with free-standing Corinthian columns and pediment, suggesting the original *Pantheon* in Rome (fig. 133).

The neoclassical revival, in France as elsewhere, associated classicism (Roman severity, the democratic Greek city-state) with the democratic aspirations of the time, as in Houdon's sculpture and David's paintings. It did not strike the late-eighteenth- and early-nineteenth-century architects as curious that ancient Greek and Roman architectural schemes were utilized for modern schools (Ecole Militaire, Paris), hospitals, govern-

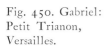

Fig. 450. Gabriel: Petit Trianon, Versailles.

Fig. 451. Soufflot: Panthéon, Paris.

ment buildings (the Mint in Paris, 1771–1775), and railroad stations — types of buildings that in some cases had never existed in ancient times. Even Christian churches such as St. Sulpice (Paris, 1732–1745) and the *Panthéon* (Ste. Geneviève, fig. 451) were erected in this rational and moral style, becoming part of the new *anticomanie*, or craze for the antique. The customs gates of Paris were designed by Le Doux as propylaea, or antique gateways, based on Etruscan and Roman models. The height of this mania produced the startling Ecole de Chirurgie, or School of Surgery (1767–1776), where a temple to Aesculapius was erected in the rear of the court, and an antique altar was set up in an amphitheater to serve as an operating table. According to André Chénier, the ill-starred poet of the period, the ideal of the time was "to make classic verses out of modern thoughts. . . ." (*Sur des pensées nouvelles faire des vers antiques*).

FRENCH PAINTING. The great contribution of eighteenth-century French art was in the field of painting. After the death of Charles le Brun in 1697 and the breakdown of the autocratic seventeenth-century art system, there emerged a series of vigorous and individual styles reflecting the various social and intellectual changes of the new century. A violent reaction against the too logical and intellectual manner of the Louis XIV period, which was found to lack *sensibilité*, or feeling, soon produced a more supple and freer art. From 1697 on, the number of portraits at the Academy *Salon* exhibitions increased markedly. The trend toward smaller buildings doomed the gigantic historical paintings, which were replaced by portraits and small genre pictures. The frequent use of

540

mirrors and more limited size of rooms left space for paintings only above fireplace mirrors, in curvilinear wall and ceiling panels, or on doors.

The earlier emphasis on line and geometric composition, the vogue of Roman and Bolognese (i.e., Carracci) styles, yielded to a preference for Venetian color and the exuberance of Rubens, who was now collected assiduously. His paintings in the Luxembourg of the life of Marie de Médicis became a sort of academy for French artists of the eighteenth century (Watteau and Fragonard copied many of these) as the galleries of the Carracci in the *Farnese Palace* had been in the seventeenth century. Dutch influence was also felt; Fragonard frequently made copies of Rembrandt, while the lesser masters and landscapists of Holland came in for a good deal of attention, as from Chardin.

The painting of the Regency period with which this century began is marked by a certain effervescence, a liveliness of form and color in transitional artists like Hyacinthe Rigaud (1659–1743). His *Portrait of Président Hébert* (fig. 452) shows a new type of personality in France, a representative of the upper middle class, who appears with happy clarity

Fig. 452. Rigaud: Portrait of Président Hébert. Washington, D.C., National Gallery of Art, Kress Collection.

Fig. 453. Watteau: Embarkation for Cythera. Paris, Louvre.

542

of countenance and color. Although this painting is symptomatic of changes that are to come, the art of the Regency is still primarily on a courtly aristocratic level.

Watteau. Antoine Watteau (1683–1721), short-lived genius of the early eighteenth century, is in many ways the best artistic representative of upper-class French society and its attitudes. His art, more freely designed than was possible during the Louis XIV period, embodies the social graces of his day or at least an idealized version thereof. Working with the colors of Rubens but in a more restrained fashion, he demonstrates the difference not only between the lustiness of the Fleming and his own somewhat diffident manner, but more important, between the former vital and decisive role of the aristocracy and its increasingly useless and negligible function in the eighteenth century. Watteau portrays aristocrats engaged in elegant idling, listening to music, having conversations in parks whose peculiarly sensitive landscapes are influenced by the tonalities of Leonardo and the rhythms of Rubens, and — most characteristic of the age — making delicate and skillful love.

As in the plays of Marivaux (1688–1763), that arbiter of the fine art of courting, Watteau depicted a theater-influenced, highly artificial concept of love in which conversation plays a leading role. Rubens's *Garden of Love* (fig. 408) with its full-blown women and impressive cavalier men may be set against Watteau's *Embarkation for Cythera* (fig. 453) with its attenuated figures and decorative sensitivity. This is the difference between two ages and cultures, between the inherent vigor of the Baroque style and the charming gallantry of the Rococo. The robustness of the Flemish master is counterbalanced in Watteau's style by the subtlety of the Venetians, especially Veronese and Titian. Pictures like *The Concert* offer a close-up view of the elegance and distinction of Watteau's characters, their aristocratic gestures, and that typical fuzzy landscape developed out of the hazes of Leonardo and the rhythmic swings of Rubens.

The celebrated *Embarkation for Cythera* sums up the essentially theatrical character of this art, in the eighteenth-century Marivaux sense of word play, of love as a game. Watteau's apprenticeship to Claude Gillot, who had lived in the milieu of the Italian comedy, lent a playful make-believe quality, the feeling of an imaginary world in which his characters wander. His lovers typify the contemporary fondness for graceful conversation and fine attitudes; in this particular painting he seems to have transposed an actual play to canvas. Beginning at the right, the first courting couple, representing the first step in the game of love,

Fig. 454. Watteau: Gilles.
Paris, Louvre.

sits in the shadow of the symbolic armless herm of Venus bedecked with flower offerings. To their immediate left the next couple is shown in the second step as the gentleman raises the lady to her feet. Again to the left, approaching the brow of the little hillock, a third pair stands; the lady casts a backward glance while the man gently urges her down toward the others who are waiting to embark for the mythical island of love, an invisible spot sensed in the misty distance. The doll-like figures in glistening satins, the men with high-heeled shoes and walking sticks, are not actual people but symbols of the behavior approved by this courtly society, which was now less interested in building up the country than in having an elegant and sophisticated good time.

Watteau's art, however, is not joyous. Partly because of the languid character of his pictured romances and partly from the melancholy induced by an incurable lung disease, he portrays an aristocratic sadness, a spiritualized gallantry. There is in his art, as in the music of Mozart (1756–1791), a characteristic blending of sad and gay. His famous clown *Gilles* (fig. 454), like many other treatments of characters from the Italian comedy, shows a gaily dressed creature in an emotionally restrained attitude, with distinct overtones of sadness (cf. Watteau's *Le Mezzetin*, Metropolitan Museum).

544

Watteau's influence was felt all over Europe — as far east as Russia and as far west and north as Britain and Scandinavia. (It is obvious in Gainsborough's fuzzy landscapes.) In France there were many direct imitators — Pater, perhaps his only student; Lancret, a fellow-student in Gillot's atelier, who later received some advice from Watteau; and De Troy — all of whom repeated the formulas of the master with little of his original *élan* and sensitivity.

Boucher. In the Louis XV period proper, after the Regency, the Rococo took on a more mundane quality with less effervescence and mobility, best seen in the work of François Boucher (1703–1770), who was far from a great painter, although very popular and successful in his time. His art was partly derived from Watteau, whose *Caractères* he engraved, and even more from the contemporary Italian decorator Tiepolo, whose work he saw during his Italian trip. He returned to Paris to become a great social success. As a protégé of the king's friend Mme. de Pompadour, whose portrait he painted several times, Boucher was

Fig. 455. Boucher: Toilet of Venus. New York, Metropolitan Museum of Art.

able to exploit his considerable decorating talents in the design of murals, Gobelin and Beauvais tapestries (he became director of the Gobelins in 1755), Sèvres porcelains, and book illustrations (Molière and La Fontaine).

Specializing in mythological and pastoral scenes, Boucher made plain the basically decorative nature of Rococo art and the great though debased influence of Watteau, whose feeling for a colorful surface is retained, if considerably vulgarized in sentiment. Boucher's *Vulcan Presenting to Venus the Arms of Aeneas* or his *Toilet of Venus* (fig. 455) illustrates the shallowness of the painter's Italianate borrowings, the superficial sensuousness of the Venus (a thinned-out Rubens type), and the fantastic idea of antiquity held by Rococo artists. Mythology had long been a standard theme, but the classicism of painters like Boucher is merely elegant and luxurious decoration, compared with the grandiose formal works of Le Brun under Louis XIV or, later, the marbled paintings of David in the 1780s. Boucher's religious pictures, e.g., *Rest on the Flight,* occupy the same ambiguous Rococo position; and the many pastorales depict groups of so-called peasants straight out of the opera of the time. These shepherds and shepherdesses are carefully manicured and barbered creatures, like the court ladies who played at this occupation in the time of Marie Antoinette.

Nattier. The eighteenth-century vogue for portraits had appeared in Rigaud, the best practitioner of the late Louis XIV period, as Jean Marc Nattier (1685–1766) was of the Louis XV era. Although Nattier had the opportunity to work for Peter the Great of Russia, he stayed in Paris to become the society portraitist *par excellence.* He specialized in a mythological approach, as in *Princesse de Condé as Diana* (fig. 456), a chic but far from characterful estimate of the noble lady. As in the portraits of Boucher, the accent here is on the decorative, the elegant and fashionable. The princess wears a tiger skin over a satin dress, and her carefully powdered coiffure surmounts the conventional doll-like eighteenth-century face.

La Tour. A remarkable contrast exists between the superficial portrayals of Boucher and Nattier and those of Maurice Quentin de La Tour (1704–1788). In spite of the latter's place in the Louis XV period (in 1750 he was made Painter to the King), he has certain striking un-Rococo qualities. La Tour is one of the great artists of the century (together with Watteau, Chardin, and Fragonard), distinguished for his brilliant, psychologically penetrative pastel portraits (fig. 457). Using what was then an unconventional medium (he does not seem to have done much oil painting), he left a remarkable gallery of aristocratic and

546

Fig. 456. Nattier: Princesse de Condé as Diana. New York, Metropolitan Museum of Art.

Fig. 457. La Tour: Mme. de Pompadour. Paris, Louvre.

intellectual figures of his day, done in the pastel chalk. Interested only in faces, this eminently sympathetic man probed into the character of his sitters and "carried them away in their entirety." In the magnificent draftsman's tradition of Holbein, the Clouets, and the later Ingres and Degas, he produced portraits of the royal family far different from those of his contemporaries, as well as vivid and exciting studies of Rousseau, Voltaire, d'Alembert, and others of the literary, musical, and theatrical world he frequented. He was a good businessman, who declined the offer of a title of nobility and had the independence to tell the Dauphin that his children were badly brought up and to advise him on his duties to the country.

The assiduous and penetrating technique of La Tour may readily be contrasted with the decorative manner of Rococo portraiture when the same subject appears in each. For example, both La Tour and Boucher did portraits of Mme. de Pompadour. The latter painted a typical artificial, empty creature of the time; but La Tour surrounded her with books, engravings, and music in a characteristically vivid and alert view of her real personality, for she was a talented woman.

Chardin. Within the Louis XV and Boucher period came the first important bourgeois painter in France, Jean-Baptiste Simeon Chardin (1699–1779). This son of a carpenter first showed his work in the open-air exhibitions of the Place Dauphine (1728), a space reserved on one day each year for those who could not — or would not — show in the

Fig. 458. Chardin: Boy with Teetotum. Paris, Louvre.

official exhibitions. Here he set out a dozen still-life pictures, his first specialty, which attracted attention because of the great popularity of Flemish painting at the time (e.g., Snyders), although Chardin himself stemmed from the Dutch school. Almost immediately received into the French Academy, he exhibited again in the Place Dauphine in 1734 with his first genre scenes. These pictures of domestic life, such as the *Boy with Teetotum* (fig. 458), *The House of Cards,* and *The Washerwoman,* combine Dutch-derived homey interiors with the grandeur and sympathy of the Le Nain tradition. It is interesting evidence of the changing tastes of the period that by the 1740s Chardin achieved considerable fame among collectors of painting, who wanted "typical" Chardins and demanded certain subjects again and again. He was very popular in Germany, Austria, Sweden, and Russia as well as in certain circles in France; yet it should be made clear that this artist was considerably ahead of his time in his serious and sympathetic portrayal of ordinary people.

Chardin's "little people at home" differ from those of the Dutch school in a delicacy of execution that allies them with the period of which he was still a part, e.g., *The Housewife* (Louvre). The proportions of the figures to the picture space, moreover, give the French characters (descendants of the Le Nains) a certain monumentality in which the Dutch were less interested. His *Boy with Teetotum* illustrates Chardin's remarkable ability to fill a picture space in a simple yet powerful way with figures that engage our attention by virtue of their absorption. His constructive genius and his modern manner of painting are seen in the many still-life pictures (fig. 459), where impressionistic reflections go from object to object and pure colors are placed side by side on the canvas. Above all, the reasoned and effective geometric relationship among objects gives these pictures an abstract quality that attracted Cézanne much later.

The painter's portraits, many in pastels and done at the end of his life, are products of the next period in the eighteenth century, e.g., *Self-portrait with Eye Shade* and *Madame Chardin* (both in the Louvre), the latter generally considered his masterpiece. These straightforward unflattering studies fulfill the bourgeois development of the century and add to the luster of one of its greatest artists.

By 1760–1765 the *petite-manière* of the Louis XV period lost ground; curve and countercurve yielded to simpler, straighter lines in architecture and furniture, as ancient art had renewed effect. The wit and satire of the *salons* were now replaced by honest sentiment. The Abbé Prevost (1697–1763) translated Richardson's *Pamela* and *Clarissa Harlowe* and afterwards wrote finer novels of his own. Rousseau's *La*

Fig. 459. Chardin: Still Life. Paris, Louvre.

Nouvelle Héloise (1761), the German Goethe's *Sorrows of Young Werther* (1774), and other ultrasentimental works added to the tender feelings and moralism which emerged separately and together in many pictures, books, and plays of the Louis XVI period. There was also a return to nature (the influence of the English and again Rousseau, whose *Nouvelle Héloise* takes place among Swiss Alps and glaciers); the French went from the *salons* into the fields. Marie Antoinette played with her so-called milkmaids at "The Hamlet" of the *Petit Trianon* in Versailles; and the irregular (i.e., natural) English park became popular. Thus the Louis XVI style, while continuing the Rococo *fêtes galantes,* contributed a new sentiment, a return to nature, and a return to the antique.

Fragonard. Love was celebrated by such painters as Jean Honoré Fragonard (1732–1806) in a manner quite different from the sensitivity of Watteau and the would-be titillations of Boucher. To be sure, there are still deliberately naughty scenes like Fragonard's *The Swing* (Wallace Collection); but these are far exceeded by out-and-out sentimental works such as his series of panels in The Frick Collection that bears an elaborate literary title which sets the story's tone, *The Romance of Young Love*. This was a typical effusion of an age that gave rise to the "tearful comedy" of La Chaussée and the moralistic middle-class tragedies of Diderot. It represents a curious mingling of Rococo charm, decorativeness, and appreciation of feminine beauty with the new sentiment that became so fashionable in all circles on the eve of the Revolution. The dexterous Fragonard's panels (originally done for Mme. du Barry) have all the superficial attractiveness of the earlier style plus the element of virtue — sometimes added, it is true, at the very last minute.

An episode in this artistic-literary saga of love and suffering (fig. 460) shows the backgrounds of fuzzy landscape and symbolic sculpture that go back to the Regency period, as do the decorative doll-like characters. Their gestures and attitudes are quite different, however, from those in the Watteau *Embarkation*. Now everything is sentiment and sincerity; love is pure and earnest, without the fine Rococo passages-at-words.

After 1770 Fragonard turned to idyls and pastorales of various

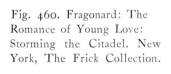

Fig. 460. Fragonard: The Romance of Young Love: Storming the Citadel. New York, The Frick Collection.

kinds, repeating the somewhat sticky morality of Greuze, the great apostle of middle-class virtue and Diderot's favorite painter. An era whose ideal was to be sensitive and to have "an open heart" fell easily into the trap of exaggerated sentimentality; plays, novels, pictures, and even tombs of deceased dogs were burdened with these feelings. Subjects were necessarily sought that would lend themselves to this kind of expression, while portraiture and landscape took on the same coloration. The consequences of this exaggerated attitude in painting were histrionics, large groups, and lower-pitched colors, with somber violets, mauves, and grays. Literary content and anecdotal painting were most evident. Sometimes subjects were taken directly from the theater of the time, which afforded the middle class such a good outlet for its emotions. The main emphasis on virtue and sentiment drove out completely the *galant* attitude and conversation.

Greuze. The chief painter in this mode was Jean-Baptiste Greuze (1725–1805). His career of storytelling pictures began in 1755 with *A Father Explaining the Bible to His Family.* The concept of the paterfamilias as the center of family life and its chief moral arbiter strikes the keynote of Greuze's work. As in many other paintings, the *petit-bourgeois* Greuze discloses not only a moral and sentimental attitude and a predilection for literary content, but also the curious idea that the subject is more important than the painting itself. In many cases, if one does not know the title of the work, it is impossible to understand the picture. His great triumph was the *Village Betrothal* (Louvre) where everyone

Fig. 461. Greuze: The Father's Curse. Paris, Louvre.

552

is gathered around the venerable father as he gives advice to the young couple — the upstanding young man and shy maiden who may be contrasted with the characters in the first scene of Hogarth's earlier *Marriage à la Mode*, whose virtue was questionable and whose bad manners were satirized. Physically, Greuze's types here and in his paintings of sentimental young women have not changed substantially from the Boucher kind, but the "open heart" effect is quite different.

Emotionally and melodramatically, his wildest effects are achieved in the pair of pictures dealing with *The Father's Curse* (fig. 461) and *The Son's Punishment*. In the first scene a quarreling father and son are kept apart by a group of frantic females aided by the little brother (Boucher's Cupid in middle-class clothes). The young man is driven from the paternal hearth for the unspeakable crime of joining the army without his father's consent. The sinister figure at the right is the recruiting sergeant. In the second episode the prodigal returns to find the old man dead, surrounded by the same hysterical women, a group of bourgeois Niobes whose contorted faces and waving arms point out to the son his crime against the paterfamilias. As a second-rate curtain scene typical of the emotional orientation of the time, this story — for it is a story rather than a picture — is perhaps without parallel.

Many paintings of this sort endeared Greuze to the otherwise sensible Diderot. The artist is also responsible for a considerable number of apparently sentimental country girls (the taste for rusticity) whose pearly flesh and coyness exhibit a distinctly false innocence. In such examples as *The Broken Pitcher, The Milkmaid, Young Woman and Lamb*, and *The Dead Bird*, the sensuousness of the Rococo (and of the painter himself) still comes through.

The renewed taste for nature, especially sentimental nature, was expressed in the works of Louis Gabriel Moreau (1740–1806), who has been considered a pioneer in the Romantic landscape, and Joseph Vernet (1714–1806), noted for his pathetic marine pictures, e.g., *A Shipwreck*. In the archaeological landscapes of Hubert Robert (1733–1808) the feeling for nature is combined with the taste for classical ruins, giving a sentimental rather than grandiose total effect, e.g., *Pont du Gard* (Louvre).

David. A more impressive version of the grandeur of antiquity (as seen in the architecture of the late eighteenth century) was rendered by Jacques Louis David (1748–1825), leading painter of the French Revolutionary period. Like the neoclassical architects of that day, he presented a more realistic antiquity based on recently acquired archaeological knowledge from Herculaneum, Pompeii, Greece, and Hadrian's Villa at Rome. The research done by the Comte de Caylus in costumes, small objects, and the general background of ancient times is clearly reflected in many of David's paintings. As their primary object, these works express a moral attitude; but in the eighties (after a period as a Rococo and historic-sentimental painter) David's morality changed from the familial to the patriotic. The characters in his famous *Oath of the Horatii* (1784, fig.

Fig. 462. David: Oath of the Horatii. Paris, Louvre.

462) still wave their arms as they surround the father of the family, but the latter no longer exhorts them to bourgeois virtue; he is now inspiring them to go out and fight against their brothers-in-law from a neighboring city, with which they are at war. The welfare of the state becomes more important than the family or individual, as the Horatii swear on their swords to do their fullest duty to the nation.

Such pictures as David's *Oath of the Horatii, Death of Socrates,* and *Brutus Mourning the Death of His Sons* (fig. 463) possess this politically virtuous character and, though commissioned by the government, may be

554

reckoned among the many factors leading to the Revolution of 1789. The bourgeois, who hitherto felt themselves the custodians of social morality, now became the upholders of political virtue and took these works as antiroyalist statements; according to Brutus, one's own sons must be executed if it will help the state.

Aesthetically, these paintings of David aspire to a Roman bas-relief quality; their color is generally harsh and unattractive, their gestures extremely rhetorical. Although David was capable of producing strong realistic works, e.g., *The Death of Marat*, and outstanding portraits, he helped to place the stamp of authority on the neoclassical style, thus snuffing out the realist tendencies of that century (as Chardin) and in a sense retarding the development of art during the early nineteenth century. Pictures like the *Brutus* exploited an accuracy of archaeological detail, which made them more effective propaganda vehicles in their time but had little to do with the progress of painting as such. In the minds of the public, the success of the Revolution was associated with the neoclassical style in which its triumphs were first expressed; this association helped fasten that style on Europe and America for a long time. Its rectitude and formality satisfied the triumphant bourgeoisie as convenient symbols, especially since they had no particular tradition of their own.

FRENCH SCULPTURE. Sculpture in France during the eighteenth century was less original than painting for two reasons: the Academy of

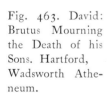

Fig. 463. David: Brutus Mourning the Death of his Sons. Hartford, Wadsworth Atheneum.

Sculpture and the French Academy in Rome (both founded in the late seventeenth century) made it mandatory for students to copy the antique; and the very nature of the medium made it less able to respond immediately to current changes of taste. For these reasons, the heavy seventeenth-century Baroque style continued its influence, as in the emotive yet elegant tombs of Jean Baptiste Pigalle (1714–1784), e.g., those for *Marshal de Saxe* (fig. 464) and *Marshal D'Harcourt*. Pigalle's tombs have a pompous melancholy that tends toward melodrama, revealing some elements of sentiment and the higher emotional expression of the time.

A good deal of eighteenth-century French sculpture is Rococo in feeling; decorative and ingeniously carved nymphs, cupids, satyrs, and the like parallel the pictorial production of that era. Etienne Maurice Falconet (1716–1791), Augustin Pajou (1730–1809), and Claude Michel, called Clodion (1738–1814), exemplify this nonmonumental trend. Typical are Falconet's *Bather* (Louvre) with its Sèvres porcelain quality, the melting flesh of Pajou's *Psyche* (Louvre), and the nervous Fragonardlike sensuousness of Clodion's *Nymph and Satyr* (Metropolitan Museum).

Houdon. The greatest sculptor of the century is Jean Antoine Houdon (1741–1828), who represents a return to seriousness in the period immediately before the Revolution. His penetrating psychological analyses compare only with the pastels of La Tour. Houdon's chief interest

Fig. 464. Pigalle: Tomb of Marshal de Saxe. Strassburg, Cathedral of St. Thomas.

556

is personality, emerging in the sardonic glance of Voltaire, the vividly expectant Diderot, the arrogant and unprepossessing Mirabeau, or the sympathetic charm of the *Comtesse de Cayla* (fig. 465). The draping of the aged *Voltaire* (Paris, Théâtre-Français, 1781) in a classical toga is a concession to the neoclassical taste of the time. Houdon's portraits of famous Americans of the Revolutionary period — Washington (Virginia State Capitol), John Paul Jones, Franklin, Jefferson, and others — done during a visit to this country, are in most cases magnificent studies of those individuals. Sober, realistic, and sympathetic, these works, like his French portraits, typify the upper-middle-class liberal elements of the end of the century.

ITALIAN MASTERS. The story of eighteenth-century European art is scarcely complete without mention of its Italian masters, especially the painters. Architecture in Italy was affected by reverse

Fig. 465. Houdon: Comtesse de Cayla. New York, The Frick Collection.

academic influences from France and England, and sculpture felt the neoclassicism stemming from archaeological investigations in Italy and elsewhere, e.g., Antonio Canova (1757–1822). Italian painting, however, had an original and often exciting quality.

Although Italy had long since passed the zenith of its power, the momentum of previous centuries now produced the brilliant decorator Giovanni Battista Tiepolo, fine painters of spectacles and architecture such as Francesco Guardi and Antonio Canaletto, and genre painters like Pietro Longhi. No longer important politically or economically, eighteenth-century Italy had become an essential part of the education of both nobility and upper middle classes from the rest of Europe and was already

Fig. 466. Tiepolo: Institution of the Rosary. Venice, Church of the Gesuati.

the tourist center of the continent. This was especially true of Venice where a gay and splendid art was newly fashioned, an art dedicated to pleasure and yet suitable to the traditions of that city in its heyday.

Tiepolo. Italy's great Rococo master, Tiepolo (1696–1770), with his typical blues, pinks, and yellows, far exceeds the French prototypes in the verve of his decorative sense and the absolute refinement of form, color, and pattern applied to religious and secular themes. Churches and public buildings of Venice display his figures floating through the air in a modernized version of Tintoretto's dynamics. The *Institution of the Rosary* (fig. 466) is an unusually effective ceiling decoration, Rococo in its color handling but more Baroque in its excitement and sense of movement, the kind of *élan* that would appeal to Goya in Spain slightly later.

Since everything in Venice was geared to pleasure, scenes of entertainment are frequently seen in its art. Guardi (1712–1765) offered pictures like *The Marriage of Venice and the Adriatic* (fig. 467), a charming scene of life and movement set against the typical Venetian canalscape, which he often painted for its own sake to exploit his interest in fuzzy

Fig. 467. Guardi: The Marriage of Venice and the Adriatic. Courtesy, Museum of Fine Arts, Boston.

Fig. 468. Canaletto: Grand Canal. London, Wallace Collection.

atmospherical effects. In this latter area Canaletto (1697–1768) is most noteworthy. His Venetian canals and architecture (fig. 468), filled with the play of light across the surface of the water, are important in the tradition of atmospheric landscape painting as well as influential for the English architectural paintings of the eighteenth century. Longhi (1702–1785) is the Italian equivalent of the Rococo painter of manners, showing the wealthy at home with frequent dashes of spice.

GERMAN ARTS. Germany, responding like England and France to the bourgeoisation of eighteenth-century culture, was relatively unimportant in the realm of the plastic arts because it lacked either the centralized patronage of France or the aesthetic tradition of Italy. The German contribution to the period lay more in the fields of music, literature, and philosophy, all of which mirrored the increasing democratization of Europe, especially the "storm and stress" movement at the end of the century. Artistically, Germany followed in the wake of France for the most part, utilizing the Rococo manner in palaces and churches, as indicated previously, and repeating academically the various formulas of French painting. Nevertheless the Rococo used in German and Austrian churches, e.g., Domenikus Zimmermann's *Church at Die Wies* in Bavaria (figs. 469–470), has an exuberant quality, grace, and coloristic excitement that are quite individual in character. German sculpture of the period, e.g., the brilliant work of Ignaz Guenther (fig. 471, 1774), suggests in general the style of Coustou in France and the Baroque fountain decorators of Italy; but it has a unique stimulating and colorful nature.

560

Fig. 469. Zimmermann: Church at Die Wies (Bavaria). Choir and High Altar.

Fig. 470. Zimmermann: Church at Die Wies. Exterior view.

Fig. 471. Guenther: Pietà.
Nenningen, Cemetery Chapel.

The new era best announced itself in Germany through the middle-class tragedy and comedy of the theater (*Minna von Barnhelm* and *Miss Sara Sampson* by Lessing, as well as his tolerance play *Nathan the Wise*) and the great democratic plays of Schiller (*Wilhelm Tell, The Robbers, Wallenstein,* etc.). It is in this area rather than the plastic arts that the Germans — however temporarily — reflect the spirit of free thought that characterized the eighteenth century.

24 / ART IN THE MODERN
WORLD: *The Nineteenth Century*

THE dynamics of a changing world generated basic contrasts and contradictions in nineteenth-century life: theories of social progress opposed to economic privilege and colonial exploitation; new scientific health standards contrasted with the actual conditions; industrial accomplishment based on miserable working conditions; cultural progress battling entrenched conservatism. Fundamental innovations had been brought about by the Industrial Revolution through the transition from handicraft to machine production, irrevocably altering methods of production, travel, communications, farming, and almost every way of life and initiating the increasingly dynamic character of modern existence.

With the amazing expansion of the business world came the factory system, concentration of capital and capitalization (e.g., the modern corporation), and a new nationalistic rivalry based on commerce. Not only the outward forms were changed, but even the methods of thinking. The absolute necessity for immediate and greater profits to keep the machines going brought an ascendancy of the materialistic spirit that for a long time limited mankind's benefits from the great mechanical and scientific achievements.

One of the most significant effects of the new production system was the growth of large cities and factory towns that transformed man's social and psychological outlook. The contrast between advancing medical knowledge and the unhealthy conditions under which workers had to live became tragically evident. At the same time, scientific advances reduced the death rate and made possible the huge population increase that marked the nineteenth century, helping to fulfill the need for a larger labor force. In this environment, whether from the bourgeois or the labor side, many artists of modern times were to emerge; from here also came the more urban art of the nineteenth century.

Socially, the most striking factors in this initial stage of modern culture were, first, the triumph of the middle class; then, a mounting re-

563

action from the working groups that attempted through organizations of various kinds to wrest from that triumph some betterment for themselves. The middle classes, now the leaders in democratic government as in business, became the new patrons of the arts, either on a small scale as buyers of portraits or more significantly as collectors and, finally, as founders of public museums. The new art patron inevitably resisted the progressive development of the artist, who was prophet and would-be interpreter of the dynamic age. For one thing, a relative newcomer to the world of art, this patron's power depended not on traditional but on recent and commercial factors. To dignify his status, he favored the retention of proved older styles (at that particular moment, the neoclassicism of the Revolutionary period). Furthermore, the same practicality and common-sense approach that distinguished his production of merchandise also affected his attitude toward literature, art, and music. Culture was expected to be standardized; conformity and easy understandability in the arts were rewarded, while nonconforming and less obvious or novel and individualistic efforts were penalized economically and socially. Naturally these very restrictions would breed rebellion in creative personalities.

The tensions of the age were expressed socially through so-called economic liberalism, a doctrine which (unlike present-day liberalism) defended the new capitalism against the reforms that repressed groups were struggling to bring about. In art, the conflict was between the tradition-bound official Academy — reestablished after the French Revolution — and those artists who attempted to find a new expression. This conflict was at first manifest in the differing approaches of the neoclassicists and the Romantics; it was sharpened by the development of competition as a part of the social order.

PROBLEMS OF THE ARTIST. As society passed from monarchical to bourgeois control, the earlier patronage of Church and monarchy or aristocracy could no longer offer the artist the same degree of employment. In the course of the nineteenth century, the artist was driven completely into the market place — a process that had begun somewhat earlier, first in Holland and then in England. The shift from absolute monarchies to limited monarchies or republics also altered the character of public works. In keeping with the trend toward democratization, new types of public buildings and business structures took the place of the earlier palaces, châteaux, or churches. Schools, hospitals, museums, and the like appeared relatively early in this period, to be followed by railroad stations, libraries, factories, office buildings, and similar facilities, as the new age reached its first climax after the middle of the nineteenth century. In the designing of these structures and in their pictorial or sculptural decoration, the question of traditional versus newer styles became important.

The representational arts made much greater progress than the buildings themselves. Architecture, by its very nature as an official or business medium, had to conform to the established viewpoint; but painting and sculpture could and did develop, however slowly, in a less hampered personal milieu. An independent painter or sculptor could choose to do something that might or might not sell; on the other hand, the architect, who was automatically an employed person, had to produce something "acceptable," so that an architectural style expressive of the new industrial era was a long time in coming. Painting from the very beginning of the century was involved in the battle of styles and advanced relatively quickly into more contemporary modes of expression; and sculpture began to move forward during the second half of the century.

Under these circumstances the nonconforming artist, especially the painter, found himself working for a very limited market, sometimes almost nonexistent. He was completely at the mercy of the middle class, which preferred for a long time the neoclassical style that symbolized both its triumph as a class and the association with tradition and respectability. Only in the latter part of the nineteenth century did the middle class furnish a moderate number of art lovers with a new attitude.

But neither at that point nor in the twentieth century was the modern artist to find a market sufficient for his needs. Other considerations apart, the collapse of the old guild system had meant that there was no limit to the possible number of artists. The problem was aggravated by the appearance of a multitude of educated and semieducated people who practiced the arts as a graceful and interesting leisure activity. This must be regarded as part of the modern democratization of culture, which had begun in eighteenth-century Britain, first with the general extension of education to the middle class and artistically with the great popularity of amateur water-color painting. Although professional standards were maintained during the nineteenth century, these were usually confined to academies which followed traditional art and held that theirs was the only valid manner of expression. If an artist wished to exhibit, he had to win the approval of these groups who, because of their official or semi-official status, controlled the public avenues of exhibition. In commercial galleries the artist was dependent on the vogue of a particular moment — sentimental landscape, formal portrait, or historical and other narrative. When more enlightened patrons appeared at the end of the nineteenth century, the commercial galleries responded, since they were now able to sell the new art, however limited its public.

Compared to the situation in former epochs, the position of the modern artist during the past century and a half has not been an enviable one. With the overwhelming emphasis placed on individual enterprise in modern society, intellectual individualism was also inevitable in spite of the conservative cultural strictures. With the fading of rigid political institutions and the excitement of social ferment, the incentives for self-expression were greater than ever before. The fact that the modern writer, painter, or other creator has come to think of himself as an important, even influential, individual, that the public since the late eighteenth century has been increasingly aware of the "genius" as a type is an indication of what has happened. It was unavoidable that painters and sculptors of the new age should have tried to find some satisfactory method for projecting their reactions to this changing dynamic period; and it was equally inescapable that the traditionalists should have resisted. As successive rebellious artists were rejected time and again by the conservative press and public, they found themselves outside the social pale; their increasingly personal and experimental series of techniques widened the breach even further. This isolation may be looked upon as basic in the emergence of an art that although it expressed the character of modern society was not generally accepted by that society.

USES OF THE PAST AND DISTANT PRESENT. Among the most typical developments of the nineteenth century (and to a certain extent of the twentieth) was the artist's constant search amidst the styles of the past and the geographically distant present for suitable outlets for his own creativity. Since the initially entrenched neoclassical style was incompatible with the need for greater expressiveness, the individualistic artist turned to other forms. In the early nineteenth century, he wandered through the halls of the newly founded Louvre Museum (formerly the king's residence, fig. 417), confronted with the riches of both old master and exotic art. Most of the past styles (except the primitive and the pre-colonial American) were to be found in this museum and were primary sources of help and inspiration. As European horizons broadened with expanding foreign trade and colonialism, artists were brought freshly into touch with the Japanese and Chinese (this had already happened to a limited degree in the eighteenth century) as well as African, Oceanic, and other primitive cultures. These forms in their several fashions would serve the needs of the painter, sculptor, graphic artist, and designer during the late nineteenth and the twentieth centuries.

Each artistic personality moved toward one style or another, seeking his own creative level. For the conservative nineteenth-century architect and sculptor, Greek and Roman motifs still lent the required air of dignity and tradition. To the nonconformist Romantic painter, the emotionalism of the Baroque or the Middle Ages, the exoticism of the Near East, were desirable. Academic or conservative painters and sculptors leaned heavily on the art of the Renaissance for precise draftsmanship, stable closed compositions, etc., while sensuously inclined artists had recourse either to the Rococo of Fragonard and Boucher or to the vitality of Rubens's Baroque.

Although the Western tradition remained the chief source throughout most of the nineteenth century, the end of that era showed the introduction of Japanese and Chinese ideas in Impressionist and post-Impressionist painting, industrial design, and even in later functional architecture. Egyptian and Indian ideas appeared (as in Gauguin), while African, Persian, Oceanic, and precolonial American forms are important to the Cubists, Fauves, and Expressionists of the twentieth century. It should be noted, however, that in either century those arts can be utilized academically (as pure repetition) or creatively — in the sense that the artist handles the material in a fresh and individual manner. For instance, the insipid and saccharine treatment of Bouguereau's *Virgin of Consolation* (see fig. 489) may be contrasted with the nobility of the similar *Pietà* by Michelangelo (fig. 349); or, on the other hand, the sensitive Puvis de Chavannes's *Poor Fisherman* (see fig. 496) may be compared with its prototype, Fra Lippo Lippi's *Adoration* (fig. 331). Both nineteenth-century painters relied to a great extent on the Italian Renaissance for their technical inspiration; yet in Bouguereau's *Virgin* there is merely bathos, whereas the *Poor Fisherman* has an original mood and excitingly handled space and linear contour.

NEOCLASSICAL ARCHITECTURE. Nowhere was the element of revivalism so evident as in the field of architectural design and decoration. The multiplicity of available past styles gave birth to Classical, Gothic, Renaissance, Baroque, Romanesque, and other adaptations in the course of the nineteenth and early twentieth centuries. The Classical phase (perhaps the most tenacious) had stemmed from the exact archaeological examples of the late eighteenth century in the architecture of England, France, and the United States (e.g., figs. 433, 445, 450, 451). For the eighteenth-century monarchy, the Classical style had augmented the glory of the royal house; for the eighteenth-century growing spirit of democracy, the style had been associated with the ancient spirit of individualism, as in the case of Jefferson's design for the University of Virginia.

Throughout the nineteenth century the Classical style appeared in a long, almost unending, series of incarnations. Some were associated with the glory of Napoleon, others with the widespread surge of nationalism,

Fig. 472. La Madeleine, Paris.

and the majority with the need of the new democracies for traditional respectability. In the first category, in Paris the church of *La Madeleine* (1807–1842, fig. 472), a large Roman-style temple building, was dedicated to the glory of the Emperor Napoleon, as were also the memorial column in the Place Vendôme (cf. fig. 130) and the arches of triumph known as the Arc du Carrousel and the *Arc de Triomphe de l'Etoile* (1806–1836, fig. 473). Nationalistic monuments are represented by the Walhalla in Regensburg, Germany (1830–1842), modeled after the *Parthenon* (fig. 85). Bourgeois democratic buildings include such examples as the Edinburgh High School (1825–1829) and the New York Subtreasury Building (now Customhouse, 1834–1841). After the Napoleonic period the emphasis shifted from Roman to Greek borrowings, as in the Edinburgh High School.

NEOCLASSICAL SCULPTURE. Neoclassical sculpture arrived at its most archaeological and derivative level with such men as the Italian Canova and the Danish Bertel Thorwaldsen (1770–1844), the former drawing from Rome, the latter from Hellenistic Greece. The innumerable instances of such adaptations with their unoriginal forms and saccharine expressions (this applied to all the arts) inevitably led to a reaction against neoclassicism. At a later period one of the rebels against this kind of art would exclaim: "Who will deliver us from the Greeks and the Romans?"

Under the pervasive influence of the antique, sculptors of the early nineteenth century executed some rather preposterous works in which

568

Napoleon either appears nude, as in Canova's version, or is dressed in a Roman toga, as in the work of Antoine Denis Chaudet (1763–1810) and in Cortot's *Triumph* (fig. 474) on the left side of the *Arc de l'Etoile*. The Cortot relief presents Napoleon in the costume of a Roman emperor, balanced on one side by a Victory that suggests the Venus of Milo and on the other by an allegory of a conquered city that brings to mind the Hellenistic figure *City of Antioch* (fig. 110). The general tone of this group, with the classical flying figure that closes the composition, conveys a dignified, balanced, clear, and even ponderous quality characteristic of neoclassicism.

This static and declamatory coronation of Napoleon contrasts with its dynamic and agitated companion relief by François Rude (1784–1855, fig. 475) on the right side of the *Arc de l'Etoile*. Finished in 1837, the latter represents not merely another period but another point of view as well. Rude's soldiers are still ancient warriors, both Romans and Greeks — they are certainly not dressed in the costume of the French Revolution or of Napoleon's time — yet this *Song of Departure* moves along with an irresistible *élan* and confidence that sum up the ardor and excitement of the year 1793, when France flew to the defense of the Revolution at Valmy. In this work Rude projects the pictorial symbol

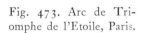

Fig. 473. Arc de Triomphe de l'Etoile, Paris.

Fig. 474. Cortot: Triumph of Napoleon. Paris, Arc de Triomphe de l'Etoile.

of *La Marseillaise* (as the figure overhead, leading the soldiers, is known): *Aux armes, citoyens!* Whereas Cortot sums up the self-conscious dignity of the neoclassical approach, Rude embodies a spirit that, in spite of its still classical garb, bespeaks a new attitude. This is the so-called Romantic spirit of revolt and independence, of dynamic rather than static expression, of irregular contours rather than well-balanced and clear forms, of warm rather than cold colors, of the right of the individual over the demands of a not always sympathetic society.

The development of the libertarian spirit — built up during the eighteenth-century Age of Reason and climaxed in the French Revolution — had been interrupted by Napoleon with his conquering surge of militaristic nationalism. In the post-Napoleonic period, the modern mercantile development really got under way, but political control fell into the hands of extreme reactionaries, creating for the intellectual a distasteful environment from which he tried in various ways to escape. Even the neoclassicists, remaining on the more conservative side of social expression through their formal and relatively stiff manner, were at odds

Fig. 475. Rude: La Marseillaise. Paris, Arc de Triomphe de l'Etoile.

with the repressive spiritual climate of that day. A sense of disillusionment was expressed through their "escape" toward a seemingly calm and ordered antiquity, just as the opposing Romantics tried to escape in the direction of the emotive and mysterious Middle Ages or the exotic and exciting Near East.

"CLASSICAL" PAINTING: *Ingres.* Still more arresting is the fact that so conservative a painter as J. A. D. Ingres (1780–1867), leader of the so-called Classical school for many years, did a considerable number of pictures whose subject matter must be considered Romantic. The real difference between Ingres and the Romantics is in the manner of expression, rather than what is portrayed. In technical approach, the clarity, tight linear contour, cold color, and relative unemotionality of Ingres's *Odalisque* (fig. 476) may be contrasted with any like "exotic" figure in the painting of Delacroix (as leader of the dissident Romantic group in France), e.g., the seminudes in the *Massacre at Scio* (see fig. 481). Paintings like the *Massacre* are executed so as to stress the dynamic over the static, the coloristic rather than the linear, warm instead of cold color, and the emotional over the objective. Moreover, while Ingres's *Odalisque* — an Eastern subject with escapist meaning — is classical in execution, the situation is reversed when Delacroix employs a classical subject, e.g., the *Medea* (Louvre), and carries it out with a dash and excitement that are completely unclassical.

Fig. 476. Ingres: Odalisque. Paris, Louvre.

Ingres's *Odalisque*, despite its exotic or faraway theme, its reference to the Near East, is tied to the linear technique of the High Renaissance, particularly Raphael. The calculated linear rhythms of Raphael's *Madonna of the Chair* (fig. 356) are suggested in Ingres's conception, where the elegant curve of the back parallels that of the arm, continued in the drapery at the right. These two lines are exaggerated in length and curvature in the interest of a swinging effect; they are contrasted with the simple angularity of the left elbow and left knee, which offer another form of parallelism. There is again reference to Raphael's Madonna in the features and headdress of the odalisque. The validity of Ingres's borrowing from the Renaissance cannot be questioned in a period given to adaptations of earlier styles, nor can the effectiveness of his design, but other artists felt that the dynamics of the new age demanded another type of expression.

THE ROMANTIC SPIRIT. The anticlassical or anti-Renaissance trend had appeared as early as the end of the eighteenth century (especially in

England where the Romantic movement began) in a tendency toward the picturesque, the macabre, and the Gothic. Side by side with the classical revival that was an integral part of the culture of the rising middle class, there emerged this parallel yet opposed tendency to irregularize, to dramatize, to personalize, and to escape in another direction, namely, toward the Middle Ages. Both areas, the ancient and the medieval, represented an unattainable ideal, a place to which the increasingly unhappy intellectual could retire in his imagination — or, in specifically artistic terms, in painting, sculpture, architecture, poetry, drama, and music. Indeed it was often possible for the same artist or writer to have recourse to both classical and Gothic (or Near Eastern) material. Ingres used the Oriental, the classical, and the medieval, as did his opposite number, the Romantic Delacroix. Goethe in Germany and Keats in England revealed in their dramas and verse the same ambivalent approach to the intellectual's problem of finding a more congenial environment.

Anticlassical Romanticism appeared simultaneously in the works of the English "graveyard poets," in the supernatural plays and novels of that time, and in picturesque paintings and prints featuring the uneven and dramatic aspects of nature — rushing rivers, jagged rocks, and interesting ruins. A good deal was made of the new forms in landscape gardening, where the earlier formal gardens of the seventeenth century (cf. fig. 418) gave way before a more "natural," irregular, and freely growing state of nature that approximated the popular idea of charm. During the first stages of Romanticism, both ancient and medieval culture were considered picturesque because they were known to the eighteenth century either as ruined buildings (Gothic abbeys, Roman aqueducts, etc.) or through glamorized and romanticized historical books. This helps explain how it was possible for the same artists, even at a later date, to use both classical and Gothic ideas. As time went on, however, the Roman and Greek material, especially in architecture, became standardized into rules as the classicists tried to "reform" and regulate the unclassical habits of Renaissance-derived architecture.

The uncompromising rules of these followers of antiquity were arrayed against an increasingly picturesque and insubstantial kind of Gothic architecture. From the Strawberry Hill of Horace Walpole around the middle of the eighteenth century to such later examples as the rather formal *Houses of Parliament* (1840–1860, fig. 477) of Sir Charles Barry, there was a continuous stream of decoratively rather than functionally planned buildings, maintaining this insubstantial and even retrogressive character down to its end in the Victorian period. Its classi-

Fig. 477. Barry: Houses of Parliament, London.

cal opponent, moving further and further along the lines of standardization, still continues in the dusty adaptations of contemporary official architecture in various parts of the world.

The anticlassical trend in sculpture has been noted in the work of François Rude. The forceful and effective animal sculptures of Antoine Louis Barye (1796–1875) also represent in both subject matter and style a part of the new Romantic spirit. Like many painters of the early nineteenth century, Barye expressed himself sculpturally in Baroque terms; like many of them, he utilized a specifically exotic material which, although modeled from tigers, lions, and other creatures in the Paris zoo, was meant to be Oriental in flavor as well as symbolic of the power of nature.

Goya. In the field of painting, as in sculpture, France took the lead. A number of the French developments, however, were prefigured in the work of the Spanish Francisco Goya (1746–1828). Goya projected a series of brilliant aquatint etchings and oil paintings that were his imaginative reflections on personalities and abuses in the still medieval and very corrupt Spain of his day. They also show his great indignation at

574

the sufferings of Spaniards in the French invasion under Napoleon. And they reveal an awareness of the turbulence of modern times. These works can be considered both as a reaction against the classical movement in Spain and as a foreshadowing of such French movements as Romanticism, Impressionism, and even Surrealism.

Goya's aquatint series known as *Los Caprichos* (*The Caprices*) dates from the very end of the eighteenth century, 1796–1797, and presents a rational and socially critical view of his era like that of the eighteenth-century Hogarth. But the Spaniard's works are expressed in a symbolic and macabre mood and technique suggesting the literature of horror and mystery of that period, e.g., Walpole's *Castle of Otranto*. The strange, demonic, and picturesque elements in such a print as *Mala Noche* (Bad Night) ally Goya to the beginning Romantic movement of the late eighteenth century. The mysterious light-and-dark contrasts, sense of fear, and irregular contours all are part of that style.

Goya's later paintings and prints, such as the oil painting *Execution of the Citizens of Madrid* (fig. 478) or the frightening *Disasters of War* aquatints, not only reflect the painter's violent response to the immediate

Fig. 478. Goya: Execution of the Citizens of Madrid, May 3, 1808. Madrid, Prado.

political situation and the oppression of his people, but also embody the second step in the Romantic development. Here arises a distinction between two phases of Romantic usage: the protest art of Goya's *Execution of the Citizens of Madrid* and the glorifying character of a contemporary French picture by Baron Gros (1771–1835), *Napoleon among the Plague-stricken at Jaffa* (1804, fig. 479).

The Goya painting is concerned with the hours immediately after a Spanish uprising against the invading troops of Napoleon. Civilians are being rounded up indiscriminately and shot down by the French soldiers. Goya shows this as a menacing night scene filled with the powerful dark-and-light contrasts that are typical for a Romantic artist's expression of individual and mass suffering (his own or other people's). From the group of the dead and the condemned a startlingly bold figure stands out, arms thrust wildly into the air, challenging the anonymous and menacing grenadiers to shoot. A strong line of the hill in the background sweeps right to be crossed by the flattened arc of the soldiers' hats and guns moving in the opposite direction. Basically, Goya's method is naturalistic in the seventeenth-century sense of Velásquez, Hals, and other masters of visual truth. He reveals the individual figure in terms of what the artist can see as the light strikes it, silhouetting the form against a contrasting background. This vivid use of outline may well be related to the eighteenth-century Rococo decorative tradition exemplified in Tiepolo (with whom Goya had worked for a time in Madrid, cf. fig. 466); but here, utilized for visual and emotive excitement, it takes on a more brutal and explosive quality.

Gros. Gros's painting, on the other hand, although filled with a similar sense of suffering, heroism, light-and-dark effects, and vivid color, is the reverse side of the Romantic coin. Dedicated to the glory of the Emperor for whom Gros was official painter, this picture shows Napoleon as a benign conqueror. He stands Christlike among the sufferers in the pesthouse, daring the horrible threat of disease by touching a patient's sore with his bare hand. Although this gesture can hardly serve any useful purpose, it seemingly reveals the leader's kindness. Together with his officers and the native doctors at the left, he is presumably alleviating the misery (for which, of course, the conquerors were in great measure responsible). At every possible point, Gros stresses the element of pathos: the macabre figure with his head in his hands at the left; the pitiful corpse face down in the foreground; the young officer in the right-hand corner whose germ mask has slipped off his face; and the horribly pathetic blind man directly behind, fumbling his way toward the center of pity represented by the emperor.

This element of emperor worship, consciously fostered as a propa-

576

ganda device, was popular on its own account in accordance with the Romantic glorification of the heroic individual and interest in nationalism, both symbolized by Napoleon. Writers like Stendhal and Heine (whose *Two Grenadiers* revives his childhood view of Napoleon and the retreat of the Grande Armée from Russia), musicians like Beethoven, and many other intellectuals felt the impact of this overwhelming personality who ranged so widely, bringing Europeans into contact with far-off places like the Near East, Russia, and Egypt. Gros's painting takes place in the courtyard of a mosque, and many of its personages are dressed in Oriental costume — factors which also appealed to the exotic interests of the Romantics.

Fig. 479. Gros: Napoleon among the Plague-stricken at Jaffa. Paris, Louvre.

Géricault. The conditions of post-Napoleonic France are represented by the works of Théodore Géricault (1791–1824) and Eugène Delacroix (1798–1863). In the well-known *Raft of the Medusa* (1819, fig. 480) Géricault sums up a protest against the corruption of a government that had allowed a ship in bad condition to leave port. After being wrecked off the coast of Africa, the crew were abandoned on a raft by their officers.

Fig. 480. Géricault: Raft of the Medusa. Paris, Louvre.

For this scene of suffering the painter, like many other Romantics, brings to bear the techniques of dramatic spotlighting and dynamic diagonals inherited from Baroque art. Two pyramids — one dark, the other light — lead from the despair of the left side with its dead and dying figures to the hope and excitement of the right, where the sailors hoist one of their number to their shoulders so that he may be seen by a ship they have sighted. The constant struggle between man and nature, symbolized by this work, is another feature of Romantic thinking and feeling.

Delacroix. Although Géricault's painting exhibits the violent movements and torsions of Baroque art, it is rather dark in color, i.e., brownish. It is not until Delacroix, as in the *Massacre at Scio* (1824, fig. 481), that the fully developed brilliant colors of Romantic painting appear. In that picture Delacroix was stimulated to a certain extent by the increasingly clear and broken colors of the English school — notably Constable — and took the first step toward a much higher color range than that of Gros or Géricault. In later works his color intensity grows even stronger. His pictures after 1830, though less dynamic in social meaning, intensify the sensation of color movement and looseness; this feeling for the object in constant motion is one of the many differences between Delacroix and his colder, more static neo-Renaissance contemporaries (cf. Ingres, fig. 476).

578

While its theme resembles other works of the period, the *Massacre* is no mere literary or escapist effort but a violent and personal demonstration of the painter's indignation against the killing and torturing of Greeks, who were attempting to free themselves from the Turks at that time. Like many early-nineteenth-century intellectuals (e.g., Byron), the artist felt great sympathy for these struggling people — Géricault

Fig. 481. Delacroix: Massacre at Scio. Paris, Louvre.

had painted a similar subject — although Delacroix's protest is more restrained in mood and action than the *Raft of the Medusa* had been. Yet the unconventional bright coloring, the deliberately unbalanced character of the composition, the fact that it differed so markedly from accepted standards, made this work unpopular with critics and public.

Like the painting of Gros and Géricault, this picture stresses the element of human suffering, a locale in a far-off place, deliberate touches of naturalistic horror to make it more interesting and convincing, together with Baroque effects of light and dark and diagonality of motion. The left side of the painting is quieter and light-colored, the people resigned to their sufferings; the right side, darker in color, is more dynamically composed. It moves strongly upward toward the climax of the Turk engaged in slaughter and cruelty. The lush young body at the extreme right writhing upward presents a contrast to the *Odalisque* of Ingres (fig. 476), which has cold colors, lineal rhythms, and objective nonemotionality. The nude figure in the lower right-hand corner, a dead mother with a child crawling over her in search of comfort and food, is one of the high points of Romantic horror and also an important element in the painter's desire to evoke sympathy. There is no one sufferer here — all humanity is tortured; and, as in the case of Goya, the painter's indignation becomes more important than anything else. It recalls too the Spanish painter's dynamism, asymmetrical balance, and dark-and-light contrasts. Delacroix had copied many of Goya's *Caprichos* and was apparently much attracted by the Spaniard's feeling for unusual effect, his great imaginativeness, and his powerful emotional approach.

After 1830 the political situation did not permit such direct contemporary reference as Géricault's *Raft of the Medusa* or Delacroix's *Liberty Leading the People* (1831, Louvre). From that point on, the latter had recourse to numerous Oriental scenes like *Algerian Women in Their Apartment* (1834, Louvre), inspired by his own trip to Algiers; scenes from Romantic literature, e.g., the *Abduction of Rebecca*, from Scott's *Ivanhoe* (1846, Metropolitan Museum); or medieval subjects such as the *Entry of the Crusaders into Constantinople* (1840, Louvre).

These various ways of escaping from the present into the past or the distant locale included a variety of classical themes treated in the dynamic, shadowy, irregular, personal, and colorful manner that characterizes the Romantic approach. The classicists in their turn utilized a wide range of material including Orientalia and medieval and Renaissance themes. They continued in the formal Renaissance manner established by Ingres but became far more academic (i.e., imitative and unoriginal) than their master. By the second half of the century, both groups (the followers of Delacroix and of Ingres) had outlived their function. They produced primarily anecdotal and photographic pictures without either the dynamic glow of the original Romantic impulse or the elegant linealism of Ingres. This deterioration is demonstrated in the Renaissance-derived, photographic, and ultrasentimental Bouguereau *Virgin of Consolation* (1877, see fig. 489).

ENGLISH PAINTING. Wherever French Romantics like Géricault and Delacroix had shown nature in their works, as in the *Raft of the Medusa*, it had necessarily been given a wild and tempestuous quality against which the protagonists were pitted or into which they were in some way absorbed. But an art of landscape painting as such had not existed in France since the seventeenth century (figs. 415–416). That tradition had been developed in England later, as in the landscapes of Wilson and Gainsborough (figs. 436–437). At the approach of the nineteenth century, England was to continue her contributions with such landscapists as John Constable (1776–1837) and J. M. W. Turner (1775–1851).

Constable. Hampstead Heath with a Rainbow (fig. 482) may be considered from both the naturalistic and the Romantic points of view. In regard to the former, Constable appears to have been the first artist

Fig. 482. Constable: Hampstead Heath with a Rainbow. Worcester Art Museum.

to appreciate fully the movement of nature — its rippling waters, changing cloud effects, and sparkling sunshine, each in its way affecting the appearance of objects. This interest fostered a spontaneous technique for rendering such qualities — the piling up of spot upon spot of paint, the use of small areas of white to reinforce the effect of bold dashes of red or vivid and differentiated greens. Constable evidently felt very strongly about nature; in a revolutionary and original (Romantic) fashion, he sketched out of doors, finishing his paintings in the studio. This in itself represented a sharp break with traditional landscape, which had almost invariably been done indoors. Moreover, he departed from the static notion of nature (as in Poussin), developing the more emotive side stemming from the Dutch (fig. 428) and already attempted by Wilson and Gainsborough. Confronting here the drama of the moment after a storm, with the landscape still in violent movement, the feelings of the Romantic painter are reflected in the sweeping arc of the rainbow and the tiny little figures in the foreground overwhelmed, as it were, by this power.

Turner. Turner's well-known *Fighting Téméraire* proceeds from a naturalistic and anecdotal event, but is transformed by moving reflections

Fig. 483. Turner: Rain, Steam, Speed. London, National Gallery.

and distances into a symbol of the passing of an epoch. The picturesque old ship is being towed to her last dock by a puffing little tug, a sign of the new industrial age (1839), while the setting sun casts its reflections diagonally across the water. Turner was much less the naturalist than Constable and made more poetic use of nature to express his feelings. The subject becomes a vehicle for his own emotions rather than a glorification of nature's power and movement. His expression of abstract force, as in the famous *Rain, Steam, Speed* (fig. 483) or the *Whale Ship* (Metropolitan Museum), is even less structural than in the *Fighting Téméraire;* the forms dissolve in a mist of steam or spray, leaving a total impression of abstract power or movement. Both Constable and Turner were to appeal to the Impressionist painters of the 1870s; Constable himself gave strong impetus during his lifetime to the French Barbizon school of 1820–1850.

Blake. Contemporaneous with the two English landscapists, though entirely unique in his flight from increasing materialism, was the poet-artist William Blake (1757–1827). He was a mystic idealist, prophesying the coming of a better world in terms that exalt the spiritual above the physical. His approach is shown in the water-color sketch for the engraving *When the Morning Stars All Sang Together* (fig. 484), a theme inspired by the Book of Job. It has been assumed that Blake's style is related to Michelangelo's, but it seems far closer to the Mannerism of the mid-sixteenth century (figs. 377, 381) in its emphasis on dematerialized types with exaggerated proportions and gestures, upward movements, and flattened two-dimensional space effects. Whether or not Blake actually went to those particular sources, his work is clearly animated by a similar unease and desire to reject his environment.

A contemporary of David and Goya, Blake was fired by the excitement of the French Revolution of which he was a violent partisan. With self-conscious democratism, he refused to truckle to patrons or to accept a post as drawing teacher with the royal family. In addition to writing his own poetry and illustrating it with colored engravings, Blake illustrated the Bible (as above) and such contemporary works as the *Night Thoughts* of Young, one of the most significant examples of Romantic literature. In 1803 he had begun to engrave the macabre-Romantic designs of the Swiss Henry Fuseli (1741–1825), who had come to England. Through Fuseli, Blake came into contact with the mysticism of the physiognomist Lavater, whose personal approach to Christianity attracted the Englishman.

The exaltation and other-worldliness of the Book of Job illustrations, among the artist's last works, their aspiration toward some other sphere,

Fig. 484. Blake: When the Morning Stars All Sang Together. New York, The Pierpont Morgan Library.

must be regarded as the essence of Blake's spirit. His Christianity is basic and genuine; it remains quite apart from the religious reactions against the French Revolution which led some contemporary Frenchmen, both writers and artists, to look backward instead of upward.

FRANCE: *The Barbizon Group.* The landscape art of England was mirrored in France slightly later by the works of the Barbizon school. This group began to function in the late 1820s, continuing into the latter part of the century. It represented another withdrawal from the city; most of its members chose to live in the country near Fontainebleau. There they could practice landscape painting, which was still unwelcome in a France dominated by the figure art of the neoclassical tradition. Under the influence of Constable — but far less lively in color — are the works of Théodore Rousseau (1812–1867), whose studio-painted *Edge of the Woods* (fig. 485) reveals that artist's rugged and powerful conception of nature. Whereas Constable utilized different gradations of green, complementary colors, and other naturalistic effects, Rousseau and his colleagues were still under the spell of the brownish tones of Dutch landscape color. Yet Rousseau managed to give his tree a certain monumental power and even personality and, in displaying his own feelings, utilized nature as a vehicle for his emotions. In this latter sense he may be compared to many Romantic poets.

Other members of this group include the lyrical Camille Corot (1795–1875) with his fuzzy poetic landscapes and more sharply focused city views; the picturesque and colorful Diaz de la Peña (1809–1876); the tumultuous Jules Dupré (1812–1889); and the poetic Charles Daubigny (1817–1878). Like other aspects of Romantic painting, the Barbizon school contains a strong naturalistic component (as in Rousseau) which inevitably connects it with the French Realist movement of the fifties and sixties and finally with the Impressionism of the seventies. Indeed, Jean François Millet (1814–1875), although a regular member of this group, is generally classified with Gustave Courbet (1819–1877) and Honoré Daumier (1808–1879) as part of the Realist school.

REALISM. The various Barbizon painters had in common their chosen location, their poverty, and, most of them, their unwelcome art. The leading Realists, however, were three individuals coming from dif-

Fig. 485. Rousseau: Edge of the Woods. New York, Metropolitan Museum of Art.

Fig. 486. Millet: The Sower. Courtesy, Museum of Fine Arts, Boston.

ferent parts of France and equally distinct backgrounds. They communicate the intensifying economic and social conflicts of the nineteenth century as well as its growing insistence on material values. The realistic technique of these and other painters mirrors a greater interest in the tangible and yet is in revolt against it.

Millet. Millet's peasants are a sincere recollection of his small farming community in northern France and of a simple home life in which religion played a large role. Lacking the advanced social attitude of his fellow Realists, his art is unquestionably sympathetic to the strivings of the people he knew and loved and whom he depicted in a dignified, even noble, manner. To that extent it was inevitably suspect in an era when classical drawing and form, Renaissance-derived but academic idealizations, or pseudomedieval histories were the requirements.

Today we realize that paintings like *The Sower* (fig. 486) have a Michelangelesque nobility. The powerful and generalized form moves along scattering seed with a magnificent gesture that matches the painting of the High Renaissance. Millet's self-taught adaptations of this earlier standard were combined with a brownish color, which was far from advanced when the newer art was beginning to clean up its palette. In spite of this color conservatism, his art was disapproved for its emphasis on what was felt to be the commonplace and probably also for its social implications. Although allied to the Barbizon school because of his interest in nature and its emotive treatment, Millet's landscape is subordinated to the human element. The latter is treated in broad terms, as here — i.e., realistically rather than naturalistically. This factor brings him within the orbit of such painters as Courbet and Daumier.

Courbet. Gustave Courbet was a middle-class individual from the provinces who emerged as leader of the Realist forces around the middle of the century, aggressively determined to paint whatever he pleased and presumably only what he could see. Millet had been ignored for the most part, but Courbet because of his dynamic attitude became a focus for conservative attacks. From the café tables where he harangued his young admirers, he launched his *réaliste* theories exalting the virtues of everyday subject matter. Again it was content rather than technique that was objected to, inasmuch as Courbet also depended on traditional methods, especially those of the seventeenth century.

My Studio (fig. 487) is a large-scale presentation of the painter's life, showing him at the easel with a typically unidealized (i.e., Realist) model, flanked at left by other models and at right by intellectual friends and patrons. This painting aroused the critics to verbal violence; not only were the various characters portrayed matter-of-factly (except for

Fig. 487. Courbet: My Studio. Paris, Louvre.

the idealized painter himself), but the huge size of the picture was a further offense. Although there was no specific social subject matter in most of Courbet's works, his attitude was so uncompromisingly individualistic and advanced that he was attacked on political grounds and ultimately was forced into a position of political leadership.

It would be a mistake, however, to think of Courbet as a sociologist in paint who depicted the nature of society with complete objectivity; subjects like his early *Stone Breakers* (Louvre) are very rare. It is, rather, his leadership among the Realist artists that gives his career meaning. In *My Studio* and most other works, in spite of the loving care with which the texture of a woman's skin or of drapery may be rendered to transmit a wonderful tactile quality, his people — and he himself — are imbued with a perceptibly thoughtful and even sentimental air. Like his many self-portraits, this work in some ways asserts the developing role of the artist in modern culture, his function as an intellectual and social leader.

Daumier. The art of Honoré Daumier portrays less flamboyantly and perhaps more effectively an artist's awareness of the inequities of society and his obligation to reveal these circumstances. Though a product of the same period as Courbet, Daumier's painting was not a public issue in spite of its admittedly higher social content and significance. He was a full-time newspaper illustrator for more than forty years of his life, painting in his spare hours for himself and a few appreciative friends. In the illustrations he presented a week-to-week picture of the life of the French people from the 1820s through the 1860s, attacking dishonesty in government and law courts as long as political circumstances permitted and satirizing injustice and hypocrisy wherever he found them. As a painter, Daumier was less topical in subject, dealing with broad truths and generalized views of ordinary people (especially the poor), men and women of the circus, his much-disliked lawyers and judges, and moral or philosophical themes often derived from literature.

His sympathies are expressed in such works as the well-known *Third Class Carriage* (fig. 488), where a group of monumentalized and idealized simple people have been brought together in a train compartment. Like Millet, Daumier glorifies his figures to a certain extent, while also giving them a general rather than specific form — the Realist rather than naturalist approach. The strength and patience which ennoble these ordinary folk lend them the importance that sacred subjects held in the past. Form is created through the light that enters the windows, silhouetting those figures near the windows and lingering on those further away, who assume greater roundness with the strong and abrupt transitions from light to dark, somewhat in the Goya manner. Although preeminently a

were also chiefly concerned with the appearance of things; but while the earlier painters had idealized their conceptions in many ways, giving them a feeling of permanence, the Impressionists attempted to render subjects in temporary and instantaneous terms. The opposition to what they had to offer would be primarily against their technique rather than subject matter.

Impressionist subjects are landscape, river, and street scenes as well as a wide variety of indoor themes, such as café and theater scenes. In color, and often in mood, these paintings make a very pleasant picture of the life of the time. The reality may not have been as attractive, but Impressionist works represent a striving toward the ideal and in that sense they are a reaction to the period. Furthermore, the rapid and impermanent tone of most of these pictures suggests the new tempo of the late nineteenth century, the view that one gets from a bus, train, or other rapidly moving vehicle — fragmentary and fleeting. Impressionism, therefore, signifies a new way of looking at things.

Manet. The titular leader of the Impressionist group during the sixties was Edouard Manet (1832–1883), who among other innovations, called attention to the function of natural light as it made the figure visible in the interior of a studio. He thus took an important step away from the soupy colors of the academicians and the dark effects of his Realist predecessors. Actually, Manet's offense against traditional art was twofold: in continuing the straightforward and matter-of-fact attitude of Courbet, he became subject to the same kind of abuse as a *réaliste*; and in working out a revolutionary new technique, he assumed an added burden and a leadership in his own generation. The new technique reversed the traditional procedure that had built the figure from a dark underpainting on which a series of lighter glazes created the highlights that described the form. Contrariwise, in order to obtain a maximum light effect, Manet began with a light-colored underpainting to which darks and half-darks were added, maintaining a bright undersurface from which light would constantly be reflected back into the eye of the spectator.

The *Execution of Maximilian* (fig. 490), an unusual recording of a contemporary event rather than an everyday scene, shows the typical light-charged atmosphere with which Manet surrounds his figures and against which they appear as silhouettes of form rather than three-dimensional entities. In this regard they are reminiscent of Goya (fig. 478) but with the significant difference that the Impressionist painter presents a study of color areas in place of the violent emotional reactions of the Spaniard. This is art of a deliberate objectivity, much prized among Realist writers and others of the period and best expressed by such painters as

Fig. 490. Manet: Execution of Maximilian. Mannheim, Kunsthalle.

Manet and Degas. The execution by Mexican patriots of Archduke Maximilian (who had been placed on the throne of Mexico by the French Emperor Louis Napoleon) was a sensational occurrence in its time (1867). But it is portrayed in such a matter-of-fact way that the spectator gets no inkling of the emotive meaning of the moment either for the disillusioned Archduke or the French public. In spite of the stylistic references to Goya (the figure at the left and the bull-ring spectators looking over the wall) this painting remains an outstanding instance of the artist as a recorder of what he sees rather than what he feels. Yet, like Géricault's earlier and more violent *Raft of the Medusa,* this work was also banned.

Monet. The Impressionism of Claude Monet (1840–1926), equally concerned with the appearance of objects under natural light, differs from that of Manet in a number of important particulars. It is, first, an outdoor instead of an indoor art and therefore occupied primarily with sunlight and outside atmosphere rather than studio light. Second, it derives its luminosity not from the charged underpainting but from bringing together small dots of pure (i.e., unmixed) color that, because of their

592

complementary relationship (e.g., red-green, blue-orange), reinforce or strengthen each other and simulate the effect of real sunlight.

Product of an age that witnessed remarkable advances in the physical sciences, the outdoor Impressionism of painters like Monet, Renoir, and Pissarro parallels the interest in physics (especially optics) of various investigators in France, Germany, and the United States. Although this kind of painting has often been referred to as scientific, it would be fallacious to consider that laboratory measurement of wave lengths of pure light and the possibilities involved in their mixture could be matched by comparatively impure pigments placed spontaneously on the canvas in accordance with general principles. It is true, however, that vibrations are set up in the eye as it adjusts to the manifold stimuli of differently colored and irregularly shaped paint spots. This gives such pictures as Monet's *Houses of Parliament* (fig. 491) a shimmering moving appearance in keeping with the momentary effect desired by the painter. It im-

Fig. 491. Monet: Houses of Parliament. Washington, The National Gallery of Art, Chester Dale Collection.

parts the impression of a form bathed in colored atmosphere — an exaggeration of the actual visual phenomenon — colored in accordance with the particular time of day it was "caught" and with the reflections cast upon it by adjacent objects and vice versa.

This preoccupation with the light enveloping an object rather than the object itself leaves a good deal of outdoor Impressionist painting (especially that of Monet) in a relatively formless and even amorphous state. The various parts of the picture are tied together by the atmosphere but not by any opposition of forces or forms. It is noteworthy that in contrast to the stability of the classical landscape (cf. figs. 415–416), the Impressionist landscape (or other subject) is a partially seen theme. Monet's view might be obtained while passing by; it represents a particular moment in time and a particular fragment of space.

Renoir. This outdoor technique was developed by Monet and Pierre Auguste Renoir (1841–1919), working together during the early seventies. Although Renoir did a good many landscapes, boulevard pictures, and similar subjects, he is best known for the scenes of relaxation and enjoyment that typify the Impressionist approach as much as its urge to explore the suburbs and the countryside. His art highlights the desire of the modern city dweller to get away from the noise and strain, to return to a more placid and natural environment from which he or his ancestors have been drawn. Paintings like the *Luncheon of the Boating Party* (fig. 492) have been referred to as "vacation pictures," first appearing as a type in the late fifties in such examples as Courbet's *Young Women on the Banks of the Seine* (1856, Paris, Petit Palais) and soon seen in works by Manet, Monet, and others. No one else, however, manages to convey the essence of pure physical enjoyment, the lyricism, projected by Renoir with his good-looking young men and women.

In this sense Renoir is surely not objective but discloses his own exuberant reaction to life — in terms of the clean colors of his and Monet's new rainbow palette, the fragmentary aspect, spontaneity of vision, and the Japanese-derived "vantage-point perspective" of all Impressionist artists (cf. fig. 172). The popular Japanese print was known in France since the 1850s, because of the expansion of trade to the Far East. It lent to works of this kind (and to Degas, Lautrec, Van Gogh, and many others) an unusual view from close on, high up, and to the side, adding to the qualities of unexpectedness, unawareness, and informality so prized by the men of this group.

Renoir's *Luncheon* is as casual as possible, showing men in boating shirts and straw hats, a man in the foreground straddling a chair, a lovely girl playing with a puppy on a disordered table, and similar details that

594

suggest the feeling of ease and contentment. The spectator looks down into this scene from one side, witnessing the various conversations and flirtations, the carefree poses. The Japanese vantage-point view gives the composition its diagonal movement from lower left to upper right — as in the arrangement of veranda and table lines — which recurs in many other Impressionist works. The figures are generally more substantial than Monet's, because of Renoir's inheritance from the joyousness and physical vitality of Fragonard and Rubens, which have been embellished with the clean tonalities of the new painting.

In spite of the informal and spontaneous elements, however, the paintings of Renoir (also of Manet and Monet) have a still and suspended quality, as though the painter could not set them in movement. While the little dots of color are placed together so the eye may fuse the respective stimuli, the figure has to stand still to allow these effects to take place and the natural light to form. Even though Impressionism demanded a sense of motion, those artists could not actually accomplish it, lest the figures fall apart.

Fig. 492. Renoir: Luncheon of the Boating Party. Washington, D.C., The Phillips Collection.

Degas. The apparent paradox was solved by Edgar Degas (1834–1917), who used neither the small spots of outdoor Impressionism nor yet the transparent effect of Renoir's figure pieces. Degas's technique was based on a conservative but individualistic draftsmanship learned from the study of such old masters as Holbein, Clouet, and Cranach. Through it the problem of movement was to be solved. This rigid drawing was first applied by Degas to carefully composed historical scenes of great naturalism (e.g., *Young Spartans Provoking Each Other to Combat*), parallel in significance to the historical novels of his contemporary, Flaubert. From there he proceeded to tightly constructed individual and group portraits of great psychological penetration, using a newer and looser, more powerful line. Degas turned more and more to contemporary Realist themes in illustrations from problem novels or pictures like his *Cotton Exchange at New Orleans.* He adopted at the same time the oblique angle and high view of current Impressionist-Japanese perspective and a matter-of-factness and objectivity like that of Manet. He went on to depict the life of the theater, the ballet, the café, the race track, and the shop.

Degas painted with what he felt was complete sociological objectivity, and he tried to give the impression of observing the many different types without being observed himself. *Dancers Practicing at the Bar* (fig. 493) illustrates his startling perspective effects and the dynamic asymmetry by means of which the characters are placed at one side and balanced by a

596

long expanse going in the opposite direction. It also demonstrates the fact that through his marvelously tense drawing, Degas succeeded in setting the figure in motion; while through thinning out his paints, he achieved an increasingly luminous effect. The final step was taken when the artist adopted the pastel technique, which in later works gave him the absolute maximum of brilliant Impressionist color and the rough, tense linear movement that he preferred.

Toulouse-Lautrec. Technically analogous to the works of Degas are the paintings, lithographs, and posters of Henri de Toulouse-Lautrec (1864–1901). The painting *At the Moulin Rouge* (fig. 494) shows his personal linear approach. Instead of Degas's presumable objectivity, Lautrec employed a mordant and bitter irony in this presentation of the well-known Montmartre cabaret and its depressing habitués. Characteristic features and attitudes are exaggerated by bold flat color and by manipulation of a constantly weaving, organic line, typical of the end-of-the-century Art Nouveau (new art). As in many of this artist's works,

Fig. 494. Lautrec: At the Moulin Rouge. Courtesy, Art Institute of Chicago.

Fig. 495. Rodin: Balzac (plaster). Paris, Musée Rodin.

there is not so much an interest in a particular moment of time and space as an attempt to reduce the personages to symbols of their special sphere.

RODIN. A sculptural counterpart to the Realist-Impressionist style exists in the work of the one man who saves nineteenth-century sculpture from oblivion: Auguste Rodin (1840–1917). After the neoclassical and neo-Baroque efforts of the early years (e.g., Cortot and Rude), sculpture in the rest of the century, with the exception of Rodin, generally shared the academic eclecticism of the paintings of Bouguereau. Rodin, on the other hand, evinces a simple and powerful naturalism (with Romantic overtones), as in his famous *Age of Bronze,* which in his day impressed opponents as a studio cast rather than an original study. On the Romantic side there are works like his *Burghers of Calais,* a larger-than-life-size group of the medieval citizens of Calais who offered their lives to the English in exchange for the safety of their city. Inspired by this patriotic incident from the Hundred Years' War, the work is related to Romanticism through its nationalistic spirit and the realistic manner of its execution, as in Géricault and Delacroix.

More specifically contemporary and Realist in the Courbet-Daumier sense is the almost 10-foot-high, full-length *Balzac* (fig. 495). The great realistic novelist is pictured in his dressing gown striding up and down, as though in the act of creation. Because of the more conservative requirement of monumental sculpture, Rodin's works, especially those referred to here, were not enthusiastically received. Yet from the present point of view, no other sculptor gives so complete a cross section of the aesthetic impulses of the century — its Romanticism, Realism, eclecticism of styles, and in the last example a certain symbolic dynamism of movement, while a flickering light suggests Impressionism as well. The latter effect is created by the motion of the figure, its informality of pose, and the twinkling lights that play over the deeply indented surface.

PUVIS DE CHAVANNES. Impressionist interests are also reflected in the *Poor Fisherman* of the philosophically minded painter Pierre Puvis de Chavannes (1824–1898, fig. 496), at least to the extent that it shows the influence of the all-pervasive Japanese wood-block-print perspective and design. Yet this painting indicates too the continuity of the Renaissance element in its formal drawing and meticulous detail, qualities that in the hands of the skillful Puvis de Chavannes give the work a unity of composition which is foreign to the contemporary (1881) works of many Impressionists.

In addition, it implies a degree of religious, even mystical, feeling, expressive of the spiritual needs of the late-nineteenth-century middle class in France (and those of England and Germany with their respective pre-Raphaelite and neo-Christian movements). It represents the con-

Fig. 496. Puvis de Chavannes: Poor Fisherman. Paris, Louvre.

servative side of a general spirituality in which the progressive forces also share. This emerges as part of the modern movement in the symbolism and mysticism of Gauguin, Van Gogh, Munch, Hodler, and other artists, in transition from the end of that century to the beginning of the present one. Similarly, Puvis's sense of compositional form parallels that of many advanced painters at the end of the century, such as Gauguin and Cézanne, who attempt to overcome the relative formlessness of Impressionism.

Puvis de Chavannes is also connected with the practice of mural painting for the many public buildings that symbolize the growth of democratic ideals and necessities — e.g., inside the *Panthéon* (fig. 451), the Sorbonne, and the Boston Public Library. His abstract decorativeness and strong generalization of form through tight outlines and pale tonalities, derived from Renaissance art, combine to make him the most effective decorator of public buildings under the French Third Republic.

LATER ARCHITECTURE. The new buildings, as indicated earlier, usually held to older traditional forms and styles in spite of modern and fresh purposes. Such instances as the British *Houses of Parliament* (fig. 477) in Gothic style are perhaps less incongruous than the Romanesque railroad stations in so many parts of the United States. Even when newer methods and materials emerged, they were surrounded by decorative elements from the Renaissance, Baroque, and other past periods. This some-

Fig. 497. Garnier: Opera House, Paris.

Fig. 498. Garnier: Opera House. Main staircase.

what confused and eclectic situation in the nineteenth century appears in outstanding examples like the Paris *Opera House* (figs. 497–498) by Charles Garnier (1825–1898), built between 1861 and 1874 at the time of the Realist-Impressionist movement in painting.

While the latter movement struggles to find a technique expressing the new highly industrialized and urbanized era, the Baroque-derived *Opera House* reflects the attitude of the middle class, intent on securing surroundings of impressive and respectable luxury in which it can display itself to the best advantage. This does not deny the skillful blending of parts in the opulent arches, columns, and staircase of the lobby or the relationship between the stage, auditorium, and corridors, whose proportions and richness have become a world wide model for similar buildings. It simply indicates that, as late as the last quarter of the nineteenth century, architecture in Europe and the United States was still primarily traditional and to a great extent unaware of what was being accomplished in technology and science.

There are some exceptions, however, that signify the growing intru-

Fig. 499. Labrouste: Bibliothèque Ste. Geneviève. Reading Room.

sion of these newer factors. Beginning around 1840, cast iron had been used in the construction of buildings, to be followed a half century later by the introduction of steel, both resulting from the increased use of these materials in industry. The *Bibliothèque Ste. Geneviève* (fig. 499) by Henri Labrouste (1801–1875), one of the first important public libraries, constructed between 1843 and 1850, symbolizes the new type of democratic necessity (education, health, and public welfare and utility buildings). It is also symptomatic of the slowly changing character of architecture in the age of industrialism.

The exterior, although functional to the extent that its sections indicate the interior divisions between reading area, book stacks, etc., is still basically within the stylistic framework of Renaissance forms. Inside, in the reading room, Labrouste has turned to the new modern materials, iron and glass, that enable him to offer a suitable high well-lighted space. Barrel vaults stretch the length of this interior, based on arched iron girders (pierced by classical floral patterns) resting on a row of slender metal columns of the Corinthian type. The architecture of traditional sentiment is utilized inconsistently with respect to modern material and functional needs. This disparity lasted well into the twentieth century in both Europe and the United States.

602

25 / ART IN THE MODERN WORLD: *The United States in the Nineteenth Century*

THE early artistic development of the United States had run parallel with Europe in historical meaning and style. Direct stimuli from that source had fostered the colonial and Federal, i.e., neoclassical, types of architecture (see figs. 442–445). These ideas continued to be popular through the first half of the nineteenth century, as expressed in the neoclassical sculpture of such men as Horatio Greenough (1805–1852) and Hiram Powers (1805–1873). Greenough's gigantic seated seminude and toga-wrapped figure of *Washington* (Smithsonian Institution) and Powers's delicate undraped young girl in chains, *The Greek Slave,* are conventional and academic works, representing the hold of the Classical style during this period. After a group of Ohio clergymen had passed on the possible moral dangers of Powers's figure (which because of its chained hands could not shield its nudity), it became in reproductions the most popular piece of American sculpture of the century.

ARCHITECTURE: *Richardson.* Toward the middle of the nineteenth century, neoclassicism's popularity was challenged by other eclectic forms, the neo-Gothic and neo-Romanesque, again paralleling European trends. The first is illustrated in New York's Trinity Church, built between 1839 and 1846 by Richard Upjohn (1802–1878), an English-born architect who was well able to reproduce the spirit of the English parish church. The neo-Romanesque style in the United States was primarily the contribution of Henry H. Richardson (1838–1886), who felt that its ruggedness and power were suited to the expression of American ideals. It is perhaps best represented in *Trinity Church* at Boston (1877, fig. 500), in which a number of different sources have been tapped. The architect has added a rustication of the stone to increase the appearance of strength.

Richardson's independent thinking is indicated in the effective group-

603

ing of various elements which, however suggestive of their French, Spanish, or German origins, move from one mass to another in climactic and dramatic fashion. In the post-Civil War era of quick expansion and financial success, the architecture of Richardson struck a warning note against the too common and shallow imitations of European styles. It served as an example to many good architects at the end of the century who were to follow this kind of thinking in other style areas. Architects of this newer type might use a Greek, Renaissance, or any other model from the past, but they would absorb its spirit rather than imitate in empty fashion its external forms. This unacademic borrowing is exemplified in the Modernized Classic style produced by the Columbian Exposition at Chicago in 1893.

From such beginnings, Richardson went on to increasingly simplified and utilitarian forms, as in his *Marshall Field Warehouse* in Chicago (1885–1887, fig. 501). Here a long rectangular building, without any eclectic historical reference, features rusticated stone for its exterior as well as rhythmically arranged, round-arched windows of varying heights — the total expressing a functional and simple, but powerfully composed, entity, making this architect an important pioneer of the modern school. One result of Richardson's influence is to be seen in the unrealized skyscraper design by L. S. Buffington (1847–1931), done in 1887–1888, a decade after completion of the Boston *Trinity Church*, and deriving

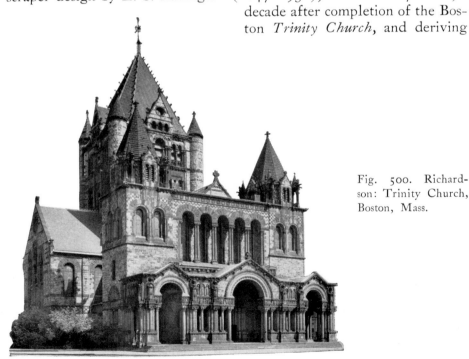

Fig. 500. Richardson: Trinity Church, Boston, Mass.

Fig. 501. Richardson: Marshall Field Warehouse, Chicago, Ill.

its square Romanesque towered form from that source. Yet the beneficent effect of Richardson's work was outweighed for a long time by the tremendous popularity of his Romanesque designs, however inadequately understood, among the medievalists of the last quarter of the century. They were finally superseded at the end of the century by the Modernized Classic, which carried over into the next era. The medieval trend may be said to represent the respectability — or the desire therefor — of the American business world in the great climax of post-Civil War expansion.

Sullivan. The more progressive or functional side of American architecture, proclaimed by Richardson (and Buffington), was to develop very slowly indeed. At the Columbian Exposition there had appeared the work of a young man whose designs were to fertilize this development: Louis Sullivan (1856–1924). In his Transportation Building, avoiding the already outmoded Romanesque and the (to him) all too facile modernized classicism of his colleagues, he enunciated the since famous dictum that "form follows function." By this, Sullivan meant that the architect should consider each building in terms of the use to which it is put. Its ultimate form should be determined by that use or function instead of by imitation of the past. The various elements of architecture — columns, windows, walls, etc. — should be placed with a functional rather than merely decorative purpose. Materials such as wood, stone, or metal ought to be utilized in a manner consistent with their separate characters. Finally, the rooms, doorways, and other spatial areas should be planned

in terms of their actual employment and not for reasons of impressiveness
or other traditional values.

The skyscraper. During the latter part of the nineteenth century, following the turn toward metal (e.g., fig. 499), building technology advanced to a point that made possible the construction of taller and taller
edifices. These had become necessary — or so the business world felt —
because of the rapid growth of cities and the consequent scarcity of space.
Nevertheless, although metal construction made the skyscraper possible,
not until the development of the elevator was it feasible to project a
building vertically upward. Actually, the two went hand in hand, but
only the later high-speed, electrically driven elevator made the skyscraper a universal American phenomenon. European cities, for reasons of
different industrial tempos and geographical features (softer foundations,
etc.), have not evolved along this line.

Buffington's pioneer twenty-eight-story skyscraper design had never
been carried out. The first skyscraper was built in Chicago, the Home
Life Insurance Building (1883–1885), a somewhat crudely planned ten-
story structure employing the principle of skeleton iron construction.
When architects applied themselves to the problem of making the early
skyscraper look like a cohesive structure rather than a series of packing

boxes, the still powerful eclectic tradition forced them into a compromise with Gothic or late-nineteenth-century Modernized Classic. Again it was Sullivan who projected the first answers to this dilemma in such examples as his Wainwright Building in St. Louis (1890–1891) or the *Guarantee (Prudential) Building* in Buffalo (1896, fig. 502).

In both of these, Sullivan's exterior design stressed the fact that the bulk of the weight was carried by the vertical elements of the skeleton, which gave the composition an upward-moving quality through the continuity of the piers from bottom to top. Walls, which in a metal skyscraper construction lose their traditional function of supports, become supplementary rather than structural elements. Although the fenestration here is uniform, variations occur at the top and bottom where service areas and stores, respectively, give the windows different shapes and proportions. The functional and expressive character of such a building was a good generation ahead of its time. For many years afterward, eclecticized designs still predominated, such as the *Woolworth Building* of 1913 by Cass Gilbert (1859–1934, see fig. 551), in which the inherent verticality of the tall building was filtered through Gothic and other adaptations (see Chapter 27).

PAINTING: *Landscape and genre*. Painting in America during this period, however tied to European styles, showed a number of local vari-

Fig. 503. Cole: Dream of Arcadia. The Toledo Museum of Art.

ants, but by and large it did not keep pace with the rapid advances of the latter part of the century abroad. In the first half of the nineteenth century, succeeding the portrait tradition, two distinctive forms had appeared — a Romantic type of rugged landscape picture and an equally popular type of genre work. Both may be related to European developments and constitute the less original part of our nineteenth-century production.

Landscape painting in the United States at this time corresponded roughly to the Romantic landscape in Europe (figs. 482, 485) and may be represented by such works as the *Dream of Arcadia* (fig. 503) by Thomas Cole (1801–1848). This parallels in form the picturesque-Romantic landscape produced in Europe since the time of Rubens and continued in the work of Gainsborough (fig. 437) and later Barbizon painters (fig. 485). But the intent of American artists like Cole was to project the feeling of a still untamed wilderness, the forests and mountains that remained to be explored in the Americas of the 1840s. This literary-philosophic intention is underlined here by the fact that the *Dream of Arcadia* is part of a series of pictures entitled *The Voyage of Life*. The English-influenced Cole had been an itinerant signboard painter who spent a good deal of time traveling about in the Catskill mountain country, much as earlier British landscapists had done in Scotland and other picturesque localities. But the wilderness art of Cole, Asher B. Durand, and others (together with their equivalent in American literature) is unique. The spirit of the frontier, the vastness of our geographical horizons, have ultimately affected life on this continent in a way that is still not fully measured.

If these sentimental landscapes leave something to be desired in the way of form and color, the same cannot be said of the landscapes of Thomas Moran (1837–1926) and F. E. Church (1826–1900), who

Fig. 504. Moran: The Teton Ridge. New York, Metropolitan Museum of Art.

608

abandoned this imitative Barbizonism in favor of a new power and grandeur. Although once more there were earlier examples of the grandiose in nature, pictures such as Moran's *The Teton Ridge* (fig. 504) or Church's paintings of the mountains of South America are composed with a solid feeling for form and emotive color and present an outlook on nature that combines realism with overwhelming drama.

Fig. 505. Bingham: Fur Traders Descending the Missouri. New York, Metropolitan Museum of Art.

The genre side of early American art is represented by George Caleb Bingham (1811–1879) and his *Fur Traders Descending the Missouri* (fig. 505). Though again there is a general relationship with the corresponding European style, this painting is far superior in abstract qualities of form and compositional asymmetry to most contemporary (1845) works across the Atlantic — except for Daumier. The stimulus for a superior expression here also would seem to come from the inspiration of the frontier. The picture's simplicity and sense of the monumental, its feeling for the endless movement of the boat, are combined with the

Fig. 506. Homer: Storm in the Bahamas. New York, Metropolitan Museum of Art.

realization of the character of the American types portrayed. The blue-green of one shirt, the red of the other, and the dark color of the chained fox in the bow stand out against the light-green water and somewhat darker green trees. Although the balance appears to be toward the right, the boat and the design as a whole move to the left through the direction of water reflections, the background trees, and the sensation of limitless distance that is conveyed.

Homer. If there were echoes of Dutch genre here and of eighteenth-century spatial conceptions in Bingham's many political pictures, bringing him within the scope of the European tradition, other American painters of this period offered a native and even untaught quality: Winslow Homer (1836–1910) and Albert P. Ryder (1847–1917). Homer's early genre pieces are in the same general category as those of Bingham, Mount, and other practitioners of this form. His sense of realism was developed by long experience as an illustrator for *Harper's Weekly* and especially by his work for that paper as a Civil War artist, from which derive such paintings as his *Rainy Day in Camp* and *Prisoners from the Front*. These sober and serious works, carefully composed, dark in tonality, may be considered as parallel in historical position with the burgeoning Realist tradition in Europe — but independent of its influence.

610

His brilliant water-color papers like the *Storm in the Bahamas* (fig. 506) show a vividness and spontaneity, a realization of the power of nature, and an instinctive arrangement of forms and colors that are unique in our culture. Racing clouds and wind-tossed branches are projected with economy of means and selectivity, equaled by the flattened outlines of the houses below. As Homer developed, he became less interested in the relationship of man to nature in the Romantic sense and more pre-occupied with the sheer majesty and overwhelming force of nature, which filled the works of his later life.

Ryder. Ryder's art is another example of the development of an un-taught painter, in his case of a solitary mystic dedicated to the portrayal of symbolic ideas. Perhaps the most original American painter of the century, Ryder brought forth a series of hitherto unknown images and formal concepts destined to influence later painters of the United States, e.g., Marsden Hartley. His art may be compared in a general way with that of the late-nineteenth-century European symbolists, to whom, how-

Fig. 507. Ryder: The Race Track. Courtesy, The Cleveland Museum of Art, J. H. Wade Collection.

Fig. 508. Eakins: The Thinker. New York, Metropolitan Museum of Art.

ever, he owes nothing. Like them, he made a spiritual protest against a highly materialistic age.

The Race Track (fig. 507), like his other works, deals in large masses of throbbing dark color, de-emphasizing outline in the conventional sense but giving the broadly massed contours the desired effect of an ominous sky and a barren land. Against this background, Death rides on his pale horse — an image that, together with the symbolic serpent in the foreground, underlines the tragic meaning of this painting, which was inspired by the death of a friend, a poor man who had lost his savings at the race track. In attempting to formulate his emotions and inner conflicts, in foregoing the meticulous realism of most of his contemporaries and concentrating on the intangible values of existence, Ryder became one of the earliest Expressionists.

Eakins. Thomas Eakins (1844–1916) represents the third stream of nineteenth-century American painting, in which native directness, seriousness, and integrity (as in Copley, Bingham, and Homer) are combined with the techniques of European art. Between his anatomical studies at the Jefferson Medical College in Philadelphia and the period spent in Paris during the 1860s absorbing the principles of academic realism at various ateliers, Eakins was perhaps the best-trained American painter of his generation. With this background he produced a carefully calculated and sober type of composition in which the figure of man or woman is seen in a subdued studio light, convincing in form without meticulous detail, and serious in tone.

His *The Thinker* (fig. 508) illustrates the concentrated, inward-turning solemnity characteristic of Eakins, the sense of the individual's worth and independence of mind, that reflect so well the character of the painter himself. This is especially true of late works of this type (1900) which

612

approximate the feeling of sturdy independence that emanates from so many of Copley's eighteenth-century paintings. More than that, however, Eakins ennobled the thinking man or woman or the creative scientist, as in the mood-filled *The Gross Clinic* (fig. 509). His works are a direct reflection of the ideals of American culture and in strong contrast to the glorifications of American social life produced by his more popular contemporaries, the dashing society portraitists like John Singer Sargent (1856–1926).

The contribution of Eakins extends beyond his own painting to his influence on the following generation of American painters. His struggle to assert the validity of the commonplace subject by elevating its importance was unsuccessful from the standpoint of contemporary critics and public, who were as reluctant as their opposite numbers in Europe to accept this idea; but it was destined to bear fruit in the works of early-twentieth-century painters. From his pictures of medical clinics, prize fights, boat races, and other genre, the so-called Philadelphia Group, in-

Fig. 509. Eakins: The Gross Clinic. Philadelphia, Jefferson Medical College.

cluding John Sloan (1871–1951), William Glackens (1870–1938), Robert Henri (1865–1929), and George Luks (1867–1933), derived a good deal of their original stimulation.

Sloan. John Sloan's painting, like that of many contemporaries, is considerably looser and more casual in style than the formalized and monumental forms of Eakins — the latter's realism was now treated with the looser brush of Manet and the Impressionists. Sloan's *The Wake of the Ferry* (fig. 510) falls within the chronological compass of the twentieth century, and yet by style and technique it belongs to the French movement in the last quarter of the preceding century. Its close-on and high-up view (vantage point), its stressing of the foreground silhouette, the atmospheric effect that carries the eye across the intervening space to the boats in the distance, are typical Impressionist elements (cf. figs. 491–492).

In pictures like this, during the latter part of the nineteenth century and the early part of the twentieth, America responded strongly to the impact of the new "clear painting." James A. M. Whistler (1834–1903), Mary Cassatt (1845–1926), Childe Hassam (1859–1935), and many

Fig. 510. Sloan: The Wake of the Ferry. Washington, D.C., The Phillips Collection.

other Americans indicate this trend quite plainly. But while those artists represent for the most part the European side of American painting, Sloan, Luks, Henri, Glackens, and later Bellows and others signify the adaptation of foreign methods to United States purposes. This was to be the outstanding quality of American painting in the twentieth century during the period following upon and deriving from the post-Impressionist era in Europe.

26 / ART IN THE MODERN WORLD: *Twentieth-century Painting and Sculpture*

THERE is no precise point at which one may say the contemporary period began. The effects of nineteenth-century materialism, nationalism, colonialism, and social differences carried over into the twentieth century, the various stresses becoming increasingly powerful, and produced the climactic wars and revolutions of our epoch. To the extent that the modern artist had been isolated from his environment, his art at the end of the nineteenth century tended to reflect that milieu less directly than had the Realism and Impressionism of previous years.

PAINTING

The painting of the post-Impressionists was preoccupied with plastic and aesthetic problems (Cézanne and Seurat) or was psychologically escapist in character (Van Gogh and Gauguin — one retreating into the mind, the other abandoning civilization for the "unspoiled" South Seas). These two trends had in some measure been apparent even earlier in the nineteenth century in the aesthetics of Impressionism, which was as much concerned with the method of painting as with its subject matter, and in Romantic (and other) rejection of materialism. The men of the end of the era continued and further developed those trends; they transmitted to the twentieth century the augmented plastic and psychological impulses that produced the various pre-World War I movements. The latter, in their turn, formed the basis of contemporary art.

In the years immediately preceding 1914, the various art movements in France, England, Germany, and Italy showed the effects of the tensions of the time. Although at the moment of their birth many of these aesthetic manifestations seemed to a large section of the public and critics little more than mad shriekings, they can be looked back upon as outgrowths of the reactions of sensitive individuals to the pressures and strains of their day. This had happened in many ages to one degree or another. Michelangelo had responded to the anguish of his transitional epoch in later works such as the *Pietà* of the Florentine Cathedral. El Greco had expressed the essence of the religious morbidity of his period. Rembrandt, in a highly material environment, had dematerialized his forms in protest against what was crushing him as an individual. Yet in all these cases the reaction of the artist had still been in the line of traditional art and was recognizably part of the historical stream, while in the modern situation this was apparently not so.

ISOLATION OF THE ARTIST. In the late nineteenth and early twentieth century the artist reached a high point of isolation from the public, working for himself or for a limited number of art lovers who maintained private collections insulated from general scrutiny. From the time of the Impressionists on, the rejected artist had taken refuge in discussions and experiments. Deprived of the traditional patronage that had made him responsible in some measure to a public, he fell back on the approval of the few like-minded individuals he could find, the few who would accept his increasingly nonrepresentational formulations.

Even worse than the active opposition to Realists and Impressionists in the third quarter of the nineteenth century was the ensuing shift from a violent reception to ultimately no reception at all. The post-Impressionists and later artists mostly existed in a vacuum. This was true at first primarily in France, where various branches of the modern movement (except for Expressionism and socially conscious art) had their origin. As modern art then appeared in other areas during the early twentieth century, it again created the furor that had been the misfortune of Monet and his colleagues in the nineteenth century; in Belgium, Scandinavia, Germany, and the United States there were violent press and public outcries against local variants of modernism. Subsequently, however, the twentieth century (until recently) has tended to ignore rather than attack the modern artist, treating him as a negligible factor in the social scene. Such was the case in the 1920s and 1930s, except in fascist and communist countries where the modern artist, because of his individualism, fell under direct attack once more — modern art was driven out of Russia and strangled in Germany. In the democracies, this period was also marked by the development of private art galleries and small museums of modern art catering to a new and necessarily still limited public.

Modern art in the meantime had gone through the later phases of Cubism, Fauvism, Expressionism, neo-Romanticism, and Surrealism —

to name some of the major movements that will be surveyed. In post-Revolutionary Mexico (i.e., after 1920) and depression-ridden United States in the 1930s, a new kind of socially conscious art had arisen, together with attempts to offer government aid and sponsorship to artists. As World War II approached, painters in different countries responded to the times with the cruelties and sadism of Surrealism, the activism and political awareness of Social Realism, and the new wave of escapist abstraction of the late thirties and early forties. After World War II in the late forties and early fifties the artistic center of the Western world seemed to hover between Europe and the United States. The depression of the thirties and the war had hit French art very badly, while Nazism and Fascism had done the same to German and Italian modern art. During the Nazi-Fascist and war period, the United States had turned from Social Realism to modernism in its own expression and received the benefits of refugee European artists, who arrived in considerable numbers. America's position thereby improved to such a point that many regarded it as the heir to the artistic tradition of modern Europe.

In this same postwar era, however, the situation of art in France and Italy was to revive considerably, so that there would again be a vital French movement and an exciting new Italian phase. The United States was to produce a more or less new formulation — a mixture of Surrealism, Abstract Expressionism, and Dadaism that, however escapist and nihilistic, would have real meaning for a fear-filled period. Especially important in recent years would be the contribution of the United States (and Italy and Britain) to sculpture and the development of architecture in the United States. All these factors comprise the story of contemporary art, which may be traced from post-Impressionism.

POST-IMPRESSIONISM. The majority of critics agree that modern painting began with Paul Cézanne (1839–1906); most painters of the first decade of the twentieth century — Fauves, Cubists, Vorticists, Expressionists, and others — would respond to his new space and color treatment. His formulations were part of the general trend of the 1890s, called post-Impressionism since it was based on and reacted against Impressionism, and advanced by Cézanne, Seurat, Gauguin, and Van Gogh. Although they may be grouped in name only and were not organized like the Impressionists, these men had certain ideas in common which sprang from the aesthetic conditions of the late nineteenth century.

Without knowing of each other's work, Cézanne and Seurat (and Gauguin), for example, agreed that Impressionism lacked form and structure. And working for the most part independently of each other, Gauguin and Van Gogh agreed that the earlier art lacked feeling and ideas. Not only did these four recognize that Impressionism had "deficiencies"; they

618

were opposed as well to conventional academic art of the late nineteenth century. Academic painting, in the process of becoming a photographic vehicle for superficial sentiment and narration (see fig. 489), had lost the form or design quality that all painting (whether Renaissance, Baroque, or medieval) must have in order to justify its existence as art.

Most post-Impressionists felt that Impressionist art in its search for the momentary and evanescent light quality had neglected both the compositional structure of the canvas and the solidity of the figure; but had it not been for Impressionism's brighter tonality and clean sparkling colors applied directly to the surface, the new post-Impressionist art would not have been possible. In the same way, the sense of formal patterning and design in Cézanne, Seurat, Gauguin, and Van Gogh was a development of the Japanese influence experienced by the Impressionists and their associates, notably by Degas, Lautrec, Manet, and Renoir. Finally, in the later works of both Renoir and Degas, there is renewed emphasis on form as such and on the organization of the canvas in rhythmic relationships.

Both Cézanne and Seurat adapted the casually applied areas of broken and clean color and utilized them in a new, more systematic, almost scientific manner. Cézanne went further, however; in his art the feeling for form and space is a tangible and convincing element. Both these men typify the growing interest in technique for its own sake (the aesthetic side of modern art), already signalized by Manet. This concern with the manner of execution rather than content would become increasingly characteristic of most twentieth-century artists. The pioneers of post-Impressionist thinking also disclose the henceforth typical concern of the twentieth-century artist with the "motif" — an aesthetically suitable bit of nature, a still-life grouping, or even a human being, whose form and color are employed to convey a "form sensation."

The painting of Cézanne and Seurat is as intense in color as that of the Impressionists and perhaps even more intense, since it drops the accidental and twinkling quality. The constant shimmer of the earlier style is changed to a permanent and solid glow. No longer did the artist project a casual or unexpected view of nature or of people caught amusing themselves or dressing or dancing. More important to the painter now was a controlled and carefully planned rendition of nature, human beings, or still life (for indoor or outdoor scenes), but still with the clean color technique of Impressionism. This was used systematically to create solid form and regulated compositions rather than to seize some fugitive effect of light or movement. The Impressionists had been satisfied with an approximation of a color relationship produced in an improvisatory manner, whereas post-Impressionists of the Cézanne-Seurat type aimed for an

Fig. 511. Cézanne: Mont Ste. Victoire. Washington, D.C., The Phillips Collection.

exact relationship between one tone and another. This, they felt, would allow them to render their sensations of form in more orderly, complete, and rhythmic arrangements in the old-master sense. One of the chief goals of this newer group, then, was to achieve traditional values in composition and form, while still retaining the undeniable merit of the clean palette introduced by their immediate predecessors.

Cézanne. The *Mont Ste. Victoire* of Cézanne (fig. 511) is typical of the new method. Contrasting it with a Monet (fig. 491) or a Renoir composition (fig. 492), we see the difference between a casually and momentarily envisaged scene and an arrangement meant as a permanent interpretation. Cézanne was not interested in a particular time of day or in a limited spatial conception lifted out of its surroundings for the spectator to see at close range. Standing well away from his motif in the manner of a classical landscapist (cf. Poussin, fig. 415), he took in a sweeping and deep view of nature, seen here from between the two enclosing trees at right and left. Dropping Monet's external descriptive light and the photographic perspective that diminished the color intensity of distant objects, Cézanne (like the other post-Impressionists) concerned himself

620

with translating the chosen material into an aesthetic pattern. He stands directly in front of his subject (not at the side in the vantage-point perspective of the Impressionists), balancing one tree against the other and using them to establish his foreground plane. The right-hand tree, moreover, becomes a means of anchoring foreground to background as its branches swing to the left and fit themselves into the curve of the mountains in the rear. In this way the painter maintains his control over the scene; he often deviates from the photographic truth to suit a desired arrangement.

The end result of a system in which foreground and background are generally tied to each other is that, instead of the traditional linear or aerial perspective (or its Impressionist variant), there is a more two-dimensional space, since the background always seems to come forward to meet the foreground. There have been various pre- and post-Renaissance (and Oriental) systems in which the third dimension is played down in favor of a more decorative and flatter projection, as can readily be seen in fourteenth-century Italian painting (Duccio, fig. 301), fifteenth-cen-

Fig. 512. Cézanne: Card Players. New York, Stephen Clark Collection.

tury Flemish painting (van Eyck, fig. 311), sixteenth-century Mannerist art (Parmigianino, fig. 377), and many other, especially non-Western, formulations. We may therefore question whether the methods of projective geometry are inviolable in regard to painting, just as we may realize that Cézanne was not doing something entirely novel. According to the painter himself, he was trying "to make of Impressionism something as solid and as durable as the art of the museums."

But Cézanne's control of his motif did not come from the space relationship, however basic this may be. His rendering of a sensation of form also derived from a new manner of using clean color. Cézanne avoided the small spots of Impressionist painting in favor of small planes or tiny areas of paint. In such pictures as the *Card Players* (fig. 512) the planes change from one intensity to another as they are used to mold, actually to build up, the figure in space. This is different from the Impressionist idea of describing the light that falls in spots on a given figure; what happens now is more akin to the process of modeling, whereby small bits of clay are constantly added. While the figures of Manet or Renoir have a loosely formed and vibrating surface quality, those of Cézanne take on a solid sculpturesque character emitting a permanent inner glow.

Similarly, there is no attempt to stress the enjoyment and relaxation of Impressionist painting; here there is a seriousness and solemnity worthy of traditional paintings such as those of Le Nain or Latour (figs. 413–414). The typical tense relationship of the forms to the picture plane shows the table, tilted forward in a kind of reverse perspective, touching the front line of the canvas, while the two side figures are brought into contact with the sides of the frame, and the rear figure and curtain touch the top. This deliberately limited spatial quality (or control of the space) is increased by the solid architectonic arch formed by the three seated figures.

This formulation signified a turning point in modern painting, an aesthetic viewpoint that influenced most painters of the early twentieth century. However much he may have been affected by traditional space techniques and tensions in arriving at it, Cézanne now offered modern artists a means with which to overcome what seemed to them the defects of the nineteenth-century academic system as well as those of the preceding Impressionist school.

Seurat. In the work of Georges Seurat (1859–1891) there are similar form factors. Identified with a special group known as neo-Impressionists (also as pointillists and chromoluminarists), Seurat in *Sunday Afternoon on La Grande Jatte* (fig. 513) projects an even more straitly reasoned version of the clean-color system. Only superficially a vacation picture, it avoids the spontaneity and charm of such works as the Renoir *Luncheon of the Boating Party.* Moreover, it takes the earlier clean divided colors, which were placed in approximate rather than exact relationships, and utilizes them in a stricter, more precise manner. Now each regularly shaped spot of color is applied with exact reference to another related spot. In addition to regularizing the tonal relationships of the colors, the shape of the mosaiclike dots, and their separation by tiny white canvas spaces, Seurat and his neo-Impressionist colleagues also tried to systematize the character of the compositions they devised. Here in a scene of rest the arrangement stresses the horizontal; in a more active theme such as *The Circus* (Louvre), the effect is diagonally upward; and so on.

Fig. 513. Seurat: Sunday Afternoon on La Grande Jatte. Courtesy, Art Institute of Chicago.

As in Cézanne's work, the same depersonalized solemnity suppresses the factor of enjoyment in favor of a controlled rendition of a form and color sensation. Again, every element in this two-year-long task is arranged to contribute to total balance and compositional completeness. It moves plane by parallel plane from the color-shadowed figures in the foreground to the enclosing wall in the rear and returns step by step from one depth to another and finally back to the exact center, the point of rest, where the mother and child "stroll" immobilized toward the

Fig. 514. Gauguin: The Day of the God. Courtesy, Art Institute of Chicago.

spectator. Just as Cézanne's form emphasis is to affect often diverse masters like Matisse, Picasso, Braque, and Beckmann, the art of Seurat
touches the work of such men as Léger and Ozenfant with their later
adaptations of the traditional French idea of balanced and controlled
forms.

Gauguin. Paul Gauguin (1848–1903) and Vincent Van Gogh (1853–
1890) — the more spiritual, symbolic, and emotive representatives of
post-Impressionism — similarly employ the products of Impressionism
for their much changed and controlled versions of nature. Gauguin's *The
Day of the God* (fig. 514) clearly shows his method of reducing what he
sees to a series of arranged and decorative patterns. Here he has proceeded
from observed natural fact (the figures of the Tahitian natives and their
background) in an abstract direction, simplifying the forms into graceful
organic linear outlines balanced against each other and transforming the
ripples of water in the foreground into large bold color areas. Both the
linear designs and the coloristic patterning are arbitrary rearrangements
of the facts, like the verticalized and restricted Cézannelike space.

Not only are the various figure areas related to each other in balance

624

and form, but the color areas are so distributed throughout the canvas that a blue in one locale will be related to a blue in another, even where in the original natural situation these blues may not have existed as such. For the purposes of aesthetic design or to heighten the emotional possibilities of the scene, the artist has taken it upon himself to make this alteration to bring about the desired pictorial effect. Gauguin's version of this universally applied artistic technique (medieval, Oriental, Egyptian) will have its immediate consequences in the work of Matisse and his Fauves and in the early-twentieth-century German Expressionists.

Van Gogh. Although Van Gogh shared the general tendency of the post-Impressionists to rearrange nature, his significance for modern painting goes beyond this. Like Gauguin, his decorative emotive formulations bore fruit in French Fauve painting and particularly in German Expressionist art. The *Cornfield with Cypress* (fig. 515) illustrates both his formalizing of what he saw and his injecting into this material a profound emotional quality, far different from the classic restraint of Cézanne and Seurat or the muted symbolism of Gauguin.

Fig. 515. Van Gogh: Cornfield with Cypress. London, Tate Gallery.

Under the influence of Japanese design with its two-dimensional qualities, accentuation of linear arrangement, and upward-tilting perspective, Van Gogh has patterned the various portions of this scene — the swells of earth, the little rock forms, the trees, and the sky itself. He enters directly into this portion of nature and transforms it from the clean charm of a Monet landscape into a symbol of tortuous, writhing unhappiness. This is effected by altering the small dots of Impressionist color into long wriggles of paint, applied with an eye to color contrast rather than bland combinations and complementaries. This color excitement will be used decoratively by painters like Matisse and emotively by such painters as Schmidt-Rottluff (see fig. 525).

Both Gauguin and Van Gogh may be said to have rebelled not only against the "deficiencies" of Impressionism but against the confused and oppressive character, the increasing tensions of the late nineteenth century itself. Gauguin consciously removed himself from this society by running off to the South Seas; Van Gogh, his whole being protesting against social injustice, brought into focus the anguish of the times.

Entering upon the extremely strained conditions of the early twentieth century, a tense, nervous, doom-foreboding atmosphere had its inevitable effect on the arts. The consequences of post-Impressionism with its formal and emotive contributions appeared in Fauvism, Expressionism, Cubism, and other movements in the first decade of the new century. These developments represent heightened versions of the post-Impressionist search for structural values or emotional symbolic relationships. The crises of the beginning of this century — social unrest, revolution, and threats of war — seem to have catalyzed artistic techniques. The fragmentation of reality and space tensions of Cubism, the warlike dynamism of Italian Futurism, the tortured colors and forms of Expressionism, the chaotic impulses of English Vorticism, are evidence of what was happening in the minds of artists.

Both the infusion of works with emotional meaning and the other powerful reactions were motivated by a feeling of imminent catastrophe. The protest character of Expressionism (Rouault, Schmidt-Rottluff, Barlach) was relatively obvious; the implicit protest of Cubists like Picasso and Braque or of Fauves like Matisse might not have been quite so apparent, although the shock quality of their art was very evident. It seems clearer today, in the light of later artists' experience with the destructive possibilities of our age, that the flight from everyday reality reached its first climax in the early part of this century. As part of the psychology of that time, this flight appeared in the wildness of the Fauves, in the form analysis and destruction of the Cubists and Futurists, and in the self-destruction of the Expressionists — all these things happening almost simultaneously. The out-of-jointness of the times was proclaimed by artists, writers, and musicians, who through lack of an appreciative audience were led further and further along the path of experimentation and subjective exploration.

THE FAUVES: *Matisse*. Henri Matisse (1869–1954) was the nominal leader of the *Fauves*, or "wild beasts," as they were at first derisively termed. His relationship to the preceding post-Impressionist tradition may be traced in *The Young Sailor* (fig. 516). The alteration of the original subject toward a deliberate arrangement of space, lines, and color areas for aesthetic rather than psychological effect brings it within the modern stream initiated by Cézanne. To the controlled shallow space (henceforth typical of so many twentieth-century painters and sculptors) is added an abstract color effect that stems from Gauguin; the broad color areas become even broader and higher keyed in pictures of this type. A relationship to Van Gogh is seen in the deliberate color contrasts; this may also be attributed partly to the sophisticating influence of Persian ceramics with their highly decorative and delicate tonalities.

The modeling of the figure in broad color planes derived from Cézanne and the powerful linear outlines and flat color areas derived

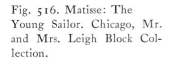

Fig. 516. Matisse: The Young Sailor. Chicago, Mr. and Mrs. Leigh Block Collection.

Fig. 517. Picasso: L'Arlésienne. New York, Walter P.
Chrysler Collection.

from Gauguin are supplemented by the color stridencies which, while dependent on Van Gogh, have gone a certain distance further. The painting
of one lip red and the other green, the contrast between green trousers
and bright blue shirt, are not mere deviations from observed facts; they
give the picture a good deal of its "wild" quality. Yet basically, however
powerful the color contrasts in these early Fauve paintings and however
violent their alteration of the outlines of the figure itself, they remain
involved with the problems of surface design, with bringing together the
various parts of the canvas. The Fauve effort, like the Cubist, being French
in origin, is still primarily a form experiment, as strange and new as it
may have appeared to the public and critics.

CUBISM: *Early Picasso.* Cubism, which began very shortly after Fauvism, is exemplified by Pablo Picasso (b. 1881) in *L'Arlésienne* (fig. 517),
which represents the early, or analytical, phase of the movement. In a
Cézannesque flattened space, the background and foreground are related
in a new and more abrupt manner. The first effect of such a picture is of
a canvas in motion, a kaleidoscopic impression of the solid portions of
the figure. This might be contrasted to the movement in Impressionist
work, which leaves only an impression of the light striking a form, an

628

external rather than analytical procedure. In early Cubism, influenced by African sculpture (figs. 7–8), the forms are broken down into a series of sharply angled, or faceted, planes.

Added to this kaleidoscopic quality is another new element. Traditionally, the painter viewed his subject from one static position outside the picture frame. Picasso and his Cubist colleagues, on the other hand, disintegrate the form into a series of simultaneously viewed but different aspects of the same subject. In order to achieve a greater understanding, or "analysis," of the figure, the Cubist painter "steps into the picture frame" and walks about the subject, observing it from various angles that strike him as significant, and recording these as his impressions of form. Although the Cubists were actually interested in greater understanding of the shapes they dealt with, one of the results of their undoubtedly startling and dynamic painting was the actual destruction of form and its reduction to a series of decorative elements. This was true in the next phase of their development, Synthetic Cubism.

Braque. The early work of Georges Braque (b. 1881) illustrates this Synthetic Cubist style, as in *Le Paquet de tabac* (fig. 518), one of his so-called pasted papers, or *papiers collés*. Here the painter begins with a package of tobacco in its environment, but instead of rendering the form impression received by "walking about" the motif, he arbitrarily joins bits of real wallpaper, playing cards, tobacco package labels, and other materials existing in the motif. These are selected not so much for form

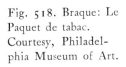

Fig. 518. Braque: Le Paquet de tabac. Courtesy, Philadelphia Museum of Art.

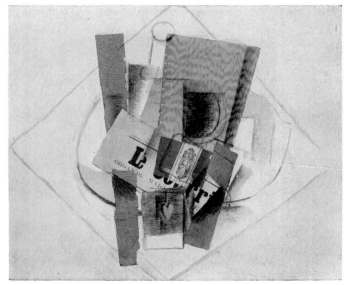

impact (as before) as for their decorative and composition-making possibilities as they are joined by a dash of line or color. There is still movement, but primarily in a surface sense rather than in the earlier and more three-dimensional manner. Where at first the Cubists tried to analyze the nature of the form, now they are more concerned with textural and decorative values.

In spite of the lack of conventional depth, these works maintain calculated and delicate color arrangements, interesting textural sensations, a unity of parts, and balanced surface structure — qualities that enable them to be considered works of art in the traditional sense. The pictures have little to do with the world at large; they stem rather from the studio, where the artists chose as motifs whatever happened to be around them.

FUTURISM. From the experiments of the Cubists came forth a considerable number of developments in painting, sculpture, architecture, and industrial art forms. One of the first was the Futurist movement begun before World War I, typified by the *Armored Train* (fig. 519) of Gino Severini (b. 1883). Futurism, primarily Italian, produced a dynamic, war-glorifying, machine-worshiping art that utilized the form-breaking

Fig. 519. Severini: Armored Train. New York, Richard S. Zeisler Collection.

techniques of Cubism in a more active, more coloristic manner on subjects involving speed, motion, and machinery. The *Armored Train,* painted during the war, conveys the movement and pace of battle and something of its emotion as well. Technically, the Futurists felt that both Impressionism and Cubism had destroyed the solidity of the object; these new activists proposed to restore it through the repetition of significant elements. This, they felt, would render an impression of form much as the Impressionists had given a sensation of light. Besides the repetition, they often added little chevrons across the surface of a canvas, directional indications called force symbols that were intended to augment the idea of motion.

Although it is questionable to what extent the Futurists succeeded in their aims, they did produce a more vividly colored and exciting version of Cubism based on themes of the outside world. Moreover, in turning the attention of artists to the mechanized nature of our society, they helped evolve an interesting facet of modern culture, the so-called machine art of the twenties and later years. Futurist influence also appears in pre-World War I English Vorticism and in the wartime Dada of France and Germany, which exalted an anti-rational and intuitive cacophony of colors and shapes.

Fig. 520. Léger: Elément mécanique. New York, Walter P. Chrysler Collection.

MACHINE ART: *Léger.* The "machine" development in painting of the twenties, which extended to sculpture, theater, and music as well, is represented by Fernand Léger (1881–1955) in *Elément mécanique* (fig. 520). While motivated by the machine aesthetic of the Futurists, Léger has here developed the style of the Synthetic Cubists with their decorative two-dimensional overlapping of parts — although with far more color excitement and with specific reference to the reduction of humanity (or anything else) to mechanical elements. The powerful human forms in other paintings of this period have the stolid impersonality of so many robots, their bodies composed of highly polished, cylindrical machine parts. These works have their starting points in specific and stimulating factual material and then become aesthetic arrangements in the Cubist sense.

Similarly, the nonrepresentational and geometric paintings of the Russian Constructivists and Suprematists and the Dutch *de Stijl* group clearly show their spiritual affinity to the machine age. A leanness of line and rigid formalistic patterns are used to relate stresses, weights, and color balances for their own sakes. In Cubist art the relationship between painting and the living world of men had become very slight. In the new nonobjective (i.e., without objects) painting, the last tenuous thread of recognizability and subject matter was finally snapped in the interests of pure design.

NONOBJECTIVE PAINTING: *Mondrian and de Stijl. De Stijl* (the style), or "neoplasticism," appears in Piet Mondrian (1872–1944) and is illustrated by his *Composition with Blue and White* (1935, fig. 521). Mondrian, a Hollander who had worked in Paris during the Analytical Cubist period, developed under the influence of the Russian nonobjectivists in a definite geometrical direction. This work is rigid and architectonic in form, simple to the point of austerity in color. The asymmetrical balancing of rectangular shapes and linear combinations creates a series of vertical and horizontal tensions. These are achieved through the shifting of proportions as the eye moves up or across the painting. At the same time, a limited and tightly controlled space quality is obtained through the overlapping of lines and the relative backward and forward effects of the

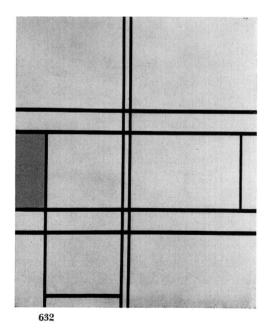

Fig. 521. Mondrian: Composition with Blue and White. Courtesy, Wadsworth Atheneum, Hartford.

632

Fig. 522. Le Corbusier: Still Life. New York, The Museum of Modern Art.

blue, black, and white color areas. An effective compositional unity results from the balancing of unequal rectangles within and around the two-armed cross that furnishes the foundation of the painting.

Kandinsky and Free Form. This geometric nonrepresentational style is paralleled by the free-form and amorphous nonobjectivity of artists like Wassily Kandinsky and his many followers in Europe and the United States (see fig. 526). This painter, who will figure prominently in our discussion of Expressionism, offers a more spontaneous counterpart to men like Mondrian. The art of Mondrian and his associates has had its consequences in the severe two-dimensional façades of the Bauhaus architectural school (1920–1933, see fig. 558) and in the industrial arts of our time — typography, poster design, advertising layout, furniture, etc. Kandinsky's painting has affected free-form, i.e., nongeometric industrial expression (as in irregularly curved table shapes and fabric patterns); and, as we shall see, certain contemporary developments in the fine arts may be attributed to Kandinsky's influence on his later adherents.

PURISM. The strictly geometric line, stemming from and related to Cubism, moves from the neoplasticism of Mondrian and his *de Stijl* school to the Purism of Le Corbusier, Ozenfant, and others. To these men the practices of Synthetic Cubism seemed too spontaneous — even capricious — and insufficient for their own rather austere purposes. They objected to the decorative emphasis of the Synthetic Cubists and tried consciously to attain a more formal, even architectonic, quality. Le Corbusier (Charles Edouard Jeanneret-Gris, b. 1888) is the distinguished Swiss-born architect whose conception of a house as "a machine for living" has influenced a whole generation of designers (see Chapter 27). His *Still Life* (1920, fig. 522) projects as mechanistic a conception as Léger's. Le Corbusier, Ozenfant (b. 1886), and their group, however, use universally significant forms that are considered necessary for "pure" art. These are either organic natural forms such as egg shapes or wing shapes (see Brancusi, fig. 544) or the machined forms of man-made objects as in the *Still Life*.

The Purists felt that paintings of this type should be able to compete with machine-made products in precision and craftsmanship. The meticulous joining of parts, precise draftsmanship, and machine smoothness of coloring bring them within the environmental framework of our modern age. Their historical importance, like that of *de Stijl* or Russian Constructivist works, lies in the speed with which their streamlined qualities have been absorbed by various industrial arts. All kinds of utilitarian objects from household appliances to automobiles, from furniture to boxes for commercial products, have been influenced by this viewpoint, which had its origin in the Cubist pre-World War I experiments. Some well-known industrial forms emerging from this stream of modern painting may be seen in the striking posters of A. M. Cassandre (fig. 523), which resemble the paintings of Le Corbusier and Ozenfant, and the packaging designs for such items as Kleenex, which derive from *de Stijl* art of Mondrian.

Fig. 523. Cassandre: Poster for the Wagon Lits. New York, The Museum of Modern Art.

This entire development, the more logical, formal, and constructionist phase of the modern movement from Cézanne through Picasso to the present day, has coexisted with another and opposed movement, the intuitive and emotional aspect of modern art. The latter, which includes the Fauves as well as the Central European and French Expressionists, owes more to the Gauguin–Van Gogh side of post-Impressionism than to the Cézanne side, though the formal elements in the work of Cézanne have had their effect on almost all schools.

ROUAULT. The genuinely "wild" aspect of Fauvism, only mildly and briefly apparent in most of its direct adherents, appears with particular force in Georges Rouault (b. 1871), whose work furnishes a link between the French and German modern schools. Rouault exhibited with the Fauves and is commonly listed as a member, but he remains considerably apart, as can be seen by comparing his *Mr. X* (fig. 524) with *The Young Sailor* by Matisse done the same year, 1905 (fig. 516). Matisse's work, with its primarily formal, decorative, and interestingly atonal quality, has relatively little psychological purpose, whereas Rouault's conception is filled with emotional meaning. It cuts through the ordinary form ideas of the period to achieve a spiritual rather than physical essence, communicated through the deliberately unbeautiful face, the wide staring eyes, and the tortured feeling conveyed by the restless movement of heavy lines. Rouault, who is an outside element in the Fauve story, can be looked upon as an Expressionist. Like his German contemporaries of 1905 in Dresden, he expresses unhappiness, emotive tortuousness, a con-

Fig. 524. Rouault: Mr. X. Buffalo, Albright Art Gallery.

stant turning inward, and an overwhelming desire to destroy reality in order to discover the emotional truth that lies behind it.

EXPRESSIONISM. Rouault is by no means typical of France; but in Germany the background of mysticism, romanticism, and powerful emotional drives makes a violent reaction understandable. The explanation of these tendencies is not a question of German native characteristics opposed to French, but of a difference in historical and social background. In France the traditions of democracy had developed naturally and gradually with the growth of the middle class; this had not happened in Germany. There one cannot speak of a nation until after 1870; there also Prussian militarism, medievalism, and political separation of provinces had gone hand in hand with a retarded economy and an underdeveloped parliamentary system. The German social order stressed duty — to church, family, and country. Most aspects of life fell into controlled patterns, beginning with the home, where the father often still exercised the rigid authority of earlier centuries, and extending into the schoolroom, the place of work, the army, and politics.

The majority of Germans, having been brought up that way, were unaware that the system bred psychic tensions; but many intellectuals found it intolerable. They rebelled in a flaming reaction that came to be known as Expressionism. In the authoritarian drum-beating Germany of pre-World War I were two distinct groups of rebellious artists: those organized in 1905 as *Die Brücke* (The Bridge), and the short-lived exhibiting society of *Der Blaue Reiter* (The Blue Rider, 1911–1913). After that war a third group, the so-called New Objectivity artists, appeared as apostles of despair and hopelessness.

Before World War I, the Expressionists represented a turning away from the unpleasant reality of the time. They denied the importance of the material and physical world with which they could not agree. But unlike the analytical and logical or the mainly atonal response of contemporary Cubists and Fauves, that of the Expressionists was turbulent and emotional in direct ratio to the repression which confronted them. Generally speaking, the pre-World War I German (and other) Expressionists divide into two main streams — the figurative and the semi-abstract — roughly corresponding to the *Brücke* and Blue Rider groups, respectively. The postwar New Objectivists were figurative and often quite naturalistic in approach.

Die Brücke. In *Die Brücke* were its intellectual leader Ernst Ludwig Kirchner (1880–1938), Karl Schmidt-Rottluff (b. 1884), Emil Nolde (1867–1956), Erich Heckel (b. 1883), Max Pechstein (1881–1955), and Otto Mueller (1874–1930). The growth of their rather homogeneous style took place under the influence of post-Impressionism (especially

636

Van Gogh and Gauguin), the linear symbolism of the Norwegian Edvard Munch, the decorative structures of Matisse, the stark power of African sculpture, and medieval German art. Their viewpoint was primitivistic and strongly emotive, with overtones of anguish, terror, and even demonic aspects. Kirchner, for example, was indebted to Van Gogh for the spasmodic character of his stroke and the deliberately harsh atonalities of his color. Like his fellows, he was concerned with inward qualities achieved through the distortion or destruction of form, color, and space. In this process, painters like Kirchner, Schmidt-Rottluff, Heckel, and the rest tried to remove the outer fact in favor of the inner truth.

Kirchner's protest is rather philosophical, as in the many versions of *Street Scene* (like the Museum of Modern Art example), which he uses as a symbol of our unhappily anonymous existence. The art of Emil Nolde, on the other hand, is particularly demonic in some of its manifestations, such as his *Magicians* (Museum of Modern Art), expressed through tortured-looking persons and frenzied religious scenes. Schmidt-Rottluff, in the *Evening by the Sea* (fig. 525) and many other works, especially his stark woodcuts, has a mystical and nonmaterial outlook. Using the substance of African primitive art (figs. 7–8), he conjures up a series of creatures from another world, with whom he identifies himself; they move lonesomely across the sharply cut canvas surface in boldly outlined and violently hacked-out unnaturalistic forms. Colors as well as

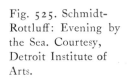

Fig. 525. Schmidt-Rottluff: Evening by the Sea. Courtesy, Detroit Institute of Arts.

forms are purposely sharp, dissonant, and abrupt in this particular version of the Expressionist desire to lose oneself in infinity, to dissolve material form in order to be absorbed into the nonworldly.

This viewpoint, usually representational or figurative, is also seen in the work of a good many independents, i.e., unaffiliated men and women of the pre-World War I period — Oskar Kokoschka (b. 1886), the brilliant Viennese painter and playwright; Ernst Barlach (1870–1938), the distinguished German sculptor, graphic artist, and dramatist (see fig. 547); and others in different parts of Central Europe. Kokoschka and Barlach, each in his own way, have achieved unique recognition for their profound understanding of the human soul. Kokoschka's continuing tortuous representations of life have had wide influence in Germany and elsewhere.

The Blue Rider; Kandinsky. The less representational side of Expressionism appears in the painters of The Blue Rider, led by the German Franz Marc (1880–1916) and the Russian Wassily Kandinsky (1866–1944), who lived in Germany. Marc is clearly related to the dynamic color and form analyses of the Futurists; Kandinsky begins from a Fauve decorative basis mingled with the linear symbolism of Art Nouveau (cf. Toulouse-Lautrec, fig. 494). From here he moves toward a nonfigurative play of lines and colors. Pictures like his *Improvisation* (1914, fig. 526) illustrate this; its musical rhythms and mystical pulsating style are de-

638

signed to create in the spectator a "state of soul." It is the ultimate in Expressionist denial of matter and substance, interested only in "a graphic representation of mood" resulting from the combinations of psychologically meaningful linear movements, form blendings, and color patterns.

By 1910 Kandinsky had already arrived at the nonrepresentational improvisatory art which offered a potential way out for the coming generation of nonobjectively inclined artists in many countries who felt an emotional inadequacy in *de Stijl*, Constructivism, or Purism. For these men the spiritual and lyrical qualities, the emotive and penetrative possibilities of Kandinsky's art, have meant a great deal. In various parts of the world, especially in America during the forties and fifties (see figs. 537, 539), this approach has proved fruitful.

Klee. The innocent animals (*Blue Horses, Red Deer, Yellow Cow*) with which Marc identifies himself, the peasants in their presumed simplicity who attract Heinrich Campendonk (b. 1889), or the boats and old buildings that draw Lyonel Feininger (1871–1956) back to his childhood tend to become part of a constantly moving and vibrating cosmos of which the Blue Rider painter is necessarily a part. Paul Klee (1879–1940) frequently used this pictorial technique, but his unique

Fig. 527. Klee: Actor's Mask. New York, Sidney Janis Collection.

lyricism and personal feeling are added, besides the unusual, even mordant, sense of humor with which he makes telling comments on man and his actions. Klee also exemplifies his group's ability to identify themselves with simple beings, in his case children or mentally disturbed people, whose art techniques he simulated in many of his works (fig. 527).

Like most of the Expressionists, Klee was drawn to primitive and generally unsophisticated art forms for the expression of a conscious naïveté that is in some ways the essence of sophistication, as in his *Actor's Mask*. This is reminiscent of African art (see fig. 7) as well as of the unlearned effects of children's drawing in which the simplicity of expression penetrates the outside of the object to some inner meaning. It leads to a fresh and exciting, sometimes vaguely disturbing, view of the object shown. Like other Blue Riders, Klee with his highly developed intuition often shares the experience of some unspoiled creature. The freshness of his imagery and the new meanings given to old ideas were of tremendous interest to the Surrealists of the 1920s and to the Abstract Expressionists of the forties and fifties.

New Objectivity: Beckmann. The third branch of the German Expressionist movement, the New Objectivity of the 1920s, was a product of the disillusionment and hopelessness that existed after World War I.

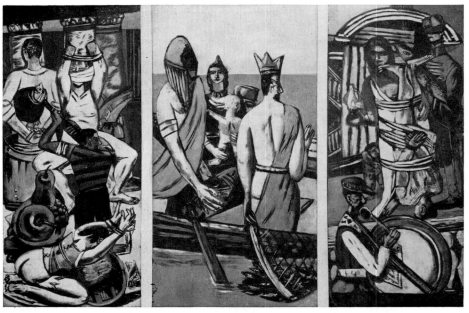

Fig. 528. Beckmann: The Departure. New York, The Museum of Modern Art.

640

Among these painters and graphic artists were George Grosz (b. 1893), Otto Dix (b. 1891), and Max Beckmann (1884–1950). Beckmann belonged to this group primarily in his early works; but in such later paintings as the famous *The Departure* (fig. 528) are still found the merciless clarity and detail, the starkness of feeling, that characterized the mid-twenties. Here, as in most of Beckmann's mature work, the penetrating, almost painful objectivity and distinctness of style carry a poetic and symbolic meaning, in place of the morbid and despairing renditions of Grosz, Dix, and many others.

Beckmann was one of the artists who were forbidden by the Nazis to exhibit or even to work. *The Departure* is an allegory on the painter's existence in Nazi Germany, expressed in the physical tortures of the left-hand panel and the psychological tortures (including the incessant propaganda drum beating) of the right-hand panel. From these cramped and bedeviled areas, the story moves into the deep calm perspective of the central portion, where the "king" and his court depart to a hopeful future. The deep spaciousness of this center panel, its clarity and visionlike mood, are qualities shared by other New Objectivists as well as by Surrealists of the twenties. But the Surrealists are concerned with psychoanalytical problems and the dream area of the mind, whereas the Expressionist Beckmann is interested in the individual soul and its relationship to the universe.

SURREALISM. During the early twenties, the development of psychiatry as a means for rehabilitating thousands of battle-shocked victims of the war led to parallel interests in literature and art. Even before the war, painters like Marc Chagall and Giorgio de Chirico in Paris had utilized similar ideas independently; in Germany, Paul Klee had attempted to project himself into the paranoiac mind. The Italian de Chirico (b. 1888) contributed to the subconscious mechanism of Surrealism a nostalgic interest in the past, probing into his own subconscious and that of his native land through long perspectives, deep shadows, and a blending of elements from past and present. The Russian-born Chagall (b. 1890) has combined the real and the unreal in a richly colorful dream manner, heightening the intensity of the experience into a new poetic super-reality.

The organized Surrealists of the twenties, exemplified by Salvador Dali (b. 1904), believing in the subconscious as a guiding factor in human activity and thinking, insisted that it was very important to free the unconscious mind from everyday restraints and inhibitions. The painters felt they could accomplish this by painting while under the influence of the subconscious or by portraying the world of dreams. In this way they tried to match the therapeutic measures of psychoanalysis and to release the individual from conflicts between his natural desires and the censoring effect of inhibition, by bringing these conflicts out into the open.

Technically, pictures like Dali's *Paranoiac Face* (fig. 529) have the meticulous clarity of a true dream experience, in which unusual or impossible things may take place with such precision of detail, such super-realism, or *surréalisme*, that they are bound to be believed at that moment.

Fig. 529. Dali: Paranoiac Face. London, Collection Edward James. Photo courtesy, The Museum of Modern Art.

It is perhaps debatable whether such naturalistic images can be rendered while the artist is under the direct influence of the subconscious. Undoubtedly, however, Surrealists have given new and fresh, even humorous, associative meanings to their subject matter by juxtaposing unrelated and incongruous items, as Jerome Bosch did (fig. 318). In the *Paranoiac Face*, Dali has presented a strange double image in which figures are both themselves and parts of something else. Thus the people seated about

642

an African kraal, when they are looked at more closely, become parts of a large head lying on its side. The line made by the person lying down at the left furnishes the bridge of the nose and one eye; the kraal itself becomes the cheek and jaw; the trees turn into hair; the jug at the right becomes the chin; and so on. This is evidence of the Surrealist painter's desire to project in concrete images the illogical, the unreal, and the spontaneous — the irrational impulses of modern man.

While painters like Dali and the more humorous Yves Tanguy (1900–1955) show the figurative side of Surrealism, other artists, more abstract in character, represent its nonfigurative aspect. Typical of this latter side of the movement are the playful, ingenious, and highly decorative works of Joan Miró (b. 1893), the dynamic restless compositions of André Masson (b. 1896), and the extraordinarily imaginative art of Matta (see fig. 539). These men are abstract in style while maintaining some reference to objects; but the free forms and soft amoebalike abstractions of Jean Arp (b. 1888) go further in the nonobjective direction. Both the figurative and nonfigurative sides of the Surrealist movement present another variant of the modern artist's attempt to avoid reality or to alter it.

PICASSO AND THE MODERN MOVEMENT. Throughout all the developments in modern art, ever since the early Cubist experiments, the creativity and personality of Picasso have been among the most powerful forces on the contemporary scene. Countless artists in every part of the world have been affected by the many transmutations of his evolution. These phases have not always been entirely his own creation, for as one artist expressed it: "He has borrowed from all of us, and yet beat us at our own game." This is at least partially true, to the extent that Picasso himself was influenced by such movements as Expressionism and Surrealism. But they were adapted and modified for his own highly individual purposes, invariably resulting in something new, something Picassoesque and very influential in its turn.

This process is illustrated with particular force by his celebrated *Guernica* (fig. 530), the painter's violent denunciation of the Fascist bombardment of an unarmed Basque city during the Spanish Civil War of 1936–1939. The basic fragmentative Cubism is combined with a flaming, soul-searching Expressionism, adding finally the fear-evoking, nightmarish quality of Surrealism. This impressively large painting with its severely limited black-gray-white palette symbolizes the suffering of Picasso's countrymen at that moment: the screaming woman at the right; the dismembered man in the foreground; the agonized and cubistically viewed horse in the center (the Spanish people); and the brutal triumphant bull at the left (the invader), standing calmly over a mother

Fig. 530. Picasso: Guernica (oil on canvas, 11′ 6″ by 25′ 8″). Owned by the artist. Photo courtesy, The Museum of Modern Art, New York.

who holds a dead child. It also foretells World War II, for which this struggle was one of the early tryouts. A naked electric light bulb casts its harsh glare over the scene into which an outraged figure (Justice) with an oil lamp thrusts its demanding arm. The great impact of this picture at the time of its creation, and its pervasive influence since then, cannot be computed mathematically, but it has surely provided a strong and fruitful source of ideas, as many derivative works in Europe and America amply prove.

SOCIAL REALISM: *United States and Mexico.* In the Americas, painting during the twentieth century has been as variegated as the diverse European currents — traditional and modern — by which it has been affected. At the same time, the traditions of native realism (figs. 505–508) have been reinforced on a new level. The late-nineteenth- and early-twentieth-century realism reappeared in the United States during the depression years after 1929 as a school of Social Realism. From Mexico, which had produced a native realism in the nineteenth-century black-and-white print, came the most significant mural movement of modern times. This art resulted from the Mexican Revolution of 1910–1920, which had overthrown the dictator Díaz; under the sponsorship of the post-Revolutionary government, mural art was intended as a didactic weapon of social reform. After its first flowering in the early 1920s, it reached a second climax in the middle thirties and also influenced realistic easel and mural painting in the United States during the depression. The example of a government-sponsored art was one of the factors leading to establishment of the United States Federal Arts Projects, as a means of helping unemployed artists (including musicians, writers, and others) through the worst depression period. This art, designed for public consumption, necessarily took on a realistic quality.

Both in the United States and in Mexico, Social Realism represented a distinct contribution to the panorama of contemporary art. In Mexico it reached a more significant level, but in the United States it was a relatively short-lived phenomenon, overwhelmed by the increasing pressure of the abstract movement. Although modernism was in abeyance during the Federal Art Project period, it was in fact, paradoxically, fostered by the Project, since actual and potential modernists were thereby enabled to exist as artists.

Most of the recent development in the United States has been in the realm of abstract and less representational art. In addition to outstanding creations in the field of modern architecture and industrial design, twentieth-century art in the United States has paralleled most of the European movements and occasionally has combined modern forms and its own native realism with great effectiveness. This has been particularly true of certain Regionalist (and Social Realist) painters of the thirties who turned to more abstract formulations. These painters, who portray the conditions and the nature of this country in the modern idiom, include such men as Jack Levine (b. 1915) and Hyman Bloom (b. 1913) of Massachusetts, Everett Spruce (b. 1908) and William Lester (b. 1910) of Texas, Ben Shahn of New York (see fig. 538), and many others.

Mexican mural movement. In Mexico the contemporary movement sprang up partly in revulsion against nineteenth-century academicism and even more in response to a specific social need of that moment. It has remained essentially representational in character and little affected by the various modern usages that have been operative in the United States. It is primarily a mural movement, and easel painting has had relatively small scope — with some significant exceptions such as Tamayo. Its four principal figures are Diego Rivera (b. 1886), José Clemente Orozco (1883–1949), David Alfaro Siqueiros (b. 1898), and Rufino Tamayo (b. 1899), the last-named striking a different and more international note.

Rivera, the most widely publicized of this group, has mainly used the Renaissance fresco medium for his publicly intentioned art, together with drawing methods and compositional arrangements from the same source. As a Paris-trained painter, however, he also shows an awareness of post-Impressionist controlled space. One of the earliest and most impressive of Rivera's mural jobs was executed in Mexico City's Secretariat

Fig. 531. Rivera: Soldier, Peasant, and Worker. Detail from Secretariat of Public Education frescoes. Mexico City.

Fig. 535. Méndez: Deportation to Death (linoleum cut). Courtesy of the artist.

MODERNISM IN THE UNITED STATES. While Mexican mural and easel paintings have been for the most part representational, this has not been true of painting in the United States. Here, since the famous Armory Show of 1913 which introduced the modern idiom to the American public, there have been successive waves of Cubist, Fauve, Expressionist, Surrealist, Purist, and other European-developed styles. Moreover, though many painters have been content to repeat the ideas gleaned from abroad, a goodly number of men and women have had the imagination to develop their own, frequently important variants. The work of several of these artists can be taken as a sampling, while it is recognized that there is actually a considerable complex of interwoven and diverse trends.

Stuart Davis (b. 1894), one of the exhibitors in the 1913 Armory Show, was first influenced by Van Gogh and Gauguin, from whom probably come his strong decorative sense and feeling for dynamic color combinations. In the early twenties he was working with the *papiers collés*, or pasted-paper techniques (cf. Braque), moving on to increasingly abstract still-life paintings. *Something on the Eight Ball* (fig. 536), like much of Davis's work, begins from a concrete subject rather than an aesthetic motif. In a manner suggesting such moderns as Léger, the material is reduced to geometric abstractions endowed with depth as well as surface

Fig. 536. Davis: Something on the Eight Ball. Philadelphia Museum of Art. Photo courtesy, Downtown Gallery, New York.

movement, coming toward the spectator in a series of attractively dissonant color combinations. Numerous other variations of the geometric approach may be found in abundance in the United States. These formulations have met with a critical acceptance and are amply represented in the exhibition catalogues of The Museum of Modern Art, the Whitney Museum of American Art, and other institutions.

The more intuitive side of modern painting that produced both Expressionism and Surrealism is also practiced by a considerable group of artists in the United States and Latin America. Paul Burlin (b. 1886), another Armory Show veteran, has gone through successive stages from figurative to semiabstract and ultimately to Abstract Expressionism. In earlier works strongly condemning injustice and stupidity, and then more mystic and symbolic in the semiabstract paintings of his next phase of Expressionism, he has lately come to the nonfigurative method that has been everywhere typical of the post-World War II period. Although paintings like the *Nude Figure* (1953, fig. 537) are in the general improvisatory tradition stemming from Kandinsky, Burlin projects a highly personal and far more violent, deliberately atonal and strident form and color arrangement.

Another, more representational type of Expressionism extremely well received in this country may be related to the German New Objectivity school of the 1920s. Many of its adherents, exemplified at a high level by Ben Shahn (b. 1898), belonged originally to the depression period of the thirties, when despair and disillusionment moved them to adopt this technique. Shahn first came to public notice with his restrained but bitter pictures on the Sacco-Vanzetti case. After assisting Diego Rivera in the Radio City mural job (1933), he participated like many others in the mural program of the Federal Art Project. Shahn early developed a precise and linear technique in which brilliance of decorative color contrasts with the social content of the pictures. Paintings such as *The Red Stair-*

way (1944, fig. 538) add a certain poetic element to the deep bitterness of the earlier works. The feeling in this scene of European devastation is no longer purely stark, but more lyric in its mourning. A figure at the right carries its burden of broken rubble, and the cripple at the left mounts the red staircase which goes up toward the sky but comes down abruptly. Characteristically, the figures exist in a deep space with emptiness and desolation all about them.

Roberto Matta Echaurren (b. 1912) is a Chilean whose connections were originally with the Paris Surrealists but who has shown widely in the United States, where his work has influenced a number of people. Matta represents the abstract side of the Surrealist movement, together with such painters as Masson and Miró. His rich coloristic imaginativeness may be traced to such diverse sources as Turner, Kandinsky, and Miró. In pictures like *The Invasion of the Night* (1941, fig. 539), softly flowing and indefinable space elements mingle with the underlying fearful and yet playful quality of Surrealist thinking. These strange, abstractly formed, suggestive, otherworldly shapes show Kandinsky's lyricism changed to a projection of neuroses and subconscious impulses. Like some other Surrealists, Matta is frequently concerned with erotic motivations, expressed in provocative and visually suggestive, though nonrepresentational, forms.

Matta's participation in the international modern movement differentiated him until recently from most of his Latin-American contemporaries who, though very much influenced by traditional European culture, had not yet fallen under the spell of the abstract school. In many coun-

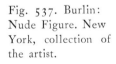

Fig. 537. Burlin: Nude Figure. New York, collection of the artist.

Fig. 538. Shahn: The Red Stairway. Courtesy, City Art Museum, St. Louis.

Fig. 539. Matta: Invasion of the Night. Mill Valley, Calif. G. Onslow-Ford Collection.

654

tries of South and Central America (as in Mexico) a twentieth-century nationalistic or, better, nativist art grew up, generally based on academic models. Exceptions to this have been painters like the Mexican Rufino Tamayo, the Guatemalan Carlos Mérida (b. 1893), the Brazilian Candido Portinari (b. 1903), and the Cuban Carlos Enríquez (b. 1900). Such men in varying ways have long responded to more advanced styles; and only in the past few years there has been a further growth of modernism in some Latin-American countries.

During the post-World War II period in the United States, besides the continuation of many geometric, Expressionist, and Surrealist styles, a series of new formulations have come forward. Among the main groupings are the so-called New York school of Abstract Expressionism, led by such artists as Jackson Pollock (1912–1956) and Willem de Kooning (b. 1904); and the mystic painters of the Northwest, e.g., Mark Tobey (b. 1890), Morris Graves (b. 1910), and Kenneth Callahan (b. 1906), centering around Seattle, Wash.

The first and more controversial school is characterized by a varying mixture of Abstract Surrealism, Abstract Expressionism, and in its most extreme form Dadaist practices involving the spontaneous and intuitive spattering of paint. Influences from Klee, Kandinsky, Masson, Matta, Miró, Arp, and similar sources may frequently be noted in this imaginative and intensely subjective art. Parallel developments have taken place in many countries in Europe and even in Latin America. The second group, the mystic painters, in their sensitive and often poetic techniques vary from the representational shapes of Callahan and Graves to the ideographic forms of Mark Tobey, with strong traceable influences from the philosophy, art, and calligraphy of the Orient. Both the New York and Northwest groupings are symptomatic of postwar sharing of modern cultural leadership by the United States and Europe. This development is even more clearly marked in the field of sculpture.

SCULPTURE

The sculpture of this century naturally has many qualities in common with its painting and architecture, as happened in earlier periods. This includes the practice of sculpture by painters such as Matisse, Picasso, and others (sculpture which necessarily is related to the general work of the artist), as well as specific sculpture movements which parallel those in the other arts.

At the very beginning of the century a good deal, if not all, of European and American sculpture followed traditional forms, primarily those of the Renaissance as adapted by the nineteenth century. This so-called humanist view is demonstrated by outstanding classicistic sculptors like Aristide Maillol (1861–1944) and Charles Despiau (1874–1946). The former with his monumentally general and serene forms (fig. 540), the latter with his equally controlled portrait heads, might be equated with the post-Impressionist phase of modern art, both combining the search for form with a meaningful emotional viewpoint. The conservative, or traditional, form viewpoint has continued to operate since the early part of the twentieth century. American sculptors like William Zorach (b. 1887, fig. 541), Chaim Gross (b. 1904), Robert Laurent (b. 1890), and many others remain productive in this stream of culture. A more mannered variant of it, akin to the symbolism of the late nineteenth century as expressed in Art Nouveau decoration and illustration, is to be found in the work of Carl Milles of Sweden (1875–1955) and Ivan Meštrović of Yugoslavia (b. 1883), now in the United States.

The American-born Jacob Epstein, living in England (b. 1880), compares with Van Gogh to the degree that both are concerned with setting the form into motion in the interests of emotive and subjective quality. Epstein in his well-known *Madonna and Child* (1927, fig. 542) uses everyday types for a presumably sacred theme, exaggerates the size of eyes, hands, and feet, and roughens the surface textures to achieve an inner probing emotionality.

Fig. 540. Maillol: Night. Courtesy, estate of Maurice Wertheim. Photo courtesy, Curt Valentin Gallery, New York.

656

Fig. 541. Zorach: Affection. Utica, N.Y., Munson-Williams-Proctor Institute. Photo courtesy, Downtown Gallery, New York.

Fig. 542. Epstein: Madonna and Child. New York, Brooklyn Museum of Art.

CUBIST AND POST-CUBIST WORKS. The sculptures of Matisse and Picasso represent their respective aesthetic attitudes at each stage. On the Cubist level, some of Picasso's early "constructions" parallel his paintings. The work of Jacques Lipchitz (b. 1891) follows first the primitivism, or Africanism, of early-twentieth-century art (cf. also Amadeo Modigliani and his African-derived forms in painting) and then goes through a number of Cubist and post-Cubist developments. Lipchitz

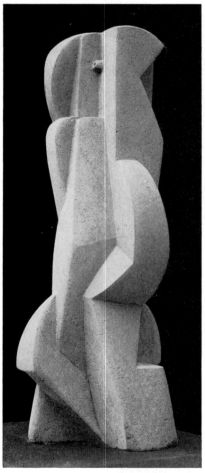

Fig. 543. Lipchitz: Seated Figure. Courtesy, Curt Valentin Gallery, New York.

Fig. 544. (Right) Brancusi: Yellow Bird (wood). Philadelphia Museum of Art, Arensberg Collection.

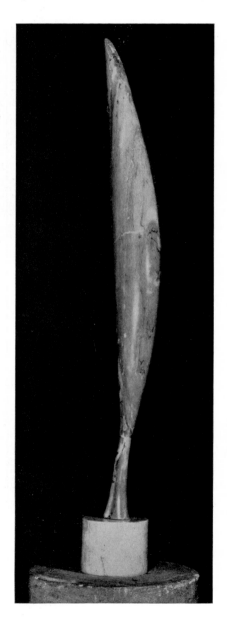

Fig. 545. Gabo: Linear Construction, Variation. Washington, D.C., The Phillips Collection.

parallels the spatial qualities of Synthetic Cubism in such works as the tightly organized limestone *Seated Figure* (1918, fig. 543). Later phases of this master's work bring into being a series of powerfully poetic narrative symbols with more rounded masses of a primordial strength, rivaling those of the British Henry Moore and exploiting the possibilities of spatial dynamics.

Post-Cubist sculpture exhibits the Purist forms of Constantin Brancusi (b. 1876) and the Constructivist arrangements of Nahum Gabo (b. 1890). Brancusi's *Yellow Bird* (fig. 544) is analogous to the paintings of Le Corbusier in which the artist offers so-called "pure" forms, either recognizable and typical shapes from nature or those of the machine. Here, in a highly polished and machined simplification in wood, the sculptor has used the universal wing shape to symbolize flight. Instead of attaching it to a representational form, he has placed it on end so as to imply both wing and bird head. It gives an irresistible sense of upward movement, to such an extent that this small figure could well be a monument to aviation.

Gabo's *Linear Construction, Variation* (fig. 545) symbolizes the contemporary interest in new industrial materials, fostered in Russian Con-

Fig. 546. Moore: King and Queen (bronze). New York, Joseph Hirschhorn Collection. Photo courtesy, Curt Valentin Gallery, New York.

structivist and German Bauhaus circles, as well as the conception of sculpture as a series of interpenetrative planes. In contrast to traditional block form (cf. fig. 540) or pictorial Baroque, the ideas of men like Gabo and his brother Antoine Pevsner (b. 1886) from the geometric side, and others like Henry Moore from the free-form side, are concerned with the penetration of the mass. Gabo accomplishes this both by the transparency of the plastic material — which brings the light into play as an agent, piercing the various transparent planes of the object — and by the literal opening up of the form itself. Works of this kind are not seen merely from the fixed point (or points) of block sculpture or as the external visual experience of Baroque pieces; here one moves visually into the shape in order to follow the artist's form sensation or form idea.

An outstanding exponent of this interior spatial viewpoint has been Henry Moore (b. 1898); and Lipchitz has also achieved very effective interpretations in this area. Moore's *King and Queen* (1953, fig. 546) has a rather impersonal quality that suggests the high polish and integration of parts in some new sort of machinery. At the same time, the various open areas give the impression of erosion that has taken place through millennia, an association that lends a certain elemental feeling, evoking the forces of nature and our desire to get close to them. These figures, which appear half-rock and half-human, are usually designed for outdoor purposes; they consist of huge masses containing limb-and-body forms with tiny heads, accentuating the effect of life emerging from the earth itself.

EXPRESSIONISM. Expressionism in its figurative aspect appeared in the sculpture of *Die Brücke* members like Schmidt-Rottluff and Kirchner and in the creations of Ernst Barlach. Barlach's sculpture (fig. 547) composes the form in the violent rhythmic movement characteristic of that school, while conveying its sense of ecstasy and obliviousness to the world. Just as in figurative Expressionist painting, the aim of the sculptor is to reach a maximum of feeling while holding the form in aesthetic control; the movements and rhythms are balanced, one part moving in one direction, another in the opposite and counterbalancing direction. Another sculptor in this same general area is Wilhelm Lehmbruck (1881–1919), whose emotional quality is introspectively lyrical rather than violent.

Among semiabstract Expressionists, the American Minna Harkavy (b. 1895) expresses a strong sympathy for humanity in meaningful form combinations. Seymour Lipton (b. 1903), also stemming from this tradition, has developed a new nickel-silver technique for poetic, semifigurative as well as abstract forms that has been widely used in connection with architecture.

Fig. 547. Barlach: Ecstatic Woman. Courtesy, Curt Valentin Gallery, New York.

RECENT TRENDS. Sculptors have greatly stimulated American art. One group stresses a complex and space-penetrative geometry, and another a more biomorphic character (i.e., based on living forms) with strong emotive power. In the first category, the precisely integrated linear structures of men like Richard Lippold (b. 1915) and Ibram Lassaw (b. 1913) deal with geometrically shaped space cages and with a delicately pre-

Fig. 548. Roszak: Fire-Bird. Chicago, Mrs. Albert H. Newman Collection. Photo courtesy, Pierre Matisse Gallery, New York.

sented subconscious interest. In the second group, men like Lipton, Herbert Ferber (b. 1906), Theodore Roszak (b. 1907), and David Smith (b. 1906) are concerned with the potent expression of intense feeling. Both groups have in common the use of newer materials such as plastics, steel, and wrought iron.

Roszak has attained brilliance in geometrical design as well as in the more Expressionist type such as his *Fire-Bird* (fig. 548). This violently

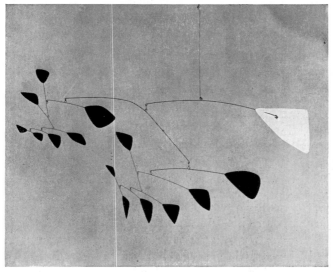

Fig. 549. Calder: 7 Red, 7 Black, 1 White. Courtesy, Curt Valentin Gallery, New York.

thrusting shape is far removed from any romantic lyricism or Brancusi-like pure form. The agitated, fierce, and jagged figure expresses the sculptor's own belief that "the world is fundamentally and seriously disquieted, and it is difficult to remain unmoved and complacent in its midst." Roszak has projected themes such as this and his *Skylark* in the tortured biomorphic style that is his statement of the apocalyptic times in which we live.

Aside from the major world trends in twentieth-century sculpture, there are other artists who defy easy classification, but who are important individually. The American Alexander Calder (b. 1898), inventor of the fascinating "mobiles" (e.g., fig. 549, 1952) contrived from lengths of wire and differently shaped and colored pieces of flat metal, presents in these works highly intuitive renderings of motion. They suggest in a general way the movements in nature, or movement in the Abstract Expressionist rhythmic and musical sense of Kandinsky.

The distinguished Italian sculptor Marino Marini (b. 1900) shares

Fig. 550. Marini: Horse and Rider. Courtesy, Curt Valentin Gallery, New York.

with many of his countrymen a certain nostalgia for the past, in his case expressed through subtle evocations of Chinese art of the T'ang period. His equestrian figures (fig. 550) have an underlying emotional content, smoothness of movement (without moving), and a conscious conveying of the eye around all sides of the figure — traits that mark the contemporary sculptor. Without reproducing the actual form of Chinese work, Marini has achieved a clear feeling of its actual presence in the timeless modernity of his own art.

27 / ART IN THE MODERN WORLD: *Twentieth-century Architecture*

THE man-centered nature of architecture has tended to keep it closer to the everyday world. It has largely avoided the flight from reality that has marked modern painting and sculpture in their movement toward the nonfigurative and subjective. As a "useful" art, architecture relates to the specific needs of people and is constructed from mundane materials in functional relationships dictated by utility as well as aesthetic need. Although both architecture and industrial design (including furniture, typography, layout, ceramics, posters, and other forms) often parallel the experiments of advanced painting and sculpture, these ideas become part of a building or industrial product, where today their demonstrable function allows them a readier public acceptance.

UNITED STATES: EARLY MODERN ARCHITECTURE. Like contemporary painting and sculpture, modern architecture had its roots in the late nineteenth century, when technological progress and sometimes social necessity made certain advances possible. In the United States, however, the fact that new design techniques were developed by architects like H. H. Richardson, Louis Sullivan, and L. S. Buffington did not necessarily mean that they would be adopted immediately. In spite of such structures as the *Guarantee (Prudential) Building* (fig. 502), the end of the nineteenth and the beginning of the twentieth century still saw revivalistic styles applied even to the new skyscraper form. Cass Gilbert's *Woolworth Building* (fig. 551), finished as late as 1913, illustrates the conflict between contemporaneity and tradition in its use of Gothic elements and adaptations to express the much desired sense of verticality (cf. fig. 266). In this 767-foot-high structure, the architect has piled a twenty-five-story tower on a thirty-story base which is divided into two parts. The upward thrust is borne by the continuity of the vertical piers, the diminishing length and bulk of the successive masses, and the repetition of vertical terminal points at the corners, culminating in a pointed spire.

Although Gilbert made this building soar powerfully upward and

Fig. 551. Gilbert: Woolworth Building, New York.

even conveyed the feeling that the weight is carried by the vertical elements of the metal framework, there are certain drawbacks. The windows are relatively small and admit a limited amount of light where light is needed. This defect is heightened by the projection of the piers, which also offer a shelter for bird droppings and other dirt accumulation, as do many of the ornamental details. The tower areas are naturally well lighted, but in the base section, because of its division into two parts, a great many rooms face a narrow interior court. Finally, in buildings of this kind, the need for upward movement has been fulfilled in a nineteenth-century fashion. Such paradoxes occurred with many painters, sculptors, and architects who resolved their new needs in terms of the museum and its traditional styles, instead of seeking a genuine contemporary solution.

Wright: early buildings. Louis Sullivan had attempted a new approach, but his effort had mainly been ignored. In the same way, the modernizing of residential and other design problems was proposed by Sullivan's great pupil, Frank Lloyd Wright (b. 1868), but his ideas were given scant attention in this country for a long time — although they were well received in Europe, where things were already stirring at the beginning of the century. Wright's functional viewpoint, first expressed in his Prairie Houses, was a nontraditional attitude that related the particular residence in form to its environment. His famous *Robie House* (fig. 552, 1907–1909) in Chicago presents a long, low outline blending into the surrounding flat landscape, with vertical accents skillfully placed against this horizontality. The overhanging shallow roof and porch eaves offer maximum shade, while the cantilevering, or projecting outward, of the same porch eaves (supported only by the framework of the building) allows the unimpeded entrance of fresh air required by summer heat.

Windows are not treated as excuses for ornamental detail but as organic parts of the plan, helping to unite interior and exterior.

Most interesting in some ways is Wright's handling here (and in later instances) of the problems of interior space. The *Robie House* does not have the traditional careful division of one room from another, but encompasses a continuous flexible area with spaces flowing into each other and arranged around fireplaces that once more relate interior to exterior. The two major rooms on each floor are brought together without doors or walls; only the main chimney and staircase act as separation. This elastic handling of interior space reappears in many examples of so-called International Style architecture in the twenties (cf. *Tugendhat House,* fig. 559).

At this early point in his career, Wright also designed new types of office buildings and churches, such as the Larkin Building at Buffalo, N.Y. (1905–1906), and the Unity Temple at Oak Park, Ill. (1905–1906). Both of them, like the *Robie House,* indicate that his architecture is no formula. Every building throughout his long career has been looked at as a problem in itself, its solution dependent on the particular needs of the client. This makes it difficult to classify him as readily as other contemporaries, but it also makes him most rewarding to observe and study. Wright's early work propounded an alternative to traditionalism even on the level of the skyscraper, in his functional design in 1912 for the San Francisco Call Building (never carried out). Nevertheless the initial ef-

Fig. 552. Wright: Robie House, Chicago, Ill.

Fig. 553. Hood and Howells: Chicago Tribune Tower, Chicago, Ill.

Fig. 554. Hood, Godley & Fouilhoux: McGraw-Hill Building, New York.

forts of progressive architects to proceed in terms of modern materials and their requirements, in terms of a building's function, remained obscured by the popular adherence to traditional formulas.

Developments in skyscraper form. The backwardness of American architecture was nowhere so dramatically illustrated as in the design competition of 1922 for the *Chicago Tribune Tower.* Out of the many designs submitted, first prize was awarded to the Hood and Howells plan (fig. 553) from which the building was constructed. Like its Woolworth predecessor, this structure consists of a series of unbroken vertical masonry lines covered with Gothic ornament wherever possible, and here culminating in a circle of flying buttresses at the top that support a Gothic shrine form. Historical interest is added by its apparent relation to the Butter Tower at Rouen, but its suitability in the modern field is questionable.

There were some in 1922 who knew better. We deduce this because the second prize in that competition was awarded to the Finnish architect Eliel Saarinen (1873–1950). In his design there was clear acceptance of Sullivan's "form follows function," an avoidance of the traditional, and a simple expression of the nature of the steel frame and its upward motion without extraneous decorative detail. Although it did not win the competition, Saarinen's design was destined to have considerable effect on the history of the American skyscraper. The impact of his ideas is demonstrated in various ways by later structures like the New York Telephone Company Building (1926), the *McGraw-Hill Building* (1931, fig. 554), and the New York *Daily News Building* (1929–1930, fig. 555). This is especially true of the first two: the solid massiveness of the Telephone Building reflects the direct simplicity of the Saarinen project; and the *McGraw-Hill Building* shows how, within a few years after the *Tribune Tower*, Raymond Hood himself (1881–1934) was influenced by the simple geometry of his competitor.

The *McGraw-Hill Building*, like the *Tribune Tower* originally designed to contain presses, reveals unusual understanding and growth on the part of its architect. His radical shift from a conservative to a progressive formulation is remarkable enough — and the later career of Mr. Hood in connection with Radio City and other buildings shows that the conversion was permanent. Even more interesting is the solution proffered here for the skyscraper problem as such. While the weight of such buildings is carried by vertical steel beams and therefore the chief accent should be on verticality, it is equally true that the structures themselves consist of superposed horizontal units, or boxes. This consideration apparently led Hood and his associates on this project (Messrs.

Fig. 555. Hood and Howells: Daily News Building, New York.

Godley and Fouilhoux) to devise a series of cubic and rectangular forms piled zigguratlike on top of each other, preserving as far as possible the horizontal accent by means of continuous horizontal bands of attractive sea-green masonry and arrangement of the windows in groups of four, divided by regular and short vertical accents.

In the *Daily News Building* (fig. 555) this rather calm and gentle solution apparently had not been suitable. Here Hood and Howells offered a powerfully upthrusting and dramatically conceived design whose verticality is only slightly ameliorated by the prescribed "setbacks." This conscious upward violence is sharply different from the equally deliberate calm of the *McGraw-Hill Building*. The two structures may even be contrasted in their individual sections. The *Daily News Building*, with its excitingly planned entrance lobby graced by a spectacular world globe sunk into the floor, giving in its constant motion a sense of contact with the world at large, is consistent with a newspaper headquarters. In the *McGraw-Hill Building*, on the other hand, there is a simple unaccented entranceway, where the dramatic yields to the constant. Perhaps the difference lies in the function and character of the clients — the newspaper dramatizing its role, the publisher presenting his products less boldly and with more permanence.

A compromise between the verticality of the Daily News edifice and the relative horizontality of the McGraw-Hill structure may be found in the elegant design of the *Philadelphia Savings Fund Society Building* (Howe and Lescaze, 1931–1932, fig. 556). This moved away to a certain extent from the "higher and higher" philosophy of immediately before and after World War I, animated by a desire to get the most out of every inch of available real estate, when business enterprise at its freest and most unrestricted had driven the skyscraper to unprecedented heights. The effects may be noted in the towering dark canyons of downtown New York City, where the buildings are set so closely together that they deprive both the pedestrians in the streets below and the occupants in the buildings above of light, air, and visual access to their surroundings. These structures of the Wall Street district sum up not so much Sullivan's dictum that a skyscraper should be "a proud and soaring thing," but the fact that it was profitable.

The negative factors mentioned and the increasing congestion of areas dominated by the mass-designed skyscrapers had led to zoning laws which produced the setback forms seen in the McGraw-Hill, Daily News, and similar structures. The ordinances specified that a building could rise di-

Fig. 556. Howe and Lescaze: Philadelphia Savings Fund Society Building, Philadelphia. Photo courtesy, The Museum of Modern Art, New York.

rectly from the street only in proportion to the width of that street, after which its façade had to be set back a certain distance before it could proceed upward. This was, however, only a partial cure for the ills of the skyscraper, which during the thirties often turned out to be economically unsuccessful as well as aesthetically unsatisfactory. The climax of the movement toward maximum height was reached in New York by such examples as the Chrysler, R.C.A., and Empire State buildings which, however spectacular and valuable as publicity, have contributed to the strain on city transportation resources.

The trend away from maximum height was signalized by such buildings as the *Philadelphia Savings Fund Society Building,* which while vertical in its main masses is equally insistent on the horizontal line. It is set on a gently curved rectangular base enclosed in glass and granite. The upper part of the building, its limestone bands alternating with gray brick between the windows, presents a handsome balancing of vertical and horizontal accents. Verticality is effected through the aluminum corner strips and the upthrusting elevator shafts fixed to the building's sides. Horizontal movement comes from the cantilevering out of the floors, which permits the architect to run continuous bands of windows across each floor, as in the *McGraw-Hill Building.* Windows of this type are necessarily more efficient than those set farther in behind dividing masonry strips as on the *Daily News Building* or the *Tribune Tower.*

In the *Philadelphia Savings Fund Society Building* verticality for its own sake no longer dominates the design, any more than in the slightly earlier McGraw-Hill structure. In both of these the wall no longer functions as a wall that encloses a mass, but as a plane surface enclosing a given volume of space. In the earlier example, however, the architect treated his problem as a series of differently shaped sections of stone piled on each other, whereas Messrs. Howe and Lescaze have produced a greater uniformity and integration in which the mass of the building is subordinated to its openness, its revealed structure. In this regard, the *Philadelphia Savings Fund Society Building* is closer in spirit to the so-called International Style, which emerged in the twenties, than to the traditional American skyscraper idea.

EVOLUTION TOWARD INTERNATIONAL STYLE IN EUROPE. The International Style, produced in post-World War I Europe, is characterized by an emphasis on the enclosure of volumes of space rather than the projection of volumes of mass. It tends, moreover, toward an irregular arrangement of parts; the resultant composition is dynamic and asymmetrical rather than symmetrical. Finally, it depends for decorative effect on the possibilities of the materials employed and the good proportions of the composition, in place of the traditional mechanism of applied ornament. Although a few American architects had envisaged such an approach at the very beginning of the century, as in the *Robie House* and other examples, it remained for European architects in England, Scandinavia, Holland, France, Austria, and Germany to provide a broader development for the style and to give it international currency during the period immediately after World War I.

A few generations earlier, the nineteenth-century Industrial Revolution in Europe had brought into being an entirely new set of social and economic circumstances, with new architectural needs such as factories, office buildings, laboratories, railroad stations, schools, hospitals, mass housing, and the many other forms that mark modern democratic society and its urban development. In these areas the traditional architect was faced with unfamiliar problems that had to be examined and solved as they arose. Ultimately he was to find that the old methods, perfectly adequate for the eighteenth-century upper-middle-class residences — or for early-nineteenth-century descendants — were not suitable for these newer needs. More than anything else, this meant that the refinements of taste and proportion which had served architects up to the modern age simply were unable to cope with such practical problems as the housing of machinery, the housing of the increasing number of workers drawn to the cities, and similar conditions. On the other hand, certain types of public buildings, such as museums, churches, hotels, and even railroad stations, could be, and were, encased in the ornamental styles of the past for a long time indeed.

It was left for European and American engineers — rather than architects — to take the first full advantage of the new materials and situations produced by the nineteenth century and to work toward a functional type of architecture, i.e., toward a type of structure that was related to the materials and necessities of our time. Both in Europe and America this development was eventually significant. Just as later the initial semifunctional structures on this side of the Atlantic profited from an imaginative handling of the new materials, those of Europe had similarly benefited. England, the home of the Industrial Revolution, can show such early examples as the 1824–1828 St. Catherine's Docks in London by Thomas Telford, a simple rectangular five-story building, decorated with round and flattened arcades in a way that suggests the later structures of Sullivan and his school. At the middle of the century there were such edifices as the Crystal Palace (1851) and the King's Cross Station (1852) in London with their generous use of glass and iron. These examples stood out against the background of constant borrowings from the past, which continued into the early twentieth century. Mid-nineteenth-century England had also produced a declassicized type of irregular but functionally arranged private house plan, destined to influence late-nineteenth-century builders — such as Frank Lloyd Wright in his early days.

Toward the end of the nineteenth century the Belgian, Dutch, and French Art Nouveau decoration was applied to the exteriors of buildings, which themselves were often designed for practical purposes with the new materials. The light, graceful, and airy Art Nouveau designs consisted of involved and swingy linear elements stemming from plant forms. They emerged simultaneously in the painting of Lautrec, Gauguin, Van Gogh, and their end-of-the-century colleagues, in the illustrative art of the same period, and finally in the architecture of many countries, including Germany, Belgium, Holland, France (the Metro stations), and the United States (Louis Sullivan). However appropriate these calligraphic undulations may have been in the symbolist painting and illustration of the late nineteenth century, in architecture they would seem to represent a reluctance to do without some form of extra ornament. By the early twentieth century, various Europeans (notably Austrians and Germans) began to react positively to steel, glass, and concrete as such, foregoing the organically twisting Art Nouveau decorations. Austrians such as Adolf Loos (Stiner House, Vienna, 1910) and Otto Wagner (Vienna Post Office Savings Bank, 1905), Germans such as Peter Behrens, indicate the strength of the new movement in Europe.

Behrens (1868–1940), who was the architect for Germany's General Electric Company, is perhaps best known for the *Turbine Factory* (1909, fig. 557), built in Berlin for his employers. Like most of the buildings he did for this company, the *Turbine Factory* was a direct avowal of the rela-

Fig. 557. Behrens: Turbine Factory for AEG, Berlin.

tionship between the modern structure and its materials. It was one of a growing number of instances in which efficiency and practicality were the determining factors. Here a single, very long chamber with large wall areas of glass is contained within angular concrete piers at the corners, its steel trusses and columns frankly expressed on the exterior. As in the later International style itself, applied ornament is avoided in favor of such intrinsic decorative elements as the color of the red-brick facing, the gray-green of the roof tiles, and the purple of the door frames. Its combination of verticals, horizontals, and diagonals, its simplicity and starkness of outline, make this one of the most impressive pre-World War I buildings. Yet since the architect treated the composition as a grouping of powerful masses in the traditional sense, it can be maintained that it does not fall within the category of the space-enclosing — rather than mass-enclosing — structures that were to characterize architecture after World War I.

INTERNATIONAL STYLE: *Gropius.* The latter viewpoint, heralded by such a transitional example as the Stuttgart Railway Station (1913–1927) by Paul Bonatz (b. 1887), emerges with forceful clarity in the work of slightly later architects in all parts of Europe. In Germany, Walter Gropius (b. 1883) and Ludwig Miës van der Rohe (b. 1886); in France, Le Corbusier; and in Holland, J. J. P. Oud (b. 1890) represent the major variants of the International style, which ultimately spread far beyond the borders of their respective countries.

Gropius, a pioneer modernist, was first noted for his leadership of the world-renowned Bauhaus workshop at Dessau, where use and understanding of modern materials and methods were developed. Here a group of designers and artists worked together in the stimulating atmosphere of the shortlived post-World War I German Republic and its advanced social aims, trying to formulate types of architecture and industrial design that would be most expressive of the modern age. In the course of the conscious attempt to bring architecture into direct relationship with the period and with its general aesthetic orientation, the Bauhaus invited a number of artists as collaborators. These included Paul Klee, Lyonel Feininger, and Wassily Kandinsky, as well as more mechanistically inclined painters such as Oskar Schlemmer, Herbert Bayer, Josef Albers, and Laszlo Moholy-Nagy, most of whom have left their mark on later industrial design.

Organized under Gropius in 1919 at Weimar (seat of the then German Republic), the Bauhaus moved in 1925 to Dessau, where it lasted until 1933 and the advent of the Nazis, who halted modern architecture, painting, and sculpture in Germany simultaneously. Many of the original adherents of the Bauhaus came to the United States, where they have stimulated the growth of industrial art as artists, teachers, and directors of design institutes.

In his emotionally stirring manifesto written on the founding of the Bauhaus in 1919, Gropius tried to instill the idea that architects, sculptors, and painters were to work together to produce an architecture in which the "artificial" distinctions between fine and applied art would be put aside. Here would be the "building of the future" which would use architecture, sculpture, and painting at the same time. However visionary this appeal may have appeared then, it is noteworthy that a good many of the collaborators at the Bauhaus developed important practical techniques in design and architecture as well as such theoretical works as Kandinsky's book *Point and Line to Plane*. From the outside, furthermore, came the stimuli of Russian Constructivism and Dutch *de Stijl*, or neoplasticism, both movements reflecting in primarily aesthetic media the character of the machine age (Chapter 26). The *de Stijl* theoretician Theo van Doesburg visited Weimar many times; El Lissitzky, an important Russian Constructivist, came to Germany frequently between 1922 and 1926, and the Russian Gabo spent most of the years between 1920 and 1933 in Germany.

Gropius's first architectural contributions belong to the pre-World War I period, when with Adolf Meyer he designed the Fagus Works at Alfeld a. d. Leine (1913) and the Exhibition Pavilion for the Deutscher Werkbund at Cologne (1914). These prefigure his most famous postwar building, the *Bauhaus Machine Shop* (1926, fig. 558), in which most of the precepts of the new architecture are represented. The steel framework here supports not walls but a screen of transparent glass panes that act as elements of space — rather than volume — enclosure. Instead of the traditional arrangement of parts around a central portal, there is a repetition of equal parts stemming from the nature of the structure itself, with the entrance thrown asymmetrically to the lower left-hand corner. No applied ornament adorns a building of this kind; the designer relies instead upon the nature of the materials, their color and texture, for decorative effect. The conception of logical function and a variety of spacing appear in the total number of Bauhaus buildings: the school, dormitory, office structure, director's house, as well as the workshop, each of them presenting a different spatial entity and geometrical form.

One of the first buildings of its kind in which the wall is totally removed in favor of the glass screen, the *Bauhaus Machine Shop* has had incalculable influence on modern development down to the forties and fifties, even in such examples as *Lever House* (see fig. 566) and the *United Nations Secretariat* (see fig. 565) in New York. Although these later examples have an *élan* of slender upthrusting proportions, they (and many contemporary buildings) ultimately owe their existence to buildings like Gropius's *Bauhaus Machine Shop*, however static the latter may seem today.

Fig. 558. Gropius: Bauhaus Machine Shop, Dessau.

Architects of the twenties, Gropius and Oud in particular, were much concerned with what they termed the sociology of modern architecture, its response to specific social needs. In that very depressed postwar period in Germany, the Social Democratic government sponsored an elaborate housing program that was planned for almost one-fifth of the country's population. To this program Gropius contributed his Siemensstadt Housing Project of 1929 in Berlin, a severe and economical design for a low-income group. Oud's spare and functional plans in this category are typified by his Hook of Holland project.

Miës van der Rohe. The geometrical logic and austerity of the Bauhaus and the designs of the other great German pioneer, Ludwig Miës van der Rohe, as exemplified by the *Tugendhat House* (1930, fig. 559), derive in many ways from the stimulus of *de Stijl* painters and

Fig. 559. Miës van der Rohe: Tugendhat House, Brno, Czechoslovakia.

architects such as Mondrian, Oud, and van Doesburg. The twinkling surface movements of horizontal and vertical lines in the *Bauhaus Machine Shop* suggest actual paintings by Mondrian during his 1914–1919 period, known as his "plus-and-minus" phase. This was later simplified by Mondrian and his colleague van Doesburg into flattened and more asymmetrical and tense arrangements, found in Mondrian's *Composition with Blue and White* (fig. 521), in the *Tugendhat House* façade itself, and in many other International-style buildings. Moreover, during the pre-Bauhaus years in Holland, various adherents of *de Stijl* had already arrived at an architectural and interior-design formulation consisting of just such dynamic arrangements of verticals and horizontals treated with large blocks of primary colors. These ideas van Doesburg brought to the Bauhaus school after the war and to German architecture generally.

In the case of Miës van der Rohe and his followers — as illustrated in the *Tugendhat House* — it has led to a precise, cold, and occasionally forbidding architecture, in which clarity of form in the pictorial sense may become even more important than utility and livableness. Two features are noteworthy in this private residence — the use of tremendous sheets of glass (in the rear of the building) to bring the inside and the outside into a continuous space relationship, and, within the same concept,

678

a continuity of interior space. The first factor implies the final negation of the wall, since the glass is now merely a transparent plane defining the interior space and offering a magnificent feeling of openness for the inhabitants of the house. This openness, on the other hand, is for many people psychologically unacceptable, if only in its lack of privacy. Architects of this school point out that such a difficulty can be overcome by curtains drawn across the windows to mask the exposure and exclude the summer sun; but then one loses the view and the openness. The uninterrupted interior spaces — as in the connected living room and library, which are divided only by a translucent onyx screen supported by chrome-steel posts — although beautifully articulated, do not always offer the most feasible solution for the practical problems of family living.

The *Tugendhat House* is far from the most extreme instance of this exceedingly influential trend in modern residential building. Set in the city of Brno, Czechoslovakia, its situation is different from those of the later chic country homes for which it has been adapted. Here the architect has treated the wall facing the street as an almost windowless arrangement to keep out the street noises, somewhat in the ancient Mediterranean fashion. In contrast he offers the interior openness with its positive and negative aspects. Finally, this extraordinary craftsman, originally trained as a furniture designer, has enriched his interior with a tasteful combination of such textures as glass, chromium-faced posts, amber-colored onyx, and gray floor linoleum. For architects opposed to Miës's formulations, buildings of this sort seem the very negation of space, since as treated here it has little character beyond its endlessness. Such opponents (primarily from the Frank Lloyd Wright school) claim this is formlessness and actual lack of a third dimension.

Le Corbusier. A third method in the International group that developed in the twenties was that of the painter-architect Le Corbusier, generally associated in architecture with his cousin Pierre Jeanneret. One of the best known of their early residences is the *Savoye House* at Poissy-sur-Seine (1929–1930, fig. 560). Just as the architecture of Gropius or Miës is aesthetically related to Dutch *de Stijl* art, so that of Le Corbusier is related to his own and Ozenfant's Purism formulated in 1918 (Chapter 26). To the same extent that Purism insisted on the relationship between modern technology and painting, the architecture of Le Corbusier continues this viewpoint in the idea of "a machine for living" conceived as early as 1923.

Apart from the apparent similarity in actual forms between the *Still Life* (fig. 522) and the windbreak top of the *Savoye House*, there is also a parallelism in the kind of colors used in both. These Purist colors lean

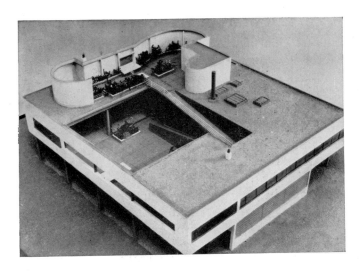

Fig. 560. Le Corbusier: Model of the Savoye House. Poissy-sur-Seine. Courtesy, The Museum of Modern Art, New York.

toward light pinks, blues, and dark brown — in contrast to *de Stijl's* bolder use of the primaries, red, blue, and yellow. Finally, in the precise adjustment of straight and curved emphases, the *Savoye House* follows fairly closely the character of the *Still Life.* As in other parallel formulations (e.g., Bauhaus and *de Stijl*), it is not a question of which came first, the painting or its architectural equivalent, but that they were both part of the same aesthetic trend. This kind of relationship was also felt in the architecture of Eric Mendelsohn and other designers of the pre- and postwar period who paralleled the development of the Expressionist idea, e.g., the Einstein Tower at Potsdam, and in the earliest work of the Bauhaus stimulated by the Expressionists Feininger, Klee, and Kandinsky.

The *Savoye House* shows a stimulating and artistically effective combination of horizontal, vertical, and round accents. The vertical columns are arranged with reference to the window divisions; the wind shelter combines in its round-straight form the general horizontality of the building and the cylindrical quality of the columns and the downstairs area. Various parts of the building are colored differently to distinguish their respective functions: the lower garage story is in dark green that relates it to the ground; the second, or living-room, floor (where the French prefer to live) is cantilevered out from the substructure in sober buff-colored cement; while the play function of the sunbathing shelter on the roof is shown in rose and blue. Le Corbusier is occupied with these aesthetic details in many of his exciting productions. To him, as indeed to many modern architects, the building must be a work of art above all, and modern living should rise to its level. The intense concentration of space effects for their own sake is part of this attitude, as is the frequently encountered interest in façades set up like a Mondrian painting with one or two dramatic openings in an otherwise bare wall. Le Corbusier also adds the somewhat dehumanizing function of the carefully tooled "machine for living." The opponents of this viewpoint assert that a house should not be a machine, and that living in an efficiently functioning residential machine might eliminate more desirable personal factors.

AMERICAN DEVELOPMENT: *Wright.* While Le Corbusier, Miës van der Rohe, and Gropius represent in their several ways the International aesthetic of the twenties and thirties, which has further evolved in all parts of the world since then, the American Frank Lloyd Wright has constantly striven for an altogether different approach. For him the house has never been an aesthetic unit sufficient unto itself, but rather a conception stemming from the particular needs of the individual or family. In addition, he has preached and practiced the idea of a house (or building of

Fig. 561. Wright: Kaufman House ("Falling Water"), Bear Run, Pa. Photo courtesy, The Museum of Modern Art, New York.

any kind) integrally related to the natural background in which it is placed. Strongly opposing the "machine" viewpoint, he feels that modern man is threatened by the machine and should try to subordinate it to his own needs.

The function and locale of Le Corbusier's house (fig. 560) may be opposed to those of Wright's *Kaufman House* (1936, fig. 561), known as "Falling Water," built at Bear Run, Pa. The *Kaufman House* is constructed partly from local rough stone and partly from smooth reinforced concrete, which offer effective contrast. It is perched on a series of stone ledges overlooking a waterfall, illustrating Wright's principle that buildings should grow from their sites. Instead of standing aloof and isolated from its background like the *Savoye House,* Falling Water shows the relationship between the lower concrete block, cantilevered out over the waterfall, and the chief stone ledge, while the block laid across at right angles follows the movement of the water itself. The rough stone forms reflect the rest of the background. In Wright's own terms, this and all his residences going back as far as the *Robie House* (fig. 552) are organically integrated with their environment. His structures, moreover, are not conceived in the idealized and nonmaterial manner of International architecture, whose large window areas or pseudo walls bind space volumes. In his construction, blocklike masses are related and superposed, treated almost sculpturally. Wright's orientation as an architect might be referred to the art climate of our time by comparing his work to the form ideas of Constructivism (fig. 545), which are concerned with the interpenetration of volumes, their overlapping and reciprocal movements.

In spite of his acidulous criticism of the International style, more than a generation ago Wright himself contributed to it by devising a continuous and flexible interior space, as in the *Robie House*. In this area as in the use of textures rather than applied ornament, deliberate asymmetry rather than balance, and frank expression of the nature of the materials used, Wright undoubtedly was one of the first to state the ideas which were later developed and varied by the International school. Whether or not he was the very first, it is important to realize that the architectural climate of the early twentieth century produced many of these phenomena more or less simultaneously. Without denying the great contribution of the Sullivan-Richardson school and its influence on Wright and his followers, this same historical stream had its parallels abroad, as noted above.

Wright is not only a great pioneer in modernizing the individual residence; he has also done the same for factories and offices, as in the Larkin Building at Buffalo in 1905–1906, or churches, as in Unity Temple at Oak Park, Ill., in 1905–1906, where he showed the possibilities of breaking away from traditional formalized plans, materials, and decorations in the solution of modern building problems. A later example of his factory units is the *Johnson Wax Company Administration Building* (fig. 562) at Racine, Wis., completed in 1939 at a time of mounting interest in Wright's work after long neglect by his countrymen. This is another effective illustration of the highly individualistic planning and use of materials that give Wright's architecture its romantic flavor. Externally, a rich red brick is used in carving out a sweepingly curved, flat, square structure, topped by diminishing circular accents upon one end. Inside, glass neon tubing in the ceiling provides a diffused lighting system as well as textural contrast with other materials. Below this attractive stretch of glass, the red-brick balconies sweep down to the floor, from which a series of up-tapering hollow concrete columns rise to reminiscently Egyptian exaggerated flat capitals. The slimness of these columns leaves ample floor space for the continuous 400-foot area, in which long oval-shaped desks offer a transition from the round to the straight lines that comprise the building's chief structural accents.

Ten years later, Wright added his spectacular *Laboratory Tower* (1949, fig. 563) to the Johnson Wax Company complex at Racine. This sixteen-story tower is one of the most imaginative and beautiful build-

Fig. 562. Wright: Administration Building (right) of the Johnson Wax Company, Racine, Wis.

Fig. 563. Wright: Laboratory Tower, Johnson Wax Company, Racine, Wis. Photo courtesy, Guggenheim Museum.

ings of our day. The architect has alternated a series of square and round balcony floors which have been cantilevered out from a central vertical core containing elevator, staircase, and other facilities. The whole is enclosed by red-brick bands, bringing the building within the color scheme of the entire factory, and by two-story-high window expanses of pyrex glass tubing. The *Laboratory Tower* is tied to the rest of the structure by a covered walk bordered with pools. From a functional viewpoint, its arrangement allows the tower to be divided into separate two-story laboratories (each with one round and one square floor) which are lighted from the window walls. Aesthetically the effect of the various contrasting surfaces seen directly in the sunlight, indirectly with the sun behind the structure and revealing its treelike aspect, and finally at night when it takes shape in another form through artificial lighting, affords one of the truly exciting experiences in modern architecture.

There is little question that in Wright's office and factory structures he has been interested and able (because of the unlimited expense budget, as in this case) to keep in mind the needs of the people working there. These needs have often been realized with great effectiveness, which has been taken to indicate a social attitude, especially since Wright has also ventured into the field of sociological thinking and pronunciamento. But this extraordinary designer is a great individualist whose architecture is not basically a product of community spirit so much as a glorification of the individual and his fulfillment. For the most part, Wright's houses have been for the wealthy, the limited few rather than the masses of people. In general, the same applies to anti-Wrightians of the Miës–Le Corbusier-Gropius persuasion.

684

During the past generation, especially in the period after World War II, many variations of the two design approaches have continued side by side. The *Johnson Wax Company Laboratory Tower* achieves one of the climaxes of an art that includes Wright's brilliant spiral plan for the Guggenheim Museum in New York, his fancifully intriguing 1949 Morris store in San Francisco, the sculpturesque Bartlesville, Oklahoma, skyscraper (fig. 564, 1953–1956), and other examples by Wright and by those he has influenced. The latter include such men as Harwell H. Harris, William W. Wurster, and John E. Dinwiddie. Harris's house for Ralph Johnson in Los Angeles (1951) testifies to this influence.

International trend in America. In the opposite group, the postwar period has brought a number of advanced ideas by Miës van der Rohe, most notably the austere Farnsworth House (1950) in Plano, Ill., and the machinelike Lake Shore Drive apartments in Chicago (1951). The latter consist of twin buildings, twenty-six floors high, in steel-enclosed concrete frames set at right angles to each other on the shores of Lake Michigan. The steel beams act as window mullions, with the glass areas repeated endlessly over the façade. The outer uniformity of these window surfaces is made even greater by the gray curtains with which each tenant is furnished (inside they may install anything they like). All the

Fig. 564. Wright: Price Tower, Bartlesville, Okla. Photo courtesy, H. C. Price Company.

Fig. 565. United Nations Secretariat, New York.

steel elements are painted black, in contrast to the aluminum window frames and gray curtains.

A variant of this approach is the development of the slab building, a flattened rectangle of glass-enclosed spaces rising high into the air. Such outstanding examples as the *United Nations Secretariat* (1950, fig. 565) and *Lever House* (fig. 566), both in New York, present a somewhat similar solution to the problem of monumentalization. These buildings are analogous to Miës's glass-cage structure in Chicago and derive from the same common source — the post-World War I products of architects like Gropius (fig. 558). Both the *Secretariat* and *Lever House* are office buildings, however different their ultimate spiritual purposes, and to that extent their functions, necessities of circulation, air, and light, may be equated.

The internationally designed *Secretariat* overlooking New York's East River is thirty-nine stories high and is planned to accommodate some four thousand people. On the east and west, it is enclosed in blue-green glass set in aluminum frames, the mass twinkling in the reflected and shimmering light from the river. The narrow, windowless north and south sides are faced with white marble. A perhaps more successful variant of the slab formula is achieved in *Lever House,* built for the Lever Brothers soap company by Skidmore, Owings, and Merrill in 1950–1952 — unhampered by the conflicting interests of the many architects of different nationalities who planned the United Nations building. Here a relatively

Fig. 566. Skidmore, Owings, and Merrill: Lever House, New York. Gordon Bunschaft, chief designer.

Fig. 567. Rockefeller
Center, New York
(center, R.C.A.
Building, 1932).

low twenty-four-story building (indicating the trend away from monster
skyscrapers of the past) is set back gracefully from the street on a one-
story, glass-enclosed base, placed over walks and a garden designed for
public use. More than fourteen hundred panes of blue-green, heat-re-
sistant glass are held in a stainless-steel frame.

The fact that *Lever House* and the *United Nations Secretariat* are
treated not as part of a beehive city, but rather as free-standing entities
surrounded by air and space, results from both the theoretical dicta of Le
Corbusier and from a practical demonstration offered by the remarkable
assemblage of buildings known as *Rockefeller Center* (1931–1947, fig.
567). The fifteen structures in this magnificent complex in the heart of
New York City are spread out over a four-block-square area in which the
units do not interfere with each other's light, air, or space. When seen
from different heights, the arrangement presents differing but equally
stimulating views. From the air — and surely modern architecture may
be viewed from the air also — *Rockefeller Center* has the appearance of

688

intersecting vertical and horizontal plus and minus signs that once more bring to mind the geometry of Mondrian. Seen from adjacent structures, these elongated blocks take on something of the slab form of the later *Lever House* or *United Nations Secretariat* (to some extent most skyscrapers give this effect). But where the R.C.A. Building slab is irregularized by its setbacks, the others in the complex have smooth edges, since the space around them makes setbacks unnecessary.

In the evolution of the modern skyscraper concept, it is as though the piled-on units of Gropius's *Bauhaus* have been rearranged and drawn upward into the general outline of the *Lever House* or United Nations building. This concept has come a long way from the Equitable Building of 1915 and similar edifices that rushed upward, unheeding the disastrous results of unregulated construction. Today's *Lever House* and the new Socony Building (1955–1956), designed by Harrison and Abramovitz, represent a broader and, it is hoped, more lasting attitude in their landscaped towers and their willingness to sacrifice some of the ground space in the interests of their own beauty and visibility and the city's welfare.

ARCHITECTURE AND MODERN MAN. Only in a limited way does modern architecture express the ideals of modern man as Gothic or Baroque did of their epochs. These great structures represent the power and technology of our time in a proud and soaring manner, but our ideals do not stop at power and technology or the glorification of commerce. Yet an architecture which began from primarily practical considerations cannot perhaps be expected to reveal our spiritual outlook to the same extent as painting, sculpture, or literature. The *United Nations Secretariat* seems no more symbolic than the even better designed *Lever House*.

In private homes the situation is somewhat easier, since here the questions of impressiveness and technology for their own sakes do not loom as important. Here man can be put into a more comfortable and unmechanistic environment. On the other hand, the bulk of good examples, whether by the individually minded Wright or his International competitors, are homes for the rich, like the *Kaufman House* (fig. 561). The avowed aim of many of these buildings is to bring man once more into touch with nature, however romantically Wrightian or endlessly spatial the concept that effects this joining. But this merely emphasizes the dilemma of urban living, a dilemma which today is solved only by spending a relatively large sum of money or by moving a considerable and inconvenient distance away from one's work.

For the average man overwhelmed by the big city with its noise, dirt, and crowding, neither the optimistic skyscraper nor the escapist country castle of glass offers any real solution. The serious degree of self-strangu-

Fig. 568. Apartment-house developments. Facing Guanabara Bay, Rio de Janeiro.

lation that has been reached in our cities has brought about an increasing number of urban and suburban housing developments geared to the earnings of middle- or low-income groups. Here the accomplishments of mass production are harnessed for the good of a greater number; in many cases the public or private sponsors of these enterprises have been able to provide decent dwelling units with light, air, and space at modest prices. This problem, too, has been solved by the modern functional architect where the opportunity has offered itself, generally during times of stress when something had to be done — the post-World War I period in Germany, the depression thirties, and the projects of recent years arising from the choked conditions of our cities.

Many examples of successful apartment-housing plans have appeared since the period after World War I, including early ones like Gropius's Berlin Siemensstadt Project of 1929. In the thirties there were such instances as the Highpoint Flats in London by the Tecton group (1935); the Cité de la Muette in Drancy, France, by Beaudoin and Lods (1934); and the Williamsburg Houses in Brooklyn, N.Y., built under a group headed by R. H. Shreve (1937). Many others have been and are being erected, down to the present day, such as the recent striking examples on Guanabara Bay in Rio de Janeiro (fig. 568) or the 1955–1956 Gratiot-Orleans plan for rebuilding blighted areas of industrial Detroit (fig. 569). The Brazilian example typifies the suburban approach to the mass-

690

housing problem; the Detroit example, designed by Victor Gruen, Minoru Yamasaki, and Oskar Stonorov, proposes an intracity solution. In the latter case a badly deteriorated area in a large city has been cleared for redevelopment in a program that will try to reverse the increasing movement toward the suburbs by building suburbs within the city. The non-profit corporation handling this project hopes ultimately to change the face of Detroit by offering a number of architecturally and socially attractive features. These include a high quality of housing at a reasonable figure, a layout planned to meet the needs of the automobile age (ready access, off-the-street parking, etc.), and a varied pattern of accommodation. Many-storied and differently shaped apartment buildings, set on lawns, mingle with six-family court units, arranged around common gardens and playgrounds to help avoid the deadly monotony that often accompanies reasonably priced housing in other areas.

Buildings like these furnish a clue to what modern architectural methods can accomplish for the welfare of man, and how in the final analysis they may express his social aspirations. Besides housing projects, there are religious centers, hospitals, schools, theaters, rest homes, and other facilities that are being built in all parts of the world. A few measures of the new trend have been R. J. Neutra's primary school in Puerto Rico (1944); the Thomsen Dock Workers' Service Center in Rotterdam, Holland (1947, Brinkman, Van den Broek, and Bakema); O. Niemeyer's

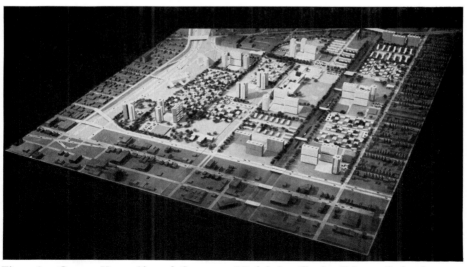

Fig. 569. Gruen, Yamasaki, and Stonorov: Model for Gratiot-Orleans Redevelopment Project, Detroit, Mich.

stunning theater in Belo Horizonte, Brazil (1947); the Maimonides Health Center by Eric Mendelsohn in San Francisco (1950); and Eero Saarinen's soaringly curved auditorium at the Massachusetts Institute of Technology (1954).

Technology by itself is not the answer to the problems of twentieth-century man. But when it is linked with a broad humanitarian outlook and responds directly to the needs of our time, it harnesses itself to the burden of man's progress. Perhaps in this sense, contemporary architecture begins to symbolize the dreams and hopes of modern man for a better world.

BIBLIOGRAPHY

The following bibliographies are confined to titles in the English language. The General Bibliography, comprised largely of works of the survey type, is followed by bibliographies of more detailed works, arranged by chapters of this book.

GENERAL BIBLIOGRAPHY

Borenius, Tancred: *Italian Painting Up to Leonardo and Raphael*, London, Avalon Press, 1946.

Chase, G. H., and C. R. Post: *A History of Sculpture*, New York, Harper, 1925.

Craven, Thomas: *A Treasury of Art Masterpieces*, New York, Simon and Schuster, 1939.

Fletcher, Sir Banister: *A History of Architecture on the Comparative Method*, New York, Scribner, 1938.

Flexner, James Thomas: *A Short History of American Painting*, Boston, Houghton Mifflin, 1950. (New York, Pocket Books, 1950: *The Pocket History of American Painting*.)

Fromentin, Eugène: *The Masters of Past Time: Dutch and Flemish Painting from Van Eyck to Rembrandt* (ed. by H. Gerson), New York, Phaidon, 1948.

Gardner, Helen: *Art through the Ages* (3d ed.), New York, Harcourt, Brace, 1948.

Gombrich, E. H.: *The Story of Art*, New York, Phaidon, 1950.

Hamlin, Talbot: *Architecture through the Ages*, New York, Putnam, 1940.

Hauser, Arnold: *A Social History of Art* (2 vols.), New York, Knopf, 1951.

Hind, A. M.: *History of Engraving and Etching*, Boston, Houghton Mifflin, 1923.

Larkin, Oliver W.: *Art and Life in America*, New York, Rinehart, 1949.

Leicht, Hermann: *History of the World's Art*, London, Allen and Unwin, 1952.

Myers, Bernard S. (et al.): *Encyclopedia of Painting* (rev. ed.), New York, Crown, 1957.

Myers, Bernard S.: *Fifty Great Artists*, New York, Bantam Books, 1953.

Newton, Eric: *An Introduction to European Painting*, New York, Longmans, 1949.

Read, Herbert: *Art and Society*, New York, Macmillan, 1937.

Robb, David M.: *The Harper History of Painting*, New York, Harper, 1951.

Sewall, John Ives: *A History of Western Art*, New York, Holt, 1953.

Upjohn, E. M., P. S. Wingert, and J. G. Mahler: *History of World Art*, New York, Oxford, 1949.

Waterhouse, Ellis Kirkham: *Painting in Britain, 1530–1790*, Baltimore, Penguin, 1953.

Whitaker, C. H.: *Rameses to Rockefeller*, New York, Random House, 1934.

Zigrosser, Carl: *Six Centuries of Fine Prints*, New York, Covici, 1937.

693

PREHISTORIC AND MODERN PRIMITIVES

Adam, Leonard: *Primitive Art*, Baltimore, Penguin, 1949.
Bataille, Georges: *Lascaux: or, The Birth of Art*, New York, Skira, 1955.
Brodrick, A. H.: *Prehistoric Painting*, London, Avalon Press, 1948.
Christenssen, Ernest O.: *Primitive Art*, New York, Crowell, 1955.
Firth, Raymond: *Art and Life in New Guinea*, New York, Studio, 1936.
Frobenius, Leo, and D. C. Fox: *Prehistoric Rock Pictures in Europe and Africa*, New York, The Museum of Modern Art, 1937.
Goddard, Pliny E.: *Indians of the Northwest Coast*, New York, American Museum of Natural History, 1939.
Guillaume, Paul, and Thomas Munro: *Primitive Negro Sculpture*, New York, Harcourt, Brace, 1926.
Hooper, J. T., and C. A. Burland: *The Art of Primitive Peoples*, New York, Philosophical Library, 1954.
Linton, Ralph, and Paul S. Wingert: *Arts of the South Seas*, New York, The Museum of Modern Art, 1946.
Obermaier, Hugo, and Herbert Kuhn: *Bushman Art*, New York, Oxford, 1930.
Osborn, H. E.: *Men of the Old Stone Age: Their Environment, Life and Art*, New York, Scribner, 1921.
Raphael, Max: *Prehistoric Cave Paintings* (trans. by Norbert Guterman), New York, Pantheon, 1945.
Sadler, Sir Michael Ernest: *Arts of West Africa*, New York, Oxford, 1935.
Segy, Ladislas: *African Sculpture Speaks*, New York, Wyn, 1952.
Trowell, Margaret: *Classical African Sculpture*, London, Faber, 1954.
UNESCO: *Australia: Aboriginal Paintings* (introd. by Sir Herbert Read), New York, New York Graphic Society, 1954.
Vaillant, George: *Indian Arts in North America*, New York, Harper, 1939.
Wingert, Paul S.: *An Outline Guide to the Art of the South Pacific*, New York, Columbia University Press, 1946.
——: *The Sculpture of Negro Africa*, New York, Columbia University Press, 1950.

ANCIENT EGYPT

Aldred, Cyril: *Middle Kingdom Art in Ancient Egypt, 2300 to 1590 B.C.*, London, A. Tiranti, 1950.
——: *New Kingdom Art in Ancient Egypt during the Eighteenth Dynasty, 1590 to 1315 B.C.*, London, A. Tiranti, 1950.
——: *Old Kingdom Art in Ancient Egypt*, London, A. Tiranti, 1949.
Baikie, James: *The Life of the Ancient East*, New York, Macmillan, 1923.
Breasted, James H.: *Ancient Times* (2d ed. rev.), Boston, Ginn, 1935.
Childe, Vere G.: *The Most Ancient East*, New York, Knopf, 1929.
Lange, K., and M. Hirmer: *Egypt, Architecture, Sculpture, Painting in Three Thousand Years*, New York, Phaidon, 1956.
Mekhitarian, Arpag: *Egyptian Painting* (trans. by Stuart Gilbert), New York, Skira, 1954.
Murray, Margaret A.: *Egyptian Sculpture*, New York, Scribner, 1930.
Smith, E. Baldwin: *Egyptian Architecture as Cultural Expression*, New York, Appleton-Century-Crofts, 1938.
Smith, William Stevenson: *A History of Egyptian Sculpture and Painting in the Old Kingdom*, New York, Oxford, 1946.

694

UNESCO: *Egypt: Paintings from Tombs and Temples* (introd. by Jacques Vandier), Greenwich, Conn., New York Graphic Society, 1954.

Weigall, Arthur E. P. B.: *The Life and Times of Akhenaton, Pharaoh of Egypt* (rev. ed.), New York, Putnam, 1923.

ANCIENT MESOPOTAMIA AND PERSIA

Baikie, James: *The Life of the Ancient East*, New York, Macmillan, 1923.

Breasted, James H.: *Ancient Times* (2d ed. rev.), Boston, Ginn, 1935.

Childe, Vere G.: *The Most Ancient East*, New York, Knopf, 1929.

Frankfort, Henri: *Sculpture of the Third Millennium B.C. from Tell Asmar and Khafājah*, Chicago, University of Chicago Press, 1939.

——: *The Art and Architecture of the Ancient Orient*, Baltimore, Penguin, 1955.

——: *The Birth of Civilization in the Near East*, Bloomington, Indiana University Press, 1951; New York, Doubleday (Anchor), 1956.

Grousset, René: *The Civilizations of the East* (trans. by C. A. Phillips, 4 vols.), New York, Knopf, 1931–1934, vol. I.

Hall, Harry Reginald Holland: *Babylonian and Assyrian Sculpture in the British Museum*, London, British Museum, 1928.

——: *The Ancient History of the Near East* (8th ed. rev.), New York, Macmillan, 1932.

Harcourt-Smith, Simon: *Babylonian Art*, London, Benn, 1928.

Herzfeld, Ernst: *Iran in the Ancient East*, New York, Oxford, 1941.

Woolley, Sir Leonard: *The Excavations at Ur*, New York, Crowell, 1954.

CRETE AND MYCENAE

Baikie, James: *The Sea Kings of Crete* (3d ed.), London, A. & C. Black, 1920.

Bell, Edward: *Pre-hellenic Architecture in the Aegean*, London, G. Bell, 1926.

Breasted, James H.: *Ancient Times* (2d ed. rev.), Boston, Ginn, 1935.

Forsdyke, Edgar J.: *Minoan Art*, London, H. Milford, 1929.

Mosso, Angelo: *The Palaces of Crete and Their Builders*, London, T. F. Unwin, 1907.

Swindler, Mary H.: *Ancient Painting*, New Haven, Conn., Yale University Press, 1929.

CLASSICAL ART: GENERAL BIBLIOGRAPHY

Agard, Walter Raymond: *Classical Myths in Sculpture*, Madison, Wis., University of Wisconsin Press, 1951.

——: *The Greek Tradition in Sculpture*, Baltimore, Johns Hopkins University Press, 1930.

Bossert, H. Th., and W. Zschietzschmann: *Hellas and Rome; the Civilization of Classical Antiquity*, New York, Weyhe, 1936.

Gardner, Ernest A.: *A Handbook of Greek Sculpture* (2d ed.), New York, Macmillan, 1929.

Swindler, Mary H.: *Ancient Painting*, New Haven, Conn., Yale University Press, 1929.

THE COMING OF GREEK ART

Anderson, W. J., and R. P. Spiers: *The Architecture of Ancient Greece* (rev. by W. B. Dinsmoor), London, Batsford, 1927.

Carpenter, R.: *The Esthetic Basis of Greek Art of the Fourth and Fifth Centuries, B.C.*, New York, Longmans, 1921.

Dickinson, G. L.: *The Greek View of Life* (15th ed.), New York, Doubleday, 1924.

Gardner, E. A.: *Art of Greece*, New York, Studio, 1925.

———: *Six Greek Sculptors*, New York, Scribner, 1915.

Lane, Arthur: *Greek Pottery*, New York, Van Nostrand, 1949.

Pfuhl, Ernst: *Masterpieces of Greek Drawing and Painting*, New York, Macmillan, 1926.

Richter, Gisela M. A.: *The Sculpture and Sculptors of the Ancient Greeks*, New Haven, Conn., Yale University Press, 1930.

———: *Three Critical Periods in Greek Sculpture*, New York, Oxford, 1951.

Rodenwaldt, Gerhart: *The Acropolis, Photographed by Walter Hege, Described by Gerhart Rodenwaldt*, Oxford, Blackwell, 1930.

Seltman, Charles Theodore: *Approach to Greek Art*, New York, Studio, 1948.

FROM HELLENISTIC TO ROMAN WORLD EMPIRE

Anderson, W. J., and R. P. Spiers: *The Architecture of Ancient Rome* (rev. and rewritten by Thomas Ashby), London, Batsford, 1927.

Bieber, Margarete: *The Sculpture of the Hellenistic Age*, New York, Columbia University Press, 1955.

Dickinson, Guy: *Hellenistic Sculpture*, New York, Oxford, 1920.

Fyfe, Theodore: *Hellenistic Architecture; An Introductory Study*, New York, Cambridge, 1936.

Goldscheider, Ludwig: *Etruscan Sculpture*, New York, Phaidon, 1941.

Lawrence, Arnold W.: *Later Greek Sculpture*, New York, Harcourt, Brace, 1927.

Maiuri, Amadeo: *Roman Painting*, New York, Skira, 1953.

Pallottino, Massimo: *Etruscan Painting*, New York, Skira, 1952.

Richter, Gisela M. A.: *Roman Portraits*, New York, Metropolitan Museum of Art, 1948.

Riis, Poul Jorgen: *An Introduction to Etruscan Art*, Copenhagen, E. Munkgaard, 1953.

Rivoira, G. T.: *Roman Architecture* (trans. by G. McN. Rushforth), New York, Oxford, 1925.

Robathan, Dorothy M.: *The Monuments of Ancient Rome*, Rome, "L'Erma" di Bretschneider, 1950.

Showerman, Grant: *Rome and the Romans*, New York, Macmillan, 1931.

Strong, Eugenie Sellers: *Art in Ancient Rome* (2 vols.), New York, Scribner, 1928.

———: *Roman Sculpture from Augustus to Constantine*, New York, Scribner, 1907.

Swindler, Mary H.: *Ancient Painting*, New Haven, Conn., Yale University Press, 1929.

Walters, H. B.: *The Art of the Romans*, London, Methuen, 1911.

THE ART OF INDIA

Anand, M. R.: *The Hindu View of Art*, London, G. Allen, 1933.

Codrington, K. de B.: *An Introduction to the Study of Medieval Indian Sculpture*, London, Goldston, 1927.

Coomaraswamy, Ananda Kentish: *History of Indian and Indonesian Art*, New York, Weyhe, 1927.

———: *The Dance of Shiva; Fourteen Indian Essays*, Bombay, Asia Publishing House, 1948.

Grousset, René: *The Civilizations of the East* (trans. by C. A. Phillips, 4 vols.), New York, Knopf, 1931–1935, vols. I–II.

Havell, Ernest B.: *The Ancient and Medieval Architecture of India*, New York, Scribner, 1915.

——: *The Ideals of Indian Art*, New York, Dutton, 1921.

Rowland, Benjamin: *The Art and Architecture of India: Buddhist, Hindu, Jain*, Baltimore, Penguin, 1953.

Singh, Madanjeet: *India; Paintings from Ajanta Caves*, New York, New York Graphic Society, 1954.

Smith, Vincent A.: *A History of Fine Art in India and Ceylon* (2d ed. rev. by K. de B. Codrington), New York, Oxford, 1930.

Vogel, J. P.: *Buddhist Art in India, Ceylon and Java*, New York, Oxford, 1936.

Zimmer, Heinrich Robert: *The Art of Indian Asia, Its Mythology and Transformations*, New York, Pantheon, 1955.

CHINA AND JAPAN

Bachhofer, Ludwig: *A Short History of Chinese Art*, New York, Pantheon, 1946.

Binyon, Laurence: *Painting in the Far East*, London, E. Arnold, 1934.

——: *The Flight of the Dragon*, London, J. Murray, 1943.

Bushell, Stephen W.: *Chinese Art* (2 vols.), New York, Brentano's, 1924.

Cohn, William: *Chinese Painting*, New York, Phaidon, 1948.

Davidson, J. Leroy: *The Lotus Sutra in Chinese Art*, New Haven, Conn., Yale University Press, 1954.

Fry, Roger (et al.): *Chinese Art*, New York, Weyhe, 1925.

Hillier, Jack Ronald: *Japanese Masters of the Colour Print*, New York, Phaidon, 1954.

Honey, William Bowyer: *The Ceramic Art of China and Other Countries of the Far East*, London, Faber, 1945.

Kuo Hsi: *An Essay on Landscape Painting* (trans. by Shio Sakanishi), New York, Dutton, 1936.

Okakura, K.: *Ideals of the East*, London, J. Murray, 1905.

Priest, Alan: *Aspects of Chinese Painting*, New York, Macmillan, 1954.

Rowley, George: *Principles of Chinese Painting*, Princeton, Princeton University Press, 1947.

Sadler, Anthony Lindsay: *A Short History of Japanese Architecture*, London, Angus and Robertson, 1941.

Sickman, Laurence, and Alexander Soper: *The Art and Architecture of China*, Baltimore, Penguin, 1956.

Silcock, Arnold: *Introduction to Chinese Art and History*, New York, Oxford, 1948.

Siren, Osvald: *Chinese Sculpture from the Fifth to the Fifteenth Century* (4 vols.), New York, Scribner, 1925.

Soper, Alexander Coburn: *The Evolution of Buddhist Architecture in Japan*, Princeton, Princeton University Press, 1942.

Warner, Langdon: *The Enduring Art of Japan*, Cambridge, Mass., Harvard University Press, 1952.

ART AND CULTURE OF THE EARLY AMERICAS

Archaeology in Mexico Today (prep. by Arturo Cesar Castillo), Mexico, D.F., Petroleos Mexicanos, n.d., ca. 1954.

Blom, Frans F.: *The Conquest of Yucatán*, Boston, Houghton Mifflin, 1936.

Bushnell, G. H. S.: *Peru* (*Ancient Peoples and Places* series, ed. by Glyn Daniel), New York, Praeger, 1957.

Covarrubias, Miguel: *Indian Art of Mexico and Central America*, New York, Knopf, 1957.

Groth-Kimball, Irmgard: *The Art of Ancient Mexico* (109 photographs by Irmgard Groth-Kimball; text and notes by Franz Feuchtwanger), New York, Thames and Hudson, 1954.

Kelemen, Pal: *Medieval American Art* (2 vols.), New York, Macmillan, 1943.

Means, Philip A.: *Ancient Civilizations of the Andes*, New York, Scribner, 1931.

Pre-Columbian Art, Dallas, Dallas Museum of Fine Arts, 1950.

Radin, Paul: *Indians of South America*, New York, Doubleday, 1942.

Spinden, Herbert J.: *Ancient Civilizations of Mexico and Central America* (3d ed. rev.), New York, American Museum of Natural History, 1943.

Twenty Centuries of Mexican Art, New York, The Museum of Modern Art, 1940.

Vaillant, George: *The Aztecs of Mexico*, New York, Doubleday, 1941.

MEDIEVAL ART: GENERAL BIBLIOGRAPHY

Chapters 10–12; 14

Davis, William S.: *Life on a Medieval Barony*, New York, Harper, 1933.

Davison, James A.: *An Outline of Medieval Architecture*, London, Cassell, 1949.

Evans, Joan: *Art in Medieval France: 987–1498*, New York, Oxford, 1948.

Ferguson, George Wells: *Signs and Symbols in Christian Art*, New York, Oxford, 1954.

Gardner, Arthur: *English Medieval Sculpture*, New York, Cambridge, 1951.

——: *Medieval Sculpture in France*, New York, Cambridge, 1931.

Herbert, J. A.: *Illuminated Manuscripts*, New York, Putnam, 1911.

Lethaby, W. R.: *Medieval Art* (rev. by D. Talbot Rice), New York, Nelson, 1949.

Lowrie, Walter: *Art in the Early Church*, New York, Pantheon, 1947.

Megrew, Alden F.: *Outline of Medieval Art*, Dubuque, Iowa, W. C. Brown, 1949.

Morey, Charles Rufus: *Christian Art*, New York, Longmans, 1935.

——: *Medieval Art*, New York, Norton, 1942.

Porter, A. K.: *Medieval Architecture*, New Haven, Conn., Yale University Press, 1912.

Sewall, John Ives: *A History of Western Art*, New York, Holt, 1953.

Swarzenski, Hanns: *Early Medieval Illumination*, New York, Oxford, 1952.

Taylor, H. O.: *The Medieval Mind* (2 vols., 4th ed.), New York, Macmillan, 1925.

EARLY CHRISTIAN AND BYZANTINE ART

Butler, Howard C., and E. B. Smith: *Early Churches in Syria*, Princeton, Princeton University Press, 1929.

Byron, Robert: *The Byzantine Achievement*, New York, Knopf, 1929.

Dalton, O. M.: *Byzantine Art and Archaeology*, New York, Oxford, 1911.

Demus, Otto: *Byzantine Mosaic Decoration; Aspects of Monumental Art in Byzantium*, London, Routledge, 1948.

Frothingham, Arthur L.: *Monuments of Christian Rome*, New York, Macmillan, 1908.

Grabar, André: *Byzantine Painting; Historical and Critical Study*, New York, Skira, 1953.

Lowrie, Walter: *Monuments of the Early Church*, New York, Pantheon, 1947.

Meyer, Peter: *Byzantine Mosaics*, New York, Oxford, 1952.

Morey, Charles Rufus: *Early Christian Art* (2d ed.), Princeton, Princeton University Press, 1953.

Rice, David Talbot: *Byzantine Painting and Developments in the West before A.D. 1200*, London, Avalon Press, 1948.

Simson, Otto Georg von: *Sacred Fortress; Byzantine Art and Statecraft in Ravenna*, Chicago, Chicago University Press, 1948.

Strzygowski, Josef: *Origins of Christian Church Art* (trans. by Dalton and Baumholtz), New York, Oxford, 1923.

Swift, Emerson H.: *Hagia Sophia*, New York, Columbia University Press, 1940.

THE EARLY MIDDLE AGES IN THE WEST

Coffey, George: *Guide to the Celtic Antiquities of the Christian Period*, Dublin, Royal Irish Academy, 1910.

Herbert, J. A.: *Illuminated Manuscripts*, New York, Putnam, 1911.

Hinks, Roger P.: *Carolingian Art: Painting and Sculpture in Western Europe; A.D. 800–900*, London, Sidgwick & Jackson, 1935.

Millar, Eric G. (ed.): *The Lindisfarne Gospels*, New York, Oxford, 1924.

Morey, Charles Rufus: *Early Christian Art* (2d ed.), Princeton, Princeton University Press, 1953.

Oppenheimer, Sir Francis: *Frankish Themes and Problems*, London, Faber, 1952.

Rice, Tamara Talbot: *The Scythians* (*Ancient Peoples and Places* series, ed. by Glyn Daniel), New York, Praeger, 1957.

Sullivan, Sir Edward: *The Book of Kells* (5th ed.), New York, Studio, 1952.

ROMANESQUE EUROPE

Belloc, Hilaire: *The Book of the Bayeux Tapestry*, New York, Putnam, 1914.

Clapham, A. W.: *Romanesque Architecture in Western Europe*, New York, Oxford, 1936.

Crichton, George Henderson: *Romanesque Sculpture in Italy*, London, Routledge, 1954.

Evans, Joan: *Cluniac Art of the Romanesque Period*, New York, Cambridge, 1950.

Hammett, Ralph Warner: *The Romanesque Architecture of Western Europe: Italy, France, Spain, Germany and England*, New York, The Architectural Book Publishing Co., 1927.

Porter, A. Kingsley: *Romanesque Sculpture of the Pilgrimage Roads* (2 vols.), Boston, Marshall Jones Co., 1923.

Ricci, Corrado: *Romanesque Architecture in Italy*, New York, Brentano's, 1925.

Saxl, Fritz: *English Sculptures of the Twelfth Century* (ed. by Hanns Swarzenski), London, Faber, 1954.

ISLAMIC CIVILIZATION

Arnold, T. W.: *Painting in Islam*, New York, Oxford, 1928.

Binyon, Laurence: *The Court Painters of the Grand Moguls*, New York, Oxford, 1921.

Briggs, Martin Shaw: *Muhammedan Architecture in Egypt and Palestine*, New York, Oxford, 1924.

Creswell, K. A. C.: *Early Muslim Architecture*, New York, Oxford, 1924.

Dimand, Maurice: *Handbook of Muhammedan Art*, New York, The Metropolitan Museum of Art, 1944.

Gray, B.: *Persian Painting*, London, Benn, 1930.

Koechlin, Raymond, and Gaston Migeon: *Oriental Art: Ceramics, Fabrics, Carpets, etc.* (trans. by Florence Heywood), New York, Macmillan, 1928.

Pope, Arthur Upham: *A Survey of Persian Art* (6 vols.), New York, Oxford, 1938–1939.

——: *An Introduction to Persian Art since the Seventh Century A.D.*, London, Davies, 1930.

Richmond, Ernest Tatham: *Moslem Architecture, 623 to 1516; Some Causes and Consequences*, London, The Royal Asiatic Society, 1926.

FROM CASTLE TO COMMUNE: THE RISE OF GOTHIC ART

Adams, Henry: *Mont St. Michel and Chartres*, Boston, Houghton Mifflin, 1904.
Arnold, Hugh: *Stained Glass of the Middle Ages in England and France*, New York, Macmillan, 1940.
Bunt, Cyril George Edward: *Gothic Painting*, London, Avalon Press, 1947.
Cambridge, S.: *A Guide to English Gothic Architecture*, New York, Cambridge, 1922.
Coulton, G. C.: *Art and the Reformation* (2d ed.), New York, Cambridge, 1953.
Crichton, George H. and Elsie R.: *Nicola Pisano and the Revival of Sculpture in Italy*, New York, Macmillan, 1938.
Harvey, John Hooper: *The Gothic World, 1100–1600; A Survey of Architecture and Art*, New York, Batsford, 1950.
Jackson, T. G.: *Gothic Architecture in France, England and Italy* (2 vols.), New York, Cambridge, 1915.
Mâle, Emile: *Religious Art in France: XIII Century* (3d ed., trans. by D. Nussey), New York, Dutton, 1913.
Marriage, Margaret S. and Ernest: *The Sculptures of Chartres Cathedral*, New York, Putnam, 1909.
Meiss, Millard: *Painting in Florence and Siena after the Black Death*, Princeton, Princeton University Press, 1951.
Natanson, Joseph: *Gothic Ivories of the 13th and 14th Centuries*, London, A. Tiranti, 1951.
Offner, Richard: *Studies in Florentine Painting; The Fourteenth Century*, New York, F. F. Sherman, 1927.
Sabatier, Paul: *Life of St. Francis of Assisi* (trans. by L. S. Houghton), New York, Scribner, 1927.
Siren, O.: *Giotto and Some of His Followers*, Cambridge, Mass., Harvard University Press, 1917.
Toesca, Pietro: *Florentine Painting of the Trecento*, New York, Harcourt, Brace, 1929.
Weigelt, Curt H.: *Sienese Painting of the Trecento*, New York, Harcourt, Brace, 1930.

THE DECLINE OF FEUDALISM: FIFTEENTH-CENTURY FLANDERS

Baldass, Ludwig von: *Jan van Eyck*, New York, Phaidon, 1952.
Cartellieri, Otto: *The Court of Burgundy*, New York, Knopf, 1926.
Elst, Joseph J. M. I. van der, Baron: *The Last Flowering of the Middle Ages*, New York, Doubleday, 1945.
Fromentin, Eugène: *The Masters of Past Time: Dutch and Flemish Painting from Van Eyck to Rembrandt* (ed. by H. Gerson), New York, Phaidon, 1948.
Huizinga, J.: *The Waning of the Middle Ages*, London, Arnold, 1924; New York, Doubleday (Anchor), 1954.
Panofsky, Erwin: *Early Netherlandish Painting, Its Origins and Character* (2 vols.), Cambridge, Mass., Harvard University Press, 1954.
Puyvelde, Leo van: *The Flemish Primitives*, Brussels, Marion Press, 1948.
——: *The Genius of Flemish Art*, New York, Phaidon, 1949.
Weale, W. H. J., and M. W. Brockwell: *The Van Eycks and Their Art*, London, Lane, 1913.

700

RENAISSANCE: GENERAL BIBLIOGRAPHY

Anderson, W. J., and A. Stratton: *The Architecture of the Renaissance in Italy*, New York, Scribner, 1927.

Berenson, Bernard: *Florentine Painters of the Renaissance* (3d ed.), New York, Putnam, 1909.

———: *Italian Painters of the Renaissance*, New York, Phaidon, 1952.

———: *Venetian Painters of the Renaissance*, New York, Putnam, 1905.

Brown, A. V. V., and William Rankin: *A Short History of Italian Painting*, New York, Dutton, 1914.

Burckhardt, J. C.: *The Civilization of the Renaissance in Italy*, New York, Oxford, 1944.

Byron, Robert, and Talbot Rice: *The Birth of Western Painting*, New York, Knopf, 1931.

Edgell, G. H.: *A History of Sienese Painting*, New York, Dial Press, 1932.

MacLagen, Eric: *Italian Sculpture of the Renaissance*, Cambridge, Mass., Harvard University Press, 1935.

Mather, Frank Jewett, Jr.: *A History of Italian Painting*, New York, Holt, 1923.

Schmeckebier, Laurence: *A Handbook of Italian Renaissance Painting*, New York, Putnam, 1938.

Scott, Geoffrey: *The Architecture of Humanism* (2d ed.), New York, Scribner, 1924.

Taylor, H. O.: *Thought and Expression in the Sixteenth Century*, New York, Macmillan, 1920.

Vasari, Giorgio: *The Lives of the Painters, Sculptors and Architects* (trans. by A. B. Hinds, 4 vols.), New York, Dutton, 1927. (Everyman's Library.)

Venturi, Adolfo: *A Short History of Italian Art* (trans. by Edward Hutton), New York, Macmillan, 1926.

Wölfflin, Heinrich: *Classical Art: An Introduction to the Italian Renaissance* (trans. by Peter and Linday Murray), New York, Phaidon, 1952.

THE RISE OF HUMANISM: FIFTEENTH-CENTURY ITALY

Antal, Frederick: *Florentine Painting and Its Social Background . . . XIV and XV Centuries*, London, Routledge, 1948.

Bazin, Germain: *Fra Angelico*, New York, Hyperion, 1949.

Bode, Wilhelm von: *Florentine Sculptors of the Renaissance*, New York, Scribner, 1909.

Clark, Sir Kenneth: *Leon Battista Alberti on Painting*, London, G. Cumberledge, 1946.

———: *Piero della Francesca*, New York, Phaidon, 1951.

Crutwell, M.: *Andrea Mantegna*, London, G. Bell, 1908.

Goldscheider, Ludwig: *Donatello*, New York, Phaidon, 1941.

Horne, A. P.: *Alessandro Filipepi, Commonly Called Sandro Botticelli*, London, G. Bell, 1908.

Pope-Hennessy, John: *Fra Angelico*, New York, Phaidon, 1952.

———: *The Complete Work of Paolo Uccello*, New York, Phaidon, 1950.

Richter, George Martin: *Andrea del Castagno*, Chicago, University of Chicago Press, 1943.

Valentiner, Wilhelm R.: *Studies of Italian Renaissance Sculpture*, New York, Oxford, 1950.

Venturi, Lionello: *Italian Painting: The Creators of the Renaissance*, New York, Skira, 1950.

Yashiro, Yukio: *Sandro Botticelli* (3 vols.), Boston, Medici Society, 1925.

THE RISE OF HUMANISM: EARLY-SIXTEENTH-CENTURY ITALY

Clark, Sir Kenneth: *Leonardo da Vinci, an Account of His Development as an Artist* (2d ed.), New York, Cambridge, 1952.

Conway, Sir Martin: *Giorgione*, London, Benn, 1929.

Cook, H. F.: *Giorgione*, London, G. Bell, 1900.

De Tolnay, Charles: *The Medici Chapel*, Princeton, Princeton University Press, 1948.

Fischel, Oscar: *Raphael* (trans. by Bernard Rackham), London, Routledge, 1948.

Goldscheider, Ludwig: *Michelangelo Drawings*, New York, Phaidon, 1951.

——: *Michelangelo: Paintings, Sculptures, Architecture*, New York, Phaidon, 1953.

Heydenreich, Ludwig Heinrich: *Leonardo da Vinci* (2 vols.), New York, Macmillan, 1954.

Holroyd, Sir Charles: *Michael Angelo Buonarroti* (2d ed.), New York, Scribner, 1911.

Leonardo da Vinci: *The Notebooks of Leonardo da Vinci* (trans. by Edward MacCurdy, 2 vols.), New York, Reynal & Hitchcock, 1938.

Popham, Arthur E.: *The Drawings of Leonardo da Vinci*, New York, Reynal & Hitchcock, 1945.

Ricci, Corrado: *Architecture and Decorative Sculpture of the High and Late Renaissance in Italy*, New York, Brentano's, 1923.

——: *North Italian Painting of the Cinquecento*, Paris, The Pegasus Press, 1929.

Siren, O.: *Leonardo da Vinci, the Artist and the Man*, New Haven, Conn., Yale University Press, 1916.

Tietze, Hans: *Tiziano Vecelli; Paintings, Drawings*, New York, Phaidon, 1950.

THE REFORMATION

Burkhard, Arthur: *Matthias Grünewald*, Cambridge, Mass., Harvard University Press, 1935.

Dickinson, H. A.: *German Masters of Art*, New York, Stokes, 1914.

Panofsky, Erwin: *Albrecht Dürer* (2 vols.), Princeton, Princeton University Press, 1943.

Schilling, Edmund (ed.): *Dürer: Drawings and Water Colors*, New York, Harper, 1949.

Schoenberger, Guido (ed.): *The Drawings of Matthis Gothart Nithart Called Grünewald*, New York, Bittner, 1948.

Stange, Alfred: *German Painting, XIV–XVI Centuries* (ed. by André Gloeckner), New York, Hyperion, 1950.

Taylor, H. O.: *Thought and Expression in the Sixteenth Century* (2d ed., 2 vols.), New York, Macmillan, 1930.

Waetzoldt, Wilhelm: *Dürer and His Times*, New York, Phaidon, 1950.

THE MANNERIST CRISIS

Barker, Virgil: *Pieter Brueghel the Elder: A Study of His Paintings*, New York, New York Arts Publishing Corp., 1926.

Bertram, Anthony: *Hans Holbein the Younger*, New York, Studio, 1948.

Bronstein, Leo: *El Greco*, New York, Abrams, 1950.

De Tolnay, Charles: *The Drawings of Pieter Brueghel the Elder* (2d ed.), London, Zwemmer, 1952.

Freedberg, Sidney: *Parmigianino: His Works in Painting*, Cambridge, Mass., Harvard University Press, 1950.

Friedlaender, Walter: *Mannerism and Anti-Mannerism in Italian Painting*, New York, Columbia University Press, 1957.

Ganz, Paul: *The Paintings of Hans Holbein*, New York, Phaidon, 1950.

Goldscheider, Ludwig: *El Greco*, New York, Phaidon, 1949.

Newton, Eric: *Tintoretto*, New York, Longmans, 1952.

Réau, Louis: *French Painting in the XIV, XV, and XVIth Centuries*, New York, Hyperion, 1939.

Tietze, Hans: *Tintoretto: The Paintings and Drawings*, New York, Phaidon, 1948.

Trapier, Elizabeth Du Gué: *Luis de Morales and Leonardesque Influence in Spain*, New York, Hispanic Society of America, 1953.

Ward, W. A.: *Architecture of the Renaissance in France* (2 vols.), London, Batsford, 1926.

THE BAROQUE AGE

Berenson, Bernard: *Caravaggio, His Incongruity and His Fame*, London, Chapman & Hall, 1953.

Blunt, Anthony: *Art and Architecture in France, 1500 to 1700*, Baltimore, Penguin, 1954.

Dupont, Jacques: *The Seventeenth Century; The New Developments in Art from Caravaggio to Vermeer*, New York, Skira, 1951.

Fokker, T. H.: *Roman Baroque Art* (2 vols.), New York, Oxford, 1938.

Furness, S. M. M.: *Georges de la Tour of Lorraine*, London, Routledge, 1949.

Harris, E.: *Spanish Painting*, New York, Hyperion, 1937.

Hinks, Roger P.: *Michelangelo Merisi da Caravaggio: His Life, His Legend, His Works*, London, Faber, 1953.

Mather, Frank Jewett, Jr.: *Western European Painting of the Renaissance*, New York, Holt, 1939.

McComb, A. K.: *The Baroque Painters of Italy*, Cambridge, Mass., Harvard University Press, 1934.

Meier-Graefe, Julius: *The Spanish Journey*, New York, Harcourt, Brace, 1926.

Ricci, Corrado: *Baroque Architecture and Sculpture in Italy*, London, Heinemann, 1922.

Sitwell, Sacheverell: *Southern Baroque Art*, London, Duckworth, 1931.

——: *Spanish Baroque Art*, London, Duckworth, 1931.

Stevenson, R. A. M. (ed.): *Rubens Paintings and Drawings*, New York, Oxford, 1939.

Sutro, Esther: *Nicholas Poussin*, Boston, The Medici Society, 1923.

Trapier, Elizabeth Du Gué: *Ribera*, New York, Hispanic Society of America, 1952.

——: *Velásquez*, New York, Hispanic Society of America, 1948.

Waterhouse, Ellis K.: *Baroque Painting in Rome*, New York, Macmillan, 1937.

Weisbach, Werner: *Spanish Baroque Art*, New York, Macmillan, 1941.

Wilenski, R. H.: *French Painting*, Boston, Hale, Cushman and Flint, 1931.

THE PROTESTANT BAROQUE

Benesch, Otto: *Rembrandt Harmenszoon van Rijn, 1606–1669. Selected Drawings*, New York, Oxford, 1947.

Fromentin, Eugène: *Masters of Past Time* (ed. by H. Gerson), New York, Phaidon, 1948.

Gowing, Lawrence: *Vermeer*, London, Faber, 1952.

Lucas, E. V.: *Vermeer of Delft* (2d ed.), New York, Doran, 1922.

Martin, Wilhelm: *Dutch Painting of the Great Period, 1650–1697*, London, Batsford, 1951.

Mather, Frank Jewett, Jr.: *Western European Painting of the Renaissance*, New York, Holt, 1939.

Rosenberg, Jakob: *Rembrandt* (2 vols.), Cambridge, Mass., Harvard University Press, 1948.

Trivas, N. S. (ed.): *The Paintings of Frans Hals*, New York, Oxford (Phaidon Series), 1942.

Wilenski, R. H.: *Dutch Painting*, New York, Beechhurst, 1955.

FROM ABSOLUTISM TO FREE THOUGHT: ENGLAND AND THE UNITED STATES IN THE EIGHTEENTH CENTURY

Barker, Virgil: *A Critical Introduction to American Painting*, New York, Whitney Museum of American Art, 1931.

Beckett, R. B.: *Hogarth*, London, Routledge, 1949.

Bertram, Anthony: *William Blake*, New York, Studio, 1948.

Borenius, Tancred: *English Painting in the XVIIIth Century*, New York, Hyperion, 1938.

Constable, W. G.: *Richard Wilson*, Cambridge, Mass., Harvard University Press, 1953.

Dutton, Ralph: *The Age of Wren*, New York, Batsford, 1951.

Flexner, James Thomas: *America's Old Masters*, New York, Viking, 1939.

———: *John Singleton Copley*, Boston, Houghton Mifflin, 1948.

Gaunt, William: *British Painting from Hogarth's Day to Ours*, London, Avalon Press, 1946.

Hagen, Oskar F. L.: *The Birth of the American Tradition in Art*, New York, Scribner, 1940.

La Follette, Suzanne: *Art in America*, New York, Norton, 1934.

Lees-Milne, James: *The Age of Adam*, New York, Batsford, 1947.

Lipman, Jean: *American Primitive Painting*, New York, Oxford, 1942.

Major, Howard: *The Domestic Architecture of the Early American Republic*, Philadelphia, Lippincott, 1926.

Morrison, Hugh Sinclair: *Early American Architecture from the First Colonial Settlement to the National Period*, New York, Oxford, 1952.

Richardson, Albert Edward: *Georgian Architecture*, New York, Pellegrini & Cudahy, 1950.

Tallmadge, T. E.: *The Story of England's Architecture*, New York, Norton, 1914.

Wilenski, R. H.: *Masters of English Painting*, Boston, Hale, Cushman and Flint, 1934.

Woodall, Mary: *Thomas Gainsborough, His Life and Work*, New York, Chanticleer Press, 1949.

FROM ABSOLUTISM TO FREE THOUGHT: FRANCE, ITALY, AND GERMANY IN THE EIGHTEENTH CENTURY

Blomfield, Sir Reginald T.: *A History of French Architecture from the Death of Mazarin till the Death of Louis XV, 1661–1774* (2 vols.), London, G. Bell, 1921.

Dilke, Lady E. F. S.: *French Architects and Sculptors of the XVIII Century*, New York, Macmillan, 1900.

Fosca, François: *The Eighteenth Century: Watteau to Tiepolo*, New York, Skira, 1952.

Furst, H. E. A.: *Chardin*, New York, Scribner, 1911.

Gradmann, Erwin: *French Master Drawings of the Eighteenth Century*, New York, Harper, 1949.

Kimball, Sidney F.: *The Creation of the Rococo*, Philadelphia, Philadelphia Museum of Art, 1943.

Lopez-Rey, José: *Francisco Goya*, New York, Harper, 1950.

Poore, Charles: *Goya*, New York, Scribner, 1939.

Rocheblave, S.: *French Painting of the Eighteenth Century* (trans. by George F. Lees), New York, Hyperion, 1937.

Sitwell, Sacheverell: *German Baroque Art*, London, Duckworth, 1927.

———: *German Baroque Sculpture*, London, Duckworth, 1938.

Vallentin, Antonina: *This I Saw: The Life and Times of Goya*, New York, Random House, 1949.

Wilenski, R. H.: *French Painting*, Boston, Hale, Cushman and Flint, 1936.

ART IN THE MODERN WORLD: THE NINETEENTH CENTURY

Behrendt, Walter C.: *Modern Building*, New York, Harcourt, Brace, 1937.

Bell, Clive: *Landmarks in Nineteenth Century Painting*, New York, Harcourt, Brace, 1927.

Berger, Klaus: *Géricault and His Work*, Lawrence, University of Kansas Press, 1955.

———: *French Master Drawings of the Nineteenth Century*, New York, Harper, 1950.

Cheney, Sheldon: *The Story of Modern Art*, New York, Viking, 1941.

Friedlander, Walter F.: *David to Delacroix* (trans. by Robert Goldwater), Cambridge, Mass., Harvard University Press, 1952.

Frost, Rosamund: *Renoir*, New York, Hyperion, 1944.

Hitchcock, Henry-Russell: *Modern Architecture*, New York, Payson, 1929.

Lassaigne, Jacques: *Daumier* (trans. by E. B. Shaw), London, Heinemann, 1938.

———: *Eugène Delacroix*, New York, Harper, 1950.

Mack, Gerstle: *Gustave Courbet*, New York, Knopf, 1951.

———: *Toulouse-Lautrec*, New York, Knopf, 1938.

Myers, Bernard S.: *Modern Art in the Making*, New York, McGraw-Hill, 1950.

Pach, Walter: *Ingres*, New York, Harper, 1939.

Rewald, John: *The History of Impressionism*, New York, The Museum of Modern Art, 1946.

Rich, Daniel Catton: *Edgar Hilaire Germain Degas*, New York, Abrams, 1951.

Sloane, Joseph C.: *French Painting between the Past and the Present*, Princeton, Princeton University Press, 1951.

Story, Somerville: *Auguste Rodin*, New York, Oxford (Phaidon Series), 1939.

ART IN THE MODERN WORLD: THE UNITED STATES IN THE NINETEENTH CENTURY

Barker, Virgil: *American Painting: History and Interpretation*, New York, Macmillan, 1950.

Baur, John I. H.: *American Painting in the XIX Century*, New York, Praeger, 1953.

Cahill, Holger, and Alfred H. Barr, Jr.: *Art in America*, New York, Reynal & Hitchcock, 1935.

Flexner, James Thomas: *A Short History of American Painting*, Boston, Houghton Mifflin, 1950. (New York, Pocket Books, 1950: *The Pocket History of American Painting*.)

Goodrich, Lloyd: *John Sloan*, New York, Whitney Museum of American Art, 1952.

——: *Thomas Eakins*, New York, Whitney Museum of American Art, 1934.

——: *Winslow Homer*, New York, Whitney Museum of American Art, 1944.

Hamlin, Talbot: *Greek Revival Architecture in America*, New York, Oxford, 1944.

Hitchcock, Henry-Russell: *The Architecture of H. H. Richardson*, New York, The Museum of Modern Art, 1936.

Isham, Samuel: *History of American Painting* (new ed. with supplementary chapters by Royal Cortissoz), New York, Macmillan, 1927.

La Follette, Suzanne: *Art in America*, New York, Norton, 1934.

Larkin, Oliver W.: *Art and Life in America*, New York, Rinehart, 1949.

Lipman, Jean: *American Primitive Painting*, New York, Oxford, 1942.

Mumford, Lewis: *The Brown Decades*, New York, Harcourt, Brace, 1931.

Richardson, Edgar P.: *The Way of Western Art*, Cambridge, Mass., Harvard University Press, 1939.

ART IN THE MODERN WORLD: TWENTIETH-CENTURY PAINTING AND SCULPTURE

American Federation of Arts: *German Watercolors, Drawings and Prints, 1905–1955*, Washington, D.C., 1956.

Apollinaire, Guillaume: *The Cubist Painters: Aesthetic Meditations, 1913*, New York, Wittenborn Schultz, 1949.

Barr, Alfred H., Jr.: *Cubism and Abstract Art*, New York, The Museum of Modern Art, 1936.

——: *Fantastic Art, Dada, Surrealism*, New York, The Museum of Modern Art, 1936.

——: *Masters of Modern Art*, New York, The Museum of Modern Art, 1954.

——: *Matisse, His Art and His Public*, New York, The Museum of Modern Art, 1951.

——: *Picasso, 50 Years of His Art*, New York, The Museum of Modern Art, 1946.

——: *What Is Modern Painting?* New York, The Museum of Modern Art, 1943.

Baur, John I. H.: *Revolution and Tradition in Modern American Art*, Cambridge, Mass., Harvard University Press, 1951.

Bell, Clive: *Since Cézanne*, New York, Harcourt, Brace, 1924.

Brown, Milton W.: *American Painting from the Armory Show to the Depression*, Princeton, Princeton University Press, 1955.

Casson, Stanley: *XXth Century Sculptors*, New York, Oxford, 1930.

Cheney, Sheldon: *The Story of Modern Art*, New York, Viking, 1941.

Duthuit, Georges: *The Fauvist Painters*, New York, Wittenborn Schultz, 1950.

Fry, Roger: *Cézanne: A Study of His Development* (2d ed.), London, Leonard and Woolf, 1932.

Giedion-Welcker, Carola: *Contemporary Sculpture*, New York, Wittenborn Schultz, 1955.

Goldwater, Robert J.: *Primitivism in Modern Painting*, New York, Harper, 1938.

Grohmann, Will: *Paul Klee*, New York, Abrams, 1955.

Guggenheim, Peggy (ed.): *Art of This Century*, New York, Art of This Century, 1942.

Helm, MacKinley: *Man of Fire: J. C. Orozco*, New York, Harcourt, Brace, 1953.

706

Hess, Thomas B.: *Abstract Painting; Background and American Phase*, New York, Viking, 1951.

Hope, Henry Radford: *The Sculpture of Jacques Lipchitz*, New York, The Museum of Modern Art, 1954.

Mondrian, Piet: *Plastic Art and Pure Plastic Art*, New York, Wittenborn Schultz, 1948.

Museum of Modern Art, The: *Art in Our Time*, New York, The Museum of Modern Art, 1946.

——: *Twentieth Century Italian Art* (ed. by J. T. Soby and A. H. Barr, Jr.), New York, The Museum of Modern Art, 1949.

Myers, Bernard S.: *Mexican Painting in Our Time*, New York, Oxford, 1956.

——: *Modern Art in the Making*, New York, McGraw-Hill, 1950.

——: *The German Expressionists: A Generation in Revolt*, New York, Praeger, 1957.

Raynal, Maurice: *History of Modern Painting* (3 vols.), New York, Skira, 1949–1950.

Read, Sir Herbert: *Art Now*, London, Faber, 1948.

Rebay, Hilla (ed.): *Kandinsky*, New York, Guggenheim Museum, 1945.

Rewald, John: *Gauguin*, New York, Hyperion, 1938.

——: *Georges Seurat*, New York, Wittenborn Schultz, 1946.

——: *Post-Impressionism*, New York, The Museum of Modern Art, 1956.

Ritchie, Andrew C.: *Abstract Painting and Sculpture in America*, New York, The Museum of Modern Art, 1951.

——: *Sculpture of the Twentieth Century*, New York, The Museum of Modern Art, 1952.

Schaefer-Simmern, Henry: *Sculpture in Europe Today*, Berkeley, University of California Press, 1955.

Soby, James Thrall: *After Picasso*, New York, Dodd, Mead, 1935.

Sweeney, James Johnson: *Plastic Redirections in 20th Century Painting*, Chicago, University of Chicago Press, 1934.

Terrasse. Charles: *French Painting in the XXth Century*, New York, Hyperion, 1939.

Uhde, Wilhelm: *Vincent van Gogh*, New York, Oxford, 1941.

Wilenski, R. H.: *Modern French Painters*, London, Faber, 1944.

——: *The Meaning of Modern Sculpture*, New York, Stokes, 1933.

——: *The Modern Movement in Art*, London, Faber, 1945.

ART IN THE MODERN WORLD: TWENTIETH-CENTURY ARCHITECTURE

Bayer, Herbert, Walter Gropius, and Ilse Gropius (eds.): *Bauhaus. 1919–1928*, New York, The Museum of Modern Art, 1938.

Behrendt, Walter C.: *Modern Building*, New York, Harcourt, Brace, 1937.

Fitch, James Marston: *American Building, the Forces That Shape It*, Boston, Houghton Mifflin, 1948.

Giedion, Siegfried: *A Decade of New Architecture*, Zurich, Editions Girsberger, 1951.

——: *Space, Time and Architecture*, Cambridge, Mass., Harvard University Press, 1941.

Gropius, Walter: *The New Architecture and the Bauhaus*, New York, The Museum of Modern Art, 1937.

Hitchcock, Henry-Russell, and Arthur Drexler: *Built in U.S.A.: Post-war Architecture*, New York, The Museum of Modern Art, 1953.

Le Corbusier: *Towards a New Architecture* (trans. by F. Etchells), London, Rodker, 1931.

Mumford, Lewis: *The Culture of Cities*, New York, Harcourt, Brace, 1938.

Pevsner, Nikolaus: *An Outline of European Architecture*, Baltimore, Penguin, 1942.

——: *Pioneers of the Modern Movement*, New York, Stokes, 1937.

Richards, J. M.: *An Introduction to Modern Architecture*, Baltimore, Penguin, 1940.

Wright, Frank Lloyd: *An American Architecture* (ed. by Edgar Kaufmann), New York, Horizon Press, 1955.

——: *When Democracy Builds*, Chicago, University of Chicago Press, 1945.

INDEX

Allegorical art (*see* Greek art, Hellenistic period; Roman art; Rubens; Van Dyck)
Altamira paintings, 3–5, 9 (fig. 3)
Altarpiece of the Lamb (*see Ghent Altarpiece*)
Altdorfer, Albrecht, 434, 435, 457, 461
    Rest on the Flight into Egypt, 435 (fig. 372)
Alternating system, 264, 265 (fig. 233)
Amalaka, 165 (fig. 150)
Amalienburg Castle (Munich), 537
Amazon (Polycleitos), 94
Ambulatory, 258, 311 (figs. 227, 272)
Amenophis IV (Akhenaton) *and His Wife*, 39 (fig. 32)
America, Central, Baroque art, 459, 473, 479, 480, 528
    Latin, 480, 528
        graphic and easel art, 650, 653, 655
        modern art and nationalism, 655
    North, European influences on, 528
    South, Baroque art, 459, 473, 479, 489, 528
        nativist art, 655
    Spanish, Baroque art, 479, 480, 528 (fig. 405)
    United States, Abstract Impressionism, 618
        architecture, colonial, 528–531 (figs. 442–445)
            Federal style, 532
            modern, 665–672, 681–692 (figs. 551–556, 561–569)
            neo-Gothic, 603
            neo-Romanesque, 603–605
            nineteenth century, 603–607 (figs. 500–502)
        Armory Show (1913), 651
        contemporary abstraction, 645
        depression period (1930s), 617
        Dutch colonies, 513
        Expressionism and Surrealism, 652, 655
        Federal Arts program, 645
        influence on, of English architecture, 528, 529, 531
            of English painting, 532–534
            of French philosophy, 535
            of Kandinsky, 633
            of Manet and Impressionism, 613, 614
            of post-Impressionism, 615
            of Spanish Baroque, 528
        neoclassicism, 519, 531, 532, 555
        painting, eighteenth-century, 532–534 (figs. 446, 447)
            nineteenth-century, 607–615 (figs. 503–510)
            twentieth-century, 617, 618, 633, 645, 646, 655
        parallels to Europe, 603, 607, 608
        portraiture, 528, 532–534
        post-World War II, 655

America, United States, precolonial art, 566, 567
    (*See also* Americas, early)
    refugee artists, 618
    regional abstractionists, 645, 646
    revolutionaries, 515, 531, 534
    sculpture, modern, 656, 661, 662
        nineteenth-century, 603
    Seattle group, 655
    shift to, 618
    skyscraper, 606, 607
    social realism, 645, 646
        vs. abstraction, 645
    waves of modernism, 651
Americas, early, Aztec Empire, 200–202 (fig. 176)
    art, 201, 202 (fig. 176)
    founding of Tenochtitlán (Mexico City), 200
    human sacrifice, 202
    Maya, early, 202–205 (figs. 177–180)
        area, 202
        ceremonial places, 203
        character of architecture, 204
        compared with Oriental sculpture, 205
        culture vs. Aztec brutality, 205
        later, general culture, 208
        important centers, 206
        paintings, 206, 207
        Toltec influence, 206
    Mexico, 1, 194–208, 480 (figs. 173–182, 405)
        common cultures, 194–196
        Valley of, 194–196, 199, 200, 202, 206, 209
    Middle, culture of, 1, 9, 20, 195, 196, 203, 204, 208, 212
    South America, 208–212
        Incas, 210–212
        pre-Inca groups, 208, 209
    Teotihuacán culture, 195–199 (figs. 173, 174)
    Toltecs at Tula, 199, 200 (fig. 175)
Amiens Cathedral, 299, 308, 321, 328
    Beau Dieu, 303, 309, 310, 318–321, 323 (fig. 278)
    compared with Chartres, 321
    interior of nave (fig. 270)
    St. Firmin, 321 (fig. 285)
    Signs of Zodiac, 321 (fig. 286)
    Vierge Dorée, 314, 323, 324, 326 (fig. 279)
Amphitheatre, 140, 141, 262 (figs. 131, 132)
Amphora, 77 (fig. 67)
Amsterdam, 507
Anacreon, 78
Anastasis (*Descent into Limbo*), 233
Anatolia, 229
Anatomy Lesson of Dr. Tulp (Rembrandt), 505–507

Carracci family, method, 463
Carthage, 115
Carthusian monastery, 347
Carved club head (Marquesas Islands, South Pacific), 15 (fig. 11)
Carved house post (Maori, New Zealand), 15, 16 (fig. 12)
Casket with mythological scenes, 229 (fig. 204)
Caspian Sea, 238
Cassandre, A. M., compared with Le Corbusier, 634
  Poster for the Wagon Lits, 634 (fig. 523)
Cassatt, Mary, 614, 615
Castagno, Andrea del, 382, 385, 400
  Crucifixion (Sant' Apollonia), 385
  Last Supper (Sant' Apollonia), 385, 401
  Pippo Spano, 385 (fig. 336)
Castle of Otranto (novel by Walpole), 575
Catacombs (Rome), 214–216
Catalonian sculptors, 333
Cathedral of Florence, 367, 368 (fig. 319)
Catholic art and Catholicism, 176, 426, 428, 440, 456, 481, 501
  Baroque, 480, 481, 502
  monarchical, 461, 462, 473
Cavallini, Pietro, 338
Cave painting (eastern Spain), 3, 4 (fig. 1)
  (Lascaux, France), 5, 6 (fig. 4)
Ceiling painting (catacomb of SS. Peter and Marcellinus, Rome), 214, 215 (fig. 188)
Cella, 98, 100 (fig. 88)
Celtic art, 77, 238, 247, 276, 277
  (*See also* Early Middle Ages, Irish art)
Celts, 236, 241
Centaur and Maiden (Olympia, *Temple of Zeus*), 92 (fig. 78)
Centralized periapsidal church (*see* Ravenna, San Vitale)
Ceremonial mask (Belgian Congo), 10, 11 (fig. 7)
Ceylon, 152
Cézanne, Paul, 181, 549, 600, 618–622
  vs. academic painting, 619
  Card Players, 621 (fig. 512)
  color methods, 622
  compared, with Monet and Renoir, 620–622
    with Poussin, 620
    with traditional art, 621, 622
  composition, 620–622
  extension of Impressionism, 619, 620
  vs. Impressionism, 618, 619
  influence of, 622, 624
  influence on, of Japanese art, 619
  Mont Ste. Victoire, 620 (fig. 511)
  new artistic reality, 622
  pioneer modernist, 618
  preoccupation with form, 616, 618

Chagall, Marc, ancestor of Surrealism, 641
  poetic quality, 641
Chambord, Chateau of, 451 (fig. 383)
Champmol (monastery), 347
Chansons de geste, 300
Chapel of Henry VII (Westminster Abbey, London), 331–333 (figs. 296, 297)
Chapingo, Mexico, Agricultural College murals (Rivera), 647
Chardin, J-B. Simeon, 491, 533, 541, 546, 548, 549, 555
  Boy with Teetotum, 548 (fig. 458)
  House of Cards, 549
  Housewife, the, 549
  Mme. Chardin, 549
  Self-portrait with Eye Shade, 549
  Still Life, 550 (fig. 459)
  Washerwoman, 549
Charlemagne, 246, 363
  (*See also* Carolingian art)
Charles I (England), 481
Charles V (Spain), 394
Charles V and Jeanne de Bourbon (Louvre, Paris), 346, 347
Chartres, *Cathedral*, 303, 309, 318–320 (*color plate 1*)
  main portal, 318 (fig. 281)
  Notre Dame de la Belle Verrière (stained glass), 313
  plan, 307 (fig. 272)
  St. Theodore (detail), 320, 321, 375 (fig. 284)
  saints and royal personages (west façade), 319 (fig. 282)
  shepherds of the nativity, 362 (fig. 269)
  view from west, 317 (fig. 280)
  University of, 300
Chaucer, Geoffrey, *Canterbury Tales*, 257
Chaudet, Antoine Denis, *Napoleon*, 569
Chenier, André, 540
Chenonceaux, Chateau of, 451
Cheops, Pyramid of, 24, 25 (fig. 18)
Chephren, Pyramid of, 24 (fig. 18)
Chevet, 311 (fig. 274)
Chiapas (Mexico), 202, 204
Chiaroscuro, 383, 385 (figs. 334, 335)
Chicago, *Chicago Tribune Tower*, 669 (fig. 553)
  Columbian Exposition, 604
  Home Life Insurance Building, 606, 607
  Lake Shore Drive apartments, 685
  Robie House, 666, 667 (fig. 552)
Chichén Itzá, *building*, 204 (fig. 178)
  El Castillo, 203 (fig. 177)
  Hall of a Thousand Columns, 207 (fig. 181)
  Temple of the Warriors, 207 (fig. 181)
Chichester, *House in West Street*, 518 (fig. 432)
Child, 323, 379, 412, 413, 432, 445, 492

716

Dutch art, in seventeenth century, 500, 501, 514, 519 (figs. 422–430)
in sixteenth century, 436, 437 (fig. 374)
(*See also* Holland)
Dutch colonies, 513
Dutch East India Company, 513
Dutch revolt from Spain, 456, 480
Dying Gaul, 124, 125, 238 (fig. 115)
Dying Lioness, 53, 175 (fig. 45)

Eakins, Thomas, 612–614
compared with Copley, Bingham, Homer, 612, 613
contrast with society portraitists, 613
The Gross Clinic, 613 (fig. 509)
influence of, 613, 614
The Thinker, 612 (fig. 508)
Early Christian art, 148, 213–222, 285, 369 (figs. 187–196)
architecture, compare *Hagia Sophia*, 225
basilicas, influence of, 217, 218
beginnings of book, 221
catacomb painting (Rome), 214–216
anticlassicism, 215, 216, 221
pagan symbolism, 215, 216
centers, 214
circular buildings, 220
decay in Merovingian art, 245
Early East Christian, 221–223 (figs. 195, 196)
end of Roman Empire, 213, 214
influence on Renaissance, 365
vs. Irish tradition, 241, 245
mosaics, influence on Italian Gothic, 335
Poussin and, 493
prayers for dead, 216 (figs. 187, 188)
revived in Carolingian period, 247, 249
Romanesque cloister and atrium, 263
sculpture and antiquity, 216, 217 (fig. 189)
Early Middle Ages (early medieval art), barbarian art vs. Christian art, 240, 241
Carolingian period, 247–251
changes since Rome, 236
compared with Romanesque, 251
cultural revival, 247
imperial aims, 247
influence of Early Christian and early medieval art, 249, 250
reorganization of Europe, 247
Irish art, 241–245 (figs. 215–218)
abstract qualities, 242
compared with Merovingian, 246
early Eastern contacts, 241
media, 242–245
Neolithic influences, 241
Merovingian style, 245–247
Irish abstraction plus Christian figurativism, 245

Early Middle Ages, Merovingian style, little sculpture or architecture, 246, 247
relative aridity, 246
population shifts since Minoan times, 236–238
Scythian-Sarmatian influence, 239, 240
wandering of nations, 238–241
Neolithic and Eastern influences on, 238
East India Company, 460
Easter Island (*see* Primitive art, Oceanian)
Eastern abstraction, 225, 233, 238
Eastern Empire, 215, 236
Eastern religions, 213, 214
Ecce Homo (Gossaert), 438 (fig. 375)
Echinus, 90, 97, 99, 100 (figs. 76, 84, 87)
Eclecticism, 482, 483, 498, 527, 598, 599
United States nineteenth-century, 603–605, 607 (fig. 500)
(*See also* Carracci)
Ecôle de Chirurgie (School of Surgery), Paris, 540
Ecôle Militaire, Paris, 539
Economic liberalism, 564
Ecstasy of St. Theresa (Bernini), 469 (fig. 396)
Ecuador, 479, 480
Eden, 384
Edge of the Woods (Rousseau), 584, 585 (fig. 485)
Edinburgh High School, 568
Egypt, ancient, 21, 22, 29, 31, 39, 40, 41 (map), 43, 170, 171, 177, 223, 228, 229, 289, 567, 577
Christian, 214
Hellenistic, 115, 152
Moslem, 283, 285, 292, 297
Ptolemaic, 115
Egyptian art, 21–39
Akhenaton period, temporary naturalism, 38, 39 (fig. 32)
background, general, 22
beginnings, 21, 22, 27
Christian Egypt, 214, 221, 222
Middle Kingdom and Empire, 29–37
cliff tombs, 29
compared with modern viewpoint, 37, 38
formalism of, vs. Old Kingdom naturalism, 36–38 (fig. 31)
great temples, 31–35 (fig. 26)
vs. Greek and Gothic architecture, 33–36
mortuary temples, 29–31, 35 (figs. 24, 25)
sculpture, 35, 36 (fig. 30)
Old Kingdom, formalism vs. naturalism, 26, 27
frontality, 27
painting and reliefs, 27, 28 (figs. 22, 23)

Expressionist art and Expressionism, reaction
to times, 626, 636
Rouault as, 635, 636
sculpture, 661–663
(See also Blue Rider; Die Brücke; New
Objectivists)
Expulsion from Paradise (della Quercia),
375 (fig. 325)
(Hildesheim bronze doors), 273 (fig. 243)

Fabliaux, 301
Façade towers, 222 (fig. 196)
Fagus Works (Alfeld a.d. Leine, Gropius
and Meyer), 676
Fa-hsien, 175
Falconet, Etienne Maurice, Bather, 556
Fall of Man (Michelangelo), 406–408 (fig.
351)
"Falling Water" (see Kaufman House)
Farnese Palace (Rome, San Gallo), 397, 398
(fig. 345)
Carracci murals, 463, 541
Farnsworth House (Plano, Ill., Miës van der
Rohe, 685
Fates (Parthenon, Athens), 103 (fig. 93)
Father Explaining the Bible to His Family
(Greuze), 552
Father's Curse (Greuze), 553 (fig. 461)
Fauves and Fauvism, 567, 617
influence on, of Cézanne, 618
of Gauguin, 625
of Van Gogh, 625
"Feathered serpent" (Quetzalcoatl), 196, 198
(fig. 174)
Federal Art Project (United States), 645
Federal style (United States), 531, 532, 603
Feininger, Lyonel, at Bauhaus, 675, 680
probing into past, 639
Feke, Robert, Isaac Royal and His Family,
533
Ferber, Herbert (Abstract Expressionist sculp-
tor), 662
Ferrara, 439
Fête Champêtre (Giorgione), 420, 460 (fig.
361)
Fêtes galantes, 550, 552
Fibula, 239, 240 (fig. 212)
Fight between a Man and a Tiger, 174, 175
(fig. 157)
Fighting Téméraire (Turner), 582, 583
Fillet Binder (Polycleitos), 94
Fire-Bird (Roszak), 662 (fig. 548)
First Baptist Meeting House (Providence),
531 (fig. 444)
First Cause, 516
Flanders, and Flemish art, 324, 346, 347,
349, 365, 366, 453, 456, 473, 481,
485–488, 491, 500, 505, 522, 543,
549

Flanders, and Flemish art, Baroque painting,
480–488, 519, 526 (figs. 406–411)
fifteenth-century painting, 348–362
(figs. 311–318)
influence on, of Franco-Flemish sculpture, 347
of International Gothic, 347
influence on German Reformation art,
427, 431, 434
Gothic art, 301 (fig. 266)
influence on eighteenth-century France,
541, 543
Mannerism, 438, 456–458 (figs. 388,
389, 375)
seventeenth-century, 480–488 (figs. 406–
411)
sixteenth-century painting, 438 (fig.
375)
people of, 344–346, 349, 351, 456, 462,
480, 481
extensive commerce, 345
independence, 345
influence of, 427
revolt from Spain, 456, 480, 481
Flaubert, Gustave, 596
Flavian period, 144
Flora, 382 (fig. 333)
Florence (Italy), 336, 359, 364, 367, 370,
371, 378, 381, 382, 385, 393, 394, 401,
404, 417, 423, 439, 440
Baptistery, 269 (fig. 239)
Cathedral, 269 (fig. 319)
dome, 367–369
compared, with Gothic, 368
with Pantheon (Rome), 368
with St. Peter's, 411
dukes of, 440, 441, 442
(See also Medici)
Laurentian Library, 411
painting, 378–386, 398–403, 441–445
Palazzo Vecchio, 367
Paradise Gates (Baptistery), 373–375 (figs.
323, 324)
Pazzi Chapel (Santa Croce), 368–370 (fig.
320)
San Lorenzo Church, 369
San Miniato al Monte Church, 269
Santissima Annunziata Church, 416
Florentine tradition, 338, 370, 371
Florida, 528
"Flowery Kingdom," 170
Flutings, 99, 101 (figs. 87, 89)
Flying buttresses, 306–310 (figs. 271, 274)
"Flying comb," 204, 206
Font-de-Gaume paintings, 6
Fontainebleau, 584
Chateau, 451
Italo-French school, 453
School, 440, 451

Fundamentalism, 426
Fur Traders Descending the Mississippi
  (Bingham), 609, 610 (fig. 505)
Fuseli, Henry, 583
Futurism, *Armored Train* (Severini), 630
  (fig. 519)
  character of, 630, 631
  compared with Cubism, 631
  influence of, 631
  influence of Cubism on, 630
  opposition to Impressionism and Cubism,
    631
  reaction to times, 626

Gabo, Nahum, Bauhaus interests, 660, 667
  Constructivist influence, 659, 660
  Linear Construction, 659 (fig. 545)
  new approach to sculpture, 660
  penetration of mass, 660
Gabriel, Jacques-Ange, *Petit Trianon* (Ver-
  sailles), 539 (fig. 450)
Gainsborough, Thomas, 487, 524–527, 545,
  581, 582
  Cottage Door, 525
  Honorable Frances Duncombe, 525 (fig.
    438)
  Landscape, 524 (fig. 437)
  The Mall, 525
  Market Cart, 525
  Mrs. Graham, 526
Galen, 283
Galilei, Galileo, 460
Gallery, 225, 264
Gandhara (India), influence of Greek art on,
  115, 116, 158 (fig. 145)
Ganymede and the Eagle (Rembrandt), 505
Gard, *St. Gilles*, 263
Garden of Love (Rubens), 485 (fig. 408)
Garnier, Charles, *Opera House* (Paris), 601
  (figs. 497, 498)
"Gathering of the grapes" type, 216
Gattamelata (Donatello), 377 (figs. 328,
  329)
  compared, with Mantegna, 387
    with Masaccio, 383
Gauguin, Paul, 37, 567, 600, 624
  vs. academic painting, 619
  aestheticism, 624, 625
  alteration of Impressionism, 624
  compared with Cézanne, 624
  Day of the God, 624 (fig. 514)
  escapism, 616, 626
  vs. Impressionism, 618, 619, 626
  influence of, on Expressionism, 625
    on Matisse, 625
  influence of Japanese art on, 619
  interest in emotions, 618
Gaul, 275
Gaul Killing His Wife and Himself, 124

Gauls, 124, 125, 236, 238
Gautama (Buddha), 151, 176
Geertgen tot Sint Jans, 360
Geese of Medum, 26, 27 (fig. 22)
Genji Monogatari (Sotatsu), 190, 191 (fig.
  171)
  courtly romance, 190
Genoa, 298
George Gisze (Holbein), 454
Georgian period, 517–519, 529
  (*See also* Adam brothers)
Gerard of Cremona (Jewish scholar), 297
Géricault, Théodore, 577–581, 598
  influence of Baroque on, 578
  Raft of the Medusa, 580, 581, 592 (fig.
    480)
German art, Carolingian, 247–251
  German successors of, 252
  early Middle Ages, 240, 241, 247–251
  eighteenth-century, architecture, 537, 560
    (figs. 469, 470)
    sculpture, 560 (fig. 471)
  fifteenth-century painting, 355, 356, 358
  Gothic, 273, 300, 328, 329, 404 (fig. 292)
  Mannerism, painting, 440, 454–456 (fig.
    387)
  Ottonian, 252–254
  Reformation, architecture, 426, 427 (fig.
    366)
    painting, 427–436, 441 (figs. 367–373)
  Romanesque, 270–273
    compared with Byzantine, 233
  seventeenth-century, 519
  twentieth-century, architecture, 674–679
    (figs. 557–559)
    painting, 636–641 (figs. 525–528)
German and Germanic peoples, 236, 238, 252,
  255, 326, 425, 431, 433, 499
Germanic-Christian spiritualism, 247, 425
Germany, deterioration of financial position,
  501
  increased town life, 344
  influence of Mantegna, 388
  International Gothic, 344
  Nazism, effects of, 618
  neo-Christian movement, 599
  neoclassicism, 519
  Reformation, 439
  Romanticism, 573
  Social Democratic government, 677
Germigny-des-Prés, 249
Ghent, 359
Ghent Altarpiece (Jan and Hubert Van Eyck)
  351–355, 381, 384 (figs. 311, 312)
Ghiberti, Lorenzo, 300, 373–375, 383
  compared, with Fra Angelico, 379
    with Gothic, 375
  Paradise Gates (*The Creation*), 372, 373
    (figs. 323, 324)

Vishnu (Hindu deity), 161–163
Visigoths, 238–240, 246, 249, 283, 286
Visitation, Reims Cathedral, 322 (fig. 287)
Vistula River, 236
Voltaire, 548, 557
   Lettres philosophiques, 535
Voltaire (Houdon), 557
Volute, 99, 101 (figs. 87, 89)
Voragine, 316
Vorticists, influence on, of Cézanne, 618
   of Futurism, 631
   reaction to times, 626
Vouet, Simon, 489
Voyage of Life series (Moran), 608 (fig. 503)

Wagner, Otto, Post Office Savings Bank (Vienna), 674
Walhalla (Regensburg), 568
Walpole, Horace, *Castle of Otranto* (novel), 575
   Strawberry Hill, 573
Walter von der Vogelweide (medieval German poet), 326
Warrior Figure (Temple of Aegina), 85, 86 (fig. 72)
Washerwoman (Chardin), 549
Washington, George (Houdon), 557
Watteau, Antoine, 525, 541, 543–546, 550
   Caractères, 545
   The Concert, 543
   Embarkation for Cythera, 551 (fig. 453)
   Gilles, 544 (fig. 454)
   influence of, 545
   influence of Rubens on, 543
   Le Mezzetin, 544
Wedding Dance (Brueghel), 457, 458 (fig. 389)
Well of Moses (Sluter), 347, 349, 351 (fig. 308)
Wells Cathedral, 329, 331 (figs. 293, 294)
West, Benjamin, 518
   president of Royal Academy, 534
West Christian art, 225
   (*See also* Early Christian art)
Western Happy Heaven, 176
Western World, 283
   expansion of, 459, 515
Westminster Abbey (London), 333
   Chapel of Henry VII, 331–333 (figs. 296, 297)
Westover (Virginia), 529
   influence of Gibbs on, 531
Whale Ship (Turner), 583
When the Morning Stars All Sang Together (Blake), 583 (fig. 484)
Whistler, J. A. M., 614, 615

Whitehall Palace (London), paintings by Rubens, 481
Whitney Museum of American Art (New York), 652
William the Conqueror, 266
William of Rubruques (medieval explorer), 298
William James (Hogarth), 520–522 (fig. 435)
Williamsburg Houses (Brooklyn, Shreve, R. H., et al.), 690
Wilson, Richard, 523, 524, 581, 582
   On the Wye, 523 (fig. 436)
   River, 523
Winchester School (manuscripts), 276, 277
Wine vessel shaped like an eared owl, 171, 172 (fig. 156)
Winged Victory of Samothrace, 118, 119 (fig. 108)
Wittenberg, 426
Wolfram von Eschenbach (medieval German poet), 326
Woman (Tanagra statuette), 121 (fig. 112)
Woman on Horseback (Persian pottery), 295 (fig. 263)
Women Putting Away Their Clothes (kylix), 106 (fig. 97)
Woods family (architects), 518
Worms Cathedral, 270, 271 (figs. 240, 241)
Wren, Sir Christopher, 518, 529
   St. Mary-le-Bow, 531
   St. Paul's Cathedral, 517 (fig. 431)
   compared with *Panthéon,* 539
Wright, Frank Lloyd, 666–669, 681–685
   antimachine viewpoint, 681, 682
   compared, with International style, 682
      with Savoye House, 682
      with Tugendhat House, 682
   early difficulties, 666
   Guggenheim Museum, 685
   heir of Louis Sullivan, 666, 682
   homes for wealthy, 684, 689
   Johnson Wax Company Administration Building, 683 (fig. 562)
   Kaufman House, 681, 684 (fig. 561)
   Laboratory Tower, 684 (fig. 563)
   Larkin Building (Buffalo), 667, 682
   modern English architecture, 674
   Morris Store (San Francisco), 685
   prairie houses, 666
   Price Tower (Bartlesville, Okla.), 685 (fig. 564)
   Robie House (Chicago), 667 (fig. 552)
   San Francisco Call Building, 667
   sculptural aesthetic, 682
   sites, importance of, 682
   space in, 667
   Unity Temple (Oak Park), 667, 682